Oklahoma Breeding Bird Atlas

George Miksch Sutton Avian Research Center
P.O. Box 2007
Bartlesville, OK 74005
United States of America

(918) 336-7778 or (918) 336-BIRD
FAX: (918) 336-7783
www.suttoncenter.org

*"finding cooperative conservation solutions for birds and
the natural world through science and education"*

Founded 1983

Grateful appreciation is expressed to the following people for their involvement with the George Miksch Sutton Avian Research Center from 1997 through 2003, the years during which the Oklahoma Breeding Bird Atlas was researched and compiled.

Current and Former Board of Directors

Oklahoma
Biological
Survey

OKLAHOMA BREEDING BIRD ATLAS

DAN L. REINKING, EDITOR

Project administrated by the George M. Sutton Avian Research Center and the Oklahoma Biological Survey

University of Oklahoma Press
Norman

This project was administrated by the George M. Sutton Avian Research Center and the Oklahoma Biological Survey, with thanks to major project sponsors: Helmerich Foundation, National Fish and Wildlife Foundation, Phillips Petroleum Company, U.S. Fish and Wildlife Service, and Williams.

As project administrators, the George Miksch Sutton Avian Research Center and the Oklahoma Biological Survey, units of the College of Arts and Sciences at the University of Oklahoma, would like to sincerely thank The Helmerich Foundation, the National Fish and Wildlife Foundation, ConocoPhillips, the U.S. Fish and Wildlife Service, and Williams for major support. Without their vision, dedication, and generosity, this historic volume could not have been completed with the degree of quality and attention to detail that was achieved.

The Helmerich Foundation

Library of Congress Cataloging-in-Publication Data

Oklahoma breeding bird atlas / Dan L. Reinking, editor.
     p. cm.
  "Project administrated by George M. Sutton Avian Research Center and the Oklahoma Biological Survey."
  Includes bibliographical references (p.).
  ISBN 0-8061-3409-7 (alk. paper)—ISBN 0-8061-3614-6 (pbk. : alk paper)
   1. Birds—Oklahoma. 2. Birds—Oklahoma—Geographical distribution. 3. Birds—Oklahoma—Geographical distribution—Maps.
I. Reinking, Dan L. II. George Miksch Sutton Avian Research Center.

QL684.O5O45 2004
598'.09766—dc22

          2003065031

The paper in this book meets the guidelines for permanence and durability of the Committee on Production Guidelines for Book Longevity of the Council on Library Resources. ⊗

Dedicated to the birders of Oklahoma and beyond, who made this project possible

Contents

Acknowledgments

Thank you. Those two seemingly insignificant words are insufficient to convey the message of gratitude for the assistance that was readily given by so many people and organizations in so many ways. Breeding bird atlas projects are by nature volunteer efforts, even when, as in the case of the Oklahoma Breeding Bird Atlas (OBBA), a sponsoring organization or agency takes the lead in coordinating the effort. It is difficult to know where to begin the acknowledgment process, but it seems appropriate to first thank the landowners of Oklahoma, who generously allowed access to their properties and who often provided useful information about birds on their land. I will now attempt to go through the stages of the project chronologically, from planning, fund-raising, organization, fieldwork, authorship, collection of photographs, and finally publication.

First, thanks must go to Steve K. Sherrod, executive director of the George Miksch Sutton Avian Research Center (GMSARC or Sutton Center). Steve is a man of vision, ambition, and persistence, who when presented with the idea for the OBBA was quick to recognize the value of the project and agree that it was a worthwhile endeavor for the Sutton Center to take the lead role on. Steve championed the project and was able to locate the significant amount of funding needed for the project thanks to major support from The Helmerich Foundation, National Fish and Wildlife Foundation, Phillips Petroleum Company, the U.S. Fish and Wildlife Service Region 2 office, and Tulsa-based Williams. Additional financial or in-kind support specifically for OBBA was received from M. Frank Carl, Indian Nations Audubon Society, Oklahoma Wildlife Federation, Sebastian Patti, Carl and Nan Reinking, Dan Reinking, Brian and Pamela Ufen, and Don and Joyce Varner. Without the generous support of these foundations, companies, agencies, organizations, and individuals, this project would not have been possible.

A number of people were particularly helpful during the planning and early implementation stages of the OBBA, including Raymond Adams, Jeanette Bider, William Busby, Ian Butler, Daniel Hough, Brad Jacobs, Wayne Mollhoff, Richard Peterson, Gary Schnell, Steve Sherrod, Kim Smith, Dave Shuford, David Wiedenfeld, James Wilson, Donald Wolfe, and John Zimmerman. Gary Schnell, then director of the Oklahoma Biological Survey (OBS), was instrumental in bringing the expertise of the OBS to the atlas project, and later in helping accomplish the affiliation of the Sutton Center with the OBS. Daniel Hough, also of OBS, designed the database used for atlas project data and provided invaluable help with atlas mapping arrangements and project website creation.

Fieldwork was conducted by a full-time seasonal employee during each year of the project. These dedicated and skilled individuals accomplished much throughout each season, including surveying blocks and entering the voluminous data collected during the course of the project. Jeanette Bider assumed this role during the first three seasons of the OBBA and contributed immeasurably to the sometimes tedious work involved in getting the project off the ground and keeping it running smoothly throughout her tenure. Kimberly Score stepped into this role during 2000, and Michael Drenth in 2001, both continuing the fine performance given by Jeanette and helping ensure that the project would be completed on time. They were the real road warriors of this project, logging over 10,000 miles in a truck each season visiting far-flung blocks all around the state. During the final year of the project, Scott Carleton was hired for a two-week run at finishing up a number of blocks, which he did well.

Despite the concerted efforts of the OBBA staff, it was volunteers who completed surveys in the majority of blocks. Over 100 of these dedicated birders gave generously of their time and travel budgets to faithfully inventory atlas blocks, some of which were close to home while others, especially in the latter years of the project, were many miles from home. Most atlasers hailed from Oklahoma, but their ranks were swelled by participants from Arkansas, Colorado, Illinois, Kansas, Missouri, and Texas. It seems that once an atlaser, always an atlaser!

It is with sincere appreciation that the block surveying participants, both staff and volunteer, are listed here, organized by the number of blocks they completed or helped complete.

1–5 blocks: Virginia Anderson, Robert Bastarache, Ned and Gigi Batchelder, Michael Bay, Karla Beatty, Patricia Bergey, Sarah P. Brennan, Vicki Byre, M. Frank Carl, Guyla Carnes, John Carter, William Carter, Dick Clapp, John Couch, Jeff Cox, Melinda Droege, Kenneth Dueck, Mickle Duggan, Stephen Gast, Walter Gerard, Claudia and Don Glass, Billy Graham, Denise Grudier, Joe Grzybowski, Thomas Haner, Jim Harmon, Laura Harris, Lawrence Herbert, Melynda Hickman, J. Isbell, Rhett Jackson, Pete Janzen, Gene and Kaye Jenkins, George and Martha Kamp, June Ketchum, Lynn Kisinger, Nathan Kuhnert, Hope McGaha, Amy Lambert, Dan Lashelle, Loyd and Glenda Leslie, Neely Lowrie, Dustin Lynch, Deborah Maas, Larry Mays, Helen C. Miller, Greg Mills, Marion Norman, Owasso Science Club, Royce Pendergast, Galen Pittman, Bill Radke, Mia Revels, Justin Roach, Aline Romero, Gary Schnell, Thomas Shane, Jerry Sisler, Glenda Smith, Sam Smith, Eddie Stegall, Barbara Tarbutton, Michelle Ternes, Jim Thayer, Olen Thomas, Laurel Upshaw, Robert Versaw, Jan Ward, Carl and Dora Webb, George and Francis Webb, Melissa Wiedenfeld, Ernie Wilson, Carl Wisk, Don Wolfe, Eugene Young. David Arbour submitted a significant number of Special Interest Species reports from Red Slough. Salt Plains National Wildlife Refuge also provided helpful information.

6–10 blocks: Ben Anderson, James Arterburn, Cyndie Browning, Jerry Cooper, John Dole, Mark Howery, David Gill, Berlin Heck, Jo Loyd, Jeri McMahon, Jim Norman, Clarence and Susie Ruby, Patricia Seibert, John Sterling, Don and Joyce Varner, Alan Versaw, David Wiedenfeld, Paul Wilson.

11–20 blocks: Scott Carleton (staff), Janet Duerr, Bonnie Gall, Patti Muzny, Steve Schafer, Jimmy Woodard, Phil Floyd.

21–30 blocks: Richard Stuart, Kimberly Wiar, Sebastian Patti.

31–50 blocks: Michael Drenth (staff), Dan Reinking (staff), Kimberly Score (staff), Nancy Vicars (the most ambitious volunteer of them all!).

Over 100 blocks: Jeanette Bider (staff).

Authorship of the species accounts was also largely dependent upon volunteers. These contributors briskly signed up for species they were interested in writing about, ensuring that no species would go unremarked. Take note of the author credit accompanying each species account. Thank you to Ken Andrews, James Arterburn, Michael Bay, Charles Brown, Vicki Byre, Carolee Caffrey, Guyla Carnes, William Carter, John Dole, Melinda Droege, David Fantina, Bonnie Gall, Walter Gerard, Joseph Grzybowski, Jerome Jackson, M. Alan Jenkins, Mark Howery, Nathan Kuhnert, Sebastian Patti, Mia Revels, Kimberly Score, John Shackford, Thomas Shane, Gregory Smith, Richard Stuart, Don Varner , Alan Versaw, David Wiggins, Paul Wilson, Donald Wolfe, and Eugene Young. Special thanks to Bruce Hoagland for preparing the chapter on Oklahoma's vegetation and for assistance with the vegetation map. Thanks to Derek Arndt and the Oklahoma Climatological Survey for the map of Oklahoma rainfall. Thanks also to John Brock and Salt Plains National Wildlife Refuge for providing information on nesting birds at the refuge and John Skeen and Brandon Brown of the Oklahoma Department of Wildlife Conservation for information on Red-cockaded Woodpeckers.

Not to be outdone by the many who surveyed blocks and prepared species accounts, photographers too answered the call for help. Professional and amateur photographers from Oklahoma as well as Arizona, Colorado, Florida, Georgia, Kansas, Mississippi, and Texas generously contributed their outstanding and hard-won bird photos. These images add immeasurably to the beauty and educational value of this book. Take note of the photo credit accompanying each photo. Thank you to James Arterburn, Giff Beaton, Jim

Burns, M. Frank Carl, James Flynn, Michael Gray, Bob Gress, Joseph Grzybowski, Bill Horn, Steve Metz, Arthur Morris, Ike Raley, Joel Sartore, John Shackford, Colin Smith, Alan Versaw, Gerald Wiens, Wildlifedepartment.com, and Warren Williams.

Mapping of survey data was accomplished using ArcView GIS software by Environmental Systems Research Institute, Inc., with the crucial help of Jeanette Bider, Daniel Hough, and David Wiedenfeld.

Michael Carter and Donna Dittmann provided thoughtful and constructive comments on the manuscript. Debbie Self, John Coghlan, and the editors and staff at the University of Oklahoma Press performed invaluable services.

Finally, a number of people have provided advice and assistance throughout the project. Some have been mentioned already, but deserve mention again, and others have yet to be recognized. The staff of the Sutton Center have provided help in many ways, from maintaining project finances, preparing bulk mailings of project newsletters, organizing final hard copies of the book manuscript, and a myriad of other behind-the-scenes needs. These staff members included M. Alan Jenkins, Karen Kilbourne Steve K. Sherrod, David A. Wiedenfeld, and Donald H. Wolfe. Daniel J. Hough was always on call for technical assistance with databases, ArcView software, and other issues. Volunteer Bonnie Gall cheerfully assisted with many tasks along the way. I thank the Sutton Center Board of Directors for its continuing support of this organization. I also thank my family for their support and interest throughout this long project.

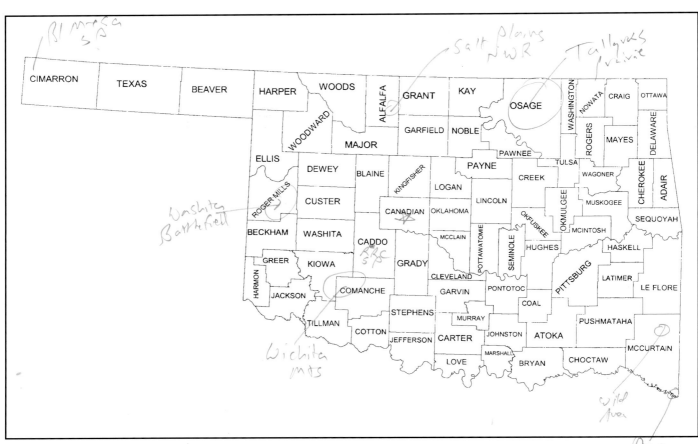

The 77 counties of Oklahoma

Oklahoma Breeding Bird Atlas

Introduction

Breeding bird atlases are being employed worldwide to provide an important benchmark against which to evaluate changes in bird populations and distributions over time. An accurate inventory of breeding bird populations in any given region is an essential first step in determining and implementing appropriate conservation actions designed to sustain and promote the existing diversity of that region's bird life. The widespread dearth of such information is evidenced by the number of Breeding Bird Atlas Projects (over 40) that have been completed or are currently in progress in the United States. All six of Oklahoma's neighboring states have either initiated or recently completed atlas projects. During planning stages for the Oklahoma Breeding Bird Atlas (OBBA), it was felt that completion of an atlas project in Oklahoma would enhance both local and regional understanding of breeding bird distributions, and subsequently would help facilitate improved decision making with regard to conservation actions.

Oklahoma has been fortunate in receiving the attentions of prominent bird researchers, including George M. Sutton and Margaret Nice. Their work and the work of others have greatly fostered and clarified our knowledge of avian occurrences and distributions within the state. As in most other states, however, current knowledge regarding the distribution of Oklahoma's bird life is rather broad in nature and not well quantified. Prior to the OBBA, existing information on the breeding distribution for most bird species in Oklahoma was limited to general statements of occurrence within broad regional areas. This information was also based on many decades of information, both opportunistic and anecdotal. The use of a standardized and proven atlasing methodology to systematically survey the entire state within the relative confines of a five-year period provides an accurate snapshot of breeding bird distribution within the state. This information will help evaluate future changes in breeding bird distribution in the context of land-use change and other processes currently impacting bird populations.

The George M. Sutton Avian Research Center (GMSARC) in Bartlesville initially proposed and began to organize the OBBA in late 1996, and the Oklahoma Biological Survey (OBS) at the University of Oklahoma was quick to express interest and a desire to help. In the fall of 1997, after the first atlas project field season, GMSARC became affiliated with the OBS, bringing even tighter integration to the effort.

The North American Ornithological Atlas Committee (NORAC) has developed a standardized set of instructions, the *Handbook for Atlasing American Breeding Birds,* published by the Vermont Institute of Natural Science, for the completion of atlas projects in North America. We considered adherence to these guidelines important, not only to ensure a well-designed and scientifically valid survey, but also to complement and augment similar surveys completed or ongoing in all six of Oklahoma's neighboring states. Such standardization enables natural resources personnel to evaluate breeding bird populations over larger regional areas; this is an important consideration as political boundaries are not perceived or recognized by birds.

The sampling unit used for the OBBA and for many other state atlas projects was the standard U.S. Geological Survey 7.5-minute quadrangle map. Using a method described by NORAC as stratified random sampling, one-sixth of every other quadrangle map (or one-twelfth of every 2 adjacent quad maps) was selected for surveying, resulting in 583 blocks, each approximately 25 km^2 in size (fig. 1). The atlas block selected for coverage from each adjacent pair of quad maps was chosen randomly with the following strictures: (1) If greater than 50 percent of a chosen block's land area fell outside of the state of Oklahoma, or (2) If a chosen block shared a common border with a previously selected block, then an alternate block was selected at random from the remaining blocks within

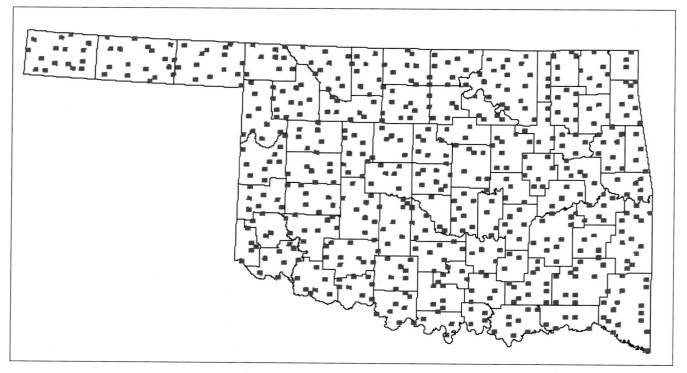

Figure 1. The 583 atlas blocks selected for coverage in Oklahoma from 1997 to 2001.

the two quads. Only the Oklahoma portions of blocks overlapping another state were surveyed. This occurred primarily in blocks along the Red River, Oklahoma's southern border with Texas.

A decidedly low-tech method was used to produce block location maps for volunteers. A transparency sheet was sized to equal one-sixth of a 7.5-minute Oklahoma quadrangle map. This sheet was overlaid onto the randomly selected sixth of each quad map chosen for coverage. The locations of the four corners of the transparency sheet formed the boundaries of the block, and were manually transferred to detailed county maps published and provided to the OBBA by the Oklahoma Wildlife Federation (1991). Block boundaries were drawn in orange marker on these county maps, which were then sent to volunteers along with project data forms and instructions.

A project web site showed the location of each block in the state, as well as its survey status. Volunteers could examine this map and select any unsurveyed blocks they wished to visit. An online sign-up form was also provided. Additional volunteer recruitment occurred at the annual fall meeting of the Oklahoma Ornithological Society. Printed versions of the current block status maps from the web site were brought to

these meetings each year for scrutiny by volunteers.

The time frame for completing atlas surveys of the 583 selected blocks was set at five years, the most commonly used interval for statewide projects such as the OBBA. Fieldwork began in 1997 and was completed on schedule in 2001, with only a handful of blocks remaining unsurveyed. The completion of fieldwork for the OBBA required personnel and time far in excess of that available from any government or private research organization in the state. As in all statewide atlas projects, volunteers contributed most of the field labor throughout the five years of data collection. Dan Reinking, a biologist with GMSARC, served as atlas coordinator throughout the project, helping to recruit and deploy volunteer atlasers and a hired, full-time seasonal field coordinator in each year of the project (Jeanette Bider for 1997–1999, Kimberly Score in 2000, and Michael Drenth in 2001) who surveyed blocks throughout the state.

Volunteers were recruited through visits to bird clubs around the state, as well as through notices posted in bird club newsletters and on the OBBA web page on the GMSARC web site (www.suttoncenter.org). Over 100 birders from Oklahoma and six other states responded to the call for participation in the OBBA.

Many of these came from the ranks of the Oklahoma Ornithological Society and from enthusiasts who had worked on atlas projects in other states and were not ready to give up atlasing just because their home state had already been surveyed.

Volunteers were provided with a 27-page *Handbook for Atlasers* (Reinking 1997, 1998), which gave detailed instructions on atlasing methods and filling out data forms (copies of data forms are provided in Appendix 2). Data were collected using a standard NORAC classification system for observations of birds within atlas blocks. Each time an observer recorded a bird species within an atlas block, it was placed within one of four categories based on the level of breeding evidence seen. The observation was further classified within each category based on the specific behavior or subject observed. Observers were encouraged to upgrade as many species as possible to the highest category possible, that of Confirmed breeder. The categories and codes used for the OBBA are as follows (as provided in Reinking 1998):

Code Description

"OBSERVED" CATEGORY (OB)

O   The species (male or female) was *Observed* during the breeding season, but *is not believed to be breeding in the block.* Contrast this with the "Possible" category. The "Observed" category can include species suspected to not breed within the defined block (such as a Great Blue Heron flying over). Nonbreeding vagrants and obvious migrants were not recorded.

"POSSIBLE" CATEGORY (PO)

X   A *singing* male was present in suitable nesting habitat.
S   *Safe Dates*: The species (male or female) was observed in suitable nesting habitat during its breeding season (see Reinking 1998). This code was used *for species that may breed in the block,* as opposed to the "Observed" category (which was for birds believed *not* to be breeding in the block). The date of observation was listed on the Species List form.

"PROBABLE" CATEGORY (PR)

M   *Seven or more singing Males* were present *on one day* in suitable nesting habitat during their breeding season.

Applies primarily to passerine species; some birds do not sing, such as ducks or swifts, and cannot be recorded using this category.

P   A *Pair* (male and female) was observed in suitable nesting habitat during their breeding season.
T   A breeding *Territory* was presumed, because an adult male was defending it (e.g., chasing other birds, or singing at the same location on at least two occasions a week or more apart).
C   *Courtship* behavior or copulation was observed, including things such as a display or food exchange, the courtship flight of male hummingbirds, or the bill-tilt display of cowbirds.
V   A bird was observed *Visiting* a probable nest site (e.g., a Great Crested Flycatcher entering a tree cavity).
A   Adult(s) exhibited *Agitated* behavior or gave anxiety calls that suggested they had a nearby nest, including such things as flushing a ground nesting bird into a bush where it repeatedly gave a distressed call, or a pair of birds flying at or circling closely above the observer. This code did not include agitated behavior induced by pishing or using tape-recorded calls. Contrast this code with code DD below.
N   *Nest* building by *wrens* or excavation of holes by *woodpeckers*. These species may build nests they never use for breeding. See also code NB below.

"CONFIRMED" CATEGORY (CO)

The presence of Brown-headed Cowbird eggs or young is confirmation of breeding for *both* the cowbird and the host species.

DD   Adult(s) gave a *Distraction Display* or feigned injury, indicating a nearby nest. Several species, especially ground nesters, will flutter, apparently helpless, and try to draw predators away from their nest. Examples include the broken wing act of Killdeer or Mourning Dove.
PE   *Physiological Evidence* of breeding based on a *bird in hand.* This included a female with a highly vascularized, edematous incubation (brood) patch or an egg in the oviduct. A single male with a cloacal protuberance did not qualify as a Confirmed breeder.
NB   *Nest Building* by all species *except woodpeckers and wrens.* See also code N above.
ON   *Occupied Nest:* Adult(s) watched entering or leaving nest site in circumstances indicating an occupied nest. Generally, this was used for high nests or holes, the contents of which could not be seen, where the adult may have been incubating eggs or brooding young. If the contents of the nest could be seen, the codes below were used.

NE *Nest* with *Egg*(s).

NY *Nest* with *Young* seen or heard.

UN *Used Nest* or eggshells found. These had to be carefully identified and were used only for unique or unmistakable nests.

AY *Attending Young:* Adult was seen carrying food for young or feeding recently fledged young or carrying a fecal sac away from the nest. This code was used carefully because some species, especially corvids and raptors, carry food some distance before eating it themselves. Generally, this code was used only if the nest or young were not found. If the nest or fledglings were found, one of the other codes in this section was used.

FL Recently *FLedged* young (of altricial species such as songbirds and raptors), or downy young (of precocial species such as ducks, shorebirds, and quail).

In addition to the surveys of the randomly selected blocks that formed the core of the atlas project, a list was developed of species for which additional information was considered desirable. These were referred to as Special Interest Species (SIS; see Appendix 2). Reports of these SIS were solicited from anywhere in the state of Oklahoma, even if the report was not from within an atlas block. This helped to better define the Oklahoma breeding distribution for species that are rare or local in occurrence and are therefore not well measured by standard atlasing survey methods.

The OBBA season lasted from February 15 through August 15 of each year. This protracted season afforded atlasers the opportunity to confirm early nesting species such as Great Horned Owl, as well as late nesting species such as American Goldfinch. May through July were the most productive months for confirming the largest number of species, and observers were encouraged to concentrate their efforts during this time. At the end of each season, data were submitted to the atlas coordinator for review. Obvious errors in identification or coding were corrected, and additional supporting details were requested in some cases. Data were then further reviewed by the field coordinator during entry into a Microsoft Access database developed by Daniel Hough of OBS.

During data review, blocks were classified as either complete or in need of further survey work. Those blocks needing further work were targeted by volunteers or OBBA staff in subsequent years. Standards were established for determining when a block was considered complete, but some flexibility was allowed in applying these standards. A goal of at least two visits and ten hours of survey time was set for each block. In some cases where high numbers of birds and breeding confirmations were achieved in less than ten hours, or when homogenous, unproductive habitat such as agricultural fields covered entire blocks, some leeway was allowed with the ten-hour rule. Additionally, the atlas coordinator used some discretion in evaluating whether the number of species recorded in each block seemed adequate given the area of the state in which the block was located. Volunteers were also encouraged to get at least one-third of the species recorded in the block into the Confirmed breeder category.

An optional request involved providing the number of individuals of each species observed in each block using three categories: 1–2 birds observed, 3–30 birds observed, or more than 30 birds observed. It was hoped that this would provide a rough measure of abundance of each species statewide. This information remains on file but has not been provided in this book, partly due to concerns about the consistency and accuracy of reporting these numbers among various observers.

LIMITATIONS

Perhaps the most obvious limitation of the OBBA is that only about one-twelfth of the total land area was surveyed. More populous states and those with smaller land areas have been surveyed more completely. Nonetheless, the OBBA sample is believed adequate to provide a good representation of the current distribution of most breeding birds in Oklahoma. Additional limitations of the OBBA as well as most other state atlas projects include a bias toward low detection of owls and other nocturnal species, low detection of rails and other marsh species that occur in very local habitats often not present or not discovered in atlas blocks, low confirmation rates of species that nest very early or very late in the season, and low detection of other rare and locally distributed species that may not be present in the randomly selected blocks. This latter problem was somewhat ameliorated by encouraging the submission of SIS reports from wherever these species were observed. Finally, the skill and ability of observers varies widely. Whenever possible, blocks that appeared to be short on species or confirmations were later revisited by other volunteers or OBBA personnel in an attempt to increase these totals.

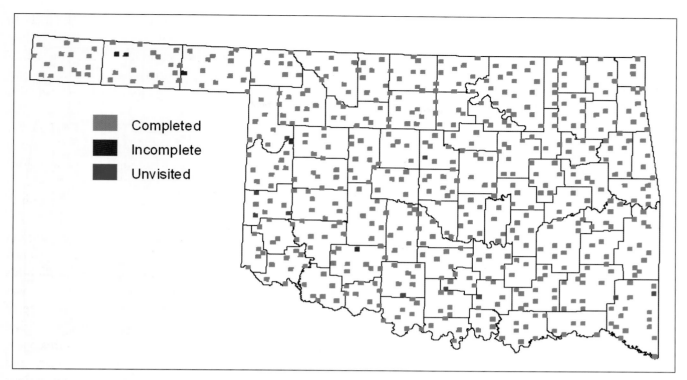

Figure 2. Final status of surveys in each atlas block from 1997 to 2001.

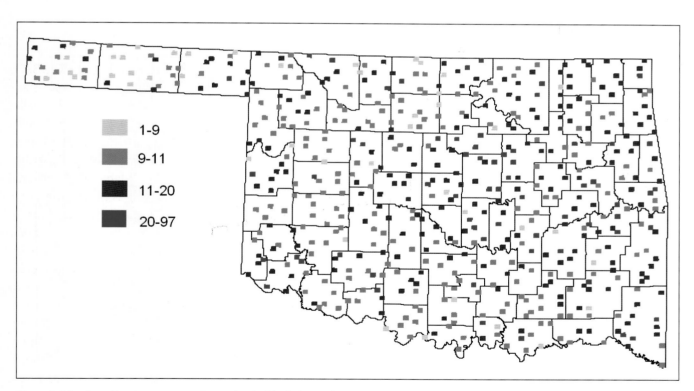

Figure 3. Number of hours spent surveying each atlas block during the period 1997–2001.

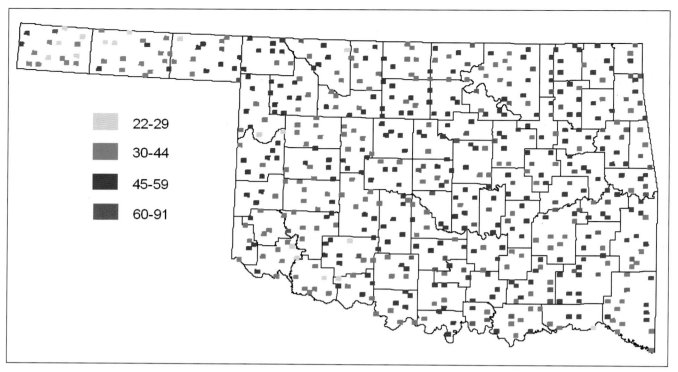

Figure 4. Number of Possible, Probable, and Confirmed breeders recorded in each atlas block from 1997 to 2001.

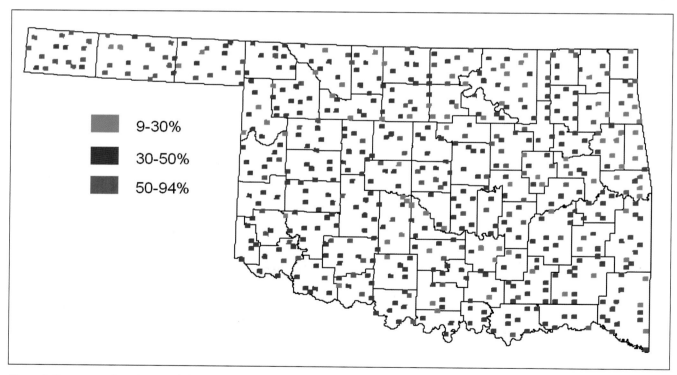

Figure 5. Percentage of species recorded in each atlas block that were scored in the Confirmed Breeder category.

RESULTS

Of the 583 blocks initially selected for coverage, 573 were visited and 568 were scored as complete, resulting in a completion rate of over 97 percent (fig. 2). The unvisited blocks occurred due to inability to get land access and to a small shortage of survey help. From 1997 to 2001, volunteer atlasers and OBBA personnel spent over 7,985 hours surveying 573 atlas blocks (fig. 3). On average, each visited block received about 13 hours of survey time.

Two hundred and twelve species were detected in atlas blocks during the project years, of which 198 were recorded with a breeding status of Possible, Probable, or Confirmed. Of these, 160 species were confirmed in atlas blocks. A number of additional species were confirmed during project years within Oklahoma but outside of atlas blocks. The total number of species recorded as Possible, Probable, or Confirmed in each block is shown in Figure 4. The percentage of Confirmed breeders recorded in each block is shown in Figure 5. Table 1 shows the ten species recorded in the largest number of blocks. Mourning Dove was detected in the most blocks, 567 out of 573 blocks that were visited. Table 2 shows the ten species that were confirmed in the most atlas blocks. Barn Swallow was confirmed more often than any other species, in 474 blocks, due to its abundance, its wide distribution, and its nest site location on easily observed bridges and other human structures. Mourning Dove, Barn Swallow, Scissor-tailed Flycatcher, and Red-winged Blackbird made appearances on both top-ten lists, indicating their widespread abundance and easily located nests.

The total number of species known or assumed to have nested in Oklahoma (including extinct and extirpated species) numbers nearly 230.

MAPS

The maps generated for each breeding species in Oklahoma form the core of the information gathered during the OBBA. As in most published breeding bird atlases, species recorded as Possible, Probable, or Confirmed have been mapped, while most species recorded in the Observed category have been omitted due to the lack of breeding evidence. There are some species that are common but hard to confirm, such as herons and egrets that are wide-ranging but nest in

Table 1. Ten Species Recorded in the Largest Number of Blocks

Species	Number of blocks (percent of visited blocks)
Mourning Dove	567 (99)
Brown-headed Cowbird	555 (96.9)
Northern Mockingbird	551 (96.2)
Barn Swallow	550 (96)
Red-winged Blackbird	540 (94.2)
American Crow	532 (92.8)
Northern Bobwhite	529 (92.3)
Scissor-tailed Flycatcher	529 (92.3)
Dickcissel	524 (91.4)
Yellow-billed Cuckoo	522 (91)

Table 2. Ten Species Confirmed in the Largest Number of Blocks

Species	Number of blocks (percent of visited blocks)
Barn Swallow	474 (82.7)
Scissor-tailed Flycatcher	418 (73)
Eastern Bluebird	410 (71.6)
House Sparrow	404 (70.5)
European Starling	359 (62.7)
Lark Sparrow	355 (62)
Eastern Phoebe	335 (58.5)
Mourning Dove	333 (58.1)
Red-winged Blackbird	333 (58.1)
Northern Cardinal	327 (57.1)

local colonies, and others such as vultures for which few of the standard breeding status codes are applicable. In these cases, records in the Observed category have been mapped using orange rectangles to better illustrate the true summer distribution of these species in Oklahoma. For most other species, only records in the higher-ranking categories are mapped.

Blocks in which a species was recorded as a Possible breeder are shown as green rectangles on the maps. Blocks in which a species was recorded as a Probable breeder are shown as blue rectangles on the maps. Blocks in which a species was recorded as a Confirmed breeder are shown as red rectangles on the maps.

Nesting confirmations for many of the SIS, as well

as for species which have nested in Oklahoma in the past but were not recorded during OBBA project years, have been mapped using colored dots to distinguish these extra records from the standardized survey data shown using colored rectangles. Nesting records outside of atlas blocks from 1997 to 2001 are shown using blue dots; these extra records were included only when they provided significant additional distribution information not evident from the standard atlas survey data. Nesting records from prior to 1997 are shown using pink dots and are referred to in the Historical section of each species account text. These data were mapped for species with limited nesting records in Oklahoma, because seeing information on a map is often more instructive and easier to interpret than simply reading a text description of former nesting locations. The word "Nests" is used in the map legends to define the dots, but in some cases these dots may represent other proof of nesting, such as recently fledged young, rather than an actual observation of a nest. In most cases, these dots were placed on maps manually based on location descriptions that varied in terms of precision.

All maps were produced from data in the OBBA Microsoft Access database using ArcView GIS software (version 3.2) by the Environmental Systems Research Institute.

TEXT

Beyond providing the important distribution information revealed by the maps and resulting from the standardized OBBA surveys, the publication of this book was seen as an opportunity for public education about Oklahoma's birds. While the maps are of primary importance to natural resources personnel and serious birders, it was recognized that many people would benefit greatly from some basic information regarding each breeding species in the state. The information presented in each species account is divided into short sections, making retrieval of specific information, such as clutch size, easy in any and all species accounts. The information is presented from an Oklahoma perspective whenever possible. For example, within the Breeding Habitat sections, only those habitats which occur in Oklahoma are listed. The fact that Virginia Rails also nest in coastal salt marshes is not mentioned because this habitat does not occur in Oklahoma

The first paragraph of each species account provides an interesting fact or two about the species or a summary of its occurrence in the state. The Description section provides a brief description of males and females, songs or calls, and mention of similar-looking species. The Breeding Habitat section summarizes the preferred breeding habitat for the species in Oklahoma, while the Nest section describes the placement and construction of nests by that species in Oklahoma. The Nesting Ecology section gives the range of months during which most nesting activity in Oklahoma takes place for that species (it does not represent the extreme nesting dates), the usual number and color of eggs laid by that species (these may often vary beyond what is described), the incubation and fledging times for each species, and the sex roles for care of eggs and young by adults of each species.

If a species is known to regularly hybridize with another species in Oklahoma, mention of this is made in a Hybridization section not included in all species accounts. The Distribution and Abundance section provides a brief summary of the worldwide range of each species and its migratory status (Rangewide section), its distribution and abundance in Oklahoma as reported in sources published prior to the OBBA (Historical section), and its current distribution as shown on the accompanying OBBA distribution map for that species (Current section). Comparisons of the Historical and Current sections sometimes reveal interesting changes in distribution that have occurred over part or all of the past century. The Population Trend section provides a summary of any information available regarding the population trend of the species in North America and in Oklahoma. Most of this information comes from the Breeding Bird Survey, another volunteer-dependent bird inventory project coordinated by the U.S. Geological Survey. Population trends are described in this section as significant at an alpha level of $P = 0.10$, but the P values are included for readers who wish to use an alternate value in interpreting trends.

The References section provides a list of key references used in preparing the species account, as well as useful sources for the reader to turn to for more information about the species. Special attention was given to sources particularly pertinent to Oklahoma, but broader scale references have been included as well. Several key references are cited in nearly every species account, while other references are specific to one particular species. It is hoped that the reader will find this section helpful in pursuing additional questions regarding a given species.

Just as the OBBA survey data were collected by a number of volunteers, so too were the species accounts prepared primarily by volunteer authors, many of whom also surveyed atlas blocks. Each author was provided with specific instructions on preparing the species accounts, which were later edited for content and for uniformity of presentation by the atlas editor. Any errors in content are attributable to the editor.

PHOTOS

Humans are visually oriented creatures, and for the majority of people color is one of the most significant features of vision. Birds provide color in variety and abundance and are so much a part of our everyday life that one need not be a birder or scientist to notice or appreciate them. Volunteers have come through in this portion of the project as well, with many professional and amateur photographers from several states generously contributing their images. It is with great pleasure that this book is presented to you in full color and includes a photo of each species for your enjoyment, education, and reflection.

THE FUTURE

Breeding bird atlas projects such as the OBBA are most valuable within the context of time. First, as mentioned above, these data represent a "snapshot" of bird distribution during a five-year period. This is useful because most distribution information is accumulated over many decades, is hard to accurately interpret and revise, and is often not current. Bird distributions change constantly, perhaps faster now than ever before due to the wholesale changes to the planet resulting from our ever-growing human population. This carefully collected information straddling the turn of the most recent century will enable measurement and analysis of changes in bird distribution over the coming years. A fundamental precept of atlas projects is that they be repeated at intervals ranging from 10 to 25 years. Revisiting these blocks for the second OBBA in, say, 2012, and using the same standardized methods will enable us to document changes in bird distribution during the intervening years. In some cases these changes are occurring at a pace fast enough to witness and record from year to year, such as the range expansions of Black-bellied Whistling-Duck and Eurasian Collared-Dove that began during the five years of Oklahoma's atlas project. Other changes are slower and less noticeable from one year to the next, but are equally important to document and understand. When the time comes to undertake another breeding bird atlas project in Oklahoma, I hope the current generation of atlasers will have a new generation of people interested in birds to help them. May this book contribute to that endeavor.

Dan L. Reinking

Vegetation of Oklahoma

Bruce W. Hoagland

Oklahoma is a state of diverse vegetation types. The distribution of vegetation in the state is affected by both patterns of climate and local geology. Oklahoma is situated along the boundary of the Temperate Continental and the Subtropical Humid climate types (Trewartha 1968). Weather patterns are influenced by the Rocky Mountains and the Gulf of Mexico. Average annual precipitation decreases with longitude, from 1,303 mm (52 in) in McCurtain County in southeastern Oklahoma to 411 mm (16 in) in Cimarron County (fig. 6). Statewide, average annual precipitation is 848 mm (33 in; Oklahoma Climatological Survey 2002). Droughts tend to occur at 20-year intervals. Major droughts occurred from 1909 to 1918 and from 1950 to 1956 (Johnson and Duchon 1995).

Temperature and growing season decrease latitudinally in Oklahoma (Johnson and Duchon 1995). The statewide average annual temperature is 16°C (61°F).

The lowest mean temperatures occur in Ottawa County (0.39°C [33°F]; Oklahoma Climatological Survey, 2002) and the highest occur in the south-central counties of Jefferson and Carter (4.7°C [41°F]; Oklahoma Climatological Survey 2002). The highest average monthly temperature occurs in July (Oklahoma Climatological Survey 2002).

The local occurrence of vegetation types is a product of geologic substrates and soils. The surface geology of Oklahoma is composed primarily of sandstone formations. Deeply eroded Permian sandstone in Canadian and Caddo counties harbor disjunct populations of sugar maples (*Acer saccharum*) (Little 1939; Rice 1960). The limestone formations of the Arbuckle Mountains produce alkaline, clay soils, which support calciphilic species such as black dalea (*Dalea frutescens*), shortlobe oak (*Quercus breviloba*), and ashe juniper (*Juniperus asheii*). Gypsum deposits of the

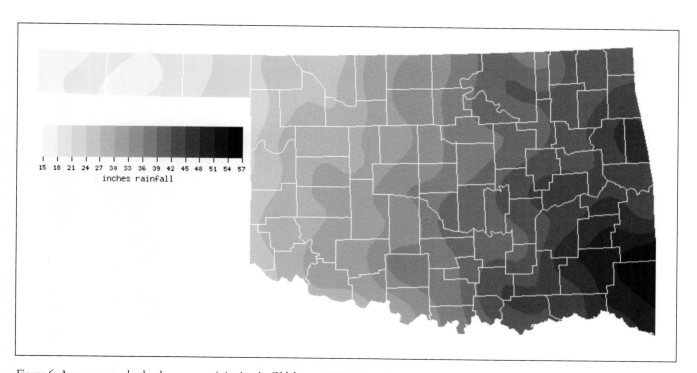

Figure 6. Average annual calendar year precipitation in Oklahoma, 1971–2000. *Map courtesy of Oklahoma Climatological Survey.*

Permian age support salt-tolerant plants such as red-berry juniper (*Juniperus pinchotii* and woolly paper-flower *Psilostrophe villosa*).

Fire is another environmental factor influencing the structure and distribution of vegetation. Fire maintains woodland vegetation, which will become closed canopy forests in the absence of fire. Fire is also a key factor in the maintenance and diversity of grassland communities. Eastern red cedar (*Juniperus virginiana*) is one of several woody plants that will encroach into grasslands following fire suppression (Engle et al. 1997).

The best reference map for Oklahoma vegetation was compiled by Duck and Fletcher and was published by the State of Oklahoma Game and Fish Department in 1943 (fig. 7). Descriptions of the game types were published in Duck and Fletcher (1945). The map serves as a potential vegetation map (i.e., portraying the distribution of vegetation in the state in the absence of human intervention), even though it is titled "A game type map of Oklahoma." There are several fine-scale vegetation associations within each Duck and Fletcher game type. The remainder of this chapter will review each Duck and Fletcher vegetation type, moving from east to west, and list representative vege-

tation associations. The description of vegetation associations follows Hoagland (2000).

BOTTOMLAND FOREST TYPE

This category, as mapped by Duck and Fletcher, extends from eastern to western Oklahoma along major rivers. However, there is a great deal of longitudinal variation of vegetation associations within this type. Common bottomland forest associations in eastern Oklahoma include silver maple (*Acer saccharinum*)–boxelder (*Acer negundo*) and river birch (*Betula nigra*)–sycamore (*Platanus occidentalis*) along the borders of stream channels. In stable floodplain areas, pecan (*Carya illinoensis*)–hackberry (*Celtis laevigata*), blackgum (*Nyssa sylvatica*)–red maple (*Acer rubrum*)–sweetgum (*Liquidambar styraciflua*), pin oak (*Quercus palustris*)–pecan (*Carya illinoensis*), and willow oak (*Quercus phellos*)–water oak (*Q. nigra*) are common vegetation associations. Woody understory species include false indigo (*Amorpha fruticosa*), giant cane (*Arundinaria gigantea*), rattan vine (*Berchemia scandens*), hornbeam (*Carpinus caroliniana*), parsley hawthorn (*Crataegus marshallii*), deciduous holly (*Ilex*

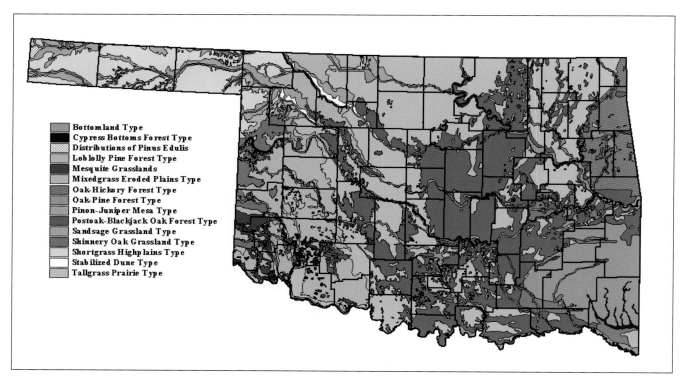

Figure 7. Potential natural vegetation in Oklahoma (based on Duck and Fletcher 1943).

decidua), and spicebush (*Lindera benzoin*). Herbaceous understory species include false nettle (*Boehmeria cylindrica*), various sedge species (*Carex spp.*), and inland sea oats (*Chasmanthium latifolium*).

The number of bottomland forest vegetation associations decreases in central and western Oklahoma (Rice 1965; Hefley 1937). Bottomland forest associations common in central Oklahoma include American and/or red elm (*Ulmus americana, U. rubra*)–hackberry and/or sugarberry (*C. occidentalis*)–green ash (*Fraxinus pennsylvanica*). Associated woody species include bitternut hickory, pecan (*C. illinoensis*), black walnut (*Juglans nigra*), bur oak (*Quercus macrocarpa*), shumard oak (*Q. shumardii*), and soapberry (*Sapindus drummondii*). Herbaceous understory species include green dragon (*Arisaema dracontium*), inland sea oats (*Chasmanthium latifolium*), elephant's foot (*Elephantopus caroliniana*), Virginia wild rye (*Elymus virginicus*), and wood germander (*Teucrium canadense*).

The eastern cottonwood (*Populus deltoides*) forest association is common in central Oklahoma and extends into the Panhandle. Associated woody species include buttonbush (*Cephalanthus occidentalis*), peachleaf (*Salix amygdaloides*), sandbar (*S. exigua*) and black (*S. nigra*) willows. Structurally, this vegetation association varies from closed canopy forests to open canopy woodlands. There has been considerable debate about the historical extent and density of this forest association. Studies along the Arkansas River in Kansas have shown a marked increase in the number of eastern cottonwood trees in the floodplain.

CYPRESS BOTTOMS FOREST TYPE

The cypress bottoms forest type is limited to the Little River drainage in McCurtain County, where it occurs in sloughs, backswamps, and other deepwater habitats (Little 1980). The dominant tree is bald cypress (*Taxodium distichum*) with associated woody plants such as hazel alder (*Alnus serrulata*), buttonbush, nutmeg hickory (*Carya myristiciformis*), water elm (*Planera aquatica*), and American snowbells (*Styrax americana*). Herbaceous associates include numerous floating-leaf and emergent species, including duckweed (*Lemna spp.*), pennywort (*Hydrocotyle umbellata*), and water crowfoot (*Ranunculus longirostris*). The overcup oak (*Quercus lyrata*)–water hickory (*Carya aquatica*) forest association occurs in areas adjacent to baldcypress vegetation but with a shorter period of inundation.

LOBLOLLY PINE FOREST TYPE

The loblolly pine (*Pinus taeda*) forest type is restricted to the Coastal Plain physiographic province of McCurtain County. Given the logging history of the area, there are probably no undisturbed forest remnants remaining. Loblolly pine is planted extensively in pine plantations, many of which are located beyond the historic range of this species.

OAK-PINE AND OAK-HICKORY FOREST TYPE

The oak-pine and oak-hickory forest types occur primarily in the Ouachita Mountains and Ozark Plateau, although oak-pine forest outliers can be found in western McIntosh County. Although these two forest types have distinct differences, there are many similarities as well. For example, the common oak and hickory species in both forests are essentially the same; southern red (*Q. falcata*), white (*Q. alba*), northern red (*Q. rubra*), and black (*Q. velutina*) oaks and shagbark (*C. ovata*), black (*C. texana*), and bitternut (*C. cordiformis*) hickories (Rice and Penfound 1959).

Shortleaf pine (*Pinus echinata*) is the dominant conifer in the oak-pine type. The structure of shortleaf pine forests tend to intergrade with closed canopy, pine-mixed oak stands to open canopy woodlands of predominately shortleaf pine. Fire was a key ecological factor in determining the degree of canopy closure. It was not until the late nineteenth century that the Ouachita shortleaf pine forests were logged at a large scale.

Common forest associations in the oak-pine type include shortleaf pine–white oak in mesic habitats, and shortleaf pine–southern red oak–black oak and shortleaf pine–post oak (*Quercus stellata*)–blackjack oak (*Quercus marilandica*) forest associations on xeric slopes. Associated species include serviceberry (*Amelanchier arborea*), mockernut hickory (*Carya alba*), highbush blueberry (*Vaccinium arboreum*), and lowbush blueberry (*V. pallidum*).

In the oak-hickory forest type, sugar maple–white oak–mockernut hickory and chinquapin oak (*Quercus muehlenbergii*)–sugar maple (*Acer saccharum*) forest associations are common vegetation associations on mesic slopes. Associated woody species include bitternut hickory, shagbark hickory, hackberry, flowering dogwood (*Cornus florida*), green ash, hop hornbeam (*Ostrya virginica*), mockorange (*Philadelphus pubescens*), and bladderpod (*Staphylea trifoliata*). On mesic to xeric slopes the southern red oak–mockernut hickory forest association predominates. Associated species include serviceberry, black hickory, post oak, black oak, and lowbush and highbush blueberry.

POST OAK–BLACKJACK OAK FOREST TYPE

The post oak–blackjack oak forest types is known colloquially as the cross timbers. The region mapped is best characterized as a mosaic of forest, woodland, and tallgrass and mixedgrass prairie vegetation (Hoagland et al. 1999). The cross timbers represent the westernmost extension of the oak-hickory forest association. In cross timbers forests, up to 90 percent of the canopy cover and 50 percent of the basal area are contributed by post oak–blackjack oak.

Both species are slow growing, low in stature, intolerant of shade, and frequently reproduce from root sprouts following disturbance. Black oak and black hickory are species of secondary importance. Other associated species include gum bully (*Bumelia lanuginosa*), redbud (*Cercis canadensis*), roughleaf dogwood (*Cornus drummondii*), mexican plum (*Prunus mexicana*), winged sumac (*Rhus copallina*), smooth sumac (*R. glabra*), buckbrush (*Symphoricarpos orbiculatus*), and blackhaw (*Viburnum rufidulum*). Understory herbaceous species are similar to those species found in adjacent grasslands, including big bluestem (*Andropogon gerardii*), pussytoes (*Antennaria parlinii*) poverty grass (*Danthonia spicata*), hairy sunflower (*Helianthus hirsutus*), trailing lespedeza (*Lespedeza procumbens*), beebalm (*Monarda fistulosa*), little bluestem (*Schizachyrium scoparium*), and purpletop (*Tridens flavus*).

Duck and Fletcher followed the traditional classification of grasslands by recognizing the shortgrass highplains type, the mixedgrass eroded plains type, and the tallgrass prairie type. Big bluestem, little bluestem, Indiangrass (*Sorghastrum nutans*), and switchgrass (*Panicum virgatum*) are the major grass species in Oklahoma and can be found in every county (Harlan 1957). Members of the legume and sunflower families are also abundant in the prairies. Much of Oklahoma grasslands are either hayed or grazed, or have been converted to nonnative species or crop production.

TALLGRASS PRAIRIE TYPE

The tallgrass prairie is the most widely distributed grassland type in Oklahoma. It intergrades with the oak-hickory forests in central and eastern Oklahoma and the mixedgrass prairie to the west. The four grasses listed above are the dominant species. In the absence of fire, or following land abandonment, tallgrass prairie will readily give way to woodland and forest vegetation. In some areas, geology plays a role in limiting the conversion of tallgrass prairie to forest. The bottomland forest species in the tallgrass prairie are similar to those in surrounding vegetation types.

Numerous herbaceous vegetation associations occur in the tallgrass prairie type (Buck and Kelting 1962), the most prevalent of which is the big bluestem–little bluestem–Indiangrass herbaceous association. In northeast Oklahoma, remnants of this vegetation association persist as native hay meadows surrounded by areas converted to fescue pastures. This association is prevalent in the Osage Hills and scattered remnants can be found throughout central and southern Oklahoma. Associated species include lead plant (*Amorpha canescens*), Indian plantain (*Arnoglossum plantagineum*), heath aster (*Aster ericoides*), small panic grass (*Dichanthelium oligosanthes*), pallid coneflower (*Echinacea pallida*), ashy sunflower (*Helianthus mollis*), switchgrass (*Panicum virgatum*), and Missouri goldenrod (*Solidago missouriensis*). In moist to wet habitats, remnants of the prairie cordgrass (*Spartina pectinata*)–spikerush (*Eleocharis spp.*) herbaceous association may persist. Associated species include toothcup (*Ammania coccinea*), field paspalum (*Paspalum laeve*), camphorweed (*Pluchea odorata*), and western ironweed (*Vernonia baldwinii*).

MIXEDGRASS ERODED PLAINS TYPE

Little bluestem–Indiangrass is the predominate vegetation association in the mixedgrass–eroded plains type. Grass species such as dropseeds (*Sporobolus* spp.) and sideoats grama (*Bouteloua curtipendula*) are also important. Native grasses in much of this area, as well as the western extent of the tallgrass prairie, have been converted to wheat production or cotton cultivation in the southwest.

On shallow, rocky soils in the mixedgrass eroded

plains region the hairy grama (*Bouteloua hirsuta*)–sideoats grama herbaceous association is common. Variants of this association can also be found in the tallgrass and shortgrass prairie region. Associated species include rushfoil (*Crotonopsis elliptica*), least daisy (*Chaetopappus asteroides*), lace cactus (*Echinocereus reichenbachii*), bladderpod (*Lesquerella ovalifolia*), gromwell (*Lithospermum tenellum*), plains prickly pear (*Opuntia phaeacantha*), little bluestem, and threadleaf (*Thelesperma filifolia*).

SANDSAGE GRASSLAND, STABILIZED DUNE, SHINNERY OAK GRASSLAND TYPES

The sandsage (*Artemisia filifolia*) grassland, shinnery oak (*Quercus havardii*) grassland, and stabilized dune types can be considered subtypes of the mixedgrass eroded plains type. Each of these four types readily intergrades and are often hard to distinguish. The shinnery oak grassland type is restricted to western Oklahoma. Shinnery oak reproduces asexually by root sprouts and forms mottes that range from 10 to 200 cm (4 to 79 in) in height. The stabilized sand dune type is characterized by sparse vegetation composed of giant sand reed (*Calamovilfa gigantea*), sand bluestem (*Andropogon hallii*), and various shrubs and vines. Silky prairie clover (*Dalea villosa*), spectacle pod (*Dimorphocarpa palmeri*), skunkbrush (*Rhus aromatica*), sand dropseed (*Sporobolus cryptandrus*), little bluestem, bush grape (*Vitis acerifolia*), and soapweed (*Yucca glauca*) are commonly associated species in deep sand habitats.

MESQUITE GRASSLAND TYPE

The mesquite grassland type is most prevalent in western Oklahoma, but extends along the Red River as far east as Jefferson County. The seeds of mesquite are readily transported in the digestive tract of cattle, and isolated populations can be found as far east as Tulsa County. Associated grasses include silver bluestem (*Bothriochloa saccharoides*) and little bluestem. Common associates include western ragweed (*Ambrosia psilostachya*), broomweed (*Amphiachyris dracunculoides*), and plains prickly pear. Soils tend to be sandy or clay loams. Based upon historical records, it is clear that the abundance and extent of mesquite has increased markedly in recent years. Randolph Marcy reported extensive areas of mesquite along the Red River in 1853.

General Land Office surveyors mapped a "mesquite brush prairie" south of the North Fork of the Red River in the 1870s.

SHORTGRASS HIGH-PLAINS TYPE

The shortgrass high-plains type reaches its greatest extent in the Panhandle. Although much of the shortgrass prairie has been converted to wheat and milo production, large areas persist in pastures on shallow soil underlain by caliche. The blue grama (*Bouteloua gracilis*)–buffalograss (*Buchloë dactyloides*) herbaceous association predominates in these habitats. Associated species include western ragweed, vine mesquite (*Panicum obtusum*), tansy aster (*Machaeranthera tanacetifolia*), plains blackfoot (*Melampodium leucanthum*), ring muhly (*Muhlenbergia torreyi*), sand dropseed, and plains zinnia (*Zinnia grandiflora*). Black grama (*Bouteloua eriopoda*) becomes increasingly common in northwestern Cimarron County. On coarse soils, the sideoats grama–hairy grama herbaceous association is common.

Playa lakes are a unique habitat type in the shortgrass high plains. The majority of playas have been altered, either by plowing for wheat or pitting to collect irrigation runoff. The western wheatgrass (*Pascopyrum smithii*)–buffalograss herbaceous association predominates in playa pastures. Wedgeleaf frogfruit (*Phyla cuneifolia*) and beakpod evening primrose (*Oenothera canescens*) are important secondary species. Other associates include bur ragweed (*Ambrosia grayii*), saltgrass (*Distichlis spicata*), snow-on-the-mountain (*Euphorbia marginata*), poverty weed (*Iva axillaris*), and vine mesquite (Hoagland and Collins 1997).

The pinyon pine–juniper mesa type is found in the northwest corner of the Panhandle in the Black Mesa region. The oneseed juniper (*Juniperus monosperma*)–sideoats grama woodland vegetation association predominates in the region. In some areas, oneseed juniper is codominant with pinyon pine (*Pinus edulis*). The habitat for these vegetation associations is talus slopes with rocky and thin soils. Common associates include silver bluestem, hairy, black, and blue grama, mountain mahogany (*Cercocarpus montanus*), cholla (*Opuntia imbricata*), skunkbrush, and soapweed. Many plants common in the western United States reach their easternmost extent in Cimarron County. For example, ponderosa pine is known from only one location in the region (Rogers 1953; Little 1996).

SPECIES ACCOUNTS

Pied-billed Grebe
Podilymbus podiceps

Jerome A. Jackson

Courtesy of Bill Horn

Oklahoma's most common breeding grebe can be found on the quiet waters of streams, ponds, and lakes throughout the state during summer and in ice-free waters in winter. A nocturnal migrant, these grebes are rarely seen in flight, but they are masters of their aquatic environment.

Description: Both males and females are brown above and silvery, silky white below, have a chicken-like bill, and lobed feet set far back on the body. The Pied-billed Grebe is a stocky bird with a small head that blends in with its thick neck to give the partially submerged bird an almost snake-like appearance. During the breeding season, adults have a black throat and a black band around the bill; in winter both the bill band and black throat are absent. Vocalizations include a spectacular and easily recognized performance that begins with low *wup* notes followed by a series of *kow* notes that are at first soft and slow, increasing in volume and tempo, and sometimes ending with an alternating series of drawn-out *kowooo* notes and "gulping" *gow* notes.

Breeding Habitat: Nests on quiet waters that are deep enough for a diving escape, that do not fluctuate drastically in water level, and that have patches of emergent vegetation.

Nest: A platform of decaying vegetation brought up from the bottom; may be floating and attached to emergent vegetation or may be built up from the bottom. The incubating adult typically covers the eggs with vegetation as it leaves the nest.

NESTING ECOLOGY

Season: May–July. Single-brooded, but will renest if first clutch is lost.

Eggs: Usually 4–8; chalky bluish white, later becoming stained brown and polished.

Development: Incubation is by both sexes for 23–27 days. Young are precocial and are provisioned by both sexes through independence at 28–68 days.

DISTRIBUTION AND ABUNDANCE

Rangewide: Breeds from northern Canada through the West Indies and Americas to southern South America.

Historical: Described as a rare summer resident, more common in migration and winter.

Current: The Pied-billed Grebe's probable presence as a breeding bird throughout the state in wetlands with emergent vegetation is barely suggested by the low proportion of blocks in which it was recorded. Its habitats and secretive nature add to the difficulty in documenting its presence. Some Probable Breeder blocks could be the result of birds seen during migration. Confirmation of breeding in western counties almost certainly represents an expansion of the species' range as a result of creation of reservoirs and farm ponds.

Population Trend: Breeding Bird Survey data for 1966–2000 show an increase of 2.1 percent per year rangewide for North America ($P = 0.05$). No trend data are available for Oklahoma. Creation of ponds and impoundments in western Oklahoma have probably resulted in population increases; destruction of wetlands in eastern Oklahoma may have resulted in losses.

References: Baumgartner and Baumgartner 1992; Harden 1977; Jackson 2001; Martin and Storer 1999; Messerly 1984; Sauer et al. 2001; Seibert 1991; Shackford 1981; Sutton 1967

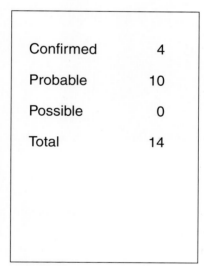

Confirmed	4
Probable	10
Possible	0
Total	14

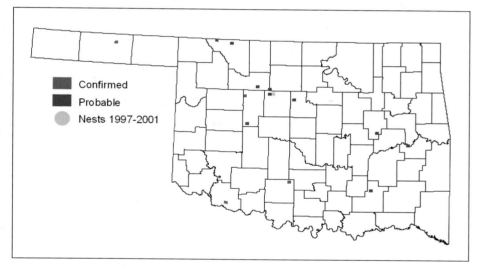

- ■ Confirmed
- ▨ Probable
- ● Nests 1997-2001

Eared Grebe

Podiceps nigricollis

John S. Shackford

The Eared Grebe in breeding plumage is striking, easy to identify, and so radically different from its nonbreeding plumage that one might wonder if the two plumages are different species. Remarkable aspects of its biology include a postbreeding migration of most of the population to hypersaline Mono Lake, California, or Great Salt Lake, Utah, to consume brine shrimp and alkali flies. While there, flight muscles atrophy and digestive organs increase to an extreme extent. By December or January, this process is reversed and birds fly nonstop to wintering areas. Similar cycles occur three to six times per year, rendering this species flightless for up to nine to ten months per year. Only recently found to nest in Oklahoma, it is at the margin of its breeding range here.

Description: Sexes similar. In breeding plumage, adults are black on upperparts, with bright rusty flanks on the breast. On the head, fans of yellowish feathers spread out from behind bright red eyes. In nonbreeding plumage, the top of the head and back are black, while the cheeks are whitish and the neck is, usually, dusky gray. The very similar winter-plumaged Horned Grebe tends to be whitish on the front of the neck and upper breast. Its song is rendered as *ooEEK* or *ooEEKa*, along with some chittering.

Breeding Habitat: Shallows of marshy lakes and ponds with emergent vegetation and lots of macroinvertebrates.

Nest: Constructed of floating, decaying debris such as cattails or reeds. Built on bent-over reeds or anchored to emergent or submergent vegetation. Nests are sometimes built singly, but are usually placed in dense colonies.

NESTING ECOLOGY

Season: May–August rangewide, but Oklahoma records are from June. Single-brooded.
Eggs: Usually 2–4 but highly variable; dull bluish or greenish white.
Development: Incubation is by both sexes for 20–22 days. Young are semiprecocial but are fed by both parents for a week and spend this time on the backs of adults. Young reach independence at about 20 days.

DISTRIBUTION AND ABUNDANCE

Rangewide: Breeds from south-central British Columbia eastward to south-central Manitoba in Canada southward to northwestern New Mexico and westward to central California. Winters from the southwestern United States southward to northern Central America. Also occurs in parts of the Old World.

Historical: Until recently considered a transient statewide. Not known to nest in Oklahoma prior to 1984. Two breeding records in recent years include young seen in Kingfisher County in 1984 and three nests found in Cimarron County in 1987.

Current: Due to its rarity, the Eared Grebe is poorly sampled by atlas methodology. The species is, at most, a very rare nester; most sightings during the breeding season are likely of nonbreeding or (still) migrating birds. To be looked for primarily in the western half of Oklahoma, but increasingly likely to be encountered as one proceeds westward in the state and through the Panhandle.

Population Trend: Breeding Bird Survey data for 1966–2000 show an increase of 6.9 percent per year rangewide ($P = 0.01$). No trend data are available for Oklahoma.

References: American Ornithologists' Union (AOU) 1998; Baicich and Harrison 1997; Baumgartner and Baumgartner 1992; Bent 1968; Cullen et al. 1999; Dechant, Johnson et al. 2002; Johnsgard 1979; Ratzlaff 1986; Sauer et al. 2001; Shackford 1988; Sutton 1967; Terres 1980

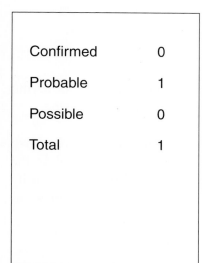

Confirmed	0
Probable	1
Possible	0
Total	1

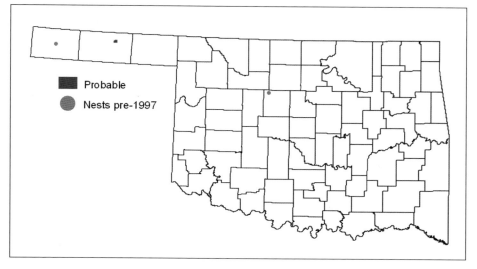

Probable
Nests pre-1997

Neotropic Cormorant
Phalacrocorax brasilianus

Dan L. Reinking

Courtesy of Jim and Deva Burns / Natural Impacts

Formerly known as the Olivaceous Cormorant, the Neotropic Cormorant was once considered a somewhat rare visitor to Oklahoma but was discovered nesting here during the atlas project. It is the only cormorant to use plunge-diving as a foraging method, although it more commonly uses the traditional cormorant foraging method of pursuing underwater prey by diving from the surface.

Description: Sexes similar. A small cormorant with a long tail and a small yellow throat patch with a white border. Usually silent, but may give a variety of frog-like noises near the nest.

Breeding Habitat: Lakes and reservoirs with water deep enough for diving, adequate perches for drying waterlogged plumage, and small trees for nesting.

Nest: A platform of sticks placed in the fork of tree limbs and lined with twigs, leaves, or grass. Built by the female from materials brought by the male. Usually placed 1–6 m (3–20 ft) above the ground or water surface.

NESTING ECOLOGY

Season: Primarily April–July, but may be earlier or later. Single-brooded, but will replace lost clutches.
Eggs: Usually 3–4; sky blue with chalky white markings and nest stains.

Development: Incubation is probably by both sexes and lasts about 25 days. Young are provisioned by both sexes, begin swimming and diving at 8 weeks, and are fed by adults for another 3 weeks.

DISTRIBUTION AND ABUNDANCE

Rangewide: Breeds in east Texas, Louisiana, and locally in New Mexico. Also breeds in Mexico, Central America, and South America. Postbreeding dispersal often brings birds much farther north.

Historical: First recorded in Oklahoma in 1950, it was considered a summer and fall visitant by 1967. No nest records prior to the atlas project.

Current: Not recorded in any atlas blocks, but an adult carrying a stick was seen at Ward Lake in southeastern McCurtain County in 2000, and two occupied nests were observed at the same location in 2001. These records represent the first nesting of this species known for Oklahoma. The large mixed-species rookery at Ward Lake was abandoned in 2002.

Population Trend: After population declines in the 1960s, this species has increased its population size and expanded its range inland over the past 30 years.

References: Baumgartner and Baumgartner 1992; Johnsgard 1993; National Geographic Society 1999; Newell and Sutton 1982; Sutton 1967; Telfair and Morrison 1995

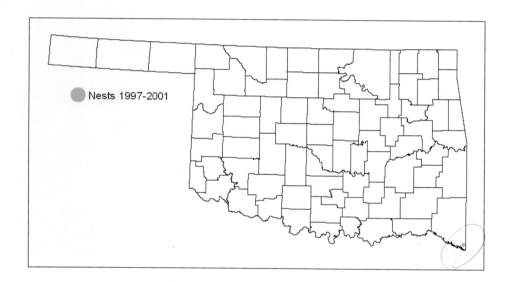

Nests 1997-2001

Double-crested Cormorant
Phalacrocorax auritus

David E. Fantina

Courtesy of Gerald Wiens

Unlike most cormorants, which are strictly coastal and are seldom found on inland waters, the Double-crested Cormorant has found a home on the man-made lakes of Oklahoma. They are a recent addition to the summer landscape, and their fish diet often places them at odds with people who fish, although the bulk of the fish consumed by Double-crested Cormorants are not sport species.

Description: Adults are large, dark, heavy-bodied birds with orange throat patches. Despite their name the crests are a very poor field mark as they are rarely visible except at close range. Young birds are browner and have a contrasting pale breast. Cormorants are often seen flying low over the water or perched on piles of dead trees at the water's edge. They sometimes fly high in a V formation. The much rarer Neotropic Cormorant is smaller and has a longer tail.

Breeding Habitat: This species nests colonially (sometimes in large heron colonies) in trees or on the ground near lakes, rivers, and swamps.

Nest: The male builds the foundation of twigs and other coarse material. The female finishes the construction and lines the nest with finer materials.

NESTING ECOLOGY

Season: April–July. Single-brooded.

Eggs: Usually 3–4; chalky pale blue.

Development: Incubation is by both sexes for 25–28 days. Young are provisioned by both sexes, are capable of flight at about 6 weeks, and can dive before they can fly.

DISTRIBUTION AND ABUNDANCE

Rangewide: The Double-crested Cormorant breeds wherever there is appropriate habitat from Alaska and Newfoundland south to Mexico and Florida. Because of its reliance on large water bodies it is somewhat locally distributed throughout its vast range. It winters as far north as it can find open water.

Historical: Until the 1940s, Double-crested Cormorants were known in Oklahoma only as migrants. However, from 1945 to 1950 a small colony nested at the Salt Plains National Wildlife Refuge. Since then it has been found nesting at Kerr Lake in Haskell County in the 1970s, and again at Salt Plains, and was reported to be a rare and local summer resident and an uncommon to abundant migrant in 1992.

Current: The highly visible Double-crested Cormorant often can be easily seen perched on piers or flying low over the water. Therefore, it is not surprising that it was readily observed on lakes and rivers in several blocks throughout the eastern two-thirds of the state. However, the only breeding activity noted was on Lake Eufala in Pittsburgh County and at Salt Plains NWR. Records scored as Observed are mapped to provide a better picture of cormorant distribution in the state.

Population Trend: Breeding Bird Survey data for 1966–2000 show an increase of 10.1 percent per year rangewide (P = 0.00). Low densities and local occurrence in Oklahoma do not allow trend estimation.

References: AOU 1998; Baicich and Harrison 1997; Baumgartner and Baumgartner 1992; Campo et al. 1993; Custer and Bunck 1992; Dolbeer 1991; Esler 1992; Haller 1973; Hatch and Weseloh 1999; Johnsgard 1993; Koenen et al. 1996; Norton 1973; Sauer et al. 2001; Sutton 1967

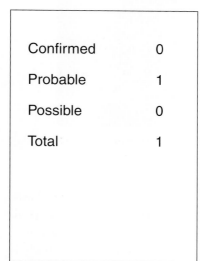

Confirmed	0
Probable	1
Possible	0
Total	1

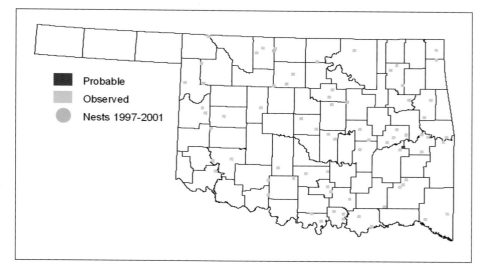

Probable
Observed
Nests 1997-2001

Anhinga
Anhinga anhinga

Bonnie L. Gall

This unique bird appears to be a cross between a wading bird like the heron and a diver like the cormorant or grebe. The Anhinga's numerous nicknames include *snakebird* for its long, thin neck that sticks out of swampy water as it pursues its favorite prey; *black darter* for its color and way of moving; and *water turkey* for its resemblance to a slender wild turkey. The Anhinga is not a common Oklahoma bird and breeding has depended on the existence of suitable habitat—remote, swampy areas in the southeastern part of the state. Protection of these areas is critical if we wish to continue to find breeding Anhingas in our state.

Description: Male is black with greenish tone above and silver spots and streaks on wings and upper back. Female has buffy neck. Immature is browner overall. Other recognizable features include a long sharp bill, heron-like neck, and fan-shaped tail. In water, body is completely submerged and only the thin snake-like neck and head are visible. Frequently sits on branches with wings extended to dry waterlogged feathers. Cormorants most closely resemble the Anhinga but have heavier bodies and bills.

Breeding Habitat: This colonial nester prefers sheltered, quiet waters in swamps, sloughs, marshy lakes, and river backwaters.

Nest: Constructed of twigs and sticks and lined with

leaves or twigs with attached leaves. Usually nests in clusters of 8–12 pairs in bald cypress, willows, or buttonbush, 1.5–6 m (5–20 ft) above water. May reuse nest from year to year or use nests of other waders. Will associate with other colony nesters such as herons, ibises, and cormorants.

NESTING ECOLOGY

Season: The few records in Oklahoma include active nests in April through June, and young in nests during August. Single-brooded.

Eggs: Usually 3–5. The pale bluish-green shell initially has a chalky coating but becomes glossy and nest stained during incubation.

Development: Incubation is by both sexes for 25–28 days beginning before clutch is complete. Young in nest often differ widely in size. Young are provisioned by both sexes, begin to leave the nest for nearby branches at 3 weeks, and begin flying at 6 weeks.

DISTRIBUTION AND ABUNDANCE

Rangewide: Breeding range includes tropical and subtropical regions of North and South America. In the United States, the northern ranges include central Texas, southeastern Oklahoma, eastern Arkansas, central Alabama, and southern North Carolina. Has nested north of this range and may wander farther west and north during other seasons.

Historical: Rare and irregular in eastern and central Oklahoma from April to November. The small number of breeding records in Oklahoma include 1937 in McCurtain County, 1971–1972 at Sequoyah National Wildlife Refuge in Sequoyah County, and at McCurtain County's Little River National Wildlife Refuge in 1991–1993.

Current: The Anhinga is a very rare and local nester in Oklahoma. During the atlas project, nesting activity was not recorded in any atlas block, but was confirmed in McCurtain County in 1997, 1998, and 2001 outside of atlas blocks.

Population Trend: Breeding Bird Survey data for 1966–2000 do not show a conclusive population trend rangewide (0.8 percent per year, P = 0.79). This species' currently small population in Oklahoma, while at the northwestern margin of the breeding range, may well become established provided that proper habitat is maintained.

References: Allen 1961; Baumgartner and Baumgartner 1941; Baumgartner and Baumgartner 1992; Bent 1964c; Frederick and Siegel-Causey 2000; Harrison 1975; Heck 1991, 1994; Johnsgard 1979; National Geographic Society 1999; Nice 1938; Norton 1973; Sauer et al. 2001; Sutton 1967; Wood and Schnell 1984

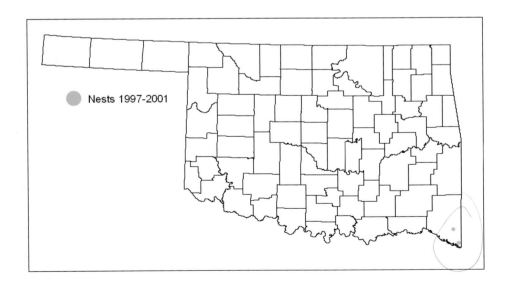

Nests 1997-2001

American Bittern
Botaurus lentiginosus

Richard A. Stuart

Courtesy of Colin Smith

A master of camouflage, the American Bittern can easily be overlooked in the marshy haunts it calls home. It is best detected by voice. When disturbed, it stands erect with head pointed upward, its plumage markings blending very well into the surrounding vegetation of cattails, reeds, rushes, or grass.

Description: The sexes are alike, being heavy-bodied wading birds with relatively long necks tapering to pointed greenish-yellow bills. The upperparts are brownish, and the long neck is boldly marked with longitudinal brown streaks on the underside. In flight, the wings show dark primaries and secondaries, with paler coverts; flight is low and direct. The song is a deep, gulping, pounding, or pumping *BLOONK-Adoonk* or *OONK-A-lunk*. When flushed, a rapid, deep *kok kok kok* is given, and in flight a loud hoarse squawk may be emitted. The American Bittern can be distinguished from night-herons by its longer, more tapered bill, more tapered and broadly streaked neck, and its habits.

Breeding Habitat: American Bitterns are normally found in cattail marshes, weedy lake shores, moist prairies, or other wet areas with tall, emergent vegetation.

Nest: A flimsy platform about 14 inches in diameter made from nearby plant material placed on dry ground or on a mound a few inches above water or mud.

NESTING ECOLOGY

Season: May–August. Single-brooded.
Eggs: 2–7; unmarked brownish buff to olive buff.
Development: Incubation is by the female for 24–28 days. Young are provisioned by the female, leave nest at about 2 weeks, but remain near the nest until they fledge; age at fledging is unknown.

DISTRIBUTION AND ABUNDANCE

Rangewide: Breeds across most of the United States and southern Canada south to the lower one-third of U.S. states. Northern populations move south for winter. Also breeds throughout Mexico and much of Central America.
Historical: Considered a transient, rare winter resident, and local breeder in 1931. Considered a local and irregular breeder throughout the state in 1967, with nest records from Grady, Harper, Oklahoma, Tulsa, Wagoner, Woods, and probably Beaver counties. Midsummer records have been reported from Alfalfa, Bryan, Cleveland, Creek, LeFlore, Love, and Payne counties, again indicating widespread if irregular and local occurrence.
Current: Nesting was confirmed at Red Slough Wildlife Management Area in McCurtain County in 2002, but not during the five years of atlas project surveys. Several records of birds observed in blocks have been mapped.

Population Trend: Breeding Bird Survey data for 1966–2000 does not provide a conclusive population trend rangewide (-1.2 percent per year, P = 0.19) The population is not well measured in Oklahoma.

References: AOU 1998; Baicich and Harrison 1997; Baumgartner and Baumgartner 1992; Dechant, Sondreal, Johnson, Igl, Goldade, Zimmerman, and Euliss 2001; Gibbs et al. 1992; Harrison 1975; Lewis 1930; National Geographic Society 1999; Nice 1931; Sauer et al. 2001; Sibley 2000; Stokes and Stokes 1996; Sutton 1967

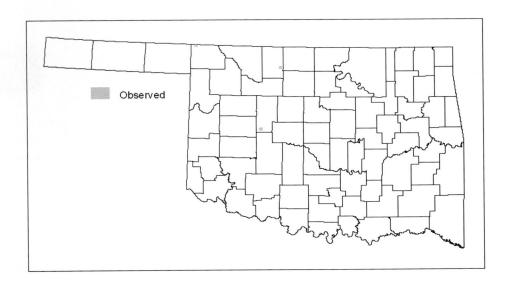

Observed

Least Bittern
Ixobrychus exilis

Nathan R. Kuhnert

Courtesy of Warren Williams

The Least Bittern, the smallest member of the heron family, is seldom seen due to its uncommon to rare status, its shy behavior, and the difficulty of accessing and navigating through its breeding habitat comprised of tall, dense, emergent vegetation. Like the American Bittern, it too will freeze and point its bill up with feathers compressed and eyes directed forward when spotted. It can also gracefully slip away undetected by walking or climbing through reeds. These traits make it all the more exciting when it is discovered by hearing the soft series of *ku* notes given only on the breeding grounds.

Description: When flushed, it barely flutters above the vegetation with its legs dangling behind before quickly dropping back down in the marsh. The dark primaries contrasting with its buff and chestnut wing patches are diagnostic, and when coupled with the light, faintly streaked underparts, identification confusion should be eliminated with the larger and bulkier Green Heron. Although sexes are similar in size, the back of the male is black and that of the female is browner. The most familiar vocalization is the dove-like or cuckoo-like cooing given by the males on the breeding ground. This song usually consists of three or four soft *ku*s at infrequent intervals.

Breeding Habitat: Both freshwater and brackish marshes with emergent, dense, and tall growths of aquatic or semiaquatic vegetation several feet in height.

The ratio of emergent vegetative cover to open water is usually equal. Cattails seem to be one of the most common species of emergent vegetation associated with Least Bittern breeding habitat, especially in Oklahoma. Stable water level also seems to be a component in habitat selection. A nesting colony was monitored in central Oklahoma from 1994 to 1997. The birds primarily nested in large patches of emergent willows before using the cattails, which replaced the willows in just a few years.

Nest: Usually a platform constructed by the male and comprised of both live and dead stalks of vegetation that are bent down or where a natural base already exists. Short stems and sticks are added on top in a spoke-like manner. The nest is usually 15–61 cm (6–24 in) above the water and near the edge of the vegetation. Semicolonial nesting occurs in the Least Bittern under certain circumstances, especially in highly productive habitat. One small colony discovered in 1994 contained up to 4 bittern territories in an approximately 4-ha (10-ac) oxbow lake off of the Canadian River, which was created by a significant flood from the previous year.

NESTING ECOLOGY

Season: May–August. Occasionally double-brooded.
Eggs: Usually 4–5; pale blue, blue white, or green.
Development: Incubation is by both sexes for 17–20 days. Young are provisioned by both sexes and leave the nest after about 13–15 days, but may continue to be fed by adults for up to 30 days.

DISTRIBUTION AND ABUNDANCE

Rangewide: Breeds across much of the eastern United States and parts of the west. Winters in south Florida and Texas south to Central America.
Historical: Described as a rare and local summer resident west to Woodward and Tillman counties. Has nested as far west as Comanche County. Largest numbers of nest records are from Alfalfa and Bryan counties.
Current: The apparent absence of this species within atlas blocks is partially the result of the Least Bittern being overlooked due to its secretive behavior and the inaccessibility of its breeding habitat. In southeastern Oklahoma, the recently established Red Slough Wildlife Management Area in McCurtain County represents one of the strongholds for this species, as up to 16 individuals and fledglings were reported in 2001. Additional nesting reports include up to 4 pairs in McClain County between 1994 and 1997.

Population Trend: Breeding Bird Survey data for 1966–2000 show no conclusive trend rangewide (-1.2 percent per year, P = 0.59) but this survey does not measure this species effectively. No trend data are available for Oklahoma.

References: AOU 1998; Baicich and Harrison 1997; Baumgartner and Baumgartner 1992; Bent 1926; Giffs et al. 1992; Kuhnert, N. R. pers. observ.; Kushlan 1973; Sibley 2000; Sutton 1936, 1967; Terres 1991; Tyler 1994d; Weller 1961

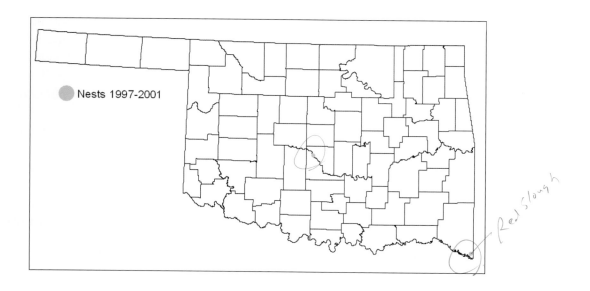

Nests 1997-2001

Great Blue Heron
Ardea herodias

Eugene A. Young

Courtesy of Warren Williams

The largest heron in Oklahoma, the Great Blue, is known for its usually solitary behavior except during the breeding season when it can be found in large colonies. These colonies are frequently associated with other species of herons and are used year after year. Like most herons, the Great Blue can be found feeding in shallow aquatic areas of streams, rivers, marshes, wetlands, and farm ponds, and can even occasionally be observed feeding on invertebrates and small vertebrates in upland prairie away from water. It is sometimes referred to as Blue Crane by locals.

Description: Sexes are similar, being long legged and having a large straight bill, blue-gray wings and body, long neck that is usually a paler gray to white mottled with brown, a distinct black mark extending behind the eye, and a black-and-white-striped cap that may be solid in juveniles. In flight this species can be told from the similarly colored Sandhill Crane by its habit of flying with its head and neck arched back in an S-shaped position typical of herons. It has a slow, steady wingbeat with downward arching wings. Commonly gives a deep *fraaaaahnk* or *braak* call when taking to flight.

Breeding Habitat: Rookeries are usually in isolated areas of tall trees that have many vertical branches. Typically located along streams and rivers in riparian woodlands, towns, swamps, and even islands associated with large lakes.

Nest: A platform of sticks and twigs occasionally lined with leaves and grasses, 0.5–1.2 m (1.6–4 ft) in diameter, usually located in trees up to 30 m (98 ft) or more above ground; sometimes in shrubs or bushes, usually in colonies, rarely as a single isolated nest. Built by the female from materials brought by the male.

NESTING ECOLOGY

Season: March–July. Single-brooded, but may replace lost clutches.
Eggs: Usually 3–5; pale bluish green to pale olive.
Development: Incubation is by both sexes for 27–28 days. Young are provisioned by both sexes and fledge in 50–80 days, but will continue to be fed for an additional 2–3 weeks.

DISTRIBUTION AND ABUNDANCE

Rangewide: Breeds from southeast Alaska and coastal British Columbia east through Nova Scotia and throughout most of the United States. Winters throughout the United States (except in the Rocky Mountains and the southwestern desert region), south to Central America and Venezuela.
Historical: Described as a locally nesting resident throughout Oklahoma.

Current: Although the Great Blue Heron has a statewide distribution, there is a low number of records of Confirmed and Probable breeders due to the localized, clumped distribution of nesting colonies. During the nesting season Great Blues travel great distances from the nesting colony to obtain adequate food for their young. As with most wetland species, there are fewer records in the Panhandle's more arid environment. Records in the Observed category have been mapped to better illustrate the distribution of this species.

Population Trend: Breeding Bird Survey data for 1966–2000 show an increase of 2.4 percent per year rangewide (P = 0.00) and a similar increase in Oklahoma (2.7 percent per year, P = 0.07).

References: AOU 1998; Baicich and Harrison 1997; Baumgartner and Baumgartner 1992; Bent 1926; Butler 1992; Heck 1994; Lish 1974; Mock 1976; Pratt 1970; Pulich 1988; Robbins and Easterla 1992; Sauer et al. 2001; Sibley 2000; Stephens 1980; Stokes and Stokes 1989; Terres 1991; Tveten 1993; Tyler 1994b; Zimmerman 1979

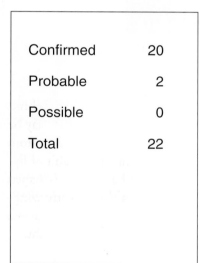

Confirmed	20
Probable	2
Possible	0
Total	22

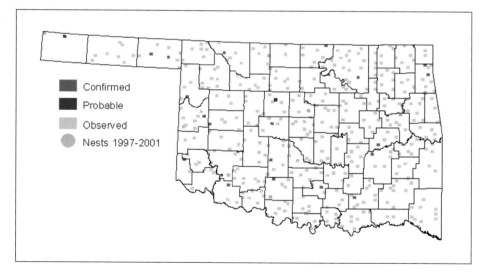

Great Egret
Ardea alba

David E. Fantina

Courtesy of Bill Horn

Like the Snowy Egret, the Great Egret was once nearly exterminated by hunters because of its plumes. The existence of this beautiful species is due mainly to the efforts of the National Audubon Society and other conservation groups that fought for an end to the plume trade in the early twentieth century. Now it is once again a locally common summer resident around large lakes and rivers in the eastern part of the state.

Description: The Great Egret is a very large all-white heron with a yellow bill and black legs. The similar Snowy Egret is much smaller and has conspicuous yellow feet and a black bill.

Breeding Habitat: This species usually nests in large mixed-species colonies in mature woodlands near bodies of water. It often nests in wooded swamps or on islands in reservoirs.

Nest: A large stick platform, built singly or in colonies. In mixed-species heronries, the Great Egret often builds higher in trees than the other species.

NESTING ECOLOGY

Season: April–June. Single-brooded, but may replace lost clutches.
Eggs: Usually 3, but variable; pale greenish blue.
Development: Incubation is by both sexes for 23–26 days. Young are provisioned by both sexes, are able to

fly short distances in about 5 weeks, and reach independence at about 9 weeks.

DISTRIBUTION AND ABUNDANCE

Rangewide: Breeds locally from southern Canada throughout the United States south to South America and also in Europe and Asia. It withdraws from the northern part of its range in winter. In late summer Great Egrets (and many other herons) wander far north of their breeding area.

Historical: The Great Egret was considered common around large lakes and rivers in eastern Oklahoma in the middle of the nineteenth century but became rare for many years due to excessive hunting. By the 1940s their numbers had started to recover significantly. Fifty nests were counted at Salt Plains National Wildlife Refuge in 1995.

Current: The Great Egret's reliance on aquatic habitats explains its widespread occurrence in the eastern part of the state and its complete absence from the Panhandle. The only two confirmed breeding records from atlas blocks were both associated with large lakes; Grand Lake O' the Cherokees in Delaware County and Altus Lake in Kiowa County. The high proportion of blocks scored as Observed is probably due to the fact that this bird is easily seen foraging in open habitats, often far from its breeding colony. These observations are mapped to better illustrate the distribution of Great Egrets in the state.

Population Trend: Breeding Bird Survey data for 1966–2000 show an increase of 2.2 percent per year rangewide (P = 0.02), but no conclusive trend in Oklahoma (3.8 percent per year, P = 0.23).

References: AOU 1998; Baicich and Harrison 1997; Baumgartner and Baumgartner 1992; Bent 1963c; Custer et al. 1992; Grover 1978; James and Neal 1986; Koenen et al. 1996; Mock 1978; Nice 1931; Sallee 1982; Sauer et al. 2001; Stancill et al. 1988; Sutton 1967; Winton and Leslie 1999

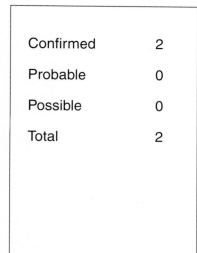

Confirmed	2
Probable	0
Possible	0
Total	2

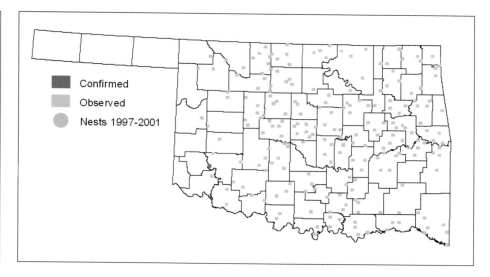

Snowy Egret
Egretta thula

David E. Fantina

Courtesy of Bill Horn

The beautiful Snowy Egret was once hunted nearly to the brink of extinction because of its plumes. These plumes, which were used to adorn women's hats, were twice as valuable as gold in the late nineteenth century. Thanks to laws enacted to protect it, this species has now recovered and has even extended its range beyond its historical boundaries.

Description: Both males and females are, as the name implies, snow-white, medium-sized herons with slender black bills, black legs, and yellow feet. In the height of the breeding season the feet turn orange. This species could be confused with the immature Little Blue Heron, which lacks the black legs and bill. The Great Egret is much larger and has a yellow bill.

Breeding Habitat: This species nests colonially (at times in huge mixed-species heronries) in trees near freshwater swamps, rivers, and inland lakes.

Nest: A shallow, flat platform of twigs generally 2–3 m (5–10 ft) high in trees but sometimes as high as 10 m (30 ft).

NESTING ECOLOGY

Season: May–June. Single-brooded, but may replace lost clutches.

Eggs: Usually 3–5; greenish blue.

Development: Incubation is by both sexes for about 23 days. Young are provisioned by both sexes and leave the nest after several weeks.

DISTRIBUTION AND ABUNDANCE

Rangewide: Disjunct breeding range includes parts of the Gulf Coast and along rivers north to Kansas and Missouri, parts of the Great Basin, and scattered locations throughout the Great Plains and the Southwest. Although many Snowy Egrets winter in the Gulf states, birds breeding in Oklahoma apparently spend the winter in Mexico and Central America. After breeding, some individuals disperse north as far as 340 km (220 mi) during the late summer. Also breeds in Mexico south to South America.

Historical: Described in 1931 as a formerly abundant summer visitant, now rare. Very rare between about 1900 and 1930 due to excessive hunting nationwide from 1880 to 1910. By the 1940s it had increased noticeably. It was first found breeding in the state in Oklahoma County in 1951 and eventually became fairly common in appropriate habitat in the eastern and central portions of the state.

Current: Like the larger Great Egret, the conspicuous Snowy Egret was readily observed in scattered wetland habitats throughout the eastern two-thirds of Oklahoma. The fact that no breeding activity was observed in blocks may be due to its localized breeding in inaccessible wet areas. It was reported with less frequency in the more arid western part of the state and was absent from the Panhandle. All reports coming from atlas blocks were scored as Observed, and these are mapped to better illustrate the distribution of Snowy Egrets in the state.

Population Trend: Breeding Bird Survey data for 1966–2000 show an increase of 3.8 percent per year rangewide (P = 0.00), but show no conclusive trend in Oklahoma (-1.0 percent per year, P = 0.84).

References: AOU 1998; Baicich and Harrison 1997; Baumgartner and Baumgartner 1992; Bent 1963c; Custer et al. 1992; Grover 1978; Hughes 1952; James and Neal 1986; Koenen et al. 1996; Parsons and Master 2000; Roberts 1971; Sallee 1982; Sauer et al. 2001; Sutton 1967; Winton and Leslie 1999

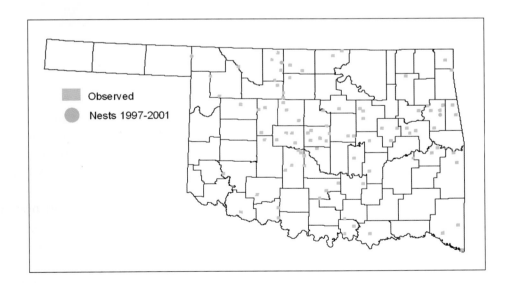

Observed
Nests 1997-2001

Little Blue Heron

Egretta caerulea

David E. Fantina

The Little Blue Heron is the only heron that exhibits distinct, age-related color morphs, with first-year birds being white and adults slate blue. Because of its lack of extensive breeding plumes, it was not hunted to nearly the same extent as many other herons during the late nineteenth and early twentieth centuries. Even today it can be overlooked because of its dark adult plumage and secretive nature.

Description: The adult Little Blue Heron is a medium-sized, slate-blue heron. During the height of the breeding season, its head and neck become reddish purple. The immature is snow white and can be confused with the similar-sized Snowy Egret. However, the immature Little Blue Heron has a gray-based bill, dull gray lores, and more extensively yellow-green legs. Birds molting from immature to adult plumage have a curious, pied appearance.

Breeding Habitat: Nests colonially (sometimes on the outskirts of mixed heronries) in mature woods near bodies of water. It prefers bottomlands, lake and pond edges, marshes, and forested wetland sites.

Nest: A flat structure made of twigs and finer materials (often reeds or grasses) generally 2–5 m (8–15 ft) high in trees or shrubs.

NESTING ECOLOGY

Season: April–July. Single-brooded.
Eggs: Usually 3–5; pale greenish blue.
Development: Incubation is by both sexes for 22–23 days. Young are provisioned by both sexes and are capable of sustained flight at about 35 days.

DISTRIBUTION AND ABUNDANCE

Rangewide: Breeds along the Atlantic Coast from southern Maine to Florida, along the Gulf Coast, and locally in the interior north to Kansas, Indiana, and Illinois. Also breeds in California, Mexico, and the West Indies. Some Little Blue Herons winter in the southeastern United States, but birds banded in Oklahoma as fledglings are consistently found from Mexico to South America in winter. Like many herons, juveniles disperse considerably to the north of the breeding areas in late summer.

Historical: Described in 1931 as a summer visitant. It was first found breeding in the state in Oklahoma County in 1951. By 1992 it was considered locally common in eastern and central regions, decreasing westward. The impoundment of rivers in the early part of the twentieth century created nesting areas for this species and many other herons. More recently, the arrival of Cattle Egrets in Oklahoma may be reducing the population of Little Blue Herons, because Cattle Egrets are more aggressive and can out-compete them for nesting sites.

Current: The Little Blue Heron's habitat requirements and breeding distribution in the state are similar to those of several other herons. It was often observed in wet locations throughout the eastern half of the state and was absent from the more arid northwest and the Panhandle. Breeding was only confirmed within two atlas blocks, plus several locations outside of atlas blocks. Additional records scored as Observed are mapped to better illustrate the distribution of this species in the state.

Population Trend: Breeding Bird Survey data for 1966–2000 show a decline of 3.0 percent per year rangewide (P = 0.04), but show no conclusive trend in Oklahoma (-1.4 percent per year, P = 0.33). In several recent studies in Oklahoma it was outnumbered by Cattle Egrets by more than 20 to 1.

References: AOU 1998; Baicich and Harrison 1997; Baumgartner and Baumgartner 1992; Bent 1963c; Burger 1978; Carl 1982; Dusi 1968; Grover 1978; Hanebrink 1968; Heitmeyer 1986; Hellack 1974; Hughes 1952; James and Neal 1986; Koenen et al. 1996; Nice 1931; Rodgers and Smith 1995; Sallee 1982; Sauer et al. 2001; Stancill et al. 1988; Sutton 1967; Tomer 1955; Winton and Leslie 1999

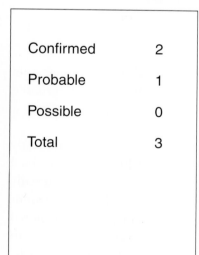

Confirmed	2
Probable	1
Possible	0
Total	3

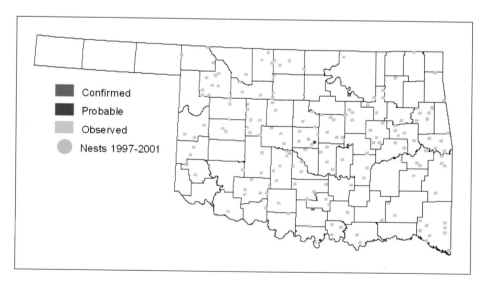

Tricolored Heron
Egretta tricolor

John M. Dole

Courtesy of Warren Williams

The strikingly colored Tricolored Heron is an exciting bird to see in Oklahoma. This heron is rare but regular in a few select locations in north-central and southeastern Oklahoma, and also wanders farther north in spring and summer.

Description: Sexes similar. A medium-sized heron with a white belly and foreneck and long yellow bill. Adult has blue-gray wings, back, neck, and head. In breeding plumage, the lower back is overlaid with long buffy feathers, and the lower neck is washed in chestnut. Note the white belly and slender yellow bill to separate Tricolored Heron from other dark herons.

Breeding Habitat: Primarily a coastal breeder, in Oklahoma Tricolored Herons utilize islands or areas of higher ground that support small trees or shrubs and are surrounded by wetland habitat.

Nest: A shallow platform of sticks constructed mostly by the female with material brought by the male; lined with thin twigs, grass, and plant stems, and normally placed 0.14–4.0 m (0.5–13 ft) high in willows or brushy thickets in or near marshes. The Tricolored Heron often nests in large rookeries in association with other heron species.

NESTING ECOLOGY

Season: April–June. Probably single-brooded.

Eggs: Usually 3–4; pale greenish blue and unmarked.
Development: Incubation is by both sexes for 22–23 days. Young are provisioned by both sexes and make first flights at 25–30 days, reaching independence at 50–56 days.

DISTRIBUTION AND ABUNDANCE

Rangewide: Resident of coastal salt marshes and mangroves from Long Island, New York, south along the east coasts of North, Central, and South America to northern Brazil, along the west coast from central Baja California, Mexico, south to Ecuador, and along the Gulf Coast of North America. Very local but expanding breeder inland or north of indicated range. Populations north of Florida and the Gulf Coast migrate south to the coast during the winter. The Tricolored Heron is also a resident of many Caribbean islands. Late summer dispersal and vagrancy, especially of juvenile birds, occurs north and inland to much of the eastern United States and southern California, Arizona, and New Mexico.

Historical: Since it was first recorded in Oklahoma in Payne County in 1922, it has become a rare but regular summer visitor. Recorded in all regions of Oklahoma, except for the Panhandle; it is most frequently seen in north-central and southeastern Oklahoma.

Current: The lack of Tricolored Heron records in the atlas blocks illustrates its rarity in Oklahoma. The first breeding record for the state occurred in 1998 at Salt Plains National Wildlife Refuge in Alfalfa County.

Population Trend: Breeding Bird Survey data for 1966–2000 show no conclusive trend rangewide (0.3 percent per year, P = 0.83). No trend data are available for Oklahoma.

References: AOU 1998; Baicich and Harrison 1997; Baumgartner and Baumgartner 1992; de Hoyo et al. 1992; Feirer and Sheppard 1999; Frederick 1997; Howell and Webb 1995; Kaufman 1996; Melvin et al. 1999; Moore 1927; National Geographic Society 1999; Sauer et al. 2001; Sutton 1967

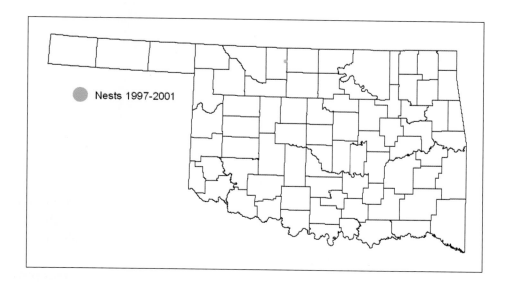

Nests 1997-2001

Cattle Egret
Bubulcus ibis

John M. Dole

Courtesy of Bill Horn

Cattle Egrets are well named as they are often found far from water feeding on insects stirred up by moving livestock. Cattle Egrets are native to the Old World and were first observed in South America around 1880. The species spread with astonishing rapidity throughout the Americas. Oklahoma's first record occurred in 1962 and nesting was recorded in 1963. The Cattle Egret is now common and well established in Oklahoma.

Description: Cattle Egrets are small, stocky, white herons with yellow to orange bills and legs. The adults are distinctively rusty orange on the crown, back, and forenecks during the breeding season. Nonbreeding Cattle Egrets are distinguished from other species by their short height and yellow bills. Cattle Egret sexes are similar in appearance. Calls include a nasal quack.

Breeding Habitat: Small tracts of isolated trees, wooded islands, or marshes, usually within heronries of other species. Forages in aquatic environments, but frequently also in terrestrial areas including pastures and rangeland, cultivated fields, parks, sports fields, road edges, lawns, and city dumps.

Nest: A shallow depression of twigs, sticks, dead reeds, or other vegetation lined with smaller twigs. Nests are usually placed 2–4 m (6–13 ft) high, occasionally higher. Both sexes build the nest, with the female doing most construction from material brought by the male. Nests colonially with other heron species.

NESTING ECOLOGY

Season: Primarily May–August; single-brooded, but will replace clutches lost early in season.
Eggs: Usually 3–4; pale sky blue and unmarked.
Development: Incubation is by both sexes for 23–24 days. Young are provisioned by both sexes, leave the nest at 20 days, begin flying at 30 days, and become independent at 45 days. Sibling aggression in nests is common, but siblicide is rare.

DISTRIBUTION AND ABUNDANCE

Rangewide: The Cattle Egret occurs from the United States and southern Canada (in a few limited areas) south through Central America to northern Chile and Argentina. Worldwide range also includes Africa, southwest Europe, south and east Asia, New Zealand, Australia, and many islands. It is less common in the northern and western United States. Most of the population leaves the United States during winter, except in Florida, the Gulf Coast, and southern California where it is resident year round.
Historical: This species was unrecorded in the New World prior to 1877. The first U.S. sighting occurred in south Florida in 1941. First recorded in Oklahoma in 1962 at the Salt Plains National Wildlife Refuge, and first known to nest in 1963 near Tulsa. Described

as locally common in eastern and central counties, uncommon to rare in western areas but expanding rapidly. In 1995, 19,199 Cattle Egret adults were estimated to be at Salt Plains NWR, up from an estimate of 1,000 adults in 1982. In 1987, 1,624 Cattle Egret nests were estimated in a mixed rookery at Grand Lake in Delaware County.
Current: While the Cattle Egret was observed over much of the state, the small number of nest records from atlas blocks indicates the local nature of its rookeries. The Cattle Egret is well established in Oklahoma, with its greatest population density in central Oklahoma. Records scored as Observed have been mapped to better illustrate the distribution of this species in the state.

Population Trend: Breeding Bird Survey data for 1966–2000 show no conclusive trend rangewide (0.9 percent per year, P = 0.34) and an increase of 9.5 percent per year in Oklahoma (P = 0.03), though most of this increase in Oklahoma occurred prior to 1980.

References: AOU 1998; Baicich and Harrison 1997; Baumgartner and Baumgartner 1992; de Hoyo et al. 1992; Howell and Webb 1995; Kaufman 1996; Koenen et al. 1996; Maddock and Geering 1994; Mock and Ploger 1987; National Geographic Society 1999; Newell 1969; Ploger and Mock 1986; Sauer et al. 2001; Shackford 1984; Stancill et al. 1988; Sutton 1967; Telfair 1994; Tomer 1967; Williamson 1973; Winton and Leslie 1996

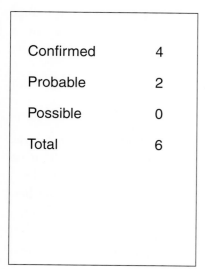

Confirmed	4
Probable	2
Possible	0
Total	6

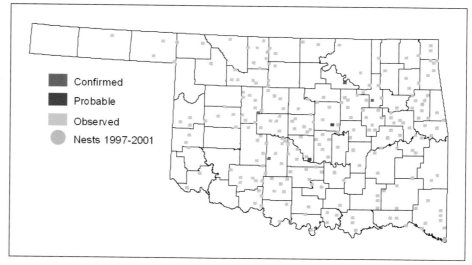

Green Heron
Butorides virescens

Richard A. Stuart

Courtesy of Warren Williams

The "Fly-up-the-creek" as it is sometimes known is probably the most common heron regularly found along small streams and creeks. The Green Heron's patience and stealth appear to be unsurpassed as it stalks its prey. If it had not been noticed as one is quietly fishing along a creek bank, one might become startled by the departure of this, another fisher, as it takes off to another site.

Description: A small heron about the size of a crow, the Green Heron has a dark cap that is sometimes raised into a crest, especially when disturbed, a dark blue-green back, a cinnamon-brown neck with a whitish stripe down the front, and yellow to orange legs. The call is a high-pitched coarse *kew* and a repeated *kluk-kluk*.

Breeding Habitat: Woodlands or scattered trees near water.

Nest: A flimsy platform, sometimes bulky after reuse, consisting of twigs, reeds, and vines with little or no lining of finer material. It is placed from ground level to 18 m (60 ft) above ground in trees and bushes. Usually a solitary nester.

NESTING ECOLOGY

Season: April–July. Often double-brooded.
Eggs: 3–5; pale blue green to mostly green.
Development: Incubation is by both sexes for 19–21 days. Young are provisioned by both sexes, leave the nest at 16–17 days, and become independent at about 30 days.

DISTRIBUTION AND ABUNDANCE

Rangewide: Breeds throughout the eastern United States as well as along the West Coast and parts of the Southwest. Winters along the western and southern coasts and somewhat inland. Also breeds in Mexico and Central and South America and in parts of the Old World.
Historical: Described as common in eastern parts of the state and gradually decreasing westward, and not known to nest in the Panhandle.
Current: The Green Heron is common, though not abundant, wherever water and trees are found throughout the main body of the state. Because Green Herons do not sing, and because the Safe Dates code could not be used for this species, there are no records in the Possible category. For this reason, blocks in which it was merely observed are mapped as well, to provide a fuller picture of its distribution.

Population Trend: Breeding Bird Survey data for 1966–2000 show a decline of 0.8 percent per year rangewide (P = 0.00) and a decline of 4.3 percent per year in Oklahoma (P = 0.00).

References: AOU 1998; Baicich and Harrison 1997; Baumgartner and Baumgartner 1992; Davis and Kushlan 1994; Harrison 1975; Koenen et al. 1996; National Geographic Society 1999; Peterson 1963; Sauer et al. 2001; Sibley 2000; Stokes and Stokes 1996; Sutton 1967

Confirmed	8
Probable	52
Possible	0
Total	60

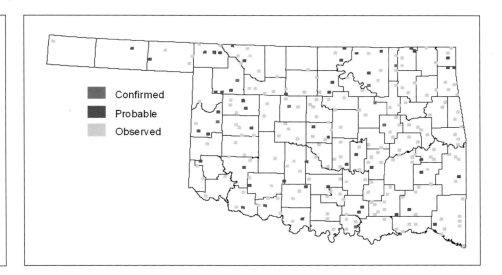

Confirmed
Probable
Observed

Black-crowned Night-Heron
Nycticorax nycticorax

David E. Fantina

Courtesy of Bill Horn

The Black-crowned Night-Heron is the most widespread and one of the most abundant herons in the world. In Oklahoma it is a locally common summer resident especially in the central part of the state. However, it is easily overlooked due to its coloration and its inconspicuous and largely nocturnal habits.

Description: A grayish, short-necked, short-legged, stocky heron with a black crown, black back, yellow legs, and dark bill. The adult plumage takes three years to acquire. Juveniles are streaked brown birds that can be easily confused with juvenile Yellow-crowned Night-Herons. These young birds can best be separated by the Black-crowned Night-Heron's browner upperparts, bolder white spotting, chunkier shape, and more evenly colored upperwing in flight. In flight the Black-crowned Night-Heron's legs extend just barely beyond the tail, while the Yellow-crowned Night-Heron's legs extend considerably farther. The call is a loud, coarse *quock.*

Breeding Habitat: This species nests colonially, alone or with other heron species, in a wide variety of natural and man-made wetland habitats including lakes, ponds, marshes, and other wet areas.

Nest: A shallow platform of twigs and leaves that can be placed anywhere from the ground to more than 30 m (100 ft) high in a tree. The nest is a heavier structure than that of other herons.

NESTING ECOLOGY

Season: May–July. Single-brooded, but may renest if first nest fails.

Eggs: 3–5; pale greenish blue; begin fading after laying.

Development: Incubation is by both sexes for about 23 days. Young are provisioned by both sexes, leave the nest for nearby perches after 3–4 weeks, and are capable of flight after 6 weeks.

DISTRIBUTION AND ABUNDANCE

Rangewide: The Black-crowned Night-Heron is nearly cosmopolitan, breeding on every continent except Australia and Antarctica. In North America it is found throughout most of the lower 48 states, wherever there are wetlands, and into parts of southern Canada. Short-distance migrants, Black-crowned Night-Herons can disperse far north of their breeding area in late summer before heading south to wintering grounds in the southern United States, the Carribean, and Mexico.

Historical: This species was generally considered a rare summer resident in Oklahoma until the 1930s when several rookeries were established or discovered. It was first reported nesting in the central part of the state in 1951, and is recorded as having nested in considerable numbers in Alfalfa, Canadian, Grant, Kay, Oklahoma, and Woods counties, and in smaller numbers in Caddo, Greer, Muskogee, Okmulgee, Sequoyah, and Tulsa counties.

Current: In light of its preference for aquatic habitats, it is surprising that the Black-crowned Night-Heron was found breeding at several locations within the comparatively dry Panhandle. This appears to represent a range expansion for this species in the state. Not surprisingly, it was also found at several widely scattered locations in the eastern part of Oklahoma.

Population Trend: Breeding Bird Survey data for 1966–2000 show an increase of 6.9 percent per year rangewide (P = 0.02) and a very large decline in Oklahoma (-30.5 percent per year, P = 0.10). A twelve-fold increase in the number of nesting birds (20 to 253) was recorded from 1982 to 1995 at the Salt Plains National Wildlife Refuge.

References: AOU 1998; Baicich and Harrison 1997; Baumgartner and Baumgartner 1992; Bent 1963c; Custer et al. 1992; Davis 1993; Grover 1978; Hughes 1952; James and Neal 1986; Koenen et al. 1996; Nice 1931; Sallee 1982; Sauer et al. 2001; Sutton 1967; Winton and Leslie 1999

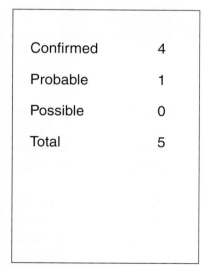

Confirmed	4
Probable	1
Possible	0
Total	5

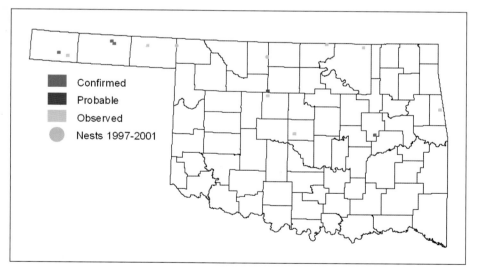

Confirmed
Probable
Observed
Nests 1997-2001

Yellow-crowned Night-Heron
Nyctanassa violacea

David E. Fantina

Courtesy of Bill Horn

Despite its name, the Yellow-crowned Night-Heron is not strictly nocturnal and is often active during the day. It is somewhat shy and retiring, however, and generally stays deep in shady swamps and thickets. Therefore, it is not a conspicuous part of Oklahoma's bird life.

Description: The adult Yellow-crowned Night-Heron is a medium-sized, stocky heron with a slate-gray body, black face with white cheeks, buffy-white crown, and yellow legs. It takes three years to acquire the adult plumage. Juvenile birds are dusky gray-brown overall with white mottling. They are difficult to separate from juvenile Black-crowned Night-Herons unless seen well in good light. They have less conspicuous white spots than the Black-crowned Night-Heron, a less chunky shape, more contrasting upperwings, and, in flight, their legs extend considerably farther behind the tail.

Breeding Habitat: This species nests alone or in small colonies in swamps, forested wetlands, and forested uplands near water. It will even nest in residential areas that have open understories and park-like areas near water.

Nest: A substantial platform of twigs and sticks generally built 10–15 m (30–45 ft) high in trees. Rarely, it nests it large mixed-species colonies.

NESTING ECOLOGY

Season: April–July. Single-brooded, but may replace lost clutches.

Eggs: Usually 3–4; very pale green.

Development: Incubation is by both sexes for about 25 days. Young are provisioned by both sexes and leave the nest after 5–6 weeks.

DISTRIBUTION AND ABUNDANCE

Rangewide: A migratory species, breeding along both coasts from Baja California and Massachusetts to Central America and inland as far north as eastern Iowa, southern Minnesota, and the lower Ohio Valley and west to northeastern Texas and Oklahoma. Birds from the interior apparently winter in Central and South America. As with most herons, juveniles may move considerably north of the breeding range in late summer.

Historical: Described in 1931 as a summer resident in northwestern and central Oklahoma. By 1967, described as a transient and summer resident throughout the main body of the state.

Current: Because it is not as conspicuous as many other herons, the Yellow-crowned Night-Heron was found at comparatively few locations in the eastern and southern parts of the state. It was completely absent from the northwest where it was considered a summer resident in 1931. The only blocks in which it was confirmed were in McCurtain, LeFlore, and Tillman counties. Additional records scored as Observed are mapped to better illustrate its true distribution.

Population Trend: Breeding Bird Survey data for 1966–2000 show no conclusive trend rangewide (-0.7 percent per year, P = 0.72) and a very large, 26.5 percent, per year decline in Oklahoma (P = 0.01), although data for the latter trend are not robust.

References: AOU 1998; Baicich and Harrison 1997; Baumgartner and Baumgartner 1992; Bent 1963c; Ehrlich et al. 1988; James and Neal 1986; Laubhan and Reid 1991; Nice 1931; Sallee 1982; Sauer et al. 2001; Sutton 1967; Watts 1995

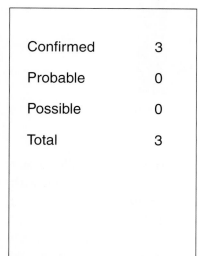

Confirmed	3
Probable	0
Possible	0
Total	3

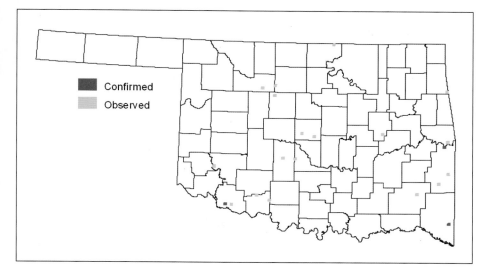

White Ibis

Eudocimus albus

James W. Arterburn

Courtesy of Warren Williams

Only very recently established as a breeding species in Oklahoma with the discovery of two nests, the White Ibis population is concentrated in and around Ward Lake and the Red Slough Wildlife Management Area in far southeastern McCurtain County.

Description: Sexes similar. White Ibis are medium-sized wading birds with all-white plumage, a long decurved bill, and long legs. The facial skin, bill, and legs are pinkish, but turn scarlet in the breeding season. The black tips to the primaries are easily seen in flight. Immatures are brownish with varying amounts of white as molting progresses, with a conspicuous white rump.

Breeding Habitat: Wetlands with stands of trees, espe-cially willows, and other vegetation with shallow water nearby for feeding. Nests in colonies, usually with herons, egrets, and other waterbirds.

Nest: A sturdy cupped structure of dead sticks, fresh twigs with leaves, and other plant material; usually placed low in live woody vegetation.

NESTING ECOLOGY

Season: Few data for Oklahoma, but April–July in other areas. Possibly double-brooded.
Eggs: Usually 2–3; bluish, greenish, or pale buff, vari-ably marked with spots, speckling, and irregular blotches of light to dark blown.

Development: Incubation is by both sexes for 21–23 days. Young are provisioned by both sexes, fledge at about 3 weeks, and fly at about 5 weeks.

DISTRIBUTION AND ABUNDANCE

Rangewide: Breeds along the Atlantic Coast from Virginia south through Central America, the West Indies, and northern South America, and winters from coastal South Carolina south over the rest of the breeding range. The White Ibis has slowly been expanding its range from coastal south Louisiana and coastal Texas into northwestern Louisiana and into northeastern Texas. It has also been expanding its range up the Atlantic Coast into Virginia.

Historical: First observed in Oklahoma in 1951 in Bryan County, it was later considered a rare visitant west to Alfalfa County.

Current: The White Ibis is limited in its Oklahoma distribution to a small area of far southeastern Oklahoma, thus making it poorly sampled by atlas project methods. The first nest records for the state occurred during the atlas project, in 2000 (2 nests) and 2001 (1 nest) at Ward Lake in southeastern McCurtain County.

Population Trend: Breeding Bird Survey data for 1966–2000 show no conclusive trend rangewide (3.9 percent per year, P = 0.17). No trend information are available for Oklahoma, but northward range expansion from Louisiana and Texas is evidently taking place

References: AOU 1998; Baicich and Harrison 1997; Baumgartner and Baumgartner 1992; Bent 1963c; DeGraaf and Rappole 1995; Ehrlich et al. 1988; Kushlan and Bildstein 1992; Pulich 1988; Sauer et al. 2001; Sutton 1967; Wiedenfeld and Swan 2000

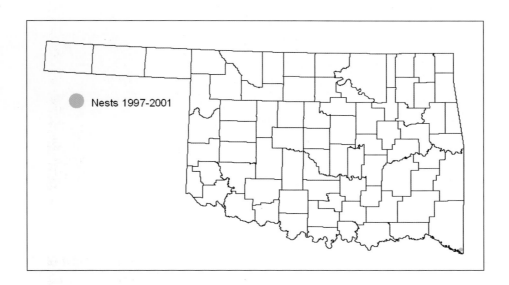

Nests 1997-2001

White-faced Ibis
Plegadis chihi

Alan E. Versaw

Courtesy of Colin Smith

Few birds suffer more from lack of an appropriate name than the White-faced Ibis. Like the unfortunate Red-bellied Woodpecker, the White-faced Ibis labors under a name that describes a barely distinguishable feature. Unlike the Red-bellied Woodpecker, though, the White-faced Ibis retains its namesake feature for only a couple months of the year.

Description: Both sexes are best recognized by long legs, long, decurved bill, and chestnut-bronze plumage. Those features still do not distinguish it from its close relative, the Glossy Ibis, which is a rare vagrant in Oklahoma. During the breeding season, though, an adult White-faced Ibis may be distinguished from its

close cousin by its all-red legs, red eye, and red facial skin at the base of its bill.

Breeding Habitat: Shallow marshes with localized areas of emergent vegetation. Bulrush and cattail marshes are both utilized extensively by the species. Time spent in shallow, flooded areas with emergent vegetation or flooded agricultural fields is typically for foraging rather than breeding purposes.

Nest: Constructed in emergent vegetation or low in trees or shrubs standing over shallow water, occasionally atop an abandoned muskrat lodge. Inland nest sites are made by constructing a supporting platform upon which to weave the base and rim of the nest. Nest materials include the vegetation growing at the nest site as well as items retrieved from short distances around the nest. Nest size, composition, and construction vary widely from site to site. Gregarious, and nests colonially with herons and egrets.

NESTING ECOLOGY

Season: May–July. Single-brooded, but may replace lost clutches.
Eggs: Usually 3–4; greenish blue.
Development: Incubation is by both sexes for 20–26 days. Young are provisioned by both sexes and begin to leave the nest after 10–12 days, but require up to 2 months to leave the colony.

DISTRIBUTION AND ABUNDANCE

Rangewide: Widely distributed along the Texas and Louisiana coastlines, but populations are spread much more sporadically through the Great Plains, the Great Basin, and the Rocky Mountain regions. Closest known breeding sites prior to discovery of breeding in north-central and southwestern Oklahoma were in central Kansas and east-central New Mexico. Retreats to Mexico, the Gulf Coast, and southern California in winter.
Historical: Long regarded as a migrant and summer

visitant prior to discovery of nesting in Oklahoma in Caddo County in 1993 and at Salt Plains National Wildlife Refuge in 1995.
Current: At once both highly visible and highly mobile, the White-faced Ibis defies easy categorization as a breeder in Oklahoma. The sheer number of summer records suggests a greater level of breeding than has been detected to this point in time. Further muddying the picture is the fact that confirmation of breeding generally requires access to areas deep within large marshes, a license usually neither sought by nor available to atlas fieldworkers or the public in general, and typically involving disturbance to sensitive species. As a result, the atlas block survey data shed little new light on the breeding range and status for this species. Two additional reports confirmed breeding in Alfalfa and Kingfisher counties, both well within the species' known summer range in Oklahoma.

Population Trend: Breeding Bird Survey data for 1966–2000 suggest a large increase of 29.9 percent per year rangewide (P = 0.01), but data are not robust for this species. No trend data are available for Oklahoma.

References: Baicich and Harrison 1997; Baumgartner and Baumgartner 1992; Davis 1989; Kaufman 1990; Koenen et al. 1996; Ryder and Manry 1994; Sauer et al. 2001; Shepperd 1996; Sutton 1967

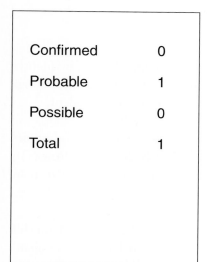

Confirmed	0
Probable	1
Possible	0
Total	1

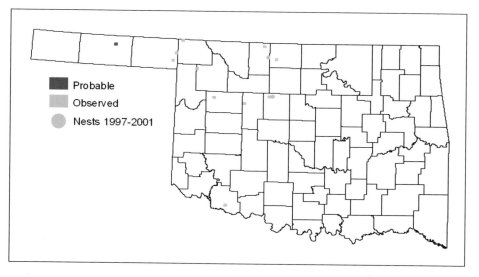

Probable
Observed
Nests 1997-2001

Black Vulture

Coragyps atratus

Kenneth D. Andrews

Courtesy of Colin Smith

Much more communal than the Turkey Vulture, this scavenger and sometimes predator is commonly seen in groups. The Black Vulture is also more aggressive than the Turkey Vulture and less efficient at finding carrion because it lacks the well-developed sense of smell possessed by its not-so-close relative. Black Vultures often hunt and feed in groups and will sometimes take over a Turkey Vulture's find. Courtship may involve an aerial flight of the male chasing a female, which begins with a rapid, prolonged spiral.

Description: Sexes are similar, black with white tips or patches on the underside of each wing tip. Bare heads are gray to black. Feet extend to the edge or beyond the short tail in flight. Wings are shorter and broader than the Turkey Vulture, and are flapped more frequently during flight, which is usually at a low altitude. Wings are held nearly level when soaring. Mostly silent.

Breeding Habitat: Breeds in dense woodlands but forages in open lowlands and garbage dumps. Roosts in undisturbed stands of tall trees. Frequently seen in savanna and second-growth areas.

Nest: No nest is built. Eggs are laid on bare rock on cliff ledges or in a cave. Hollow logs, rock crevices, or abandoned buildings may also be used. Sometimes found in openings amid dense vegetation. Breeding density may be limited by the number of suitable nest sites.

NESTING ECOLOGY

Season: February–May. Single-brooded.

Eggs: 2; pale gray green with brown or chocolate splotches. Deposited gently to avoid breakage from the hard nest substrate.

Development: Reported incubation period widely variable but probably 38–39 days by both sexes taking alternating 24-hour shifts. Eggs are placed one on each foot of the incubating adult. Young are provisioned by both sexes and fledge at about 80 days. A prolonged period of juvenile dependence may last weeks to months.

DISTRIBUTION AND ABUNDANCE

Rangewide: Resident from southern Arizona and western Texas to southern Illinois, southern Indiana, and New Jersey south to the Gulf Coast, southern Florida, and Central and South America to Argentina. May retreat from northern range limits in winter, with some individuals migrating as far as Panama. Generally found in warmer climates than Turkey Vulture.

Historical: Uncommon residents found in southeastern Oklahoma. Once found in northeastern Oklahoma north to Tulsa and Osage counties, but now confined to heavily wooded relict areas farther south. Rarely found in western plains, but may once have been more common west of contemporary range.

Current: The Black Vulture is limited to the southeastern region of Oklahoma where its favored deciduous forests are located. This species' secretive nesting habits and absence of nest building make it difficult to confirm in a block. Few of the atlasing codes apply to this species, resulting in most sightings of it (usually seen soaring) being placed in the Observed category. These observations have been mapped to better illustrate the true distribution of the species in the state.

Population Trend: Breeding Bird Survey data for 1966–2000 show an increase of 2.7 percent per year rangewide (P = 0.00), but no conclusive trend in Oklahoma (24.7 percent per year, P = 0.35).

References: Baumgartner and Baumgartner 1992; Brown and Amadon 1989; Buckley 1999; DeGraaf and Rappole 1995; Ehrlich et al. 1988; Jackson 1983; Mays 1971; McHargue 1981; National Geographic Society 1983; Rappole and Blacklock 1994; Sauer et al. 2001; Sutton 1967; Udvardy and Farrand 1997; Walters 1994; Wilbur and Jackson 1983

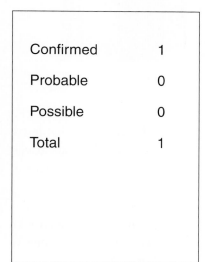

Confirmed	1
Probable	0
Possible	0
Total	1

Turkey Vulture
Cathartes aura

Kenneth D. Andrews

Courtesy of Warren Williams

Popularly called a buzzard by inhabitants of the southern United States, the Turkey Vulture is one of the two common North American vultures. It is frequently seen soaring, though in early morning it may be seen roosting with other vultures in a tall, dead snag, waiting for the formation of the warm air currents which carry it aloft. It uses a remarkably well developed sense of smell to locate the carrion on which it feeds.

Description: Males and females are black with naked, red-skinned heads, long tails, and silvery flight feathers that give a characteristic two-toned, black-and-gray pattern. Wings are commonly held in a slight V shape when soaring. Immature have a dark or black head.

Breeding Habitat: Uses a wide variety of habitats, from open areas to forest. It is commonly seen over deciduous forests and woodlands, as well as adjacent farmlands.

Nest: No nest is made. The eggs are laid on bare rock, in caves or hollow stumps of trees, in abandoned buildings, or on the ground in dense shrubs.

NESTING ECOLOGY

Season: April–June. Single-brooded.
Eggs: 2; dull white or cream with spots or blotches of brown.

Development: Incubation is by both sexes for 38–41 days. Young are provisioned by both sexes and fledge gradually over 66–88 days.

DISTRIBUTION AND ABUNDANCE

Rangewide: Breeds from southern British Columbia, western Ontario, and Massachusetts south throughout the remaining continental United States to South America. North American individuals winter from northern California, Arizona, Texas, Nebraska, the Ohio valley, and Pennsylvania south to the Gulf Coast, Florida, and northwestern South America.

Historical: Described as an uncommon to common summer resident, also wintering in southeastern Oklahoma.

Current: The Turkey Vulture is a common summer resident throughout Oklahoma. Its secretive nesting habits and absence of nest building make it difficult to confirm in a block. Few of the atlasing codes apply to this species, resulting in most sightings of it (usually seen soaring) being placed in the Observed category. These observations have been mapped to better illustrate the true distribution of the species in the state.

Population Trend: Breeding Bird Survey data for 1966–2000 show an increase of 1.5 percent per year rangewide for North America (P = 0.00), but no conclusive trend in Oklahoma (1.6 percent per year, P = 0.14).

References: Baumgartner and Baumgartner 1992; Brown and Amadon 1989; Clark and Ohmart 1985; DeGraaf and Rappole 1995; Ehrlich et al. 1988; Jackson 1983; National Geographic Society 1999; Rappole and Blacklock 1994; Sauer et al. 2001; Sutton 1967; Udvardy and Farrand 1997; Walters 1994; Wilbur and Jackson 1983

Confirmed	17
Probable	7
Possible	0
Total	24

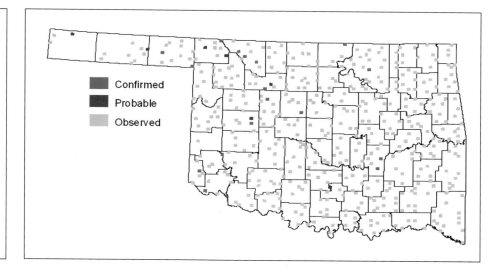

Black-bellied Whistling-Duck
Dendrocygna autumnalis

James W. Arterburn

Courtesy of Warren Williams

Black-bellied Whistling Duck is only very recently established as a breeding species in Oklahoma, with localized populations pioneering in the southeast, northeast, and central parts of the state. This advancement of the range of the Black-bellied Whistling-Duck corresponds with the spread of this species in the south over the past century. Some of this range expansion may be due to escaped captive birds in northeastern Oklahoma as well as raised birds released at refuges in southeastern Louisiana.

Description: Sexes similar. The most erect of ducks, with long neck and legs. Face and upper neck gray with white eyering, red bill. Breast and lower neck cinnamon-brown; black streak extends up the hindneck to the cinnamon-brown crown. The back is cinnamon-brown, and the wing shows a large white patch. Belly and flanks black with white undertail coverts spotted with black. Legs pink.

Breeding Habitat: Swamps, marshes, and cultivated areas with small reservoirs or cattle stock ponds. Black-bellied Whistling-Ducks return with fidelity to their breeding areas. Highly gregarious and nonterritorial.

Nest: Found in tree cavities, nest boxes, and on the ground amid low vegetation. Cavity nests are usually unlined, while ground nests are composed of dead grasses woven into a shallow cup. Tree cavity nests are 2.4–9 m (8–30 ft) high.

NESTING ECOLOGY

Season: May–August; possibly later. Single-brooded.
Eggs: 8–12, sometimes up to 18; white to creamy white. Eggs are regularly laid in the nests of other hens, sometimes up to 101 in communal "dump nests."
Development: Incubation is by both sexes for 27–28 days. Young are precocial but are brooded by both parents, fly at 2 months, and stay with parents for up to 4 more months.

DISTRIBUTION AND ABUNDANCE

Rangewide: The northern population of the Black-bellied Whistling-Duck breeds from Arizona, Texas, Oklahoma, and Louisiana south through Mexico and Central America. Also breeds in South America.
Historical: Few Oklahoma records prior to 1990s. Has been expanding its range north from the Gulf Coast into central to northern Texas and southern to central Oklahoma as well as expanding east into Louisiana.
Current: The Black-bellied Whistling-Duck was first recorded as breeding in Oklahoma during the atlas project, in 1999. The currently rare and local distribution of Black-bellied Whistling-Duck in Oklahoma makes it poorly sampled by atlas methodology. The only atlas block in which this species was found was in the central part of the state. Reports of confirmed breeding outside of atlas blocks came from central, southeastern, and northeastern parts of the state.

Population Trend: Breeding Bird Survey data for 1966–2000 show an increase of 7.8 percent per year rangewide in North America ($P = 0.01$). Having only recently colonized Oklahoma, there are no reliable trend data, but it seems likely to increase here.

References: AOU 1998; Baicich and Harrison 1997; Baumgartner and Baumgartner 1992; Bellrose 1976; Bent 1962b; DeGraaf and Rappole 1995; Heck and Arbour 2001; James and Thompson 2001; Kamp and Loyd 2001; Madge and Burn 1988; Norman and Hayes 1988; Palmer 1976; Sutton 1967; Todd 1996; Wiedenfeld and Swan 2000

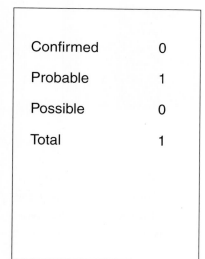

Confirmed	0
Probable	1
Possible	0
Total	1

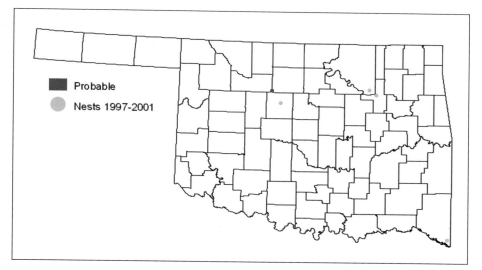

Probable
Nests 1997-2001

Canada Goose
Branta canadensis

Eugene A. Young

These large "honkers," as locals affectionately call them, declined as a breeding species and have been restored throughout the region. Once nearly extirpated from the wild, a small population of the Giant Canada Goose subspecies was found in Minnesota in 1962 and became the nucleus for successful reintroductions throughout the United States. A rather gregarious species that forms monogamous pair bonds, they have become fairly common in urban areas, especially along golf courses and parks with suitable water habitats. To many folks, the northward movement of Canada Geese serves as the harbinger of spring.

Description: Sexes are similar, large dark-bodied geese mottled with browns and grays, with a black head,

dark eye, white cheek patch, black bill, feet, and legs. Call is described as a *honk* or *ahonk,* with the male's call usually done in two syllables and the female's in a single syllable. They can reach weights of 18 pounds or more.

Breeding Habitat: Utilizes a variety of habitats near water, including ponds, marshes, and reservoirs. Nesting territories are less than 0.5 ha (1.24 ac), but once young are hatched family groups will combine and occupy larger areas.

Nest: Near water, usually on the ground on a ridge or elevated place, frequently on muskrat and beaver dens, on nest platforms; constructed of a stick foundation lined with a bulky pile of grasses, cattails, and feathers; built by the female.

NESTING ECOLOGY

Season: March–July. Single-brooded.
Eggs: Averages 5–6, ranges from 2–12; dull white to creamy white.
Development: Incubation is by the female for 25–30 days. Young are precocial and capable of flight in about 9 weeks. Young are brooded for the first few days, after which they can walk, swim, and feed on their own, relying on parents only for protection. Will remain with parents until the following spring as a family group. Adults will adopt foreign gosling clutches that have been abandoned.

DISTRIBUTION AND ABUNDANCE

Rangewide: Breeds in Alaska through Canada, south through the northern half of the United States. Winters throughout the United States to Mexico.
Historical: Described as a common transient, wintering locally, throughout the state. A few breeding records existed for Salt Plains and Tishomingo National Wildlife Refuges prior to 1951, but were mostly dismissed as crippled or captive birds. A nest discovered at Lake Texoma in 1951 was tended by two geese capable of flight. Prior to the 1950s, populations declined throughout the United States, but from 1955 to 1974 populations throughout the Central Flyway increased by 70.6 percent.

Current: The high proportion of blocks with confirmed nesting may be attributed to their ability to tolerate urban and agricultural environments, their use of small wetlands, and their frequent use of constructed nesting platforms. The lack of records for the Panhandle reflects its more arid environment, with diminished wetlands. The paucity of records in the southeast can be attributed to the heavily forested habitats there.

Population Trend: Breeding Bird Survey data for 1966–2000 show an increase of 10.5 percent per year rangewide (P = 0.00) and a very large 17.7 percent per year increase in Oklahoma (P = 0.07).

References: AOU 1998; Baicich and Harrison 1997; Baumgartner and Baumgartner 1992; Bellrose 1976; Busby and Zimmerman 2001; Collias and Collias 1984; Collias and Jahn 1959; Hansen 1965; Riggs and Starks 1951; Skutch 1999; Stokes and Stokes 1979; Sutton 1967; Terres 1991; Tveten 1993

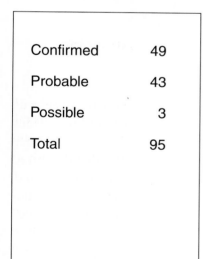

Confirmed	49
Probable	43
Possible	3
Total	95

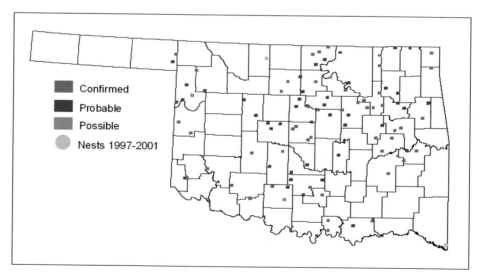

Wood Duck
Aix sponsa

Richard A. Stuart

Courtesy of Bill Horn

The male Wood Duck is one of the most colorful of ducks. Westward expansion of settlers depleted much of the required habitat of this species, which along with excessive hunting greatly reduced populations. Wood Ducks are now recovering through placement of nest boxes and enforced hunting regulations. There exists an 1875 report of a Wood Duck nesting in an Ivory-billed Woodpecker hole in Atoka County; Wood Ducks have since prospered while the Ivory-bill has not.

Description: Both sexes are crested and have blue speculums on darkish wings. The male has a reddish bill and eye, black head with two white bars extending upward on either side of a white throat, a chestnut breast speckled with white, and yellowish-brown sides edged with black-and-white "zebra" stripes just under the wings. In contrast, the female is dull brown-gray with white spots or short streaks on the breast and sides, the bill is grayish with yellowish edging, and the eyes are surrounded by white "teardrops" extending to the rear.

Breeding Habitat: Woodlands usually near water.

Nest: In natural cavities and man-made nest boxes 1–18 m (3–60 ft) high. The cavity is lined with wood chips and down from the female's breast.

NESTING ECOLOGY

Season: April–July. Sometimes double-brooded.

Eggs: 6–15; unmarked, dull white to pale buff. Occasional "dump nests" may contain large numbers of eggs from several females.

Development: Incubation is by the female for 28–31 days. Young are precocial and jump from the cavity to follow the female to water, remaining together for a month or more.

DISTRIBUTION AND ABUNDANCE

Rangewide: Breeds throughout most of the eastern United States and southern Canada, as well as parts of the west. Northernmost populations move south for winter. Since the enactment of the Migratory Bird Treaty Act in 1918, this species has flourished.

Historical: Described in 1931 as once common, now rare. Early in the twentieth century this species as well as many other cavity nesting species became very rare due to loss of habitat, nest sites, and uncontrolled hunting. Beginning in the 1930s, hunting controls were initiated and a program for installing nest boxes was established. These successes meant that by 1992 Wood Ducks were described as uncommon over eastern and central Oklahoma, and rare westward.

Current: Because the Wood Duck prefers woodlands near water, it is rare in nonwooded areas of Oklahoma. Elsewhere it may be considered uncommon. Some of the Probable Breeder blocks may be the result of pairs seen prior to the end of spring migration.

Population Trend: Breeding Bird Survey data for 1966–2000 show an increase of 5.2 percent per year rangewide (P = 0.00), but no conclusive trend in Oklahoma (-4.6 percent per year, P = 0.34).

References: AOU 1998; Baicich and Harrison 1997; Baumgartner and Baumgartner 1992; Bellrose 1976; Gooders and Boyer 1986; Harrison 1975; Hepp and Bellrose 1995; Holmgren 1981; National Geographic Society 1999; Nice 1931; Peterson 1963; Sauer et al. 2001; Shurtleff and Savage 1996; Sibley 2000; Stokes and Stokes 1996; Sutton 1967, 1978; Williams 1973

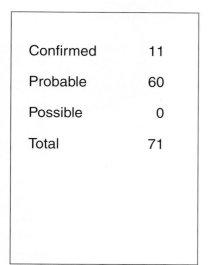

Confirmed	11
Probable	60
Possible	0
Total	71

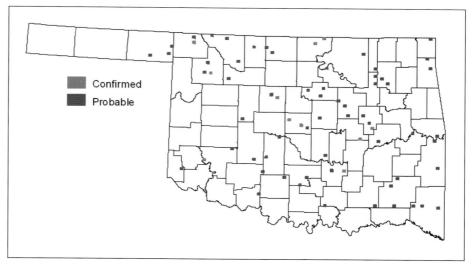

Gadwall
Anas strepera

Joseph A. Grzybowski

Courtesy of Bill Horn

A familiar winter bird, as many a waterfowl hunter could attest, the Gadwall seems to frequent those reservoirs in Oklahoma with the highest silt loads. At a distance a superficially drab duck, the plumage of males in-the-hand displays browns, grays, and black (even some chestnut) in patterns of intricate detail. Females are more drab, but share the common trait of white specula. Curiously, more than 90 percent of the females are mated the fall before breeding, indicating a highly monogamous mating structure. While Oklahoma provides the "honeymoon" backdrop for many a Gadwall pair, few actually nest in this state.

Description: A medium-sized dabbling duck, the males are mostly vermiculated with gray, brown, and tan anteriorly, scapulars and tertials are sepia to gray, some wing coverts chestnut, and with distinctively black rump and undertail coverts. Bill black to slate gray, with some muted orange at sides in nonbreeding periods. Females maintain drab, mottled gray-brown plumage typical of many dabblers, with varying amounts of brown on the belly. In females, the bill is a mix of horn and drab orange, the latter more evident on sides of bill. Legs and feet are generally orange to yellow. White specula, outlined by black in males, separate it from all other North American dabbling ducks.

Breeding Habitat: Breeds extensively in prairie potholes, usually with significant cover, and grassy wetland settings, occasionally using stock ponds or lagoons when natural wetlands are limited. First documented breeding in Oklahoma occurred in a sewage lagoon.

Nest: A scrape lined with vegetation and down feathers plucked from the female's breast and concealed in dense vegetation.

NESTING ECOLOGY

Season: April–August, primarily early May to mid-July, generally later than other ducks. Single-brooded, but can renest after nest failure.

Eggs: Usually 7–12; dull white to grayish green. Interspecific parasitism documented by Lesser Scaup, Redhead, and Ring-necked Pheasants. Intraspecific parasitism also occurs, but in low frequency.

Development: Incubation is by the female for about 26 days. Young are precocial, are brooded by the female for up to 14 days, and are tended by the female for 7–9 weeks after hatching.

DISTRIBUTION AND ABUNDANCE

Rangewide: Breeds primarily in mid-latitude zones of the Northern Hemisphere. Widespread in western North America from eastern British Columbia through Manitoba and south to southern California and Nebraska. Breeds sparingly in coastal southeastern Alaska and the Aleutians, recently and locally in eastern North America to Great Lakes, Quebec, the Maritime Provinces, and coastal New Jersey. Winters mostly in the southern United States and Mexico north locally to coastal Maine, Great Lakes, southern Minnesota, southwestern Canada, and coastal southeastern Alaska. In Palearctic, to western Europe, eastern Africa, northern India, southern China, and southern Japan.

Historical: One breeding record from Boise City Sewage Ponds, Cimarron County, in 1985. Summer vagrants occur most years. Common in migration and winter.

Current: Without direct evidence, the atlas detections of Gadwall are difficult to distinguish from those of mere summer vagrants. Observations occurred in two Panhandle counties, one the location of the only confirmed historical nesting.

Population Trend: Breeding Bird Survey data for 1966–2000 show an increase of 5.8 percent per year rangewide (P = 0.00). No trend data are available for Oklahoma.

References: AOU 1998; Baumgartner and Baumgartner 1992; Belrose 1976; Cramp and Simmons 1977; Grzybowski 1987; Hines and Mitchell 1984; LeSchack et al. 1997; Nice 1931; Oring 1969; Sauer et al. 2001; Sutton 1967

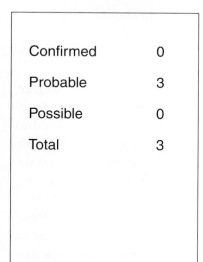

Confirmed	0
Probable	3
Possible	0
Total	3

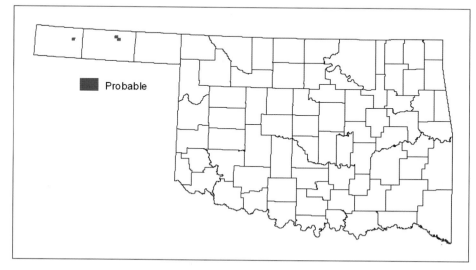

Probable

Mallard
Anas platyrhynchos

Eugene A. Young

Courtesy of Colin Smith

The Mallard is one of the most abundant and most recognizable ducks in the Northern Hemisphere and has the most extensive breeding range of any duck in North America. Mallards are most common in Oklahoma during migration and the winter months. They are often observed feeding with head submerged and rump and tail bobbing on the surface of the water, typical "dabbling duck" behavior.

Description: Male is easily identified by its glossy metallic-green head, white, gray, and black body with a bright chestnut breast separated by a white neck collar, bright orange to red legs, and yellow to green bill. Females are drab brown like most female ducks, but can usually be identified by bill shape and color (orange blotched with black), white outer tail feathers, and violet-blue speculum bordered by white on both the front and back, as in the male. Females can be confused with female Gadwall. The female *quack,* usually repeated in a series, is one of the most recognizable calls of any waterfowl species.

Breeding Habitat: Grassy areas usually associated with wetlands, hayfields, cattail marshes, sloughs, lakes, and reservoirs. Nesting may take place some distance from water in pastures and alfalfa fields.

Nest: A hollow on the ground, with sufficient cover of tallgrasses, reeds, cattails, rushes, or crops, lined with nearby grass-like vegetation and down from the female.

NESTING ECOLOGY

Season: April–July. Single-brooded.

Eggs: Usually 8–12; bluish green, buff green, whitish, pale green, or pale blue with no markings.

Development: Incubation is by the female for 26–29 days. Young are precocial and can fly in about 7–8 weeks.

DISTRIBUTION AND ABUNDANCE

Rangewide: Breeds from northern Alaska, east through Canada and southern Maine, and south through the northern United States. Winters throughout the United States south through Mexico.

Historical: Described as a rare to local summer resident, mostly in northern counties. More common in winter.

Current: As with many species of ducks, the Mallard's preference for nesting near wetlands associated with grasslands accounts for its greater abundance in western Oklahoma. A number of the Probable Breeder records may represent pairs seen prior to the end of spring migration.

Population Trend: Breeding Bird Survey data for 1966–2000 show an increase of 1.8 percent per year rangewide (P = 0.00) and an increase of 15.1 percent per year in Oklahoma (P = 0.02), although the Oklahoma data are not robust.

References: AOU 1998; Baicich and Harrison 1997; Baumgartner and Baumgartner 1992; Bellrose 1976; Bent 1923; Johnsgard 1968; Sauer et al. 2001; Shackford 1982; Stancill et al. 1989; Stokes and Stokes 1979; Sutton 1967; Terres 1991; Tveten 1993

Confirmed	30
Probable	95
Possible	0
Total	125

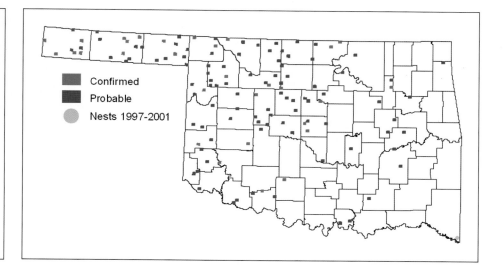

Confirmed
Probable
Nests 1997-2001

Blue-winged Teal
Anas discors

Eugene A. Young

The small Blue-winged Teal is closely related to the Cinnamon Teal and the Northern Shoveler but is restricted to breeding in North America. Females and males in eclipse plumage during the fall may be virtually indistinguishable from Cinnamon Teal. These species have been known to hybridize, further complicating identification in areas where both may occur. Uncommon for North American waterfowl, Blue-winged Teal have traveled up to 6,437 km (4,000 mi) from summer to winter grounds.

Description: Small dabbling duck; wing pattern similar to Northern Shoveler and Cinnamon Teal; male distinguished from other species by dark blue-gray head with a white half-moon crescent between eye and bill. Females are drab brown similar to Green-winged Teal and Cinnamon Teal. In fall, males don't molt into their more colorful breeding plumage until November.

Breeding Habitat: Usually near ponds, potholes, marshes, or wet meadows, occasionally in cropland, abandoned fields, on muskrat dens, and in grasslands.

Nest: A well-concealed hollow in the ground, up to 17.8–20.3 cm (7–8 in) in diameter, filled with grasses and weed stems, lined with down; nearby cover may be arched over nest for concealment.

NESTING ECOLOGY

Season: May–August. Single-brooded.

Eggs: Usually 8–12, range 6–15; slightly glossy, dull or creamy white or with pale olive tint.

Development: Incubation is by the female for 23–27 days. Young are precocial and can fly in about 35–49 days. Only females tend the young.

DISTRIBUTION AND ABUNDANCE

Rangewide: Breeds from Alaska, east to New Brunswick and Nova Scotia, south to North Carolina, west to southern Texas, central Nevada, and northeastern California. Winters in the southern United States, south to central Argentina.

Historical: Rare to occasional nester, chiefly in northern counties. Common early fall migrant and late spring migrant when numbers make this a dominant waterfowl species.

Current: The Blue-winged Teal's preference for nesting near wetlands associated with grassland habitat may account for its more westerly distribution in Oklahoma. The high number of Probable Breeder blocks is likely the result of pairs being seen prior to the end of spring migration.

Population Trend: Breeding Bird Survey data for 1966–2000 show no conclusive trend rangewide (-0.4 percent per year, P = 0.53) and suggest a 3.6 percent per year increase in Oklahoma (P = 0.02), but this latter trend is based on just six Oklahoma BBS routes.

References: AOU 1998; Andrews and Righter 1992; Baicich and Harrison 1997; Baumgartner and Baumgartner 1992; Bellrose 1976; Bent 1923; Bolen 1979; Robbins and Easterla 1992; Sutton 1967; Terres 1991; Thompson and Ely 1989; Tveten 1993

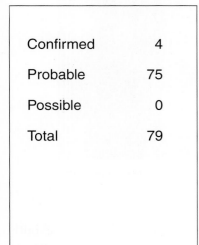

Confirmed	4
Probable	75
Possible	0
Total	79

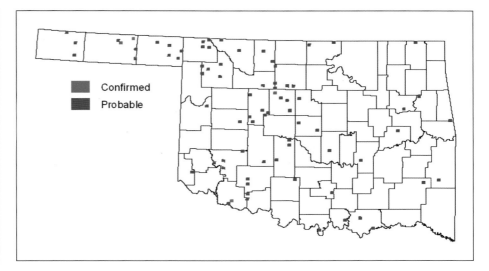

Cinnamon Teal
Anas cyanoptera

Alan E. Versaw

Courtesy of Gerald Wiens

From the uniforms of a state university's football team to the color of the soil, shades of red dominate everyday life in Oklahoma. It seems only appropriate then, that the Cinnamon Teal should establish a breeding toehold in a state dominated by a sister species utterly lacking in red, the Blue-winged Teal.

Description: The rusty plumage and red eye of the drake Cinnamon Teal set it apart from all North American ducks. Cinnamon Teal hens, however, are virtually indistinguishable in the field from the closely related Blue-winged Teal. The surest means of distinguishing eclipse males and female Cinnamon Teals from their Blue-winged counterparts is the somewhat longer bill of the Cinnamon Teal, and the somewhat

warmer tones to the plumage. Both sexes of both species wear blue upperwing-coverts and green speculums.

Breeding Habitat: Potential breeding habitat includes all manner of freshwater wetlands, including stock ponds, reservoirs, and expansive marshes. Preferred sites are those with extensive emergent vegetation. The Cinnamon Teal appears more tolerant of alkaline marsh habitat than the Blue-winged Teal.

Nest: Nests are usually constructed close to shallow water, but records of nests well away from water exist. The nest itself is a hollow lined with grasses and down constructed in dense vegetative cover. When threat of flooding exists, the nest may be built up by adding additional material to the nest.

NESTING ECOLOGY

Season: Mostly May–July. Single-brooded.
Eggs: Usually 8–12; off-white to buff in color.
Development: Incubation is by the female for 21–25 days. Young are precocial and are led by the hen to water within 24 hours of hatching. The female accompanies the young until they fledge at 7 weeks.

DISTRIBUTION AND ABUNDANCE

Rangewide: The North American subspecies of the Cinnamon Teal breeds extensively from southwestern Canada well south into Mexico. Abundant at widespread sites throughout the western states. Highest breeding density occurs in the vicinity of Great Salt Lake, Utah. Winter range extends from northern California through most of Mexico.

Historical: Probably a very rare and localized breeder in Oklahoma since permanent settlement. Actual breeding frequency may be hidden by female's similarity to her Blue-winged counterpart. Possible breeding record from Salt Plains National Wildlife Refuge in 1959.
Current: The handful of reports for this species in addition to the sole record from within an atlas block came from Texas and Cimarron counties. Atlas fieldworkers were unable to confirm breeding for the species anywhere within the state. The difficulty of differentiating between Blue-winged and Cinnamon hens and ducklings should frustrate all but the most tentative identifications of the breeding range for Cinnamon Teal within the state for the foreseeable future.

Population Trend: Breeding Bird Survey data for 1966–2000 show no conclusive trend rangewide (-0.3 percent per year, P = 0.64). Extremely low density in Oklahoma reveals no trends.

References: AOU 1998; Baicich and Harrison 1997; Baumgartner and Baumgartner 1992; Bellrose 1980; Bolen 1979; Gammonley 1996; Madge and Burn 1988; Ryser 1985; Sauer et al. 2001; Sutton 1967

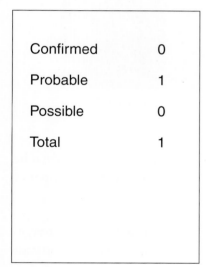

Confirmed	0
Probable	1
Possible	0
Total	1

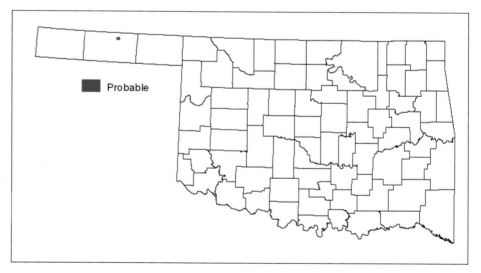

Probable

Northern Shoveler

Anas clypeata

Eugene A. Young

Courtesy of Bill Horn

The Northern Shoveler is the most widespread of all shovelers in the world, with a holarctic distribution, although they reach the southern edge of their breeding range in northern Oklahoma. It is the most territorial of North American dabbling ducks.

Description: Usually distinguishable from all other ducks by its long "spoonbill" or spatula-shaped bill and flat-headed appearance in both sexes. Females most closely resemble female Mallards but can usually be told by shape of bill and smaller size. Males resemble male Mallards, but are distinguished by large bill, chestnut flanks or sides, white breast, and smaller size.

During flight, both male and female shovelers can be separated by their powder-blue wing pattern in front of the speculum.

Breeding Habitat: Marshy areas with emergent vegetation and wetlands with adjacent tallgrass or shortgrass prairie.

Nest: Well concealed on the ground in a depression of grasses and lined with feathers and down. Usually placed near water but will also nest in prairies some distance from water.

NESTING ECOLOGY

Season: May–August. Single-brooded.

Eggs: Usually 8–12; pale olive buff to pale green gray, similar to Mallard and Northern Pintail.

Development: Incubation is by the female for 22–26 days. Young are precocial and can fly in about 50 days. As in most ducks, only the female tends the young.

DISTRIBUTION AND ABUNDANCE

Rangewide: Breeds throughout much of western North America, and locally in southeast Canada and the eastern United States. Primarily winters along the east and west coast states, southern United States, and south to Central America.

Historical: Described as a rare and local summer resident breeding irregularly in small numbers at Salt Plains National Wildlife Refuge and in the Panhandle.

Uncommon to common in migration and winter; more common west.

Current: The scarcity of records for Northern Shoveler is not surprising, given that northern Oklahoma is at the southern edge of the species' breeding range. Many of the Probable Breeder records may be the result of pairs being seen prior to the end of spring migration.

Population Trend: Breeding Bird Survey data for 1966–2000 show an increase of 2.1 percent per year rangewide (P = 0.01). No trend data are available for Oklahoma.

References: AOU 1998; Baicich and Harrison 1997; Baumgartner and Baumgartner 1992; Bellrose 1976; Dubowy 1996; Heitmeyer and Vohs 1984; Jacobs and Wilson 1997; Sauer et al. 2001; Sutton 1967; Terres 1991

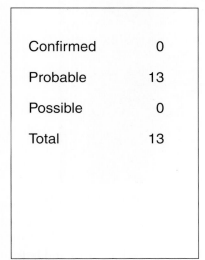

Confirmed	0
Probable	13
Possible	0
Total	13

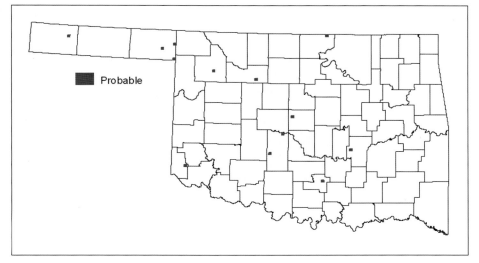

■ Probable

Northern Pintail

Anas acuta

David E. Fantina

Courtesy of Bill Horn

The Northern Pintail is well known to hunters in Oklahoma because it is one of the most abundant of waterfowl in the state during migration. However, it is very rare here as a breeding bird, as most move on to the prairie pothole region of Canada and the northern United States to nest. Its habit of nesting in agricultural fields has caused many nests to be destroyed, and its numbers have declined considerably in the past few decades.

Description: The handsome male Northern Pintail is unmistakable with its chocolate-brown head, white neck, gray body, and long streamer tail. The female is a mottled brown bird with a gray bill that can best be told from other female ducks by its long neck and large size.

Breeding Habitat: Grasslands and cultivated fields near lakes, rivers, and ponds.

Nest: The female makes a hollow in the ground and lines it with plant material.

NESTING ECOLOGY

Season: April–June. Single-brooded.
Eggs: Usually 7–9; yellow green to greenish blue.
Development: Incubation is by the female for 22–24

days. Young are precocial and fledge in about 4–6 weeks.

DISTRIBUTION AND ABUNDANCE

Rangewide: A widespread species breeding in the Western Hemisphere from northern Alaska and Canada as far south as Arizona, New Mexico, the Oklahoma Panhandle, and Kentucky. Winters throughout much of North America south to northern South America. Also occurs in Europe and Asia.

Historical: Described as an abundant migrant and uncommon to common winter resident, with a few nest records. Nests have been found in Alfalfa, Harper, Beaver, and Cimarron counties.

Current: The map of the Northern Pintail's distribution has to be viewed with caution because some records scored as Probable may actually represent late migrants observed as pairs. However, two sighting of fledglings in Texas County in July of 2001 continues a historical trend of sporadic breeding in the Panhandle.

Population Trend: Breeding Bird Survey data for 1966–2000 show a decline of 3.3 percent per year rangewide (P = 0.00), but no conclusive trend in Oklahoma (13.5 percent per year, P = 0.42). The Northern Pintail's North American population has declined severely from about 6 million birds in the 1970s to approximately half that number 20 years later. Losses are attributed to a variety of factors including farming operations, predation, and drought. New conservation measures appear to be helping the population to recover.

References: AOU 1998; Austin and Miller 1995; Baicich and Harrison 1997; Baumgartner and Baumgartner 1992; Bellrose 1976; Heflebower and Klett 1980; Sauer et al. 2001; Sutton 1967; U.S. Fish and Wildlife Service and Canadian Wildlife Service 1989

Confirmed	0
Probable	8
Possible	0
Total	8

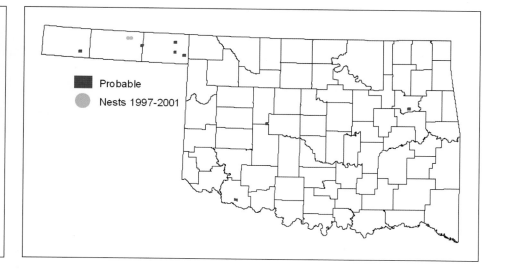

Probable
Nests 1997-2001

Redhead
Aythya americana

Alan E. Versaw

Courtesy of Warren Williams

Among Oklahoma's breeding ducks, the Redhead stands as the lone representative of the genus *Aythya*. While most of these diving specialists depart for more northern climes during the breeding season, Redheads linger a bit farther south than their cousins. Even so, the handful of Redheads that breed in Oklahoma range at least five degrees south of the species' normal breeding range at this longitude.

Description: The smoothly rounded red head and yellow eye set the drake Redhead apart from all North American ducks. Other marks of the male include the black breast and grayish back and sides. The pale blue (male) or gray (female) bill is marked by a black tip. A white band around the bill of the male just above the

black tip may be seen at close range. Females are remarkably similar to the females of other *Aythya* species and are best distinguished by head shape and bill pattern. Redheads rarely vocalize and few birders are able to recognize the species by voice.

Breeding Habitat: Redheads exhibit a pronounced preference for alkaline marshlands of one or more acres in size. Within this habitat, marshes with extensive growth of bulrushes or cattails are favored, but the species may also nest in sedges or on dryland sites.

Nest: A hollow or cup invariably lined with down. Nests tend to be more substantial in wet areas than dry. When the nest is built over a wet area, the structure is anchored to emergent growth, typically bulrushes or cattails.

NESTING ECOLOGY

Season: Primarily April–July. Single-brooded.

Eggs: 9–15 in a single nest. Hens may, however, dump several more eggs in available nearby nests. Eggs are typically glossy and green or pale olive in color.

Development: Incubation is by the female for 23–29 days. Young are precocial and tended by the female for 30–40 days before they are capable of flight. Females often abandon young before they are ready to take flight.

DISTRIBUTION AND ABUNDANCE

Rangewide: Breeds from Manitoba to British Columbia in the north and from Colorado to California in the south. Scattered populations breed as far north as Alaska and in the northeastern states and southeastern provinces of Canada. Winters across the southern tier of states into Mexico and Cuba.

Historical: Described as an uncommon winter resident. First Oklahoma breeding record from 1958 at Salt Plains National Wildlife Refuge; a few later records.

Current: The large number of Probable Breeder records may suggest something other than actual breeding activity. Redhead "pairs" continue to appear after the window of migration has safely passed for most duck species, particularly divers. Occasional non-breeding Redheads linger through the summer, underscoring the need for careful documentation of all breeding activity in Oklahoma. While breeding records do exist for this species in Oklahoma, the range of such breeding activity over a limited period of time is likely less extensive than the atlas map suggests. Never more than a marginal breeder in Oklahoma, and probably absent during many or most summer seasons.

Population Trend: Breeding Bird Survey data for 1966–2000 show an increase of 3.3 percent per year rangewide (P = 0.00). No trend data are available for Oklahoma.

References: Baicich and Harrison 1997; Baumgartner and Baumgartner 1992; Bellrose 1980; Joyner 1983; Kaufman 1996; Madge and Burn 1988; McKnight 1974; Ryser 1985; Sauer et al. 2001; Sutton 1967

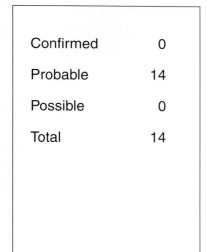

Confirmed	0
Probable	14
Possible	0
Total	14

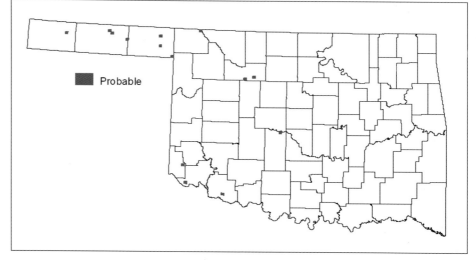

■ Probable

Hooded Merganser
Lophodytes cucullatus

Richard A. Stuart

Courtesy of Bill Horn

Oklahoma's woodland fishing duck, the Hooded Merganser, is becoming a regular summer resident of the Salt Plains National Wildlife Refuge. It often uses Wood Duck nest boxes, and eggs of both species are sometimes found together. Crayfish and aquatic insects round out its diet, and its eyes are well adapted to see its underwater prey.

Description: The male has a black head and a black-and-white crest, the white of the crest being outlined with black and appearing fan-shaped when raised. The breast is white with a black stripe extending from the black shoulders, the flanks are brownish, and the short, thin bill is black. The female is brownish overall, with the crest being reddish brown. The voice consists of low grunting or croaking sounds. Males are most easily confused with the male Bufflehead, which has white sides, a stouter bill, and a more rounded head. The female may be confused with other female merganser but has a much smaller size, a yellowish bill, and a fan-shaped crest.

Breeding Habitat: Slow-moving woodland rivers, ponds, lakes, and marshes. They may also be found nesting in nonwooded wetlands where artificial nesting cavities have been provided.

Nest: Natural cavities in trees and snags, as well as artificial nest boxes 1–27 m (3–89 ft) above ground. The cavity is lined with debris and down from the female's breast.

NESTING ECOLOGY

Season: April–June. Single-brooded.

Eggs: 6–12; pure glossy white and nearly spherical. Larger clutches sometimes result from multiple females laying in a single nest. Parasitism from and toward Wood Ducks is also common.

Development: Incubation is by the female for 29–33 days. Young are brooded by the female for the first 24 hours before leaving the nest. They are subsequently attended by the female and fledge in about 70 days.

DISTRIBUTION AND ABUNDANCE

Rangewide: A short-distance migrant breeding in southeastern Alaska, southern Canada, and the northeastern states southward and west to Missouri. They winter south to the Gulf of Mexico and in parts of the western United States.

Historical: The Hooded Merganser was first confirmed as a breeding bird in Oklahoma in May 1977 on the Sequoyah National Wildlife Refuge in Sequoyah County when a hen and 8 small ducklings were observed. A second nesting, a female and 8 ducklings, were reported in May 1981 near the headquarters of the Salt Plains National Wildlife Refuge. More recently, according to refuge personnel, Hooded Mergansers utilize nearly half of the Wood Duck nest boxes at the Salt Plains NWR.

Current: The local distribution of the Hooded Merganser makes it poorly sampled by atlas methods. They may be expanding their breeding range and could be expected to nest at slow-moving bodies of water. Several breeding confirmations reported from locations not within atlas blocks are mapped.

Population Trend: Breeding Bird Survey data for 1966–2000 show an increase of 8.2 percent per year rangewide (P = 0.09). No trend data are available for Oklahoma.

References: AOU 1998; Baicich and Harrison 1997; Baumgartner and Baumgartner 1992; Bellrose 1976; Clover 1981; Dugger et al. 1994; Gooders and Boyer 1986; Harrison 1975; National Geographic Society 1999; Norman 1977; Pearson 1936; Peterson 1963; Sauer et al. 2001; Sibley 2000; Stokes and Stokes 1996; Sutton 1967

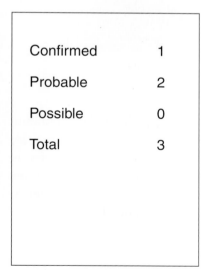

Confirmed	1
Probable	2
Possible	0
Total	3

Ruddy Duck

Oxyura jamaicensis

Alan E. Versaw

As adept in water as it is helpless on land, the Ruddy Duck ranks among Oklahoma's rarest breeding waterfowl. They may, however, be slightly more common as breeders than their reputation indicates. While summer drakes, with their white faces and sky-blue bills, are readily visible when present, the females spend much of the summer hidden by dense vegetation. Even after ducklings emerge from the nest they, like most other ducklings, are not easily identified by casual observation, although the presence of a nearby adult female can help.

Description: A small diving duck, the drake in breeding plumage is unmistakable, with his uniformly red-

dish body, black crown and nape, white face, and blue bill. The brownish hen, with a thin dark line below the eye acting as the single most distinctive character, is considerably easier to confuse with females of other small ducks. Identification of both male and female Ruddies is made easier by the fact that both sexes often hold their stiff tails at a steep angle, sometimes approaching the vertical.

Breeding Habitat: Both freshwater and alkaline marshes. Their nests are typically hidden within dense emergent vegetation of cattails, reeds, or bulrushes, but they also require marshes with enough open water to facilitate takeoffs and landings. Ideal foraging conditions are found in waters just deep enough that the bottom vegetation lies beyond the reach of dabbling ducks.

Nest: Either built up from the marsh bottom or anchored to surrounding emergent vegetation. The woven nest boasts a substantial inside diameter of up to 0.3 m (1 ft). Plants are pulled together over the nest in order to help conceal it.

NESTING ECOLOGY

Season: May–August. Single-brooded. Breeds late in season with greater regularity than most ducks.

Eggs: Usually 6–10; white, exceptionally large and round. Females of this species are notorious for egg dumping in nests of any nearby species. One hen may lay as many as 60 eggs in a single season.

Development: Incubation is by the female for 24 days. Young are precocial and are accompanied by both the female and the male, unusual among ducks. Young can fly by 6–7 weeks.

DISTRIBUTION AND ABUNDANCE

Rangewide: Breeds extensively throughout central and western North America, even as far north as the Yukon Territory and Alaska. A smaller population breeds in the area of the eastern Great Lakes. Winters in the southern and western United States south to Central America. The species has been introduced in Europe where it competes with the similar, and endangered, White-headed Duck.

Historical: Although widespread throughout Oklahoma during migration and somewhat less common during winter, the Ruddy enjoys a very limited breeding range in the state. Most summer and breeding records are from the Panhandle and northwestern corner of the state, with the first definitive nest record being from Cimarron County in June of 1978.

Current: Little is known about the breeding status and distribution of the Ruddy Duck within Oklahoma. Several observations of fledglings outside of designated atlas blocks suggest the species is more widely distributed as a breeder than previously suspected. Still, the atlas methodology is poorly suited to offering a comprehensive picture of the breeding status of relatively scarce and localized breeders such as the Ruddy Duck.

Population Trend: Breeding Bird Survey data for 1966–2000 show no conclusive trend rangewide (1.5 percent per year, P = 0.17). No trend data are available for Oklahoma.

References: Baicich and Harrison 1997; Baumgartner and Baumgartner 1992; Bellrose 1980; Johnsgard 1978; Joyner 1977, 1983; Kingery 1998; Madge and Burn 1988; Palmer 1976; Sauer et al. 2001; Shackford 1980; Sutton 1967

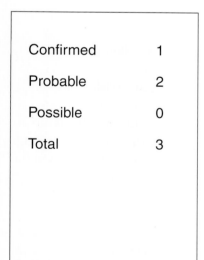

Confirmed	1
Probable	2
Possible	0
Total	3

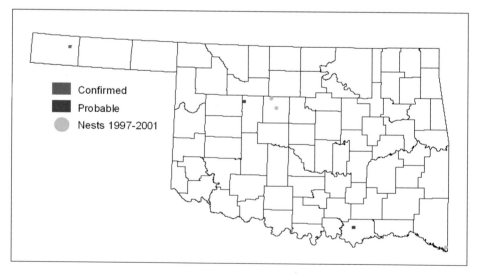

Confirmed
Probable
Nests 1997-2001

Osprey
Pandion haliaetus

Richard A. Stuart

The "Fish Hawk" is so named because of its almost exclusive diet of fish. The Osprey is very well adapted to capturing such prey and makes impressive stoops from the air to do so. Only two to three nest records exist for Oklahoma, where this species is primarily a migrant.

Description: Both the male and female are similar, with brown on the back and a brown-and-white-barred tail; the head is white with a prominent dark eye stripe; the underparts are white with brown streaking across the female's breast. The wings are narrow and bent backward at the wrist with obvious dark carpal patches. Vocalizations consist of a series of a high-pitched *keer, keer, keer* calls. When hunting, they will dive directly into the water feet first to capture their prey.

Breeding Habitat: Near water, along lakes or rivers.

Nest: A huge collection of sticks and debris up to 18.3 m (60 ft) high in a tree, cliff, platform, piling, buoy, or even on the ground, and normally reused for several years with more material added each year.

NESTING ECOLOGY

Season: March–June. Single-brooded.
Eggs: Usually 3; creamy to yellowish with dark brown spots and blotches.
Development: Incubation is by both sexes for 32–33

days. Young are fed by the female with food brought by the male and fledge in 51–59 days.

DISTRIBUTION AND ABUNDANCE

Rangewide: Nearly cosmopolitan in range except for the polar regions and New Zealand. Breeds in North America mostly in the northern and western United States and Canada. In the Western Hemisphere, winters in the southern United States to South America.

Historical: Although the Osprey is a regular migrant and there are a few summer records in Oklahoma, there are only two valid nesting records. In 1958 or 1959 a large nest was discovered below the Salt Plains Reservoir dam in Alfalfa County, where the adults were feeding young. The second record was in 1983 at the Robert S. Kerr Reservoir in Sequoyah County, where adults were observed feeding one chick. A report of nesting in Cherokee County in 1928 is considered unsubstantiated.

Current: No Ospreys with any level of breeding status were reported during the five years of the atlas project surveys.

Population Trend: Breeding Bird Survey data for 1966–2000 show an increase of 6.4 percent per year rangewide for North America (P = 0.00). No trend data are available for Oklahoma because the species is essentially accidental in summer.

References: AOU 1998; Baicich and Harrison 1997; Baumgartner and Baumgartner 1992; Bent 1961; Brown 1976; Harrison 1975; Isley and Lish 1986; Loyd 1987; McMahon, D. J., III 1989; National Geographic Society 1999; Parry and Putman 1979; Perrins and Harrison 1979; Peterson 1963; Sibley 2000; Snyder and Snyder 1991; Stokes and Stokes 1996; Stotts 1975; Sutton 1967

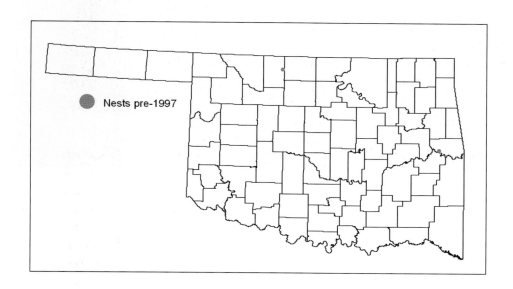

Nests pre-1997

White-tailed Kite
Elanus leucurus

Richard A. Stuart

Courtesy of Jim and Deva Burns / Natural Impacts

Formerly known as the Black-shouldered Kite, this species had a brush with extinction in the early twentieth century from which it later recovered. It has had an erratic history in Oklahoma, with sightings and nesting reports spaced over a century apart. Curiously, the type specimen egg for this species came from the 1860 nest near Fort Arbuckle.

Description: Falcon-like, the sexes are similar with white head and tail, pearl-gray upperparts, and black shoulder patches. The primaries are dark from below with a dark patch at the wrist or bend of the wings; the remaining undersides are white. The call is a short, descending whistle; also a raspy *kee-ah*. Although similar in coloring to gulls and terns, the wrist markings

will easily differentiate them, and the Mississippi Kite is never as white and also lacks the wrist markings.

Breeding Habitat: Open areas of grassland, cultivated fields, meadows, and riparian areas.

Nest: A well-concealed, loosely built but sound structure of twigs, lined with a variety of softer plant materials. Normally placed 4–18 m (12–60 ft) high in a tree.

NESTING ECOLOGY

Season: Primarily April–June. Sometimes double-brooded.
Eggs: Usually 4; white to faint buff with reddish-

brown scrawls and blotches heavier at the large end.
Development: Incubation is by the female for 30–32 days. Young are provisioned by the female with food brought by the male and fledge after 4–5 weeks.

DISTRIBUTION AND ABUNDANCE

Rangewide: Prior to the 1940s it was on the brink of extinction in the United States where it occurred in California and the southern states. Beginning in the 1960s, but especially after the 1980s, it increased dramatically in Texas. Now resident along parts of the West Coast, south Texas, Florida, and throughout much of Mexico and Central America.
Historical: Described in 1931 as "formerly a rare summer resident" based on an 1860 nest in Murray County. Two subsequent nest records are from Latimer County in 1982, over 120 years later than the other known nest record. Additional sightings occurred in Comanche, Tillman, and Tulsa counties in the early 1980s.

Current: The White-tailed Kite is a rare and erratic nester in the southeastern and south-central part of Oklahoma, to be looked for in savanna or riparian habitats. Due to its very rare and local distribution, it is poorly sampled by atlas methodology, but no reports for the species were received from any part of Oklahoma during the atlas project years.

Population Trend: Breeding Bird Survey data for 1966–2000 show no conclusive trend rangewide (5.6 percent per year, P = 0.24). Erratic occurrence in Oklahoma yields no trend information.

References: AOU 1998; Baicich and Harrison 1997; Bailey 1921; Baumgartner and Baumgartner 1992; Carter and Fowler 1992; Dunk 1995; Farrand 1988; Harrison 1975; National Geographic Society 1999; Nice 1931; Peterson 1963; Sauer et al. 2001; Sibley 2000; Stokes and Stokes 1996; Sutton 1967; Udvardy 1977

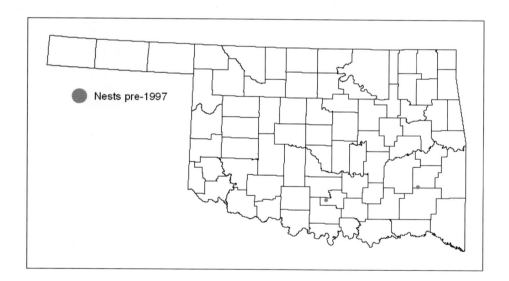

Nests pre-1997

Mississippi Kite
Ictinia mississippiensis

Victoria J. Byre

Courtesy of Gerald Wiens

The Mississippi Kite is one of the most exciting birds to watch as it swoops, dives, glides, twists, and soars in pursuit of large flying insects. Its slender body and long falcon-like wings enable it to fly with speed as well as gracefulness.

Description: Male and female Mississippi Kites are similar in size and are dark gray overall, except for black primaries and tail, and white on the uppersides of the secondaries. The adult male has a whitish head while the adult female has a somewhat duskier head but paler undersides of the primaries and tail. Immatures are heavily streaked and spotted, with pale bands on the tail. The superficially similar male

Northern Harrier has a completely different flight pattern, rounder wing tips, and an obvious white rump patch. The call of the Mississippi Kite is a high, thin whistled *yipEEEER,* or *peeTEEER,* very similar in tone to the Broad-winged Hawk's call, but descending rather than held on one pitch.

Breeding Habitat: Riverine forests, wooded streams, open woodlands, shelter belts, or groves, usually near open fields, prairies, or plains. They also nest in wooded suburbs, city parks, and golf courses.

Nest: A flimsy platform of dead twigs, lined with green leaves in a tree usually 6–10.5 m (20–35 ft) above ground, but may be higher or lower, depending on available sites. Often nests colonially. The species is sometimes aggressive in nest defense.

NESTING ECOLOGY

Season: May–July, sometimes later. Single-brooded.
Eggs: Usually 2; white or bluish white.
Development: Incubation is by both sexes for about 30 days. Young are provisioned by both sexes, fledge at about 34 days, but rely on adults for food for 6–8 more weeks.

DISTRIBUTION AND ABUNDANCE

Rangewide: Breeds in the central and southern Great Plains, scattered areas of the Southwest, and in southern states along the Mississippi River and east of it. They apparently winter in central South America, but winter records are very scarce.
Historical: Described as abundant along the Arkansas River and its tributaries in 1853, but considered a summer resident only in western Oklahoma, excluding the Panhandle, by 1931. By 1992, described as an uncommon to common summer resident in the western and central parts of the state.
Current: The Mississippi Kite's preference for nesting near open fields, prairies, and plains is documented by

its common occurrence in the central and western parts of the state and its scarcity in the more forested eastern third of the region. The high number of Confirmed and Probable nesting reports may be due in part to the kite's spectacular aerial acrobatics over its territory and its sometimes aggressive nest defense.

Population Trend: Breeding Bird Survey data for 1966–2000 show no conclusive trend rangewide (-0.5 percent per year, P = 0.70) and a decline of 4.3 percent per year in Oklahoma (P = 0.00). The species has undergone major population fluctuations since the mid-1800s, in Oklahoma and elsewhere, as a result of shooting, egg collecting, pesticide use, and habitat change. In more recent decades, since afforded legal protection and with the regulation of pesticides, the breeding range is again expanding in Oklahoma and elsewhere, and the species is commonly seen in all but the eastern regions of the state.

References: AOU 1998; Baicich and Harrison 1997; Baumgartner and Baumgartner 1992; Bolen and Flores 1993; Engle 1981; Eubanks 1971; Franson 1994; Freeman 1993; Garrison 1986; Mason 1983; Nice 1931; Parker 1999; Parker and Ogden 1979; Sauer et al. 2001; Sutton 1939, 1944, 1967; Wheeler and Clark 1999; Woodhouse 1853

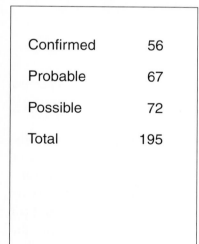

Confirmed	56
Probable	67
Possible	72
Total	195

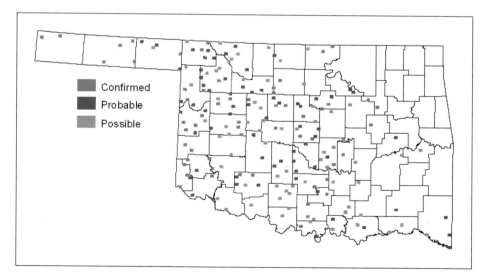

Bald Eagle
Haliaeetus leucocephalus

M. Alan Jenkins

Designated by Congress as our nation's symbol, the species has not always received the respect its high office deserves. Bounties for eagle feet were once paid in Alaska in a ill-considered attempt to improve the fishing industry there, and the use of persistent pesticides caused it to disappear from parts of its range and lower population and productivity in other parts. Luckily, there was concern in the conservation sector that led to its recovery and a recent proposal to take it off the list of threatened and endangered species. From 1984 through 1992, 275 young Bald Eagles were reared from eggs taken in Florida and released into 8 southeastern states; 90 of these were released in eastern Oklahoma, resulting in an increase from no known nesting pairs in 1990 to the current level of 33 active nests in 2002.

Description: A large diurnal bird of prey with unfeathered tarsi. Adults have a solid brown body with a white or mostly white head and tail and a yellow beak and cere. Immatures have black to brown plumage with varying amounts of white in the head, back, belly, tail, and tail coverts, as well as the underwing linings and axillaries; the beak and cere are of variable dark color becoming yellow with age. The similar-sized Golden Eagle has feathered tarsi and a black beak and is dark with golden neck hackles as an adult, with variable amounts of white in the tail and primaries as an immature.

Breeding Habitat: Large trees with open branch structure, situated in close proximity to a reservoir or large river. Rarely near smaller ponds, lakes, or creeks unless they are close to larger rivers or reservoirs.

Nest: A large structure, 6 feet or more in diameter, made of large sticks and lined with grasses or other softer vegetation to form the nest cup. The nest is usually placed in the largest, oldest tree with an open branch structure in the area. Living trees are preferred, but dead snags have been used.

NESTING ECOLOGY

Season: December–February for egg laying. Single-brooded, but may replace lost clutches.

Eggs: 1–3, 2 on average; dull white with few if any markings.

Development: Incubation is by both sexes for 35 days. Young are provisioned mostly by the male for the first 2 weeks while the female broods, but later by both sexes. Fledging occurs at 11–12 weeks of age, but there is a long postfledging dependency period that may last for 2 months or more.

DISTRIBUTION AND ABUNDANCE

Rangewide: Occurs only in North America. Generally uncommon, more common in coastal areas and Great Lakes areas, and especially common in coastal Alaska.

Historical: While some historical sources hint at the possibility of Bald Eagles nesting in Oklahoma, the first documented successful nesting took place in 1978 in Haskell County. From 1984 to 1990, 90 captive-reared eagles were released in Oklahoma by the George M. Sutton Avian Research Center as part of a larger eagle restoration program in the southeastern United States. This successful program began increasing the number of known eagle nests in Oklahoma.

Current: In Oklahoma, nesting distribution is mostly along the Arkansas River and its main tributaries from Tulsa to Arkansas, with a few nests in Osage County, at the Grand Lake of the Cherokees, at Wes Watkins Reservoir, and recently acquired reports from the Chandler area. The number of known nests in the state peaked at 33 in 2002. Because of this small number of nests in the state, only one nest was actually located within an atlas block.

Population Trend: Increasing nationally in the lower 48 states since 1990, mostly owing to reintroductions. Breeding Bird Survey data for 1966–2000 show an increase of 8 percent per year rangewide (P = 0.00). Downlisted from Endangered to Threatened in 1996. In Oklahoma, increased from zero nesting pairs to over 30 pairs in the 1990s.

References: AOU 1998; Baumgartner and Baumgartner 1992; Buehler 2000; Carmichael 1978; George M. Sutton Avian Research Center, unpublished data; Isley 1979, 1982; Jenkins and Sherrod 1993, 1994; Lish and Sherrod 1986; Palmer 1988; Sauer et al. 2001; Simons et al. 1988; Stalmaster 1987; Sutton 1967

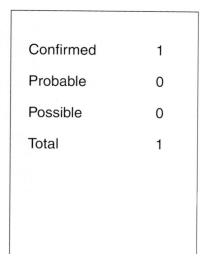

Confirmed	1
Probable	0
Possible	0
Total	1

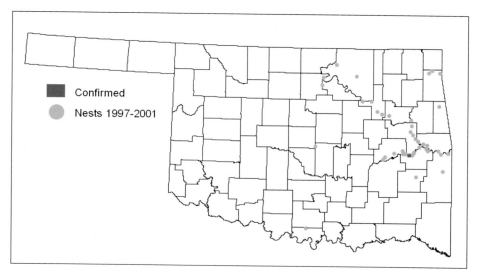

■ Confirmed
● Nests 1997-2001

Northern Harrier

Circus cyaneus

Gregory A. Smith

Gracefully gliding low over prairies and marshes, Northern Harriers are slim, medium-sized hawks with owl-like faces. Formerly known as the Marsh Hawk, Northern Harriers are the only harrier species in North America and the only ground-nesting hawk in Oklahoma. Harriers also distinguish themselves from other hawks by relying heavily on auditory cues when hunting prey, unlike most hawks, which are primarily visual hunters.

Description: Slim, medium-sized hawk with long, broad wings and long legs and tail. A characteristic facial ruff lends an owl-like appearance. Females and juvenile males are dark brown above and buffy below, with some streaking on the underparts. Adult males are gray above, white below, with wingtips edged in black. Both sexes display a characteristic white rump patch. Females are, on average, larger than males.

Breeding Habitat: Open grasslands, wetlands, marshes, pastures, old fields, and dry upland prairies.

Nest: A shallow depression in the ground lined with grass or a platform of sticks, grass, and reeds built predominately by the female with the male providing some materials. Most nests are placed in treeless, vegetated areas. Some are built up in standing water, raising it above water level.

NESTING ECOLOGY

Season: April–June. Single-brooded, but may renest if an early clutch is lost.

Eggs: Usually 4–6; light bluish fading to white after 2–4 days.

Development: Incubation is by the female for 30–32 days. Both the young and the female are provisioned by the male until the young are 10–14 days old. Young fledge in about 33 days (males) to 37 days (females).

DISTRIBUTION AND ABUNDANCE

Rangewide: Breeds widely throughout northern, central, and western North America, essentially from northern Alaska and Canada south to Baja in the west. Absent as a regular breeder in many midwestern states as well as the southeast. Primarily a short-distance migrant, wintering in the eastern and southern United States south to Central America. Much of the western United States and Great Plains have year-round populations of Harriers.

Historical: Widely dispersed and sparse breeder throughout northern and western Oklahoma. Breeding records exist from as far south as Marshall County, but no records from southeastern counties. Several nest records exist for Osage County in the early to mid-1990s.

Current: Northern Harriers are uncommon breeders in the state. Although a number of blocks recorded harriers, some of the blocks scored as Probable or Possible may be the result of birds seen prior to the end of spring migration. The only blocks in which nesting was confirmed were within the shortgrass prairies of the Panhandle, specifically Texas County. Harriers are much more common in the state during winter.

Population Trend: Breeding Bird Survey data for 1996–2000 show no conclusive trend rangewide (-0.7 percent per year, P = 0.15) and a very large 15.6 percent per year decline in Oklahoma (P = 0.00).

References: AOU 1998; Baumgartner and Baumgartner 1992; Baumgartner and Howell 1942, 1948; Bent 1961; Brown and Amadon 1968; Force 1929; Hamerstrom 1986; Harden 1972; Johnsgard 1979, 1990; Kaufman 1996; Looney 1972; MacWhirter and Bildstein 1996; Montaperto 1988; Moore 1927; Nice 1927; Palmer 1988; Peterjohn and Sauer 1999; Platt 1974; Regosin et al. 1991; Sallee 1974; Sauer et al. 2001; Silver 1952; Sutton 1967; Tate 1923, 1924; Thompson and Ely 1989; Wood and Schnell 1984

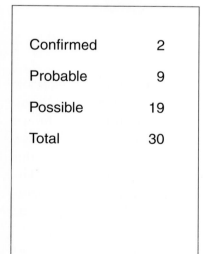

Confirmed	2
Probable	9
Possible	19
Total	30

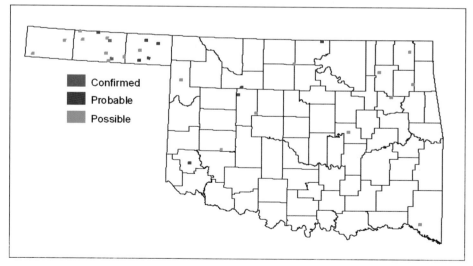

Cooper's Hawk

Accipiter cooperii

M. Alan Jenkins

The "blue darter," as the Cooper's Hawk was once called, is a furtive bird of woodlands and forests that is usually only glimpsed for short periods, if seen at all. Feeders of birds are often dismayed to see this predator zipping through their back yard. But if not for the speedy avian predators such as the accipiters, what would have caused other birds to evolve such fleetness of wing? The adult Cooper's Hawk, especially the male, is a study of deep blue and reds worthy of any birder's life list.

Description: A medium (crow)-sized, bird-hunting, woodland hawk. Like other accipiter hawks, it is secretive and usually inconspicuous. It has a rounded wing shape in flight and a long tail. Adults are brown (female) or bluish brown (male) with red barring below and have orange to red eyes and a dark crown. Juveniles are brown above and cream with brown streaks below. The nest defense call is a loud *kak, kak, kak, kak* or *ci, ci, ci, ci* challenge to intruders; this species is usually silent during most of the year. The similar Sharp-shinned Hawk is smaller, has a proportionally smaller head, and lacks the dark cap of the Cooper's Hawk.

Breeding Habitat: Extensive forest, woods 4–8 ha (10–20 ac) in size, and occasionally lone trees. More recently, this species has been known to nest in urban parks and pine plantations.

Nest: A platform of twigs placed in a deciduous or coniferous trees, 8–15 m (26–49 ft) high under a closed canopy, and often near water.

NESTING ECOLOGY

Season: April–July. Single-brooded, but will replace lost clutches.

Eggs: Usually 3–5; white or pale blue.

Development: Incubation is by the female for 34–36 days. Young are provisioned by both sexes, fledge at 27–34 days, and reach independence at about 8 weeks.

DISTRIBUTION AND ABUNDANCE

Rangewide: Breeds throughout southern Canada and most of the United States. Winters across much of the United States and south to Colombia.

Historical: Described as an uncommon winter resident and rare summer resident throughout the state in 1992. From a previous, intensive 3-year survey conducted in the Oklahoma Panhandle during the early to mid-1990s especially designed to detect raptors, it is known to nest with regularity in this area.

Current: The secretive nature of all the accipiter hawks makes them difficult to survey for and confirm as breeders, especially with general survey methods intended to detect all bird species such as the atlas protocol. The atlas surveys show that, as a nesting species, it is widely distributed in the state, but at low population levels.

Population Trend: Breeding Bird Survey data for 1966–2000 show an increase of 5.8 percent per year rangewide (P = 0.00) and an increase of 31.4 percent per year in Oklahoma (P = 0.01), although the magnitude of the actual increase is somewhat uncertain because this species is poorly monitored by this survey. Populations apparently have rebounded from the pesticide-era declines in the 1960s.

References: AOU 1998; Baumgartner and Baumgartner 1992; Droege 1989; George M. Sutton Avian Research Center 1995; Palmer 1988; Regosin 1994a; Rosenfield and Bielefeldt 1993; Sauer et al. 2001; Shackford 1984; Sutton 1967

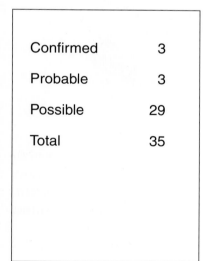

Confirmed	3
Probable	3
Possible	29
Total	35

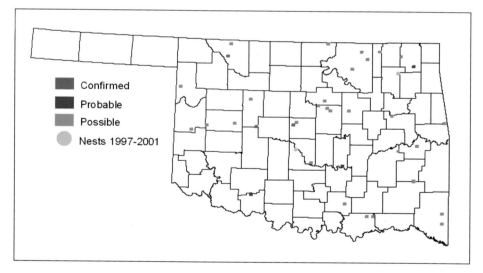

Confirmed
Probable
Possible
Nests 1997-2001

Red-shouldered Hawk
Buteo lineatus

Victoria J. Byre

The Red-shouldered Hawk inhabits lowland forests and wooded creek and river bottoms. It is known for using the same nesting territory year after year, and for the breathtaking courtship displays that are performed in the open sky high above its woodland nest sites.

Description: The Red-shouldered Hawk has relatively long wings and a longish tail for a buteo, or soaring hawk. The adults have a cinnamon-colored breast and wing linings, reddish shoulders, and, from above, bold white spots on dark wings. Three or four white bands alternate with wider black bands on the tail, and in flight, the black-and-white-checkered flight feathers show pale, crescent-shaped "windows" parallel to the dark wing tips. The slightly smaller Broad-winged Hawk, another woodland buteo, has only one obvious wide white band on its tail in adult plumage. The Red-shouldered Hawk's harsh *keyaar, keyaar* call is often superbly imitated by Blue Jays.

Breeding Habitat: Moist, mature woodlands, flooded deciduous swamps, wooded riparian areas, and even wooded suburban areas with creeks or ponds nearby.

Nest: Constructed of dead and live twigs and branches and lined with items such as leafy twigs, leaves, bark, moss, and sprigs of conifers. It is usually placed in a fork or crotch of a tree 6–18 m (20–60 ft) high.

NESTING ECOLOGY

Season: April–July. Single-brooded, but may replace lost clutches.

Eggs: Usually 3–4; light tan or bluish white with reddish brown or dark brown variably sized speckles, spots, and blotches.

Development: Incubation is by both sexes, but mostly by the female, for about 33 days per egg. Initially young are provisioned mostly by the male while the female broods. Young are capable of flight after 5–6 weeks.

DISTRIBUTION AND ABUNDANCE

Rangewide: Breeds throughout eastern North America from southern Canada through Florida and as far west as riparian woodlands of the eastern Great Plains. A western population breeds west of the Sierra Nevadas from extreme southern Oregon to northern Baja California. Only the northernmost populations are migratory, but usually do not travel far, although some may migrate to the southern edges of the breeding range or into central Mexico for winter.

Historical: Described as fairly common to rare in bottomland woods in eastern and central Oklahoma, but usually only a rare visitant to western parts of the state.

Current: The Red-shouldered Hawk prefers lowland forests and moist wooded areas and is common in the eastern half of the state. In other habitats it is almost completely absent, as in the western third of the state. The high number of atlas blocks showing this species as Possible gives evidence of the Red-shouldered's very vocal nature.

Population Trend: Breeding Bird Survey data for 1966–2000 show an increase of 2.6 percent per year rangewide (P = 0.00), but no conclusive trend in Oklahoma (7.1 percent per year, P = 0.14).

References: AOU 1998; Baicich and Harrison 1997; Baumgartner and Baumgartner 1992; Bednarz et al. 1990; Bent 1961; Byre 1995; Crocoll 1994; Palmer 1988; Sauer et al. 2001; Stokes and Stokes 1996; Sutton 1967; Tyler et al. 1989

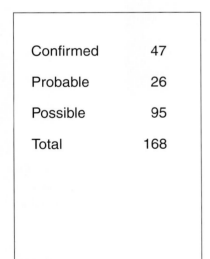

Confirmed	47
Probable	26
Possible	95
Total	168

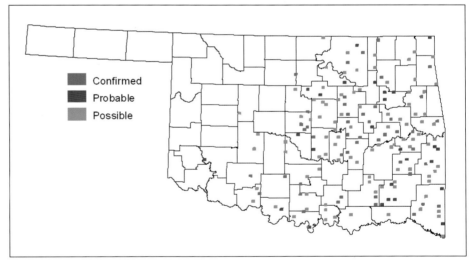

Broad-winged Hawk
Buteo platypterus

Melinda Droege

Courtesy of Gerald Wiens

Though Oklahoma misses the spectacularly large kettles of Broad-winged Hawks seen in some locales during migration, many woodlands host a nesting pair of these small secretive buteos. They spend the spring and summer beneath the forest canopy quietly raising their young and hunting the woods and streams.

Description: A small, stocky buteo about the size of a crow, the Broad-winged Hawk has white underwings outlined with dark borders. Its tail has broad black-and-white bands of equal width. Can be confused with the Red-shouldered Hawk, which in all plumages is longer tailed and longer winged with pale crescents at the base of the primaries. The Broad-winged has both broader wings and a broader, shorter tail. The call is a shrill, high-pitched whistle *p-wee-e-e-e-e* somewhat suggestive of the Eastern Wood-Pewee.

Breeding Habitat: Dense oak-hickory-pine woods of southern Oklahoma and heavily wooded bottomlands of northeastern and central Oklahoma. Always near ponds or streams.

Nest: Small and loosely built of twigs and sticks, lined with bark and lichens by both sexes; female decorates with greenery throughout incubation and nestling stage. Nest is built usually in main crotch of deciduous (occasionally coniferous) tree 7.3–12.2 m (24–40 ft) from ground and near water. Often an old nest of other birds or squirrels may be used.

NESTING ECOLOGY

Season: April–June. Single-brooded.
Eggs: Usually 2–3; dull or creamy white marked with brown or purple splashes.
Development: Incubation is primarily by the female for 28–30 days. Young are provisioned by both sexes and fledge at 5–6 weeks. Fledglings have been observed using nest as feeding and roost site up to 2 weeks after first flight and may stay on territory with siblings and adults up to 8 weeks after fledging.

DISTRIBUTION AND ABUNDANCE

Rangewide: Summer resident in eastern United States and central and southern Canada. Winters in southern Florida, Mexico, and Central America south to Bolivia and Brazil.

Historical: Uncommon summer resident in eastern Oklahoma, rare central. Nesting has been recorded west to Osage, Payne, Cleveland, and Love counties.
Current: The Broad-winged Hawk's secretive nature may explain the relatively small number of detections in atlas blocks. Confirmed and Probable observations indicate that the species may breed farther west than previously reported.

Population Trend: Breeding Bird Survey data for 1966–2000 show no conclusive trend rangewide (0.6 percent per year, P = 0.43) or in Oklahoma (-0.2 percent per year, P = 0.92).

References: AOU 1998; Baicich and Harrison 1997; Baumgartner and Baumgartner 1992; Bent 1961; Ehrlich et al. 1988; Goodrich et al. 1996; Harrison 1975; Johnsgard 1979; Matray 1974; Nice 1931; Romero and Romero 1971; Rosenfield 1984; Sauer et al. 2001; Sutton 1967

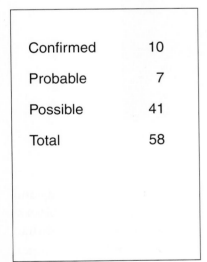

Confirmed	10
Probable	7
Possible	41
Total	58

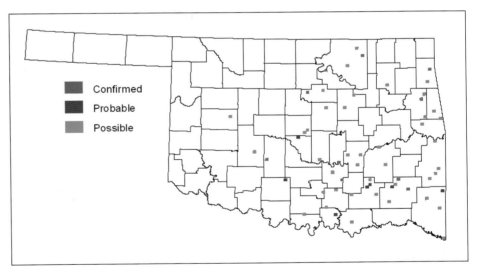

Swainson's Hawk
Buteo swainsoni

Gregory A. Smith

The Swainson's Hawk is a common hawk of plains and prairies. It undertakes the second longest migration of any raptor species, some traveling over 10,000 km (6,213 mi) each way. A highly gregarious species, flocks (or "kettles") can number into the thousands during spring and autumn migration. In October of 1954, 2,000 individuals were recorded in one day at Wichita Mountains National Wildlife Refuge in southwestern Oklahoma.

Description: A slender buteo with long, narrow, pointed wings. Plumage extremely variable, occurring in light, dark, and intermediate morphs. Light morph adults, which are the most common, are white below with a white throat patch and dark, rufous bib. Flight feathers are dark, contrasting with a white body and leading edges of underwings. Dark morph adults are brown to almost black below, with very little distinction between flight feathers and wing edges. Intermediate morphs can show any combination of these plumage characteristics but are often rufous below with a dark bib. All morphs show similar barring on the tail.

Breeding Habitat: Breeds on open plains, dry grassland, and farmland, in areas with scattered trees or bushes. Absent from dense and moist woodlands.

Nest: Conspicuous structure of twigs and grasses placed 2–20 m (6–66 ft) high in trees, rock outcrops, embankments, mesquite bushes, or giant cacti; only rarely on the ground. Nests are often lined with bark, lichens, and other plant material with leafy twigs added regularly. Both sexes help build the nest, and nests may be reused in successive breeding seasons.

NESTING ECOLOGY

Season: May–June. Single-brooded.
Eggs: 2–3; white, usually unmarked but may show some faint brown speckling.
Development: Incubation is almost exclusively by the female for 34–35 days. Young are provisioned primarily by the male, venture out of the nest at 27–33 days, and first fly at 38–46 days.

DISTRIBUTION AND ABUNDANCE

Rangewide: Breeds throughout the Great Plains and Great Basin from southern Canada to northern Mexico. Breeding populations extend from California, Oregon, and Washington in the west to western Missouri and parts of Iowa and Minnesota in the east. Highly migratory. Almost all of the North American breeding population winters in South America, primarily on the pampas of Argentina.
Historical: Described as a fairly common summer resident in western Oklahoma; local and rare farther east. At times abundant in migration.
Current: The Swainson's Hawk's preference for open,

dry plains is reflected in its breeding distribution in the state. All Confirmed atlas records occurred in the western half of the state, especially the Panhandle. Some Probable blocks could be the result of pairs seen prior to the end of spring migration. This primarily western distribution in Oklahoma is consistent with atlas data from Kansas and Texas, in which the majority of confirmed nestings bordered counties in western Oklahoma and the Panhandle.

Population Trend: Breeding Bird Survey data for 1966–2000 show no conclusive trend rangewide in North America (-0.3 percent per year, P = 0.65) and a decline of 4.5 percent per year in Oklahoma (P = 0.04).

References: AOU 1998; Baumgartner and Howell 1942, 1948; Baumgartner and Baumgartner 1992; Bechard et al. 1990; Bednarz 1988; Benson and Arnold 2002; Bent 1961; Brandt 1959; Brown and Amadon 1968; Busby and Zimmerman 2001; Dunkle 1977; England et al. 1997; Force 1929; Gilmer and Stewart 1984; Harden 1972; Heflebower and Klett 1980; Johnsgard 1979, 1990; Kaufman 1996; Keir and Wilde 1976; Moore 1927; Nice 1923, 1931; Nice and Nice 1925; Nighswonger 1977; Olendorff 1974; Palmer 1988; Parker 1976; Platt 1974; Sauer et al. 2001; Sutton 1967; Tate 1923, 1924; Thompson and Ely 1989; Thurow and White 1983; Tyler 1981; Wood and Schnell 1984; Zimmerman 1993

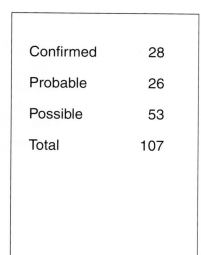

Confirmed	28
Probable	26
Possible	53
Total	107

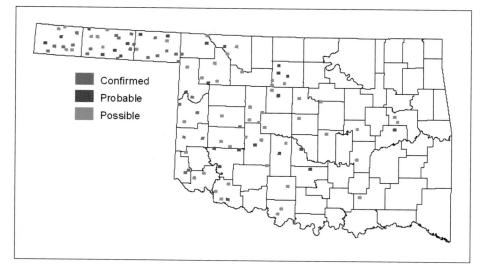

Red-tailed Hawk

Buteo jamaicensis

M. Alan Jenkins

Courtesy of Bob Gress

Not only is the Red-tailed Hawk arguably Oklahoma's most common breeding raptor, but its numbers swell in the winter as migrants from the north stop to help consume the state's abundant rodent populations. On some roads in a good year, it is not hard to see one hawk for each mile traveled. This also reflects the species' preference for roadside habitats for hunting and perching. Several fairly distinctive subspecies are represented in the winter: Krider's, Harlan's, and "western" subspecies join Oklahoma's resident "eastern" subspecies.

Description: A very common, widespread, large, soaring buteo hawk with numerous, well-marked popula-
tions and subspecies. The highly variable adults have brick-red tails, except for wintering Krider's, which have paler tails, and Harlan's, which generally lack red altogether. Juveniles have barred brown or brown-and-white tails, and like the adults, almost always have a dark bar on the underside of the leading edge of the wing. Call is a loud, harsh descending *keeeer*.

Breeding Habitat: A wide range of open areas, including woodlots, agricultural lands, forest edges, rangeland, and plains. This species will nest near human activities and habitations.

Nest: A large stick structure placed in tree or on cliffs, depending on the availability of the substrates, usually high above the ground with a commanding view and open access into the nest.

NESTING ECOLOGY

Season: March–June. Single-brooded.
Eggs: Usually 2–3; white with brownish blotches.
Development: Incubation is by both sexes for 28–35 days. Young are provisioned by both sexes, fledge at 42–46 days, and learn to hunt in about 3 more weeks.

DISTRIBUTION AND ABUNDANCE

Rangewide: Distributed throughout all of North America south of the tree line, south to Central America. Most Canadian breeders move south to the United States for winter.
Historical: This widespread buteo has always been considered a resident throughout the state.

Current: The Red-tailed Hawk is surely the most widely, and evenly, distributed breeding raptor in the state. The atlas methodology is well suited for detecting the species' distribution. The Red-tailed Hawk occupies all of Oklahoma's habitats and biomes; it is also generally tolerant of human disturbances and will nest near habitations and human activities wherever there is sufficient food and nesting trees or cliffs.

Population Trend: Breeding Bird Survey data for 1966–2000 show an increase of 2.9 percent per year rangewide (P = 0.00) and no conclusive trend in Oklahoma (0.0 percent per year, P = 1.00).

References: AOU 1998; Baumgartner and Baumgartner 1992; Carpenter et al. 1969; Palmer 1988; Preston and Beane 1993; Sauer et al. 2001; Sutton 1967

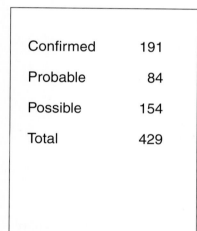

Confirmed	191
Probable	84
Possible	154
Total	429

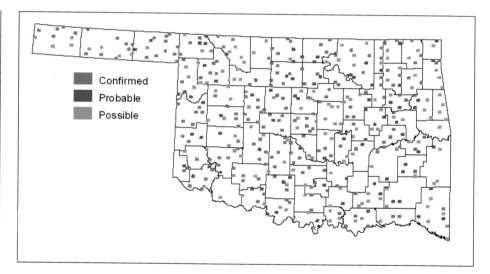

Ferruginous Hawk
Buteo regalis

Gregory A. Smith

Courtesy of Bob Gress

The Ferruginous Hawk is the largest North American buteo; in appearance, diet, nesting, behavior, and voice it may remind one of the Golden Eagle. Ferruginous refers to the color of the plumage, similar to that of iron ore. Ferruginous Hawks primarily prey on rabbits and large rodents. In winter, loose groups of five to ten hawks may congregate around prairie dog towns, with prairie dogs being a favored prey item.

Description: Largest buteo, having a large head, wide gape, robust chest, and feathered tarsi. Occurs in both a dark and light morph, with the light morph being more common. Sexes are similar in plumage, but females tend to have more pigmentation on legs and belly. Both morphs show very pale colored tails and trailing wing edges. Dark morph adults have dark upper- and underwing surfaces, back, belly, head, and tail coverts. Light morph adults have white bellies with grayish heads, rufous backs, and grayish upperwing surfaces. As in most raptors, females are generally larger than males.

Breeding Habitat: Open prairie grasslands with scattered trees or bushes. Also readily uses rocky hillside cliffs and ledges. Nest locations usually afford open views of the surrounding landscape. Avoids areas subject to direct human interference.

Nest: A bulky, conspicuous mass of sticks, bones, and debris from the ground. Lined with grass, bark, and horse or cow dung. Nests may be placed as high as 20 m (66 ft). Of the three widely nesting buteos of western North America (Ferruginous, Swainson's, and Red-tailed hawks), Ferruginous Hawk nests are usually lowest. Will use artificial nesting platforms and man-made structures such as transmission towers and utility poles as well as the occasional haystack. Both members of the pair help build or refurbish the nest. Nests are often reused annually, becoming larger with each successive nesting.

NESTING ECOLOGY

Season: May–June. Single-brooded.

Eggs: Usually 3–4, but variable; white to bluish white, finely and irregularly speckled and spotted.

Development: Incubation is by both sexes for 32–33 days and begins before the laying of the last egg. Male's involvement diminishes as incubation proceeds, as he provides food for the female and protects the nest. Young are brooded mostly by the female with the male providing food for her and the chicks. Young leave the nest at 38–50 days but stay dependent on their parents for several weeks after fledging.

DISTRIBUTION AND ABUNDANCE

Rangewide: Breeds throughout much of the Great Plains and Great Basin. Winter populations may move south into northern Mexico and west to California.

Historical: Described as a very rare summer resident in Texas and Cimarron counties and an uncommon migrant and winter resident east to Rogers County.

Current: The Ferruginous Hawk is a very local breeder in the Panhandle, principally Texas County. Some records of Possible Breeders are likely birds seen prior to the end of spring migration. Although limited in its distribution within the state, the number of confirmed nesting blocks in Texas County indicates that it is locally common there.

Population Trend: Breeding Bird Survey data for 1966–2000 show an increase of 4.3 percent per year rangewide (P = 0.00), but declines have been noted in several parts of its range. The low density in Oklahoma reveals no trends.

References: Allison et al. 1995; AOU 1998; Baicich and Harrison 1997; Baumgartner and Baumgartner 1992; Baumgartner and Howell 1942, 1948; Bechard and Schmutz 1995; Bent 1961; Blair and Schitoskey 1982; Johnsgard 1979, 1990; Kaufman 1996; Lokemoen and Duebbert 1976; Moore 1927; Nice 1931; Palmer 1988; Peterjohn and Sauer 1999; Sauer et al. 2001; Sutton 1967, 1986; Tate 1923; Thompson and Ely 1989; Thurow and White 1983; White and Thurow 1985; Wood and Schnell 1984

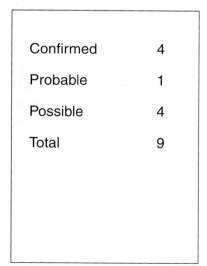

Confirmed	4
Probable	1
Possible	4
Total	9

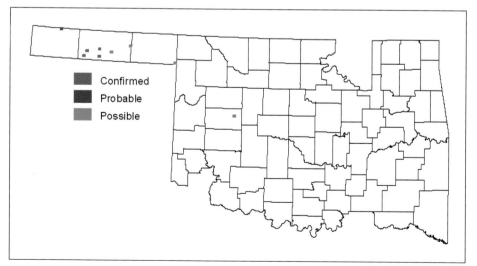

Golden Eagle
Aquila chrysaetos

M. Alan Jenkins

Courtesy of Warren Williams

The powerful Golden Eagle is always a thrill to see, although one usually must go to the western parts of the state to find it. It is a successful predator of rabbits and large rodents, but will not hesitate to take medium-sized to large birds. Anecdotes of Golden Eagles preying on pronghorns have been published. It is often wrongly blamed for livestock losses. As with many species of raptors that build stick nests, the nests of Golden Eagles grow larger each year as they are added on to, and some cliff nests reach huge proportions.

Description: A very large bird of prey with dark brown body feathers; adults have a variable amount of golden-yellow coloration on the hackles at the back of the neck

and crown. Juveniles and immatures have variable amounts of white in wings and tails, depending on age. The immature Bald Eagle and similarly sized adult Golden Eagle are separated by the distribution of white on the wings and tail. Immature Bald Eagles have white coloration mostly limited to underwing coverts and may have white elsewhere, such as on the belly. White present in an adult Golden Eagle is mottled with gray and confined to the tail.

Breeding Habitat: Remote, open country and cliffs of the western Oklahoma Panhandle.

Nest: A large, bulky stick platform usually placed on cliffs, but trees may be used where tall cliffs are absent.

Some ground nests, and nests on artificial structures, are known from other areas.

NESTING ECOLOGY

Season: April–June. Single-brooded.
Eggs: 1–3, but usually 2; white with brown spotting or blotching.
Development: Incubation is usually by the female alone for 43–45 days. Young are provisioned by the female with food brought by the male for the first 40 days, after which time both sexes deliver food. Young fledge at 63–70 days but rely on adults for food for much longer.

DISTRIBUTION AND ABUNDANCE

Rangewide: In North America, nests primarily in the western United States and Canada, northwestern Mexico, and southern Canada. Formerly nested more frequently in the Appalachian Mountains south to northern Georgia. Also occurs in much of the Old World.
Historical: Described in 1931 as a formerly common but now rare resident. More recently, still described as a rare and local resident in Cimarron County. A three-year survey prior to the atlas project found 14 active nests in the Panhandle.

Current: The Golden Eagle's nesting range in Oklahoma typifies the low nesting density of the species east of the Rocky Mountains. The atlas methodology does not sample well for this rare and locally distributed species. It is only known to nest in the western extreme of the Oklahoma Panhandle, an area which is more typical of the shortgrass semi-desert areas of the western Great Plains and very different from habitats in the main body of the state.

Population Trend: Breeding Bird Survey data for 1966–2000 show no conclusive trend rangewide (1.6 percent per year, P = 0.44). No trend data are available for Oklahoma. As with most species on the edge of their range, Golden Eagle nesting populations fluctuate greatly; and as with most predatory species its population and distribution vary, often cyclically.

References: AOU 1998; Baicich and Harrison 1997; Baumgartner and Baumgartner 1992; George M. Sutton Avian Research Center 1995; Nice 1931; Palmer 1988; Sauer et al. 2001; Sutton 1967

Observed

American Kestrel
Falco sparverius

Gregory A. Smith

Courtesy of M. Frank Carl

American Kestrels are the smallest and one of the most abundant birds of prey in North America. Known colloquially as the "Sparrow Hawk" or "Killy Hawk," kestrels are often observed hovering over fields and pastures waiting to pounce on an unsuspecting grasshopper, mouse, or small songbird. In the winter, when they are most abundant in the southern United States, one does not have to drive far to observe several of these beautiful little falcons perched along roadside power lines and telephone poles. Kestrels require nesting cavities in trees and are susceptible to biomagnification of pesticides due to their predominantly insectivorous diets during the summer.

Description: Kestrels have the typical falcon form with long, narrow, pointed wings and a long tail. Females are, on average, larger than males. The sexes also differ markedly in plumage color and pattern, a difference which is evident in nestlings. Adult females have a brown, heavily barred back, pale breast, and brown wings. The barring of the back continues along the length of the tail. Adult males have brown backs, pinkish breasts, and slate-blue wings. The tail is unbarred except for a black subterminal band and a white tip. Both sexes have a bluish-gray crown with a central rufous patch of variable size as well as a black "moustache" stripe drooping down from each eye.

Breeding Habitat: Breeds in open country with scattered trees or along woodland edges, such as grasslands, croplands, or tree groves.

Nest: Kestrels are secondary cavity nesters, nesting in holes excavated by other species or natural holes in logs or trees. They do not excavate their own cavities. Nests are simply a shallow scrape with little or no additional nesting material added. Cavities are usually between 2.5–9.5 m (8–31 ft) above ground, most often in trees, but occasionally in rock crevices, old magpie nests, or large birdhouses and artificial nest boxes, which they readily use.

NESTING ECOLOGY

Season: April–May. Probably single-brooded.
Eggs: Usually 3–5; whitish to light cinnamon or pale pink, usually with small brown spots or fine speckling throughout.
Development: Incubation is for 29–30 days principally by the female. The male will bring food to the female while she incubates. Young are provisioned by both sexes and leave the nest at 30 days.

DISTRIBUTION AND ABUNDANCE

Rangewide: A New World falcon, kestrels breed throughout North and South America, from the tree line in northern Canada and Alaska to the southern tips of Chile and Argentina, as well as numerous islands of the Caribbean. Numbers tend to increase in the southern United States during winter with the influx of migrating individuals.

Historical: Found throughout Oklahoma year round, with larger populations of resident individuals in eastern Oklahoma. Less common in summer, even rare in some areas of the state, but this may be a bit deceiving as kestrels are very secretive breeders.
Current: American Kestrels are fairly common breeders within the state, being detected in numerous atlas blocks. Their preference for open areas is reflected in their breeding distribution within the state. They are more common in atlas blocks of central and western Oklahoma, and less common in the more forested regions of the east, particularly the southeast. The large number of blocks with records no higher that the Possible category is likely a result of the very secretive breeding habits of this species.

Population Trend: Breeding Bird Survey data for 1966–2000 show no conclusive trend rangewide (0.0 percent per year, P = 0.91), but a decline of 5.2 percent per year in Oklahoma (P = 0.04).

References: AOU 1998; Baicich and Harrison 1997; Balgooyen 1976; Baumgartner and Baumgartner 1992; Baumgartner and Howell 1942, 1948; Bent 1961; Black 1976; Black 1979; Brewer and Harden 1975; Cade 1982; Carter 1968; Force 1929; Harden 1972; Howell 1950; Johnsgard 1979, 1990; Kaufman 1996; Looney 1972; McGee 1980; Messerly 1998a; Moore 1927; Nice 1931; Palmer 1988; Platt 1974; Sauer et al. 2001; Slack 1973; Snyder and Snyder 1991; Stahlecker and Griese 1977; Sutton 1967, 1977a, 1979, 1986a; Sutton and Tyler 1979; Tate 1923; Thompson and Ely 1989; Tomer 1974, 1997; Wood and Schnell 1984

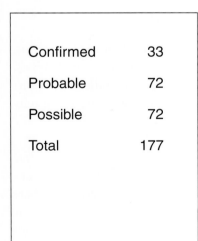

Confirmed	33
Probable	72
Possible	72
Total	177

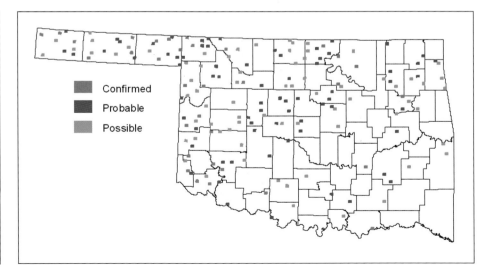

Prairie Falcon

Falco mexicanus

M. Alan Jenkins

Courtesy of M. Frank Carl

The Prairie Falcon preys mainly on ground squirrel-sized mammals and meadowlark-sized birds, with an occasional lizard and insect taken, but is capable of taking larger species. It is only mildly migratory and is restricted to western North America, primarily the United States. Nesting populations can be locally dense where the favored ground squirrel prey is abundant.

Description: A large falcon, mostly brown above and creamy white below, adults with spotted breasts and bellies, and juveniles similar with streaked breasts and bellies. Sexes are similar except for size; females average larger. Distinctive features include a narrow black malar stripe and black under the base of the wings.

Adults have yellow lore, cere, and leg skin, while juveniles are gray blue in these areas.

Breeding Habitat: Prairie Falcons nest in open plains, especially those areas having cliffs in prey-rich habitats, such as the western Oklahoma Panhandle. They don't nest in urban areas, areas lacking cliffs, or heavily forested regions.

Nest: Almost exclusively cliff nesting; very rarely a tree nester. The stick nests of other large raptors and ravens are sometimes used; otherwise, eggs are laid on the bare soil in a bowl-like depression situated on a ledge or more often in a cavity or crevice. Utilized cliffs vary from quite short to very high. Some traditional nest sites are reused for many years.

NESTING ECOLOGY

Season: April–June. Single-brooded.
Eggs: Usually 3–5; white or creamy with variable dark brown spots, splotches, or bands.
Development: Incubation is mostly by the female for 31 days. Young are provisioned by the male at first and by both sexes later. Young fledge in 38–40 days, but remain dependent on adults for another 25 days.

DISTRIBUTION AND ABUNDANCE

Rangewide: Nests from southern Canada south across the western United States to central Mexico, but is mostly absent from the Pacific coastal slopes. Winters farther east out onto the Great Plains and farther south in Mexico.
Historical: Long described as a resident of the western Oklahoma Panhandle. Raptor surveys conducted prior to the atlas project found Prairie Falcons to be a nesting species in the far western Panhandle of Oklahoma, but not elsewhere. A 1995 survey reported 7 active nests in the Panhandle.
Current: This rare and local species is not easily detected by atlas methods and was not recorded in any atlas blocks aside from a number of mostly late winter observations.

Population Trend: Breeding Bird Survey data for 1966–2000 show an increase of 3.5 percent per year rangewide (P = 0.05), although this species is not well measured by this survey. Recent studies suggest a small but stable number of pairs nesting in the Oklahoma Panhandle.

References: AOU 1998; Anderson and Squires 1997; Baumgartner and Baumgartner 1992; Cade 1982; George M. Sutton Avian Research Center 1995; Nice 1931; Palmer 1988; Sauer et al. 2001; Steenhof 1998; Sutton 1967

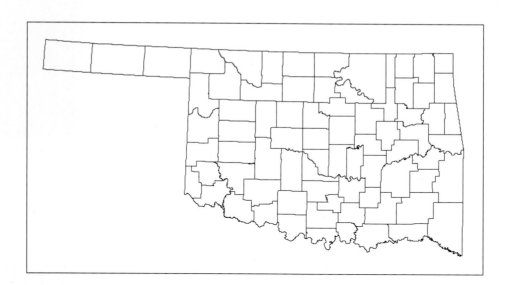

Ring-necked Pheasant
Phasianus colchicus

John M. Dole

The large Ring-necked Pheasant was first successfully introduced to the United States as a game bird in the late 1800s from Asia. Well established in the northern United States, in Oklahoma the Ring-necked Pheasant is limited in distribution to the northern third. Recent reports from Illinois indicate that Ring-necked Pheasants may be a factor in the decline of isolated groups of Greater Prairie-Chickens through nest parasitism, although this has not been found to be a problem in Oklahoma.

Description: Male Ring-necked Pheasants are mainly bronze, mottled with a variety of black, brown, buff, and green markings. The neck is boldly ringed in white, the upper neck and eartufts are iridescent greenish purple, and the large, fleshy eye patches are red. The long pointed tail is distinctive in the case of quick views as the birds run or fly away. The females also have long tails but are smaller and buff colored, mottled with dark brown and black. The female could be confused with prairie-chickens except for its larger size and long pointed tail. Call is a harsh crow or hiccup.

Breeding Habitat: Prairies, cultivated fields, abandoned fields, and open scrub areas. Often associated with agriculture.

Nest: A shallow hollow, unlined or sparsely lined with

grass, dead leaves, or nearby plants and placed on the ground. Female constructs the nest.

NESTING ECOLOGY

Season: April–July. Single-brooded, but will renest multiple times if nests fail.

Eggs: 7–15; unmarked, olive brown or more distinctly olive, brown, or blue gray. Egg dumping by several hens may result in nests with many more eggs, and eggs are sometimes laid in the nests of other species.

Development: Incubation is by the female for 23–27 days. Young are precocial, are tended by the hen, and can fly within 12 days, but remain with the hen for 70–80 days.

DISTRIBUTION AND ABUNDANCE

Rangewide: Resident (discontinuously) over much of the northern United States and southern Canada from the east to the west coast. Native to eastern and central Asia, but has been introduced to Europe, Tasmania, and New Zealand.

Historical: Introductions into Oklahoma began in 1910. Described by 1967 as locally common in Cimarron, Texas, Beaver, Harper, Woods, Alfalfa,

Woodward, Major, Ellis, and Roger Mills counties; by 1992 it was considered a resident east to western Grant, Blaine, and Custer counties.

Current: While the Ring-necked Pheasant is limited to northwestern Oklahoma, it appears to be common based on the large number of blocks in which it was recorded. The addition of records in Kay and Noble counties since 1992 indicates the species may be slowly expanding its range to the east. Possible records in Seminole and Tillman counties may represent escaped individuals, as this species is known to be held in captivity.

Population Trend: Breeding Bird Survey data for 1966–2000 show a decline of 1.0 percent per year rangewide (P = 0.00), and a large increase of 7.4 percent per year in Oklahoma (P = 0.08).

References: AOU 1998, Baicich and Harrison 1997; Baumgartner and Baumgartner 1992; de Hoyo et al. 1994; Duck and Fletcher 1944; Giudice and Ratti 2001; Howell and Webb 1995; Kaufman 1996; Lauckhart and McKean 1956; National Geographic Society 1999; Nice 1931; Sauer et al. 2001; Sutton 1967; Westemeir et al. 1998

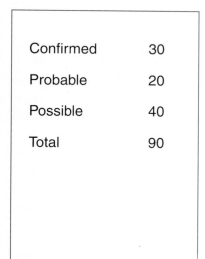

Confirmed	30
Probable	20
Possible	40
Total	90

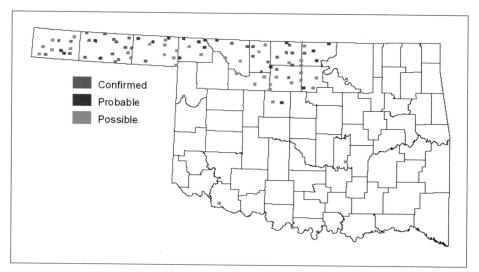

Greater Prairie-Chicken
Tympanuchus cupido

Donald H. Wolfe

Courtesy of Joel Sartore

Greater Prairie-Chickens were once abundant throughout the tallgrass and mixedgrass prairies of the eastern half of Oklahoma. One of two extant species of grouse in Oklahoma, they were once considered conspecific with Lesser Prairie-Chicken and called Pinnated Grouse. Greater Prairie-Chickens make up one of three subspecies of *Tympanuchus cupido*. The Heath Hen, once found along the Atlantic Coast of North America, became extinct in 1932. Attwater's Prairie-Chicken, found in the coastal plains of southeast Texas, is critically endangered.

Description: A medium-sized grouse with elongated feathers on the back of the upper neck called pinnae, which are much longer in males than in females, and are often held erect when displaying. During courtship displays, males show large tennis-ball-sized air sacs, usually orangish in color, which when deflated, account for the deep "booming" sound so associated with these

birds. The basic plumage for both males and females is an overall brown barred pattern. The tail of the male is usually solid gray-black, except for the inner two (occasionally four) retrices, which are barred. The entire tail of females shows the barred pattern.

Breeding Habitat: Greater Prairie-Chickens are very dependent on a large grassland mosaic of fresh burned areas and unburned areas with residual tall grasses, often with a sizable forb or shrub component.

Nest: Nests can range from a shallow scrape lined with sparse grass to large built-up bowls. Nests are commonly placed on slight slopes and are generally very well concealed from all angles by blackberry bushes or substantial forbs. Usually, nests are located in close proximity to burned areas, which are utilized for foraging by the hen and the successful brood.

NESTING ECOLOGY

Season: Mid-April–July. Single-brooded, but may have as many as three attempts if early nests are destroyed.

Eggs: 7–16; pale, whitish, buffy, or olive colored, occasionally with few faint reddish or brownish speckles. Known to suffer from brood parasitism by Ring-necked Pheasants in some parts of their range, but the paucity of pheasants in Greater Prairie-Chicken range in Oklahoma probably leads to little problem in this state.

Development: Incubation is by the female for 23–28 days. Young are precocial and will typically leave the nest within hours. Although capable of short flights after a couple of weeks, poults usually stay with the hen for about 12 weeks, by which time they are capable of sustained flight. Broods from two or more hens sometimes mingle after 4 or 5 weeks.

DISTRIBUTION AND ABUNDANCE

Rangewide: Range extends from northeastern and north-central Oklahoma north to Minnesota and southeastern North Dakota, west to northeastern Colorado, and east to Missouri, Illinois, and Wisconsin.

Historical: Found in prairie areas across the eastern two-thirds of Oklahoma. Transplanting birds from Osage County to Comanche County in the 1950s was largely unsuccessful.

Current: Greater Prairie-Chickens are found primarily from Payne and Noble counties north to Kay and Osage counties, and east to Craig County. They are also found in small numbers in a few counties southeast of this range, although these populations did not show up in atlas surveys. Few observations were recorded in atlas blocks, perhaps due to the local nature of remaining populations.

Population Trend: Numbers of Greater Prairie-Chickens in Oklahoma have decreased by about 80 to 90 percent over the past two decades. After reaching extremely low numbers in the mid-1990s, they have increased slightly in recent years. The Oklahoma Department of Wildlife has closed the hunting season on prairie-chickens in Oklahoma until recovery goals are met.

References: Aldrich 1963; Aldrich and Duvall 1955; Applegate et al. 2001; Baicich and Harrison 1997; Baker 1953; Baumgartner and Baumgartner 1992; Bidwell 2003; Bidwell and Peoples 1991; Bidwell et al. 1995; Bump 1963; Cannon and Knopf 1981b; Copelin 1958, 1959a; Duck and Fletcher 1944; Ellsworth et al. 1994, 1995; Evans 1968; Geary 1986; George M. Sutton Avian Research Center unpubl. data; Gross 1932; Grzybowski 1980; Hammerstrom and Hammerstrom 1961; Hammerstrom et al. 1957; Hier 1999; Horak 1985; Horak and Applegate 1998; Horton and Wolfe 1999; Jacobs 1958, 1959, 1968; Johnsgard 1973, 1979; Jones 1960, 1961, 1963a, 1963b, 1964; Martin 1978, 1980; Martin and Knopf 1980; Rue 1973; Ryan et al. 1998; Schroeder and Robb 1993; Snyder et al. 1999; Sutton 1967; Svedarsky et al. 1999; Toepfer 1988; Toepfer et al. 1990; Vance and Westemeier 1979; Vohs and Knopf 1980; Westemeier 1980; Westemeier and Gough 1999; Westemeier et al. 1998; Wiedenfeld et al. 2002; Zimmerman 1993

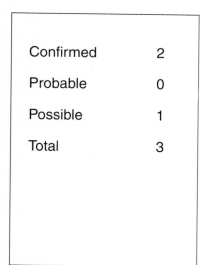

Confirmed	2
Probable	0
Possible	1
Total	3

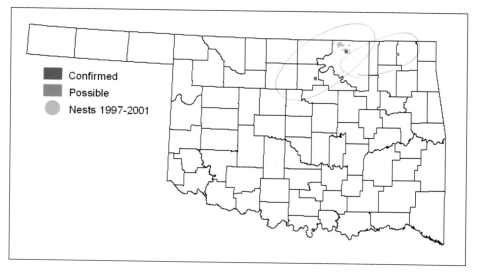

Confirmed
Possible
Nests 1997-2001

Lesser Prairie-Chicken
Tympanuchus pallidicintus

Donald H. Wolfe

Courtesy of Joel Sartore

Lesser Prairie-Chickens are the western counterpart of Greater Prairie-Chickens, primarily occupying the shortgrass prairies, sand-sagebrush prairies, and shinnery-oak prairies of northwestern Oklahoma and the Oklahoma Panhandle. One of two extant species of grouse in Oklahoma, they were once considered conspecific with Greater Prairie-Chickens and were collectively called Pinnated Grouse.

Description: A medium-sized grouse, smaller than the Greater Prairie-Chicken, having elongated feathers on the back of the upper neck called pinnae, which are often held erect when displaying. Males performing courtship displays also show large tennis-ball-sized air sacs, usually red or rose in color, which when deflated, produce the deep "booming" sound so associated with these birds. The basic plumage for both males and females is an overall brown barred pattern.

Breeding Habitat: Lesser Prairie-Chickens are depend-ent on large areas with a mixture of tall grasses and shrubs.

Nest: Ranges from a shallow scrape sparsely lined with grass, to a large, built-up bowl. Nests are generally very well concealed from all angles and are placed in tussocks of tall grasses or under dense stands of shinnery oak or sand sagebrush. Nests are almost always located within a mile of an active booming ground.

NESTING ECOLOGY

Season: April–July. Single-brooded, but second attempts are common if early nests are destroyed.

Eggs: 7–14; pale, whitish, buffy, or olive colored. Often with few faint reddish or brownish speckles. Known to suffer from brood parasitism by Ring-necked Pheasants in Kansas, and interactions between Ring-necked Pheasants and Lesser Prairie-Chickens on booming grounds in Ellis and Harper counties have been observed, but no pheasant-parasitized prairie-chicken nests have been found in Oklahoma.

Development: Incubation is by the female for 23–28 days. Young are precocial and typically leave the nest within hours. Although capable of short flights after a couple of weeks, poults usually stay with the hen for about 12 weeks, at which time they are capable of sustained flight. It is common for the broods from two or more hens to mingle at the age of 4 or 5 weeks.

DISTRIBUTION AND ABUNDANCE

Rangewide: Resident from southeastern New Mexico north to southeastern Colorado and western Kansas and east through the Texas Panhandle and northwestern Oklahoma.

Historical: Formerly found in Beaver, Beckham, Cimarron, Dewey, Ellis, Harper, Major, Roger Mills, Texas, Woods, and Woodward counties, and possibly farther east.

Current: Resident from Beaver and Harper counties east to Woods and Woodward counties and south to Ellis County. Small numbers may be present west of Beaver County. The region in which this species was found in atlas blocks probably represents the core of the range in Oklahoma at this time. While no breeding confirmations came from atlas blocks, intensive research on this species during the project years resulted in a number of known nest locations being mapped.

Population Trend: Numbers of Lesser Prairie-Chickens in Oklahoma have decreased by about 80 percent over the past two decades. After reaching extremely low numbers in the mid-1990s, however, they have increased slightly in recent years. The species is considered a "warranted but precluded" candidate for listing under the Endangered Species Act. The Oklahoma Department of Wildlife has closed the hunting season on prairie-chickens in Oklahoma until recovery goals are met. Forty-two percent of mortality in Oklahoma is attributable to collisions with fences (32 percent), power lines (6 percent), and vehicles (4 percent).

References: Aldrich and Duvall 1955; Baicich and Harrison 1997; Baumgartner and Baumgartner 1992; Bidwell 2002; Bidwell and Peoples 1991; Bidwell et al. 1995; Boyd and Bidwell 2001; Cannon 1980; Cannon and Knopf 1978, 1979, 1980; 1981a, 1981b; Cannon et al. 1982; Copelin 1959a, 1959b, 1963; Crawford 1980; Crawford and Stormer 1980; Davison 1940; Donaldson 1966, 1969; Ellsworth et al. 1994, 1995; Geary 1986; George M. Sutton Avian Research Center unpubl. data; Giesen 1998; Grzybowski 1980; Hammerstrom and Hammerstrom 1961; Horak 1985; Horton 2000; Jacobs 1968; Jamison et al. 2002; Johnsgard 1973, 1979; Jones 1960, 1961, 1963a, 1963b, 1964a, 1964b; Leslie et al. 1999; Mote et al. 1999; Rue 1973; Sands 1968; Sauer et al. 1994; Sutton 1964, 1967, 1968b, 1977b; Taylor and Guthery 1980; U.S. Fish and Wildlife Service 1998; Van Den Bussche et al. 2003; Wiedenfeld et al. 2002; Wildlife Habitat Management Institute 1999; Woodward et al. 2001

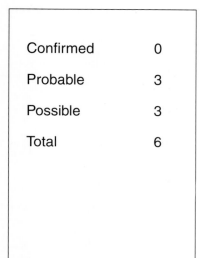

Confirmed	0
Probable	3
Possible	3
Total	6

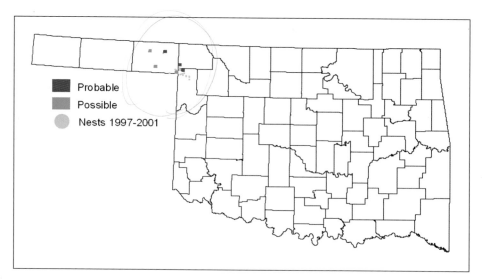

- Probable
- Possible
- Nests 1997-2001

Wild Turkey
Meleagris gallopavo

Guyla Carnes

Courtesy of Warren Williams

A success story of modern wildlife management, this species was nearly extirpated from Oklahoma by 1920. Turkeys have been reintroduced into many areas, where they are now fairly common. The male, or gobbler, gobbles in the early morning to call the hens. The turkey flies strongly for only short distances and prefers to avoid danger by running.

Description: A very large bird with long legs and a long broad tail. The males have a "beard" or "brush" of modified feathers hanging from the chest. Both sexes of adult turkeys share a bare head and neck, whereas the male has an erectile lappet that usually hangs down over the beak. Plumage is black to glossy bronze and rufous.

Breeding Habitat: Breeds in open deciduous forest, along forest edges, and in clearings.

Nest: A shallow hollow on the ground lined with vegetation or dead leaves of plants nearby.

NESTING ECOLOGY

Season: April–August. Single-brooded, but will replace lost clutches.
Eggs: Usually 8–12; pale buff or yellowish, heavily spotted and speckled overall with light to dark brown or purplish brown.
Development: Incubation is by the female for 28 days. Young are precocial and are tended by the female. The

young can fly into trees at about 2 weeks of age, and they roost on branches with the female for several weeks. Brood remains together until winter.

DISTRIBUTION AND ABUNDANCE

Rangewide: Resident throughout much of the eastern United States; more widely scattered west.

Historical: Considered an abundant resident throughout the main body of the state, and present but less common in Cimarron County during the mid-1800s, the turkey population dwindled significantly by the turn of the twentieth century. A statewide survey in 1941 documented a mere 220 birds in just six southeastern Oklahoma counties. Subsequent protection from overhunting, along with better land management practices and careful restocking efforts, have restored turkey populations statewide.

Current: Wild Turkeys are broadly distributed across the state, occurring most frequently in northwestern counties and less frequently in the northeastern and Panhandle counties.

Population Trend: Breeding Bird Survey data for 1966–2000 show in increase of 12.3 percent per year rangewide (P = 0.00) and an increase of 11.0 percent per year in Oklahoma (P = 0.00). The population increase of this species is a result of intensive wildlife management.

References: AOU 1998; Baicich and Harrison 1997; Baumgartner and Baumgartner 1992; Duck and Fletcher 1944; Eaton 1992; Logan 1970; National Geographic Society 1999; Nice 1931; Sauer et al. 2001; Schorger 1966; Sutton 1967

Confirmed	49
Probable	27
Possible	81
Total	157

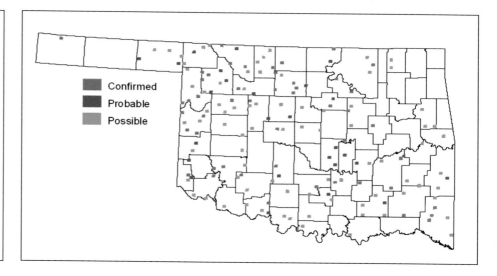

Scaled Quail

Callipepla squamata

Alan E. Versaw

Courtesy of Steve Metz

Throughout most of Oklahoma, the Northern Bobwhite is the only quail species. In the state's most arid regions, however, the handsome Scaled Quail takes center stage. In the Panhandle and southwestern corner of the state, the nasal, two-syllable call of the Cottontop reverberates from an abundance of low perches.

Description: The white-topped crest and the scaly appearance of the breast and belly feathers distinguish this quail of the arid country. Muted tones of brown and blue-gray enable the Scaled Quail to blend in against the dusty tones of the landscape. Even the bird's *Pecos, Pecos* call seems especially suited to this country,

echoing the name of the river that bisects the northern third of the species' range.

Breeding Habitat: Cactus-studded sandsage plains, brushy arroyos, and rocky hillsides provide ideal habitat for Scaled Quail. The species exploits tall cactus, idle machinery, and brush piles for cover and nesting sites. Such sites provide both shade from the sun and protection from predators. In general, the species selects sites with less cover than the Northern Bobwhite; hybridization between the two species occurs, but is rare.

Nest: Nests are shallow depressions lined with grasses

and leaves, where available. Nest lining is minimal in many cases.

NESTING ECOLOGY

Season: May–August. Later dates probably reflect replacement nests or rare second clutches.
Eggs: Usually 12–14, but variable; cream colored with pale brown speckling.
Development: Incubation is by the female for 22–23 days. Young are precocial and immediately follow both parents to forage on their own.
Hybridization: Reported with Northern Bobwhite in Harmon and Greer counties and in Kansas and Texas.

DISTRIBUTION AND ABUNDANCE

Rangewide: Permanent resident ranging from desert habitats of southeastern Colorado and northwestern New Mexico in the north to central Mexico in the south.
Historical: Described as a resident of Cimarron County in 1931. Described as resident there as well as in uncultivated parts of southwestern Oklahoma by 1967. Considered resident in Harmon, Greer, and Jackson counties in 1979. Recorded locally as far east as Love County and as far north as Beckham County in 1959. By 1992, described as common in the Black Mesa area and uncommon to rare east to Harper, Ellis, and Tillman counties. Due to the species' popularity as a game bird, there have been numerous unsuccessful attempts at introducing the species beyond its natural range in Oklahoma.
Current: The convergence of rock outcroppings and stands of cactus preferred as breeding habitat by the Scaled Quail occurs mainly, though not exclusively, in the Panhandle of Oklahoma. This species also occurs with some frequency, perhaps more than suggested by atlas results, in southwestern Oklahoma as well.

Population Trend: Breeding Bird Survey data for 1966–2000 show a decline of 2.0 percent per year rangewide ($P = 0.05$), but no conclusive trend in Oklahoma (-1.5 percent per year, $P = 0.54$).

References: Baicich and Harrison 1997; Baumgartner and Baumgartner 1992; Gietzentanner 1976; Jacobs 1960; Nice 1931; Schemnitz 1961, 1964, 1994; Sutton 1967; Tate 1923; Tyler 1979a; Webb and Tyler 1988

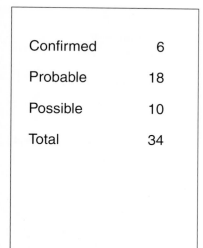

Confirmed	6
Probable	18
Possible	10
Total	34

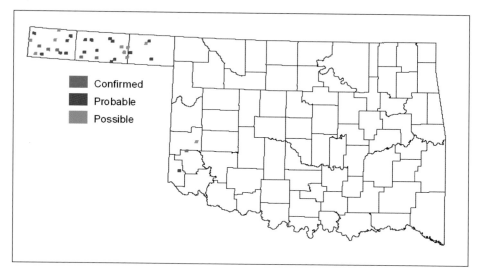

Northern Bobwhite
Colinus virginianus

Guyla Carnes

Courtesy of Steve Metz

A common game bird found across the state, the Northern Bobwhite inhabits brushy pastures, abandoned fields, and open woods. It is a chunky reddish-brown quail that forms winter flocks or coveys that burst into flight when disturbed. At night, the covey forms a tight circle on the ground with tails pointed inward.

Description: Sexes are a somewhat similar reddish-brown color, but males have a white throat and eye line whereas the female has a buff throat and eye line. The familiar *bobwhite* call is frequently heard in the spring and early summer.

Breeding Habitat: Breeds in a wide variety of habitats, but generally in early successional scrub, scattered cover in grasslands or cultivated areas, and along woodland edges.

Nest: Built by both sexes, it is a shallow hollow in the ground lined with plant material such as grasses, mosses, or pine needles, usually within 15 m (50 ft) of a clearing. Growing plants are usually pulled over the nest to hide it.

NESTING ECOLOGY

Season: April–September. Double- to triple-brooded.
Eggs: Usually 12–14; dull or creamy white.
Development: Incubation is mostly by the female for

about 23 days. Young are led to food by both sexes and may remain with adults for an extended period.

Hybridization: Reported with Scaled Quail in Harmon and Greer counties and in Kansas and Texas.

DISTRIBUTION AND ABUNDANCE

Rangewide: Resident from southwestern Wyoming and central South Dakota south and east to the Atlantic and Gulf coasts; also throughout eastern Mexico.

Historical: Considered a common resident throughout most of the state, except in dense forest and open plains.

Current: The Northern Bobwhite is common across nearly all of Oklahoma wherever grasslands and cultivated areas can be found. Its familiar and frequent calling helps ensure that its presence is recorded wherever it is found.

Population Trend: Breeding Bird Survey data for 1966–2000 show a decline of 2.9 percent per year rangewide (P = 0.00) and a decline of 0.9 percent per year in Oklahoma (P = 0.06).

References: AOU 1998; Baicich and Harrison 1997; Baumgartner and Baumgartner 1992; Brennan 1999; DeMaso et al. 1997; Robbins et al. 1983; Sauer et al. 2001; Sutton 1967; Webb and Tyler 1988

Confirmed	90
Probable	255
Possible	170
Total	515

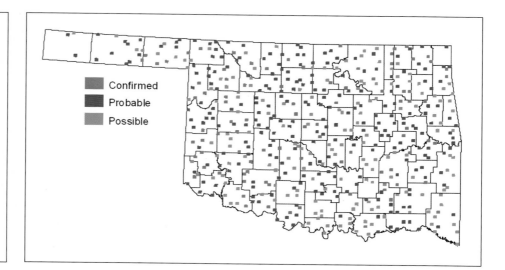

Confirmed
Probable
Possible

Black Rail
Laterallus jamaicensis

Dan L. Reinking

© Herb Clarke / VIREO

The tiny, rare, local, secretive, and nocturnal Black Rail surely qualifies as the species seen by the smallest number of people of any of the species in this book. It would be a highly prized find for many birders who wish to see one, but is seldom encountered in Oklahoma. A single nesting record exists from the Salt Plains National Wildlife Refuge, but the potential exists for isolated breeding areas to be found in the state.

Description: A tiny rail, mostly black as its name implies, but having chestnut on the back of its neck, white speckling on its upperparts, white barring on its flanks, and red eyes. Sexes similar. Calls are usually described as *kik-kee-do* and are usually given late at night.

Breeding Habitat: Marshes with emergent vegetation and perhaps wet meadows.

Nest: A deep cup of grasses and sedges, often with a canopy formed from adjacent vegetation. A ramp of dead vegetation leads to an entrance on one side of the nest.

NESTING ECOLOGY

Season: Probably late April–July, although the sole nest record in Oklahoma was of a recently fledged bird captured on 19 August.

Eggs: 5–9; white or creamy white and evenly spotted with fine brown dots.

Development: Incubation is by both sexes for 18–20 days. Young are semiprecocial but are brooded by adults. Little information on growth and development.

DISTRIBUTION AND ABUNDANCE

Rangewide: Breeds along the Atlantic and Gulf coasts, locally inland in the Great Plains and Midwest, in southwestern Arizona, and in southern and coastal northern California. Also breeds in Mexico and Central America. Winters from the southern portion of its U.S. breeding range south.

Historical: Described in 1967 as a rare transient but possible breeder. A recently fledged young bird was captured and photographed in August of 1971 at Salt Plains NWR, confirming the species as a breeder in Oklahoma. A June sighting was recorded in Osage County in 1977.

Current: No reports of Black Rails were received during atlas project years. The species may be a rare and local breeder, especially in northern Oklahoma, given this area's proximity to known breeding grounds in southern Kansas. Its secretive, nocturnal nature make it difficult to locate.

Population Trend: Very difficult to measure due to natural population cycles, local and irregular distribution, and secretive habits, but the species is believed to have declined dramatically over the past century, primarily due to loss of coastal and inland wetlands. No trend data are available for Oklahoma.

References: Baicich and Harrison 1997; Baumgartner and Baumgartner 1992; Eddelman et al. 1994; Hicks 1978; Sullivan 1976; Sutton 1967

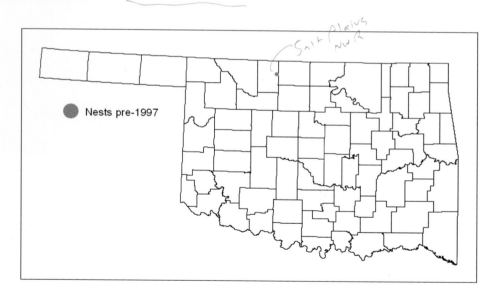

Salt Plains NWR

● Nests pre-1997

King Rail
Rallus elegans

Melinda Droege

Courtesy of James Arterburn

Oklahoma's largest rail, the King Rail is an elusive and local species. Little is known about its migratory movements, and it may often be overlooked in its favored marshy habitats. Recent wetland restoration efforts may provide a secure home for this species in Oklahoma.

Description: This large freshwater rail has a long, slightly decurved bill. The back is black with tawny streaking, the underparts are cinnamon, and the flanks have black-and-white barring. The sexes are similar with males being slightly larger in size. The King Rail is best known for its loud, harsh *kik-kik-kik* call, given night or day. This rail mostly walks or runs, but flies when flushed, provoked, or migrating; it also swims to cross creeks or ponds. The similarly sized and slightly paler Clapper Rail does not occur in Oklahoma; the Virginia Rail is much smaller.

Breeding Habitat: Freshwater marshes are preferred, but in Oklahoma the King Rail will nest along weedy riverbeds and farm ponds, in low-lying wet fields, and also near highways in the deep grass ditches and borrow-pits.

Nest: A deep basket of dead vegetation usually built by the male 15–45 cm (6–17 in) above water in a clump of cattails, rushes, or grasses that are used to form a canopy. The female observes construction and often lays the first egg before the nest is completed.

NESTING ECOLOGY

Season: May–July. Possibly double-brooded.

Eggs: Usually 10–12; creamy white to pale buff sparsely spotted with brown or dark red.

Development: Incubation is by both sexes for 21–24 days. Young are precocial but are fed by adults for 1–3 weeks and remain with adults for weeks to months.

DISTRIBUTION AND ABUNDANCE

Rangewide: Widely distributed in the eastern and midwestern United States but barely reaches Canada. Occurs west to the 100th meridian and south to central Mexico. Winters in the south-central United States and along the southern Atlantic Coast.

Historical: Described as an uncommon transient and summer resident in the main body of the state. There are several nest records for Beaver County in the Panhandle from the 1930s, but the species is no longer considered regular there.

Current: The rare, local, and secretive King Rail is poorly sampled by atlas methods. Additional reports collected during the atlas project indicate a broader distribution of this species than that shown by block surveys, including areas encompassing parts of southern, central, and western Oklahoma. Nest records were reported from Red Slough Wildlife Management Area in McCurtain County and Hackberry Flat in Tillman County.

Population Trend: Breeding Bird Survey data for 1966–2000 show a decline of 6.2 percent per year rangewide (P = 0.01). No trend data are available for Oklahoma.

References: AOU 1998; Baicich and Harrison 1997; Baumgartner and Baumgartner 1992; Bent 1963c; Delap 1979a; Ehrlich et al. 1988; Harrison 1975; Isted 1978; Johnsgard 1979; Meanley 1992; Oklahoma Bird Records Committee 2000; Sauer et al. 2001; Sutton 1938b, 1967; Tanner and Hendrickson 1956

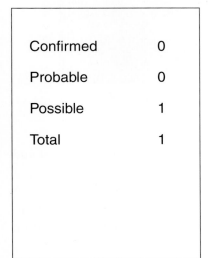

Confirmed	0
Probable	0
Possible	1
Total	1

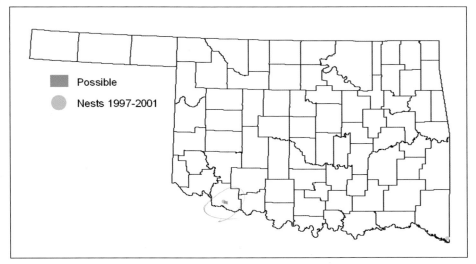

■ Possible

● Nests 1997-2001

Virginia Rail
Rallus limicola

Dan L. Reinking

Shy and secretive, the Virginia Rail is difficult to observe and has only rarely been found breeding in Oklahoma. Special feather tips on the front of its head help prevent feather wear as it penetrates dense marsh vegetation. It usually runs from danger, but will also fly or swim if necessary.

Description: A medium-size rail, blackish brown above and rich brown below, with chestnut wing patches, a gray face, and a long bill. Large feet typical of rails help with walking on soggy vegetation. A series of *kid kid kidick* calls and *oink* notes make up the vocalizations.

Breeding Habitat: Wetlands with shallow water and thick emergent vegetation.

Nest: A loosely woven basket made from readily available plant materials, often with a canopy formed from bent-over vegetation.

NESTING ECOLOGY

Season: Primarily April–June. Sometimes double-brooded.
Eggs: Usually 6–8; white or buff with sparse spotting.
Development: Incubation is by both sexes for about

19 days. Young are precocial and leave the nest 3–4 days after hatching, following parents for up to a month.

DISTRIBUTION AND ABUNDANCE

Rangewide: Breeds across much of southern Canada and the northern and western United States and in portions of Mexico and Central and South America. Most U.S. breeders winter in the southwestern United States and Mexico.

Historical: Described as a transient and rare summer resident, with breeding records from Washita County in 1860, Beaver County prior to 1930 and in 1956, Tulsa County in 1930, and the Salt Plains National Wildlife Refuge in Alfalfa County in 1961. The exact location of the Washita County nest record is uncertain. This species has also wintered locally in Oklahoma.

Current: No breeding evidence for Virginia Rails was reported during atlas project years.

Population Trend: Breeding Bird survey data for 1966–2001 show an increase of 4.2 percent per year rangewide (P = 0.00), but this species is poorly measured by this survey. No trend data are available for Oklahoma.

References: Baumgartner and Baumgartner 1992; Conway 1995; Lewis 1930; Nice 1931; Sutton 1967

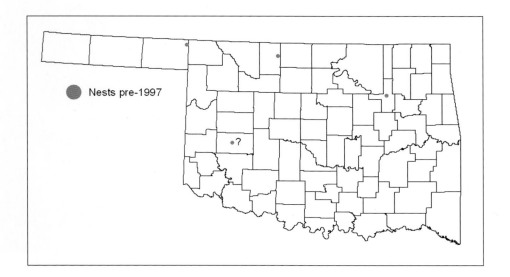

Nests pre-1997

Purple Gallinule
Porphyrula martinica

Guyla Carnes

Gallinules are somewhat rare in Oklahoma, found mainly in the eastern and central regions in marshes and ponds with dense stands of cattails and reeds. A long neck, a short bright-colored bill with a horny shield across the front of the head, and long legs with long toes give the bird an awkward appearance, but it is well equipped for darting across ponds on lily pads.

Description: The Purple Gallinule is a medium-sized marsh bird with a compact body that appears to be compressed sideways. Both male and female are similar in color, with a gaudy, bluish-purple head and underparts and an iridescent greenish sheen on the back. The species is further distinguished by a bluish-white shield that caps the scarlet bill. Vocalizations include a hen-like cluck.

Breeding Habitat: Gallinules nest in marshes from 0.3–1 m (1–3 ft) above fairly deep water in cattails and dense stands of lotus. They prefer closed-in, shadowy places and are seldom seen except when they climb vegetation to sunbathe and preen.

Nest: A bulky cup of plant material, built up well above the water

NESTING ECOLOGY

Season: May–July. Probably double-brooded.

Eggs: Usually 6–8; pale creamy buff with speckling of reddish brown.

Development: Incubation is by both sexes for 20–25 days. Young leave the nest in 1–2 days and reach independence in 8–9 weeks.

DISTRIBUTION AND ABUNDANCE

Rangewide: Breeds primarily along the Gulf Coast and inland to southern Oklahoma and Arkansas. Also breeds south through South America. Winters from south Texas and Florida southward. Wanders widely across eastern North America.

Historical: Described as a very rare and local migrant, with nesting documented in Bryan County in the 1960s.

Current: Due to the rare and local distribution of Purple Gallinule in Oklahoma, it is poorly sampled by atlas project methods. Fledglings seen at Red Slough Wildlife Management Area in May of 2001 represent the only breeding confirmation in the state during atlas project years, though one additional record of a single bird was reported from LeFlore County.

Population Trend: Breeding Bird Survey data for 1966–2000 show no conclusive trend rangewide (-7.4 percent per year, P = 0.29). No trend data are available for Oklahoma.

References: AOU 1998; Baicich and Harrison 1997; Baumgartner and Baumgartner 1992; Sauer et al. 2001; Sutton 1967; Robbins et al. 1983

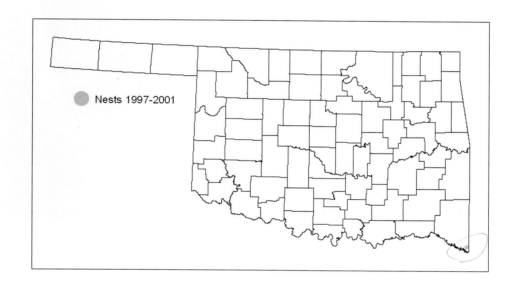

Nests 1997-2001

Common Moorhen
Gallinula chloropus

Richard A. Stuart

Common Moorhens build several nests for different uses, such as brooding, in addition to a nest used for laying eggs. This species normally begins incubating with the first egg laid, so hatching of all eggs takes place over an extended period. Because of this, the adults construct special brooding platforms for those young that hatch early. This results in one parent brooding and the other incubating at the same time.

Description: Sexes are similar with brownish back, slate body, a white flank stripe, white undertail coverts with a dark median stripe, yellowish-green legs, and a red bill and forehead shield with a yellow tip to the bill. The bill color is much brighter in breeding adults. Call is a rather high-pitched, drawn-out *kak kak kak kak*. It is most likely to be confused with American Coot, which is larger and lacks the white flank stripe and bears a white bill.

Breeding Habitat: Freshwater lakes, rivers, ponds, marshes, and even ditches. Prefers to locate nest within rank vegetation.

Nest: A platform composed of dead aquatic plants and anchored in a clump of vegetation often including shrubs in or near the water. Regularly constructs extra nests for brooding purposes.

NESTING ECOLOGY

Season: May–August. Probably multiple-brooded.
Eggs: Usually 5–11; irregular brownish spotting on grayish-white to pale buff to greenish background.
Development: Incubation is by both sexes for 19–22 days. Young are cared for by both sexes and even by older siblings from an earlier brood of the same year; young are capable of flight in 6–7 weeks.

DISTRIBUTION AND ABUNDANCE

Rangewide: Breeds from southeast Canada and the Great Lakes southward to the Gulf Coast, also throughout Mexico, and in the west from southern New Mexico and Arizona through much of California. Winters from much of the southern United States southward. Also breeds in Central and South America and in much of the Old World.
Historical: Described as a rare to uncommon summer resident, with scattered records throughout the state.

Current: Rare and local distribution makes the Common Moorhen a species that is poorly sampled by atlas methodology. Summer records of young birds indicate that Common Moorhens may nest wherever suitable habitat exists, particularly in the north-central and southeastern parts of Oklahoma.

Population Trend: Breeding Bird Survey data for 1966–2000 show no conclusive trend rangewide (3.2 percent per year, P = 0.15). Low density in Oklahoma precludes trend estimation.

References: AOU 1998; Baicich and Harrison 1997; Baumgartner and Baumgartner 1992; Cassidy 1990; Harrison 1975; National Geographic Society 1999; Peterson 1996; Sauer et al. 2001; Seibel 1977; Seyffert 1989b; Shackford 1981; Sibley 2000; Sutton 1967

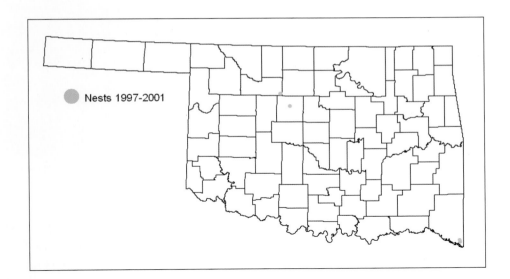

American Coot

Fulica americana

Guyla Carnes

The American Coot, or "mud hen," is a common bird found in all parts of the state, abundant during fall and spring with some remaining during winter on large impoundments. These duck-like birds are at home on open water where they swim buoyantly, with nodding head and paddle with lobed toes rather than the webbed feet of a duck. Each toe is framed by a scalloped web that aids walking on dry or marshy ground as well as swimming.

Description: The American Coot has dark, slate-colored plumage that contrasts with a stubby white bill and a white patch underneath a short tail. The immature coot is grayish overall, with a white chin and throat. The light-colored bill lacks the partial ring at the tip typical of the adult. Coots make a wide variety of calls consisting of cackles and croaks. The hen makes a clucking *Kuk-kuk-kuk-kuk-kuk*, or to call the brood together a puffy *pulque, pulque, pulque.*

Breeding Habitat: Breeds on lakes and marshes with some open water and reed or cattail cover.

Nest: The nest, a bulky cup of dead leaves and stems, is usually on the ground at water level in growing vegetation or branches lying or hanging into the water.

Extra nest platforms may be built by both sexes, with the male bringing most materials to the site and the female constructing the nest. Only one nest is used for eggs while the others may be used by young for resting.

NESTING ECOLOGY

Season: May–July.

Eggs: Usually 6–9; pale buff, marked with dark brown and black specks. Occasionally, a female will lay eggs in another coot's nest.

Development: Incubation by both sexes for 21–24 days. The young hatch over several days and are usually brooded by the female and fed by the male. Young follow adults who soon divide the brood and the feeding responsibilities. Young are able to feed themselves by 1 month and are independent by 2 months.

DISTRIBUTION AND ABUNDANCE

Rangewide: Breeds from the mid-latitudes of Canada south (except for much of the southeastern United States and the Atlantic Coast) through Mexico to northern South America. Winters throughout much of the western, midwestern, and southern states, south to South America.

Historical: Long considered a common transient and local breeder, with most nest records from western Oklahoma.

Current: The American Coot's distribution indicates a preference for western Oklahoma marshes. Some of the Probable Breeder records may be the result of birds considered paired but seen prior to the end of spring migration.

Population Trend: Breeding Bird Survey data from 1966–2000 show no conclusive trend rangewide (0.9 percent per year, P = 0.32). No trend data are available for Oklahoma.

References: AOU 1998; Ault 1977; Baicich and Harrison 1997; Baumgartner and Baumgartner 1992; Carter 1969; Felis 1975; Messerly 1969; Ray, R. E. 1973; Robbins et al. 1983; Sauer et al. 2001; Scott 1978; Shackford 1981; Sutton 1967; Tate 1923

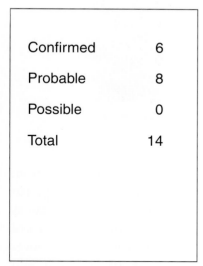

Confirmed	6
Probable	8
Possible	0
Total	14

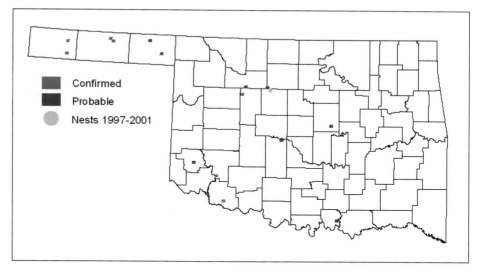

Snowy Plover
Charadrius alexandrinus

Victoria J. Byre

Courtesy of Bill Horn

The Snowy Plover is a small, inconspicuous shorebird that races along sandy beaches, sandbars, and salt flats in search of the tiny invertebrates that it eats. In Oklahoma, Snowy Plovers share habitat used by Least Terns and can often be found nesting near or within Least Tern colonies.

Description: In all adult plumages, both male and female Snowy Plovers are a pale sandy color above with a single partial neck ring, a thin, pointed black bill, and dark grayish-black legs. In breeding plumage, the male has a dark blackish bar across his forehead, a dark eye patch, and darker partial neck ring. These areas are lighter brown in breeding females, immatures and win-

ter adults. The Snowy Plover's display song, given from the ground, is a rather mellow whistled *tueeoo,* repeated several times. It also has a low whistled flight call as well as a harsh *krip krip* call. The darker brown-backed Semipalmated Plover and the very pale Piping Plover both are slightly larger than the Snowy Plover, and both have orangish or pinkish legs.

Breeding Habitat: Sandy beaches, flat barren sandbars and banks along inland rivers, and on salt flats and dry lake beds.

Nest: A shallow scrape on open bare ground, either unlined, or sparsely lined with bits of shells, small pebbles, plant fragments, or other debris. It is sometimes located close to a piece of driftwood, a clump of vegetation, or a small ridge in the sand.

NESTING ECOLOGY

Season: Late April–August. Often double-brooded and will readily renest if a nest is destroyed.

Eggs: Usually 2–3; oval, with brown, black, and gray spots and scrawls on an olive-buff or sandy-colored background.

Development: Incubation is by both sexes for 23–28 days. Young are precocial and leave the nest 1–3 hours after hatching. Both adults are active in leading the young to food. Chicks are capable of flight at 28–33 days.

DISTRIBUTION AND ABUNDANCE

Rangewide: A cosmopolitan species found in Eurasia, Africa, and India as well as North and South America. In North America, breeding populations are found along the Gulf and Pacific coasts and in the Caribbean as well as at scattered inland locations in the western and south-central United States and central Mexico. The species winters on islands and coastal areas of western and southern North America and south to southern Mexico.

Historical: In Oklahoma as well as elsewhere, the Snowy Plover has disappeared as a breeder at many historical nesting locations as breeding ranges shrank due to habitat alteration and fragmentation. It occurs as a breeder at scattered locations on salt plains in the north

and northwest parts of the state, as well as along broad sandy riverbeds and impoundment shores in western and central Oklahoma. In 1977 and 1978, 325 and 260 breeding pairs, respectively, were counted at Salt Plains National Wildlife Refuge in Alfalfa County. Thirty-eight of 52 nests (73 percent) were successful in 1977, while only 14 of 37 nests (38 percent) were successful in 1978, due largely to flooding.

Current: Because the Snowy Plover occurs locally as a breeder at scattered locations along sandy beaches and shorelines and on salt flats, its range and distribution are not well delineated by atlas project results. However, additional information collected in association with the atlas block surveys confirmed the Snowy Plover as breeding in Alfalfa, Cleveland, McClain, Texas, and Tillman counties. In 1998, 10 pairs produced 20 fledglings along a 32 km (19 mi) stretch of the Canadian River in Cleveland and McClain counties.

Population Trend: This species is not adequately measured by the Breeding Bird Survey. The current North American population is believed to be between 16,000 and 21,000, with about 87 percent of these located west of the Rocky Mountains.

References: AOU 1998; Baicich and Harrison 1997; Baumgartner and Baumgartner 1992; Boyd 1972; Byre 2000; Grover and Grover 1982; Grover and Knopf 1982; Hill, L. A. 1985, 1992, 1993; Koenen 1995; Morrison et al. 2001; National Geographic Society 1999; Page et al. 1995; Paton 1999; Purdue 1976; Sibley 2000; Sutton 1967

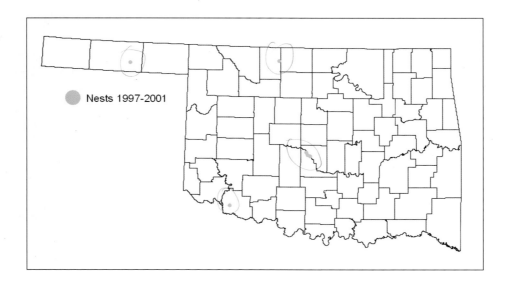

Nests 1997-2001

Piping Plover
Charadrius melodus

John S. Shackford

Courtesy of Bob Gress

The Piping Plover is a small endangered shorebird breeding on interior shorelines and northern Atlantic beaches. The male, on his breeding territory, has a fascinating slow courtship "butterfly" flight that is quite different from his usual rapid flight. Only two breeding records exist for Oklahoma, both from Optima Reservoir in Texas County.

Description: Males and females are similar in appearance, the upperparts being a light sandy brown, the underparts white. In breeding plumage, adults have a black collar around the neck and upper breast that is complete in some males, but broken on the breast of other males and females. Breeding adults also have orangish legs and bill, the latter tipped in black, which help distinguish it from the similar Snowy Plover.

Breeding Habitat: Sandy shorelines, usually above high watermark, that are totally or largely bare of vegetation.

Nest: Slight hollow in the sand that may be lined with pebbles, shells, or driftwood.

NESTING ECOLOGY

Season: May–July. Single-brooded, but will replace lost clutches.

Eggs: Usually 4, but sometimes 3; pale buff marked with dark splotches, usually thicker on the larger end.
Development: Incubation is by both sexes for about 28 days. Young are precocial, leaving nest soon after hatching, but associating with parents for some time.

DISTRIBUTION AND ABUNDANCE

Rangewide: Breeds along the northern Atlantic Coast from Newfoundland, Canada, south to North Carolina. Interior populations nest in the area enclosed by the Great Lakes south to Nebraska, northwest to east-central Alberta, eastward through southern Saskatchewan, Manitoba, and southwestern Ontario. Winters along the Atlantic and Gulf coasts from North Carolina southward into Mexico, several West Indies islands, and northern Cuba.
Historical: Only two breeding records for Oklahoma, both along shoreline at Optima Reservoir in eastern Texas County. The first record consisted of 2 adults

and 4 chicks found on 17 June in 1987, and the second record was of a nest with 4 eggs found on 25 June in 1988, a nest which later was probably flooded out.
Current: Piping Plover is (or was) an extremely rare breeder in Oklahoma and should be watched for on (nonsaline?) sandy flats adjacent to lakes and rivers, particularly those in northwestern Oklahoma and the Panhandle.

Population Trend: Listed as either Endangered or Threatened in the United States and Canada due to human disturbance and manipulation of breeding habitat.

References: AOU 1998; Baicich and Harrison 1997; Baumgartner and Baumgartner 1992; Bent 1962a; Boyd 1991; Cairns 1982; Haig 1992; Johnsgard 1979; Peterjohn and Sauer 1999; Sutton 1967; Terres 1980; Tyler 1991a

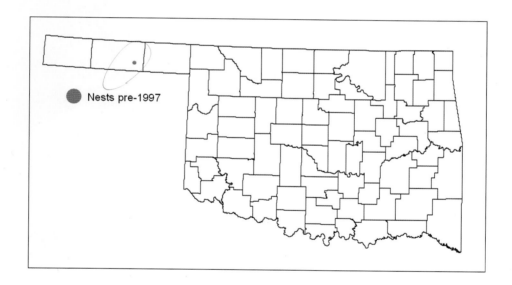

Nests pre-1997

Killdeer
Charadrius vociferus

Eugene A. Young

Courtesy of Warren Williams

The Killdeer is perhaps the most common nesting and certainly the most familiar shorebird in Oklahoma. It is easily identified due to its feigning broken-wing distraction performance near nests or young and its bright rufous orange rump. Killdeer have benefited from human alterations to habitats, increasing their range and population.

Description: Sexes similar, of medium size for plovers and having a black bill, reddish-brown eye bordered by a small red ring, white wing stripes, and a rufous-orange rump and tail with a white tip. The brown upperparts and white underparts with two distinct black chest bands, along with a white supercilium help distinguish this species from other plovers. Voice a familiar *killdeer* cry.

Breeding Habitat: Open areas with sparse vegetation (upland prairie, peanut and cotton fields, other farm fields, pasture, mudflats, airports, golf courses, farm ponds), or lacking vegetation; commonly within beds of small gravel, pebbles, or rocks (roadsides, railroads, ball fields, dumps, parking lots); occasionally nests on buildings with gravel roofs. Nests are usually placed away from water, but birds are often associated with at least some water.

Nest: Usually a scrape or slight depression on the

ground, 12.7–19 cm (5–7.5 in) wide, may be lined with grass or other debris that is commonly white or light in color. Nests are often slightly elevated above surrounding terrain. Both sexes construct the nest, usually 7–10 days before laying begins. Occasionally fake nests are used to distract predators.

NESTING ECOLOGY

Season: Mid-March–August. Single- to double-brooded.
Eggs: Usually 4; light brown to tan, yellowish gray, or gray buff, with irregular black-and-brown spotting, blotching, or scrawling.
Development: Incubation is by both sexes for 22–28 days. Young are precocial but remain with adults until they can fly, at about 20 days.

DISTRIBUTION AND ABUNDANCE

Rangewide: Breeds coast to coast from Alaska south to southern Mexico. Winters across much of the southern United States south through Central America. Also occurs in South America.

Historical: Described as a common summer resident throughout Oklahoma except in the heavily wooded eastern regions.
Current: The Killdeer is common nearly statewide, but becomes scarce in the heavily wooded habitats of southeastern Oklahoma. Its conspicuous nesting habits such as placing nests along road edges, together with its familiar broken-wing distraction display, make it easy to confirm as a breeder.

Population Trend: Breeding Bird Survey data for 1966–2000 show a decline of 0.3 percent per year rangewide (P = 0.05), but no conclusive trend in Oklahoma (-0.5 percent per year, P = 0.30).

References: AOU 1998; Baicich and Harrison 1997; Baumgartner and Baumgartner 1992; Jackson and Jackson 2000; Mitchell 1954; Pulich 1988; Sauer et al. 2001; Smith et al. 1999; Stokes and Stokes 1983; Sutton 1967; Terres 1991; Turner 1971; Tveten 1993

Confirmed	297
Probable	106
Possible	25
Total	428

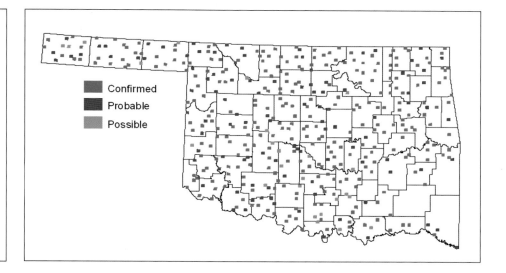

Mountain Plover
Charadrius montanus

Gregory A. Smith

Courtesy of Bob Gress

Of all North American "shorebirds," the Mountain Plover is undoubtedly the one most disconnected from the shore. This is a bird of the upland plains, nesting in shortgrass prairie, often at sites historically used by prairie dogs, bison, and pronghorn. Known as the "Prairie-Ghost," Mountain Plovers can be almost invisible on the open prairie owing to their light coloration and habit, when wary, of remaining perfectly still.

Description: Fairly large plovers, almost Killdeer size, but with longer legs and an upright posture. In breeding plumage, male and female Mountain Plovers show unbanded white underparts, distinguishing them from all other brown-backed plovers. A more extensive buffy tinge on the breast is usually evident in winter plumage.

Female plovers are slightly larger than males. Calls include low drawn-out whistles and harsh notes during the breeding season and a harsh *krrr* note on wintering grounds or during migration.

Breeding Habitat: Shortgrass prairie and arid high plains. Prefers sites dominated by blue grama and buffalograss, often in disturbed areas with patches of bare ground. Frequently associated with prairie dog towns. Plovers have also been known to nest in cultivated fields, perhaps an adaptation to changing land-use practices within recent times and the resulting loss of native prairie.

Nest: A shallow, unlined scrape in the ground dug by

the male. Nest scrapes are usually located in the open but may be situated next to cow dung, stones, or cacti. Nests are often lined with dried grass or other plant materials, dirt, cow chips, and other debris. The nest lining is deposited after the clutch is initiated, as the parents walk around the nest and toss materials into it.

NESTING ECOLOGY

Season: April–July. Often double-brooded. A female from one pair may lay two clutches, with the male incubating one while the female incubates the other.

Eggs: Usually 3; drab light olive or olive buff with fine speckles of black and gray.

Development: Incubation lasts for 28–31 days and is performed alternately by both sexes if only one clutch was laid or by the male alone on one clutch and the female on another if two clutches were laid. Young are precocial, leaving the nest within a few hours of hatching and obtaining their own food. They are usually attended by the parent that incubated them, and first flight occurs within 33–34 days.

DISTRIBUTION AND ABUNDANCE

Rangewide: Breeds throughout the western Great Plains from northern Montana and southern parts of Canada south to central New Mexico and the Texas Panhandle. Winters from north-central California south to southern Mexico. Most migratory populations move north-south but some may move east-west, spending the winter in California.

Historical: Considered a rare and local summer resident of Cimarron County.

Current: Mountain Plovers are breeders in the short-grass prairies of the High Plains, and this is reflected in their very limited breeding distribution in the western Panhandle. Although their secretive nature and well-camouflaged plumage makes them a difficult species to census using atlasing methods, this mapped distribution is likely accurate. All reported observations outside of atlas blocks were also in Cimarron County. Confirmed breeding in Morton County, Kansas, is consistent with this localized breeding distribution in Cimarron County; birds could also be looked for in northwestern Texas County.

Population Trend: Breeding Bird Survey data for 1966–2000 show no conclusive trend rangewide (-1.2 percent per year, P = 0.51), but there is concern over declining populations resulting from habitat loss in eastern portions of the western Great Plains. The species has been considered for listing under the Endangered Species Act. No trend data are available for Oklahoma.

References: AOU 1998; Baumgartner and Baumgartner 1992; Bent 1962a; Busby and Zimmerman 2001; Davis 1970; Flowers 1985; Graul 1975; Johnsgard 1979; Kaufman 1996; Knopf 1996; Knopf and Rupert 1999; Nice 1927; Peterjohn and Sauer 1999; Sauer et al. 2001; Shackford 1991, 1995, 1996; Sutton 1967; Tate 1923; Thompson and Ely 1989; Tyler 1968a; Wood and Schnell 1984

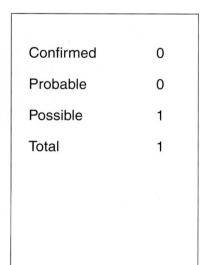

Confirmed	0
Probable	0
Possible	1
Total	1

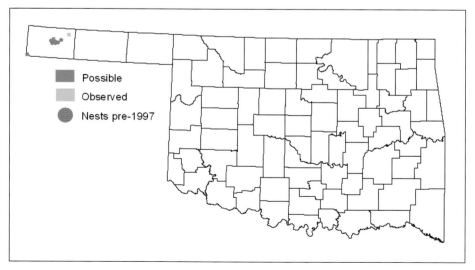

Possible
Observed
Nests pre-1997

Black-necked Stilt
Himantopus mexicanus

Mark Howery

The Black-necked Stilt is a large distinctive shore-bird most commonly observed in Oklahoma during migration. Over the past twenty years, the Black-necked Stilt has expanded its breeding range into the Texas Panhandle and western Oklahoma.

Description: The Black-necked Stilt has unusually long red legs and a moderately long thin black bill. The plumage on the back, wings, and dorsal side of the neck and head is black. The tail, belly, breast, and undersides of the neck and head are a contrasting white. The wings are long and, at rest, extend past and cover the white tail. The eyes of mature birds are red. The plumage of females has a faint wash of brown on the back.

Breeding Habitat: Shallow freshwater marshes including seasonally flooded wetlands. In Oklahoma, breeding stilts have been found in seasonally flooded, depressional wetlands in pastures and cultivated fields in several locations in northwestern Oklahoma, Hackberry Flat Wildlife Management Area in Tillman County, and in wetlands along the Red River Valley in southeastern Oklahoma.

Nest: In dry areas, the nest may be a scrape in the ground lined with a small amount of plant stems. In wetter sites, stilts may construct a mound of plant stems several inches high with a small depression within it, or they may nest on an existing tussock of grasses or sedges.

Additional nesting material may be added during incubation to build up a nest if the water level around it rises. Pairs of Black-necked Stilts may nest singly but are usually found nesting in loose associations resembling colonies.

NESTING ECOLOGY

Season: Late May–mid-July. Normally single-brooded.
Eggs: Usually 4; brownish buff in color with variable black spotting.
Development: Incubation is by both sexes for 25–26 days. The young are precocial and able to run and feed themselves shortly after hatching. Both parents care for the young until they become independent at approximately 28–32 days.

DISTRIBUTION AND ABUNDANCE

Rangewide: Black-necked Stilts are widespread across western and southern North America, Central America, the Caribbean, and South America southward to Paraguay and northern Argentina. In the United States, Black-necked Stilts are most common around shallow marshes in California, the inter-mountain west, and along the Gulf and southern Atlantic coasts. In recent years, stilts have expanded their range into the lower Mississippi River valley and the southern Great Plains.
Historical: Historical accounts of Black-necked Stilts in Oklahoma are sparse but suggest that stilts may have been a rare breeding species along the Red River in southwestern Oklahoma. First well-documented nest records for Oklahoma are from Alfalfa and Garfield counties in 1993. Since then, breeding Black-necked Stilts have been found more regularly in western and extreme southeastern Oklahoma.
Current: Black-necked Stilts are rare and occur locally in Oklahoma, probably as a result of our state's position at the eastern edge of the species' breeding range. Because of its rarity and specialized habitat preferences, a complete distribution map for the Black-necked Stilt is difficult to generate using atlas project methodology. To offset this difficulty, the Black-necked Stilt was classified as a special interest species and breeding season observations outside of atlas blocks were solicited. Based upon atlas block surveys and other observations, it appears that the Black-necked Stilt is an infrequent breeder in the western quarter of the state and in the Gulf Coastal Plain of extreme southeastern Oklahoma.

Population Trend: Breeding Bird Survey data for 1966–2000 show no conclusive trend rangewide (0.3 percent per year, P = 0.91). No trend data are available for Oklahoma, although the species anecdotally appears to be increasing. An unmeasured population increase may be facilitating the apparent range expansion in the central United States.

References: Baicich and Harrison 1997; Baumgartner and Baumgartner 1992; Davis 1985; Erlich et al. 1988; Hayman et al. 1986; Koenen et al. 1994; Robinson et al. 1999; Sauer et al. 2001; Seyffert 1989a; Sutton 1967; U.S. Shorebird Conservation Plan 2001

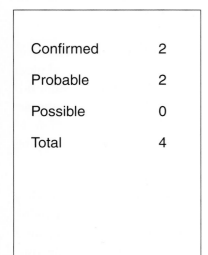

Confirmed	2
Probable	2
Possible	0
Total	4

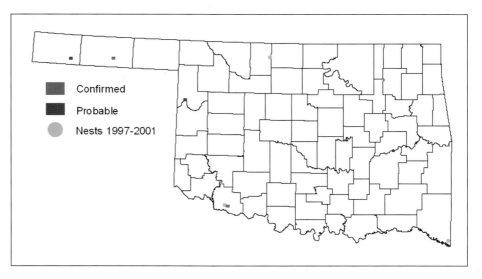

American Avocet

Recurvirostra americana

Sebastian T. Patti

Courtesy of Bill Horn

The American Avocet is a large long-legged shore-bird with a distinctive recurved bill. It is well known as an aggressive species during the breeding season, and birds often engage in "dive-bombing" attacks, diversionary antics, and loud calling when a perceived predator is present. Food is generally limited to aquatic invertebrates that are captured by the species' hallmark method of feeding: scything. This technique involves a bird walking slowly through water or mud and sweeping the bill side to side, and held at the level of the substrate.

Description: A large shorebird with long bluish-gray legs and a bold black-and-white back pattern. White below. In alternate plumage, the head and neck are a bright cinnamon rufous; in basic plumage, the head and neck are light gray. Sexes are usually separable by bill size and structure, with males' bills being longer and not as greatly recurved, while those of females are shorter and strongly recurved.

Breeding Habitat: The American Avocet breeds in alkaline marshes, prairie potholes, and ephemeral playa lakes of the western United States. Other impoundments, ponds, and lagoons can be used, and it appears that sludge lagoons at commercial swine operations in the southern Great Plains states may be a developing resource for this species.

Nest: When present, islands are selected because they provide a measure of predator protection. Otherwise, the nest will generally be placed at water's edge, amid some sparse vegetation. The nest itself is a scrape, usually slightly elevated from the surrounding area and lined with grasses or other vegetable matter, mud, pebbles or small gravel, and feathers or hair. Both sexes participate in nest construction.

NESTING ECOLOGY

Season: April–July. Single-brooded, but will replace lost clutches.
Eggs: Usually 4; pale, pinkish buff, and mottled with light and dark brown speckles.
Development: Incubation is by both sexes for 23–26 days. Young are precocial, and stay within the nest no more than 24 hours after the hatching of the last chick. Chicks feed themselves.

DISTRIBUTION AND ABUNDANCE

Rangewide: Breeds from southern Canada across the western United States to Texas. Many birds winter in Mexico and in the southeastern United States from coastal Florida north and east to Georgia, South Carolina, and North Carolina.
Historical: Described as a rare transient in Oklahoma in 1931; by 1967 it was considered a transient and summer resident, with nesting noted at Salt Plains National Wildlife Refuge in Alfalfa County. About 50 breeding pairs were estimated at Salt Plains in the late 1970s, and 19 of 23 monitored nests (83 percent) in 1977 were successful. Predation by coyotes and flooding were the main causes of nest loss. Apparent nest success for 122 nests monitored in 1982 and 1983 was 33 percent. Twenty-eight of 47 nests (60 percent) were successful during the 1995 and 1996 breeding seasons. The apparent decline in relative abundance of avocets at Salt Plains from the 1982–1983 nesting seasons to the 1995–1996 nesting seasons may be due to saltcedar encroachment.

Current: During the atlas project, the species was found in three discrete areas of the state: the Salt Plains NWR in Alfalfa County, Hackberry Flats area in Tillman County, and the Panhandle. The population at Salt Plains, historically the most important breeding area in the state, seems to have declined rather dramatically in the last decade. Because of this, Tillman County is an important breeding area for the species in the state. In the Panhandle, the species was noted in three different areas: ephemeral playa lakes, small town/village wastewater treatment lagoons, and lagoons associated with commercial swine operations. Because playas are by their very nature "ephemeral," during extended dry periods, the latter two lagoon areas may provide resources for this species in the Panhandle.

Population Trend: Breeding Bird Survey data for 1966–2000 show no conclusive trend rangewide (-0.3 percent per year, P = 0.82). No trend data are available for Oklahoma. May be declining at Salt Plains NWR, but may be increasing in other areas of Oklahoma due to habitat creation during the late 1990s.

References: AOU 1998; Baumgartner and Baumgartner 1992; Busby and Zimmerman 2001; Dechant et al. 2002; Grover and Grover 1982; Grover and Knopf 1982; Hill 1985; Koenen 1995; Nice 1931; Oberholser 1974; Robinson et al. 1997; Sibley 2000; Sutton 1967; Winternitz 1998a; Winton and Leslie 1997

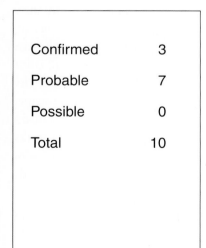

Confirmed	3
Probable	7
Possible	0
Total	10

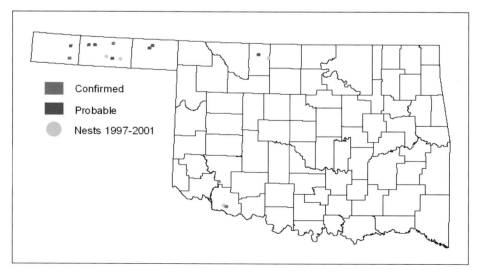

Spotted Sandpiper

Actitis macularia

Mark Howery

The Spotted Sandpiper has the most widespread breeding range of any sandpiper in North America. One of the most unusual characteristics of this species is its polyandrous breeding system in which the parental roles of the sexes are reversed. Females are larger and more aggressive than the males, while the male takes the primary parental care role. Female Spotted Sandpipers return to the breeding grounds ahead of males and establish territories. Females compete to attract and usually mate with one to three males.

Description: The Spotted Sandpiper is a small, short-necked, and long-tailed shorebird that bears distinctly different breeding season and nonbreeding season plumages. In the breeding season the head, back, and wings are brown, while the breast and belly are white with many bold, dark spots. The bill is predominantly orange in color with a black tip. In the nonbreeding season, the head, back, and wings are a grayish brown and the white breast and belly lack spots. The bill color fades to a straw or flesh color. In both seasons, the wings have dark primaries and a thin white wing stripe. The most distinguishing characteristic is the bird's behavior of bobbing and teetering its body as it walks and forages. Its characteristic flight behavior includes flying just above the ground or water with rapid, shallow fluttering wing beats.

Breeding Habitat: A wide range of wetland habitats are used by nesting birds, but they appear to prefer freshwater marshes and habitats dominated by herbaceous vegetation along the shorelines of streams, rivers, and lakes.

Nest: Normally placed within herbaceous vegetation 100 m (330 ft) or less from the shoreline of a stream, river, lake, or marsh. Constructed by both sexes, it consists of a scraped-out depression in the soil around which plant stems, grasses, and small sticks are pulled or placed. Nest material is usually collected from within a few feet of the nest

NESTING ECOLOGY

Season: May–July. The species is polyandrous, so a female may lay successive clutches for one to three males, but each male raises only a single brood per season.

Eggs: Usually 4; cream to buff in color with numerous dark speckles and a scattering of larger, blackish-brown spots.

Development: Incubation is by both sexes or by the male alone for 20–24 days. Young are precocial and capable of running and foraging within a few hours of hatching. Most brooding and parental care of the chicks is done by the male. The chicks are capable of flight at approximately 16–18 days and then may remain with the male for several weeks longer.

DISTRIBUTION AND ABUNDANCE

Rangewide: Very widespread and fairly common. The breeding range extends from the tree line in Alaska, east to Newfoundland, and south to Virginia, Missouri, Colorado, and central California. The wintering range extends from Florida, along the Gulf Coast, across southern Texas to the Pacific Coast as far north as Washington, and south through Uruguay and Paraguay.

Historical: Oklahoma lies along the southern edge of the breeding range in the central United States. Breeding has been documented only a few times, primarily along the Cimarron, Beaver, and Canadian rivers in western Oklahoma and the Panhandle.

Current: Three nesting confirmations were recorded during the atlas project years: two in atlas blocks in Bryan and Caddo counties, and one additional report from Packsaddle Wildlife Management Area. Several reports of probable breeders were recorded in atlas blocks from around the state; some of these may represent birds recorded as pairs during migration.

Population Trend: The U.S. Shorebird Conservation Plan estimates the current population at about 150,000. Population estimates are difficult to extrapolate because the species occurs at low densities over a very large area and does not congregate into large flocks during migration as other shorebirds do. Because this species is largely solitary, its population was not substantially affected by market hunting in the late 1800s. No trend data are available for Oklahoma.

References: Baicich and Harrison 1997; Baumgartner and Baumgartner 1992; Brown et al., eds. 2001; Ehrlich et al. 1988; Hayman et al. 1986; Lack et al. 1985; Oring and Davis 1966; Oring et al. 1983, 1987; Ports 1979; Sutton 1967

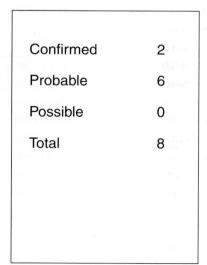

Confirmed	2
Probable	6
Possible	0
Total	8

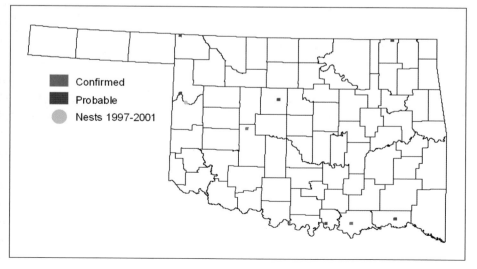

Confirmed
Probable
Nests 1997–2001

Upland Sandpiper
Bartramia longicauda

Dan L. Reinking

Courtesy of Warren Williams

Unique among Oklahoma sandpipers, the Upland Sandpiper forages and nests, as its name implies, in upland areas. Formerly abundant, populations were decimated in the late 1800s by market hunting following the loss of the Passenger Pigeon. Once again more numerous, it is an early spring migrant to northern Oklahoma prairies where many birds remain to establish nesting territories.

Description: Both males and females are pale brownish shorebirds with yellow legs, long thin necks, small heads, and large dark eyes. After landing, Upland Sandpipers often extend their wings outward and upward before folding them. Their song, usually given in flight on the breeding grounds, is a fascinating,

tremulous wolf whistle. This species could be confused with American Golden-Plover, which occurs in similar habitat during spring migration.

Breeding Habitat: This species utilizes tallgrass prairie, pastures, and airports. Preferred areas contain good grass cover and few woody plants, although fence posts or other display perches are used. Upland Sandpipers forage in areas with short vegetation such as recently burned or heavily grazed grassland, but prefer to nest in taller vegetation. They may nest at a higher density in ungrazed areas, and they require sizeable habitat patches, perhaps greater than 50 ha (124 ac).

Nest: A small hollow or depression lined with grasses,

often with surrounding grasses pulled over the nest for concealment.

NESTING ECOLOGY

Season: May–June. Single-brooded.
Eggs: Usually 4; pale buff with fine speckles.
Development: Incubation is by both sexes for 21 days. Young are precocial and are capable of flight after 30 days.

DISTRIBUTION AND ABUNDANCE

Rangewide: Long-distance migrant, breeding in parts of Alaska, north-central Canada, north-central Great Plains, the Midwest, and the Northeast, and wintering in eastern South America.
Historical: Formerly an abundant breeder on Oklahoma prairies, but reduced to a rare breeder limited to northern counties by 1931. Has nested as far southwest as Comanche County. Described as uncommon and local except in north-central counties in recent decades.

Current: The Upland Sandpiper is locally common throughout most of the northern counties and some central counties, reaching greatest abundance in the Flint Hills of Osage County. Records from southern and southwestern Oklahoma likely pertain to migrants, as this species begins fall migration starting in the mid- to late summer months.

Population Trend: Breeding Bird Survey data for 1966–2000 show an increase of 1.0 percent per year rangewide (P = 0.01), but show no conclusive trend in Oklahoma (0.5 percent per year, P = 0.08).

References: AOU 1998; Baicich and Harrison 1997; Baumgartner and Baumgartner 1992; Bent 1962a; Bowen and Kruse 1993; Dechant et al. 1999; Nice 1931; Peterjohn and Sauer 1999; Sauer et al. 2001; Sutton 1967; Zimmerman 1993

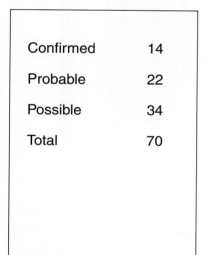

Confirmed	14
Probable	22
Possible	34
Total	70

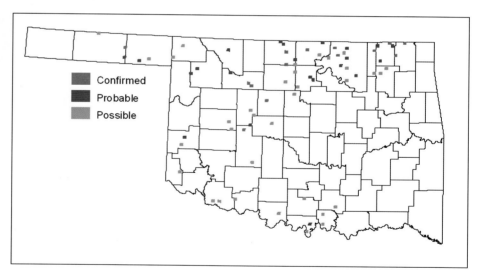

Long-billed Curlew
Numenius americanus

Gregory A. Smith

Courtesy of Warren Williams

The Long-billed Curlew is the largest of our shore-birds and can often be seen away from shore. Curlews are also known as "Sicklebills," owing to their very long, slender, downcurved bills. More than any other shorebird, curlews seem to embody the "wild, roving spirit of the vast open prairies" (Bent 1962a).

Description: Large shorebird, cinnamon-brown above, buff below. Very long downcurved bill. Patterning resembles Marbled Godwit but godwit bill is upcurved. Potentially confused with Whimbrels, Long-billed Curlews lack the dark eye stripes of that species. Call a loud, ascending *cur-leeew*. Female curlews are slightly larger and longer billed than males.

Breeding Habitat: Open grasslands, sagebrush prairie, and wet meadows. Occasionally nests on agricultural fields, usually near the edge, close to cover. May choose areas with damp low spots to provide potential feeding areas for young.

Nest: A shallow hollow in the ground, sometimes with a raised rim, especially in wet areas. Lined with grasses and debris.

NESTING ECOLOGY

Season: May–June. Single-brooded.
Eggs: Usually 4; pale green or olive with heavy brown specks and spots.

Development: Incubation is by both sexes for 27–28 days. Young are born precocial, are tended by both sexes, and first fly in 32–45 days.

DISTRIBUTION AND ABUNDANCE

Rangewide: Breeds throughout the western Great Plains from southern Canada to southern New Mexico. West of the Rocky Mountains, the breeding populations extend from southern Canada to southern Nevada but do not reach the Pacific Coast. Long-billed Curlews are short-distance migrants, with a large proportion of the population wintering in the southern United States and northen Mexico. Some east-west migration occurs, resulting in a wintering population in southern Florida.

Historical: Described as a rare summer resident of the Panhandle. Reported to have nested as far south as Washita County in 1893. Former breeder in northwestern Oklahoma counties. Occurs irregularly within the main body of the state, although breeding records are scarce. May gather in large feeding or migratory flocks.

Current: Long-billed Curlews breed in only the shortgrass High Plains region of the Oklahoma Panhandle. The records for Probable Breeder could pertain to late migrants, which can be observed in pairs. The *Texas Breeding Bird Atlas* did not record breeding individuals in Texas counties adjacent to southern or western Oklahoma. Breeding in Texas was only recorded in the northwestern panhandle, adjacent to Cimarron County, Oklahoma, and on the Gulf Coastal Plain. Therefore, there is no reason to believe that curlews were in fact breeding throughout western Oklahoma and were simply missed by atlasing methods. They are local breeders in the state.

Population Trend: Breeding Bird Survey data for 1966–2000 show no conclusive trend rangewide (-1.2 percent per year, P = 0.11) and a decline of 14.4 percent per year in Oklahoma (P = 0.04), although it is detected on few routes here, making trend analysis difficult.

References: AOU 1998; Baumgartner and Baumgartner 1992; Benson and Arnold 2001; Bent 1962; Davis 1970; Dechant et al. 2001; Graul 1971; Johnsgard 1979; Kaufman 1996; Nice 1931; Peterjohn and Sauer 1999; Sauer et al. 2001; Shackford 1994; Sutton 1967; Tate 1923; Thompson and Ely 1989; Wood and Schnell 1984

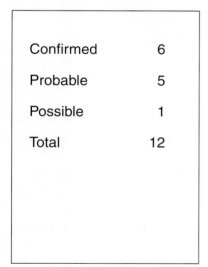

Confirmed	6
Probable	5
Possible	1
Total	12

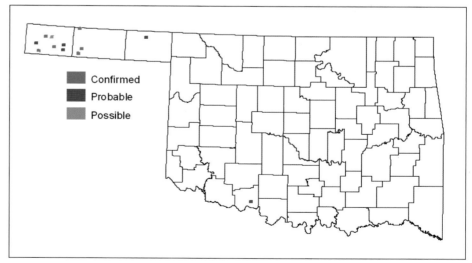

American Woodcock
Scolopax minor

Melinda Droege

Courtesy of Gerald Wiens

The courtship display of the American Woodcock is one of the first signs of spring in Oklahoma, beginning in early February, and usually on a warm moonlit night. It is still a mystery, though, as to whether all displaying individuals remain to nest or continue onward to other breeding sites.

Description: A chunky, short-necked, short-legged shorebird with a mottled dead leaf pattern on the upperparts. The American Woodcock has a distinctive long bill, rusty underparts, a barred crown, rounded wings, and large eyes set far back in the head. It could possibly be confused with the Common Snipe, which is best separated by its streaked crown and pointed wings. Distinctive also are the nasal *peent* call and the twittering whistle of the male's wings during courtship.

Breeding Habitat: The ideal habitat for woodcock is one of variety: damp woodlands near water for foraging earthworms, open dry woods near overgrown fields for courtship displays, and brushy areas and thickets for nesting.

Nest: A slight depression on the ground usually near a bush, small tree, or weeds, but sometimes in the open. Nest is lined with dead leaves and occasionally rimmed with twigs or pine needles. At least 90 m (300 ft) from display area but usually closer to feeding grounds.

NESTING ECOLOGY

Season: March–April. Single-brooded. Displays in mid- to late March are suspected to represent renesting activities.

Eggs: Usually 4; buffy pink to cinnamon blotched with brown.

Development: Incubation is by the female for 20–21 days. Young are precocial and leave the nest a few hours after hatching. They grow rapidly and can fly short distances at 14 days. By 25 days they are fully grown, fly well, and may eat their own weight in earthworms daily.

DISTRIBUTION AND ABUNDANCE

Rangewide: Breeding widely distributed in the eastern United States north to southern Canada, as well as on their winter range in southern states. Also winter in south-central Texas, the Gulf Coast, and southern Florida. Range expanding northward due to extensive forest harvesting.

Historical: Eastern and east-central Oklahoma are on the westernmost edge of its range, with nests found as far west as Pontotoc and Payne counties. As courtship flights also occur on migration and wintering grounds, this is not necessarily proof of nesting. Display sites and/or nesting activity have been cited for 23 Oklahoma counties. Woodcock broods have been recorded from 10 March to 15 April; the brood found on 10 March would have come from a nest containing eggs laid on or before 14 February, suggesting nesting may begin earlier than commonly thought.

Current: No American Woodcocks were reported from atlas blocks. The rare and local distribution of this species in Oklahoma makes it poorly sampled by atlas methodology. In addition, few observers were in the field at dusk and dawn during February and March when this species is actively displaying.

Population Trend: Rangewide population trend is not well measured, but indicates large increases in some areas and large declines in others. Little trend data are available for Oklahoma. Woodcock habitat in Oklahoma may be increasing due to farm abandonment and control of fire. Heavy grazing by cattle of wooded areas may be most responsible for loss of woodcock habitat.

References: AOU 1998; Baicich and Harrison 1997; Barclay and Smith 1977; Baumgartner and Baumgartner 1992; Bent 1962a; Brown 1981; Delap and Droege; Ehrlich et al. 1988; Harrison 1975; Johnsgard 1979; Keppie and Whiting 1994; Pettingill 1936; Sauer et al. 2001; Sheldon 1967; Smith 1974; Sutton 1967; Tyler 1972

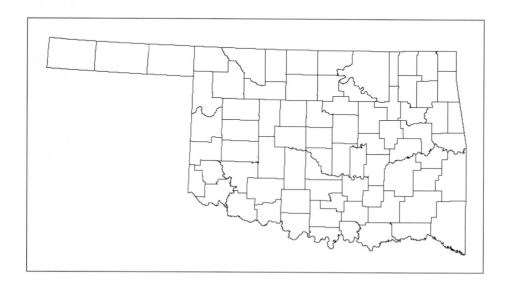

Wilson's Phalarope
Phalaropus tricolor

Bonnie L. Gall

These sleek little water birds are easy to spot during migration, as they twirl in prairie wetland ponds, to bring choice morsels to the water's surface. In Oklahoma, however, only a few records exist to suggest that they linger to nest in appropriate wetland habitat. A prime example of sex-role reversal, the female is a gadabout, laying her eggs and leaving the male to take care of the young while she finds another boyfriend.

Description: The Wilson's Phalarope is a slender, long-legged sandpiper with a small head and long, thin bill. During the breeding season, the female shows a black-ish stripe on face and neck, grayish crown, white throat, and chestnut from throat to breast. The male is

less colorful. Fall adults are pale gray above and white below, while legs can be either gray or yellow. A longer bill and fainter cheek patch differentiate this bird from other fall plumaged phalaropes. Sounds have been described as nasal or guttural, including *ernt, wa, purr,* and *chug* during courtship, and flight calls resembling *wemf, vint,* or *vimp.* One characteristic feeding habit includes spinning rapidly while swimming; this helps bring food items to the water's surface.

Breeding Habitat: Across its breeding range, this species prefers wetland habitats such as wet meadows, grassy marshes, roadside ditches, river or lake edges, and prairie playa ponds. The water can be fresh to highly saline. Vegetation in the area of the nest site is often thicker than that of other prairie-nesting shorebirds.

Nest: Usually a hollow on damp ground that has been lined with grasses, but occasionally raised 2–7 cm (1–3 in) above ground in marshy vegetation. Built by the male alone and usually well hidden.

NESTING ECOLOGY

Season: May–July in the Great Plains region.
Eggs: 3–4; slightly glossy, and buffy in color with numerous brown spots, dots, and blotches.
Development: Males often guard females during the laying period. Incubation is by the male alone for about 23 days, but timing is variable. Young are precocial and are tended by the male alone. The female abandons the male after completing the clutch to potentially breed with other males.

DISTRIBUTION AND ABUNDANCE

Rangewide: Breeding range includes wetland areas of the western United States and Canada, including the northern plains states. A number of nesting records exist east and north of this range. The species migrates to highly alkaline/salty lakes or bays in the western United States where it stages, often in huge flocks, before migrating to similar habitat for the winter, mainly in Bolivia and Argentina. Females often stage earliest, followed by males, and finally by juveniles.

Historical: The species is a relatively common Oklahoma migrant during spring and fall, especially in the central and western parts of the state. One possible nesting record exists from June 1931, when a pair was observed exhibiting nesting behavior at the Salt Plains National Wildlife Refuge in Alfalfa County. There are several records of birds in juvenile plumage in mid- to late July. Because of the difficulty of finding nests, young birds are usually not seen until they have fledged and moved away from the nesting area.

Current: Atlas efforts have resulted in three Probable and one Confirmed records for Wilson's Phalarope from the Oklahoma Panhandle. The latter record consists of fledged juveniles seen during July in association with a small flock of adults and could represent birds moving into Oklahoma after nesting elsewhere rather than a true Oklahoma breeding record. Additional efforts are encouraged to locate stronger evidence of nesting in Oklahoma.

Population Trend: Breeding Bird Survey data for 1966–2000 show no conclusive trend rangewide (-1.3 percent per year, P = 0.16). No trend data are available for Oklahoma.

References: Baumgartner and Baumgartner 1992; Bent 1927; Colwell and Jehl 1994; Harrison 1979; Johnsgard 1979; National Geographic Society 1999; Nice 1931; Oring and Davis 1966; Sauer et al. 2001; Sutton 1967

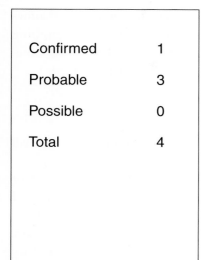

Confirmed	1
Probable	3
Possible	0
Total	4

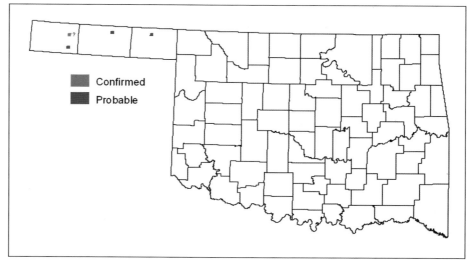

Confirmed
Probable

Least Tern
Sterna antillarum

Victoria J. Byre

Courtesy of Colin Smith

The Least Tern is the smallest North American tern. It is exciting to watch as it hovers in midair on rapid wing beats, then plunges straight down into the water for tiny fish and invertebrates. Because of widespread habitat loss to development and recreation, it is classified for protection in much of its range.

Description: The Least Tern is gray above with white underparts. In addition to its small size, it can be identified and distinguished from other terns during the breeding season by its black cap, white forehead, and black-tipped yellow bill. In flight, the black leading edges of the outer wing feathers are also distinctive. The sexes are very similar in all plumages. Least Terns utter a sharp *kaDEEK, kaDEEK* call in flight, and a sharp rising *zreek* alarm call, as well as other vocalizations.

Breeding Habitat: Least Terns breed on barren, gravelly, or sandy shores near reservoirs and lakes, along rivers with broad flat sandy banks and bars, and on salt flats that have water nearby.

Nest: Least Terns usually nest in colonies but sometimes as isolated pairs. The nest is usually nothing more than a shallow scrape in the sand or gravel, sometimes with a few pebbles or bits of debris added.

NESTING ECOLOGY

Season: May–early August. Single-brooded, but will renest if eggs are lost.

Eggs: Usually 2–3; smooth and nonglossy, buff or cream colored with blotches, speckles, and scrawls of brown, blackish-brown, and shades of gray.

Development: Incubation by both sexes for 19–22 days. Young are semiprecocial and leave nest after 1 day. They are provisioned by both adults and fledge at 19–21 days.

DISTRIBUTION AND ABUNDANCE

Rangewide: Breeds at scattered locations along the Pacific Coast from central California south to southern Baja California and Chiapas; along the Atlantic-Gulf Coast from Maine south to Florida, the Caribbean, and the beaches surrounding the Gulf of Mexico, as well as inland along the major interior rivers and salt flats of the central United States. Winters along marine coastlines of Central and South America.

Historical: Considered a summer resident at Salt Plains, western Oklahoma rivers, and the Red River in 1931. Between 1981 and 1992, Least Terns were found breeding in Oklahoma at 88 locations on major rivers, at two sites on reservoir beaches or sand spits, and at three major salt flats, and were more numerous in eastern than in western Oklahoma. A site on the Arkansas River in Tulsa is one of few with consistently high production, averaging 1.7 fledglings per pair from 1987 to 1992; a site along a 32 km (19 mi) stretch of the Canadian River in Cleveland and McClain counties averaged 1.2 fledglings per pair from 1991 to 1998. Statewide, the average production was 0.5 to 0.7 fledglings per pair from 1982 to 1992, comparable to the national average. Former breeding ranges in Oklahoma are similar to current ranges (on salt flats, along broad sandy riverbeds and sandbars, and on barren shores of impoundments throughout the state), but, due to dams and reservoirs, sand-mining operations, development, and recreational activity, colony distribution in these areas is now much more fragmented and populations much smaller.

Current: Because Least Terns nest in loose colonies at scattered locations along sandy rivers, lake shores, and salt flats, and because the species may wander widely over a day or season, its range and distribution are not well delineated by atlas project results. However, additional data collected in association with the block survey data confirm the Least Tern as nesting in a number of Oklahoma counties. The largest nesting concentration in the state is on the Salt Plains National Wildlife Refuge in Alfalfa County.

Population Trend: Difficult to measure. Current range is probably similar to historic range, but more fragmented. The national population declined substantially around 1900 due to feather and egg collecting, but rebounded after passage of the Migratory Bird Treaty Act in 1916. Habitat losses and concerns over declining populations in the last half of the twentieth century resulted in the interior population of Least Terns being listed as endangered in 1985. A 1992 population estimate for Oklahoma was 1,600 to 1,800 adults, which represented about 25 percent of the interior U.S. population.

References: AOU 1998; Archibeque 1987; Baicich and Harrison 1997; Baumgartner and Baumgartner 1992; Byre 2000; Grover and Grover 1982; Grover and Knopf 1982; Hill, L. A. 1985, 1992, 1993; Nice 1931; Pianalto 1993; Schweitzer 1994; Schweitzer and Leslie 1996; Sibley 2000; Sidle et al. 1988; Stokes and Stokes 1996; Sutton 1967; Thompson et al. 1997; U.S. Fish and Wildlife Service 1985; U.S. Fish and Wildlife Service 1990; Wood and Leslie 1992

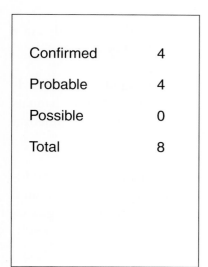

Confirmed	4
Probable	4
Possible	0
Total	8

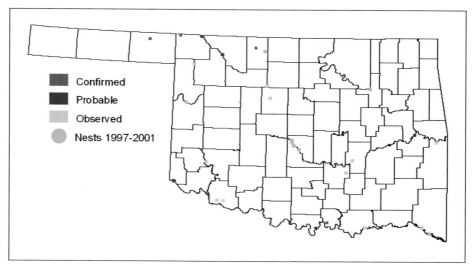

Confirmed
Probable
Observed
Nests 1997-2001

Rock Dove
Columba livia

Richard A. Stuart

A nonnative species introduced to North America in the early 1600s, the Rock Dove, or pigeon as it is often called, now inhabits nearly all of the United States and southern Canada. They are most common around urban areas and in rural settings near human habitation.

Description: Sexes similar. Typical plumage is gray, with iridescence on the neck and a white rump. Two black bars are present on the wing, the tip of the tail sports a broad black band, and the feet are red. Plumage color is highly variable, ranging from large amounts of white to almost all dark. Call consists of a variety of coos rendered *coo-cuk-cuk-cuk-coooo*.

Breeding Habitat: Commonly found on farm buildings and on buildings in urban areas. Natural habitats include cliffs, which they use in western Cimarron County.

Nest: Situated on protected ledges such as on buildings, bridges, dams, barns, abandoned houses, and, more rarely, natural cliffs. A scanty platform of grasses, straw, and other materials; nests may be reused, resulting in raised platforms of nest material, fecal matter, and other debris

NESTING ECOLOGY

Season: All year. Up to 6 or more broods per year.
Eggs: 2; white.
Development: Incubation is by both sexes for 18–19 days. Young are provisioned with "pigeon milk" by both sexes until fledging at 25–32 days in summer or up to 45 days in winter.

DISTRIBUTION AND ABUNDANCE

Rangewide: Resident throughout the lower 48 states and southernmost Canada. Native to Scandinavia and Russia south to India; now introduced nearly worldwide.
Historical: Described as a common resident; less common in forest and open plains.

Current: The Rock Dove is a common resident throughout most of Oklahoma. It is usually easy to locate due to its preference for man-made structures as nest sites, but may be difficult to confirm because nests are often in inaccessible locations. Also, the nestlings' diet of pigeon milk means that food carries cannot be observed. Flocks are often found near granaries, barns, large bridges, and multistoried buildings.

Population Trend: Breeding Bird Survey data for 1966–2000 show no conclusive trend rangewide in North America (0.2 percent per year, P = 0.44) and no conclusive trend in Oklahoma (12.5 percent per year, P = 0.25).

References: Baumgartner and Baumgartner 1992; Clements 1978; Harrison 1975; Johnston 1992; National Geographic Society 1999; Peterson 1963, 1996; Sauer et al. 2001; Sibley 2000; Stokes and Stokes 1996; Sutton 1967

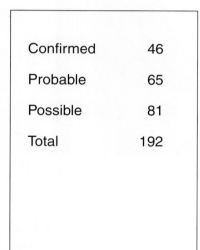

Confirmed	46
Probable	65
Possible	81
Total	192

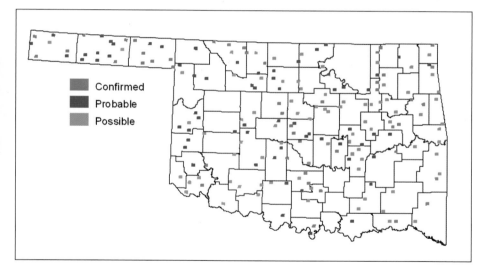

Eurasian Collared-Dove
Streptopelia decaocto

James W. Arterburn

Courtesy of Warren Williams

The first accepted report of the nonnative Eurasian Collared-Dove in Oklahoma was from Muskogee County on 16 September 1995. Since then it has spread over much of the state. This species is associated with human settlements, where food and shelter are plentiful, and it relies largely on waste grain associated with agriculture.

Description: Sexes similar. A medium-sized dove with a long tail and pale plumage. Body is pale sandy brown with buffy gray neck, head tinged with pink; underparts are brownish gray. Sides of neck have narrow black bars edged in white. Primaries are darker then the rest of wing. In flight, wings show blue gray on greater

wing coverts. Long tail is squared with black basal underside that almost reaches the gray undertail coverts. Undersides of outer tail feathers are black at the base and extending distally. Closed tail looks almost white from below. Song consists of three-syllable hooting.

Breeding Habitat: Inhabits open country with trees and scrub, usually near cultivated areas; also small towns, parks, and gardens or wherever there are dense trees for nesting.

Nest: A flat, thin platform of fine twigs and plant stems. Nest is built by the female, but the male does bring material. Placement is normally in a tree, often in an evergreen, or rarely on a building ledge. Usually 3–12 m (10–40 ft) high.

NESTING ECOLOGY

Season: Reported as usually March–August, but almost year round except autumn. Usually triple-brooded.
Eggs: 2; white, smooth and moderately glossy.
Development: Incubation is by both sexes for 14 days. Young are provisioned by both parents and fly at about 18 days, leaving the nest area at about 21 days.

DISTRIBUTION AND ABUNDANCE

Rangewide: Native to the Old World. Became established in Florida in the 1980s and is now rapidly expanding across the North American continent and the Caribbean Islands.
Historical: The Eurasian Collared-Dove was first recorded in Oklahoma in Muskogee County in 1995.

The first known nest record is from Tulsa in 1996.
Current: The Eurasian Collared-Dove has been rapidly increasing and expanding its range in Oklahoma (and throughout much of the United States), especially in the central and western areas of the state. However, the species is still uncommon enough to make it poorly sampled by atlas methodology. A nest record for Tulsa in 1997 was in the same area as the 1996 record.

Population Trend: Breeding Bird Survey data for 1966–2000 show a huge increase of 58.7 percent per year rangewide (P = 0.00), but because this species only became established in the 1980s, and is not well measured on a large number of routes, this estimate may not be numerically accurate. It is expanding and increasing rapidly, however, including in Oklahoma.

References: AOU 1998; Baicich and Harrison 1997; Kaufman 2000; Romagosa and McEneaney 1999; Sibley 2000; Smith, P. W. 1987; Svensson et al. 1999; Wiedenfeld and Swan 2000

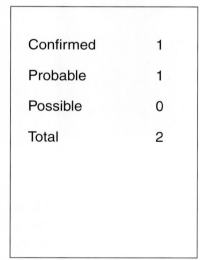

Confirmed	1
Probable	1
Possible	0
Total	2

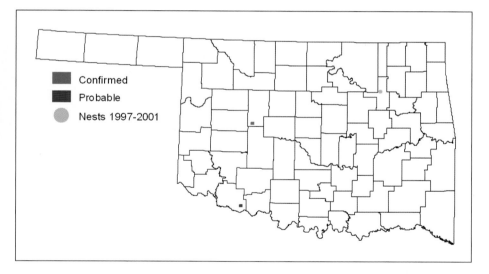

Mourning Dove
Zenaida macroura

Eugene A. Young

Courtesy of Colin Smith

A common symbol of peace, this widespread species is one of the most abundant birds across the continent and continues to spread northward in part because it has tolerated human habitat alterations so well. Like other doves and pigeons, Mourning Doves feed their young "pigeon milk," which is a semiliquid concoction of partly digested seeds prepared in the parent's crop for the first 3–4 days.

Description: Commonly identified by its long "coo call" *ooah coo-coo-coo* or *ooahoo-oo-oo-o,* which can be heard from early spring through summer. These songs are used primarily by males to attract females. The plumage of both sexes is generally a soft grayish to brownish, with short wings, a long pointed tail edged with white on the outer margin, a small rounded head, and short neck rounding out their appearance. Adults have a small blue ring around the eye. Mourning Doves are separated from other doves, especially in flight, by their size and tail length, pattern, and shape, as well as by the lack of contrasting colors on their wings.

Breeding Habitat: Cultivated land with scattered trees, bushes, and open woodland, suburbs, towns, shelterbelts, roadsides, farmsteads, arid and desert country, cemeteries, and a variety of other habitats.

Nest: A flimsy platform of twigs, oftentimes built in another species' nest. Usually in a tree or shrub, preferably in a crotch, and usually 1.5–7.6 m (5–25 ft) high; occasionally on the ground. May share nests with other species on occasion.

NESTING ECOLOGY

Season: March–August, sometimes later. Often double- or triple-brooded.
Eggs: 2; white. Occasional "dump nests" contain more eggs.
Development: Incubation is usually by the male during the day and the female at night and lasts 14 days. Young are fed "pigeon milk" by both sexes and fledge at about 15 days. Males will continue to feed young for up to 30 days.

DISTRIBUTION AND ABUNDANCE

Rangewide: Breeds from southern Canada and throughout the United States and Mexico, where it is also a permanent resident. Northern populations migrate southward depending on severity of winter.
Historical: Considered a common to abundant resident throughout the state.

Current: Mourning Doves have a statewide distribution with a high proportion of breeding confirmations, especially in the western half of the state where nests are in more open habitats. Breeding confirmations become more difficult in the heavily wooded portions of southeastern Oklahoma.

Population Trend: Breeding Bird Survey data for 1966–2000 show a decline of 0.2 percent per year rangewide (P = 0.03) and a decline of 1.7 percent per year in Oklahoma (P = 0.00).

References: AOU 1998; Baicich and Harrison 1997; Baumgartner and Baumgartner 1992; Brackbill 1970a; Dodson 1954; Downing 1959; Drobney et al. 1998; Hitchcock and Mirarchi 1984; Mirarchi and Baskett 1994; Nice 1922; Pulich 1988; Ray, G. E. 1973; Regosin 1993; Sauer et al. 2001; Skutch 1999; Stokes and Stokes 1983; Sutton 1967; Terres 1991; Thompson and Ely 1989; Tveten 1993; Westmoreland and Best 1987; Westmoreland et al. 1986; Wolfe 1994b; Zimmerman 1993

Confirmed	332
Probable	163
Possible	61
Total	556

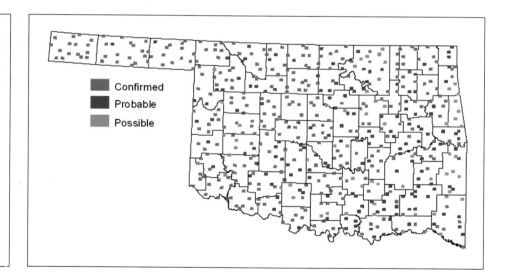

Inca Dove
Columbina inca

Sebastian T. Patti

A small dove of arid regions of the southwestern United States, Mexico, and Central America, the Inca Dove dramatically expanded its range north, east, and south into wetter areas during the twentieth century. The species has a marked affinity for human habitations and settlements, and some authors have suggested a connection between this association and the species' range expansion. It is a recent addition to Oklahoma's breeding avifauna.

Description: A small dove with brownish-gray upperparts and somewhat paler underparts. Dark-tipped feathers above and below give the bird a scaly appearance. Sexes are similar, though the female is somewhat more drab than the male. Primaries and wing linings show a rufous chestnut color in flight. Tail is long, graduated, and square tipped, with outer edges tipped white. Distinctive call is a monotonous, two-syllable *COOO-cooo,* often rendered as *No hope.*

Breeding Habitat: Generally associated with human habitation, including cities, towns, villages, and farm- and ranchyards. Inca Doves forage almost exclusively on the ground for seeds and grain; they seem particularly fond of lawns where they forage for grass seeds and are easily attracted to bird feeders.

Nest: A compact platform made of twigs, roots, stalks, grass, and leaves; over time, and with use, the nest becomes encrusted with excrement that "cements" the nest together. Usually placed in a small tree or shrub in the vicinity of a human dwelling. Construction is completed by the female from materials brought to her by the male.

NESTING ECOLOGY

Season: Nearly year round in parts of range. Two to 5 broods per year. Few data for Oklahoma.
Eggs: 2; unmarked white.
Development: Incubation is by both sexes for 13–15 days. Young receive crop milk from both sexes and fledge in 12–16 days.

DISTRIBUTION AND ABUNDANCE

Rangewide: Resident from central and southern Texas and southwestern Louisiana, southern New Mexico, central and southern Arizona and southern Nevada and southern California, south through Mexico and much of Central America. The expansion of the Inca Dove has been documented remarkably well. The species was first noted in Arizona in 1872 (Tucson) and was well established in Phoenix by 1885. The species was first recorded in Texas in 1866 (Laredo) and in San Antonio in 1890, where it was well established by 1904. First noted in New Mexico in 1924. There are many vagrant records for areas well north and east of the established breeding areas in the United States.

Historical: This species was considered a "straggler" to Oklahoma in 1992. The species was first confirmed breeding in southwestern Kansas in 1993 and in southeastern Colorado in 2000. The species may be cold sensitive, and this is probably a limiting factor in its northward expansion.

Current: First known to nest in Oklahoma in Hugo in Choctaw County in 2000. One additional observation from an atlas block in Oklahoma County is mapped. Additional summer sight records from outside of atlas blocks exist, and this species may become more common in the state.

Population Trend: Breeding Bird Survey data for 1966–2000 show an increase of 4.2 percent per year rangewide (P = 0.03). No trend data are available for Oklahoma.

References: AOU 1998; Baumgartner and Baumgartner 1992; Busby and Zimmerman 2001; Felis 1976; Hardy 1958; Heck 2001; Johnston 1960; Mueller 1992; Oberholser 1974; Sauer et al. 2001; Sibley 2000; Sutton 1967; Tyler 1974

Observed
Nests 1997-2001

Black-billed Cuckoo
Coccyzus erythropthalmus

Melinda Droege

Elusive to Oklahoma's birders, the Black-billed Cuckoo may be more numerous than assumed. Late breeding records for the Yellow-billed Cuckoo suggest that nests for the Black-billed might be looked for after the peak breeding months, as do late nesting records for adjacent states.

Description: A slender, long-tailed bird that is uniformly grayish brown above, including the primaries, and whitish below. The slightly decurved bill has a black upper mandible and gray base to the lower mandible. The adult has a reddish eye ring, while that of the immature is yellowish. The underside of the tail is gray with small white crescents. The similar and much more common Yellow-billed Cuckoo has con-spicuously rufous primaries and a strongly contrasting black-and-white tail. Song of the Black-billed is a distinctive, fast, rhythmic *cucucu, cucucu, cucucu,* which is often repeated three or four times.

Breeding Habitat: Similar to that of the Yellow-billed Cuckoo, but often inhabits denser woodlands. Uses a variety of trees, bushes, thickets, and vines for nesting; has been noted breeding in locust, riparian willow stands, and orchards and forest edges and along streams.

Nest: A loosely built cup of twigs and grasses and usually heavily lined with ferns, grass, stems, and other plant material. Usually placed 1–2 m (3–6 ft) high on a fork or horizontal branch of a deciduous tree or shrub.

NESTING ECOLOGY

Season: May–July. Presumed single-brooded.

Eggs: 2–3, rarely 4–5; greenish blue, occasionally marbled with same. Both Yellow-billed and Black-billed Cuckoos occasionally lay in one another's nests, as well as nests of other birds. Rarely parasitized by Brown-headed Cowbirds.

Development: Incubation is by both sexes for 10–11 days beginning with the first egg. The altricial young hatch at intervals and are of different sizes. Young are provisioned by both sexes. In only 6–7 days after hatching they are able to leave their nests to run along the ground or climb around the nest tree; able to fly at 3 weeks.

DISTRIBUTION AND ABUNDANCE

Rangewide: This species is more northerly in its distribution than the Yellow-billed Cuckoo, with its breeding range stretching from central Alberta east to Nova Scotia and south to north Georgia. It winters in South America, with poorly understood range limits.

Historical: Rare migrant in the wooded areas throughout the state. Nests irregularly in small numbers in the northern half. There are only five actual nesting records, but a number of additional summer observations exist, mostly in northern counties.

Current: The scarcity of observations in atlas blocks attests to the rare, local, and elusive nature of this species. Some of the records scored as Possible may be birds heard singing during migration.

Population Trend: Breeding Bird Survey data for 1966–2000 show a decline of 1.9 percent per year rangewide (P = 0.00), but show no conclusive trend in Oklahoma (-15.7 percent per year, P = 0.57).

References: AOU 1998; Baicich and Harrison 1997; Baumgartner and Baumgartner 1992; Bent 1964a; Busby and Zimmerman 2001; Dillon 1975; Ehrlich et al. 1988; Haller 1972; Harrison 1975; Johnsgard 1979; Sauer et al. 2001; Spencer 1943; Sutton 1967

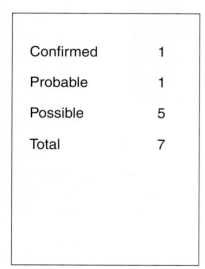

Confirmed	1
Probable	1
Possible	5
Total	7

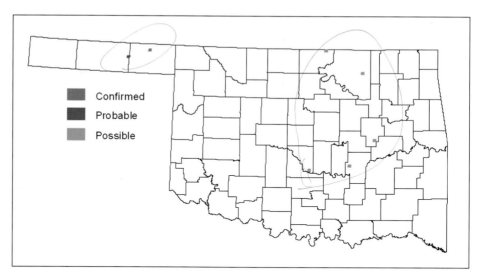

Yellow-billed Cuckoo

Coccyzus americanus

Donald H. Wolfe

Courtesy of Bob Gress

The Yellow-billed Cuckoo is one of three species of cuckoos found in Oklahoma, along with the similar Black-billed Cuckoo and the Greater Roadrunner. Unlike the parasitic cuckoos native to Europe, Asia, and Africa, North American cuckoos are not obligate nest parasites. However, some amount of opportunistic intraspecific and interspecific brood parasitism does occur.

Description: Yellow-billed Cuckoos are medium-sized, long, slender birds with white underparts, except for the primaries, which show extensive rufous from above and below. The upperparts are olive gray. While the two inner retrices are olive gray, the rest are black at the base and white on the distal end. In flight, the black

tail has large white spots at the tips of each feather. The smaller but similar Black-billed Cuckoo has a more buffy underside, and much smaller white crescents in the tail.

Breeding Habitat: Yellow-billed Cuckoos inhabit open woodlands in the east, but also riparian strips, isolated thickets, shrubby roadsides, and even single trees throughout the state. Since the mainstay of the Yellow-billed Cuckoo diet is caterpillars, they are commonly found in areas with heavy infestations of tent caterpillars.

Nest: A saucer-shaped shallow cup, usually made of twigs. Often similar to but slightly larger than Mourning Dove nests. Nests may be placed in a crotch, on a vertical limb, or within vines covering a tree, often about 2 m (6 ft) high. They are usually well concealed by leaves or debris.

NESTING ECOLOGY

Season: May–September, although the peak of nesting may be in July.

Eggs: Usually 3–4; blue, with a dull, almost powdery-looking surface. Nests are occasionally parasitized by other cuckoos and rarely by cowbirds.

Development: Incubation is by both sexes for about 10 days. Young are provisioned by both sexes. They have shiny black skin with pinfeathers at hatching. For about a week, the only difference in the appearance of the young is their size. At about a week of age, the feather sheaths break over the entire body, and the young birds leave the nest within a day, walking or hopping on nearby branches.

DISTRIBUTION AND ABUNDANCE

Rangewide: Breeding range extends from the Atlantic Coast to the Rocky Mountains, north to southern Canada, and south through Central America. Scattered populations exist west of the Rockies. Winter range extends from Colombia and Brazil south through Argentina.

Historical: Considered a common summer resident throughout the state, though less common in the Panhandle.

Current: Atlas project results mirror the historical reports, with this species being found in most blocks statewide, but less frequently in the Panhandle. Besides being common, it is quite vocal, and its presence is easy to record.

Population Trend: Breeding Bird Survey data for 1966–2000 show a decline of 1.8 percent per year rangewide (P = 0.00) and a decline of 1.1 percent per year in Oklahoma (P = 0.01). The species has a much more serious decline west of the Rockies.

References: Baicich and Harrison 1997; Baumgartner and Baumgartner 1992; Bent 1940; Clotfelter and Brush 1995; Davies 2000; Dillon 1975; Friedmann and Kiff 1985; Friedmann et al. 1977; Haller 1972; Hendricks 1975; Hughes 1999; Jennings 1983; Johnsgard 1979; Nice 1931; Sutton 1967, 1977a, 1986b; U.S. Fish and Wildlife Service 2001; Wiens 1965; Wolfe 1994b

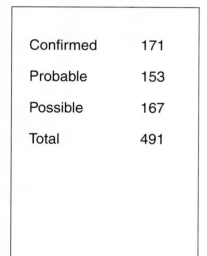

Confirmed	171
Probable	153
Possible	167
Total	491

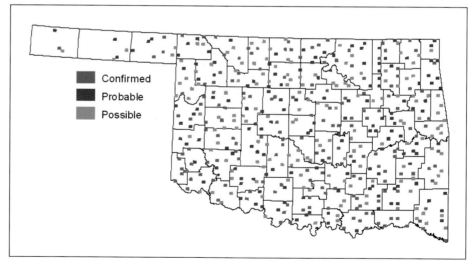

Greater Roadrunner

Geococcyx californianus

John M. Dole

Courtesy of M. Frank Carl

The roadrunner is well known outside of its range in the southwestern United States through fictionalized cartoons and writings. The real bird is even more interesting, with its rapid sprints, expressive crest, moaning voice, and diet of snakes, lizards, and scorpions. Living up to their name, roadrunners can run for long periods at speeds up to 30 km/hr (18 mph).

Description: The Greater Roadrunner is a large brown bird mottled with buff and white above. The bushy crest can be raised and lowered. The large bill and long white-tipped tail are distinctive. Sexes are similar. Song is a slow series of *cooo cooo cooos*. The Greater Roadrunner is largely terrestrial and might be confused with Ring-necked Pheasants and prairie-chickens if the view is brief or poor.

Breeding Habitat: Arid to semiarid, open to brushy habitat.

Nest: A compact cup of twigs or plant stems, lined with leaves, grass, roots, feathers, snakeskins, and seed pods. The nest is placed 1–4.6 m (3–15 ft) high in a low tree, shrubby thicket, or cactus clump. Female constructs nest, with male bringing material to the site.

NESTING ECOLOGY

Season: April–August. Single- or double-brooded.
Eggs: Usually 3–6; white to creamy white.
Development: Incubation is by both sexes for 19–20 days. Young are provisioned by both sexes and leave the nest at 14–25 days.

DISTRIBUTION AND ABUNDANCE

Rangewide: The Greater Roadrunner is primarily a southwestern species with the northern limit of its range in California, southern Nevada, southern Utah, southeastern Colorado, southern Kansas, and southwest Missouri. Arkansas and western Louisiana form the easternmost boundary. It is nonmigratory and occurs as far south as central Mexico.

Historical: Described as a resident throughout Oklahoma, but more common in the west. Sutton noted that the range appeared to be expanding northward, especially during the 1930s and later. May be negatively effected by severe winters.

Current: The southwestern nature of this species is evident in Oklahoma, with few records in the northern tier of counties and in the northeast. Though the large roadrunner is easy to distinguish, its relatively low population density probably accounts for the moderate number of records.

Population Trend: Breeding Bird Survey data for 1966–2000 show no conclusive trend rangewide (0.6 percent per year, P = 0.54) or in Oklahoma (-0.6 percent per year, P = 0.83).

References: Allen 1950; AOU 1998; Baicich and Harrsion 1997; Baumgartner and Baumgartner 1992; Beal 1978a, 1978b, 1981; Calder 1967; Colvin 1935b; de Hoyo et al. 1997; Geluso 1969, 1970a, 1970b; Howell and Webb 1995; Hughes 1996; Kaufman 1996; National Geographic Society 1999; Neeld 1972; Sauer et al. 2001; Sutton 1915, 1922, 1940, 1967, 1972

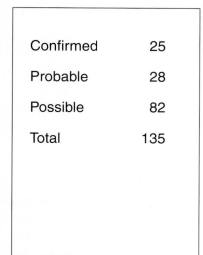

Confirmed	25
Probable	28
Possible	82
Total	135

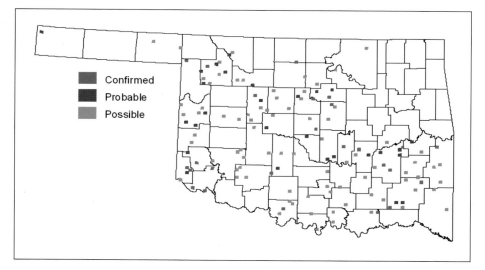

Barn Owl
Tyto alba

Paul W. Wilson

Courtesy of Warren Williams

One of the most widespread land birds in the world, the Barn Owl locates and captures its prey primarily by sound, more so than other Oklahoma owls that rely more on sight. It is a resident of Oklahoma, with a breeding territory of approximately one square mile.

Description: Colloquially identified as the "Monkey-faced Owl" or the "Heart-shaped-Faced Owl" due to the conspicuous facial discs. Upperparts are tawny to gray. Females are larger than males and tend to have a buff-colored rather than white breast as in the males. Vocalizations include hisses, screams, snores, and twittering chirps.

Breeding Habitat: This species utilizes many habitats, but stable grassland that is moderately grazed is preferred. Dense woodlands and wetlands appear to be the least preferred habitats. Crucial nesting factors for this species are open space and sufficient population prey density of small mammal species. When prey populations become low, Barn Owls may forage over several miles. Normally in Oklahoma, there is no more than one pair of Barn Owls per square mile. However, there are many observations of multiple nesting pairs at one site, with as many as four pairs nesting simultaneously in the same house. Barn Owl territories will coexist with those of other owl species.

Nest: Most commonly nest in barns and attics of abandoned houses. Other observed nest sites in Oklahoma include holes in banks, water towers, tree cavities, abandoned trucks, open spaces in buildings or structures, nesting platforms, and Barn Owl nesting houses. Nest construction is usually lacking, although they may dig into banks when using such sites. Nest success for over 500 nests monitored in Oklahoma from 1969 to 2002 ranged from 20–60 percent. Occupancy rates for nest houses and nest platforms placed for Barn Owls in Oklahoma ranged from 50–80 percent.

NESTING ECOLOGY

Season: Highest frequency of nesting is mid-March, however there are nesting records throughout the year in Oklahoma. Normally single-brooded, occasionally double-brooded, rarely triple-brooded.

Eggs: Usually 4–8; white, approximately the size and shape of a ping-pong ball.

Development: Incubation is by the female for about 30 days. The female broods and feeds the young, while the male brings food to the nest. Young first leave the nest about 45 to 60 days after hatching, but may return to roost for several more weeks.

DISTRIBUTION AND ABUNDANCE

Rangewide: All of South America, much of Europe, Madagascar, Africa, India, and Australia. Resident of the continental United States and southern British Columbia southward, except for a band from Montana to Maine. Largely sedentary.

Historical: Reported as an uncommon to rare resident throughout the state, with a noticeable decline in the 1970s.

Current: Atlas data indicate that Barn Owl distribution is common in the southwest, common to uncommon in the northwest (including the Panhandle), and rare in the northeast and the southeast, primarily due to habitat availability. Actual numbers may be higher in the northeast as well as most other parts of the state than is indicated by the data, due to the nocturnal habits of this species making it rarely encountered during typical daytime surveys.

Population Trend: Population trends are not adequately measured rangewide or in Oklahoma. Due to changes in hay storage techniques and the development of large round bales, barns with a loft are obsolete, thereby reducing the number of possible nesting sites for Barn Owls. Observations suggest that the only portion of Oklahoma where the Barn Owl population appears common and stable is in the southwest. Barn Owls will move to more favorable habitats in other areas and may temporarily abandon a territory when rodent populations crash.

References: Ault 1982; Baumgartner and Baumgartner 1944, 1992; Baumgartner and Howell 1942; Greer and Gilstrap 1970; Marti 1992; Marti et al. 1979; Nice 1931; Norman 1971; Otteni et al. 1972; PWW unpubl. data; Sheffield 1996; Stewart 1980; Sutton 1967

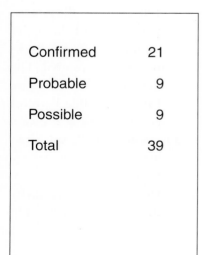

Confirmed	21
Probable	9
Possible	9
Total	39

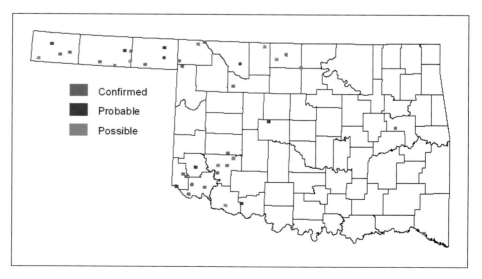

Western Screech-Owl
Otus kennicottii

Sebastian T. Patti

Courtesy of Steve Metz

The Western Screech-Owl is the common, small, low-elevation woodland owl of the western United States. It is most common in deciduous riparian habitats, but it also occurs in deserts. Its prey includes a wide variety of small animals, including birds, reptiles, and insects, but consists primarily of rodents. This species was first recognized as a separate species in 1982. Prior to that time, the Western had been treated by most authorities as conspecific with the Eastern Screech-Owl.

Description: A small grayish owl with yellow eyes and feathered ear tufts. The plumage of the Western Screech-Owl is similar to that of the Eastern, although the barring and streaking of Westerns may be more broad and distinct. Most significantly, at close range and with good light, the bill color is diagnostic. Westerns have a black bill with the tip of the upper mandible a light color; in Oklahoma, Eastern Screech-Owls have a bill that is uniformly horn colored. The species is more easily separated by voice. Westerns give the well-known "bouncing ball" call, while Easterns give the descending "whinny." Westerns also give a double trill compared to a monotone single trill given by Easterns.

Breeding Habitat: Western Screech-Owls are cavity nesters and are generally limited to riparian habitat in the northwestern part of Cimarron County.

Nest: Within a cavity excavated by woodpeckers, or in natural cavities. Cottonwoods appear to be favored whenever they are present, perhaps because of this tree species' propensity to form large natural cavities.

NESTING ECOLOGY

Season: March–June. Single-brooded, but lost clutches may be replaced.
Eggs: Usually 3–5; white.
Development: Incubation is by the female for about 30 days. Young are provisioned by the male for 3 weeks, after which time the female also helps. Fledging begins after several weeks, but young closely associate with adults for 5 weeks after fledging.

DISTRIBUTION AND ABUNDANCE

Rangewide: Resident in western North America from southern coastal Alaska and British Columbia to western Washington; from western Montana and all of Idaho south, including most of Oregon, Nevada, California, Utah, Arizona, and western Colorado and New Mexico. The species ranges south to central Mexico.
Historical: Resident in northwestern Cimarron County. Of some interest to birders and taxonomists is the proximity of the ranges of Western and Eastern Screech-Owls in the Oklahoma Panhandle. There are apparently no specimens of Easterns from Cimarron County, although the species has been recorded on the North Canadian (Beaver) River in Texas County, and Westerns have been recorded as far east as extreme southwestern Kansas on the Cimarron River. The only strong indication of nesting in Oklahoma is a female with a fully formed egg collected north of Boise City in 1966.
Current: Generally known only from the northwesternmost portion of Cimarron County, the single report of this species from an atlas block was from north of Boise City on the Cimarron River. There, as many as 8 individuals were heard calling in July of 1997. Because of the inherent sampling bias against recording nocturnal species such as owls, and because of the limited range of the species in the state, it is likely that this species was underreported during the atlas project.

Population Trend: Breeding Bird Survey data show no conclusive trend rangewide (0.0 percent per year, P = 1.00), although this nocturnal species is poorly measured by this survey. No trend data are available for Oklahoma.

References: AOU 1982, 1998; Baumgartner and Baumgartner 1992; Cannings and Angell 2001; Grzybowski 1983; Sauer et al. 2001; Sutton 1967; Thompson and Ely 1989

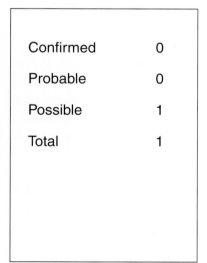

Confirmed	0
Probable	0
Possible	1
Total	1

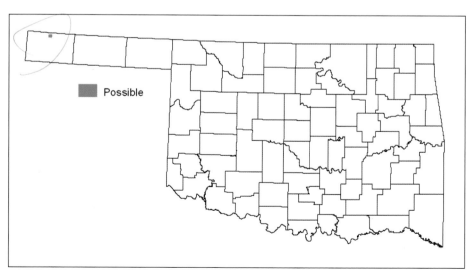

Possible

Eastern Screech-Owl
Otus asio

Eugene A. Young

The smallest tufted owl in North America can occur as either a gray phase or red phase, unique among Oklahoma owls. Phase color doesn't appear to be related to age, sex, or season, and different phases can exist in the same brood. It is probably the most nocturnal owl in Oklahoma.

Description: Sexes similar. Plumage is mottled in grays, browns, and reds; ear tufts can be erected or held flat against the head. Eyes are bright yellow with black pupils. The bill is pale greenish-yellow, helping to separate this species from the similar Western Screech-Owl, which has a black bill. Vocalizations include a horse-like whinny and a long whistled trill.

Breeding Habitat: Riparian and upland woodlands, parks, suburban yards, shelterbelts, woodlots, forest, swamps, and orchards, or any other area where trees dominate the landscape, either naturally or artificially. Commonly uses cottonwood, elm, box elder, and oak trees.

Nest: Within natural cavities of trees, stumps, or limbs; sometimes in old woodpecker cavities (usually flickers). Readily uses nest boxes as well. No material is added to the nest. Typical nest heights are 3.8–5.5 m (12.5–18 ft).

NESTING ECOLOGY

Season: March–June. Single-brooded.

Eggs: Usually 4–5; round, glossy, and white.

Development: Incubation is by the female (who is fed by the male) for about 30 days. Young are provisioned by both sexes and fledge in about 4 weeks but depend on parents for about 2 months.

DISTRIBUTION AND ABUNDANCE

Rangewide: A permanent resident east of the Rocky Mountains to the Atlantic Coast from southern Saskatchewan south through Montana, western Kansas, west Texas, and eastern Mexico.

Historical: Described as an uncommon to rare permanent resident throughout the state.

Current: The Eastern Screech-Owl has a virtually statewide distribution, though its nocturnal habits make it difficult to survey. As a result, there are few blocks where the species is recorded, especially as a confirmed breeder.

Population Trend: Breeding Bird Survey data for 1966–2000 show no conclusive trend rangewide (3.7 percent per year, P = 0.53) or in Oklahoma (64.2 percent per year, P = 0.31). The nocturnal habits of this species make it poorly measured by this survey.

References: AOU 1998; Baicich and Harrison 1997; Baumgartner and Baumgartner 1992; Carter 1967; Comer and Cooksey 1973; Gehlbach 1994, 1995; Sauer et al. 2001; Stewart 1989; Stewart and Tyler 1989; Stokes and Stokes 1989; Sutton 1967, 1986b; Terres 991; Thompson and Ely 1989; Tveten 1993

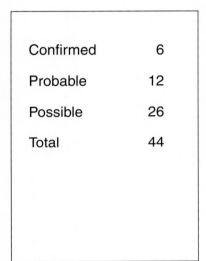

Confirmed	6
Probable	12
Possible	26
Total	44

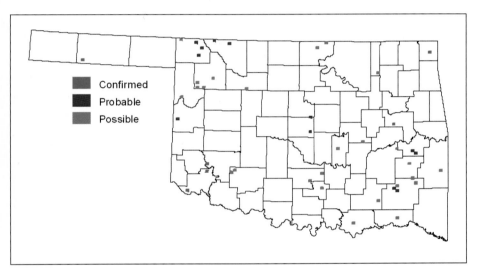

Great Horned Owl
Bubo virginianus

Kenneth D. Andrews

Courtesy of Warren Williams

The most widespread North American owl, the Great Horned Owl is a generalized, opportunistic predator of most small vertebrates. This large, silent night hunter can take animals as small as worms and as large as skunks and Great Blue Herons. About 90 percent of the diet is comprised of mammals.

Description: A large owl mottled with brown, gray, and white above. Gray to white below with bars of brown. Yellow eyes within a rusty facial disc. A white throat is not always visible, but prominent, widely spaced ear tufts are usually evident. Song is a series of deep hoots.

Breeding Habitat: Found in a wide variety of habitats including mixed and deciduous woodlands, ravines, swamps, and riparian areas.

Nest: Commonly uses abandoned nests of other birds including herons, hawks, and crows. Eggs are occasionally laid on bare rock on cliffs, in a cave, or on the ground.

NESTING ECOLOGY

Season: January–May, sometimes December. Single-brooded. Usually the earliest nesting bird in Oklahoma.

Eggs: Usually 2, but 1–5; white and spherical without markings.

Development: Incubation is by the female for 30–37 days. Young are fed by the female with food brought by the male and begin leaving the nest at 6 weeks, but continue to be fed by adults for weeks or months.

DISTRIBUTION AND ABUNDANCE

Rangewide: Found from the western reaches of Alaska all the way to the southern tip of South America. Mostly nonmigratory.

Historical: Described as an uncommon permanent resident in central and western Oklahoma; rare in eastern portions of the state.

Current: The Great Horned Owl is an uncommon permanent resident of Oklahoma. Its nocturnal habits make it a somewhat poorly sampled species in atlas projects, because few observers go out at night when the owl is most active. It is confirmed fairly often, perhaps because it is visible while incubating on its large nests early in the year before the trees leaf out.

Population Trend: Breeding Bird Survey data for 1966–2000 show no conclusive trend rangewide (-0.1 percent per year, P = 0.86) or in Oklahoma (0.6 percent per year, P = 0.81), although this nocturnal species is not well measured by this survey.

References: AOU 1998; Adamcik and Keith 1978; Baumgartner 1938, 1939; Baumgartner and Baumgartner 1992; Byre 1995; Ehrlich et al. 1988; Hume 1991; Marti 1974; National Geographic Society 1983; Rappole and Blacklock 1994; Sauer et al 2001; Seibert 1995; Udvardy and Farrand 1997; Voelker 1979

Confirmed	69
Probable	15
Possible	91
Total	175

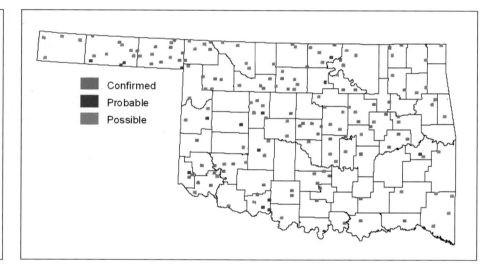

Burrowing Owl
Athene cunicularia

Thomas G. Shane

Courtesy of Bill Horn

This prairie owl was observed regularly by the naturalists of the Major Stephen Long expedition in 1820 as they traveled the Arkansas and Canadian rivers. The Native American name for the owl, "Coquimbo," was published in their final reports. This species is often associated with prairie dog towns because these colonies provide numerous holes for a family of owl fledglings to escape predators, thereby potentially increasing reproductive success compared to owls using the single nest hole of most other burrowing mammals. Vehicle collisions, severe weather, mammalian and avian predators, insecticide use, and prairie dog control are all threats to this species, which is declining in Oklahoma.

Description: Small brown owl with buffy-white spots on crown, back, and scapulars, long legs, large lemon-colored eyes, head round lacking ear tufts, and often stands on the ground, frequently bobbing and bowing. The primary song, *coo coooo,* used in courting and establishing territory, is occasionally heard in the field. The most commonly encountered vocalization is the *quick-quick-quick-quick* alarm call.

Breeding Habitat: Dry, open, shortgrass plains most often associated with a variety of burrowing mammals, including badgers, ground squirrels, and frequently prairie dogs.

Nest: Burrows vary according to the animal that made it. All include one or more turns and a mound of soil at the entrance. A typical burrow slopes down several feet to a small nest chamber that the owl may line with cow dung, feathers, grasses, and bones. Birds may rarely excavate their own burrows.

NESTING ECOLOGY

Season: Primarily May–June; single-brooded.
Eggs: Often 7–8; smooth glossy white.
Development: Incubation is by the female for 28–30 days. Young are provisioned both sexes and fledge in about 44 days.

DISTRIBUTION AND ABUNDANCE

Rangewide: Breeds in western North America from southern Canada locally south through Central and South America to Tierra del Fuego, as well as in Florida and several Caribbean islands. Largely migratory except in Florida and southern California. Winters from southern California east to north Texas and then south.
Historical: Described as formerly abundant in western Oklahoma, with some records east to central and eastern Oklahoma, now uncommon to rare, and now found primarily in the Panhandle. Numbers were greatly reduced in the state after a major prairie dog poisoning campaign in 1922. Statewide population estimated at less than 1,000 birds in the mid-1960s. Only about 1 percent of the number breeding in Oklahoma are found here in the winter.
Current: The majority of Burrowing Owls were found in the Panhandle, where fairly extensive tracts of short-grass prairie with prairie dog towns still exist. The high number of confirmed records was made possible because fledglings are easily observed huddled around a nest hole.

Population Trend: Breeding Bird Survey data for 1966–2000 show no conclusive trend rangewide (-1.6 percent per year, $P = 0.54$) and a substantial decline of 11.8 percent per year in Oklahoma ($P = 0.00$). The species appears to be declining rapidly in the Great Plains and Canada but increasing in southwestern portions of its U.S. range.

References: AOU 1998; Baicich and Harrison 1997; Baumgartner and Baumgartner 1992; Butts 1973, 1976; Butts and Lewis 1982; Dechant et al. 1999; Desmond and Savidge 1999; Haug et al. 1993; Henderson 1933; James 1823; Lincer and Steenhof 1997; Nice 1931; Sauer et al. 2001; Sheffield and Howery 2001; Sutton 1967; Tyler 1968a, 1983

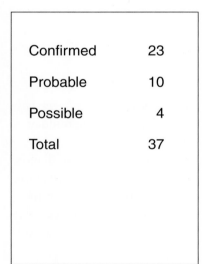

Confirmed	23
Probable	10
Possible	4
Total	37

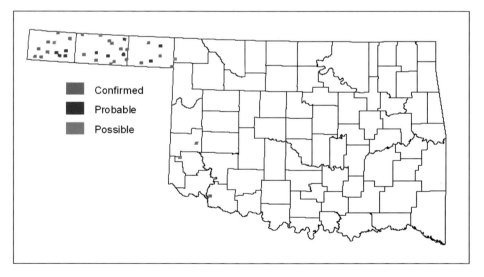

Barred Owl
Strix varia

Victoria J. Byre

Courtesy of Warren Williams

This large woodland owl is relatively tame and much less aggressive than the Great Horned Owl. It is more active during daylight hours than most owls and often can be seen as it scans the forest floor for prey from a low branch or stump.

Description: Both sexes are large and chunky with dark brown and pale buff barring on the head, neck, chest, and most upperparts, and dark brown and pale buff streaking on the belly. The eyes are dark brown, and there are no ear tufts as evident on the similar but slightly larger Great Horned Owl. The Barred Owl is one of the most vocal owls, often repeating its *who cooks for you, who cooks for you all* call even during midday.

Breeding Habitat: Barred Owls inhabit woodlands, wooded creek and river bottoms, and wooded swamps. They favor dense thick woods, especially in low-lying areas, and with only scattered clearings. They can also be found in wooded suburban areas if there are woodlots and creeks or ponds nearby.

Nest: Barred Owls nest in large natural cavities in tree trunks, in broken-off snags, in old hawk or squirrel nests, and even in appropriately sized nest boxes. They add no lining to the nest, which is usually located 4.5–9 m (15–30 ft) up.

NESTING ECOLOGY

Season: February–June. Single-brooded, but will replace lost clutches.
Eggs: Usually 2–3; white and smooth and slightly glossy.
Development: Incubation is by the female for 28–33 days. Young are provisioned by both sexes, although male does most of the hunting initially while the female broods the young. Young are capable of flight at about 6 weeks but parental care may extend beyond 4 months.

DISTRIBUTION AND ABUNDANCE

Rangewide: Resident species from central and eastern Canada south through the central and eastern United States to the Gulf of Mexico and as far west as the riparian woodlands of the eastern Great Plains. It is also found in southeast Alaska and through British Columbia and the northwestern United States. The northernmost populations are probably semimigratory depending upon prey availability.

Historical: Described as uncommon (with low-density populations) in the eastern and central regions of Oklahoma, becoming rare to local in the western third of the state. Absent from southwesternmost counties and the Panhandle.
Current: Except for the Panhandle and the southwesternmost counties, Barred Owls are found at scattered locations in suitable habitat throughout the state, but with a more dense concentration in the eastern half. The high number of blocks scored as Possible is likely a result of this species' habit of vocalizing during daylight hours. In contrast, the low number of records scored as Confirmed is probably due to the owl's well-concealed nest sites and its nocturnal activity.

Population Trend: Breeding Bird Survey data for 1966–2000 show an increase of 2.8 percent per year rangewide ($P = 0.00$) but no conclusive trend in Oklahoma (0.1 percent per year, $P = 0.97$).

References: AOU 1998; Baicich and Harrison 1997; Baumgartner and Baumgartner 1992; Bent 1961; Johnsgard 1988; Mazur and James 2000; Sauer et al. 2001; Stokes and Stokes 1996; Sutton 1967

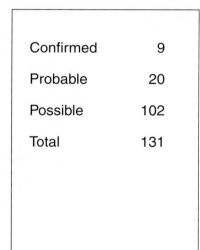

Confirmed	9
Probable	20
Possible	102
Total	131

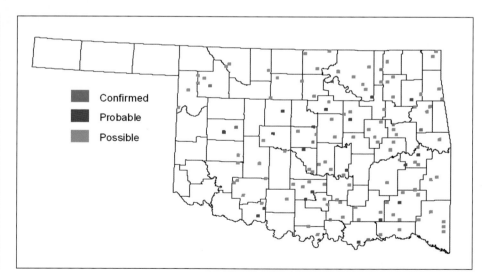

Long-eared Owl
Asio otus

Bonnie L. Gall

Courtesy of Steve Metz

This secretive nocturnal owl is most common in Oklahoma in winter when groups of owls have been found roosting in junipers and other dense woods around the state. The few nesting records in Oklahoma should encourage efforts to locate Long-eared Owls during spring and summer.

Description: A slender owl with long close-set ear tufts, rusty facial disks, and bold streaks and bars on breast and belly. Call is one or more long *hooo*s. Usually roosts on a limb close to a tree trunk.

Breeding Habitat: Dense or open evergreen or decid-uous forests (conifers preferred), wooded parks, orchards, and farm lots.

Nest: Usually uses nests of other species such as crow, hawk, magpie, or squirrel; occasionally uses tree cavities or the ground. Nests are unlined or lined sparingly with grass, green twigs, leaves, or feathers. May evict owner of an occupied nest, such as crows.

NESTING ECOLOGY

Season: March–May.
Eggs: Usually 4–5, but variable; pure white.

Development: Incubation is by the female for 26–28 days and starts after the first egg is laid, resulting in young of differing ages. Young are provisioned by both sexes and start to leave the nest at about 21 days, beginning short flights at about 35 days.

DISTRIBUTION AND ABUNDANCE

Rangewide: Breeds from central Canada south across the upper-midwest and southwestern United States. Winters erratically south and east of this range. In the winter, it may roost in flocks, especially in dense woods.

Historical: Although considered mainly a rare winter visitor to Oklahoma, nesting records or suggestion of nesting activity exist for Rogers County in 1990, Tulsa County in 1928, Creek County in 1931, Payne County in 1939, Caddo County in 1962, Comanche County in 1944, Woods County in 1922, Harmon County in 1955, Beaver County in 1923, and Cimarron County in 1913, 1937, 1955, and 1959.

Current: The Long-eared Owl is (or was) a rare and erratic breeder in Oklahoma. No records were reported during the atlas project, either inside or outside of survey blocks.

Population Trend: Declining in parts of range, but trend is difficult to measure. No trend data are available for Oklahoma.

References: Baumgartner and Baumgartner 1992; Baumgartner and Howell 1942; Bent 1961; Droege 1996; Harrison 1975; Johnsgard 1979; Marks et al. 1994; National Geographic Society 1999; Nice 1931; Sutton 1967

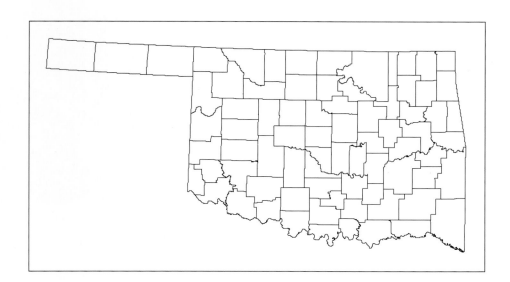

Short-eared Owl
Asio flammeus

Gregory A. Smith

Courtesy of Steve Metz

The Short-eared Owl is widely distributed worldwide. It nests on the ground in open plains and marshes, where males may be observed performing elaborate courtship flights complete with chatter calls, hoots, and wing clapping. It is also one of the most diurnal of owls on the Great Plains, often seen flying low or hovering during daylight hours in search of rodents, large grasshoppers, and the occasional small bird. Short-eared Owls often form large winter and migratory flocks sometimes numbering 200 individuals or more. Population cycles of these owls are linked closely to cycles of their mammalian prey.

Description: Medium-sized owl, about the size of a large crow. Females are slightly larger than males. In adult plumage, females are also darker than males, most noticeably on the belly and face. Adults are mottled brown and buff on the back, blending in with the dried grasses they inhabit. Their bellies are whitish to rust colored, with dense vertical streaking on the breast. They have large round heads with small ear tufts that are generally not seen. Facial disks are gray and white with black eye patches surrounding yellow eyes. They have long narrow wings with a buffy patch beyond the wrist above and a dark patch at the base of the primaries below.

Breeding Habitat: Open country, on plains, prairies, and marshes. May nest in loose colonies.

Nest: A shallow depression, or bowl, scraped out by the female and lined with grasses, weed stalks, and downy feathers. Nests are placed on the ground in areas sheltered by tall grass, reeds, or bushes.

NESTING ECOLOGY

Season: April–June. Usually single-brooded.
Eggs: Usually 4–8; cream colored or white, becoming darker over time as they are stained by nest materials.
Development: Incubation is by the female for 24–28 days. Young are fed by the female with food brought by the male, and leave the nest at 12–18 days but do not fly for another 10 days. Even after fledging, the young may depend on their parents for another 2 months.

DISTRIBUTION AND ABUNDANCE

Rangewide: Short-eared Owls are a nearly a cosmopolitan species, breeding throughout much of North America and Eurasia, in grasslands of South America, Iceland, the Hawaiian Islands, and the Galapagos Islands. In North America, breeding populations extend from northern Canada and Alaska south to middle latitudes of the United States as well as some islands in the Caribbean. Migrating individuals move south into the central to southern United States and northern Mexico.
Historical: Very rare breeder in Oklahoma. Only nest records include one from Woods County prior to 1931, two nests in Tulsa County in 1990, and one in Osage County in 1993. Transient and winter visitor throughout most of the state. During winter, can be found in large groups where rodents are abundant.
Current: Short-eared Owls are rare breeders in Oklahoma. Breeding was confirmed in only one block, located in Texas County. This species' preference for tall vegetation makes it difficult to detect. It was confirmed in few blocks in Kansas and was not confirmed in Texas, further indication that the species is truly a rare breeder in this region.

Population Trend: Breeding Bird Survey data for 1966–2000 show a decline of 4.4 percent per year rangewide for North America (P = 0.06). No trend data are available for Oklahoma, where it is rare in summer.

References: AOU 1998; Baicich and Harrison 1997; Baumgartner and Baumgartner 1992; Baumgartner and Howell 1942, 1947; Benson and Arnold 2001; Bent 1961; Blaha et al. 1995; Busby and Zimmerman 2001; Delap 1977; Eckert and Karalus 1987; Force 1929; Holt and Leasure 1993; Johnsgard 1979; Kaufman 1996; McMahon 1989; Nice 1927, 1931; Peterjohn and Sauer 1999; Ports 1974; Sauer et al. 2001; Sutton 1967; Thompson and Ely 1989; Wilson 1995; Wood and Schnell 1984

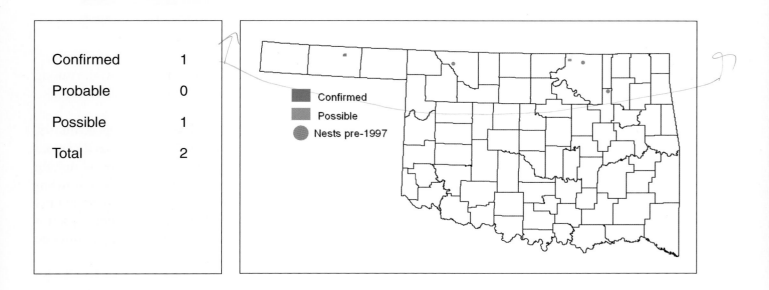

Confirmed	1
Probable	0
Possible	1
Total	2

Confirmed
Possible
Nests pre-1997

Common Nighthawk
Chordeiles minor

Dan L. Reinking

Courtesy of Warren Williams

Sometimes known as bullbats because of their erratic bat-like flight, Common Nighthawks can be heard giving their distinctive nasal calls as they forage at dusk over cities and prairies of Oklahoma. They are often attracted to the insects congregating around street lights just before dark.

Description: Common Nighthawks are grayish brown overall, with barred underparts, a notched tail, and long pointed wings with a white bar extending across the primaries, which is clearly visible in flight. Males have a white throat, while females have a buffy throat. Call is a nasal "peent," and displaying males also make

a distinctive vibrating sound produced by air rushing through the wings during a steep, rapid dive.

Breeding Habitat: Originally a bird of open country, the Common Nighthawk has in some areas adapted well to urbanization and is commonly found nesting on flat gravel roofs and asphalt parking lots in towns and cities. Other preferred areas include open prairie, burned-over woodlands, fields, and rock outcrops. It is uncommon during the breeding season in forested parts of the state.

Nest: No nest is built by Common Nighthawks; rather,

they simply lay their eggs on a flat rock, rooftop, parking lot, or bare ground.

NESTING ECOLOGY

Season: May–June. Single-brooded (rarely double).
Eggs: Almost always 2; variable in appearance but usually creamy white and heavily speckled with a variety of colors.
Development: Incubation is by the female for 19 days. Young are brooded by the female and fed by the male through regurgitation before sunrise and after sunset. Nestlings may make small ground movements prior to fledging, but begin flights at 18–23 days and become independent by 30 days.

DISTRIBUTION AND ABUNDANCE

Rangewide: The Common Nighthawk is a long-distance migrant that winters in South America, although its distribution there is poorly understood. It breeds in parts of Central America, Mexico, nearly all of the United States except portions of the southwest, and in Canada from the northen edge of the southern provinces south.

Historical: Described as common in open areas throughout the state and uncommon in forested areas. Common Nighthawks arrive late and depart early compared to most migrants, and some may still be migrating when others have begun nesting in the spring.
Current: The Common Nighthawk's preference for open areas is demonstrated by its common occurrence in northern and western parts of the state and its scarcity in forested regions of the state. The high proportion of blocks scored as Probable are likely a result of this species' aerial courtship behavior, which is both audible and highly visible to human observers.

Population Trend: Breeding Bird Survey data for 1966–2000 show a decline of 1.6 percent per year rangewide (P = 000) and no conclusive trend in Oklahoma (0.6 percent per year, P = 0.39).

References: AOU 1998; Ault 1978; Baicich and Harrison 1997; Baumgartner and Baumgartner 1992; Brigham 1989; Poulin et al. 1996; Sauer et al. 2001; Sutton 1967; Tyler and McKee 1991; Weller 1958; Whittier et al. 1999

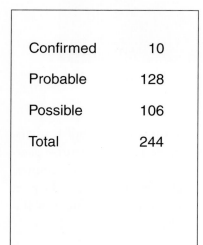

Confirmed	10
Probable	128
Possible	106
Total	244

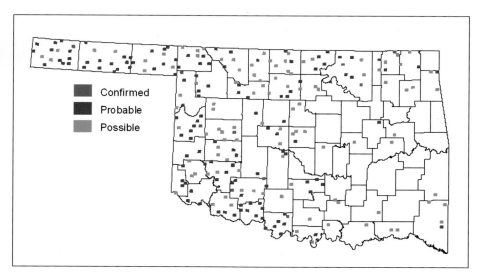

Common Poorwill
Phalaenoptilus nutallii

David A. Wiggins

Common Poorwills are the smallest of the Oklahoma caprimulgids, inhabiting dry open spaces throughout the western half of the state. Rarely seen, they are more often located during twilight hours in late spring, when males give their distinctive *poor-will* call. This species was the first bird known to enter long periods of torpor in winter. Recent studies have shown that Poorwills will use torpor during the breeding season as well, typically during cold and wet weather conditions.

Description: Sexes similar. Speckled gray, black, and brown plumage is cryptic against many backgrounds. Large head, short, compact body with relatively wide, rounded wings and white-tipped outer tail feathers. Males (and occasionally females) sing a repetitive *poor-will* repeated every few seconds for several minutes. May give a loud hissing call when disturbed at the nest. If not well seen, may be confused with Chuck-will's-widow or Common Nighthawk.

Breeding Habitat: Dry, open, rocky areas such as canyons, badlands, and lightly forested hillsides.

Nest: On bare ground, with little structure other than a very shallow scrape. Nest site often partially concealed under a bush or small rock outcrop.

NESTING ECOLOGY

Season: May–July. Double-brooded.
Eggs: 2; white, occasionally with dark spots at larger end.
Development: Incubation is by both sexes for 20–21 days. Young are provisioned by both sexes and fledge at 20–23 days.

DISTRIBUTION AND ABUNDANCE

Rangewide: Summer resident from southern British Columbia, extreme southeast Alberta and southwest Saskatchewan, south through the western Great Plains (where local), the Great Basin, California and the southwestern United States, into central and western Mexico. Year-round resident in southern portions of breeding range.
Historical: Reported as an uncommon to rare summer resident in broken, rocky country locally in western Oklahoma, most common in the Black Mesa region of Cimarron County. Nest records exist for Caddo County in 1954 and Cimarron County in 1972. A third nest record from Osage County in 1993 is by far the easternmost for Oklahoma.

Current: Common Poor-wills were found in traditional nesting areas in western Oklahoma, including the Black Mesa area and the Wichita Mountains. Possible breeders were also found in the gypsum ravine country of Jackson and Harmon counties, as well as the bluffs along the Cimarron River in Beaver, Harper, and Woods counties. However, the Common Poorwill's unobtrusive habits and fondness for rough, broken hillsides make it difficult to estimate its range with atlas methods. Thus, it may have a wider distribution in western Oklahoma than shown here.

Population Trend: Breeding Bird Survey data for 1966–2000 show no conclusive trend rangewide (3.8 percent per year, P = 0.16) or in Oklahoma (0.9 percent per year, P = 0.92).

References: AOU 1998; Baumgartner and Baumgartner 1992; Carter 1968b; Csada and Brigham 1992; Glass et al. 1994; Goard 1973; Ligon 1970; Lindsay 1985; McGee 1990; Orr 1948; Sauer et al. 2001; Sutton 1967; Weske 1973

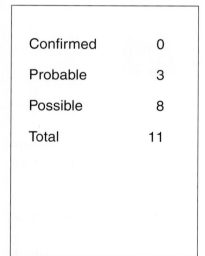

Confirmed	0
Probable	3
Possible	8
Total	11

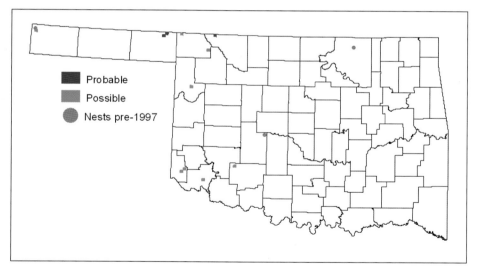

Probable
Possible
Nests pre-1997

Chuck-will's-widow
Caprimulgus carolinensis

Melinda Droege

Spring has truly arrived in Oklahoma when the Chuck-will's-widow sings. Farmers and gardeners around the state use this large nightjar as the signal to plant, forecasting no more frost. Bird students are amazed at its consistency in site fidelity and in its arrival dates. In 25 years of record keeping at the same spot in Washington County, the Chuck-will's-widow has arrived April 20–24; it has stopped singing July 16–20. The diet of this large nightjar is surprising. In addition to the expected crepuscular flying insects, including moths and beetles, it also forages on the ground for tree frogs during its late summer tail molt. This species also ingests stones and sand from the roads at night, presumably to help grind up parts of the insects. Most surprising of all is the chuck's consumption of small birds, mainly warblers, and mainly during migration.

Description: This nightjar is best identified by its loud voice, repeating its name *Chuck-will's-wid-ow* in a long series. Its cryptically patterned plumage is reddish brown mottled with black spots and streaks. The buffy brown throat contrasts with its dark breast, and both wings and tail are rounded. The similar Whip-poor-will is smaller with more grayish plumage that contrasts with its black chin. Its song is similar but faster and higher pitched.

Breeding Habitat: Inhabits dense woodland, both oak-hickory and oak-pine forests, mainly along creeks and streams.

Nest: None. Lays eggs on ground in dead leaves or pine needles, sometimes within 3 m of a previous year's nest location. Cryptic coloration of the incubating adult together with its reluctance to flush makes nest finding very difficult.

NESTING ECOLOGY

Season: May–June. Single-brooded, but lost clutches are replaced.
Eggs: 2; creamy white, mottled and spotted with gray, purple, or brown.
Development: Incubation mainly by the female for 20 days. The semiprecocial and downy young move around in short hops and fledge at about 17 days, but are dependent on adults for about another 2 weeks.

DISTRIBUTION AND ABUNDANCE

Rangewide: Main breeding range extends from northern Missouri south and west to south-central Texas and east to the Atlantic Coast south of Pennsylvania. Winters in southern Florida and Mexico south to Colombia.

Historical: Described as a common summer resident in eastern Oklahoma west to the canyons of Caddo County and Wichita Mountains. No nesting has been reported from the Panhandle.
Current: The uneven distribution of the Chuck-will's-widow in atlas blocks across the state may be due to limited survey effort during the nighttime hours when this species is most active. The small number of breeding confirmations can also be attributed to the species nocturnal habits, as well as to the difficulty in finding its nest.

Population Trend: Breeding Bird Survey data for 1966–2000 show a decline of 1.6 percent per year rangewide (P = 0.00), but no conclusive trend in Oklahoma (-0.8 percent per year, P = 0.43).

References: AOU 1998; Baicich and Harrison 1997; Baumgartner and Baumgartner 1992; Bent 1964a; Bryce 1986; Delap and Droege; Ehrlich et al. 1988; Harrison 1975; Jenkinson and Mengel 1970; Johnsgard 1979; Mengel and Henkinson 1971; Muzny 1982; Rohwer 1971; Rohwer and Butler 1977; Sauer et al. 2001; Straight and Cooper 2000; Sutton 1967; Sutton 1969

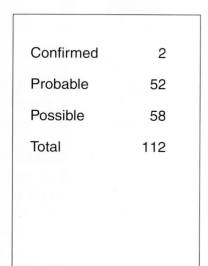

Confirmed	2
Probable	52
Possible	58
Total	112

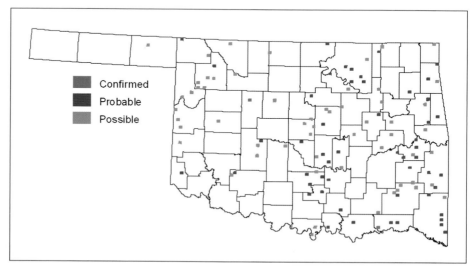

Whip-poor-will
Caprimulgus vociferus

Donald G. Varner

Almost everyone has heard of the Whip-poor-will, but few have actually heard its call in the wild, for this is a bird of the deep woods and is absent even from suburbs and many campgrounds. Some have heard the call of the more widespread Chuck-will's-widow and mistakenly thought it was a Whip-poor-will.

Description: This species is normally identified by its *Whip-poor-will* song. The birds are a mixture of brown, black, and gray colors, and the sexes are similar although the male has more white in the tail feathers. The species can be distinguished from the larger Chuck-will's-widow by call and by the unbarred white patches of the tail feathers.

Breeding Habitat: Open, mature woodlands, both deciduous and coniferous. Grazing and human disturbance usually causes birds to avoid an area.

Nest: The two eggs are laid directly on leaf-covered ground, in uneven shade. Both eggs and birds sitting on them are extremely difficult to see, and the first nest was not found in Oklahoma until 1980.

NESTING ECOLOGY

Season: May–June. Single-brooded.
Eggs: 2; white or off-white with gray and brown irregular squiggles and spots.

Development: Incubation is by the female for 17–20 days. Young are provisioned by both sexes and can fly at 14–20 days.

DISTRIBUTION AND ABUNDANCE

Rangewide: There are two distinct populations that do not come into contact with each other. The Mexican population extends into Arizona, New Mexico, Nevada, and California. The Eastern population breeds in the eastern United States from southern Canada to Gerogia and Alabama. Both populations winter from Mexico south to Central America.

Historical: Long described as a summer resident in eastern Oklahoma; more recently described as being most common in northeastern counties. First nest record not found until 1980, in Okmulgee County.

Current: Because the Whip-poor-will makes no nest, but lays eggs on the camouflaged, deep forest floor where they are seldom seen, confirmations are lacking. Nonetheless, enough birds were heard to indicate that the species is found mostly in the eastern fourth of the state, with the possibility of a few stragglers elsewhere in wooded areas.

Population Trend: Breeding Bird Survey data for 1966–2000 show a decline of 1.8 percent per year rangewide (P = 0.00), but no conclusive trend in Oklahoma (2.0 percent per year, P = 0.65).

References: AOU 1998; Baicich and Harrison 1997; Baumgartner and Baumgartner 1992; Bent 1964a; Newell 1981; Sauer et al. 2001; Sibley 2000; Sutton 1967; Wood 1982

Confirmed	0
Probable	5
Possible	6
Total	11

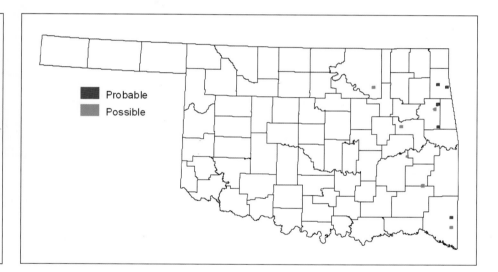

Probable
Possible

Chimney Swift
Chaetura pelagica

Alan E. Versaw

Courtesy of M. Frank Carl

The last 40 years have, in all probability, witnessed the apex of the Chimney Swift's presence in Oklahoma. The next 40 years, with the inevitable decline of suitable nest sites ushered in by urban renewal and the practice of capping chimneys, promise a sharp decline in the species' abundance. Just as we have grown fond of their chattering presence on hot summer evenings, we must prepare to bid these entertaining birds a slow adieu unless we can find some means of providing acceptable alternate nest sites.

Description: Both sexes wear a sooty-brown plumage, fading to a more pale shade of brown in the throat. In all but the best lighting, however, Chimney Swifts appear to be charcoal gray in color. Perhaps the most

distinctive character of swifts, though, are the long arcing wings. The wings beat rapidly, generating forward thrust on both upward and downward strokes. Of North American birds, only hummingbirds share with swifts this double mode of propulsion.

Breeding Habitat: Historically, a bird restricted to mature forests with large dead and broken trees suitable for nesting, Chimney Swifts are today much better known as birds of older urban areas. Rough mortar and brick, especially as found inside old brick chimneys and open well shafts, provide ideal nesting habitat.

Nest: Darkness and shelter from the elements are essential for any nest site. Also required is a rough surface to which the nest may adhere. Nest itself is shaped like a deep half saucer and constructed of small sticks cemented in place to a vertical surface with saliva. Sticks for the nest are collected in flight.

NESTING ECOLOGY

Season: May–August. Believed to be single-brooded.
Eggs: Usually 4–5; smooth and white.
Development: Incubation is by both sexes, and sometimes additional helpers, for about 19 days. Young are provisioned by both sexes (and helpers) and remain in or near the nest for about 28 days, taking short flights after 24 days.

DISTRIBUTION AND ABUNDANCE

Rangewide: Breeds across the eastern United States and southern Canada, from eastern New Mexico to extreme eastern Saskatchewan eastward. Winters in Peru, Chile, and Brazil.
Historical: Described as a summer resident as far west as Oklahoma and Cleveland counties in 1931, having expanded westward with the building of chimneys.

Expanded steadily across the western half of Oklahoma through the better part of the twentieth century, becoming well established in the Panhandle as late as the 1960s.
Current: The range of this species within Oklahoma underscores one simple fact—as long as a site has bugs and a serviceable chimney and is located somewhere between the Atlantic Ocean and the Rocky Mountains, Chimney Swifts will eventually set up shop for breeding. Although the distribution appears to thin out somewhat over the Panhandle, we must remember that so, likewise, does the occurrence of suitable nest sites in this sparsely populated region.

Population Trend: Breeding Bird Survey data for 1966–2000 show a decline of 1.5 percent per year rangewide (P = 0.00) and a decline of 2.4 percent per year in Oklahoma (P = 0.01).

References: AOU 1998; Baicich and Harrison 1997; Baumgartner and Baumgartner 1992; Fischer 1958; Jacobs and Wilson 1997; Kaufman 1996; Kingery 1998; Nice 1931; Sauer et al. 2001; Sutton 1967; Zahm 1976

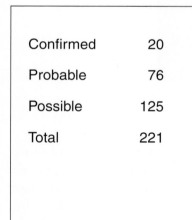

Confirmed	20
Probable	76
Possible	125
Total	221

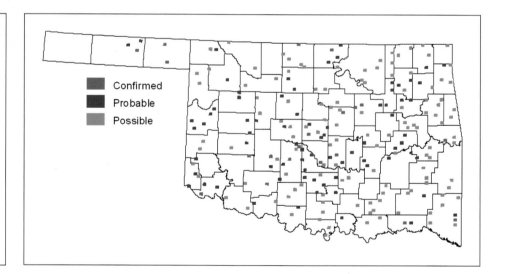

Ruby-throated Hummingbird
Archilochus colubris

Walter B. Gerard

Courtesy of Bill Horn

The genus name, *Archilochus,* can be translated from Greek to mean "first among the birds," an appropriate description for this beneficial pollinator of many plant species. Shimmering metallic colors, along with the ability to hover as well as fly laterally and backward, are among its noteworthy characteristics. Although one of the smallest birds, the Ruby-throated Hummingbird not only migrates great distances overland through Texas and Mexico, but is also capable of crossing the Gulf of Mexico in a single flight.

Description: The male and female are iridescent green above and whitish below. The male has a black chin, an iridescent red throat that can appear black as well as green or gold depending on the angle of light, and a

forked tail. The female has a whitish chin and throat while the tail is rounded with white-tipped outer feathers. Both sexes emit a rapid squeaking call in agonistic situations. In western Oklahoma, the female Ruby-throated Hummingbird can be confused with the almost identical female Black-chinned Hummingbird, which has a more grayish forehead, slightly longer and down-curved bill, broader wingtips, and tendency to pump its tail while hovering in the act of feeding.

Breeding Habitat: Deciduous or mixed woodland with proximity to water, open areas, meadows, orchards, old fields, parks, and gardens where there is access to nectar, spiders, and insects. Both sexes are highly territorial, with territory size based on the availability of food and therefore variable. Nests in Oklahoma have been recorded spaced 322 m (1,056 ft) apart.

Nest: A tiny cup placed by the female, usually 3–7m (10–23 ft) high on a downward sloping tree limb; composed of thistle and dandelion down as well as bud scales and other plant materials. The nest is fastened to the limb and held together with spider silk. It is lined with plant down and camouflaged with lichens to look like a small tree knot.

NESTING ECOLOGY

Season: May–July. Possibly double-brooded.
Eggs: 2; white.
Development: Incubation is by the female for 12–16 days. Young are provisioned by the female through regurgitation and fledge in 18–22 days.

DISTRIBUTION AND ABUNDANCE

Rangewide: A long-distance migrant, breeding in southern Canada from Nova Scotia to Alberta and in the United States from Maine to central Florida, west to the central Great Plains and east Texas. Winters from Mexico to Panama, with small numbers now recorded each year along the U.S. Gulf Coast.

Historical: Breeds in eastern and central Oklahoma. Described as a rare and irregular in the northwest (excluding the Panhandle) and southwest areas of the state. Breeding Bird Survey data indicate greater breeding densities of this species in eastern Oklahoma than in most other areas of North America.

Current: This species breeds primarily in eastern and central Oklahoma where it has access to deciduous or mixed woodland. The paucity of confirmed breeders is probably linked to the difficulty of finding nests.

Population Trend: Breeding Bird Survey data for 1966–2000 show an increase of 2.5 percent per year rangewide (P = 0.00), but show no conclusive trend in Oklahoma (3.0 percent per year, P = 0.09).

References: AOU 1998; Baicich and Harrison 1997; Baumgartner 1989; Baumgartner and Baumgartner 1992; Bent 1964; Dickinson 1999; Ehrlich et al. 1988, 1992; Garrison 1978; Harrison 1979; Johnsgard 1997; National Geographic Society 1999; Oklahoma Bird Records Committee 2000; Rickstrew 1976; Robinson, Sargent, and Sargent 1996; Sauer et al. 2001; Sibley 2000; Sutton 1967; Womack 1994

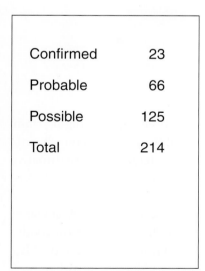

Confirmed	23
Probable	66
Possible	125
Total	214

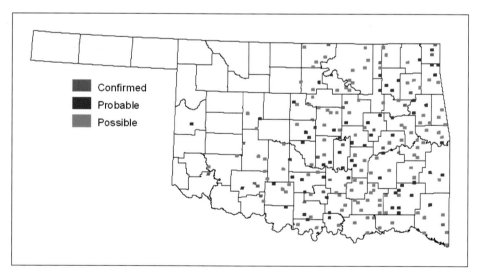

Black-chinned Hummingbird

Archilochus alexandri

Sebastian T. Patti

The Black-chinned Hummingbird is a fairly common breeding species in the western and southwestern United States. The species is highly adaptable and now regularly uses urban or suburban environments in addition to its preferred "natural" habitats. It is a congener with the Ruby-throated Hummingbird, the common breeding species of eastern North America.

Description: A small hummingbird with a slightly decurved black bill. Sexually dimorphic. Adult males are generally iridescent green above; chin and upper throat black, with the lower throat iridescent violet; underparts whitish. Adult females are iridescent dull green above, but head duller, and gray green; underparts whitish. A variety of calls are given ranging from soft to sharp in tone; warbling song rarely heard. Separating females from female Ruby-throated Hummingbirds is difficult.

Breeding Habitat: Range wide, the preferred habitat is a canyon or riparian community with cottonwoods, sycamores, willows, or *Tamarix* often present. Also present in orchards and, significantly, in urban and suburban residential areas where the species can be attracted to hummingbird feeders. The species is generally absent in agricultural areas.

Nest: Built by the female and placed in a tree, the nest is cup shaped and "fitted" to the female's body and made of plant down. Lichens, feathers, and materials such as moss, bark, or flowers are often attached to the outside of nests.

NESTING ECOLOGY

Season: April–July. Sometimes double-brooded.
Eggs: 2; unmarked white.
Development: Incubation is by the female for 12–14 days. Young are provisioned by the female through regurgitation, leave the nest at about 21 days, but continue to be fed for another week.

DISTRIBUTION AND ABUNDANCE

Rangewide: Breeds throughout much of the western United States. Winters primarily in Mexico.
Historical: First noted in Oklahoma in the 1940s. Most summer records are from western and southwestern Oklahoma, and from northwestern Cimarron County. Although little clear evidence exists, it would seem that the species has benefited from the ever-increasing numbers of humans who supply hummingbirds with feeders and flowers.
Current: The current breeding range for the Black-chinned Hummingbird is limited to the far-western

and southwestern portions of the main body of the state and to northwestern Cimarron County. Breeding was only confirmed during the atlas project period on two blocks: one in Comanche County, the other in Cimarron County. In the last several years, a number of residents in the small town of Kenton (Cimarron County) have regularly placed hummingbird feeders in their yards during the spring and summer seasons. This has led to, or made more noticeable, a number of Black-chinned Hummingbirds summering in the immediate area. This area was not located within an atlas block, and this localized population was not recorded by the project. The birds recorded in Stephens County are farther east than previously published reports on this species have indicated the range to extend.

Population Trend: Breeding Bird Survey data for 1966–2000 show no conclusive trend rangewide (1.1 percent per year, P = 0.19). No trend data are available for Oklahoma.

References: AOU 1998; Baltosser and Russel 2000; Baumgartner and Baumgartner 1992; Boyle 1998; Oberholser 1974; Sauer et al. 2001; Sibley 2000; Sutton 1967

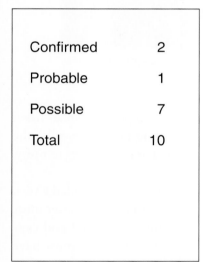

Confirmed	2
Probable	1
Possible	7
Total	10

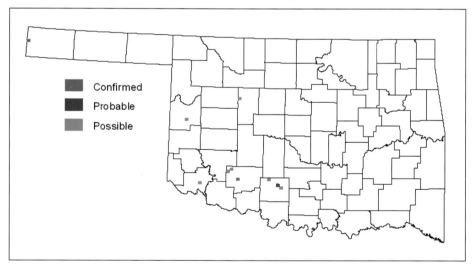

Belted Kingfisher
Ceryle alcyon

Walter B. Gerard

Courtesy of Bob Gress

Although kingfishers make up a large family of birds with a worldwide distribution, only one member of this family, the Belted Kingfisher, nests in Oklahoma. Its contrasting colors enable the Belted Kingfisher to capture its prey, mainly small fish, from a perch or hovering position with some degree of security. The dark/light countershading pattern serves to break up the bird's outline to avian predators, while the white underparts camouflage the kingfisher to its prey.

Description: The Belted Kingfisher is heavy billed with an irregular bushy crest atop a large blue-gray head. It has a white neckband and a blue-gray pectoral band that merges into the blue-gray back. The wings and upper side of the tail are blue gray while the underparts are white. The sexes are similar except the female has a rufous lower breast band. The most common call is the loud rattle, given when alarmed or proclaiming territory.

Breeding Habitat: This species prefers wooded rivers, streams with riffles, ponds, and lakes. The water must be open and clear so prey can be detected and captured. In addition, the Belted Kingfisher must have access to vertical earthen banks to excavate its burrow for nesting. Although unusual, the burrow may sometimes be located away from water or in a tree cavity. Territories are determined by competition and prey density along a body of water.

Nest: Both sexes excavate a 1–2 m (3–6 ft) long tunnel

that is 9–10 cm (3.5–4 in) wide and 7–9 cm (3–3.5 in) high, and located 0.3–0.9 m (1–3 ft) below the top of the bank. The tunnel slopes upward to a 25–30 cm (10–12 in) diameter, domed egg chamber. There is no nest, but food debris and regurgitated pellets layer the floor of the chamber.

NESTING ECOLOGY

Season: May–June. Usually single-brooded, but may replace lost clutches.

Eggs: Usually 6–7; smooth, glossy, and white.

Development: Incubation is by both sexes for 22–24 days. Young are provisioned by both sexes and fledge at 27–29 days, but continue to be provisioned by both parents at least occasionally for an additional 3 weeks.

DISTRIBUTION AND ABUNDANCE

Rangewide: Breeds locally throughout all but the northernmost areas of North America, much of the southwestern United States, and south Florida. A solitary migrant from most of Alaska and Canada, the Belted Kingfisher winters throughout much of the United States (depending on the availability of ice-free water) to northern South America.

Historical: The Belted Kingfisher breeds in all regions of the state, although it can be local and uncommon in some areas. Abundance is tied to availability of open, clear, unpolluted water; suitable cover; and access to appropriate nest sites.

Current: The Belted Kingfisher is found near open and clear water throughout the state. It is local in distribution in all parts of the state and is generally uncommon.

Population Trend: Breeding Bird Survey data for 1966–2000 show a decline of 1.6 percent per year rangewide (P = 0.00) and a decline of 3.8 percent per year in Oklahoma (P = 0.05).

References: AOU 1998; Baicich and Harrision 1997; Baumgartner and Baumgartner 1992; Bent 1964a; Droege 1987; Ehrlich et al. 1988; Hamas 1994; Harrison 1979; National Geographic Society 1999; Oklahoma Bird Records Committee 2000; Sauer et al. 2001; Sibley 2000; Silver 1952; Stokes and Stokes 1983; Sutton 1967

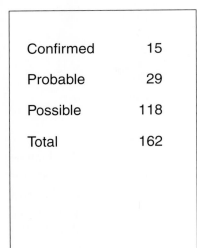

Confirmed	15
Probable	29
Possible	118
Total	162

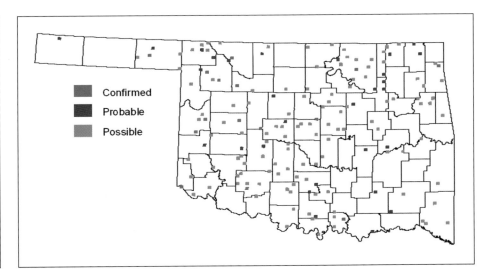

Lewis's Woodpecker
Melanerpes lewis

Alan E. Versaw

Courtesy of Steve Metz

In the world of North American woodpeckers, the Lewis's Woodpecker bears only a faint resemblance to its chisel-billed cousins. Its behavior is somewhat woodpecker-like, but, even here, the Lewis's Woodpecker brings a few surprises, such as flycatching for prey. At once both the rarest and most unusual of Oklahoma's regularly occurring woodpeckers, a sighting of this species ranks high in the memory of any Oklahoma birder.

Description: Both male and female Lewis's Woodpeckers carry the distinctive dark green back and crown, red face, and rose-colored breast. Slightly larger than its closest Oklahoma relative, the Red-headed Woodpecker, the species' dark coloration and slow, deliberate wing beats mean that the Lewis's Woodpecker may be easily mistaken for a crow. The error of such misidentifications, though, is usually revealed when the bird perches on the vertical portion of a utility pole or tree trunk. Also notable is the species' regular habit of sallying out from a perch in pursuit of flying insects.

Breeding Habitat: With the exception of a single nest in a pinon tree, the nesting habitat of Lewis's Woodpeckers found in Oklahoma has been large cottonwoods found along creek beds in western Cimarron County. In other parts of its range, the Lewis's Woodpecker nests commonly in large pines (especially ponderosa in areas of old burns) and sometimes in oak woodlands or orchards, but large cottonwoods are easily the most abundant of the accepted habitat types within the species' limited Oklahoma range.

Nest: Nests cavities are excavated in trunks or large-diameter tree limbs. In most cases, cavities are excavated into dead or diseased wood. The species will, however, appropriate existing holes of other larger-sized woodpeckers when available. Nest heights vary widely. Entrance diameter averages 6–7.5 cm (2.4–3 in).

NESTING ECOLOGY

Season: May–July. Single-brooded.
Eggs: Usually 6–7; white.
Development: Incubation is by both sexes for 12–16 days. Young are provisioned by both sexes and fledge in about 31 days but continue to receive food from adults for about 10 more days.

DISTRIBUTION AND ABUNDANCE

Rangewide: Lewis's Woodpeckers breed primarily in open pine forests and older riparian forests throughout the western United States and southeastern British Columbia. Northern populations retreat to southwestern states in winter.
Historical: Described as a rare and irregular resident of Cimarron County. Occurs sporadically throughout Oklahoma with some sight records from the eastern half of the state. All known breeding activity, however, has been in Cimarron County.
Current: The atlas data reveal nothing new or surprising about the range of the Lewis's Woodpecker in Oklahoma. Dependent as the species is on large broadleaf cottonwoods, particularly where they grow in proximity to large ponderosa pines, western Cimarron County pretty well exhausts the inventory of suitable sites for breeding. While the randomization of block selection meant that several potential breeding sites were left unsurveyed, little more detail would have been added even with complete coverage of Cimarron County. So far as breeding Lewis's Woodpeckers are concerned, it is a happy accident for Oklahomans that Cimarron County did not wind up as part of a neighboring state.

Population Trend: Breeding Bird Survey data for 1966–2000 show no conclusive trend rangewide (1.3 percent per year, P = 0.75). No trend data are available for Oklahoma.

References: Baicich and Harrison 1997; Baumgartner and Baumgartner 1992; Harris 1988; Kuenning 1998; Nice 1931; Sauer et al. 2001; Sutton 1967; Tate 1923; Tobalske 1997; Tyler 1979c; Vierling 1997

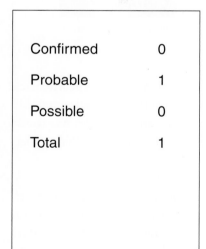

Confirmed	0
Probable	1
Possible	0
Total	1

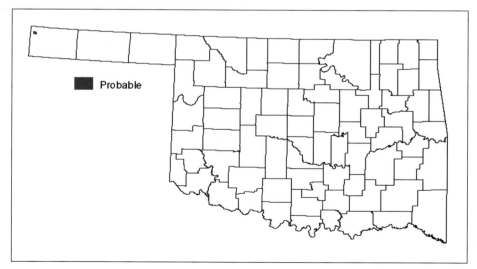

Probable

Red-headed Woodpecker
Melanerpes erythrocephalus

Alan E. Versaw

Courtesy of Bob Gress

Perhaps no Oklahoma woodpecker enjoys more widespread recognition than the Red-headed Woodpecker. The brilliant red head, combined with the bird's conspicuous flight and penchant for perching on exposed sunlit perches, affords the species a familiarity lost to other woodpecker species. Although less frequently encountered in the arid expanses of western Oklahoma, it also ranks one of the state's most widely distributed woodpeckers.

Description: The sexes are identical in appearance, although the male is slightly larger than his mate. Both male and female wear red head feathers that show as brilliant scarlet in bright sunlight. The belly, rump, and wing patches are an equally brilliant white color. These red and white colors are set off against the nearly black wings, back, and tail, giving the bird a remarkably clean and attractive appearance. Voice has been described as a wheezy *queeah,* similar to Red-bellied Woodpecker.

Breeding Habitat: In the Panhandle and western Oklahoma, Red-headed Woodpeckers rely heavily on large trees along both natural and artificial watercourses. Many are also found in cities where trees grow large under artificial conditions. In eastern Oklahoma, however, the species enjoys a greater range of acceptable habitat options, including both pines and hardwoods, and can be found in almost any relatively open woodland with a few standing snags. Red-heads prefer more open conditions and habitats with less undergrowth than Red-bellied Woodpeckers.

Nest: Almost without fail, nests are excavated in a dead branch or a dead tree from which the bark has peeled away. Occasionally, the species exploits artificial sources such as buildings or utility poles for nest sites, with the nests in creosote-treated poles often failing. Nest heights vary widely, from 2–23 m (6–75 ft).

NESTING ECOLOGY

Season: May–July. Sometimes double-brooded.
Eggs: Often 5, but sometimes 4–7 or more; white.
Development: Incubation is by both sexes, with males incubating at night, for 12–14 days. Young are provisioned by both sexes and fledge at 24–27 days but may continue to be fed by adults for some time.

DISTRIBUTION AND ABUNDANCE

Rangewide: Breeds throughout most of the United States and southern Canada east of the Rocky Mountains. The species is, however, mostly absent from New England and southwestern Texas. In winter, the species retreats from the northern tier of states and Canada.
Historical: Described as an uncommon to common summer resident statewide and as irregular in winter. Records indicate no significant range expansions or con-

tractions for this species in Oklahoma. Establishment of urban woodlands has enabled Red-headed Woodpeckers to colonize localized areas not previously suitable for the species, but this has resulted in no substantial expansion of range.
Current: It will surprise nobody to learn that Red-headed Woodpeckers enjoy a broad distribution across the state of Oklahoma. What the atlas data reveal, however, that requires closer inspection are two conspicuous gaps in breeding activity, one each in the southeastern and southwestern portions of the state. Had such a gap of records occurred in the Panhandle it might easily be explained away as a poor match between block boundaries and existing wooded plots. Such an explanation may hold true in southwestern Oklahoma, but not in southeastern Oklahoma. Whether these gaps represent statistical anomalies or legitimate holes in the population's range is one of the tantalizing questions that each atlas project seems to leave in its aftermath.

Population Trend: Breeding Bird Survey data for 1966–2000 show a decline of 2.5 percent per year rangewide (P = 0.00) and a larger decline of 5.1 percent per year in Oklahoma (P = 0.00).

References: Baumgartner and Baumgartner 1992; Jackson 1976; Ramsey 1970; Shackelford and Conner 1997; Sauer et al. 2001; Sibley 2000; Smith et al. 2000; Sutton 1967; Winkler et al. 1995

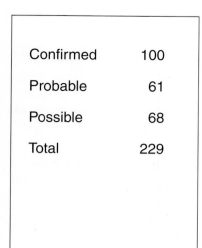

Confirmed	100
Probable	61
Possible	68
Total	229

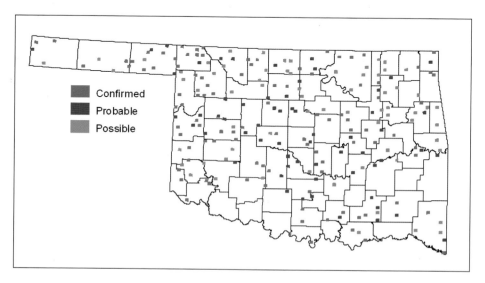

Golden-fronted Woodpecker
Melanerpes aurifrons

Dan L. Reinking

Courtesy of Bill Horn

Unknown in Oklahoma until 1954, Texas and Oklahoma are now the only states in the United States where the Golden-fronted Woodpecker can be found. Relatively little information is available on the breeding biology of this species. A few counties in southwestern Oklahoma form an area in which this species and the closely related Red-bellied Woodpecker overlap and are known to interbreed.

Description: The Golden-fronted Woodpecker is a woodpecker of medium size, with a red crown (white in females) and orange-yellow nape (both sexes), whitish underparts, strongly barred black and white wings, and a white rump. Vocal year round, common calls include a harsh, rolling *churr-churr* and a loud

kek-kek. It is similar to Red-bellied Woodpecker, in which the orange-yellow is replaced with red.

Breeding Habitat: Riparian woodlands and mesquite brushlands of southwestern Oklahoma.

Nest: Cavities are located in limbs or trunks of live or dead trees or fence posts. Cavities in south Texas average 32 cm (13 in) deep.

NESTING ECOLOGY

Season: April–July. Presumably double-brooded.
Eggs: Usually 4–5; white.
Development: Incubation by both sexes for 12–14

days. Young are provisioned by both sexes and fledge at about 30 days.

Hybridization: Reported locally with Red-bellied Woodpecker in a small zone of overlap in southwestern Oklahoma (roughly Greer, Jackson, and Tillman counties). Some birds in this area show intermediate morphology and mixed genetic composition. This is a recent occurrence due to range expansions of both species into this area.

DISTRIBUTION AND ABUNDANCE

Rangewide: The Golden-fronted Woodpecker is a year-round resident, breeding from southwestern Oklahoma south through central Texas, much of eastern Mexico, and parts of northern Central America. The northward expansion into Oklahoma occurred during the past half century.

Historical: The Golden-fronted Woodpecker was first reported in Oklahoma in 1954 in Harmon County and first confirmed nesting there in 1958. This species is established in Harmon, Greer, Jackson, and Tillman counties, and has been recorded north to Ellis and east to Comanche counties. It is believed to have come into contact with the range of Red-bellied Woodpecker in Oklahoma by 1959.

Current: Golden-fronted Woodpeckers were only recorded in the three southwesternmost counties in Oklahoma. It is unclear whether they were simply missed in Tillman County due to local distribution or whether they have diminished in number there from previous population levels.

Population Trend: Breeding Bird Survey data for 1966–2000 show no conclusive trend rangewide (-1.4 percent per year, P = 0.17) or in Oklahoma (-24.8 percent per year, P = 0.26), although the proliferation of mesquite on rangelands should have favored this species.

References: AOU 1998; Baicich and Harrison 1997; Baumgartner and Baumgartner 1992; Husak and Maxwell 1998, 2000; Payne 1970; Selander and Giller 1959; Sauer et al. 2001; Shackelford et al. 2000; Smith 1987; Sutton 1967

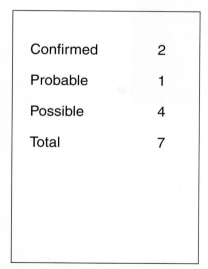

Confirmed	2
Probable	1
Possible	4
Total	7

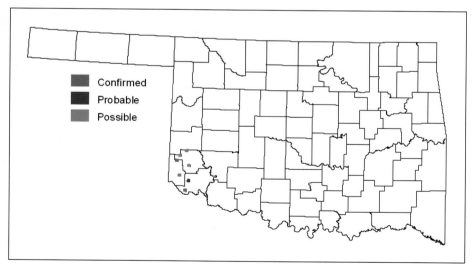

Red-bellied Woodpecker

Melanerpes carolinus

Dan L. Reinking

Courtesy of M. Frank Carl

Present across all but parts of extreme western Oklahoma, the Red-bellied Woodpecker is a common and familiar resident of wooded areas, both urban and rural. It seldom excavates wood to reach its meals, instead relying on fruit, nuts, seeds, and insects gleaned from trees. A few counties in southwestern Oklahoma form an area in which this species and the closely related Golden-fronted Woodpecker overlap and are known to interbreed.

Description: The Red-bellied Woodpecker is a woodpecker of medium size, with a red crown (white in females) and nape (both sexes), whitish underparts, strongly barred black and white wings, and a white rump. Vocal year round, common calls include a harsh,

rolling *churr* and a loud *chiff-chiff*. It is similar to the Golden-fronted Woodpecker, in which the red is replaced with orange-yellow.

Breeding Habitat: Adaptable to a variety of habitats, Red-bellied Woodpeckers generally prefer mature hardwood or mixed pine-hardwood forests. Bottomland hardwood forests are especially favored due to the abundance of mast. Large dead trees are needed for nest cavities.

Nest: Males attract a female to a completed or partially completed cavity with calls and drumming. If accepted by the female, she joins the male at the cavity and engages in nearly synchronous, slow mutual tapping.

Cavities are located in dead trees or fence posts, usually 2–18 m (6–59 ft) above the ground, are 22–32 cm (9–13 in) deep, and are about 9 x 13 cm (4 x 5 in) in size. European Starlings may out-compete Red-bellied Woodpeckers for nest cavities.

NESTING ECOLOGY

Season: April–July. Double-brooded.
Eggs: Usually 4, but sometimes 2–6; white.
Development: Incubation is by both sexes for 12 days. Young are provisioned by both sexes and fledge at 24–27 days.
Hybridization: Reported locally with Golden-fronted Woodpecker in a small zone of overlap in southwestern Oklahoma (roughly Greer, Jackson, and Tillman counties). Some birds in this area show intermediate morphology and mixed genetic composition. This is a recent occurrence due to range expansions of both species into this area.

DISTRIBUTION AND ABUNDANCE

Rangewide: The Red-bellied Woodpecker is a North American resident breeding from roughly the 100th meridian eastward and south of central Minnesota. It is mostly sedentary except for northern birds, which may retreat south in winter. The current range reflects a northward and westward expansion in the past half century, with the former due to maturing northeastern forests and backyard bird feeding, and the latter occurring mostly along wooded river bottoms extending westward through the plains, and due to maturing urban tree plantings.

Historical: Red-bellied Woodpecker is considered a common resident over much of the state, except western portions of the Panhandle and southwestern Oklahoma where it is rare to uncommon and local. It is believed to have expanded west past Major and Comanche counties in the 1930s and to have reached the range of Golden-fronted Woodpecker in Oklahoma by 1959.

Current: The Red-bellied Woodpecker is common and uniformly distributed across the main body of the state, except for the far southwestern corner, and is nearly absent from the Panhandle.

Population Trend: Breeding Bird Survey data for 1966–2000 show an increase of 0.6 percent per year rangewide (P = 0.00), but no conclusive trend in Oklahoma (0.1 percent per year, P = 0.92).

References: AOU 1998; Baicich and Harrison 1997; Baumgartner and Baumgartner 1992; Boone 1963; Jackson 1976; Jackson and Davis 1998; Sauer et al. 2001; Selander and Giller 1959; Shackelford et al. 2000; Shackford and Harden 1993; Smith 1987; Sutton 1967, 1984b

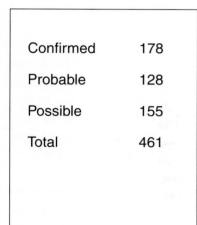

Confirmed	178
Probable	128
Possible	155
Total	461

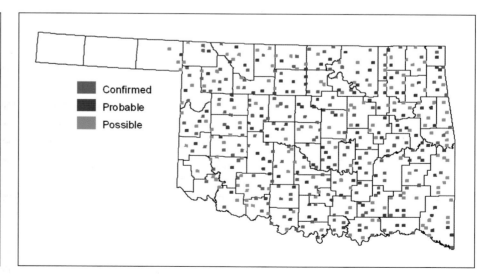

Ladder-backed Woodpecker
Picoides scalaris

Joseph A. Grzybowski

Courtesy of Bill Horn

It may not look like woodpecker habitat, but a fence row and a few yuccas in an otherwise open grassland may be all a wandering Ladder-backed Woodpecker needs. For breeding, it may take a modest patch of mesquite, perhaps a small locust grove, maybe some willows with a sugarberry or two for variety. In this sparsely wooded habitat, Ladder-backs can still be quite elusive, low on the opposite sides of gnarled mesquite trunks. Relatively little is known about the breeding biology of this species.

Description: Between the size of Downy and Hairy woodpeckers, the Ladder-backed is distinctive in having a thinly lined horizontal black-and-white pattern on its back and wings. Males have a continuous red crown and nape; this is black in females. Both have a pale auricular patch outlined in black, a dark eye line forming the upper boundary, and buff-tinted underparts, spotted on the flanks. Experienced listeners might distinguish the *pick* call as intermediate in tone between those of Downy and Hairy woodpeckers.

Breeding Habitat: Open mesquite grassland, xeric riparian areas, or isolated mottes and farmyards. May wander into open areas containing only cholla and yucca.

Nest: Cavity bored in dead wood, usually 1–5 m (3–16 ft) high.

NESTING ECOLOGY

Season: May–July. Single-brooded.
Eggs: Usually 3–4; glossy white.
Development: Incubation is by both sexes for about 13 days. Young are provisioned by both sexes. No information on fledging age. May travel in family groups after fledging.

DISTRIBUTION AND ABUNDANCE

Rangewide: Resident in southwestern United States from southeastern Colorado and central Texas west to southeastern California and southward through Mexico to Nicaragua.
Historical: Western Oklahoma forms parts of the northeastern boundary of this species' range. Found in the outer half of the Panhandle, and in northwestern Oklahoma, following the distribution of mesquite to Dewey, Blaine, and western Kingfisher counties. Perhaps most abundant in southwestern Oklahoma, east to Kiowa, Cotton, and Comanche counties, regularly to Carter County, rarely to Marshall County.

Within this area, gaps occur both in the distribution of Ladder-backs and in extant information.
Current: Although not a "faithful marriage," distribution of Ladder-backed Woodpeckers is influenced strongly by distribution of mesquite. Clearly common in mesquite areas of southwestern Oklahoma, its atlas distribution in other parts of western Oklahoma are consistent with the more localized and patchy distribution of mesquite there. Missed in Carter County where it likely breeds locally. Location in Harper County provides new breeding information.

Population Trend: Breeding Bird Survey data for 1966–2000 show a decline of 1.5 percent per year rangewide (P = 0.07) and a decline of 1.9 percent per year in Oklahoma (P = 0.01).

References: AOU 1998; Baicich and Harrison 1997; Baumgartner and Baumgartner 1992; Bent 1939; Lowther 2001; Nice 1931; Sutton 1967; Tate 1923; Winkler et al. 1995; Winternitz 1998

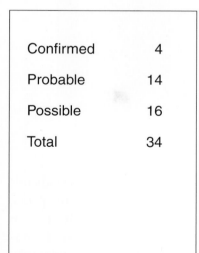

Confirmed	4
Probable	14
Possible	16
Total	34

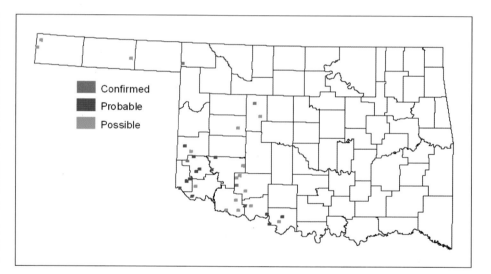

Downy Woodpecker
Picoides pubescens

Melinda Droege

Courtesy of Bill Horn

Oklahoma's smallest woodpecker, the Downy is probably also one of the best known. Common at feeding stations and on field trips, care must be taken not to confuse it with the less abundant but very similar Hairy Woodpecker.

Description: This small familiar woodpecker is patterned black and white with a narrow red patch on the upper nape that distinguishes the male. Back and underparts are white; a black eye stripe, a black mustache, and a white eyebrow are also distinctive. Calls include a soft *pik* and a rattling *ki-ki-ki-ki*. The similar Hairy Woodpecker is both larger bodied and larger billed and lacks black bars on the outer tail feathers.

Breeding Habitat: Occupies all types of woodlands from pinewoods to deciduous forests to parks, orchards, and gardens in Oklahoma. The Downy also feeds in tall vegetation such as giant ragweed, sunflower, and mullein, something that Hairy's seldom do.

Nest: A new nest hole is excavated every year by both sexes in a live or dead tree, stump, or fence post usually in rotting wood about 0.9–15.2 m (3–50 ft) above ground. The cavity opening is a perfect circle of about 3.8 cm (1.5 in), camouflaged by surrounding fungus, lichens, and moss. The cavity is 20.3–25.4 cm (8–12 in) deep and lined with chips.

NESTING ECOLOGY

Season: March–June. Double-brooded.

Eggs: 4–5, occasionally 3 or 6; pure white.

Development: Incubation is by both sexes, by the male at night, for 12 days. Young are provisioned by both sexes and can climb to the cavity entrance at 12 days. They leave the nest at 20–22 days and are dependent on the parents for up to 3 more weeks.

DISTRIBUTION AND ABUNDANCE

Rangewide: A resident from central Alaska, Canada, and most of the United States except for parts of the southwest.

Historical: Described as a resident in most of the state, decreasing westward, and becoming scarce in summer in the Panhandle. One nest record as far west as Cimarron County in 1913.

Current: The Downy Woodpecker is widely distributed across the main body of the state, though is less common in the southwestern part. No broad patterns of distributional change are evident.

Population Trend: Breeding Bird Survey data for 1966–2000 show no conclusive trend rangewide (0.0 percent per year, P = 0.97) or in Oklahoma (0.2 percent per year, P = 0.86).

References: AOU 1998; Baicich and Harrison 1997; Baumgartner and Baumgartner 1992; Bent 1964d; Ehrlich et al. 1988; Harrison 1975; Johnsgard 1979; Kilham 1974; Sauer et al. 2001; Shackford and Harden 1993; Sutton 1967; Tate 1923

Confirmed	138
Probable	99
Possible	182
Total	419

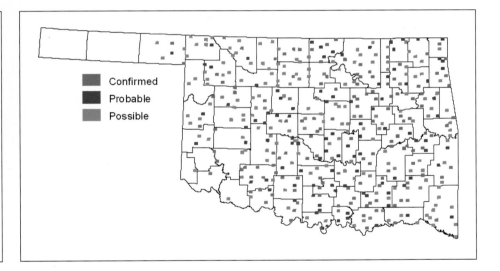

Hairy Woodpecker
Picoides villosus

Donald G. Varner

Courtesy of Gerald Wiens

Distinguished from the similar Downy Woodpecker by its larger size and proportionally longer bill, this is an uncommon bird of mature woodlands. However, individuals roam freely and can be found almost anywhere in Oklahoma where trees are present, especially in winter.

Description: Females are patterned with black and white; males are similar with the addition of red feathers near the back of the head. Juveniles of both sexes have a few red feathers on top of the head. The call is a more emphatic *peek,* but still similar to the *pik* of the smaller Downy Woodpecker, and the Hairy's drumming is also faster.

Breeding Habitat: Mature woodlands and timbered ravines with fairly large trees, often near water.

Nest: In a cavity, usually one of their own excavation. The entrance is about 5 cm (2 in) in diameter and the cavity about 0.3 m (1 ft) deep. Wood chips are the only nesting material. Generally, they excavate a hole in a dead limb or trunk quite high up the tree, but some nests are located in live trees and as low as 1.5 m (5 ft).

Occasionally they use a preexisting cavity and have been known to nest in man-made nest boxes.

NESTING ECOLOGY

Season: April–June. Single-brooded.
Eggs: Usually 4–6; white.
Development: Incubation is by both sexes for 11–15 days. Young are provisioned by both sexes and leave the nest at 28–30 days, but rely on adults for another 2 weeks.

DISTRIBUTION AND ABUNDANCE

Rangewide: Permanent resident over almost all of North America where suitable forest habitat occurs. Moves into areas adjacent to breeding habitat in winter and often makes use of suet feeders.

Historical: Described as an uncommon resident statewide; rare in the southwest and the Panhandle.
Current: This medium-sized woodpecker is found in all tree-covered areas of Oklahoma, with most confirmations occurring in the central third of the state. Individuals were even recorded in each of the Panhandle counties.

Population Trend: Breeding Bird Survey data for 1966–2000 show an increase of 1.5 percent per year rangewide (P = 0.00), but show no conclusive trend in Oklahoma (-7.2 percent per year, P = 0.24).

References: AOU 1998; Baicich and Harrison 1997; Baumgartner and Baumgartner 1992; Bent 1964d; Sauer et al. 2001; Sibley 2000; Sutton 1967

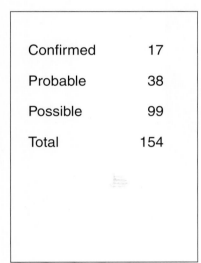

Confirmed	17
Probable	38
Possible	99
Total	154

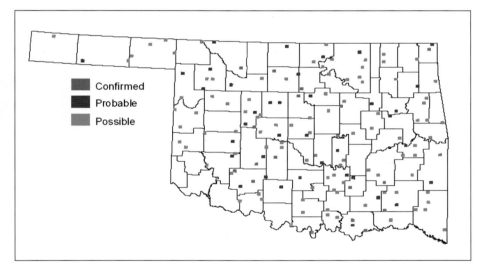

Red-cockaded Woodpecker
Picoides borealis

Jerome A. Jackson

Courtesy of wildlifedepartment.com

The Red-cockaded Woodpecker is a resident bird of old-growth fire climax pine forest ecosystems of the southeastern United States. In Oklahoma, it was once more widespread but today is known to occur only in the McCurtain County Wilderness Area. This highly social, cooperatively breeding bird has declined and is considered endangered rangewide as a result of fragmentation and loss of habitat due to short-rotation forestry, clearing for many land uses, and restriction of natural fires.

Description: Both males and females are black-and-white, white-breasted, ladder-backed woodpeckers with large white cheek patches surrounded by black. Adult males have a few tiny red feathers between the black and white on each side above the cheek patches. The red is usually hidden except during aggression or courtship. Juvenile males have visible red feathers on the forehead; juvenile females have white-tipped feathers low on the forehead. Red-cockaded Woodpeckers forage in family groups and often maintain a near constant chatter of querulous notes.

Breeding Habitat: This species is characterized as being a bird of extensive, mature, open pine forests, but in southeastern Oklahoma, where it reaches the northwestern limits of its range, it is found in relatively open areas of mixed pine-hardwood forest.

Nest: The Red-cockaded Woodpecker is a primary cavity nester that excavates nest and roost cavities in the trunks of living pines averaging 90–100 years old. Nests are typically at about 10 m (33 ft) high, usually below the lowest branch, and most often open to the south and west. Nest cavities may be used for several years, are characteristically the roost cavity of the breeding male, and are usually excavated into heartwood that has been softened by the red-heart fungus that infects older pines. Artificial cavities, called "inserts," placed in appropriate trees are readily used and are part of the management and recovery strategy for this species in Oklahoma and elsewhere.

NESTING ECOLOGY

Season: April–June. Single-brooded.
Eggs: Usually 3–5; glossy white.
Development: Incubation is by both sexes and sometimes helpers for 10–11 days. Young are provisioned by both sexes and sometimes helpers, and can fly at 26–29 days.

DISTRIBUTION AND ABUNDANCE

Rangewide: Once found from southeastern Oklahoma and east Texas east to south-central Missouri, south-central Kentucky, coastal Maryland and Virginia, and southern New Jersey south to the Gulf Coast and southern peninsular Florida. Now gone from Missouri, Maryland, Tennessee, and New Jersey; last known birds in Kentucky were relocated following a pine beetle epidemic. The species is endangered and has very fragmented populations; mostly on state and federal land.
Historical: Known from Bryan, Latimer, LeFlore, McCurtain, Pittsburg, and Pushmataha counties; possibly from Atoka, Choctaw, and Haskell counties.
Current: Known only from McCurtain County Wilderness Area, where about 9–11 nests per year have been monitored from 1997 to 2001.

Population Trend: A steady decline has occurred rangewide due to loss and fragmentation of its mature, open pine-forest habitat. In recent years, some stabilization in populations has resulted from intensive management efforts and translocation of birds among populations. A total of 33 birds were translocated to the McCurtain County Wilderness Area from 1995 to 2001, primarily from Texas. A recovery plan for Oklahoma calls for 45 active nest clusters to be achieved in the wilderness area through forest management, predator guards on nest trees, establishment of artificial cavities, and population augmentation through translocations

References: Baumgartner and Baumgartner 1992; Carter 1967; Crabb 1930; Jackson 1994; Jackson et al. 1986; Kelly et al. 1993, 1994; Masters et al. 1989, 1994; Nice 1931; Oklahoma Department of Wildlife Conservation unpubl. data; Sutton 1967; Wood 1975, 1983a, 1983b

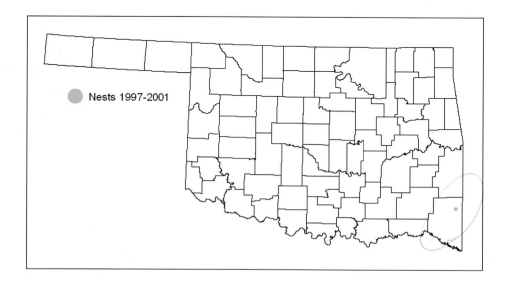

Nests 1997-2001

Northern Flicker
Colaptes auratus

Walter B. Gerard

Courtesy of Gerald Wiens

Once avidly hunted as a game bird in the United States, the Northern Flicker is today appreciated for its ecological importance in providing nest cavities for other species of birds and its useful consumption of ants as well as other insects. Among the interesting characteristics of this woodpecker are its high incidence of ground foraging, undulating flight, loose flocking during migration, and a hybrid zone including Oklahoma where two subspecies come into contact.

Description: The two forms of Northern Flicker in Oklahoma are brownish, black-barred above, with a white rump; below they are whitish tan with black spots, and a black crescent across the upper breast. The Yellow-shafted Flicker has a gray crown, tan face, red nape patch, yellow below the wings and tail, with the male distinguished by a black mustache. The Red-shafted Flicker has a brown crown, gray face, no nape patch, reddish below the wings and tail, with the male having a red mustache. The loud, prolonged *week* vocalization is associated with territoriality and courtship; it is given along with regular drumming on resonant tree trunks, limbs, and man-made objects by both sexes, although more often by males.

Breeding Habitat: Open woodlands and forest edges with snags, riparian areas, old farm fields, parks, and burned forests with damaged trees.

Nest: Excavates cavity in dead or diseased tree trunk or limb but will utilize live trees focusing on knothole as entry point. Height from ground is variable but often 2.4–7.6 m (8–25 ft). Entrance diameter is 5.1–10.2 cm (2–4 in) with a cavity depth of 17.8–45.7 cm (7–18 in), and the egg chamber is unlined except for wood chips. Also known to use nest boxes.

NESTING ECOLOGY

Season: May–June. Single-brooded.
Eggs: Usually 6–8; white.
Development: Incubation is by both sexes for 11–13 days. Young are provisioned by both sexes and fledge in 24–28 days.

DISTRIBUTION AND ABUNDANCE

Rangewide: Breeds throughout most of Canada and the United States as well as into Mexico, with a narrow hybrid zone that runs through the western edge of the Great Plains across the Canadian Rockies into southern Alaska. Northern breeders migrate south for the winter. The two other subspecies of the Northern Flicker are allopatric, with one found in Cuba and the other from southern Mexico into Central America.

Historical: Described as common in migration and winter and uncommon to common in summer. The Red-shafted group is most likely found in the more arid western part of the Panhandle, while the Yellow-shafted form occurs over most of the state. The hybrid zone is located in the western Panhandle.
Current: The Northern Flicker is found throughout the state, although it does not appear to be evenly distributed. It doesn't occur in great numbers and is in possible decline, perhaps due to a shortage of suitable cavity locations and to competition from European Starlings.

Population Trend: Breeding Bird Survey data for 1966–2000 show a decline of 2.2 percent per year rangewide (P = 0.00) and a decline of 4.5 percent per year in Oklahoma (P = 0.02).

References: AOU 1998; Baicich and Harrison 1997; Baumgartner and Baumgartner 1992; Bent 1964d; Crabb 1924; Ehrlich et al. 1988; Harrison 1979; Moore 1995; National Geographic Society 1999; Oklahoma Bird Records Committee 2000; Sauer et al. 2001; Sherrod 1972; Sibley 2000; Stokes 1979; Sutton 1967

Confirmed	23
Probable	47
Possible	90
Total	160

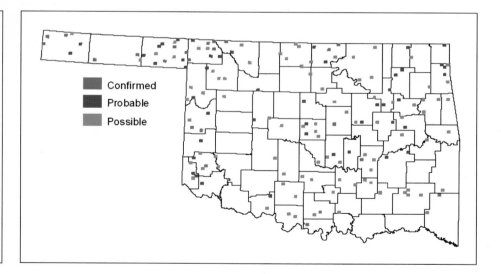

Confirmed
Probable
Possible

Pileated Woodpecker
Dryocopus pileatus

Dan L. Reinking

Courtesy of wildlifedepartment.com

Oklahoma's largest remaining woodpecker since the demise of the Ivory-billed Woodpecker, the crow-sized Pileated's loud calls and drumming echo through eastern woodlands. Pileated Woodpeckers mate for life and defend territories year round, where they feed primarily on wood-dwelling ants and beetles, but also on fruits and nuts in season.

Description: Both males and females are large, heavy-billed, mostly black woodpeckers with a red crest and black-and-white-striped face and neck. Males have a red forehead and malar stripe extending back from the bill, while in females these features are black. In flight, a large white area shows on the leading underside of the wings, and a limited amount of centrally located

white is visible in the wings from above. The most common call is a loud, repeated *cuk, cuk, cuk,* similar to that given by flickers.

Breeding Habitat: Pileated Woodpeckers are found in mature stands of deciduous and coniferous forest, as well as younger stands with scattered large dead trees. Population densities are greater in older stands with larger, denser trees and more snags. The cavity size needed by this large species for nesting and roosting requires the presence of sizeable trees, and fallen logs are frequently used for foraging.

Nest: Nest cavities are excavated by both sexes, but mostly by males, over several weeks. Cavities are typically 40 cm (16 in) deep, have a 15–20 cm (6–8 in) diameter, and have an oval-shaped entrance about 11 cm (4 in) high and 9 cm (3.5 in) wide. Some wood chips are left in the bottom of the cavity. Nest cavities are rarely reused for nesting, but may be used again for roosting.

NESTING ECOLOGY

Season: April–May. Single-brooded.
Eggs: Often 4, sometimes 3–5; white.
Development: Incubation is by both sexes during the day and by males at night for about 18 days. Young are provisioned by both sexes through regurgitation. Nestlings fledge at about 28 days, and siblings may leave the nest up to 3 days apart.

DISTRIBUTION AND ABUNDANCE

Rangewide: Resident in forested areas from the Great Plains east in North America, west across forested Canada to British Columbia, and south along the West Coast and Sierras to central California.
Historical: Fairly common resident in eastern bottom-land woodlands and both deciduous and coniferous forests; becoming rare and local west to a line from Alfalfa to Love counties, and increasing in western portions of this Oklahoma range since the mid-1960s. Pileated Woodpeckers are recorded nesting as far west as Boiling Springs State Park in Woodward County, and have been observed during June at Wichita Mountains National Wildlife Refuge in Comanche County.
Current: The Pileated Woodpecker is broadly distributed across the eastern half of the main body of the state, reflecting its preference for forest and large woodlands. It probably occurs somewhat farther west than shown by the map, but only locally, explaining why it may have been missed in those areas by atlas project sampling.

Population Trend: Breeding Bird Survey data for 1966–2000 show an increase of 1.4 percent per year rangewide (P = 0.00), but show no conclusive trend in Oklahoma (-0.6 percent per year, P = 0.69).

References: AOU 1998; Baicich and Harrison 1997; Baumgartner and Baumgartner 1992; Bull and Jackson 1995; Carter 1974; DeVore 1979; Ely 1990; Hobbet and Hobbet 1988; Hoyt 1957; McGee and Neeld 1972; Moore 1984; Powders 1986; Renken and Wiggers 1993; Sauer et al. 2001; Sutton 1967

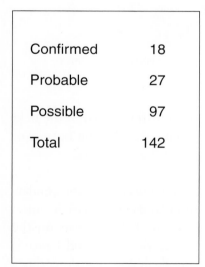

Confirmed	18
Probable	27
Possible	97
Total	142

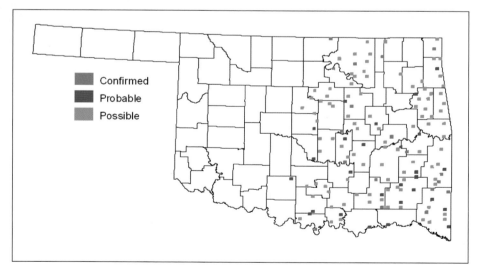

Western Wood-Pewee
Contopus sordidulus

Alan E. Versaw

Courtesy of Bob Gress

Although a common breeding species in neighboring Colorado and New Mexico, the Western Wood-Pewee ranks as one of Oklahoma's most uncommon breeders. The species' familiar burry *peer* note is regularly heard in Oklahoma only in the westernmost parts of Cimarron County.

Description: Sexes similar. The Western Wood-Pewee has a dark olive-gray back with faint wing bars and no eye ring. It spends much of the day hunting from dead or bare lower tree branches. Western Wood-Pewees are virtually indistinguishable from their eastern cousins. Although coloration tendencies differ slightly between individuals in fresh plumage, Western and Eastern Wood-Pewees can be safely distinguished in the field only by voice, and then only with caution outside of the normal breeding ranges for each species.

Breeding Habitat: A variety of deciduous and coniferous (especially pines) woodlands and riparian zones. Although some potential pine habitat exists on the slopes of the Black Mesa, the Western Wood-Pewee is recognized as a breeder in Oklahoma only along riparian zones in western Cimarron County. Tree plantings around rural homesites in the region may provide additional breeding habitat.

Nest: An open cup of grass, fibers, and other material

placed well toward the outer edges of the host tree. Usually placed in the fork of nearly horizontal branches at least 5 m (16 ft) high.

NESTING ECOLOGY

Season: May–August. Single-brooded, but will replace lost clutches.

Eggs: Usually 3; cream to pale yellow and spotted or blotched with deep reddish or purple. The species is a somewhat infrequent cowbird host, and few cowbirds fledge from nests of this species.

Development: Incubation is by the female for about 15 days. Young are provisioned by both sexes and fledge at about 16 days.

DISTRIBUTION AND ABUNDANCE

Rangewide: Breeds throughout forested and riparian areas of Mexico and the western United States and Canada. Eastern extent of breeding range barely reaches central South Dakota and central Kansas. Winter range includes southern Central America and northern South America. Full extent of winter range poorly known due to difficulty in separating from the Eastern Wood-Pewee.

Historical: Described as a rare summer resident in Cimarron County, with the first and only nest noted in 1920.

Current: The Western Wood-Pewee would be a fine addition to the list of regularly breeding species in Oklahoma were it not for its predilection for habitats occurring almost entirely outside of the state. Only at the western end of the Panhandle does the species find conditions sufficiently like those found from the Rocky Mountains westward to support an occasional breeding venture. The species' distinctive and oft-repeated song ensures that it was not overlooked by atlas fieldworkers.

Population Trend: Breeding Bird Survey data for 1966–2000 show a decline of 1.4 percent per year rangewide (P = 0.00). No trend data are available for Oklahoma.

References: Baicich and Harrison 1997; Baker 1998; Baumgartner and Baumgartner 1992; Bemis and Rising 1999; Chace et al. 1997; Sauer et al. 2001; Sutton 1967

Confirmed	0
Probable	2
Possible	0
Total	2

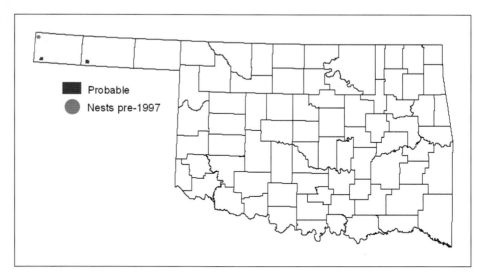

Probable
Nests pre-1997

Eastern Wood-Pewee
Contopus virens

Bonnie L. Gall

Throughout the summer the Oklahoma woods ring with the song of the Eastern Wood-Pewee, which proudly announces itself by name with a plaintive *pee-a-wee*. It can wake you up in the morning and still sing into the twilight. The nest is hard to find, being only a little knob on an outstretched branch. A helpful Blue Jay located one nest for this author, however, as the resident pewee vigorously defended its nest from this notorious egg robber.

Description: Dark grayish-olive above, dull white throat, darker breast, and whitish or yellowish underparts. Bill of adult has a dark upper mandible and dull orange lower mandible. Bill of the immature is all dark. The primary song is a clear, slow *pee-a-wee* with the second note lower in tone, while a second song is a downslurred *pee-yer*.

Breeding Habitat: Eastern Wood-Pewee's prefer woodland habitats, including mature forests, farm woodlots, orchards, parks, borders of fields, clearings, and roads primarily in eastern and central Oklahoma.

Nest: A thick-walled, shallow cup built by the female of grasses, weed stems, plant fibers, spider webs, and hair, lined with finer pieces of the same materials, and covered with lichens on the outside. Located on a horizontal limb of a fairly big tree 3.7–16.6 m (12–54 ft) above a path or open ground. It is usually well out from the tree trunk.

NESTING ECOLOGY

Season: Late May–July. Probably single-brooded.

Eggs: Usually 2–4; not glossy, oval, creamy white, and wreathed with brown blotches or spots. Regularly parasitized by Brown-headed Cowbirds, but no records of parasitism from Oklahoma.

Development: Incubation is by the female for 12–13 days. Young are provisioned by both parents and fledge in about 15–18 days.

DISTRIBUTION AND ABUNDANCE

Rangewide: Summer resident over the eastern United States west to the central plains states. Absent from south Florida and south Texas. Winters in northern South America.

Historical: One of the last spring arrivals, the Eastern Wood-Pewee is a summer resident statewide except in the Panhandle from late April through September. It has been described as a common migrant and summer resident in the eastern regions, decreasing in abundance toward the west.

Current: Atlas project data show that the Eastern Wood-Pewee was commonly detected east of I-35, the main interstate highway that bisects the state from north to south. West of this line, suitable woodland breeding habitat declines significantly. The current distribution mirrors the historical data.

Population Trend: Breeding Bird Survey data for 1966–2000 show a decline of 1.7 percent per year rangewide (P = 0.00), but show no conclusive trend in Oklahoma (-0.3 percent per year, P = 0.81).

References: AOU 1998; Baumgartner and Baumgartner 1992; Bent 1963b; Carter 1967; Craig 1943; Harrison 1975; Johnsgard 1979; McCarty 1996; National Geographic Society 1999; Sauer et al. 2001; Sutton 1967

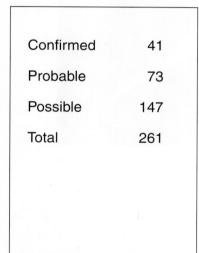

Confirmed	41
Probable	73
Possible	147
Total	261

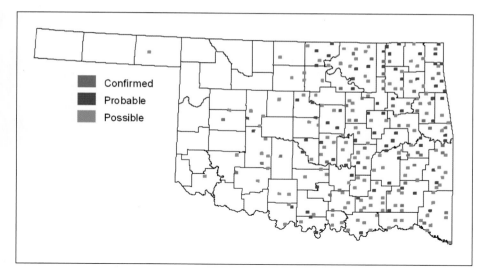

Acadian Flycatcher
Empidonax virescens

Richard A. Stuart

Courtesy of Joseph A. Grzybowski

The Acadian Flycatcher is a bird of eastern forests that is found in moist Oklahoma woodlands west to central Oklahoma. It can be easily identified during the breeding season by habitat and voice. A molting *Empidonax* flycatcher seen during the late summer and early fall in Oklahoma would likely be of this species, because most flycatchers in this family molt on the wintering grounds.

Description: Male and female Acadian Flycaytchers are alike, with greenish backs and light yellowish flanks. Like most *Empidonax* flycatchers, they have two light-colored wing bars and a pale eye ring. The Acadian is best distinguished by habitat and voice. The song is an explosive *pit-sah* or *pit-see,* differing from the

songs of other species in this family. The Willow Flycatcher is the only other *Empidonax* flycatcher that nests in eastern Oklahoma, although migrants of other species may pass through the state going northward through mid-June and returning southward in July.

Breeding Habitat: Dense woodlands, streamside forests, hardwood swamps, and wooded ravines.

Nest: Normally situated on a lower limb of a large tree out away from the trunk usually 2.4–6 m (8–20 ft) above ground, often over water or dry streambeds. The nest is a rather frail saucer-shaped basket hung between forked twigs of a smallish limb, attached with caterpillar silk. It is composed of various plant materials including weed stems, dead leaves, and grasses, and a good deal of material attached to strands of caterpillar silk is often allowed to hang from the nest giving it a rather unkempt or shaggy appearance.

NESTING ECOLOGY

Season: May–June. Single-brooded.
Eggs: 2–4, but often 3; cream to buffy white, marked with a few small brownish spots.
Development: Incubation is by the female for 13–14 days. Young are provisioned by both sexes and fledge at 13–14 days but continue to be fed for about 12 more days.

DISTRIBUTION AND ABUNDANCE

Rangewide: Breeds from Iowa and southern Wisconsin southward to central Texas and eastward to the Atlantic Ocean. Winters in Central America and northern South America.

Historical: Common in appropriate habitat in the eastern part of state, but becoming more local to rare westward to central Oklahoma.
Current: The Acadian Flycatcher's preference for moist eastern woodlands is reflected by its absence from central and western Oklahoma. Some of the Possible Breeder records may pertain to migrants singing prior to the end of spring migration, which is generally late in *Empidonax* flycatchers.

Population Trend: Breeding Bird Survey data for 1966–2000 show no conclusive trend rangewide (0.1 percent per year, P = 0.67) or in Oklahoma (-0.3 percent per year, P = 0.97).

References: AOU 1998; Baicich and Harrison 1997; Baumgartner and Baumgartner 1992; Bent 1963b; Grula 1974; Harrison 1975; National Geographic Society 1999; Peterson 1996; Sauer et al. 2001; Sibley 2000; Stokes and Stokes 1996; Sutton 1967; Weske 1974

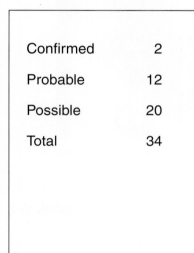

Confirmed	2
Probable	12
Possible	20
Total	34

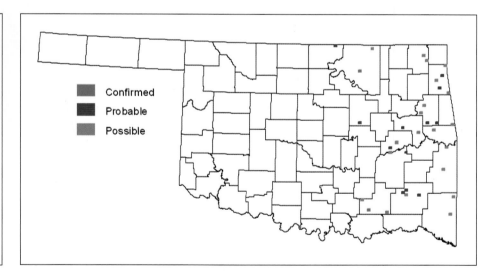

Willow Flycatcher
Empidonax trailii

David E. Fantina

Courtesy of Jim and Deva Burns / Natural Impacts

One of an array of confusingly similar, small brownish-olive flycatchers of the genus *Empidonax,* the Willow Flycatcher was only officially recognized as distinct from the Alder Flycatcher in 1973. It arrives in late spring and spends only about three months on its breeding grounds; the remainder of the year is spent in the tropics.

Description: Males and females are small olive-brown birds with long tails, white throats, olive breasts, and yellow bellies. They are virtually identical in appearance to Alder Flycatchers. The two can only be safely separated by voice; the Willow sings a sneezy, two-note *fitz-bew,* while the Alder sings a buzzy, three-note *fee-bee-o.* Even here, the observer has to be careful because the Alder Flycatcher's third note is not always audible at a distance.

Breeding Habitat: Moist, brushy thickets, open second growth, and riparian woodland, especially where willow and buttonbush are present.

Nest: A compact cup of various plant materials built 2–7 m (5–20 ft) high in a shrub or tree. The nest often has a cottony appearance similar to that of the Yellow Warbler.

NESTING ECOLOGY

Season: May–July. Single-brooded.

Eggs: Usually 3–4; white with brown spots near the larger end. Not reported to be parasitized by the Brown-headed Cowbird in Oklahoma but is commonly parasitized in many other states.

Development: Incubation is by the female for 13–14 days. Young are provisioned by both sexes with the female playing the major role; fledges at 13–15 days.

DISTRIBUTION AND ABUNDANCE

Rangewide: A long-distance migrant, breeding from southern Canada south to Georgia, Tennessee, and northeastern Oklahoma. Winters in Central America and northern South America.

Historical: The fact that until recently this species and the Alder Flycatcher were considered one species (Traill's Flycatcher) clouds the interpretation of historical information. However, it is clear that the Willow Flycatcher has always been a somewhat rare and local summer resident in the state. Historical breeding records come from Craig County in 1912 and Tulsa County in 1927 (3 nests) and 1956 (fledgling observed).

Current: Only a small number of records for Willow Flycatcher were received. Some Willow Flycatchers can still be migrating north in June, and some southward movement begins in July. Therefore, some Possible Breeder blocks may actually represent transient birds. It is too rare and too locally distributed to be appropriately sampled by atlas project methodology. The species is considered a rare summer resident of Craig and Ottawa counties. A 2001 nest record from Red Slough Wildlife Management Area in McCurtain County is well south of the normal breeding range for this species.

Population Trend: Breeding Bird Survey data for 1966–2000 show a decline of 1.2 percent per year rangewide ($P = 0.01$). No trend information are available for Oklahoma. The southwestern subspecies was recently placed on the federal endangered list due to habitat loss and heavy parasitism by Brown-headed Cowbirds.

References: AOU 1998; Baicich and Harrison 1997; Baumgartner and Baumgartner 1992; Brown 1994; Melhop and Tonne 1994; Sauer et al. 2001; Schweitzer et al. 1998; Sedgewick 2000; Sedgewick and Knopf 1988; Stoleson and Finch 1999; Sutton 1967

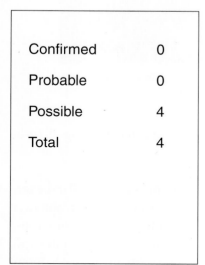

Confirmed	0
Probable	0
Possible	4
Total	4

■ Possible
● Nests 1997-2001

Eastern Phoebe
Sayornis phoebe

Eugene A. Young

Courtesy of Bill Horn

The Eastern Phoebe is a common and conspicuous flycatcher around bridges, culverts, and dwellings. It is very hardy, being one of the first species to return in early spring and one of the last to leave in late fall, and a few even winter in parts of Oklahoma.

Description: A medium-sized flycatcher, males and females look alike with black bill, dull brownish-gray upperparts that are slightly darker on head and tail, and whitish to yellow-olive underparts, especially along the sides. It is similar to the smaller *Empidonax* flycatchers and Eastern Wood-Pewee. Often seen perched and performing its typical tail wagging or flipping behavior, while singing its characteristic song of *fee-o-bee* or *fee-be fee-bee*.

Breeding Habitat: Open woodlands, woodland edge, associated with streams or other nearby water; also near fence rows, farms, towns, cliffs and rocky outcrops, bridges and culverts near water, eaves and rafters of barns and sheds. Commonly nests in similar habitats with other species such as Barn Swallows and Cliff Swallows. Will occupy the same site in successive years.

Nest: A sturdy construction of mud and vegetation lined with hair and fine grass built by the female in

3–14 days; often reuses the same nest the following year, or it may build on top of an old Barn Swallow nest.

NESTING ECOLOGY

Season: March–July. Double-brooded, rarely triple-brooded.

Eggs: Usually 4–5; white, although a few may be spotted. Mean clutch size for 28 nests in Osage County from 1992 to 1996 was 4.4. Regularly parasitized by Brown-headed Cowbirds (9 of 55 nests in Osage County from 1992 to 1996).

Development: Incubation is by the female for 14–17 days. Young are provisioned by both sexes and fledge in about 16 days.

DISTRIBUTION AND ABUNDANCE

Rangewide: A short-distance migrant that breeds from northeast British Columbia, south through the prairie provinces of Canada, east to Nova Scotia, south through the United States to central Georgia, and northeast New Mexico. Winters in the southeastern United States and Texas, south through eastern Mexico.

Historical: Described as common in the eastern portion of the state, less common westward, rare in the Panhandle.

Current: Eastern Phoebe's have a statewide distribution, though they occur with much less frequency in the more arid Panhandle. The high number and proportion of blocks in which phoebes were confirmed as breeders is a reflection of this species' nesting habits, namely a preference to use human structures, especially bridges, near water.

Population Trend: Breeding Bird Survey data for 1966–2000 show a increase of 1.2 percent per year rangewide (P = 0.00) and an increase of 3.4 percent per year in Oklahoma (P = 0.02).

References: AOU 1998; Baicich and Harrison 1997; Baumgartner and Baumgartner 1992; George M. Sutton Avian Research Center unpubl. data; McGee 1978; Murphy 1994; Sauer et al. 2001; Schukman 1974; Sibley 2000; Smith 1942; Stokes and Stokes 1983; Sutton 1967; Terres 1991; Thompson and Ely 1992; Tveten 1993; Weeks 1994

Confirmed	331
Probable	57
Possible	82
Total	470

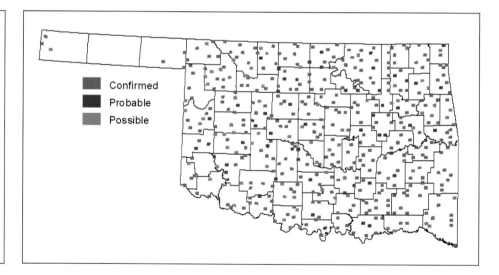

Say's Phoebe
Sayornis saya

David A. Wiggins

Courtesy of Steve Metz

Say's Phoebes are typically found in open country and are characteristic birds of western ranches and farms. Relatively quiet birds, they typically sit on low, exposed perches from which they make short, sallying flights after insects.

Description: Sexes are similar, with dull, gray-brown plumage on the head, back, and upper chest, and rich cinnamon/ochre on the belly and undertail coverts. The male sings a simple, whistled two-note song.

Breeding Habitat: Prefers open habitats such as prairie, sagebrush, and arid canyonlands. It is often found nesting around ranch and farm buildings.

Nest: A cup built by the female and consisting of a mixture of twigs, grasses, leaves, and mud, lined with hair and fine grass. Nest is typically placed under building eaves, in abandoned buildings, under bridges, or on cliff ledges. Will also build on old Barn Swallow and Cliff Swallow nests.

NESTING ECOLOGY

Season: May–July. Often double-brooded.
Eggs: Usually 4–5; pure white, rarely with reddish-brown spots. Rarely parasitized by Brown-headed Cowbirds; one erroneous record is published from Oklahoma.
Development: Incubation is by the female for 14–17 days. Young are provisioned by both sexes and fledge in 14–17, but continue to be fed mostly by the male while the female prepares to nest again.

DISTRIBUTION AND ABUNDANCE

Rangewide: Summer resident throughout western North America, from northern Alaska through western Canada, the western Great Plains, the Great Basin and the southern Rocky Mountains, while permanent resident in southern regions of California, Nevada, Arizona, and New Mexico, as well as southwestern Texas. Resident in northern Baja, and north-central regions of Mexico.

Historical: Described in 1931, 1967, and 1992 as a rare to uncommon summer resident of western Cimarron County. One nest record for Beaver County in 1983 was the first reported outside of Cimarron County.

Current: During the atlas period, Say's Phoebes were found breeding widely throughout the Panhandle region, which is surprising given that they were formerly considered common only in Cimarron County, and were rarely found breeding eastward to Texas and Beaver counties. It therefore appears that the species has undergone a range expansion and now occupies suitable habitat (e.g., abandoned farms, bridges) throughout the shortgrass prairie region of the Panhandle.

Population Trend: Breeding Bird Survey data for 1966–2000 show no conclusive trend rangewide (1.2 percent per year, P = 0.17) or in Oklahoma (7.1 percent per year, P = 0.54). This apparent increase in Oklahoma is supported by the expanded range of this species in the state over the past 20 years.

References: Baicich and Harrison 1997; Baumgartner and Baumgartner 1992; Dunn 1984; Johnsgard 1979; Nice 1931; Sauer et al. 2001; Schukman and Wolf 1998; Sutton 1967; Tate 1923; Tyler and Dunn 1984

Confirmed	20
Probable	4
Possible	1
Total	25

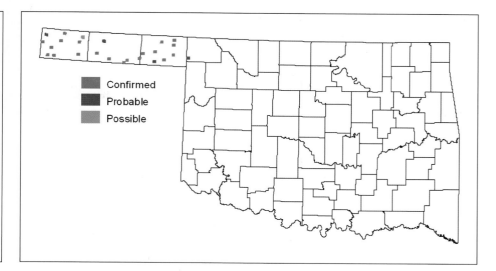

Confirmed
Probable
Possible

Vermilion Flycatcher
Pyrocephalus rubinus

John S. Shackford

Courtesy of Bob Gress

The brilliantly colored adult male Vermilion Flycatcher is truly a wonder of nature, one of North America's most striking species. In spite of the male's remarkable color, this small, somewhat retiring species is easily overlooked. In Oklahoma, it is a rare breeder, primarily in northwestern Cimarron County.

Description: The male in full adult plumage has a brilliant red head, throat, and breast, black on the wings and back, as well as a black eye stripe from nape to bill. The female is brownish-gray above and has a whitish breast finely streaked with gray and a rose wash on the belly. Immature males are similar to adult females and show variable and increasing amounts of red as they mature. Song consists of high, sharp notes and a trill.

Breeding Habitat: Most frequently selects cottonwood, willow, or mesquite trees, usually near water.

Nest: Shallow cup composed of small twigs, rootlets, weeds, etc., and lined with finer material such as hairs, spider webs, and feathers. Usually placed in the fork of a horizontal limb about 2.5–6 m (8–20 ft) high.

NESTING ECOLOGY

Season: April–June. Apparently double-brooded.
Eggs: Usually 2–3; buffy or pure to creamy white,

238

boldly blotched with dark brown and lavender, especially near the larger end. Infrequently parasitized by the Brown-headed Cowbird.

Development: Incubation is by the female for 13–14 days. Young are provisioned by both sexes and fledge at 14–16 days. Males may take charge of fledged young while the female begins a new nest.

DISTRIBUTION AND ABUNDANCE

Rangewide: Normally breeds from southern California and Nevada, central Arizona, southern New Mexico, and western and southern Texas south to Central America. In winter, tends to retire from northern portion of range, also moving eastward into southeastern Texas and eastern Mexico.

Historical: First seen in Oklahoma in Tulsa in 1949. Described in 1992 as an irregular summer resident. Nesting records are from Major County in 1956 (two nests), Lincoln County in 1960 (two nests), and Cimarron County in 1982 (two nests), 1985, and 1990. A "family group" was reported in August of 1972 in Washington County.

Current: A very rare breeder in the Black Mesa area of Cimarron County. Elsewhere, widespread nestings are possible but extremely rare. A pair nested at Black Mesa State Park in Cimarron County in 2002, one year after the close of atlas project fieldwork.

Population Trend: Breeding Bird Survey data for 1966–2000 show no conclusive trend rangewide (-3.5 percent per year, P = 0.14). No trend data are available for Oklahoma.

References: AOU 1998; Baicich and Harrison 1997; Baumgartner and Baumgartner 1992; Bent 1963b; Johnsgard 1979; Matthews 1974; Peterjohn and Sauer 1999; Sauer et al. 2001; Sutton 1967; Terres 1980; Tomer 1983; Webster 1990; Wolf and Jones 2000

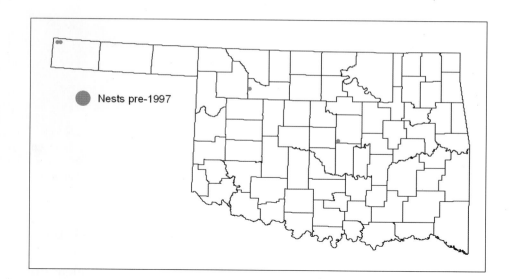

Nests pre-1997

Ash-throated Flycatcher
Myiarchus cinerascens

Sebastian T. Patti

A medium-sized pale *Myiarchus* of the western and southwestern United States, the Ash-throated Flycatcher is often referred to as the "aridland counterpart of the Great Crested Flycatcher." The Ash-throated inhabits riparian woodlands, pinyon-juniper woodlots, and mesquite-cactus desert grasslands. It is, as are all its congeners, a cavity nester.

Description: Sexes similar. The identification of *Myiarchus* flycatchers can be very difficult. The Ash-throated is somewhat smaller and considerably slimmer than the Great Crested Flycatcher. The upperparts are brownish gray, the throat whitish, the upper breast pale gray, and the remainder of the underparts are very pale

yellow, compared to the larger and darker Great Crested that has brighter yellow underparts. The flight feathers have considerable rufous that can be seen even when the bird is at rest. The familiar call is a two-syllable *ka-BRICK!*

Breeding Habitat: Open stands of cottonwoods, willows, mesquite, or saltcedar. Also pinyon-juniper woodlands. Dense woodlands are avoided by this species.

Nest: A cup placed in a natural or artificial cavity and constructed of plant materials such as stems, roots, or grasses. The nest is rarely higher than 6 m (20 ft) above ground. Woodpecker holes or natural cavities in cottonwoods, junipers, or pinyons are most often used, but nest boxes are readily used as well.

NESTING ECOLOGY

Season: May–July. Single-brooded.
Eggs: Usually 4–5; cream or buff colored with purple-brown longitudinal streaks or lines.
Development: Incubation is by the female for 13–15 days. Young are provisioned by both sexes and leave the nest at 16–17 days.

DISTRIBUTION AND ABUNDANCE

Rangewide: Breeds from southeastern Washington south and east to Colorado, parts of western Kansas and Oklahoma, and central Texas, and south to central Mexico. Migratory throughout the United States' portion of the species' range, except in southwestern Arizona, where it may be found year round. Also winters in south Texas and Mexico.
Historical: Considered a summer resident in Cimarron

County, as well as several other counties in southwestern Oklahoma. Evidence of nesting reported from Beckham, Cimarron, Comanche, Harmon, Jackson, Kingfisher, and Tillman counties.
Current: This species is limited in its breeding range to the far-western portions of the state. The species was located during the atlas project period in all three Panhandle counties, several far-western counties in the main body of the state, and in several counties in southwestern Oklahoma. The only confirmed breeding for the species came from a block in Cimarron County.

Population Trend: Breeding Bird Survey data for 1966–2000 show an increase of 1.2 percent per year rangewide (P = 0.01) and a very large increase in Oklahoma (27.7 percent per year, P = 0.10), although the data are not robust for this species.

References: AOU 1998; Busby and Zimmerman 2001; Baumgartner and Baumgartner 2001; Dexter 1998; Oberholser 1974; Sauer et al. 2001; Shackford and Harden 1989; Sibley 2000; Sutton 1967; Thompson and Ely 1992

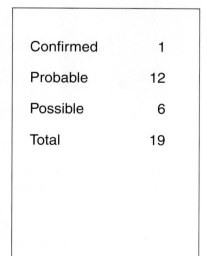

Confirmed	1
Probable	12
Possible	6
Total	19

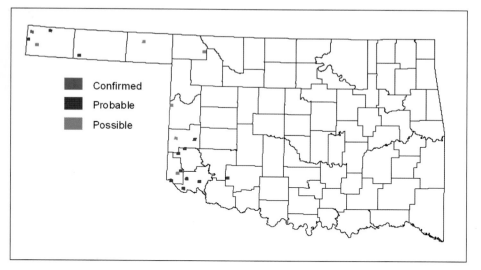

Great Crested Flycatcher
Myiarchus crinitus

Melinda Droege

One of Oklahoma's two cavity nesting flycatchers, the Great Crested Flycatcher has chosen some interesting and sometimes perilous nest sites, including a hollow section of abandoned steel farm equipment standing in full sun in one McCurtain County atlas block. Its loud calls are the best indication of its presence in open woodlands of Oklahoma.

Description: This large, noisy flycatcher arrives in Oklahoma early in April with its unmistakable whistled *whee-eep* call and demanding *prrr-eet* chatter. It is distinctive with its olive-brown back, dark gray throat and breast, bright yellow belly and undertail coverts, and rufous wings and tail. Topped with a bushy crest and a large bill, this species can be confused with the Ash-throated Flycatcher, with which it overlaps to some extent in western Oklahoma.

Breeding Habitat: This species prefers open deciduous woodlands, old orchards, parks, and towns in central and eastern Oklahoma. At the western edge of its range it is limited to river valleys.

Nest: Built in a natural cavity or abandoned woodpecker hole about 3–6 m (10–20 ft) up in either a live or dead tree. Often uses birdhouses, drain spouts, and other artificial structures. Both sexes fill the cavity with twigs, leaves, hair, fibers, fur, and other trash, which almost always includes snakeskin or cellophane. A small cup for the eggs formed in the bulky mass is lined with finer material and feathers.

NESTING ECOLOGY

Season: May–June. Single-brooded, but may replace lost clutches.

Eggs: Usually 5, but variable; creamy white to yellowish heavily streaked with purple or lavender.

Development: Incubation is by the female for 13–15 days. Young are provisioned by both sexes and leave the nest at 14–15 days, but remain with parents for up to 3 weeks.

DISTRIBUTION AND ABUNDANCE

Rangewide: Summer resident over the eastern United States and southern Canada to approximately the western edge of the plains states. Winters in south Florida, Mexico, and south to northern South America.

Historical: Described as a common summer resident of eastern and central Oklahoma and in smaller numbers westward; rare in the Panhandle.

Current: Widespread throughout the main body of the state, the Great Crested Flycatcher is easily detected due to its conspicuous behavior and vocalizations. It has apparently been extending its range westward in recent years, as seen in its frequency of occurrence in western Oklahoma and the eastern Panhandle.

Population Trend: Breeding Bird Survey data for 1966–2000 show no conclusive trend rangewide (0.0 percent per year, P = 0.87) or in Oklahoma (-0.3 percent per year, P = 0.77).

References: AOU 1998; Baicich and Harrison 1997; Baumgartner and Baumgartner 1992; Bent 1963b; Ehrlich et al. 1988; Harrison 1975; Johnsgard 1979; Lanyon 1997; Mousely 1934; Sauer et al. 2001; Stauffer and Best 1980; Sutton 1967

Confirmed	89
Probable	184
Possible	145
Total	418

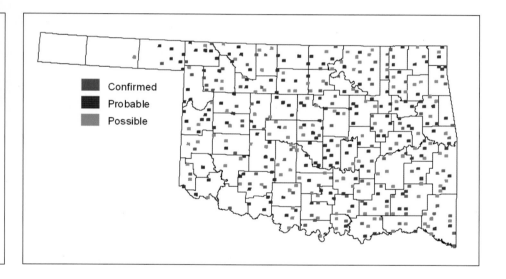

Cassin's Kingbird
Tyrannus vociferans

Sebastian T. Patti

Courtesy of wildlifedepartment.com

A large, vocal flycatcher primarily found in the southwestern United States, Cassin's Kingbird is superficially similar to the more-widespread Western Kingbird, with which it overlaps geographically in the western portion of its range. Often more aggressive than other members of the genus, Cassin's Kingbirds may "rule the roost" and will exclude other tyrannid flycatchers, at least in suboptimal habitats, from selected foraging areas.

Description: Sexes similar. A large flycatcher with a lemon-yellow lower breast, belly, and undertail coverts. The head, nape, back, throat, and upper breast are a dark bluish gray, contrasting sharply with a clean white malar and chin. Wings are brownish, and the tail

blackish with a pale tip. The call is a clean, loud *CHICK-keeer,* often repeated in a series slowly descending in tone. This species may be confused with the Western Kingbird, which has a paler head and throat and white edges to the outer tail feathers.

Breeding Habitat: Riparian woodlands, pinyon-juniper woodlots, grasslands, and rural shelterbelts are all occupied by the species. Large cottonwoods are often used as nest sites. There may be overlap with Western Kingbirds in these areas, and the two species may nest near each other.

Nest: Constructed by the female of materials gathered from the ground such as twigs, roots, plant stalks, bark, and the like. Pieces of string, leaves, or even rags are often worked in. The inner portion of the nest is usually lined with softer materials such as grasses, feathers, and cottonwood seeds. The nest is "saddled over" a horizontal branch, often 6–12 m (20–40 ft) up.

NESTING ECOLOGY

Season: Primarily May–June. Single-brooded, but failed nests are often replaced.

Eggs: Usually 3–4; slightly glossy in texture, and white with brown spots usually concentrated at the large end. The species is a rare host of the Brown-headed Cowbird; not known in Oklahoma.

Development: Incubation is by the female for 14–16 days, while the male guards the nest. Young are provisioned by both sexes and fledge in about 14 days.

DISTRIBUTION AND ABUNDANCE

Rangewide: Breeds from southeastern Montana through extreme eastern Wyoming, far-western Nebraska, and in southwestern South Dakota. Largest portion of range extends from southeastern and southwestern Colorado and the northwestern part of the Oklahoma Panhandle south and west through central and western New Mexico, west Texas, southern Utah, northern and eastern Arizona, and south through southern Mexico. Also in central and southern California. U.S. populations winter in Mexico.

Historical: First record in Oklahoma was a nesting bird found in Cimarron County in 1935. Since described as a transient and uncommon summer resident, primarily in Cimarron County, with a few non-breeding observations east of the Panhandle.

Current: Generally limited to riparian woodlands and farm/ranch yards with cottonwoods in northwestern Cimarron County. The species was confirmed as breeding on 4 atlas blocks located in this part of the state. Because Cassin's and Western kingbirds often nest close to one another, one observation from a block on the Cimarron River north of Boise City in 1997 seems significant. An adult Cassin's Kingbird was watched repeatedly feeding a young Western Kingbird.

Population Trend: Breeding Bird Survey data for 1966–2000 show no conclusive trend rangewide (0.6 percent per year, P = 0.63). No trend data are available for Oklahoma.

References: AOU 1998; Baicich and Harrison 1997; Baumgartner and Baumgartner 1992; Colvin 1939; Jones 1998; Oberholser 1974; Sauer et al. 2001; Seyffert 2001; Sutton 1967; Thompson and Ely 1992; Tweit and Tweit 2000

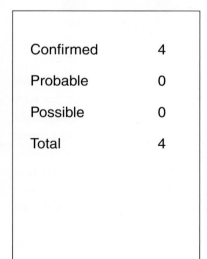

Confirmed	4
Probable	0
Possible	0
Total	4

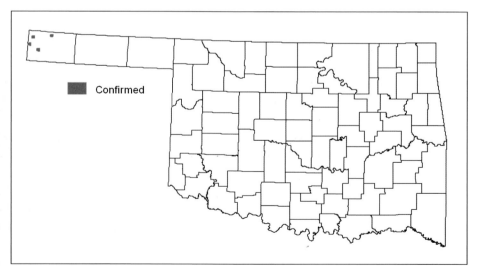

Western Kingbird
Tyrannus verticalis

Thomas G. Shane

Courtesy of Bill Horn

If the Eastern Bluebird is the harbinger of spring in the east, the Western Kingbird holds the position on the Great Plains. Its arrival is announced by a nearly constant chatter. It is a tyrant both in rural areas as well as cities and towns, where it is often seen chasing hawks or dive-bombing pet cats. Young Eleanor Henderson, while collecting data in and around her home in Texas County for her master's thesis in the early 1930s, periodically checked a kingbird nest in her parent's farmyard. Thereafter, the pair would dive at her each time she departed the house, but would never dive at her parents.

Description: A large flycatcher, both sexes having a black bill, pale gray head and breast, sulphur-yellow underparts, brownish-black wings, and a black tail with white outer edges. One must rise early, an hour or more before sunrise before any other species begins to sing, to hear the Western Kingbird give its most lovely vocalizations of the day, described as a complex series of high-pitched notes. The rest of the day is all chatter.

Breeding Habitat: Most often in open riparian woodlands or in urban areas with trees.

Nest: An open cup, usually placed on a utility pole, in a deciduous tree, and occasionally in a pine; made of forb stems, grasses, rootlets, fine twigs, cotton, and other plant fibers. Often includes a variety of man-made items.

NESTING ECOLOGY

Season: May–August. Normally single-brooded.

Eggs: Usually 4; creamy white with blotches of brown most prominent near the large end. Rarely parasitized by the Brown-headed Cowbird.

Development: Incubation is by the female for 14 days. Young are provisioned by both sexes and fledge at 13–19 days.

Hybridization: Rare with Scissor-tailed Flycatcher.

DISTRIBUTION AND ABUNDANCE

Rangewide: Breeds from British Columbia and Manitoba south through California and Oklahoma to Sonora, Mexico, and southern Texas. Winters primarily on the Pacific slope from Mexico to Costa Rica.

Historical: Described in 1931 as a summer resident in the western half of the state, having greatly expanded its range eastward in the preceding 25 years. By 1992, described as a common to abundant summer resident in western and central Oklahoma and decreasing eastward.

Current: The Western Kingbird has been making advances eastward for many decades and will most likely continue its range expansion. The high percentage of blocks with confirmed breeding records is likely due to the ease of finding nests on utility poles and in dead trees, along with the conspicuous and vocal fledglings seen later in the nesting cycle.

Population Trend: Breeding Bird Survey data for 1966–2000 show no conclusive trend rangewide (0.2 percent per year, P = 0.31) and a decline of 4.8 percent per year in Oklahoma (P = 0.00).

References: AOU 1998; Baicich and Harrison 1997; Baumgarten and Baumgartner 1992; Davis and Webster 1970; Gamble and Bergin 1996; Grzybowski 1981; Henderson 1933; Nice 1924, 1931; Sauer et al. 2001; Sheffield 1993; Sutton 1967, 1986; Tyler and Parkes 1992

Confirmed	137
Probable	71
Possible	67
Total	275

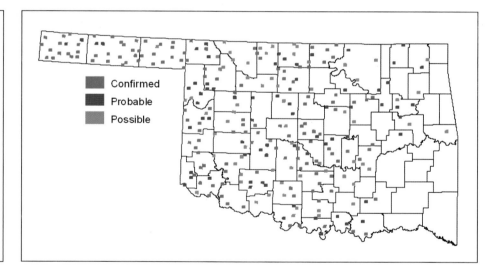

Eastern Kingbird

Tyrannus tyrannus

Gregory A. Smith

Courtesy of M. Frank Carl

"Tyrannus" means tyrant, despot, or king. Eastern Kingbirds, and kingbirds in general, are certainly deserving of this name. They are aggressive defenders of their territories and nests. Hawks, crows, jays, snakes, cats, and dogs are soon made aware of this quality when they wander into a kingbird-protected area. Often seen sallying forth from shrubs or fences, kingbirds are highly beneficial insectivores, ridding the countryside of numerous flying pests.

Description: Sexes similar. Fairly large tyrant flycatchers with contrasting black upperparts and white underparts and a faint gray chest band. There is a slight crest on a dark black head with a small central concealed patch of colored feathers varying from orange or red to yellow. The tail is black with a terminal white band. Typical song is a series of sharp, rasping notes ending with a descending buzz. Common calls include a sharp, buzzy *kzeer.*

Breeding Habitat: Open areas with scattered trees or tall shrubs, hedgerows, orchards, shelterbelts, and forest areas with uneven canopies providing foraging vantage points.

Nest: Large deep cup built by the female and composed of twigs, weed stems and other plant material, straw, twine, feathers, string, cloth, or wool, with loose material on the outside. Lined with finer materials such as dry grass, rootlets, and hair. Nests are placed in open areas near the end of a horizontal tree branch, away from the trunk, sometimes on stumps or posts; very often over water. Nest height varies but is usually below 8 m (26 ft).

NESTING ECOLOGY

Season: May–July. Single-brooded, but may replace lost clutches.

Eggs: Usually 3–4; creamy white or pinkish, speckled or spotted with reddish brown or gray. Markings may be bold and concentrated at the larger end. Mean clutch size of 150 nests in Osage and Washington counties from 1992 to 1996 was 3.4. Cowbird parasitism does occur, but kingbirds are very efficient at detecting and rejecting cowbird eggs.

Development: Incubation is by the female for 14–17 days. Young are brooded by the female for about 10 days with both parents sharing feeding duties. Young leave the nest at 16–17 days and remain with their parents in a family group for 30 days or more.

DISTRIBUTION AND ABUNDANCE

Rangewide: Eastern Kingbirds have the most extensive breeding range of all North American flycatchers. They breed from northwestern and southeastern Canada south to southern Texas and the southeastern United States. They occur throughout most of the western United States except for the desert southwest. They winter in South America.

Historical: Described as a summer resident statewide, less common in the southwest and Panhandle.

Current: The Eastern Kingbird is a conspicuous breeder throughout the state, with numbers diminishing somewhat in the far-western Panhandle. The breeding displays and territorial behavior of this species make it difficult to miss within a block.

Population Trend: Breeding Bird Survey data for 1966–2000 show a decline of 0.9 percent per year rangewide (P = 0.00) and a decline of 2.3 percent per year in Oklahoma (P = 0.00).

References: AOU 1998; Baicich and Harrison 1997; Baumgartner and Baumgartner 1992; Baumgartner and Howell 1942, 1947; Baumgartner and Lawrence 1953; Bay 1996; Bent 1963b; Carter 1961; Force 1929; George M. Sutton Avian Research Center unpubl. data; Johnsgard 1979; Kaufman 1996; Messerly 1972; Moore 1927; Murphy 1996; Nice 1923, 1927, 1931; Norman 1976, 1982, 1987; Ortenburger 1926; Parmley 1974; Sheffield 1993; Sauer et al. 2001; Saunders 1926; Silver 1952; Sutton 1967, 1977; Tate 1923; Thompson and Ely 1992; Tyler 1994; Wood and Schnell 1984

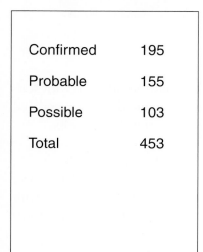

Confirmed	195
Probable	155
Possible	103
Total	453

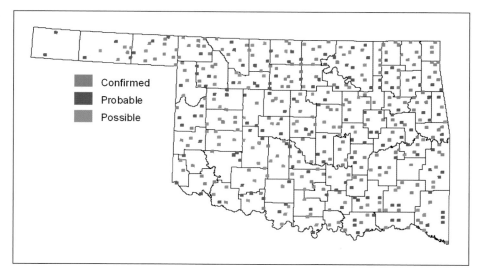

Scissor-tailed Flycatcher
Tyrannus forficatus

John M. Dole

Courtesy of Bill Horn

The state bird of Oklahoma, the Scissor-tailed Flycatcher is also one of the most beautiful birds in the United States. Oklahomans eagerly await the annual return of the Scissor-tail in late March and early April.

Description: The head, back, and chest are pearl gray; the throat is white; wings and extremely long tail are dark brown to black. The tail is deeply forked and the outer edges and tips are white. The lower belly, under-tail coverts, and wing linings are washed in salmon pink and the wing axillaries are dark reddish salmon. The red crown patch is rarely visible. Sexes are similar, but females have shorter tails than males.

Breeding Habitat: Open prairies and fields with scattered trees and shrubs. Also found along woodland edges and hedgerows and occasionally in towns.

Nest: A loose cup built by the female of thin twigs, rootlets, weed stems, husks, twine, cotton, plant down, wool, paper, rags, and other debris, and lined with rootlets, hair, and cotton. Located 1.5–15 m (5–50 ft) high in trees or on utility pole cross members.

NESTING ECOLOGY

Season: April–July. Rarely double-brooded.
Eggs: Usually 4–5; white, creamy white, or slightly

pinkish, blotched and spotted with brown, dark red, or purple. Rarely parasitized by Brown-headed Cowbirds.
Development: Incubation is by the female for 14–15 days. Young are provisioned by both sexes and leave the nest in 14–17 days.
Hybridization: Rare with Western Kingbird.

DISTRIBUTION AND ABUNDANCE

Rangewide: The limited breeding range of this species extends from southwestern Missouri, Arkansas, and western Louisiana west to southeastern Colorado and southeastern New Mexico. Southern Nebraska is the northern limit and northeastern Mexico is the southern edge of the breeding range, although its range appears to be expanding eastward. Winters from southern Mexico south to Costa Rica; some birds also winter in southern Florida.
Historical: Occurred in all regions of Oklahoma. Described as most common in central and western Oklahoma.
Current: Found virtually throughout the state, the Scissor-tailed Flycatcher's range abruptly stops in Texas County in the Panhandle. The remarkably high number of nesting confirmations for this species is due to the fact that it often nests in isolated trees which are readily visible and to the fact that young birds retain their distinctively short tails for a long period of time and perch conspicuously in family groups as fledglings. Population density appears to be lower in southeastern Oklahoma, probably due to lower availability of open habitat.

Population Trend: Breeding Bird Survey data for 1966–2000 show no conclusive trend rangewide (0.0 percent per year, P = 0.97) and a decline of 2.4 percent per year in Oklahoma (P = 0.00).

References: AOU 1998; Baicich and Harrison 1997; Baumgartner and Baumgartner 1992; Davis and Webster 1970; Freeman 1993; Howell and Webb 1995; Kaufman 1996; National Geographic Society 1999; Parmley 1978; Regosin 1993, 1994a, 1994b, 1998; Regosin and Pruett-Jones 1995; Sauer et al. 2001; Sutton 1967; Tyler 1979; Tyler and Bechtold 1996; Tyler and Parkes 1992; Withgott 1991

Confirmed	415
Probable	77
Possible	23
Total	515

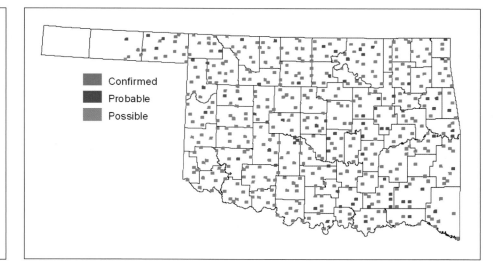

Loggerhead Shrike
Lanius ludovicianus

Gregory A. Smith

Courtesy of Bill Horn

The Loggerhead Shrike is the only shrike species occurring exclusively in North America. More raptor-like in habits, the presence of this species is often given away by the sight of a grasshopper, mouse, lizard, or small bird impaled along a barbed-wire fence or on a thorn. "Butcherbird," as it is sometimes known, seems an appropriate moniker.

Description: Sexes similar. Medium-sized passerines, resembling Northern Mockingbird in size and coloration. More compact than a mockingbird, shrikes have stout, hooked bills, bluish-gray backs and heads, and white or grayish-white underparts with faint barring in juveniles. Distinctive black masks are present on the face, extending through the eye and across the top of the bill. The wings are black with large white patches. Vocalizations are limited but generally given as a series of two-syllable phrases such as *krrrDI* or *JEEuk*.

Breeding Habitat: Open country with scattered trees or shrubs, shelterbelts, cemeteries, farmsteads, or hedgerows. Uncommon to rare in heavily wooded areas.

Nest: A bulky cup of twigs, weeds, and rootlets. Most are lined with plant matter, bark, fur, roots, or feathers. The female is responsible for most nest-building chores, although the male will help gather nest material. Nests are placed 1.2–6.1 m (4–20 ft) above ground in a variety of trees and shrubs, usually concealed by twigs and foliage. In Oklahoma, Osage orange is a preferred nesting tree, along with hackberry and Chinese elm.

NESTING ECOLOGY

Season: March–June. Double- to triple-brooded.

Eggs: Usually 4–5; creamy white or faintly tinted buff or gray with various speckling and blotching of browns or purples. Large markings are often concentrated at the larger end. Cowbird parasitism has been documented, although it is rare and has not been reported in Oklahoma. Shrikes will actively defend nests approached by cowbirds.

Development: Incubation is by the female for 16 days. Young are provisioned by both sexes and fledge at about 18 days. Young shrikes learn impaling techniques by 30 days, but remain dependent on their parents for 40–45 days.

DISTRIBUTION AND ABUNDANCE

Rangewide: Breeds from central Alberta south throughout much of the United States. However, breeding populations are absent from the northeastern United States, eastern Canada, western Canada, and far-northen Canada and Alaska. Northern populations are migratory and move into southern latitudes of the United States and Mexico in winter.

Historical: Described as an uncommon summer resident and common winter resident throughout Oklahoma, but less common in wooded areas of eastern Oklahoma.

Current: Shrikes are common breeders throughout the state except for the heavily forested southeastern region, where they are nearly absent. Their well-hidden nests may account for the large numbers of blocks scored as Possible or Probable rather than Confirmed. The large number of blocks throughout the state with shrike records is a positive result for a species that has been on the decline.

Population Trend: Breeding Bird Survey data for 1966–2000 show a decline of 3.6 percent per year rangewide (P = 0.00) and a decline of 5.4 percent per year in Oklahoma (P = 0.00). The Loggerhead Shrike is currently listed as a species of special concern in several states, including the subspecies that occurs as a migrant in Oklahoma.

References: AOU 1998; Baicich and Harrison 1997; Baumgartner and Baumgartner 1992; Baumgartner and Howell 1942, 1947; Bent 1965b; Black 1976, 1985; Comer and Freeland 1980; Cooksey 1968; Dirck 1986; Force 1929; Frings and Frings 1976; Johnsgard 1979; Kaufman 1996; Leppla and Gordon 1978; Moore 1927; Nice 1923, 1927, 1931; Sauer et al. 2001; Saunders 1926; Shannon 1921; Silver 1952; Smith 1991; Sutton 1967, 1977a, 1986a; Sutton and Tyler 1978; Tate 1923, 1924; Tomer 1974; Tyler 1987, 1991b, 1992c, 1994e; Tyler and Bechtold 1996; Josef 1996; Wood and Schnell 1984

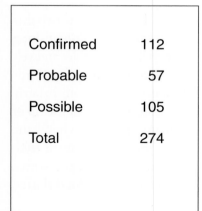

Confirmed	112
Probable	57
Possible	105
Total	274

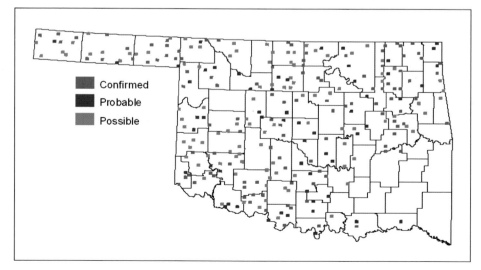

White-eyed Vireo
Vireo griseus

Mark Howery

The White-eyed Vireo is a vocal yet easily over-looked songbird that can be locally common during the spring and summer in moist thickets across much of eastern Oklahoma. White-eyed Vireo is classified as a Neotropical migrant, and much of the U.S. population migrates to Mexico and Central America during the winter months. This is one of the first migrants to return to Oklahoma in the spring, and males can be heard proclaiming their territories as early as the end of March, as the thickets in which they will nest are just beginning to leaf out.

Description: White-eyed Vireos are small songbirds with greenish plumage on the head, back, wings, and tail. The breast and belly are predominately white with

a yellowish wash on each side. Each wing has two distinct white wing bars. The vireo's most distinguishing plumage characteristics are its yellow spectacles and yellow feathering on the lores. Additionally, adult birds have white eyes. The White-eyed Vireo's bill is fairly thick for its size, and there is a slight hook on the tip of the upper mandible. Like many species of vireos, the males are very vocal and are more easily heard than seen. The song is loud and repetitious. It begins with a pronounced chip note followed by several loud slurred notes.

Breeding Habitat: Dense, deciduous thickets. In central Oklahoma, White-eyed Vireos are most often found along streams in dense second-growth forests and riparian forests with dense understory thickets. In eastern Oklahoma they favor thickets along streams and in flood plains and other low-elevation sites, but they also occupy moist second-growth forests such as those that develop following the abandonment of pasture land or after clear-cutting.

Nest: A cup constructed of grass, roots, and small twigs bound together by spider webbing and fine plant fibers. It is placed in a hanging position from the fork of a branch on a small tree or shrub, often 1.5–4.5 m (5–15 ft) high. Usually difficult to find due to placement among dense branches and tangles of briars and vines.

NESTING ECOLOGY

Season: April–July. Often double-brooded.
Eggs: Usually 4; white with dark brown speckling.
Development: Incubation is by the female for 13–16 days. Young are provisioned by both sexes and fledge at 10–13 days, but remain under the parents' care for an additional 3–4 weeks. White-eyed Vireo nests are commonly parasitized by Brown-headed Cowbirds.

DISTRIBUTION AND ABUNDANCE

Rangewide: The White-eyed Vireo is found throughout the southeastern United States from the Ohio Valley and Ozark Plateau southward. They are summer residents across most of their range, but are year-round residents in Florida, portions of the Caribbean, and along the Gulf Coast. The wintering range extends through eastern Mexico to Honduras.

Historical: Described as a common to uncommon summer resident in the eastern half of the state, and rare and local west to Washington, Caddo, Comanche, and Love counties.

Current: The White-eyed Vireo's preference for moist and/or low-elevation thickets is evident in its decreasing frequency across central Oklahoma and its near absence in the western part of the state. Because this species is vocal and therefore easily detected on roadside censuses, atlas project volunteers probably located it in most blocks in which it occurred. However, because of its preference for thickets and dense cover, it was not frequently confirmed as a breeding species. Some of the western records may represent errant spring migrants rather than breeding individuals.

Population Trend: Breeding Bird Survey data for 1966–2000 show no conclusive trend rangewide (0.1 percent per year, P = 0.78) or in Oklahoma (1.4 percent per year, P = 0.49).

References: Baicich and Harrison 1997; Baumgartner and Baumgartner 1992; Bradley 1980; DeGraaf and Rappole 1995; Ehrlich et al. 1988; Grzybowski 1994; Hopp et al. 1995; Sauer et al. 2001; Sutton 1967

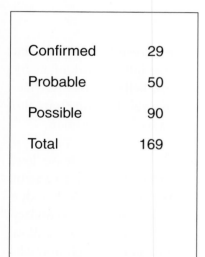

Confirmed	29
Probable	50
Possible	90
Total	169

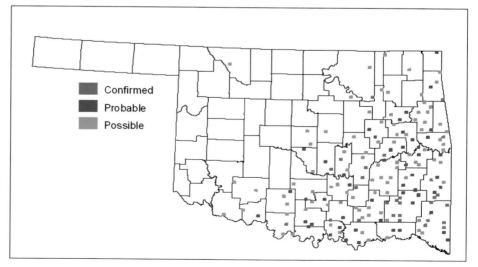

Bell's Vireo
Vireo bellii

Victoria J. Byre

Courtesy of Bill Horn

The nondescript and lively but rather hard to see Bell's Vireo is more active than most vireos as it bustles about, foraging in low shrubs and occasionally even darting out to catch insects in midair. It is also very aggressive in defense of its nest, though cowbirds are not deterred.

Description: Both sexes are grayish or greenish gray above and whitish or yellowish white below, with a white line above the eye. Field marks include an indistinct whitish eye ring and two whitish wing bars, the upper one faint and sometimes absent. Bell's Vireo is distinguished from the Warbling Vireo by its different shape and somewhat brighter colors, wing bars, and preferred habitat. It is distinguished from the Ruby-

crowned Kinglet, which can be seen in similar habitat during migration, by its larger bill and lack of a dark area below the lower wing bar. Bell's Vireo's easily recognizable, rapid, harsh but musical chattering song also helps give away its identity as well as its location.

Breeding Habitat: Bell's Vireos breed in dense, low, shrubby vegetation that is generally characteristic of early successional areas. River bottom lands that, due to periodic flooding, continually produce secondary vegetation such as 2–3 m (6.5–10 ft) high willow thickets are favored, as are mesquite, low plum thickets, and shrubby roadside growth.

Nest: A small but deeply rounded cup suspended from

a twig fork by the rim. It is constructed of grass and leaf fragments, bark strips, and sometimes feathers, and is bound together with spider's webs and cocoons. It is lined with fine grasses, thin weed stems, and hair and is usually located about 1 m (3 ft) above ground, but occasionally higher or lower.

NESTING ECOLOGY

Season: Primarily May–July. Possibly double-brooded in Oklahoma.

Eggs: Usually 3–5, often 4; white with sparsely scattered brownish specks. Commonly parasitized by Brown-headed Cowbirds, which greatly reduces vireo nesting success and productivity. Twenty-two of 31 Marshall County nests (71 percent) and 18 of 61 Payne County nests (30 percent) were observed to be parasitized in the early 1960s. Ten of 21 nests (48 percent) in Osage and Washington counties from 1992 to 1996 were observed to be parasitized.

Development: Incubation is by both sexes for 14–15 days. Young are provisioned by both sexes and fledge at 10–12 days.

DISTRIBUTION AND ABUNDANCE

Rangewide: In the United States, breeds locally in the north-central Great Plains, the Midwest, and south through the south-central and southwestern states including southern California. It also breeds locally throughout much of Mexico and winters as far south as Honduras and northern Nicaragua.

Historical: Described as once abundant in northeastern and central Oklahoma and in some localities westward and as rare in the Panhandle and heavily wooded eastern areas. A reduction in numbers since the 1960s has been noted. Although populations of this species are generally in decline, they can be locally abundant in suitable habitat.

Current: Bell's Vireos are found in suitable habitat at scattered locations throughout the state except in the western Panhandle. The high proportion of blocks scored as Possible is likely a result of the vireo's distinctive and persistent territorial singing.

Population Trend: Breeding Bird Survey data for 1966–2000 show a decline of 3.0 percent per year rangewide (P = 0.00) and a decline of 7.2 percent per year in Oklahoma (P = 0.00).

References: AOU 1998; Baicich and Harrison 1997; Barlow 1964; Bent 1965b; Brown 1993; Byre and Kuhnert 1996; Ely 1957; Franzreb 1989; George M. Sutton Avian Research Center unpubl. data; Harris 1986; Hellack 1969; Nice 1929, 1931; Overmire 1962, 1963; Sauer et al. 2001; Stokes 1996; Sutton 1967; Wiens 1963

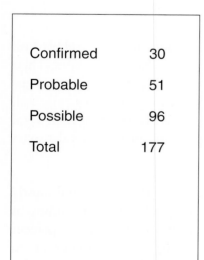

Confirmed	30
Probable	51
Possible	96
Total	177

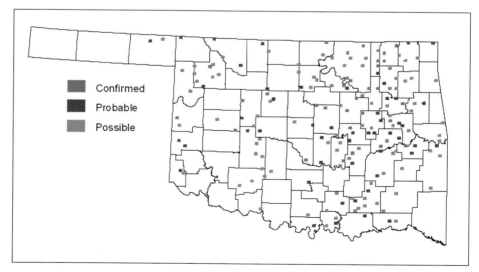

Black-capped Vireo
Vireo atricapillus

Joseph A. Grzybowski

The Black-capped Vireo is an active foliage-gleaning songbird of early successional shrubby habitats. It is unique among vireos in exhibiting plumage differences in cap color between males and females, delayed-plumage maturation in yearling males, and an exceptionally large syllable repertoire for its songs. Formerly a locally common species in much of its range, its numbers have been reduced by habitat loss (primarily from fire suppression and consequent vegetation maturation) and cowbird parasitism. It can now be found in Oklahoma only in the Wichita Mountains, plus a few in isolated outposts elsewhere.

Description: Adults have black (males) or gray (females) caps with broad white spectacles interrupted above eye, green backs, two pale wing bars, white throats, olive to yellowish sides, red eyes, and blackish legs and feet. Yearling males have gray napes. Their songs are made up of a series of 2–5 note phrases, some notes clear, others raspy. Males sing persistently well into the heat of the day, generally becoming more vocal in midmorning when singing of other local species wane.

Breeding Habitat: Low-growth shrubby and mostly deciduous habitat with spaces between clumps of woody vegetation (generally more than 50 percent open) where ample aproning of vegetation occurs to ground level. Areas of persistent habitat occur most frequently in rocky terrain or eroded hillsides or gullies. Tends to invade areas within a few years of burning where oaks resprout from their roots.

Nest: Pendant nest of dead grass, leaves, and spider silk is placed in the fork of a branch most frequently only a meter (3 ft) high, and hanging into a more open enclave of the vegetation. The cup tends to be deeper than that of other vireo nests.

NESTING ECOLOGY

Season: Late April–early July, a few later. Can be double-brooded.

Eggs: 3–4; white (unusual among vireos). Frequent host of Brown-headed Cowbird. Observed levels of parasitism for the 1950s and 1980s in Caddo County involved 47 percent and 100 percent of nests found, respectively. Cowbird control is now used around some nesting populations.

Development: Incubation is by both sexes for 14–17 days. Young are provisioned by both sexes and fledge at 9–12 days; post-fledgling care generally for 35–40 days, sometimes only 28, or more than 50.

DISTRIBUTION AND ABUNDANCE

Rangewide: A Neotropic migrant, breeding from west-central Oklahoma, through central Texas, and west to Big Bend National Park and northern Coahuila, Mexico. Winters on Pacific slope of Mexico from southern Sinaloa to Jalisco, possibly east to Oaxaca.

Historical: Range in Oklahoma always limited to a strip in central and west-central areas. Some early accounts describe birds as locally common, but historical record very sketchy. Never widely distributed. As recently as the 1950s and 1960s was locally uncommon in several west-central counties.

Current: Atlas blocks sampled two of the three known breeding areas in Oklahoma determined from extensive previous surveys for this species. A Possible singing male noted in Woods County could not subsequently be relocated. Vireos are present over a wider area in Comanche County than indicated by block sampling. A small group in Cleveland County went undetected by atlas sampling, but nesting confirmation was reported from this site. Although other small groups may have gone undetected, atlasing generally confirmed the extirpation of this species over much of its previous range in central and west-central Oklahoma. The species is currently endangered and now found in only a few isolated areas. Restoration efforts through cowbird trapping and burn programs have increased the population on federal lands in the Wichita Mountains to over 650 pairs in 2001, but potential for maintaining two other small and isolated groups in Blaine and Cleveland counties is tenuous.

Population Trend: Not well measured by Breeding Bird Survey data. Species listed as Endangered by the U.S. Fish and Wildlife Service in 1987 due to substantial reduction in range and numbers and to disappearance over much of its former range in Oklahoma and north-central and central Texas. Population currently increasing at Wichita Mountains National Wildlife Refuge with intensive management.

References: AOU 1998; Bent 1950; Bunker 1910; Graber 1957, 1961; Grzybowski 1995a; Grzybowski et al. 1986, 1994; Nice 1931; Oberholser 1974; U.S. Fish and Wildlife Service 1991

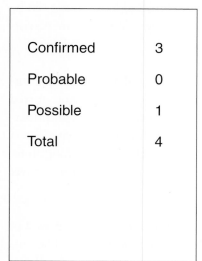

Confirmed	3
Probable	0
Possible	1
Total	4

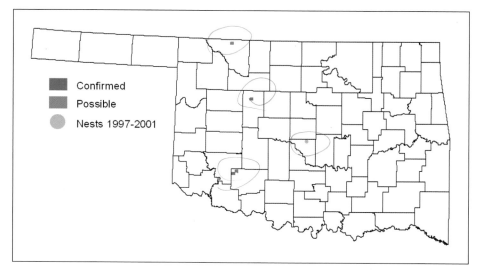

Confirmed
Possible
Nests 1997-2001

Yellow-throated Vireo
Vireo flavifrons

Nathan R. Kuhnert

Courtesy of John Shackford

The Yellow-throated Vireo is perhaps the most color-ful in the vireo family. Its slow and deliberate song is usually heard before the bird is seen. More common in eastern North America, it has however been known to nest in far-western Oklahoma on one occasion.

Description: Both male and female Yellow-throated Vireos have bright yellow, spectacle-like eye rings and two prominent white wing bars that contrast with their greenish head and back and gray rump. The underparts consist of a bright yellow throat and breast and an all-white belly. The male's low and hoarse song is slower than other vireos with longer pauses between phrases often described as *three-eight, three-eight.* They repeat this song over and over again and in a regular order.

The more common call note consists of a rapid, harsh series of *cheees.* The Yellow-throated Vireo's song can be easily overlooked by the Red-eyed Vireo's more persist-ent song.

Breeding Habitat: Yellow-throated Vireos inhabit bot-tomland and upland mature deciduous and mixed forests with open understory, near clearings and ripar-ian areas. Although typically associated with forest edge, they may require large blocks of intact forest inte-rior habitat or high percentages of regional forest cover to successfully breed.

Nest: A very neat, deep, rounded cup, comprised of plant fibers, spiders' webs, and cocoon fibers. The outside is covered with lichen flakes and the inside lined with fine grass-heads or thin pine needles. Typically constructed by the male and lined by the female, it is usually suspended from a fork 6–18 m (20–60 ft) above the ground and near the top of a tall, living, deciduous tree. Nests are typically lower to the ground near the western edge of its range.

NESTING ECOLOGY

Season: May–July. Single-brooded.
Eggs: 3–5; white or creamy white to pinkish white, strongly spotted at large end with black, browns, or lavender. Frequent host of cowbird eggs.
Development: Incubation is by both sexes for 13–15 days. Young are provisioned by both sexes and leave the nest at about 13 days.

DISTRIBUTION AND ABUNDANCE

Rangewide: Breeds throughout the eastern United States and parts of southernmost Canada. Winters from Mexico south to Central America. Generally common throughout most of its range but typically a low-density nester.

Historical: Described in 1853 as "Very abundant in Texas, New Mexico, and the Indian Territory." Described in 1931 as a summer resident throughout eastern Oklahoma. In 1992, described as an uncommon summer resident in eastern Oklahoma; rare and local west to Osage, Cleveland, and Johnston counties. One nest record for Cimarron County in 1986.
Current: Widely distributed across eastern Oklahoma, the Yellow-throated Vireo sings less frequently than other vireos and may occur farther west in local areas. The small number of breeding confirmations is probably a result of its tendency to nest high in the canopy.

Population Trend: Breeding Bird Survey data for 1966–2000 show an increase of 0.8 percent per year rangewide (P = 0.04), but show no conclusive trend in Oklahoma (1.2 percent per year, P = 0.80).

References: AOU 1998; Baicich and Harrison 1997; Baumgartner and Baumgartner 1992; Bent 1950; Cornell Laboratory of Ornithology 1993; Friedman 1963; Graber et al. 1985; James and Neal 1986; National Geographic Society 1999; Rodewald and James 1996; Sauer et al. 2001; Shackford 1992b; Sibley 2000; Sutton 1967; Terres 1991

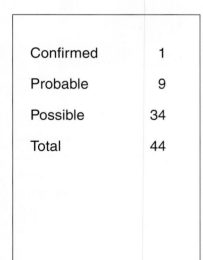

Confirmed	1
Probable	9
Possible	34
Total	44

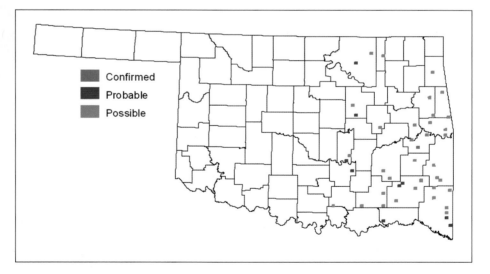

Warbling Vireo
Vireo gilvus

Joseph A. Grzybowski

Courtesy of Jim and Deva Burns / Natural Impacts

The sweetly rolling song from even a small group of cottonwoods can call one's attention to the treetops hoping for a glimpse of a subtly colored Warbling Vireo. Although this species' songs have been well studied, its nesting ecology has yet to be adequately quantified. The eastern subspecies may be the smallest host to successfully puncture-eject cowbird eggs placed in their nests.

Description: Adults are generally a nondescript olive gray above and whitish below that can be washed slightly with yellow on the mid- to lower underparts. There is a whitish superciliary line. The bill, eye, and legs are dark. Ornithologists so inclined have given an array of chatty phonetics to describe its rambling war-

ble of a song, including *If I sees you, I will seize you, and I'll squeeze you till you squirt.* This species can be confused most easily with migrant Philadelphia Vireos, particularly in the fall, but the Warbling seldom shows any yellow wash on its throat, while even a pale Philadelphia will show some yellow there.

Breeding Habitat: Generally a bird of mature mixed deciduous woodlands, especially cottonwood-dominated riparian areas. Can be found in isolated cottonwood trees in the wheat fields of western Oklahoma.

Nest: A rounded, hanging cup of fine fibers, grasses, bark, and silk suspended from forks of horizontal twigs, most frequently placed high in the canopy.

NESTING ECOLOGY

Season: May–July. Probably double-brooded, but uncertain in Oklahoma populations.

Eggs: 3–4; sparingly spotted white eggs. Frequently parasitized by Brown-headed Cowbirds.

Development: Incubation is by both sexes for 12–14 days. Young are provisioned by both sexes and fledge at 13–14 days, but continue to be fed for about 2 weeks.

DISTRIBUTION AND ABUNDANCE

Rangewide: Breeds broadly across middle portions of North America from southern McKenzie Territory (Canada) to Nova Scotia, south to mid-Atlantic states and Midwest to southern California, and in the highlands of Mexico, with a few outpost groups in Baja California. Winters in southern Mexico.

Historical: Described as a summer resident in 1931, breeding locally in eastern and central Oklahoma; uncommon in the Panhandle. Later considered a widely distributed breeding species, though less common in the Panhandle and southwestern Oklahoma. Specimens indicate the breeding subspecies to be of the nominate race—*V.g. gilvus*.

Current: Probably benefiting from the fire suppression and "foresting" of western Oklahoma since dust-bowl days, atlasing shows the Warbling Vireo with a dispersed but statewide distribution. Notable voids occur within the Panhandle, and in the central Osage Prairie. Although easy to detect by song, its generally dispersed detections depict its low general abundance. The high proportion of blocks in which it was recorded as Possible emphasizes its low density, but also its difficult-to-locate nests high in the canopy.

Population Trend: Breeding Bird Survey data for 1966–2000 show an increase of 1.2 percent per year rangewide (P = 0.00). Trend analyses for Oklahoma are more difficult to interpret, as the general pattern for 1966–2000 indicates a modest increase, while the trends for each of the two halves of the survey period depict declines, indicating poor-quality data for this species.

References: AOU 1998; Baumgartner and Baumgartner 1992; Bent 1950; Gardali and Ballard 2000; Howes-Jones 1985a, 1985b, 1985c; Nice 1931; Oberholser 1974; Sealy 1996; Sutton 1967; Tate 1923; Voelker and Rowher 1998

Confirmed	6
Probable	24
Possible	105
Total	135

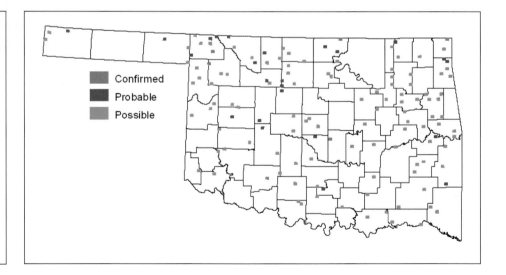

Red-eyed Vireo
Vireo olivaceus

Richard A. Stuart

Courtesy of Joseph A. Grzybowski

One of the most persistent bird songsters in North America, the Red-eyed Vireo has been called the Preacher Bird in some circles. In every woodland area within its range, one will hear it singing nearly continuously from within the treetop foliage. Except when it may be perched or feeding on the outer fringes of the tree, it is often quite difficult to observe.

Description: Sexes similar. One of the largest vireos in Oklahoma, it is olive green above, lacks wing bars, has a gray crown separated from a white supercilium by a black stripe, and has a red eye with a black eye stripe. The song consists of phrases that resemble *Hear me? Here I am. See me? Here I am* and are repeated almost constantly. This vireo can most easily be confused with the Warbling Vireo, which is smaller, grayer overall, and has a supercilium without the dark upper and lower margins and a yellowish wash on the flanks.

Breeding Habitat: Deciduous woodlands, mixed deciduous-coniferous forest, and wooded parks and residential areas.

Nest: A suspended cup structure supported by forked horizontal twigs and composed of fine grasses, bark strips, rootlets, and birch bark when available. It is bound by spider webs and spider egg cases. The location is usually 2.5–4.5 m (8–15 ft) high in a shrub or tree.

NESTING ECOLOGY

Season: May–July. Sometimes double-brooded.

Eggs: 3–5; white with scattered fine spots of browns or black. Very frequently parasitized by Brown-headed Cowbirds.

Development: Incubation is by the female for 11–14 days. Young are provisioned by both sexes and fledge at 10–12 days.

DISTRIBUTION AND ABUNDANCE

Rangewide: Breeds throughout the eastern and northern United States and southern Canada where deciduous woodlands are found. Winters in South America.

Historical: Described as a common to abundant summer resident in eastern Oklahoma, rare and local westward, and absent as a breeder in far-western Oklahoma and the Panhandle.

Current: The Red-eyed Vireo can be considered common in the eastern and more heavily wooded areas of Oklahoma, but it becomes uncommon to rare in the western part of the state. Because of its persistent singing it is not difficult to locate, but its treetop nesting habits make it very difficult to confirm. Particularly in the west, some of the Possible Breeder blocks may be the result of birds heard singing prior to the end of spring migration.

Population Trend: Breeding Bird Survey data for 1966–2000 show an increase of 1.3 percent per year rangewide (P = 0.00), but show no conclusive trend n Oklahoma (2.4 percent per year, P = 0.11).

References: AOU 1998; Baicich and Harrison 1997; Baumgartner and Baumgartner 1992; Cassidy 1990; Farrand 1983; Harrison 1975; National Geographic Society 1999; Pearson 1936; Peterson 1963, 1996; Pyle 1997; Sauer et al. 2001; Sibley 2000; Stokes and Stokes 1996; Sutton 1949, 1967

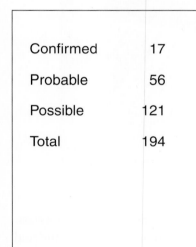

Confirmed	17
Probable	56
Possible	121
Total	194

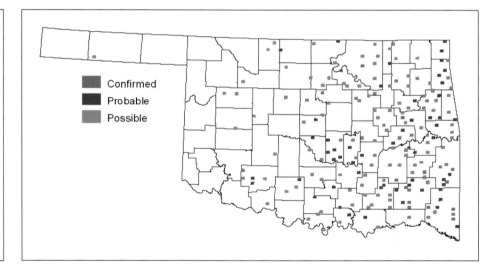

Blue Jay
Cyanocitta cristata

Dan L. Reinking

Courtesy of M. Frank Carl

Bold, aggressive behavior, bright plumage, and loud calls make Blue Jays conspicuous in yards, in woodlands, and at feeders. Blue Jays do not defend traditional nesting territories; instead they merely guard the immediate area around their nest from other intruding jays. Their reputation for eating eggs and nestlings of other birds, while not without merit, may be overestimated in terms of the damage it does.

Description: Both male and female Blue Jays have a blue crest, back, wings, and tail, and white underparts with a black necklace. The tail is barred with black, while the wings show both black bars and white patches. Commonly heard calls include a strident *jay*

jay jay, a much more musical *weedle-eedle,* and a passable imitation of the scream of a Red-shouldered Hawk.

Breeding Habitat: Blue Jays nest in a variety of wooded habitats, including forests, woodlands, parks, and suburbs. They readily occupy areas of human habitation, including residential areas with mature trees.

Nest: The nest is built by both sexes and is constructed of live and dead twigs, bark, grasses, stems, feathers, and paper or cloth debris. The nest cup is lined with finer plant materials. Nests are usually found between 3–12 m (10–40 ft) up in trees or shrubs.

NESTING ECOLOGY

Season: April–July. Sometimes double-brooded.

Eggs: Usually 4–5, but ranges from 2–6. Color is variable, but usually pale olive, buff, or bluish-green, spotted and blotched with brown, olive, gray, or purple.

Development: Incubation is by the female for 17–18 days, during which time she is fed by the male. Young are provisioned by both sexes but are brooded by the female alone. They leave the nest after 17–21 days but continue to be fed for about 3 weeks.

DISTRIBUTION AND ABUNDANCE

Rangewide: The Blue Jay is largely a resident species from the western Great Plains eastward in the United States, and over much of southern and eastern Canada west to central Alberta and eastern British Columbia. Some individuals (<20 percent) migrate south from breeding areas for the winter, and most parts of the breeding range contain birds year round. The breeding range has expanded westward in the past 30–60 years due to urbanization and associated tree planting, and the proliferation of bird feeders in these areas.

Historical: Described as common over most of the main body of the state where trees are present, but less common in the Panhandle.

Current: The Blue Jay is broadly distributed across Oklahoma, though less common in the southwest and Panhandle than elsewhere. Its secretive habits during the nesting season make it a moderately difficult species to confirm.

Population Trend: Breeding Bird Survey data for 1966–2000 show a decline of 1.1 percent per year rangewide (P = 0.00) and a decline of 1.5 percent per year in Oklahoma (P = 0.00).

References: AOU 1998; Baicich and Harrison 1997; Batcheller 1980; Batcheller et al. 1984; Baumgartner and Baumgartner 1992; Bock and Lepthien 1976; Conant 1972; McGee and McGee 1972; Oberholser 1921; Sauer et al. 2001; Smith 1978; Stewart 1982; Sutton 1967; Tarvin and Woolfenden 1999

Confirmed	127
Probable	91
Possible	197
Total	415

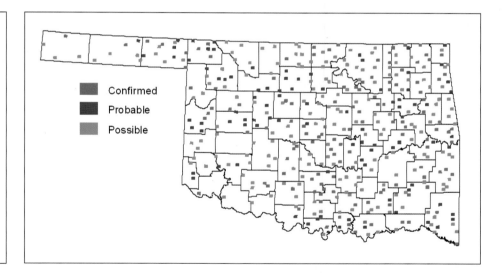

Western Scrub-Jay
Aphelocoma californica

David A. Wiggins

Courtesy of Steve Metz

Western Scrub-Jays are common and conspicuous throughout much of their range, which barely reaches the western Oklahoma Panhandle. They remain in small family flocks throughout the fall, winter, and early spring and are often easily located by their loud calls given from exposed perches. During the breeding season, however, they become quiet and secretive, especially in the vicinity of the nest.

Description: Scrub-Jays are largely bluish gray on the back, nape, and crown, with bright blue wing and tail, and dirty gray-white underparts and throat. The face is typically dark gray. Sexes are similar. Calls are typically raspy, jay-like notes. Similar to the Pinyon Jay, but has a much longer tail and is more often found in small flocks or pairs.

Breeding Habitat: Pinyon-juniper, scrub-oak, and ponderosa-pine woodlands.

Nest: A bulky twig structure typically less than 3 m (10 ft) from the ground and typically well hidden in a pinyon, juniper, or other conifer. Built by both sexes.

NESTING ECOLOGY

Season: April–May. Single-brooded.

Eggs: 2–4, sometimes more; pale green, pale blue, or reddish, with black spotting.

Development: Incubation is by the female for about 16 days. Young are provisioned by both sexes and are thought to leave the nest at about 18 days. They remain with their parents for an extended though unknown period after fledging.

DISTRIBUTION AND ABUNDANCE

Rangewide: Resident from southern Washington south through the Great Basin, east to the Rocky Mountain foothills, and south to north-central Mexico.

Historical: Described in 1992 as a common resident restricted to the Black Mesa region of northwestern Cimarron County, straying (during winter) only very rarely away from this area. Few actual nest records reported.

Current: Restricted to pinyon-juniper habitat and generally secretive during the nesting season, the Western Scrub-Jay is not an easy species to document with atlas methods. The two records during the atlas period suggest that the species continues to nest in its historical breeding range in extreme northwestern Cimarron County.

Population Trend: Breeding Bird Survey data for 1966–2000 show an increase of 0.9 percent rangewide (P = 0.00). No trend data are available for Oklahoma.

References: Baicich and Harrison 1997; Baumgartner and Baumgartner 1992; Johnsgard 1979; Nice 1931; Sauer et al. 2001; Sibley 2000; Sutton 1967; Tate 1923

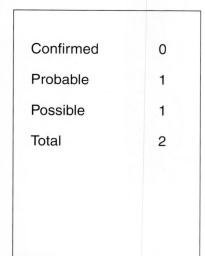

Confirmed	0
Probable	1
Possible	1
Total	2

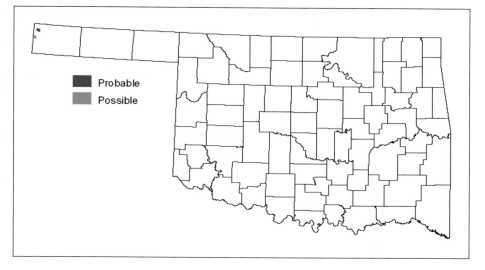

Probable
Possible

Pinyon Jay
Gymnorhinus cyanocephalus

David A. Wiggins

Courtesy of Michael Gray

Pinyon Jays occur throughout the interior west, moving about in large flocks in the fall and winter, and breeding semicolonially in family groups. At the margin of its range in Oklahoma, the Pinyon Jay occurs only in western Cimarron County, where its favored pinyon-juniper woodlands exist.

Description: A large, compact, dark blue jay with a pale throat and characteristically short tail. Call is a relatively high-pitched, descending *kaa-eh*. If not seen clearly, may be confused with Scrub-Jay, which has a much longer tail.

Breeding Habitat: Dry pine forests and pinyon-juniper woodlands.

Nest: Constructed of twigs and lined with hair or feathers. Built by both sexes. Located 2–6 m (6–20 ft) high in pine or juniper tree. Often nests colonially, but not known for Oklahoma.

NESTING ECOLOGY

Season: April–early June. Single-brooded.
Eggs: Usually 3–5; bluish white with brown spots.

Development: Incubation is by the female for 17 days. Young are provisioned by both sexes and sometimes by helpers. Young fledge at about 3 weeks and receive post-fledging parental care for several months.

DISTRIBUTION AND ABUNDANCE

Rangewide: Resident throughout the Great Basin, the central and southern Rocky Mountains, and the eastern foothills of the Rockies, south to south-central Arizona and New Mexico.

Historical: Described as an uncommon to common resident of the Black Mesa area of Cimarron County.

Current: The single breeding record (a pair with two fledglings) for the atlas period was in pinyon-juniper habitat in extreme northwestern Cimarron County, in the same general area as historical nesting records. Restricted all year to the pinyon-juniper mesas in extreme northwestern Cimarron County, the Pinyon Jay can be easily overlooked as it occurs in low densities and is secretive during the nesting season.

Population Trend: Breeding Bird Survey data for 1966–2000 show a decline of 3.1 percent per year rangewide (P = 0.02). No trend data are available for Oklahoma.

References: Baicich and Harrison 1997; Baumgartner and Baumgartner 1992; Sauer et al. 2001; Sutton 1967; Tate 1923

Confirmed	1
Probable	0
Possible	0
Total	1

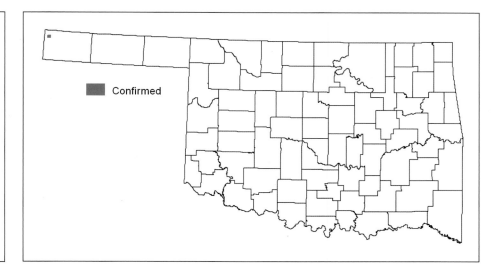

Confirmed

Black-billed Magpie
Pica hudsonia

John M. Dole

The Black-billed Magpie is bold in color and behavior. This large Panhandle resident commands attention with its long black tail and striking black and white wings. Often moving around in small groups the birds can be noisy, making a variety of calls. Birds may move further south and east during the winter.

Description: The head, back, chest, tail, and vent are black. The belly is white and the wings are white and black. The wings and tail are iridescent green in proper light. Sexes are similar and immatures have shorter tails and more white below than adults. The Black-billed Magpie could be confused with few other species in Oklahoma with the exception of partial albino crows and ravens.

Breeding Habitat: Riparian thickets, often near open areas.

Nest: A large, rounded structure, generally 75 cm (30 in) high and 50 cm (20 in) across with one or more entrances. New nests may be built on old nests resulting in structures several meters high. The interior cup is composed of thick twigs and heavily lined with mud or dung. A layer of thin weeds, rootlets, and hair lines the cup. The nest is constructed by both sexes and is usually located 7–9 m (15–30 ft) high in a tree or tall shrub. Multiple pairs may nest in a small area.

NESTING ECOLOGY

Season: April–July. Single-brooded, with occasional second brood only if first brood is lost.

Eggs: Usually 6–7; pale greenish blue to tan, heavily spotted with dark brown to gray which sometimes rings blunt end.

Development: Incubation is by the female for about 18 days, with the male providing her with food. Young are provisioned by both sexes and leave the nest 24–30 days after hatching.

DISTRIBUTION AND ABUNDANCE

Rangewide: The Black-billed Magpie occurs from Alaska east to southwestern Ontario and northwestern Minnesota and south to northwestern Oklahoma, northern New Mexico, northern Arizona, and northeastern California. The Black-billed Magpie also occurs in northern Europe and Asia, but some authorities consider it to be a different species than that in North America.

Historical: First noted in Oklahoma (in Cimarron County) in 1919 when three nests were found, and has been a locally common resident in Cimarron County since the early 1930s. Occasionally strays eastward. Two dead nestlings were found in a heronry in Creek County in 1979.

Current: The relative rarity of this distinctive bird is evident in that it was restricted to only a few records in the Oklahoma Panhandle. The large nest typically placed high up in trees and tall shrubs allows easy nesting confirmation, but the wide ranges of individual pairs reduces the chance that a nest will be found in a specific block.

Population Trend: Breeding Bird Survey data for 1966–2000 show a decline of 0.7 percent per year rangewide ($P = 0.04$). No trend data are available for Oklahoma.

References: AOU 1998; Baicich and Harrison 1997; Baumgartner and Baumgartner 1992; Birkhead 1991; Bock and Lepthien 1975; Erpino 1968; Kaufman 1996; National Geographic Society 1999; Sallee 1980; Sauer et al. 2001; Sutton 1934, 1967; Tate 1923, 1925b, 1927, 1933; Trost 1994

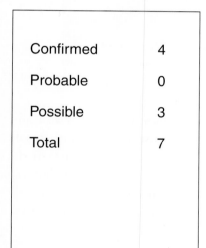

Confirmed	4
Probable	0
Possible	3
Total	7

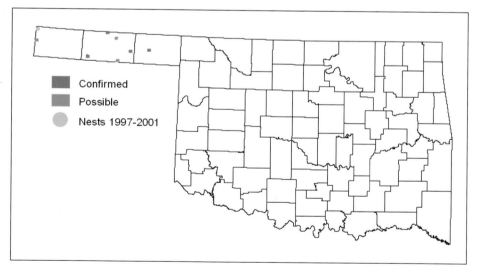

Confirmed
Possible
Nests 1997-2001

American Crow
Corvus brachyrhynchos

Carolee Caffrey

Courtesy of Bill Horn

Clever, cunning, curious, and vocal, seemingly bold but actually very wary, these opportunists are one of our most familiar birds. The groups of 2–14 crows seen year round are "families"; offspring may stay with their parents for 1–4 years before dispersing, unusual among birds. Crows breed "cooperatively" in that a breeding pair is assisted in raising young by nonbreeders, which are often older offspring of the pair. Yet, family groups also regularly include individuals that have moved in from other families—a very unusual social organization. Crows in Stillwater, Oklahoma, have been observed to modify and use tools.

Description: Large, glossy black passerine with stocky bill and fan-shaped tail. Sexes similar; males slightly larger than females. Individuals in their first year are identifiable by duller, brownish, ragged feathers of wings and tail. Vocal repertoire is large and varied, including calls that sound like cat meows, goose honks, and dog barks. Most common calls are variations of familiar *caw*. Nestlings and incubating females give nasal *waah* begging calls.

Breeding Habitat: Crows are territorial and will breed in a wide variety of settings, including areas of human habitation, as long as foraging habitat and access to water are available nearby. Nest trees include deciduous species, but are more often evergreen (such as conifers, cedars, and magnolias). Forages primarily on ground in open areas of low-growing vegetation, especially grass.

Territories of rural groups are much larger than those of urban and semiurban groups.

Nest: Large cup nest about 48–56 cm (19–22 in) outside diameter, constructed of twigs, and lined with mud, grass, strips of bark, mammal fur, and other soft materials. Nests may be placed anywhere in nest tree, but are usually built into some kind of supporting crotch.

NESTING ECOLOGY

Season: February–June. Single-brooded, but may renest if first attempt fails.
Eggs: 4–5; very variable in color and shape. Commonly pale green blue with variable brown markings.
Development: Incubation is by the female for 17–21 days. Young are provisioned by breeders and helpers of both sexes and fledge after 30–35 days.

DISTRIBUTION AND ABUNDANCE

Rangewide: Breeds across the southern half of Canada and across most of the United States. In winter, withdraws from northern extremes; occurs from southern parts of Canadian provinces to southern limits of breeding range.
Historical: Presence in the Panhandle has increased from uncommon to common since the early 1900s, but otherwise described as a common summer and winter resident throughout the state. In winter, crows from more northern latitudes join our residents and contribute to the large foraging flocks seen during those months, and probably comprise the majority of the hundreds of thousands of crows that may occur in any of the communal roosts scattered throughout Oklahoma from November through February.
Current: The flexibility of crows with respect to nesting habitat is evidenced by their occurrence across the state; they're everywhere! That they have not been confirmed breeding in all blocks is likely due to their surprising secrecy with regard to nest locations, although the begging of incubating females and older nestlings is unmistakable to those familiar with this vocalization.

Population Trend: Breeding Bird Survey data for 1966–2000 show an increase of 1.1 percent per year rangewide (P = 0.00) and an increase of 1.6 percent per year in Oklahoma (P = 0.00).

References: Baumgartner and Baumgartner 1992; Caccamise et al. 1997; Caffrey 1992, 1999, 2000a, 2000b, 2001, 2002a, 2002b; Freeman 1993; Good 1952; Kilham 1989; Moore and Switzer 1998; Sauer et al. 2001; Stouffer and Caccamise 1991; Sutton 1967; Verbeek and Caffrey 2002

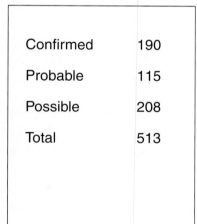

Confirmed	190
Probable	115
Possible	208
Total	513

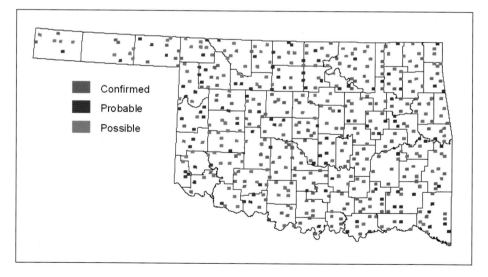

Fish Crow
Corvus ossifragus

Richard A. Stuart

This smallish crow is a relatively recent addition to Oklahoma and is usually associated with rivers or shorelines where it scavenges for food, as well as with heron rookeries, which it raids for eggs and nestlings. Its association with herons may have facilitated range expansion inland from the coasts. Two reports from the 1800s described this species taking dead fish floating on the water using its feet rather than its bill.

Description: The sexes are indistinguishable; the plumage is a glossy black resembling a slightly smaller version of the nearly identical appearing American Crow. The voice is a very nasal, somewhat high-pitched *ca* or *ca-ha,* the former resembling some call notes of young American Crows but ending more abruptly. The latter, two-note call is not given by American Crows.

Breeding Habitat: River bottom woods, marshes, and lakes are typically used. They may also be found in the vicinity of heron rookeries, which are often placed in similar habitats.

Nest: Constructed of sticks, twigs, bark fiber, soil, and other plant materials, and lined with softer plant materials. Located in treetops 1.5–27.5 m (5.5–90 ft) above ground. Nesting is either solitary or in loose colonies. Because of the depth of the nest, an incubating female may not be visible from the ground.

NESTING ECOLOGY

Season: April–June. Single-brooded, but may replace a lost clutch.

Eggs: 4–6; blue to gray green with scattered spotting of browns and grays.

Development: Incubation is by the female for 18–21 days. Young are provisioned by both sexes, but mostly by the male for the first 10 days while the female broods the young. Young fledge at 32–40 days, but are fed by the parents for several more weeks.

DISTRIBUTION AND ABUNDANCE

Rangewide: Resident throughout most of the coastal plain of the East and Gulf coasts of the United States east of eastern Texas. Spreading north and northwestward up the Mississippi, Red, and Arkansas rivers to south-central and northeastern Oklahoma into southeastern Kansas and eastern Missouri.

Historical: Possibly paralleling the resurgence of herons and egrets in the 1940s, the Fish Crow has gradually increased its range northward and westward from the Gulf Coast. They crossed into Oklahoma in the Fort Smith area in 1954. By the mid-1980s they had spread up the river valleys to Choctaw County along the Red River and to Bartlesville, presumably following the Verdigris and Caney rivers. It is now known to winter in southeastern Oklahoma.

Current: The Fish Crow is slowly expanding its range from southeastern Oklahoma to the north and west along the rivers of Oklahoma. Wherever large lakes and rivers exist, at least in the eastern portions of the state, we might expect to eventually find breeding populations of this species.

Population Trend: Breeding Bird Survey data for 1966–2000 show an increase of 1.5 percent per year rangewide (P = 0.02), but show no conclusive trend in Oklahoma (12.5 percent per year, P = 0.31), although its range expansion in Oklahoma has undoubtedly increased its numbers here in recent decades.

References: AOU 1998; Angell 1978; Baicich and Harrison 1997; Baumgartner and Baumgartner 1992; Cassidy 1990; Goodwin 1976; Easterla 1965; Harrison 1975; McNair 1984; National Geographic Society 1999; Pearson 1936; Peterson 1963; Sauer et al. 2001; Sibley 2000; Stokes and Stokes 1996; Sutton 1967; Taylor 1972; Wilhelm 1960; Wilmore 1977

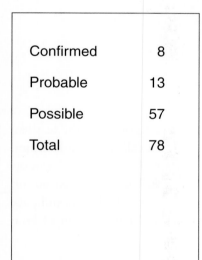

Confirmed	8
Probable	13
Possible	57
Total	78

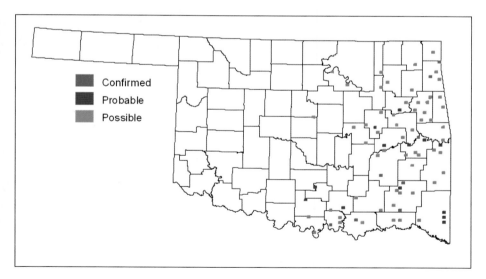

Chihuahuan Raven
Corvus cryptoleucus

Sebastian T. Patti

Courtesy of Jim and Deva Burns / Natural Impacts

Intermediate in size between the Common Raven and the American Crow, the Chihuahuan Raven is a "flat lander," in contrast to the Common Raven, which prefers rough and rocky country. It was formerly known as the White-necked Raven because of the white-based feathers on the species' nape and neck. The specific name, *cryptoleucus,* means "hidden white" in Greek. The species is often regarded as sedentary, but it seems clear that many, if not most, birds withdraw from the northern portions of the species' range during the colder winter months.

Description: Both males and females are unicolored black corvids with a wedge-shaped tail and stout bill. The diagnostic white feathers of the neck can some-

times be seen when a bird preens or when the feathers are disturbed by the wind. The calls of adult birds are generally higher pitched than those of the Common Raven, but are still best described as croaks; young birds give calls that are higher pitched still, and that can almost sound scream-like. Identification of lone ravens can be quite difficult.

Breeding Habitat: Chihuahuan Ravens are residents of grasslands, deserts, and agricultural lands of the arid southwestern United States and inhabit the shortgrass plains and farmland of extreme western Oklahoma and the Panhandle.

Nest: Usually placed 2–12 m (7–40 ft) up in solitary

trees, but these birds also make use of man-made structures such as windmills, water towers, or even power poles. Nest is a bulky, open structure made of large twigs and small branches, lined with leaves, grasses, fur, or hair. This species has a well-known fondness for barbed, baling, or fence wire, and these materials can usually be found in its nests.

NESTING ECOLOGY

Season: April–early July. Single-brooded.
Eggs: Usually 5–7; pale green with streaks and spots of brown and grayish purple.
Development: Incubation is by both sexes for about 21 days. Young are provisioned by both sexes and take first flight at about 30 days.

DISTRIBUTION AND ABUNDANCE

Rangewide: This species apparently underwent a range expansion during the nineteenth century and then suffered a range contraction during the early twentieth century. It is clear that the species no longer ranges as far north as it once did, currently occurring from southeastern Colorado and southwestern Kansas, south through the Oklahoma and Texas Panhandles, southwestern Oklahoma and southwest through west Texas, southern New Mexico and Arizona, and northern and central Mexico. Birds largely withdraw from the northern reaches of the breeding range in winter.

Historical: Described as a rare resident in southwestern Oklahoma and the Panhandle in 1931. Reported to be a resident in the Panhandle and western fifth of the main body of the state by 1967, and considered a common summer resident in southwestern Oklahoma, less common in the Panhandle, by 1992.

Current: Restricted to the grassland areas of the Panhandle and the far-western and southwestern portions of the main body of the state, although it was not recorded in the latter region during the atlas project, perhaps due to local or diminishing distribution there. During the project period, the species was only recorded in Cimarron, Texas, and Woodward counties; breeding was confirmed in 4 blocks in Cimarron and Texas counties.

Population Trend: Breeding Bird Survey data for 1966–2000 show no conclusive trend rangewide (-1.6 percent per year, P = 0.25) or in Oklahoma (-3.9 percent per year, P = 0.35).

References: AOU 1998; Baicich and Harrison 1997; Baumgartner and Baumgartner 1992; Busby and Zimmerman 2001; Nelson 1998; Nice 1931; Oberholser 1974; Sauer et al. 2001; Sibley 2000; Sutton 1967; Tyler 1968b

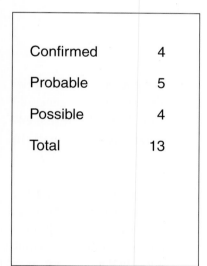

Confirmed	4
Probable	5
Possible	4
Total	13

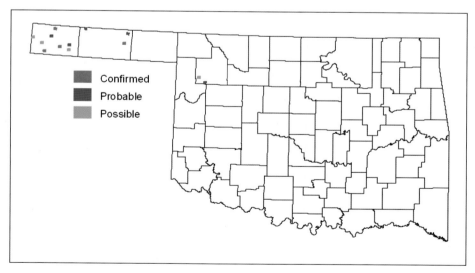

Common Raven

Corvus corax

Sebastian T. Patti

Courtesy of Gerald Wiens

The largest passerine in North America, the Common Raven is a corvid that is culturally significant for many peoples around the world, and is known, anecdotally, for its intelligence. The species suffered a significant decline in its distribution in the central and eastern United States from the 1800s through the early 1900s. Although the species is social, Common Ravens tend to be more solitary than other members of the genus *Corvus*.

Description: A large, glossy black corvid with a distinctive wedge-shaped tail and very large bill. Larger and heavier than a Red-tailed Hawk. Common Ravens have elongated throat feathers that are often referred to as "hackles." Sexes not easily separable, though females

average smaller than males in some body characteristics. Adult calls, though highly variable, can generally be described as deep *croaks* usually rendered sequentially. Can be difficult to separate from Chihuahuan Raven.

Breeding Habitat: Ecologically and geographically, the Common Raven is one of the most widespread species in the world, and it inhabits a broad array of habitats. There is a preference for "rough" areas that have significant contours that provide updrafts and thermals that these birds can use for long-range foraging and food detection. In Oklahoma it is found in the steep, rocky mesa country of northwestern Cimarron County.

42 Birds — Canadian Cty, OK (eve)

Rock Wren   (c it)
(Chimney Creek)
BlCp Vireo   (sc)
W Kingbird
Vermillion Flyc (2.e)
Common Poorwill (is)

Roadrunner
Upland Sandpiper   — mc
Sw Hawk   — mv

Cassin's Sparrow
Lark B/h — ln
W Mead

} Bison pr Dog
   Prairie
   Opera

10. **SOPHISTICATED HULA**, composed by Sol K. Bright – entire cast

Each company will dance their own choreography to the same fun mele—e hoʻonanea pū kākou—let's enjoy!

Please join us in singing HAWAIʻI ALOHA (composed by Lorenzo Lyons):

E Hawaiʻi, e kuʻu one hānau ē
Kuʻu home kulāiwi nei
ʻOli nō au i nā pono lani ou
E Hawaiʻi aloha ē

Hui (Chorus); *repeat 2x*:
E hauʻoli e nā ʻōpio o Hawaiʻi nei
ʻOli ē! ʻOli ē!
Mai nā aheahe makani e pā mai nei
Mau ke aloha no Hawaiʻi (*repeat at end of second time through*)

Nest: Usually placed on a cliff ledge or in a tree. Construction is apparently completed by the female, though the male may assist by bringing materials. General composition is of sticks and small branches placed on a flat substrate; an inner cup is created by smaller twigs and branches, the bottom of which may be lined with mud, bark, grasses, fur, or hair. Often makes use of old nests.

NESTING ECOLOGY

Season: April–June. Single-brooded, but may replace lost clutches.

Eggs: Usually 4–6; greenish, and streaked or splotched with brownish.

Development: Incubation is by the female for 20–25 days; male often "stands guard" while female incubates. Young are provisioned by both sexes and fledge when 5–6 weeks old. Young birds generally stay in the vicinity of the nest for at least a week, though sometimes significantly longer, and are attended by the parents during this time.

DISTRIBUTION AND ABUNDANCE

Rangewide: Resident from Alaska through most of Canada, the northeastern United States, the Appalachians, most of the western United States, and most of Mexico to parts of Central America. Also resident throughout much of the Old World.

Historical: For the past century or more, only known from the Black Mesa area of Cimarron County. Reported in 1931 to have been formerly abundant throughout the state in the 1800s, but in 1967 it was convincingly asserted that most birds were probably Chihuahuan Ravens, although an 1852 record of nesting Common Ravens as far east as Nowata County was considered believable. A 1935 published record of a nest on a windmill in Cimarron County was likely a Chihuahuan Raven instead. There were no reported nests in Oklahoma from 1908 to 1967.

Current: Now known only from the roughest part of northwestern Cimarron County, where the species is not uncommon. The species was recorded, and breeding confirmed, on one of three blocks established by the atlas project in the Black Mesa country.

Population Trend: Breeding Bird Survey data for 1966–2000 show an increase of 2.9 percent per year rangewide (P = 0.00). Extremely local and low-density population in Oklahoma reveals no trends. By the early part of the twentieth century, this species had retreated from many areas in which it had been common in the 1800s.

References: AOU 1998; Baicich and Harrison 1997; Boarman and Heinrich 1999; Baumgartner and Baumgartner 1992; Colvin 1935a; Langford 1970; Nice 1931; Sauer et al. 2001; Sibley 2000; Sutton 1967; Tate 1923; Winn 1998

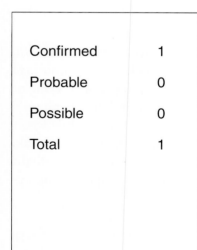

Confirmed	1
Probable	0
Possible	0
Total	1

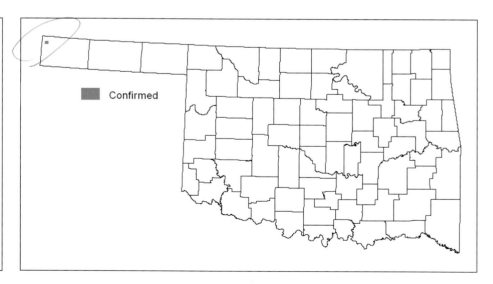

Confirmed

Horned Lark
Eremophila alpestris

Gregory A. Smith

Courtesy of Bob Gress

The Horned Lark is the only member of the lark family, Alaudidae, native to North America. It is a common, widespread bird of open country that often gathers in large, mixed-species flocks in winter. Arguably the most abundant bird on the high plains of our Panhandle, Baumgartner and Baumgartner likened them to "leaves blown around by the wind" as they flitted about in front of their vehicle during a spring drive. Winter populations are even more numerous and at times it seems these little passerines are everywhere.

Description: Small, ground-dwelling songbirds with distinctive feather tufts, or "horns," above each eye. The head is marked with black lores, cheek, and breast patches alternating with yellow eyebrow stripes, ear coverts, and chin. The upperparts are generally brown, streaked with dusky brown or black. The outermost tail feathers on either side are black, tipped with white or gray. The breast and belly are white or sometimes a shade of cinnamon. Overall, males are slightly larger and darker than females. Typical song includes a weak, tinkling warble often given by males during in-flight courtship displays. Flight calls are a simple, lisping *see-tu* or *see-titi.*

Breeding Habitat: Breeds in open habitats with very short, sparse vegetation, including grazed prairie grassland and cultivated fields.

Nest: Nests are placed on the ground, usually in the

shelter of a tuft of grass or stone. The nest is constructed by the female and begins as a shallow depression in the ground, one she digs herself or adapts from a natural depression. Inside this scrape is woven a cup of grass, roots, and stems lined with finer materials such as down, fur, feathers, and rootlets. Often, an array of peat, dung, and pebbles will be placed around the outside of the nest.

NESTING ECOLOGY

Season: March–July. Double- to triple-brooded.
Eggs: Usually 2–5; pale greenish white with fine brown or buff speckling throughout. Horned Larks are infrequently parasitized by Brown-headed Cowbirds, except in the central plains, where rates of parasitism are higher.
Development: Incubation is by the female for 11 days. Young are provisioned by both sexes and fledge in about 10 days, but are fed by the adults for another week.

DISTRIBUTION AND ABUNDANCE

Rangewide: A holarctic species, Horned Larks occur from the Arctic south to central Asia and Mexico. They can be found at any time of the year throughout the United States except for some areas of the northeast and southeast where they occur irregularly. They are more common breeders in the central and western United States than in the east. Northernmost populations are migratory and population sizes may increase dramatically in central and southern areas of their range as northern individuals move south

Historical: Described as a common to abundant resident in the open plains of western Oklahoma, decreasing eastward. Uncommon to rare in wooded areas of the southeast.

Current: The Horned Lark's nesting habitat preference for open prairie is indicated by its western breeding distribution and high density in the Panhandle. Horned Larks are most abundant in the shortgrass regions of the Panhandle, while breeding is rare in the more forested eastern portions of the state. Nests of this species may be difficult to locate at times, but the conspicuous breeding displays of males make this species a good candidate for detection by atlasing methods.

Population Trend: Breeding Bird Survey data for 1966–2000 show a decline of 2.0 percent per year rangewide (P = 0.00) and a decline of 3.7 percent per year in Oklahoma (P = 0.10).

References: AOU 1998; Baicich and Harrison 1997; Baumgartner and Baumgartner 1992; Baumgartner and Howell 1942, 1947; Beason 1995; Beason and Franks 1974; Bent 1963b; Dinkins et al. 2001; Force 1929; Johnsgard 1979; Kaufman 1996; Moore 1927; Nice 1927, 1931; Parker 1973; Peterjohn and Sauer 1999; Reinking et al. 2000b; Rohwer 1969; Sauer et al. 2001; Saunders 1926; Silver 1952; Sutton 1967; Tate 1923; Thompson and Ely 1992; Wood and Schnell 1984

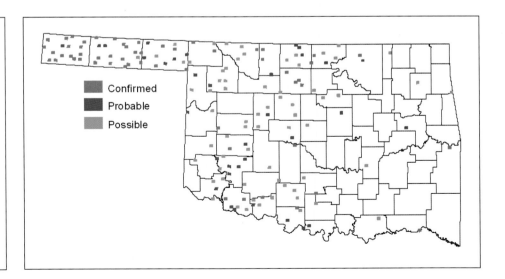

Confirmed	56
Probable	34
Possible	67
Total	157

Purple Martin
Progne subis

Charles R. Brown

Courtesy of Bill Horn

The Purple Martin is one of the most popular back-yard birds in Oklahoma and throughout much of the eastern United States. Originally the species used abandoned woodpecker holes and natural cavities in dead trees, but east of the Rocky Mountains martins have switched almost entirely to multicompartment birdhouses or gourds in backyards. This switch to artificial housing was virtually complete in Oklahoma before the beginning of the twentieth century; the last nest in a natural site reported in the state was in 1914. Intense competition for nesting sites has selected for early spring arrival, and consequently Purple Martins are among the first summer residents to return in the spring, often in February.

Description: The Purple Martin is the largest North American swallow; males are uniformly glossy bluish black. Females are gray to grayish white on the under-parts and show a mixture of dark brown and bluish black on the upperparts. Females tend to show a brownish or grayish collar around the nape. Yearling males resemble females in color pattern but show variable amounts of bluish-black feathering on the head and underparts. Yearling females tend to be whiter on the underparts and have less bluish black on the upper-parts than older females. The adult male's uniformly dark underparts, and the large size of both sexes, distinguish the Purple Martin from all other swallows in Oklahoma.

Breeding Habitat: The Purple Martin is found primarily in cities and towns where suitable birdhouses occur in backyards.

Nest: Cavity in birdhouse or (rarely in Oklahoma) dead snag. Cavity is usually filled by an evenly spread, loose mat of twigs, dead leaves, and grass. Mud is sometimes placed across the nest in front of the entrance hole, and fresh green leaves are used to line the nest cup around the eggs.

NESTING ECOLOGY

Season: April–July. Usually single-brooded.
Eggs: 3–6; pure white.
Development: Incubation is by the female for 15–18 days. Young are provisioned by both sexes and fledge at 27–29 days, but are typically fed by their parents for several days afterward.

DISTRIBUTION AND ABUNDANCE

Rangewide: The Purple Martin is common throughout most of the United States and extreme southern Canada east of the Rocky Mountains; it is uncommon in New England. Smaller, more isolated populations occur in the mountains of the western United States and Mexico. Purple Martins winter primarily in Brazil.

Historical: Prior to European settlement of Oklahoma, Purple Martins were probably relatively uncommon in the state, restricted to swamps and river bottoms where dead snags with suitable woodpecker holes could be found. The species likely is now much more widespread and more common with its adoption of backyard birdhouses as nesting sites. Described in 1992 as a common summer resident in eastern and central regions, decreasing westward.
Current: Purple Martins are found throughout the eastern two-thirds of the state wherever there are cities and towns. They are rare and local in the western counties and absent in the Panhandle. Being entirely a backyard bird in Oklahoma, the martin is easily surveyed and easily confirmed, and few colonies were likely missed.

Population Trend: Breeding Bird Survey data for 1966–2000 show no conclusive trend rangewide (-0.1 percent per year, P = 0.64), with increases in parts of its range and decreases in others. Data for Oklahoma show an increase of 3.2 percent per year (P = 0.00).

References: Baumgartner and Baumgartner 1992; Brown and Wolfe 1978; Brown 1997; Brown and Brown 1998; Davis and Brown 1991; Davis 1998; Mays 1987; Peterjohn and Sauer 1995; Phillips 1986; Sauer et al. 2001; Strawn 1992; Sutton 1967

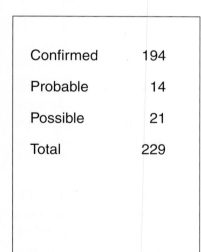

Confirmed	194
Probable	14
Possible	21
Total	229

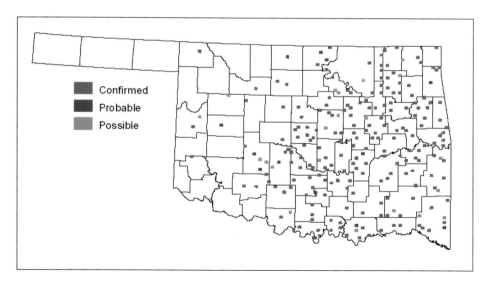

Tree Swallow
Tachycineta bicolor

Charles R. Brown

Courtesy of Bill Horn

Commonly breeding in nest boxes throughout much of the northern United States and well studied as a consequence, Tree Swallows have only recently begun nesting in Oklahoma. The species has taken advantage of dead timber standing in the upper reaches of relatively recently created reservoirs, primarily in eastern Oklahoma, and the birds are now found each year breeding in areas of Oklahoma, western Arkansas, and northeastern Texas where they had not previously been known to nest.

Description: Males and older females are iridescent greenish blue on the upperparts and white on the underparts; yearling females show a mixture of brown and greenish blue on the upperparts. The Tree Swallow is a medium-sized swallow with a moderately forked tail; its overall proportions and flight pattern are most similar to Purple Martin, but the much smaller size of the Tree Swallow easily distinguishes it from the martin.

Breeding Habitat: Tree Swallows are usually found in open habitats, often near water, in areas with standing dead trees that provide nesting cavities. Recent breeding in Oklahoma has been primarily in snags in or near lakes and ponds, but the birds have used nest boxes in a variety of habitats.

Nest: A cavity in a dead tree or nest box. Nest cup within the cavity is made of grasses, rootlets, aquatic vegetation, or other plant materials, and lined with feathers of waterfowl, gulls, or poultry.

NESTING ECOLOGY

Season: May–July. Usually single-brooded.
Eggs: 4–7; pure white.
Development: Incubation is by the female for 14–15 days. Young are provisioned by both sexes, fledge at 21–24 days, and typically are fed by their parents for several days afterward.

DISTRIBUTION AND ABUNDANCE

Rangewide: Breeds throughout much of northern and central North America, with its breeding range extending north to the tree line. Isolated populations breed south to central Arizona and New Mexico. The species winters primarily along the Gulf Coast and in Florida, but may occur as far south as the Caribbean coast of South America in winter.
Historical: Tree Swallows were not known to nest in Oklahoma until 1979, when they were found at Lake Etling in Cimarron County. The number of breeding pairs in the state has increased annually since then, primarily in areas near eastern Oklahoma reservoirs.

Current: Birds seem to be responding to the availability of cavities in dead snags in the upper reaches of the artificial reservoirs and impoundments that were built in (primarily eastern) Oklahoma in the 1950s. As breeding populations grow, birds are now moving into a wider variety of habitats where they occupy nest boxes installed for bluebirds. However, the species is still so rare and local that it can often be missed, especially by atlas surveys, and it probably occurs in more eastern Oklahoma counties than shown.

Population Trend: Breeding Bird Survey data for 1966–2000 show no conclusive trend rangewide (0.5 percent per year, P = 0.19), although it is believed to be increasing over most of its range. The species remains primarily a migrant in Oklahoma at present, but Tree Swallows have started to use bluebird boxes in some areas, and thus they may continue to increase as a breeding bird in the state.

References: Baumgartner and Baumgartner 1992; Heck 1999; Long and Long 1997; Neeld 1993; Price et al. 1995; Robertson et al. 1992; Sauer et al. 2001; Sutton 1967

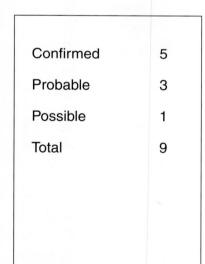

Confirmed	5
Probable	3
Possible	1
Total	9

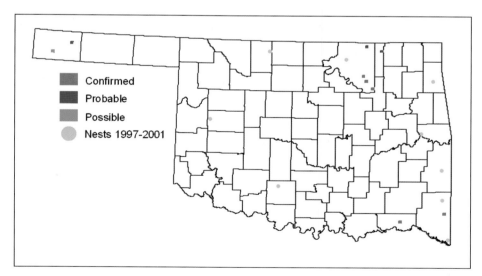

Northern Rough-winged Swallow
Stelgidopteryx serripennis

Charles R. Brown

Courtesy of Ike Raley

Named for the rough leading edge of the outer primary feather which lacks terminal interlocking barbules, the nondescript Northern Rough-winged Swallow is widely distributed throughout all of North America. Unlike most swallows, this species usually nests solitarily, and rarely does more than a single pair nest within sight of each other. Some of the highest-density nesting known for the species anywhere occurs in southern Oklahoma, however, where 10–20 pairs sometimes nest in relatively close proximity to one another in sandy banks on the north side of Lake Texoma. The Northern Rough-winged Swallow is the least studied of the swallows regularly occurring in Oklahoma, and most of what we know about its breeding biology comes from a single study in Michigan in the early 1960s.

Description: The Northern Rough-winged Swallow is grayish brown on the upperparts and dull creamy white on the underparts, with a pale grayish-brown wash on the chest, sides, and flanks. The throat tends to be paler and is sometimes tinged with buff or cinnamon. Its tail is less forked than all other swallows except the Cliff Swallow. The Northern Rough-winged

Swallow can be distinguished from the similar Bank Swallow by the former's lack of a clearly defined breast band and markedly slower flight.

Breeding Habitat: The Northern Rough-winged Swallow occurs in a variety of habitats, but it seems to prefer open areas, including open woodlands, associated with rocky gorges, sandy banks, roadcuts, railroad embankments, gravel pits, or other exposed substrates that provide nesting sites.

Nest: The typical nest is a burrow in the side of a cliff or sandy bank, but Northern Rough-winged Swallows have been known to use a variety of cavities and crevices in vertical surfaces, including gutters, drainpipes, mailboxes, sides of buildings, wharves, boats, and semitrailers. The birds do not excavate their own burrows and use either naturally occurring ones or those dug by kingfishers, Bank Swallows, or small mammals. The terminal end of the burrow is lined with a variety of materials, including twigs, grass, straw, leaves, moss, mud, hair, string, and dung. Feathers are rarely used.

NESTING ECOLOGY

Season: April–July. Single-brooded.
Eggs: 4–7; pure white.
Development: Incubation is by the female for 16 days. Young are provisioned by both sexes, fledge at 18–22 days, and typically are fed by their parents for several days afterward.

DISTRIBUTION AND ABUNDANCE

Rangewide: Breeds throughout the United States and southern Canada. The northern limit of the range extends farther north in the west (north-central British Columbia) than in the east (southeastern Quebec). Breeding also occurs in Mexico and Central America. The birds winter along the Gulf Coast and Rio Grande Valley, and (mostly) in Mexico south to Panama.
Historical: Described as an uncommon summer resident statewide. There are no documented changes in the Northern Rough-winged Swallow's distribution in Oklahoma, although the species is possibly more numerous now than 100 years ago with the widespread creation of sandy banks along the shorelines of man-made lakes and reservoirs.
Current: This species' willingness to use a variety of habitats for nesting is reflected in its relatively even distribution across most of Oklahoma. The bird appears to be uncommon only in southwestern Oklahoma, and even there, it may have been overlooked.

Population Trend: Breeding Bird Survey data for 1966–2000 show no conclusive trend rangewide (0.1 percent per year, P = 0.89) or in Oklahoma (2.5 percent per year, P = 0.42).

References: Baumgartner and Baumgartner 1992; DeJong 1996; Lunk 1962; Price et al. 1995; Sauer et al. 2001; Sutton 1967

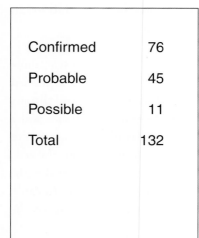

Confirmed	76
Probable	45
Possible	11
Total	132

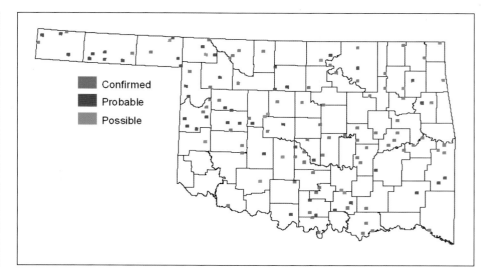

Bank Swallow
Riparia riparia

Charles R. Brown

Courtesy of Bob Gress

Found worldwide, the burrow-nesting Bank Swallow is one of the two highly colonial North American swallows. Colonies in some parts of North America reach 3,000 or more nests. In the Western Hemisphere, Bank Swallows breed primarily in central and northern North America, and breeding occurs rarely as far south as Oklahoma. Colonies have occurred in sandy banks along the Arkansas River in northeastern Oklahoma and in isolated sites elsewhere, but successful breeding was not known to have occurred in the state until 1980. Birds apparently nested in eroded heaps of coarse gravel mine tailings in Ottawa County from 1976 to at least 1983. Banks suitable for nesting tend to be vulnerable to erosion, flooding, and human dis-turbance, and consequently breeding populations in Oklahoma are small and ephemeral.

Description: The Bank Swallow is the smallest swallow found in Oklahoma. Sexes similar; both are grayish brown on the upperparts and have clear white throats and underparts, a prominent brown breast band, and a slightly forked tail. The breast band and clear white underparts distinguish the Bank Swallow from the ecologically and morphologically similar Northern Rough-winged Swallow; Bank Swallows also are noticeably smaller and more delicate in appearance than rough-wings and have a faster flight.

Breeding Habitat: Bank Swallows are found primarily in lowland areas near rivers, streams, lakes, and road-cuts that provide vertical sandy banks for nesting, but the birds also use commercial gravel pits, piles of mine tailings, and other substrates that offer suitable soil for digging burrows.

Nest: Horizontal burrow in sandy bank, excavated by the birds themselves. Burrows tend to be parallel to the ground and perpendicular to the bank face. Burrow depth averages 58–90 cm (23–35 in) in different parts of North America and was about 83 cm (33 in) in colonies in Ottawa County. The terminal end of the burrow is enlarged slightly and lined with a mat of grass, feathers of domestic fowl or other large birds, straw, leaves, or rootlets. Multiple burrows are usually placed in close proximity; single burrows are infrequent, and if found, are more likely to be those of the Northern Rough-winged Swallow.

NESTING ECOLOGY

Season: May–July. Single-brooded in North America.
Eggs: 3–6; pure white.
Development: Incubation primarily by the female for 14–16 days; both sexes feed the nestlings; young fledge at 19–23 days of age, and typically are fed by their parents for several days afterward.

DISTRIBUTION AND ABUNDANCE

Rangewide: Breeds across much of northern and central North America from western Alaska to eastern Newfoundland. Southern limit of breeding range is reached in southern Colorado and northern New Mexico, northern Oklahoma, southern Missouri, and the Ohio River Valley. Isolated breeding populations occur along the Rio Grande River in southern Texas, Tamaulipas, and Coahuila. Bank Swallows winter throughout most of South America south to northern Argentina. Also occurs in much of the Old World.

Historical: Although successful breeding was not documented in Oklahoma until 1980, the Bank Swallow has probably always been a rare nesting species in the state, and it is unlikely that its populations have changed much in Oklahoma in the last 100–200 years. Burrow construction or nesting has been reported from Cimarron, Logan, Muskogee, Ottawa, Sequoyah, and Tulsa counties.

Current: The Bank Swallow's rare and local distribution means it is poorly sampled by atlas methodology. Its current breeding distribution generally matches the areas it has been reported from since the late 1970s and early 1980s.

Population Trend: Breeding Bird Survey data for 1966–2000 show no conclusive trend in North America (-0.9 percent per year, P = 0.23). Little or no trend data are available for the small Oklahoma margin of this species' range, although the rare and local breeding population here probably has not changed much in number.

References: Baumgartner and Baumgartner 1992; Evans 1995; Garrison 1999; Price et al. 1995; Sauer et al. 2001; Sutton 1967; Wilson 1981

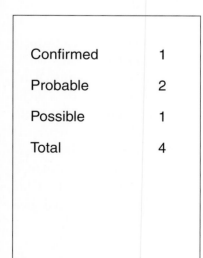

Confirmed	1
Probable	2
Possible	1
Total	4

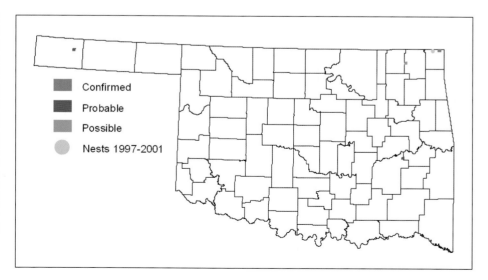

Confirmed
Probable
Possible
Nests 1997-2001

Cliff Swallow
Petrochelidon pyrrhonota

Charles R. Brown

Courtesy of Bill Horn

The Cliff Swallow is one of the most social landbirds in North America, with some colonies reaching up to 3,500 nests in size. The birds often stack their mud nests together closely, and they forage, nest build, mob predators, migrate, and spend the winter in large groups. Historically, this species nested on the sides of steep cliffs and canyon walls underneath vertical overhangs, and large numbers of birds still do so in the Rocky Mountains, the Sierra Nevadas, and the Cascades. Cliff Swallows have also readily adopted artificial nesting sites such as the sides of buildings and bridges, and these alternative sites have allowed them to expand their range into areas where they formerly did not occur or were found only rarely. Their highly social lifestyle has led to the evolution of some complex behavioral traits, including intraspecific brood parasitism by physically transferring eggs between nests, a sophisticated vocal system for identifying their own young among the others in a colony, and transfer of information about food sources through use of specific food-related calls.

Description: Cliff Swallows can be identified by their white forehead, grayish-blue upperparts with white streaking on the back, prominent orange rump, chestnut throat, cream-colored underparts with a light rufous wash, and square tail. The sexes are not safely distinguishable by plumage. The birds can be separated from the ecologically similar Barn Swallow by the latter's deeply forked tail and its absence of an orange rump and white forehead patch. Juvenile Cliff Swallows show extensive variability in color and degree of white speckling on the throat and forehead.

Breeding Habitat: Cliff Swallows are found in a wide

variety of habitats, including grasslands, towns, broken forest, riparian edge, open canyons, foothills, escarpments, and river valleys. Breeding habitat always contains some sort of vertical substrate with a horizontal overhang for nest placement and usually also includes open areas for foraging and a water source for collecting mud.

Nest: A gourd-shaped completely enclosed nest made entirely of mud pellets attached to a vertical wall underneath an overhang. The entrance is usually narrowed into a relatively small opening, often with a tubular "neck" pointing downward. Adjacent nests often share walls. Unlike the Barn Swallow, Cliff Swallows do not incorporate any grass into their mud pellets. The inside of the nest has variable amounts of grass stems; feathers are not used, and some nests have relatively little lining. Nests are placed on natural cliff faces, under bridges, in highway culverts, or (more rarely in Oklahoma) under the eaves of buildings.

NESTING ECOLOGY

Season: April–July. Single-brooded.

Eggs: 3–5; ground color creamy white or pinkish white with speckling of various shades of light and dark browns.

Development: Incubation is by both sexes for 13–15 days. Young are provisioned by both sexes, fledge at 23–26 days of age, and typically are fed by their parents for several days afterward.

DISTRIBUTION AND ABUNDANCE

Rangewide: The Cliff Swallow's breeding range extends from close to the Arctic Ocean in northeastern Alaska south through the Yukon, across most of the Prairie Provinces to central Quebec and Nova Scotia, and south throughout the United States and much of central Mexico. Cliff Swallows winter in southern South America, primarily southwestern Brazil, Uruguay, and northern and central Argentina.

Historical: Cliff Swallows historically were more abundant in western Oklahoma, where they used natural cliff sites such as the Caddo Canyons in Caddo County. With the adoption of bridges and culverts, the species has expanded its range throughout the state, especially in the eastern half. For example, the number of colonies increased markedly in the Stillwater and Tulsa area during the 1990s, and this range expansion and population increase will likely continue in most parts of the state.

Current: The Cliff Swallow remains most common in the western half of Oklahoma, generally west of Interstate 35. However, it continues to increase in the eastern half of the state, being least often reported in the easternmost counties, which are also the most forested and least suitable for the species. The use of bridges and culverts as nest sites makes Cliff Swallows very easy to confirm.

Population Trend: Breeding Bird Survey data for 1966–2000 show no conclusive trend in North America (2.9 percent per year, P = 0.14) or in Oklahoma (-1.1 percent per year, P = 0.76).

References: AOU 1998; Baumgartner and Baumgartner 1992; Brown 1986; Brown and Brown 1995, 1996; Emlen 1954; Oliver 1970; Price et al. 1995; Sauer et al. 2001; Sutton 1967

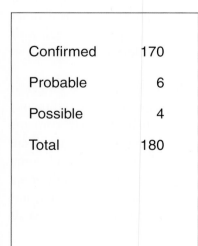

Confirmed	170
Probable	6
Possible	4
Total	180

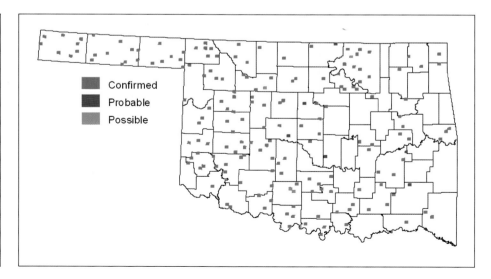

Barn Swallow
Hirundo rustica

Charles R. Brown

The Barn Swallow is the most widely distributed and thoroughly studied swallow in the world. Originally nesting in caves, Barn Swallows began to switch to artificial nesting sites such as the eaves of buildings as soon as European settlement of North America began. This switch was virtually complete by the middle of the twentieth century, and nesting in natural sites is rarely seen anywhere today. No records of Barn Swallows using natural nesting sites have ever been reported in Oklahoma.

Description: The Barn Swallow can be identified by its deeply forked tail with white spots on the inner webs, steely blue upperparts, rufous underparts, and chestnut forehead. The sexes appear similar, but males have longer outer tail streamers and tend to be darker chestnut on the underparts. Barn Swallows can be told from all other swallows in Oklahoma by their deeply forked tail with white spots and their extensive rufous underparts.

Breeding Habitat: Barn Swallows occur in a variety of habitats, including agricultural areas, cities and towns, and along highways. Breeding habitat usually contains open areas (fields, meadows) for foraging and a nest site with a vertical or horizontal substrate underneath some type of roof or ceiling. The species commonly nests under the eaves of buildings, bridges, and culverts, and are usually found as solitary breeding pairs or in small colonies of 5–25 nests.

Nest: A semicircular or cup-shaped nest made of mud pellets attached to a vertical wall or on top of a horizontal platform of some type. Fine pieces of grass are sometimes incorporated into the mud. The inside of the nest contains grass, fine rootlets, or horsehair, and is often profusely lined with large feathers from waterfowl or poultry. Nests are placed underneath eaves of or inside buildings, under bridges, inside highway culverts, on bolts protruding from a wall, and on many other types of artificial structures. Of 156 bridge and culvert nests monitored in Osage County from 1992 to 1996, 84 (54 percent) were successful.

NESTING ECOLOGY

Season: April–August. Double-brooded.
Eggs: 3–6; ground color creamy white with small spots and fine dots of reddish brown, dark brown, or purplish brown. Rarely parasitized by Brown-headed Cowbirds (1 of 157 nests in Osage County from 1992 to 1996).
Development: Incubation is by both sexes, but mostly by the female, for 13–16 days. Young are provisioned by both sexes, fledge at 19–24 days, and typically are fed by their parents for several days afterward.

DISTRIBUTION AND ABUNDANCE

Rangewide: Barn Swallows breed throughout most of Europe and Asia and are widely distributed in North America, where the breeding range includes nearly all of the United States and southern Canada. Also breeds throughout much of central Mexico. Barn Swallows winter uncommonly from Mexico southward through Central America, but the bulk of the population apparently winters throughout South America.

Historical: In Oklahoma, as in other parts of North America, Barn Swallows were probably uncommon and restricted to nesting in a relatively few suitable caves or hollow trees prior to European settlement. With the appearance of buildings and other human structures on the landscape, the birds greatly expanded their range and breeding populations in the state. Reported as common statewide except for the Panhandle, where they are slightly less common.

Current: The Barn Swallow is found as a common breeder throughout the state. Partly as a result of its close association with human habitations and other sorts of artificial structures such as roads, it is an easy species to survey and confirm and was rarely missed by atlas workers.

Population Trend: Breeding Bird Survey data for 1966–2000 show a decline of 0.6 percent per year rangewide for North America (P = 0.00), but show no conclusive trend in Oklahoma (-0.6 percent per year, P = 0.13).

References: Baumgartner and Baumgartner 1992; Brown and Brown 1999; George M. Sutton Avian Research Center unpubl. data; Oliver 1970; Phillips 1986; Sauer et al. 2001; Sutton 1967; Thompson 1961; Withgott and McMahon 1993; Wolfe 1994

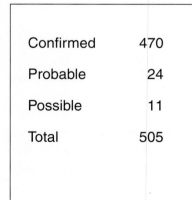

Confirmed	470
Probable	24
Possible	11
Total	505

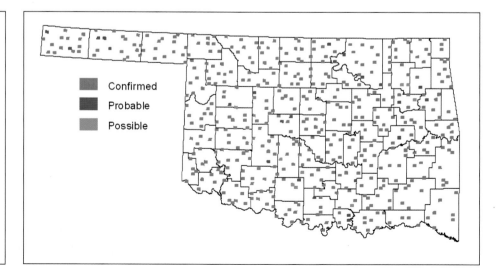

Carolina Chickadee
Poecile carolinensis

Richard A. Stuart

Courtesy of Bill Horn

A human favorite among backyard birds for its ready acceptance of feeders, its acrobatics, and its boisterous personality, the Carolina Chickadee makes a beautiful nest containing a thick layer of moss which retains moisture and remains green during most of the nesting period. On rare occasions, if its nest appears to be in jeopardy, it has been known to carry nestlings off to a safer location.

Description: Sexes similar, gray and white overall with a black cap and bib and a whitish cheek patch. Sounds include a rapid, high-pitched *chick-a-dee-dee-dee-dee* and a song consisting of *fee-bee, fee-bay,* the first set is usually lower than the second set. Very similar in appearance to Black-capped Chickadees, which are rare visitors to northern Oklahoma.

Breeding Habitat: Open woodlands, forests, parks, and residential areas with mature trees, almost anywhere cavities are available.

Nest: May be located in a tree cavity in decayed wood, which the male and female excavate, used woodpecker cavities, a cavity in a fence post, or a nest box, usually 1.2–4.5 m (4–15 ft) up. The nest consists of a thick cushion of moss and other soft materials including hair, fur, and plant down.

NESTING ECOLOGY

Season: March–July. Usually single-brooded.
Eggs: 3–9, usually 6; whitish and evenly spotted with reddish brown concentrated at the large end.
Development: Incubation is by the female for 11–14 days. Young are provisioned by both sexes and fledge at 16–17 days.

DISTRIBUTION AND ABUNDANCE

Rangewide: Nonmigratory, occurring from New Jersey to the Texas Panhandle and southward to the Gulf Coast.
Historical: Described as common over the main body of the state, less common in the counties adjoining the Texas Panhandle, and rare or absent from the Oklahoma Panhandle.
Current: The Carolina Chickadee's choice of nest cavities in or near woodlands restricts it to the main body of the state where it is common and readily noticed because of its constant activity and vocalization. There are very few records for the Oklahoma Panhandle where trees are much less plentiful. The proportion of confirmations is high, perhaps because of the conspicuous begging engaged in by recently fledged young.

Population Trend: Breeding Bird Survey data for 1966–2000 show a decline of 0.9 percent per year rangewide (P = 0.00), but show no conclusive trend in Oklahoma (1.5 percent per year, P = 0.21).

References: AOU 1998; Baicach and Harrison 1997; Baumgartner and Baumgartner 1992; Brewer 1961; Gall 1989; Goertz and Rutherford 1972; Harrison 1975; National Geographic Society 1999; Peterson 1963; Sauer et al. 2001; Sibley 2000; Stokes and Stokes 1996; Sutton 1967

Confirmed	278
Probable	101
Possible	95
Total	474

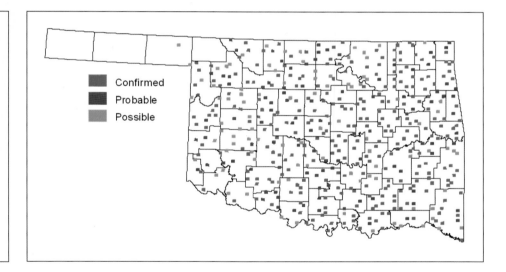

Juniper Titmouse
Baeolophus ridgwayi

David A. Wiggins

Courtesy of Jim and Deva Burns / Natural Impacts

The Juniper Titmouse is a permanent resident of pinyon-juniper woodlands and is rarely found outside this habitat. Although it is a relatively common breeding bird throughout much of the southwestern United States, this drab little titmouse is easily overlooked, has received little study, and much of its natural history remains unknown. Formerly known as the Plain Titmouse, it was recently split into two species, the western Oak Titmouse and the interior Juniper Titmouse.

Description: Sexes similar. Drab, grayish plumage, slightly lighter gray on the belly, with a small crest. Song and calls are chickadee-like, including a rapid, bouncing *tsicka-dee-dee*.

Breeding Habitat: Largely restricted to pinyon-juniper woodlands, rarely in nearby riparian woodland.

Nest: In an old woodpecker cavity or natural hole in tree, with a preference for the latter, or in a nest box. Nest height typically low, 1–2 m (3–6 ft), in pinyon-juniper woodlands.

NESTING ECOLOGY

Season: April–June. Usually single-brooded.
Eggs: Usually 6–7; white, occasionally with minute reddish-brown speckling. No reports of brood parasitism by Brown-headed Cowbirds.
Development: Incubation is by the female for 14–16

days. Young are provisioned by both sexes and fledge at about 17 days, but continue to be fed by adults for several weeks.

DISTRIBUTION AND ABUNDANCE

Rangewide: Resident from the northern Great Basin east to the Rocky Mountain foothills and south to the U.S.-Mexico border.

Historical: First recorded in Oklahoma in 1920 and described in 1931 as a rare winter visitant in Cimarron County, but was found nesting there in 1936. No Oklahoma reports exist from 1938 to 1952, but by 1967 the species was considered a resident. More numerous in winter.

Current: Juniper Titmice occur at relatively low densities and are confined to the pinyon-juniper country of extreme northwestern Cimarron County. As with other species that are restricted to this habitat in Oklahoma, they are probably poorly censussed with traditional atlas project methods. Although no breeding records were recorded from within atlas blocks, about 12 nests in nest boxes were found near Kenton from 1998 to 2001.

Population Trend: Breeding Bird Survey data for 1966–2000 show no conclusive trend rangewide (-0.2 percent per year, P = 0. 94). No trend data are available for Oklahoma.

References: Baicich and Harrison 1997; Cicero 2000; Nice 1931; Sauer et al. 2001; Sutton 1936, 1967; Tate 1923, 1924; Wiggins 1979

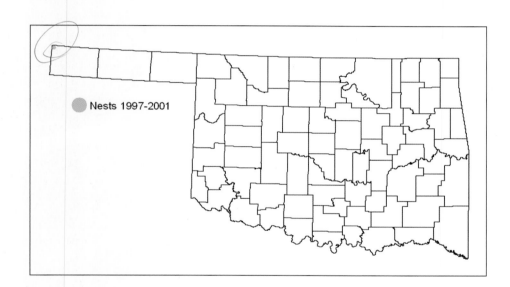

Nests 1997-2001

Tufted Titmouse
Baeolophus bicolor

Black-crested Titmouse
Baeolophus atricristatus

Richard A. Stuart

Courtesy of Bill Horn

These interesting birds sometimes launch "hair raids" on live animals, including humans, to use their hair or fur in nest construction. In spite of being such a bandit, they have endeared themselves to many of us, as they often take advantage of our generosity at feeding stations and nest boxes. Black-crested Titmouse was elevated to full species status only after breeding bird atlas surveys were completed, and any titmouse records from southwestern Oklahoma, where it may occur, were reported as Tufted Titmouse.

Description: Sexes similar. Both have gray upperparts with whitish underparts and peachy orange on the flanks. The crested crown is gray, and the forehead is black in the northern or eastern form, while the crest is black and the forehead is gray in the southern form.

The song is a clear whistled *pete-pete-pete* or *peter-peter-peter*. The Black-crested Titmouse, as its name suggests, has a black crest. The Juniper Titmouse occurs in the northwestern Panhandle where its range does not overlap with either the Tufted or Black-crested Titmouse.

Breeding Habitat: A variety of woodlands and treed suburbs, favoring riparian areas.

Nest: Uses natural cavities, woodpecker holes in dead trees and rotten snags, and nest boxes, usually 0.3–27 m (1–90 ft) above the ground. Bottom of cavity is lined with bark strips, leaves, moss and grass and padded with fur, hair, string, cottony materials, and sometimes snake skins.

NESTING ECOLOGY

Season: March–June. Single-brooded.
Eggs: Usually 3–6, but variable; white or cream speckled with small spots; some concentration of spots at the large end.
Development: Incubation is by the female for 12–14 days; young are provisioned by both sexes and fledge in 15–16 days.

DISTRIBUTION AND ABUNDANCE

Rangewide: Year-round resident throughout woodlands of the eastern half of the United States except the extreme northern areas near the Canadian border.

Historical: Described as abundant in riparian woodlands of eastern Oklahoma, less so in upland woods, becoming scarce in western Oklahoma and absent from the Panhandle. Black-crested Titmouse, or hybrids, have been recorded in Beckham, Cotton, Greer, Harmon, Jackson, Kiowa, and Tillman counties in southwestern Oklahoma.

Current: The Tufted Titmouse is common throughout most of the state in riparian woodlands and uncommon in upland woodlands. Mirroring the historical distribution, population densities decrease in the western part of Oklahoma, where it becomes rare to absent. The conspicuous begging of fledged young make it an easy species to confirm. Because Black-crested Titmouse was not differentiated from Tufted Titmouse, no distribution data resulted from atlas efforts.

Population Trend: Breeding Bird survey data for 1966–2000 show an increase of 1 percent per year rangewide (P = 0.00), but show no conclusive trend in Oklahoma (1.7 percent per year, P = 0.13).

References: AOU 1998; Baicich and Harrison 1997; Baumgartner and Baumgartner 1992; Brackbill 1970; Grubb and Pravosudov 1994; Harrison 1975; National Geographic Society 1999; Offutt 1965; Peacock 1969; Peterson 1963; Sauer et al. 2001; Sibley 2000; Stokes and Stokes 1996; Sutton 1967; Van Tyne 1948

Confirmed	208
Probable	80
Possible	120
Total	408

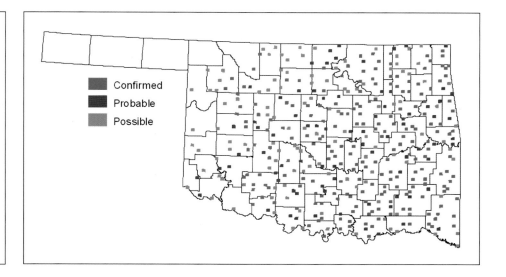

Verdin
Auriparus flaviceps

Guyla Carnes

Courtesy of Bill Horn

A rare and local resident or former resident in Jackson County, this cousin of the chickadees and titmice has a unique habit of building numerous nests for both nesting and winter roosting. Verdin can be found in mesquite and other desert scrub, where it actively feeds by gleaning insects.

Description: Sexes similar, though males are brighter in color. A tiny gray bird with a yellow head and throat and chestnut shoulders. Calls include a high, piercing note and a longer whistle.

Breeding Habitat: Arid areas with sparse, thorny scrub such as mesquite or cactus.

Nest: Spherical, made of thorny twigs, grasses, and spider's silk, lined with feathers and plant down. Usually placed at the end of a low branch in a shrub, cactus, or tree. The entrance to the nest is at the side. Male constructs most of outer shell, while the female does the lining. Smaller nests are built for winter roosting, and nest construction may take place in any month.

NESTING ECOLOGY

Season: April–July. Double-brooded.

Eggs: Usually 4; pale blue or greenish blue; finely speckled with reddish brown, often concentrated at or around the larger end. Rarely parasitized by Brown-headed Cowbirds; not known from Oklahoma.

Development: Incubation is by the female for 14–18 days. Young are provisioned by the female for the first week and later by both sexes. Young leave the nest at about 3 weeks, but continue to roost in any available nest with the male for 2 weeks.

DISTRIBUTION AND ABUNDANCE

Rangewide: Resident from southern Nevada and California through southern Arizona, New Mexico, and Texas south to central Mexico.

Historical: First reported and observed nesting in Oklahoma in Jackson County in 1971. Since described as a rare and local summer resident of Jackson County. One empty nest was found on the ground in Harmon County in 1977, but it may have been a winter dormitory rather than a breeding nest.

Current: No Verdins were reported during the five years of atlas surveys.

Population Trend: Breeding Bird Survey data for 1966–2000 show a decline of 3.7 percent per year rangewide (P = 0.02). No trend data are available for Oklahoma.

References: AOU 1998; Baicich and Harrison 1997; Baumgartner and Baumgartner 1992; National Geographic Society 1999; Owen and Leuck 1978; Seyffert 1972

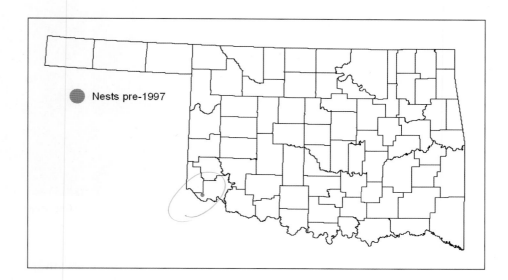

Nests pre-1997

Bushtit
Psaltriparus minimus

David A. Wiggins

Bushtits are relatively common throughout most of western North America in oak woodlands on the Pacific Coast or pinyon-juniper woodlands in the interior, but they just reach Oklahoma in the northwestern corner of the Panhandle. They spend much of the year in large flocks, keeping in constant contact with high, buzzy calls. Bushtits are occasionally cooperative breeders, with one or more helpers assisting the parents at the distinctive, pendulous nest.

Description: One of North America's smallest passerines, Bushtits are plain gray to grayish-brown birds with long tails. Males have dark eyes while females have pale eyes. Both sexes call frequently, with high, buzzy contact notes. Unlikely to be confused with any other species in pinyon-juniper habitat.

Breeding Habitat: Interior populations, including those in the Oklahoma Panhandle, are largely restricted to pinyon-juniper woodlands. They may also occur in scrub oak and along the margins of low- to mid-elevation pine (e.g., ponderosa) forests.

Nest: Finely woven, pendulous sac some 25 cm (10 in) deep constructed by both sexes of grasses and other plant material held together with spider webs. Usually placed 2–5 m (6–15 ft) high in pinyon, juniper, scrubby oak, or hackberry. Construction takes 2 weeks to 2 months. Because of this significant time invest-ment, cooperative breeding behavior in Bushtits is driven by competition for existing nest sites. Failed breeders may attempt to take over an existing nest, or join with the pair as helpers, and try to contribute eggs to a second nesting attempt.

NESTING ECOLOGY

Season: April–June. Single- or possibly double-brooded.

Eggs: 4–6, sometimes more; dull white. Few records of parasitism by Brown-headed Cowbird, and none in Oklahoma.

Development: Incubation is by both sexes for 12–13 days. Young are fed by both parents and occasionally by 1 or more helpers, which are often failed breeders. Young fledge at approximately 14 days.

DISTRIBUTION AND ABUNDANCE

Rangewide: Resident along the Pacific Coast, from southern British Columbia south to Mexico and east to the central Rocky Mountain foothills and west-central Texas.

Historical: Described as a resident in northwestern Cimarron County where it is restricted to rough mesa country. Has occasionally strayed eastward to north-western and southwestern Oklahoma, but there are no nest records for these areas. A number of nest records exist for northwestern Cimarron County.

Current: In Oklahoma, Bushtits are restricted to pinyon-juniper habitats in the Black Mesa region of extreme northwest Cimarron County. While no Bushtits were recorded in atlas blocks, one active nest was found in 1999 and two in 2000 not far from Kenton.

Population Trend: Breeding Bird Survey data for 1966–2000 show no conclusive trend rangewide (-1.9 percent per year, P = 0.13). No trend data are available for Oklahoma.

References: Baicich and Harrsion 1997; Baumgartner and Baumgartner 1992; Humann 2001; Johnsgard 1979; Kaufman 2000; Nice 1931; Sauer et al. 2001; Sloane 1996, 2001; Sutton 1967

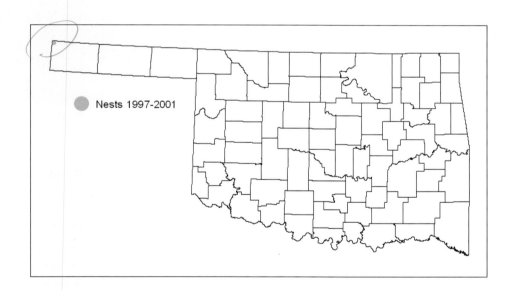

Nests 1997-2001

Red-breasted Nuthatch
Sitta canadensis

John S. Shackford

Courtesy of Bob Gress

The small, handsome Red-breasted Nuthatch is a delightful visitor to Oklahoma in the nonbreeding season. It is usually seen then at bird feeders and in coniferous trees. As a breeding species in the state, only two known or probable nesting records exist.

Description: The upperparts are gray, except for black on the crown and eye line, while the underparts are rusty in the male and slightly paler in the female. On the face, a white eyebrow surrounded by black distinguishes it from other nuthatches. Call is a high-pitched, nasal, *yank-yank-yank*.

Breeding Habitat: Mature coniferous forest, especially balsam fir, spruce, and pine forests in the northern and western United States and the southern one-third of Canada.

Nest: Excavated cavity, with nest of grass, bark strips, and pine needles lined with fur, feathers, hair, or fine plant materials. Evergreen pitch is smeared around nest entrance, possibly to reduce competitive or predatory interactions.

NESTING ECOLOGY

Season: April–July. Single-brooded.
Eggs: Usually 6; white, spotted profusely with brown.
Development: Incubation is by the female for 12–13 days. Young are provisioned by both sexes and fledge at

18–21 days, but are fed by the adults for another 2 weeks or more.

DISTRIBUTION AND ABUNDANCE

Rangewide: Resident in coniferous forests over much of Canada and southeastern Alaska, south to the northern United States, as well as southward into mountainous regions of the eastern and western United States. In recent years, the southern edge of this species' range appears to be expanding somewhat to the south and east. Winters irregularly far south of normal range.

Historical: Described as a rare and erratic winter resident. No early breeding records for Oklahoma. First record of probable nesting reported from Oklahoma County in 1970, and a second, confirmed report came from Ponca City in Kay County in 1981.

Current: An extremely rare nester in the northern half of Oklahoma. The increase of trees, including evergreens, on the Great Plains in recent decades may be responsible for an occasional rare nest as far south as Oklahoma.

Population Trend: Breeding Bird Survey data for 1966–2000 show an increase of 1.2 percent per year rangewide (P = 0.00). No trend data are available for Oklahoma.

References: AOU 1998; Baicich and Harrison 1997; Baumgartner 1992; Baumgartner and Baumgartner 1992; Bent 1964b; Ghalambor and Martin 1999; Johnsgard 1979; Sauer et al. 2001; Sutton 1967; Terres 1980; Vacin 1972

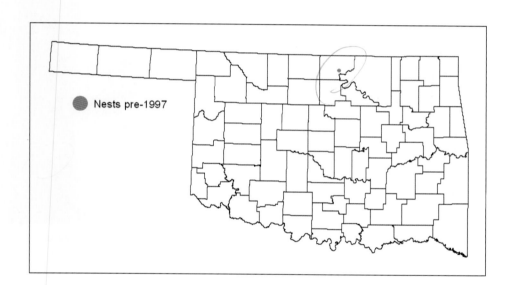

● Nests pre-1997

White-breasted Nuthatch
Sitta carolinensis

Mickle D. Duggan and William A. Carter

Courtesy of Bill Horn

A delightful acrobat, the White-breasted Nuthatch is often first identified by its behavior. The ability to seemingly defy gravity allows it to move about both above and below branches in any direction. Tool use by this species has been recorded only once in the state.

Description: A small, compact bird with short legs and very long toes, often seen perched upside-down or moving down the trunk of a tree head first closely hugging the tree. White-breasted Nuthatches have white underparts and cheeks with white completely circling the eye; back is blue gray. The crown and extreme upper back is black, but may show dark bluish gray to dull black in young and females. Flanks may appear rusty. Tail is short and wings extend almost to the end of the tail. Both wing and tail feathers are blackish showing blue-gray markings. Bill is long and may appear to be slightly upturned. Nasal *yank, yank* call notes are distinctive.

Breeding Habitat: Areas with mature deciduous trees, including mixed deciduous and coniferous trees, urban parks, and woodland edge areas. Pairs remain together for life and on nesting territory all year.

Nest: As secondary cavity nesters, White-breasted Nuthatches use naturally occurring cavities or old woodpecker holes and, rarely, nest boxes. They may, however, perform some excavation work on a cavity. Nest height varies from 3–18 m (10–60 ft). Nest is a simple cup of plant material (wood fibers and chips, bark strips, twigs, and grasses) forming the base, lined with hair, fur, and feathers and is built by the female.

NESTING ECOLOGY

Season: March–April. Single-brooded.

Eggs: 5–9; white, and spotted reddish-brown, spotting concentrating on large end. May show a pinkish tint and have lavender markings. Brown-headed Cowbird parasitism is rare and has not been reported in Oklahoma.

Development: Incubation is by the female for 12–14 days. Young are provisioned by both sexes and fledge at about 26 days, but remain with parents for several more weeks.

DISTRIBUTION AND ABUNDANCE

Rangewide: Resident from southern Canada, throughout the United States, and much of Mexico in appropriate habitat.

Historical: Described as a common resident in woodlands of the eastern half of state, less common in western part of state.

Current: White-breasted Nuthatches are common residents in woodlands of the eastern half of the state. In western Oklahoma, their numbers decrease as acceptable woodland habitat diminishes and they are restricted to riparian corridors. In areas such as this where they are found only locally, atlasing methods may not accurately reflect their distribution. White-breasted Nuthatches are single-brooded, and young of the year are not easily distinguished from adult females, making confirmation of breeding difficult.

Population Trend: Breeding Bird Survey data for 1966–2000 show an increase of 2.2 percent per year rangewide (P = 0.00) and an increase of 3.1 percent per year in Oklahoma (P = 0.07).

References: AOU 1998; Baicich and Harrison 1997; Baumgartner and Baumgartner 1992; Droege 1993; Kaufman 1996; Mitchell 1993; Pravosudov and Grubb 1993; Sauer et al. 2001; Sutton 1967

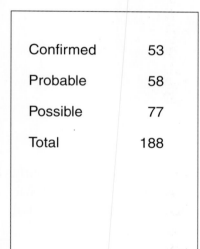

Confirmed	53
Probable	58
Possible	77
Total	188

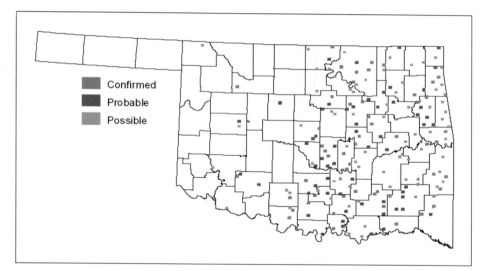

Brown-headed Nuthatch
Sitta pusilla

Mickle D. Duggan and William A. Carter

Courtesy of Ike Raley

Small, active Brown-headed Nuthatches are often heard before they are seen. Their constant, tiny squeaking is given as they work in groups of two or more along branches and trunks of conifers. Brown-headed Nuthatches share the acrobatic traits of the nuthatch family and are usually seen busily scrambling about gleaning insects from tree bark in the small portion of southeastern Oklahoma in which they occur. They also use bark as a prying tool to expose insect larvae and are one of the few cooperatively breeding birds found in North America.

Description: Sexes similar. A brown cap extends down to a narrow dark eye line. The back is grayish blue with a white spot at the neck line. Underparts are buffy white. Both wing and tail feathers are grayish and may show some brownish markings. Calls include nasal squeaks.

Breeding Habitat: Open, mature, old-growth pine woods with standing snags.

Nest: A cavity excavated by the pair and helpers; several excavations may be started before one is finished. The cavity is usually in standing rotting wood such as a stump or old fence post, or occasionally in old woodpecker holes and birdhouses. Nest is unusually low to the ground for a cavity nester, frequently about 1.2 m

(4 ft), although nests may be constructed much higher. Nest composed of bark fibers, wood chips, pine seed wings, and other materials.

NESTING ECOLOGY

Season: March–May. Usually single-brooded, but may renest after failure of first nest. There are few documented dates for nesting in Oklahoma. Young male helpers may attend pair from the time of cavity excavation through fall.

Eggs: Usually 4–6; white and heavily spotted red brown with some blotching at the larger end. Not known to be parasitized by Brown-headed Cowbirds in Oklahoma and very rarely reported elsewhere.

Development: Incubation is by the female for 14 days; male may feed incubating female and roost at night in cavity. Both parents and helpers feed nestlings through fledging at 18–19 days and thereafter for 3–4 weeks.

DISTRIBUTION AND ABUNDANCE

Rangewide: Endemic in pine woods of the southeastern United States, from southeastern Oklahoma and east Texas to southern Maryland.

Historical: Formerly more common in southeastern Oklahoma pine forests before timber cutting removed many of the old-growth pines. Rare and local resident in scattered areas of preferred habitat in Atoka, Latimer, LeFlore, McCurtain, and Pushmataha counties.

Current: Oklahoma's rare, scattered pockets of Brown-headed Nuthatches are not readily detected by atlas project methodology. This species may be regularly located at known sites in the counties named above. Oklahoma populations of the Brown-headed Nuthatch should be carefully monitored as continued removal of old-growth pine forests eliminates the required habitat of the remnant population here at the northwestern-most limits of its range.

Population Trend: Breeding Bird Survey data for 1966–2000 show a decline of 2 percent per year rangewide (P = 0.01). Insufficient trend data are available for Oklahoma, but undoubtedly fewer birds exist here today than in presettlement times due to timber harvesting and dam construction.

References: AOU 1998; Baicich and Harrison 1997; Baumgartner and Baumgartner 1992; Carter 1972; Kaufman 1996; McNair 1984b; Halloran and Conner 1987; Oklahoma Bird Records Committee 2000; Sauer et al. 2001; Sutton 1967; Withgott and Smith 1998

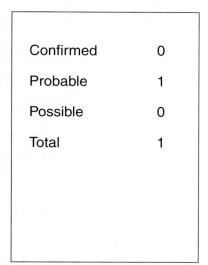

Confirmed	0
Probable	1
Possible	0
Total	1

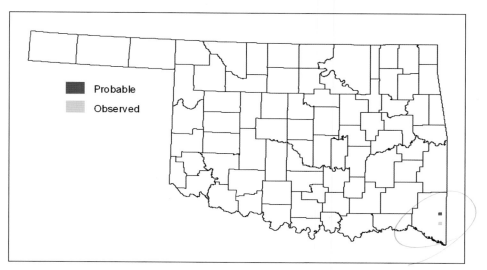

Rock Wren

Salpinctes obsoletus

Thomas G. Shane

Courtesy of Alan Versaw

From Black Mesa, the Glass, Quartz, and Wichita mountains, to the Tenkiller Dam, as its name implies, this wren is most often found in areas with significant rock outcrops or rocky slopes where it may set up a nesting territory. This magnificent songster is more often heard than seen. Once located it is often observed on top of a high rocky point in its territory, pouring out its memorable song and performing its familiar bob.

Description: Sexes similar. Both are a light grayish-brown with some fine speckles of black and white on the back, black barring on the tail, and a contrasting cinnamon rump. An individual male can have over 100 songs in its repertoire, many of which appear to be learned from neighboring males.

Breeding Habitat: Rock outcrops and fractured cliffs, often with a talus slope below containing large boulders, grasses, and occasional shrubs. Sometimes uses holes in a dirt bank of a gulch. These locations are often surrounded by prairie.

Nest: In holes and crevices in rock cliffs, in holes under large boulders, and in holes in dirt banks. Male and female often build a pavement of stone leading to and into nest hole and then carry sticks and stones into hole for nest base. Female builds nest of fine dry grasses lined with hair or wool, with male occasionally gathering materials and bringing them to her.

NESTING ECOLOGY

Season: April–July. Double- to triple-brooded.
Eggs: Usually 5–6, but variable; white speckled and spotted with reddish-brown around the larger end. Sometimes parasitized by the Brown-headed Cowbird in the Great Plains; one report for Oklahoma.
Development: Incubation is by the female for 12–15 days. Young are provisioned by both sexes and fledge at 14–16 days. The male continues to tend the fledglings for about 1 week while the female begins a new nest.

DISTRIBUTION AND ABUNDANCE

Rangewide: Breeds from southern Alberta south across the western United States to Central America. Winters in the southern two-thirds of the breeding range.
Historical: Described as an uncommon resident of western Oklahoma. Small numbers moved into eastern Oklahoma to nest during the 1950s and 1960s, most likely in response to the construction of large rock-covered dams.
Current: The Rock Wren is generally restricted to the areas of large rock formations and outcrops in the western part of the state. Consequently, these isolated rock formations are often missed by the random placement of atlas blocks. The true distribution of the species is therefore not accurately depicted with atlasing methods. This, perhaps, was the reason for the apparent absence of the species from Comanche County. Confirmation of breeding can also be difficult given the often rugged, rocky habitat.

Population Trend: Breeding Bird Survey data for 1966–2000 show a decline of 1.8 percent per year rangewide (P = 0.00). No trend data are available for Oklahoma.

References: AOU 1998; Baicich and Harrison 1997; Baumgartner and Baumgartner 1992; Lowther et al. 2000; Matiasek 1998; Sauer et al. 2001; Sutton 1967: Tyler 1979a

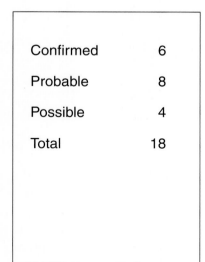

Confirmed	6
Probable	8
Possible	4
Total	18

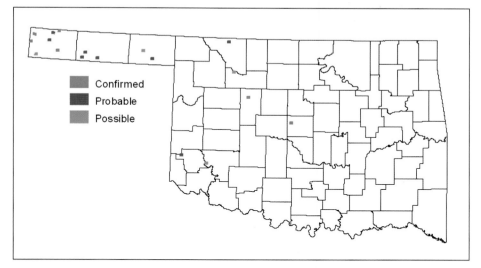

Canyon Wren
Catherpes mexicanus

Sebastian T. Patti

Courtesy of Joseph A. Grzybowski

The Canyon Wren is a large rufous-colored wren resident in rocky areas and canyonlands of the western part of the United States. It is largely restricted to rocky cliffs and rock outcrops throughout its range and is well known in these habitats by its familiar song, a series of sweet, cascading but slowing whistles, ending in several flat buzzes.

Description: Sexes similar, generally rufous above and below, with some indistinct blackish barring and white spotting; head grayish and throat and upper breast clean white. The tail is bright rufous with distinct black barring. Bill is long and slightly decurved. Next to the Rock Wren, with which it shares a similar habitat, it is the largest wren in Oklahoma.

Breeding Habitat: Requires cliffs, rocky outcrops, or boulder piles, with crevices in these areas furnishing nest sites that are often inaccessible to people.

Nest: Both sexes construct a cup-shaped structure composed of a base of twigs or other coarse material lined with softer materials such as feathers, hairs, or lichens. Placed in rock caverns, crevices, cliff faces, or banks.

NESTING ECOLOGY

Season: April–July. Probably double-brooded.
Eggs: Usually 5; white with fine speckling.
Development: Incubation is by the female for 12–18 days. Young are provisioned by both sexes and fledge at about 15 days.

DISTRIBUTION AND ABUNDANCE

Rangewide: Resident from southern British Columbia and eastern Washington and Oregon, and southwestern Idaho, south through southern Wyoming, Nevada, western and southern Colorado, Utah, California, Arizona, and New Mexico, through western Texas and the highlands of interior Mexico as far south as Oaxaca. There is a disjunct population in the Black Hills of South Dakota, Wyoming, and Montana. Mostly nonmigratory, with a few altitudinal movements noted during the winter months.
Historical: Described as an uncommon resident in the Black Mesa country of northwestern Cimarron County and in the rougher parts of southwestern Oklahoma.

Current: The Canyon Wren is limited in its distribution in Oklahoma to the northwestern part of Cimarron County and to the more rugged areas in the southwestern part of the main body of the state. The species' range seems to be restricted to those portions of the state where the topography is composed of cliffs or rugged, rocky outcrops. The species was only confirmed breeding on one atlas block, in Comanche County.

Population Trend: Poorly measured, and Breeding Bird Survey data for 1966–2000 show no conclusive trend rangewide (-2.7 percent per year, P = 0.21). No trend data are available for Oklahoma.

References: AOU 1998; Baicich and Harrision 1997; Baumgartner and Baumgartner 1992; Jones 1998; Jones and Dieni 1995; Nice 1931; Ortenburger and Little 1930; Sauer et al. 2001; Stevenson 1936; Sutton 1967

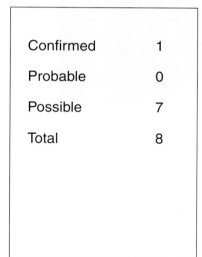

Confirmed	1
Probable	0
Possible	7
Total	8

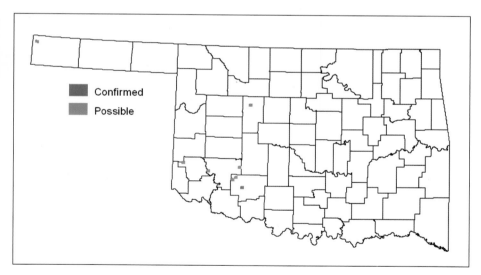

Bewick's Wren

Thryomanes bewickii

Mark Howery

The Bewick's Wren is the common nesting wren around farmyards and rural residences across western and central Oklahoma. This wren is also found in eastern Oklahoma but is much less common, especially south of the Arkansas River. The plumage color and song complexity of Bewick's Wrens varies geographically across the United States. Most Oklahoma birds appear to belong to western forms, which tend to have medium-brown to gray-brown plumage. Some birds from the Ozark region may belong to the eastern population, and eastern birds appear to winter in extreme southeastern Oklahoma.

Description: In Oklahoma, the plumage is usually a grayish-brown on the back and wings, with a contrasting white breast and belly. This species lacks wing bars, but has a bold white stripe running across each side of the head just above the eye. The tail is long and thin in proportion to the body and is often held upright at an angle between 45 and 90 degrees relative to the body. Additionally, the tail feathers have white tips that give the tail the appearance of being edged in fine white spots. Though small in size, the male Bewick's Wren's song is a loud and distinctive sequence of musical buzzes and ascending trills. Similar species include the House Wren, which is a slightly smaller species and lacks the white eye stripe, and the Carolina Wren, which is larger and has a rusty cinnamon color on the breast and belly.

Breeding Habitat: Closely associated with human habitation, dense thickets, and rocky hillsides and canyons. This is a fairly common resident of shrub borders in backyards, farmsteads, thickets, and hedgerows across most of Oklahoma, except for the Ouachita Mountains and West Gulf Coastal Plain where this species is rare. They tend to avoid heavily forested habitats and prairies that lack some form of shrub cover.

Nest: A bulky cup constructed by both sexes of an outer layer of small sticks and twigs and lined with fine grass and feathers. They are normally constructed in natural tree cavities, brush piles, and rocks, but wrens also take readily to artificial structures such as nest boxes, sheds, and fence posts. Nests are typically constructed within 1–3 m (3–10 ft) of the ground.

NESTING ECOLOGY

Season: Early March–mid-July. Frequently double-brooded.
Eggs: Usually 5–7; white with many fine brown and purplish flecks and speckles.
Development: Incubation is by the female for 12–14 days. Young are provisioned by both sexes, fledge at about 14 days, and continue to be fed by adults for another 2–3 weeks.

DISTRIBUTION AND ABUNDANCE

Rangewide: Resident from central Texas, Oklahoma, and the Ozark region of Missouri westward to the Pacific Coast. The range extends northward along the Pacific Coast to British Columbia. To the south, the range extends into southern Mexico. Scattered populations also occur between the Mississippi River and the Appalachian Mountains; however, these populations have declined substantially over the past 100 years.

Historical: Described as a resident throughout the state but less common in winter, suggesting some migration. Interestingly, Bewick's Wrens appear to be more common during the winter months in far-southeastern Oklahoma, possibly as a result of a seasonal influx of wintering birds from populations to the north and east.

Current: The Bewick's Wren was located in a large percentage of atlas blocks in western and central Oklahoma. Bewick's Wrens were commonly confirmed as a breeding species within the blocks in which they were detected, possibly as a result of their tendency to nest near human residences or in nest boxes. The atlas surveys demonstrate a dramatic reduction in the species' frequency of occurrence in the Ozark and Ouachita mountains, where the landscape is dominated by mature forest.

Population Trend: Breeding Bird Survey data for 1966–2000 show no conclusive trend rangewide (-0.2 percent per year, P = 0.67) or in Oklahoma (-0.4 percent per year, P = 0.67), although eastern U.S. populations are declining. The species is currently declining in the Ozark region and eastern Oklahoma, but there has not been a contraction in its range.

References: Baicich and Harrison 1997; Baumgartner and Baumgartner 1992; Erhlich et al. 1988; James and Neal 1986; Kennedy and White 1997; Sauer et al. 2001; Sibley 2000; Sutton 1967

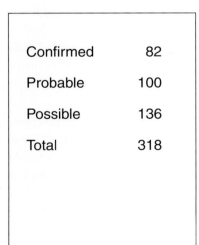

Confirmed	82
Probable	100
Possible	136
Total	318

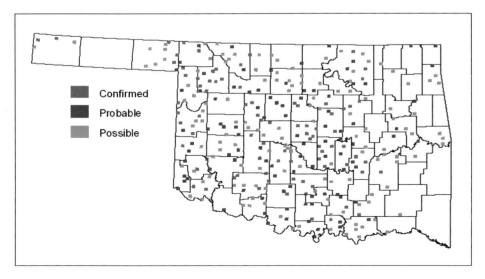

House Wren
Troglodytes aedon

John S. Shackford

Courtesy of Bob Gress

The House Wren, with its bubbly, cheerful, familiar song, is one of North America's favorite songbirds. Spring is always a little more fascinating with a pair of these wrens singing and building a nest in the yard, but its range in Oklahoma is somewhat limited, making it an extra treat here.

Description: The House Wren is dull brown above and buffy below, with a faint brown eyebrow. It has fainter dark barring on the lower belly and a longer tail than the Winter Wren, while the Carolina Wren is larger, has brighter browns, and has no such barring on the lower belly.

Breeding Habitat: Where moisture and vegetation are plentiful, House Wrens nest in a wide variety of habitats. The House Wren nests in the northern one-half of Oklahoma, tending to nest in areas with ample moisture in yards and gardens, shelterbelts, and other heavy woods, while avoiding drier upland areas.

Nest: Selects a wide variety of natural or artificial cavities, in trees (such as old woodpecker holes), nest boxes, iron pipes, etc. Outer part of the nest is made up of small sticks and twigs, while the inner lining has finer materials such as hair, feathers, or wool.

NESTING ECOLOGY

Season: May–August. Double-brooded.

Eggs: Usually 4–8; white or pinkish white and profusely speckled with small brown dots. Very rarely parasitized by Brown-headed Cowbirds; parasitism not known in Oklahoma.

Development: Incubation is by the female for 12–13 days. Young are provisioned by both sexes and fledge in about 16–18 days, but continue to be fed by adults for about 2 weeks.

DISTRIBUTION AND ABUNDANCE

Rangewide: Breeds across the northern two-thirds of the United States and well into southern Canada. Winters in the southern one-fifth of the United States southward through most of Mexico.

Historical: Oklahoma is at the southern limit of the breeding range, where it nests, usually sparingly, in the northern half of the state in towns, shelterbelts, or other heavy woodlands. Described as local and uncommon in most parts of this range. Has nested southward to Stephens, Cleveland, and Oklahoma counties.

Current: Nests primarily in the northern half of Oklahoma. Death due to overheating of young in the nesting cavity may limit, at least in part, successful nesting in southern Oklahoma. Usually a rare to uncommon breeder, it can reach moderate to high densities in heavy woodlands in Harper and Beaver counties. A number of the Possible Breeder blocks may represent nonresident birds singing during spring migration.

Population Trend: Breeding Bird Survey data for 1966–2000 show an increase of 1.1 percent per year rangewide (P = 0.00) and an increase of 5.4 percent per year in Oklahoma (P = 0.01).

References: AOU 1998; Baicich and Harrison 1997; Baumgartner and Baumgartner 1992; Bent 1964b; Brown 1985; Hunt 1986; Johns 1971; Johnsgard 1979; Johnson 1998; Peterjohn and Sauer 1999; Sauer et al. 2001; Sutton 1967; Terres 1980

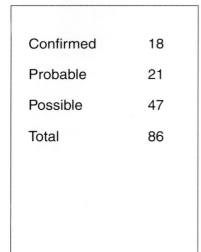

Confirmed	18
Probable	21
Possible	47
Total	86

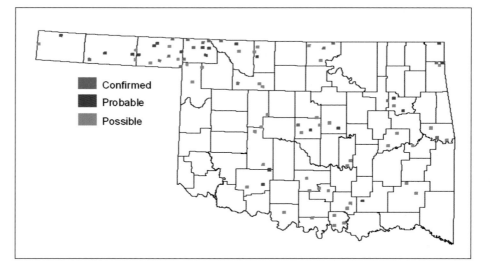

Sedge Wren
Cistothorus platensis

Sebastian T. Patti

Courtesy of Bob Gress

The Sedge Wren is a small short-billed, short-tailed wren of sedgy marshes and hay meadows. Formerly known as the Short-billed Marsh Wren, the species has a fascinating breeding phenology and sexual behavior. While breeding occurs in the northern part of the species' range as early as May, breeding is delayed until as late as August in the southern portions of its range. The species is polygynous, and males are known to build "dummy nests," possibly as decoys to avoid or reduce the effects of predation.

Description: Sexes similar. Top of head and back brownish, streaked with white. Underparts whitish, washed with warm buff. The rump is cinnamon buffy, and the wings and tail are brownish-black and boldly barred. Easily separated from all other North American wrens by its back streaks, and from the similar Marsh

Wren by its streaked crown, lack of prominent white eye stripe, and by its vocalizations. The song, delivered only by males, is a two-part composition. The first part is a series of 3–4 introductory *chapp* notes; the second part a dry, staccato chattering, or trill, of 5–7 notes. Male Sedge Wrens are known to sing at night.

Breeding Habitat: Areas with dense tall cover of grasses or sedges, such as marshes, hay meadows, and old fields. Retired croplands such as those encouraged by the Conservation Reserve Program have apparently had a beneficial effect on the species by providing new areas to colonize. Because of the ephemeral nature of these habitats, the species has relatively low site fidelity and may avoid or abandon areas that had been populated in the past. Sedge Wrens seem to avoid areas with short or sparse vegetative cover and marshes or wetlands dominated by cattails.

Nest: Built by the male, it is a globe-type structure with a side entrance; grasses and sedges are used in construction. Nests that are actually used for egg laying (as opposed to "dummy nests," which are also built) are modified by the female wren to include fur or feathers in the interior. The structure is usually placed less than 1 m (3 ft) above the ground in dense sedges or at the base of a small tree.

NESTING ECOLOGY

Season: Little information; probably July–August. In the northern part of the species' range, nesting occurs in May and June. In the southern portions of the species' range (which would include Oklahoma), nesting occurs later, in July and August.

Eggs: Usually 7; white.

Development: Incubation is by the female for 13–16 days. Young are provisioned by the female and fledge at about 12–14 days.

DISTRIBUTION AND ABUNDANCE

Rangewide: Breeds from east-central Alberta southeast through eastern Kansas and east to New York. Also breeds east and south of this range later in the summer, possibly including Oklahoma. More research is necessary to determine the origin of these late, southern breeding birds.

Historical: The only confirmed breeding record for Oklahoma is a nest found in Harper County in 1936. Birds have suddenly appeared singing in mid-July of several years in the mid 1990s in Washington County tallgrass prairie plots that had been studied all summer and had not had Sedge Wrens earlier in the year. August sightings have also been reported for Tulsa and Sequoyah counties.

Current: During the atlas project period, this species was only recorded on three widely scattered blocks. Observers in one block in Blain County reported the species as Probable for breeding, while observers in both Garfield and McIntosh counties recorded the species as Possible for breeding. The relevant literature would seem to suggest that if breeding does occur within the state, it most likely takes place after many other species have already nested: that is, in late July, August, and even early September. This may have contributed to observers not recording the species, or observers recording birds that were still migrating north. Additional fieldwork late in the breeding season may well reveal information about this very interesting species' summer distribution in Oklahoma.

Population Trend: Breeding Bird Survey data for 1966–2000 show an increase of 3.0 percent per year rangewide (P = 0.00). No trend data are available for Oklahoma.

References: AOU 1998; Baumgartner and Baumgartner 1992; Busby and Zimmerman 2001; Dechant, Sondreal, Johnson, Igl, Goldade, Zimmerman, and Euliss 2001; Herkert et al. 2001; Jacobs and Wilson 1997; Oberholser 1974; Reinking, D. L., pers. observ.; Robbins and Easterla 1992; Sauer et al. 2001; Sibley 2000; Sutton 1967; Thompson and Ely 1992

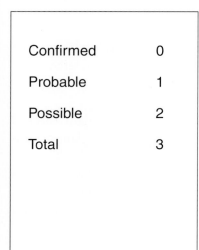

Confirmed	0
Probable	1
Possible	2
Total	3

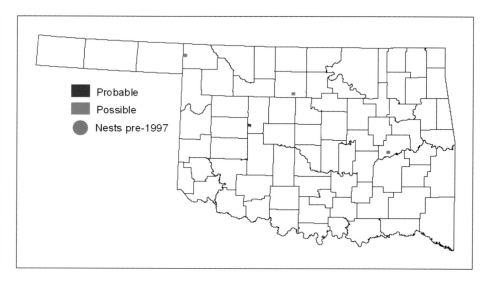

Blue-gray Gnatcatcher
Polioptila caerulea

Bonnie L. Gall

Courtesy of Bill Horn

This tiny but active bird is hard to miss in the woodlands of Oklahoma. If you don't see it busily feeding on gnats and other small flying insects, you will certainly hear it giving its fussy, wheezing call as it flits around in the branches over your head. The Blue-gray Gnatcatcher has often been described as a miniature mockingbird in color and shape.

Description: Male is blue-gray above, whitish underneath, with a black upper tail and white outer tail feathers. Female has a grayer back, but is otherwise similar. In breeding plumage, male shows a black line on side of crown. Call is a raspy *pweez* or *screez*. The song is nondescript, variously described as rapid notes and trills of high pitch.

Breeding Habitat: Oak woods, mixed forests, riparian areas, and wooded swamps, with a preference for broad-leaved trees.

Nest: The nest is cup shaped, built of tightly packed plant down, fiber, oak catkins, and other plant materials kept together with insect or spider web silk. The outside is covered with lichens and/or plant down, and the inside is lined with fine plant material or sometimes feathers. The nest is usually attached to small horizontal branches or tree forks usually less than 7.6 m (24 ft) above ground. Both sexes build the nest in 1–2 weeks, making frequent, often obvious direct flights with nest material. Gnatcatchers may tear up a completed or partially built nest and use the material to build another nest, perhaps due to disturbance or change in conditions that make the first site undesirable.

NESTING ECOLOGY

Season: Early April–early June. Single- to double-brooded.

Eggs: Usually 4–5; pale bluish or bluish white with reddish-brown spots or fine dots. Sometimes parasitized by cowbirds, in which case few if any gnatcatchers fledge.

Development: Incubation is by both sexes and averages 13 days. Young are provisioned by both sexes, fledge in 10–15 days, and are fed for another 3 weeks.

DISTRIBUTION AND ABUNDANCE

Rangewide: A summer resident from New England to Florida and across the central and southern United States to California. Populations appear to be increasing and expanding northward. A year-round resident along the coastal areas from North Carolina, Florida, southern Texas, and most of Mexico. Some winter south to Honduras.

Historical: Common in forests of eastern Oklahoma and in oak-juniper of central Oklahoma during early summer. One study in McCurtain County indicated an average of 0.14 pairs per ha (5.6 pairs per 100 ac). By late summer to fall, it is uncommon in the same areas. Although less common in the west, it has been known to breed to the western edge of the Oklahoma Panhandle. Mostly recorded from late March through September. Only a few winter records exist for the state.

Current: Blue-gray Gnatcatchers were observed in at least one atlas block in every Oklahoma county except Greer County in the southwest and Texas County in the Panhandle. This bird's noisy behavior and its use of a variety of woodland habitat types made it easy to observe. Its conspicuous nest-building behavior made it easy to confirm. The atlas project distribution mirrors the historical distribution.

Population Trend: Breeding Bird Survey data for 1966–2000 show an increase of 0.7 percent per year rangewide (P = 0.04), but show no conclusive trend in Oklahoma (1.7 percent per year, P = 0.24).

References: Baumgartner and Baumgartner 1992; Carter 1967; Ellison 1992; Harrison 1975; Johnsgard 1979; National Geographic Society 1999; Root 1969; Sauer et al. 2001; Sutton 1967; Weston 1964

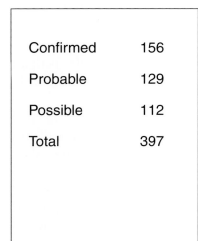

Confirmed	156
Probable	129
Possible	112
Total	397

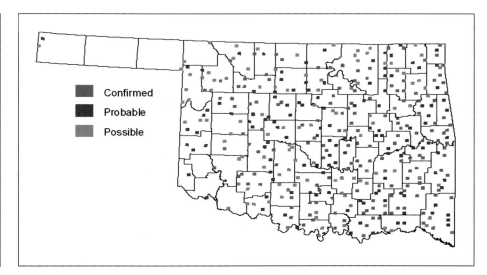

Eastern Bluebird
Sialia sialis

William A. Carter and Mickle D. Duggan

Courtesy of Bill Horn

Eastern Bluebirds have benefited from the efforts of thousands of dedicated and adoring human fans across their entire range. Hundreds of nest boxes across our state are used by bluebirds and other secondary cavity nesters. The nationwide Breeding Bird Survey data show that eastern Oklahoma has one of the highest densities of nesting Eastern Bluebirds in North America.

Description: The Eastern Bluebird male's upperparts are blue, while the throat, breast, and upper belly are rusty red, with white on the lower belly and undertail coverts. The female is grayish to dull blue on the upperparts, with a pale rusty-red breast and upper belly. The young are pale like the female, perhaps duller, with spotted breasts, but showing some blue in wings and tail.

Breeding Habitat: Prefers areas of open woodlands with little ground cover, woodland edges, parks, shelterbelts, and around rural homes.

Nest: Secondary cavity nesters, bluebirds use old woodpecker holes and natural cavities, and frequently use nest boxes. Nest is a cup of grasses lined with finer grass and built by the female. In pine lands, pine needles may be used.

NESTING ECOLOGY

Season: Nest building may begin in late February, but egg laying is usually from March through July. Usually 2, sometimes 3, broods are produced each year.

Eggs: Usually 4–5; pale blue, sometimes white. Uncommon host for Brown-headed Cowbird.

Development: Incubation is by the female for 11–19 days, usually 14. Young are provisioned by both sexes and fledge at about 19 days, but may remain in family groups for 3 weeks.

DISTRIBUTION AND ABUNDANCE

Rangewide: Found east of the Rocky Mountains from southern Canada to the Gulf Coast and from southeastern Arizona south into the Mexican highlands and into Central America. Winters from much of the southeastern United States south.

Historical: Statewide in wooded areas, more common in eastern and central parts of the state. Populations have shown steep declines in both breeding season and winter, followed by gradual increases.

Current: The Eastern Bluebird is a common resident of open woodland and woodland-edge habitats of Oklahoma. The high proportion of Confirmed records is due to the adults and young being conspicuous, and to the two to three broods that are raised each year. The lack of observations in the western Panhandle may partly result from the local distribution of this species there not being picked up well by atlas sampling methods.

Population Trend: Breeding Bird Survey data for 1966–2000 show an increase of 2.7 percent per year rangewide (P = 0.00) and an increase of 1.8 percent per year in Oklahoma (P = 0.09).

References: AOU 1998; Baicich and Harrison 1997; Baumgartner and Baumgartner 1992; Carter 1981; Gowaty and Plissner 1998; Kaufman 1996; Sauer et al. 2001; Sutton 1967

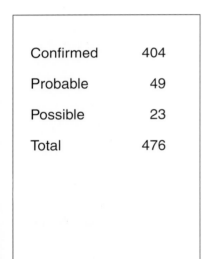

Confirmed	404
Probable	49
Possible	23
Total	476

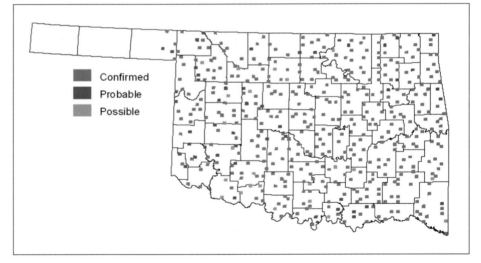

Mountain Bluebird
Sialia currucoides

William A. Carter and Mickle D. Duggan

Courtesy of Gerald Wiens

The Mountain Bluebird's stunning blue color and its easy acceptance of nest boxes has made it nearly as popular in the west as its cousin, the Eastern Bluebird, is in the east. Although it is locally common in western Oklahoma in some winters, it is only an irregular nester in the state.

Description: The male is sky blue above and paler below with a small white area on the lower belly. The female is brownish except for blue on the wings, tail, and rump. Young of the year are like the female, but with spotting on the breast. They are about the same size, but trimmer and lack the rust color found on both Eastern and Western bluebirds.

Breeding Habitat: Edges of woodland and shortgrass prairie and open areas with scattered trees.

Nest: A secondary cavity nester, it uses natural cavities, old woodpecker holes, and nest boxes. The nest cup is composed of weed and grass stems and is lined with finer stems. Most of the nest construction is done by the female.

NESTING ECOLOGY

Season: April–July. Often double-brooded.
Eggs: Usually 5–6; pale blue, occasionally white. Rarely parasitized by the Brown-headed Cowbird and

not documented in any of the few nests reported from Oklahoma.

Development: Incubation is by the female for about 13 days. Young are provisioned by both sexes, although while the female is brooding the young, she prevents the male from directly feeding them. Young fledge in about 18–21 days and remain with parents for 3 or more weeks.

DISTRIBUTION AND ABUNDANCE

Rangewide: Breeds from central Alaska through the Rocky Mountains of Canada and the United States. Winters in southern parts of the breeding range and spreads into plains of western Kansas, Oklahoma, Texas, and northern Mexico.

Historical: Described as a rare summer resident of Cimarron County and irregular in winter eastward to central Oklahoma. The few breeding records in Oklahoma are mostly from Cimarron County, but sin-gle nest records exist from Cleveland County in 1951 and Harmon County in 1954.

Current: Although equally as conspicuous as the Eastern Bluebird, the limited number of Mountain Bluebirds nesting in woodlands along the streams of Cimarron County were not detected in atlas blocks. Two confirmed nestings of this species were reported during the atlas project years, one in 1998 and one in 2001.

Population Trend: Breeding Bird Survey data for 1966–2000 show an increase of 1.9 percent per year rangewide (P = 0.01). No trend data are available for Oklahoma.

References: AOU 1998; Baicich and Harrison 1997; Baumgartner and Baumgartner 1992; Kaufman 1996; Nice 1931; Power and Lombardo 1996; Sauer et al. 2001; Schwilling and Comer 1972; Shackford and Grigsby 1993; Sutton 1967; Tate 1923

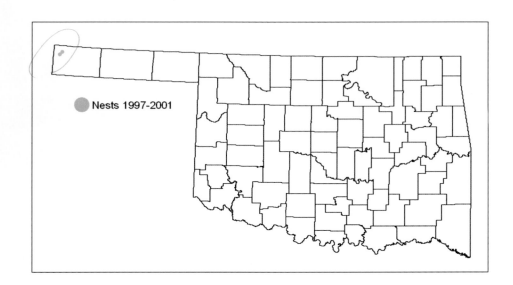

Nests 1997-2001

Wood Thrush
Hylocichla mustelina

John M. Dole

Courtesy of Michael Gray

The loud, rich song of the Wood Thrush usually announces its presence well before the bird is visible in the moist woods it prefers. Susceptible to forest fragmentation and Brown-headed Cowbird parasitism, populations of Wood Thrushes have declined in many parts of its range in eastern North America.

Description: Sexes are similar. The upperparts are warm reddish brown, except for the face, which is streaked black and white. The eye is surrounded by a white eye ring. Large dark spots mark the lower throat, breast, and sides of the belly. The lower belly and vent are white and unmarked. The upperparts of immatures are spotted in buff. During fall and spring migration when other spot-breasted thrushes are migrating

through Oklahoma, note the rusty brown upperparts and large dark spots on the underparts of the Wood Thrushes. Song is a beautiful series of flute-like notes.

Breeding Habitat: Prefers moist deciduous and mixed forest.

Nest: The deep cup has an outer layer of leaves and grass and weed stems, a middle layer of mud and dead leaves, and an inner layer of fine rootlets and dead leaves. The nest is usually located 2–5.5 m (6–18 ft) high in a shrub or tree. The nest is constructed primarily by the female, although males may occasionally assist.

NESTING ECOLOGY

Season: Late April–July. Sometimes double-brooded.
Eggs: Usually 3–4; turquoise green and unmarked. Occasional Brown-headed Cowbird host in Oklahoma, common host in other areas.
Development: Incubation is by the female for 12–14 days. Young are provisioned by both sexes and fledge at 12–15 days, reaching independence at 3–4 weeks.

DISTRIBUTION AND ABUNDANCE

Rangewide: This eastern species occurs from southern Canada to northern Florida, Louisiana, and Mississippi west to eastern Texas and the Dakotas. Wood Thrushes winter from southeast Mexico to northern Columbia.
Historical: Uncommon summer resident in eastern Oklahoma, becoming rare and local in central Oklahoma where it is limited to sheltered, heavily wooded streams. Formerly more common in central Oklahoma.
Current: The eastern distribution of the Wood Thrush is apparent, and the low number of records for Oklahoma indicates that this species is relatively uncommon. In addition, some of the records scored as Possible may be of singing individuals still migrating. The virtual lack of records for central Oklahoma may reflect the local nature of populations in that area or may indicate extirpation from that region. While this species is easy to hear during the nesting season, the difficulty of finding Wood Thrush nests is evident in the low number of confirmations.

Population Trend: Breeding Bird Survey data for 1966–2000 show a decline of 1.9 percent per year rangewide (P = 0.00), but show no conclusive trend in Oklahoma (0.0 percent per year, P = 0.99).

References: AOU 1998; Baicich and Harrison 1997; Baumgartner and Baumgartner 1992; Carrie 1999; Friesen et al. 1999a; Howell and Webb 1995; Kaufman 1996; Lane and Jaramillo 2000; National Geographic Society 1999; Roth et al. 1996; Sauer et al. 2001; Sutton 1967

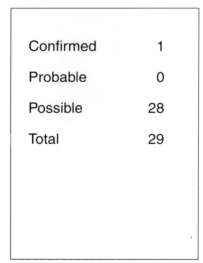

Confirmed	1
Probable	0
Possible	28
Total	29

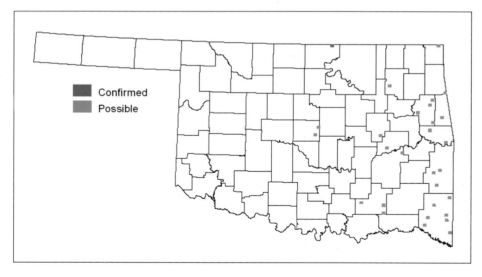

American Robin
Turdus migratorius

Eugene A. Young

Courtesy of M. Frank Carl

The American Robin is perhaps one of the best-known birds in North America, especially by its colloquial name of Robin Red-breast. Robins seem to be undaunted by towns and urban development, where they are attracted to watered lawns and gardens, though they are equally at home in natural habitats. As a result, robins appear to have expanded their range and increased in numbers since the arrival of European settlers.

Description: A large thrush, characterized by its yellow-orange bill, partial white eye ring, black head, gray-brown upperparts, wings, and tail, and brick-red underparts with white undertail coverts, and dark stripes on white throat. Sexes are similar, though males

are usually brighter reddish with blacker heads than females. Juveniles are identified by general robin shape and appearance with speckled breast and shorter tails. Their song is a series of liquid, whistled phrases.

Breeding Habitat: Commonly found in towns, farmyards, golf courses and parks, windbreaks and shelterbelts, woodlands, and less commonly in riparian and coniferous forests.

Nest: A deep cup of plant material, cloth or string, lined with a middle layer of mud followed by an upper layer of fine grasses, although the material used depends upon what is locally available. Typically in a horizontal branch of a tree or shrub, rock ledge, or ledges of human-made structures. The first nest is typically placed in evergreens for protection early in the breeding season, while the second nest may be placed in a deciduous tree. Occasionally nests on the ground. Occasionally uses nest from previous year, with new nest added on top of old. Female builds the nest in 2–7 days and males bring material. The robin has been reported sharing nest with other species. Of 99 nests monitored along Osage County roadsides from 1992 to 1996, 28 were successful.

NESTING ECOLOGY

Season: April–July. Double- to triple-brooded.

Eggs: Usually 4; bluish green and unmarked, commonly referred to as "Robin's egg blue." Uncommonly and (usually) unsuccessfully parasitized by Brown-headed Cowbirds and Yellow-billed Cuckoos. Parasitized nest noted from Pottawatomie County, and two nests in Osage County, one of which fledged a cowbird.

Development: Incubation is by the female for 11–14 days. Young are provisioned by both sexes and fledge in about 13 days, but are tended by both parents for about 3 weeks after leaving the nest.

DISTRIBUTION AND ABUNDANCE

Rangewide: Breeds from the tree line of Alaska across Canada, south to the Gulf Coast and central Mexico, west to southern California, rarely in the desert regions. Winters from southern Alaska and southern Canada, south through the United States into Mexico, but will remain in northern latitudes with favorable weather conditions and adequate food supply.

Historical: Less common in southern Oklahoma and the Panhandle and most abundant in east and central Oklahoma, nesting primarily in towns. Nested originally only in eastern and central Oklahoma, but followed plantings of trees in yards and parks as settlers moved westward, with a major range expansion to the west estimated for the period 1907–1910. Robins can occur in large flocks at roosts during migration and during the winter, with large numbers (thousands) being reported in Oklahoma and adjacent states as well.

Current: American Robins are common and widely distributed in Oklahoma, but are less common in the heavily forested southeast and arid southwest. The conspicuous nature of the robin means its presence in a block is seldom missed. Both nests and young are readily observed, making it easy to confirm breeding.

Population Trend: Breeding Bird Survey data for 1966–2000 show an increase of 0.8 percent per year rangewide (P = 0.00), but show no conclusive trend in Oklahoma (0.6 percent per year, P = 0.40).

References: AOU 1998; Andrews and Righter 1992; Baicich and Harrison 1997; Baumgartner and Baumgartner 1992; Cink 1975; Collias and Collias 1984; George M. Sutton Avian Research Center unpubl. data; Horvath 1963; Nice 1924, 1931; Purdue 1969; Raney 1939; Sallabanks and James 1999; Sauer et al. 2001; Skutch 1999; Stokes and Stokes 1979; Sutton 1967; Terres 1991; Thompson and Ely 1992; Tveten 1993; Wolfe 1994a; Young and Thompson 1995

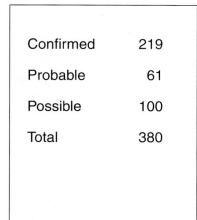

Confirmed	219
Probable	61
Possible	100
Total	380

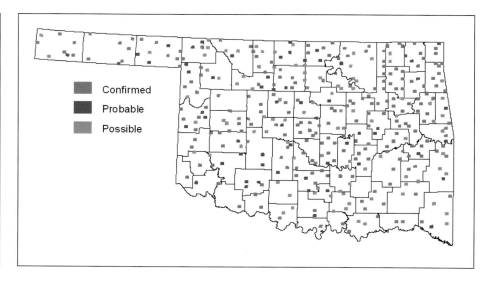

Gray Catbird

Dumetella carolinensis

Mia R. Revels

Courtesy of Bob Gress

The Gray Catbird is one of five species of "mimic thrushes" in Oklahoma, a group of elegant songsters and talented imitators. The Catbird's song can be distinguished from other mimids by its usually repeated phrases which are interspersed with harsh, guttural notes. The harsh, cat-like *mew* call for which it is named is diagnostic.

Description: Sexes similar. A distinguished, plain, gray bird with a black cap, long black tail, and bright chestnut undertail coverts. Male's song is a long series of short syllables delivered quickly. Females sing rarely and at a lower volume than the male. Gray Catbirds tend to skulk in brushy vegetation and can be difficult to observe. This species is not likely to be confused with any other species in Oklahoma.

Breeding Habitat: Areas with dense, shrubby vegetation such as thickets, briars, forest edges, and some residential areas. Most abundant in shrub-sapling stage successional habitats. Gray Catbird densities increase as shrub densities increase.

Nest: Bulky outer nest cup of twigs, leaves, and grasses built by the female and lined with much finer materials. Typically well concealed by foliage and placed 0.9–3.0 m (3–10 ft) above ground.

NESTING ECOLOGY

Season: May–August. Double- to triple-brooded.

Eggs: 3–5; deep greenish blue, unmarked. Parasitized by the Brown-headed Cowbird, but the female Gray Catbird ejects cowbird eggs from nest; parasitism not noted in Oklahoma.

Development: Incubation is by the female for 12–14 days. Young are provisioned by both sexes and usually fledge at 11–14 days, but continue to be fed by adults for up to 12 days.

DISTRIBUTION AND ABUNDANCE

Rangewide: Long-distance migrant breeding from British Columbia south and east through Idaho and Montana, most of the Great Plains, and all of the eastern United States south to the Gulf Coast states, excluding the immediate coastline. Winters along Gulf Coast south to Mexico, Central America, and the Carribean.

Historical: Described as an uncommon to common summer resident in eastern and central Oklahoma; rare in summer elsewhere. Has been recorded as an occasional winter resident or visitor.

Current: The Gray Catbird's preference for dense, shrubby, early successional habitat is shown by its near absence in the heavily forested portions of the eastern half of the state. The small number of blocks scored as confirmed may be due to the difficulty of observing nests and fledglings in the dense vegetation. Some of the blocks scored as Possible may be the result of birds seen prior to the end of spring migration.

Population Trend: Breeding Bird Survey data for 1966–2000 show no conclusive trend rangewide (-0.2 percent per year, P = 0.13) or in Oklahoma (0.7 percent per year, P = 0.83).

References: AOU 1998; Baicich and Harrison 1997; Baumgartner and Baumgartner 1992; Baumgartner and Howell 1948; Cimprich and Moore 1995; Ehrlich et al. 1988; Nice 1931; Sauer et al. 2001; Shirley 1928; Sutton 1967; Tate 1923; Whittle 1923

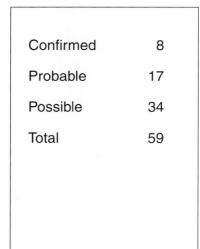

Confirmed	8
Probable	17
Possible	34
Total	59

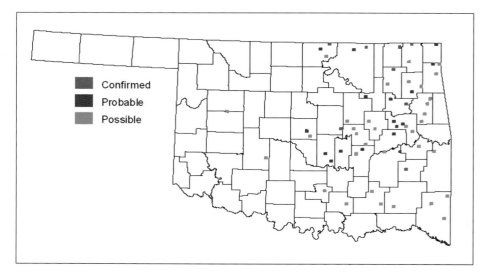

Northern Mockingbird
Mimus polyglottos

Walter B. Gerard

Courtesy of Bill Horn

The Northern Mockingbird is a familiar Oklahoma bird with the remarkable ability to learn a large number of songs throughout its life. Its scientific name means "many tongued mimic," appropriate for a bird that can mimic beautiful songs and calls of other individual mockingbirds as well as other bird species, along with a variety of additional natural and man-made sounds.

Description: Both the male and female are gray above and whitish below, having a long dark tail with white outer tail feathers. Large white wing patches are displayed when the wings are spread and during flight. Songs are varied with a phrase from an individual's repertoire given repeatedly. Males sing during the breeding season, with unmated males being more likely to sing at night, while both sexes sing during the fall when winter territories are established. Both males and females have a variety of calls, such as the *chewk* call, that expresses anxiety or territoriality. The Loggerhead Shrike looks somewhat similar to the Northern Mockingbird, but bears a black mask and a stout, hooked bill.

Breeding Habitat: Open to partly open areas with shortgrass bordered by shrubs, thickets, and woodlands. The Northern Mockingbird seems to have benefited from access to disturbed habitat such as early successional oldfields, parks, urban gardens, rural gardens, roadside shelterbelts, and scrubby woodlands.

Size of breeding territory has been reported as ranging from 0.66 ha (1.63 ac) to 2.53 ha (6.25 ac).

Nest: A bulky cup made up of an outer layer of twigs and coarse weed stems with an inner layer of bark, leaves, fine roots, grasses, and sometimes trash such as paper, string, and cloth. Usually located 1–3 m (3–10 ft) high in a tree, shrub, or thicket.

NESTING ECOLOGY

Season: May–July. Double- to triple-brooded.
Eggs: Usually 3–5; shades of blue or green ground color with brownish or reddish markings and blotches. The species is reported to be a rare Brown-headed Cowbird host. Five of 78 nests (6 percent) found from 1992 to 1996 in Comanche, Osage, and Washington counties were observed to be parasitized.
Development: Incubation is by the female for 13 days. Young are provisioned by both sexes and fledge in about 12 days.

DISTRIBUTION AND ABUNDANCE

Rangewide: Resident from southern Canada through Mexico. Due to human alteration of habitat, the Northern Mockingbird has expanded its range to the north, although there is some southward withdrawal in the winter.

Historical: Described as a common summer resident and less common winter resident throughout the state.
Current: The Northern Mockingbird is unusually easy to confirm because of its conspicuous nesting habits, often in association with human habitation. It is a confirmed breeder in every county of Oklahoma.

Population Trend: Breeding Bird Survey data for 1966–2000 show a decline of 0.8 percent per year rangewide (P = 0.00) and a decline of 1.6 percent per year in Oklahoma (P = 0.00). The Northern Mockingbird was such a popular cage bird in the United States from the late eighteenth century to the early twentieth century that local extirpation of the species was widespread. Although human alteration of habitat hastened the bird's comeback and range expansion, the species has recently declined in the southern parts of its range.

References: AOU 1998; Baicich and Harrison 1997; Baumgartner and Baumgartner 1992; Bay 1996; Bent 1948; Derrickson and Breitwisch 1992; Ehrlich et al. 1988; George 1969; George M. Sutton Avian Research Center unpubl. data; Harrison 1979; National Geographic Society 1999; Oklahoma Bird Records Committee 2000; Sauer et al. 2001; Sibley 2000; Stokes and Stokes 1983; Sutton 1967; Wolfe 1995

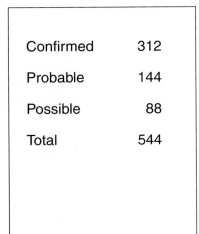

Confirmed	312
Probable	144
Possible	88
Total	544

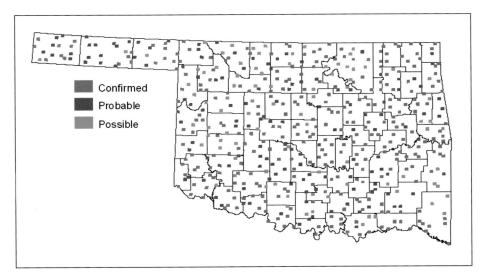

Brown Thrasher
Toxostoma rufum

Eugene A. Young

Courtesy of Warren Williams

The Brown Thrasher is a large, long-tailed, reddish-brown and white bird that is easy to recognize but seldom seen because of its secretive habits. It is perhaps best known for its song, with over 1,100 documented variations. Thrashers are usually viewed from the road or in garden areas where they consume large numbers of insects during the summer nesting period.

Description: A typical thrasher build, with a long slender body and a long tail; reddish-brown upperparts, white below with reddish-brown spotting, yellow to brown eye, and relatively short blackish bill compared to other species of thrashers found in North America. A couple of classic songs follow a definite cadence and are put into words as follows: *plant-a-seed, plant-a-seed,* *bury-it, bury-it, cover-it-up, cover-it-up, let-it-grow, let-it-grow, pull-it-up, pull-it-up, eat-it, eat-it, yum-yum,* and *hello, hello, yes, yes, who is this? who is this? I should say, I should say, how's that? how's that?*

Breeding Habitat: Commonly found in woodlands and brushy edge habitat with thickets and shrubs, hedgerows, gardens, and shelterbelts

Nest: Typically in the crotch of small trees (elm, Osage orange, eastern red cedar) or shrubs (dogwood, American plum) usually 0.3–2.1 m (1–7 ft) high, up to 4.6 m (15 ft), rarely on the ground (3 reports in Oklahoma), always well hidden. Nest is bulky, outside diameter to 30.5 cm (12 in), made of four layers: the bottom layer consists of thorny twigs, with a layer of dead leaves upon it, followed by a layer of small stems, twigs, and roots with dirt, then lined with the fourth layer of cleaned rootlets. Both sexes build the nest.

NESTING ECOLOGY

Season: April–August. Single- to double-brooded.
Eggs: Usually 4–5; bluish white or pinkish white with reddish-brown spots. Occasionally parasitized by cowbirds; sometimes removes cowbird eggs. Of 310 nests monitored in Osage and Washington counties from 1992 to 1996, 9 were observed to be parasitized (3 percent). Of the 4 parasitized nests that successfully raised any young, none raised cowbirds.
Development: Incubation is by both sexes for 11–14 days. Young are provisioned by both sexes and fledge in 10–13 days.

DISTRIBUTION AND ABUNDANCE

Rangewide: Breeds from east-central Alberta east through southern Canada, south through the eastern half of the United States. Winters in the southern and southeastern United States, including the southeastern third of Oklahoma.

Historical: Expanded westward with human settlement. Described as an uncommon to common summer resident throughout the state, but uncommon to rare in the Panhandle.
Current: Like its relative the American Robin, the Brown Thrasher is present statewide but is less common in the heavily forested southeast and in the arid west. The easily recognized song of the Brown Thrasher accounts for the high number of blocks in which it was recorded statewide, along with the high proportion of Possible Breeder blocks. The secretive nature of this species makes it difficult to confirm breeding.

Population Trend: Breeding Bird Survey data for 1966–2000 show an overall decline of 1.2 percent per year rangewide (P = 0.00), but show no conclusive trend in Oklahoma (-1.3 percent per year, P = 0.23).

References: AOU 1998; Baicich and Harrison 1997; Baumgartner and Baumgartner 1992; Bent 1948; Ehrlich et al. 1988; George M. Sutton Avian Research Center unpubl. data; Nice 1931; Snow 1994; Stokes and Stokes 1983; Sutton 1967; Terres 1991; Thompson and Ely 1992; Tveten 1993; Tyler 1994c; Zimmerman 1993

Confirmed	128
Probable	97
Possible	153
Total	378

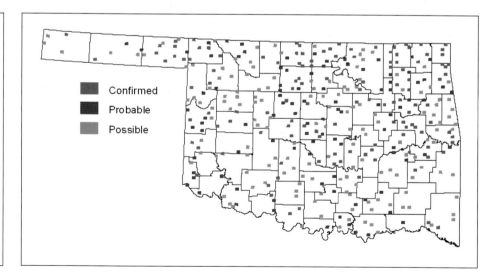

Curve-billed Thrasher
Toxostoma curvirostre

Sebastian T. Patti

Courtesy of Steve Metz

A fairly common resident of the southwestern United States, the Curve-billed Thrasher frequents both brushland and desert habitats and is relatively tolerant of human activity. Recent studies suggest that differences between Texas birds (which include Oklahoma populations, subspecies *curvirostre*) and Arizona birds (subspecies *palmeri*) may warrant species-level recognition.

Description: A robin-sized ground forager, with a slimmer body and longer tail than the familiar American Robin. It is large headed, with sturdy legs and feet, and a long black decurved bill. The sexes are similarly plumaged, being grayish brown with a dirty white throat. Curve-bills have round breast spots against a grayish-brown background and two indistinct but visible wing bars. The irides are orange-yellow in adult birds. The tail is generally brown, appearing darker than the rest of the bird in flight, and is tipped with white spots. The species' call, *whit-WHIT,* sometimes trebled, *whit-WHIT-whit,* is one of the ubiquitous and distinctive bird calls of the arid southwestern United States. This call is often imitated by Northern Mockingbirds.

Breeding Habitat: Curve-bills inhabit yucca-cholla-mesquite grasslands. They also frequent ranches and farmyards, especially when chollas are present as ornamental plantings.

Nest: Both sexes participate in the construction of the nest, which is a cup made of large twigs and lined with fine grasses or hairs. Usually placed in a cholla cactus (Cimarron County), mesquite tree (Jackson County), or thorny shrub, 0.6–2.7 m (2–9 ft) above ground.

NESTING ECOLOGY

Season: Probably April–July. Likely double-brooded and will replace lost clutches.

Eggs: Usually 3–4; light bluish green, dotted with reddish brown. Rarely parasitized by Brown-headed Cowbirds; not reported in Oklahoma.

Development: Incubation is by both sexes for about 14 days. Young are provisioned by both sexes, though mostly by the female, and fledge in about 14 days. If food is scarce, only older, larger young are fed and survive. Young reach independence by 40 days.

DISTRIBUTION AND ABUNDANCE

Rangewide: Generally regarded as a resident, nonmigratory species, but apparently underwent an expansion in the northeastern part of its range (including Oklahoma) during the 1900s, and the species has been found extralimitally in the United States as far east as the Atlantic Coast. The *curvirostre* group generally ranges from southeast Colorado (first noted in 1951) and southwestern Kansas, through the western portion of the Oklahoma Panhandle and extreme southwest Oklahoma through eastern and southern New Mexico, southeast Arizona, and western Texas, south to northern and central Mexico.

Historical: The species was first found in the Black Mesa country of Cimarron County in 1933, where it was first reported nesting in 1936. It was noted in Jackson County in 1965 and began to be found there regularly in the 1970s. It is now established in Cimarron County and in the Jackson County grasslands around Eldorado. One nest record exists for Texas County in 1988. A number of nonbreeding records have been noted from other parts of the state.

Current: Generally restricted to the central and western portions of the Panhandle and to the extreme southwestern portion of the main body of the state; the species seems to be limited to areas where the preferred nesting substrates (cholla and mesquite) are present.

Population Trend: Breeding Bird Survey data for 1966–2000 show a decline of 2.7 percent per year rangewide (P = 0.00). No trend data are available for Oklahoma.

References: AOU 1998; Ault 1984; Baumgartner and Baumgartner 1992; Busby and Zimmerman 2001; Dillon 1998b; Grzybowski 1983a; Sauer et al. 2001; Shackford 1989; Sutton 1936b, 1948, 1967, 1968a, 1968c; Tweit 1996; Tyler 1986a; Zink and Blackwell-Rago 2000

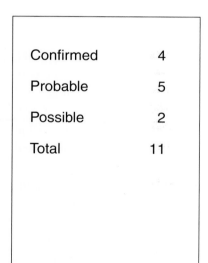

Confirmed	4
Probable	5
Possible	2
Total	11

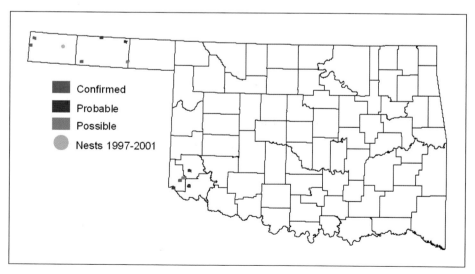

Confirmed
Probable
Possible
Nests 1997-2001

European Starling
Sturnus vulgaris

Dan L. Reinking

Courtesy of Bill Horn

From an introduction of about 100 birds to New York's Central Park in 1890 and 1891, the European Starling has successfully colonized most of the continent and now numbers some 200 million birds in North America. It competes with many native species for nest site cavities and may be partially responsible for declines of some species. An interesting feature of the starling is the musculature of its head, which provides powerful bill-spreading ability for foraging in thick grass, compared to other bird species in which muscles that close the bill are more powerful than those that open it.

Description: Sexes similar. Glossy, iridescent black with speckles, and a yellow bill during most of the year. Vocal mimics, starlings make a variety of sounds.

Breeding Habitat: Often found in close association with human-altered habitats, including urban and rural areas with access to mowed or grazed grassy lawns or fields. Often nests in and around commercial buildings, attics, farm buildings, and other structures.

Nest: Within a natural cavity or in one of a variety of cavity-like openings in buildings or other structures.

Grasses and bits of debris form the nest, which is lined with feathers, fine grass, and other materials. Green vegetation is also periodically added to the nest.

NESTING ECOLOGY

Season: Primarily April–June. Often double-brooded.
Eggs: 5–7; pale light blue. Intraspecific brood parasitism is common.
Development: Incubation is by both sexes for 12 days. Young are provisioned by both sexes and fledge at 20–22 days.

DISTRIBUTION AND ABUNDANCE

Rangewide: Native to much of Eurasia, but introduced to North America, South Africa, Australia, New Zealand, and elsewhere.

Historical: Formerly considered a winter visitant, with the first record for the state occurring in 1929. More recently considered a common resident statewide.
Current: Easily confirmed due to its conspicuous and close association with humans, the starling was found in atlas blocks statewide, although somewhat less often in heavily forested areas of southeastern Oklahoma.

Population Trend: Breeding Bird Survey data for 1966–2000 show a decline of 0.9 percent per year rangewide ($P = 0.00$), but show no conclusive trend in Oklahoma (-0.5 percent per year, $P = 0.41$).

References: Baicich and Harrison 1997; Baumgartner and Baumgartner 1992; Cabe 1993; Sauer et al. 2001; Sutton 1967, 1984b, 1985

Confirmed	358
Probable	32
Possible	51
Total	441

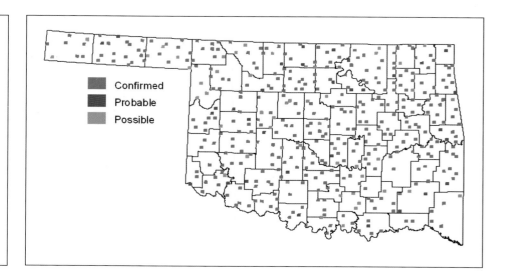

Cedar Waxwing
Bombycilla cedrorum

Bonnie L. Gall

Courtesy of Gerald Wiens

The gregarious, nomadic Cedar Waxwing is seldom seen alone. It is a delight to watch a flock wheel and turn with the precision of Blue Angel jet pilots. If the tight formation flight of the waxwing doesn't catch one's eye, their high-pitched socialization calls can alert one to a group in the treetops. Cedar Waxwing is mainly a fruit eater, and much of its behavior centers on its cooperative search for ripening fruits and berries. In Oklahoma, this bird is sporadic but relatively common during nonbreeding seasons. A few breeding records exist, however, making nest sightings of special interest for the state.

Description: A sleek, crested bird with grayish-brown plumage. Adults have a sharp, black face mask edged in white, a black chin patch, and red waxlike "droplets" on the ends of the secondaries. The belly is pale yellow, and the tail has a yellowish terminal band. The bill is small. Vocalizations include a high-pitched trill and thin whistles (*bzeee*) and a high-pitched flight call (*seee*). Juveniles are streaked on the breast but have the yellow band on the tail.

Breeding Habitat: Usually associated with deciduous open woods, orchards, suburbs, or stands of cedars or other conifers.

Nest: A loosely constructed cup of grasses, weeds, and twigs, lined with softer and finer materials; built by both sexes. Usually placed 1.2–15.2 m (4–50 ft) above ground in small trees. Social and nonterritorial year round and may nest in loose clusters.

NESTING ECOLOGY

Season: Primarily May–June in Oklahoma, later northward. Timing appears to be connected with ripening of fruits and berries. Probably double-brooded; first and second nests may overlap in time.
Eggs: Usually 4–5; pale gray with brownish spots.
Development: Incubation is by the female alone for about 12 days. Young are provisioned by both sexes, but primarily the male, which also feeds the incubating female. Young usually leave the nest at about 15–16 days. Occasionally parasitized by Brown-headed Cowbirds, but waxwings often throw out foreign eggs or abandon the nest altogether. In addition, cowbird nestlings do poorly on waxwing diets, so that few survive. Nest parasitism not noted in Oklahoma.

DISTRIBUTION AND ABUNDANCE

Rangewide: Found over most of North America during at least one season of the year. Breeding range includes much of Canada and most of the northern United States, including Missouri and parts of northwest Arkansas; Oklahoma is generally not considered within this species' breeding range.

Historical: Described as a common but erratic migrant and winter visitor statewide. The handful of pre-atlas project nesting records includes Cimarron County in 1914 and 1920, Beaver County in 1921, and Oklahoma County in 1961. Some records of apparently paired birds and juveniles also exist from Cherokee, Okmulgee, and Texas counties.
Current: Only one record of confirmed nesting was recorded in Oklahoma for the Cedar Waxwing during atlas project years. In addition to this record in extreme northeastern Oklahoma, two other June sight records came from Blaine and Pawnee counties in areas outside of atlas blocks. The rare and local distribution of this species make it poorly sampled by atlas project methods.

Population Trend: Breeding Bird Survey data for 1966–2000 show an increase of 1.4 percent per year rangewide (P = 0.00). No trend data are available for Oklahoma.

References: Baumgartner and Baumgartner 1992; Bent 1965b; Harrison 1975; Herbert 1997; Johnsgard 1979; National Geographic Society 1999; Nice 1931; Sauer et al. 2001; Sutton 1967; Tate 1923; Tyler 1993; Witmer et al. 1997

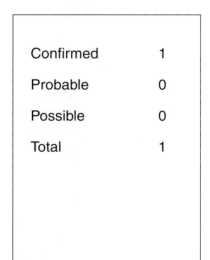

Confirmed	1
Probable	0
Possible	0
Total	1

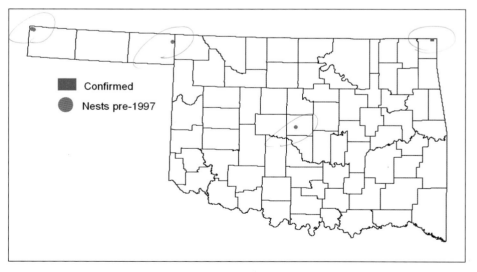

Confirmed

Nests pre-1997

Blue-winged Warbler
Vermivora pinus

David E. Fantina

© W. Greene / VIREO

One of the rarest nesting birds in the state, the Blue-winged Warbler is at the extreme western limit of its range in Oklahoma and is very seldom found breeding, often at intervals of several years. It is a tiny bird that stays deep in the dense underbrush, and it sings a quiet unobtrusive song, so it may be overlooked at times.

Description: The male Blue-winged Warbler is a very small, bright yellow bird with blue-gray wings, white wing bars, and a conspicuous thin black eye line. The female is similar but duller overall. Because of their small size and their preference for staying in the dense underbrush, their characteristic sneezy two-note *bee-buzz* song is heard much more often than the birds are

seen. The Blue-winged Warbler often hybridizes with the closely related Golden-winged Warbler, producing "Lawrence's" and "Brewster's" warblers, which are intermediate between the parent types. Both of these hybrids have been found in Oklahoma during migration.

Breeding Habitat: Nests in early- to mid-succession habitats such as overgrown pastures, forest edges and forest clearings, and other areas with low, shrubby cover.

Nest: The female builds a cup of grass, leaves, and bark strips lined with finer materials on or very close to the ground.

NESTING ECOLOGY

Season: May–July. Single-brooded, but probably replaces lost clutches.

Eggs: Usually 4–5; white with brown speckles. Commonly parasitized by Brown-headed Cowbirds in some areas; not noted in Oklahoma, but few actual nest records exist.

Development: Incubation is by the female for 11–12 days. Young are provisioned by both sexes and leave the nest at 8–10 days.

DISTRIBUTION AND ABUNDANCE

Rangewide: A long-distance migrant breeding in scattered locations throughout the northeastern United States (generally east of Oklahoma and Nebraska) and southern Canada. Winters in Mexico and Central America.

Historical: The Blue-winged Warbler was considered a rare and local migrant and breeder in Oklahoma prior to about 1955. Between 1955 and 1986, the species become even rarer, with no breeding records. In 1987, a pair was found nesting in dense bottomland woods in Delaware County.

Current: The Blue-winged Warbler's rarity in Oklahoma makes it one of the species not adequately sampled by the atlas methodology. The only record reported was of two birds apparently on territory at the J. T. Nickel Family and Nature Preserve in Cherokee County in late June of 2001.

Population Trend: Breeding Bird Survey data for 1966–2000 show no conclusive trend rangewide (-0.5 percent per year, P = 0.47). They have expanded their range considerably in the northeast and retreated somewhat from the western fringe of their range. No trend data are available for Oklahoma.

References: AOU 1998; Baicich and Harrison 1997; Baumgartner 1988; Baumgartner and Baumgartner 1992; Bent 1953; Gill et al. 2001; Morse 1989; Sauer et al. 2001; Sutton 1967

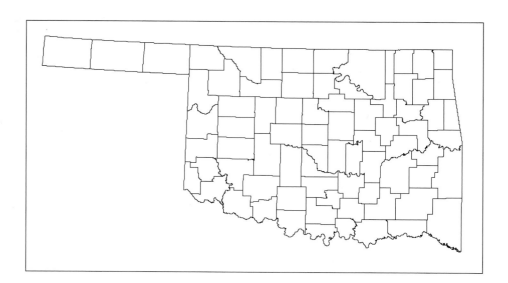

Northern Parula
Parula americana

Nathan R. Kuhnert

Courtesy of Michael Gray

The Northern Parula is one of Oklahoma's common warblers, and its distinctive ascending and buzzy song is one of the earliest to be heard in the spring. Formerly referred to as Blue Yellow-Back Warbler by Wilson and Audubon, the Northern Parula is one of the most diminutive warblers of North America.

Description: Blue above with a triangular green back patch and bold white wing bars. Underparts are whitish with yellow on the breast. Males have chestnut and black bands across the chest and are slightly larger than females. Performs two distinct song types, often designated type A and type B. Type A is an ascending trill with a separated terminal note and is typically given to advertise territories to females. Type B, given more on the edge of territories during hostile encounters with other males, is more complex and consists of a series of buzzy notes that can be confused with the rare Cerulean Warbler.

Breeding Habitat: Favors riparian areas and bottomland forests near swamps, especially where Spanish moss is found.

Nest: A cup usually built into lichen or moss; the nest can also contain dense grasses and bark shreds and is lined with plant down and fine rootlets. Nests are built by the female and are often difficult to locate, although generally only built 1.5–4.5 m (5–15 ft) high.

NESTING ECOLOGY

Season: April–June. Probably single-brooded in Oklahoma.

Eggs: Usually 3–5; white to creamy white, variably speckled and spotted with brown. Few cases of Brown-headed Cowbird parasitism; known from Delaware and Washington counties in Oklahoma.

Development: Incubation is by the female for 12–14 days. Young are provisioned by both sexes and leave the nest at 10–11 days, but continue to be fed by adults for an unknown time.

DISTRIBUTION AND ABUNDANCE

Rangewide: Breeds throughout the eastern United States and Canada except for a void ranging from southern Michigan and northwest Ohio and west through northern Indiana and Illinois, southern Wisconsin, and southern Minnesota. Winters primarily in the West Indies but can be found in Florida and possibly other southern states in addition to areas to Mexico and Central America.

Historical: Described as an uncommon to common summer resident in eastern Oklahoma, rare in central counties, and casual west.

Current: The Northern Parula's distribution is fairly widespread in the eastern half of the state, extending westward along and almost halfway between the 97th and 98th meridians, where the sharp division of eastern forests and the western prairie grasslands exists. The distribution derived by atlas methodology seems more accurate than range maps in current national field guides, which truncate the western periphery by almost a degree of longitude in several cases.

Population Trend: Breeding Bird Survey data for 1966–2000 show an increase of 0.9 percent per year rangewide (P = 0.02), but show no conclusive trend in Oklahoma (1.0 percent per year, P = 0.72).

References: AOU 1998; Baicich and Harrison 1997; Baumgartner 1992; Baumgartner and Baumgartner 1992; Bay 1999; Bent 1953; Dunn and Garrett 1997; Graber et al. 1983; James and Neal 1986; Moldenhauer and Regelski 1996; Sauer et al. 2001; Sibley 2000; Stokes et al. 1997; Sutton 1967; Terres 1991

Confirmed	15
Probable	38
Possible	91
Total	144

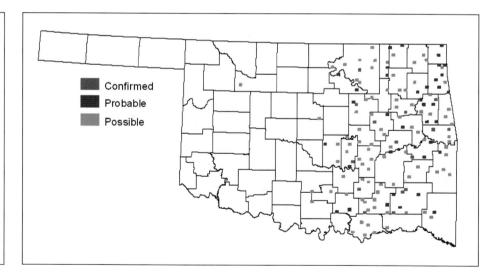

Yellow Warbler
Dendroica petechia

Nathan R. Kuhnert

The Yellow Warbler is one of the most familiar and abundant warblers of broadleaf forests and moist thickets throughout North America. In addition to its widespread range, nesting from the Atlantic to the Pacific, and from Canada to Mexico, there is extensive morphological variation, more so than within any other wood-warbler, with more than 40 recognized subspecies.

Description: The widespread eastern North American Yellow Warbler subspecies is more extensively yellow than most other wood-warblers and unique in having yellow on the inner webs of its tail feathers. Males are golden yellow with rusty streaks on the breast and flanks. Females are less vibrant and lack breast streaks.

The well-known rendition of their bright, rapid musical song is *sweet, sweet, sweet, I am so sweet.*

Breeding Habitat: In the eastern United States, the Yellow Warbler is a bird of successional vegetation. Habitats are generally moist and deciduous consisting of old fields, overgrown pastures, woodland edges, hedgerows, borders of swamps, ponds, and bogs, as well as streamsides containing various species of willows. In the west, the Yellow Warbler is more restricted to riparian habitats.

Nest: A neat and compact cup of dry weed-stem fibers, fine grass stems, wool, and plant down built by the female and lined with fine plant fibers. Typically placed low in brushy or shrubby habitat, often below 4 m (13 ft) but occasionally much higher.

NESTING ECOLOGY

Season: April–June. Single-brooded.

Eggs: Usually 4–5; white or tinted grayish or greenish; speckled, spotted, or blotched in dull brown. Brown-headed Cowbird parasitism is very common, with as many as 40 percent of nests parasitized in some studies. The Yellow Warbler has evolved a strategy to bury the cowbird eggs (along with their own eggs) by adding a nest layer, thus insulating them from incubation. Some nests have been found containing as many as six layers.

Development: Incubation is by the female for 11 days. Young are provisioned by both sexes and leave the nest at 9–12 days.

DISTRIBUTION AND ABUNDANCE

Rangewide: Breeds throughout much of North America up to the shrub and tree line in Alaska and Canada. Also breeds in the Carribean and northern South America. Winters primarily in Central and South America.

Historical: Described in 1931 as a summer resident in the northern half of the main body of the state, as well as in Cimarron County. By 1992, described as a local and irregular summer resident throughout the state, more common in northern and central counties, and not known to nest in many southern counties. In the summer of 1996 in central Oklahoma along an approximately 32 km (20 mi) stretch of the Canadian River, 21 territories were located in successional willow scrub and near a few large cottonwoods.

Current: Although appearing fairly widespread across the state based on the number of blocks in which it was reported, its density and distribution may be skewed too high. Some of the Possible Breeder blocks may be the result of singing birds recorded prior to the end of spring migration.

Population Trend: Breeding Bird Survey data for 1966–2000 show an increase of 0.5 percent per year rangewide (P = 0.00), but show no conclusive trend in Oklahoma (-4.7 percent per year, P = 0.63).

References: AOU 1998; Baicich and Harrison 1997; Baumgartner and Baumgartner 1992; Bay 1999; Bent 1953; Cornell Lab of Ornithology 2000; Dunn and Garrett 1997; Graber et al. 1983; Kuhnert, N. R., pers. observ.; Lowther et al. 1999; Moldenhauer and Regelski 1996; Nice 1931; Sauer et al. 2001; Sibley 2000; Stokes et al. 1997; Sutton 1967; Terres 1991

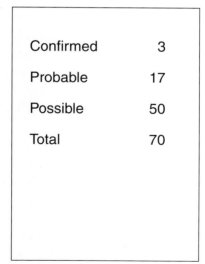

Confirmed	3
Probable	17
Possible	50
Total	70

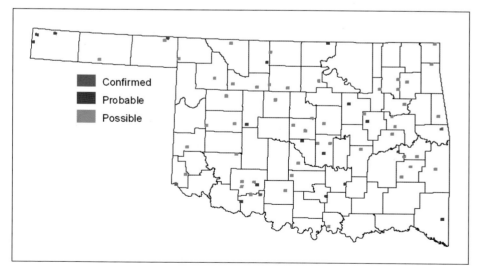

Yellow-throated Warbler
Dendroica dominica

Mark Howery

The Yellow-throated Warbler is of course named for its bright yellow throat. It is a fairly common summer resident of lowland hardwood forests and forested swamps. One of its common foraging behaviors is to creep along tree branches looking for insects, similar to the behavior of the Black-and-white Warbler. Across the northern portion of its range, the Yellow-throated Warbler was once known as the Sycamore Warbler; however, it does not appear to prefer stands of sycamores as nesting habitat in Oklahoma.

Description: Unlike many warblers, the breeding and nonbreeding plumages are similar, as are male and female plumages. The throat and upper portion of the breast are a bright yellow outlined by a contrasting thin black band that extends from the base of the bill and below the eye down the side of the neck and breast. The face is predominantly black with contrasting white markings, including a thin white stripe above the eye,

a small white crescent below the eye, and a white spot on the neck. The back, wings, and tail are gray, with two white bars on each wing. The female's plumage has a faint brownish wash, and the forehead is gray rather than black. The song begins as a series of short, rapid whistles that steadily descend in pitch, then ends with two or three ascending notes.

Breeding Habitat: Mature lowland forests in the eastern third of Oklahoma. This range includes valleys within the Ouachita Mountains and Ozark Highlands, as well as floodplain forests along the Red and Arkansas rivers and their tributaries. Yellow-throated Warblers appear to prefer mature bottomland forests that are dominated by oak, cypress, pine, and/or black gum trees. They also may be found in thinned mature forests, maturing second-growth bottomland forests, and forested suburban gardens.

Nest: A small cup-shaped structure constructed by both the male and female on the outer branches of large canopy trees. The nest is constructed of fine plant stems, plant down, and caterpillar silk, as well as Spanish moss where available.

NESTING ECOLOGY

Season: Late April–July. Usually single-brooded.

Eggs: Usually 4; grayish white and speckled or spotted with brown, reddish, and purplish markings. Infrequently parasitized by Brown-headed Cowbirds; the first report of parasitism of this species was from Oklahoma; Ohio is the only other location to report parasitism.

Development: Incubation is by the female for 12–13 days. Young are provisioned by both sexes and fledge at about 10–11 days, but remain with their parents for an additional 2–3 weeks.

DISTRIBUTION AND ABUNDANCE

Rangewide: Breeds from eastern Texas, eastern Oklahoma, and Missouri east to the Atlantic Coast and south to central Florida. Because of its preference for low-elevation forests, most populations occur in the Atlantic and Gulf coastal plains, and in the valleys of the Mississippi and Ohio rivers and their tributaries. The species occurs year round in central Florida, coastal Georgia, and South Carolina and in the Bahamas. The winter range encompasses southern Florida, the Greater Antilles, and eastern Mexico through Nicaragua. Oklahoma's breeding population winters in Mexico and Central America.

Historical: Described in 1931 as a summer resident of eastern and central Oklahoma; later described as locally uncommon to rare east and very rare and irregular to central Oklahoma. It is assumed that this species was more numerous prior to European settlement because of the substantial amount of bottomland forest habitat that has been lost over the past 300 years as a result of clearing and conversion to agricultural uses.

Current: Yellow-throated Warblers were detected primarily within the eastern one-fifth of Oklahoma and were found relatively frequently in the Ouachita Mountains and the Ozarks. Probably as a result of its very specialized habitat requirements, this species was not detected in many of the atlas blocks within its geographic range. In order to locate this species, atlas volunteers needed access to mature bottomland forests, a habitat type that is both uncommon and difficult to survey. Yellow-throated Warblers were confirmed as a breeding species in only one atlas block, underscoring the difficulty of locating and confirming this species.

Population Trend: Breeding Bird Survey data for 1966–2000 show no conclusive trend rangewide (0.7 percent per year, P = 0.23) or in Oklahoma (-21. percent per year, P = 0.59).

References: Baicich and Harrison 1997; Baumgartner 1992; Baumgartner and Baumgartner 1992; Curson et al. 1994; DeGraaf and Rappole 1995; Dunn and Garrett 1997; Ehrlich et al. 1988; Griscom and Sprunt 1979; Hall 1996; Mery 1976; Nice 1931; Sauer et al. 2001; Sutton 1967

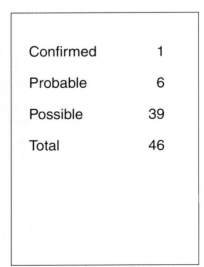

Confirmed	1
Probable	6
Possible	39
Total	46

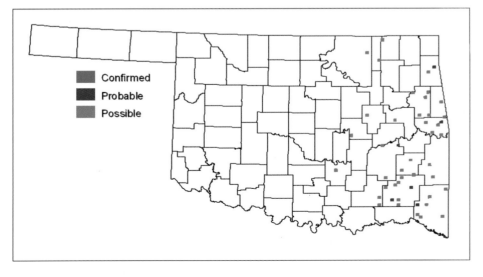

Pine Warbler
Dendroica pinus

Mia R. Revels

Courtesy of Michael Gray

The Pine Warbler is Oklahoma's only resident warbler species. It spends the entire year in the pine forests and mixed woodlands of the southeastern portion of the state. The only wood warbler known to regularly consume seeds, it is often seen at feeders in the winter.

Description: Male is olive green above with a yellow throat and breast, dark streaks on sides of breast, and white underparts. Female coloration is similar, but duller. Song is a soft, flat musical trill, which can vary considerably in rate and intensity. Pine Warblers are seldom found far from the pine trees for which they are named and can be found creeping along branches when foraging. During fall migration, Pine Warblers can be distinguished from similar Bay-breasted and Blackpoll warblers by the lack of streaking on their backs and their brighter yellow underparts.

Breeding Habitat: Open, upland pine and pine-hardwood forests. Will nest in areas of primary deciduous forest with scattered individual or small groves of pines. Density of understory may vary, but Pine Warblers are generally more abundant where understory is sparse. The species can utilize pine plantations for breeding; densities increase with increasing age of stand.

Nest: Compact cup built by female and placed on horizontal branch of a pine tree from 9–15 m (30–50 ft) high. Nest materials include stems, bark, and pine needles bound with spider silk; lined with hair, pine needles, and feathers. Usually completely hidden from below.

NESTING ECOLOGY

Season: April–July. Double-brooding suspected, but not documented.
Eggs: Usually 4, but sometimes 3–5; white or creamy white, speckled with brownish markings. Infrequently parasitized by the Brown-headed Cowbird.
Development: Incubation is by the female, and possibly the male, for 10–13 days. Young are provisioned by both sexes and fledge at 10 days.

DISTRIBUTION AND ABUNDANCE

Rangewide: A short-distance migrant, with a fragmented breeding range from southern Canada to the Gulf Coast; year round in the southeastern United States with winter populations augmented by northern birds; winter resident in southern Texas and Louisiana; rare or absent outside of pine woodlands.

Historical: Described as a local summer resident in pine-oak woods of northeastern Oklahoma; year-round resident in southeastern portions of the state.
Current: The Pine Warbler's preference for its namesake is clearly shown by its common occurrence in the southeastern pine woodlands of the state. The high number of blocks marked Confirmed is likely due to the open nature of this breeding habitat, which makes the birds fairly easy to observe. Though less common there, this species is also present in the mixed woodlands of the northeastern corner of the state.

Population Trend: Breeding Bird Survey data for 1966–2000 show an increase of 1.3 percent per year rangewide ($P = 0.00$), but show no conclusive trend in Oklahoma (4.9 percent per year, $P = 0.43$).

References: AOU 1998; Baicich and Harrison 1997; Baumgartner 1992; Baumgartner and Baumgartner 1992; Bent 1953; Ehrlich et al. 1988; Letson and Letson 1954; Nice 1931; Repenning and Labisky 1985; Rodewald et al. 1999; Sauer et al. 2001; Sutton 1967

Confirmed	26
Probable	8
Possible	13
Total	47

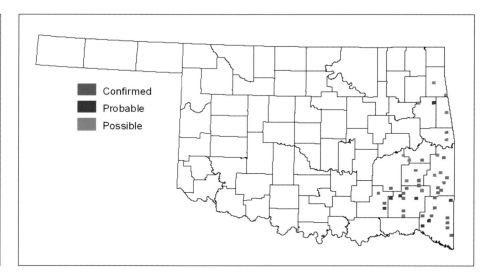

Prairie Warbler
Dendroica discolor

Michael D. Bay

Courtesy of Arthur Morris / www.birdsasart.com

With such a suggestive name, you might expect this species to be abundant throughout the prairies of Oklahoma, but instead the Prairie Warbler prefers young deciduous woodlands, brushy clearings, and oldfields, particularly those of earlier successional stages.

Description: Male and female are similar with yellow throat, cheek, and breast and olive back. Black eye and cheek markings along with black streaking along the sides characterize the species. Males have chestnut markings on the back, but they are sometimes inconspicuous. Tail wagging is typical behavior. Song is described as an upward series of z's, but is sung in two forms often designated as type A and type B. The similar Pine Warbler also has a yellow breast and some side streaking, but is considerably duller in color and also lacks the yellow cheek.

Breeding Habitat: Prefers brushy clearings, scrublands, forest edges, pine barrens, and early successional oldfields. The reduction in size and number of oldfields may have contributed to its decline in some areas.

Nest: Open cup composed of bark shreds woven with fine grasses and spider silk and situated in a fork of a bush or tree. Female builds the entire nest, which is placed from 0.3–3 m (1–10 ft) above ground.

Sometimes nest "fragments" are constructed before building a complete nest, a behavior uncommon in warblers.

NESTING ECOLOGY

Season: May–July. Single- to double-brooded.

Eggs: 3–5; white or off-white with brown markings. Common cowbird host.

Development: Incubation is by the female for about 12 days. Young are provisioned by both sexes and fledge at 9–11 days.

DISTRIBUTION AND ABUNDANCE

Rangewide: Breeds from eastern Nebraska, Kansas, Oklahoma, and northern Michigan south to east Texas, the Gulf Coast, and Florida. Winters from Florida to West Indies and Central America.

Historical: Described as an uncommon breeding resi-dent throughout eastern Oklahoma counties and as a rare breeding resident in central Oklahoma. The west-ernmost record for Oklahoma as a summer resident was in Caddo County in 1954.

Current: The Prairie Warbler is primarily limited in distribution to southeastern Oklahoma counties, where brushy forest clearings and/or oldfields are likely to be found.

Population Trend: Breeding Bird Survey data for 1966–2000 show a decline of 2.2 percent per year rangewide (P = 0.00) and a decline of 11.5 percent per year in Oklahoma (P = 0.02), although the latter esti-mate is based on few survey routes.

References: Baumgartner 1992; Baumgartner and Baumgartner 1992; DeGraaf and Rappole 1995; Ehrlich et al. 1988; Harrison 1984; Morse 1989; National Geographic Society 1983; Nolan 1978; Robbins et al. 1966; Sauer et al. 2001; Sutton 1967

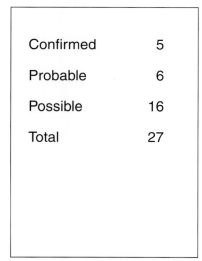

Confirmed	5
Probable	6
Possible	16
Total	27

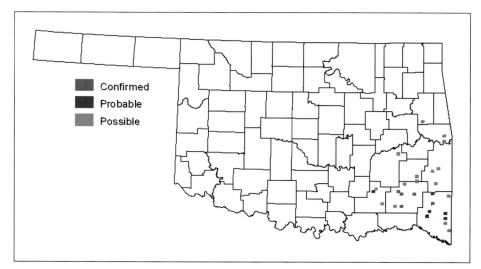

Cerulean Warbler
Dendroica cerulea

Nathan R. Kuhnert

Courtesy of Arthur Morris / www.birdsasart.com

Formerly abundant across portions of the eastern United States, the Cerulean Warbler has became so scare that in the last three decades it has been proposed for listing under the Endangered Species Act. Logging and road building both in the United States and in the bird's winter home of South America, along with nest parasitism by Brown-headed Cowbirds, are cited as reasons for its decline. Measures that include population assessments, determining the range of acceptable habitats, and development of management strategies have been initiated for recovery of this tiny and musical blue treetop warbler.

Description: Males are light blue (cerulean) on the upperparts and white below with a narrow blue-black ring that crosses the upper breast. The female is blue gray and olive green above and whitish below with a white line over the eye. Both sexes have two white wing bars and white tail spots. The Cerulean Warbler's spirited song is wheezy with rapid buzz notes like *zray, zray, zray, zray, zreee*. It can be easily confused with one song type of the Northern Parula, which occurs in similar habitat.

Breeding Habitat: Requires large, undisturbed tracts of old growth, mesic deciduous forest, primarily along rivers, streams, and swamps. Also found in upland habitats, which include extensive mature broadleaf forest. Key tree species found in Oklahoma territories of Cerulean Warbler include oak and hickory on upper north-facing slopes. In neighboring Missouri, optimal habitats contained a substantial number of large trees

(>30 cm/12 in dbh), and a high (>18 m/59 ft) closed canopy. Minimum forest-tract size varies, but may require area of 3,000 ha (7,412 ac).

Nest: Not well known. Cup constructed by the female of fine grasses, bark fibers, and hairs, decorated on the outside with gray or white materials. Placed on a lateral limb of a deciduous tree usually 4–18 m (13–59 ft) above ground.

NESTING ECOLOGY

Season: May–June. Usually single-brooded, but may replace lost clutches.

Eggs: Usually 3–5; white with brown or purple spots. Rates of parasitism by Brown-headed Cowbirds are apparently high in some areas, but are hard to measure due to the difficulty of finding nests; no records for Oklahoma.

Development: Incubation is by the female alone for 11–12 days. Young are provisioned by both sexes and fledge at about 12 days.

DISTRIBUTION AND ABUNDANCE

Rangewide: Breeding range patchily distributed from southeastern Minnesota and western New England south to the northern Gulf Coast states. Small numbers breed west to the eastern Great Plains states including parts of eastern Kansas and Oklahoma. Winters from Venezuela and Columbia south to southern Peru and northern Boliva. While much of its breeding range has been reduced, there has been some extension of its range to the north and northeast in recent decades.

Historical: Reported to be abundant in the timber of the Arkansas River and its tributaries in the mid-1850s. One nest record exists for Washington County in 1913. Extensive surveying in McCurtain County in the mid-1960s verified breeding success along the Mountain Fork River and in the McCurtain County Wilderness Area. Surveys of the Cucumber Creek watershed in southern LeFlore County revealed a number of singing birds in 1994 and 1995.

Current: Many of the former forest habitats in Oklahoma have been drastically changed and reduced, resulting in only a few small areas remaining in Delaware and LeFlore counties which may support Cerulean Warblers today. As recently as 1998, survey work in LeFlore County documented a few Cerulean Warbler territories along the steep north slope of Lynn Mountain in Ouachita National Forest.

Population Trend: Breeding Bird Survey data for 1966–2000 show a decline of 4.2 percent per year rangewide (P = 0.00). No trend data are available for Oklahoma.

References: AOU 1998; Baicich and Harrison 1997; Baumgartner and Baumgartner 1992; Bent 1953; Carter 1965; Cornell Laboratory of Ornithology 1999; Couch 1996; Dunn and Garrett 1997; Graber et al. 1983; Hamel 2000; Jacobs and Wilson 1997; James and Neal 1986; Kahl et al. 1985; Kuhnert 1998; Nice and Nice 1924; Rosenberg et al. 2000; Ruley 2000; Sauer et al. 2001; Sibley 2000; Stokes et al. 1997; Sutton 1967; Terres 1991; Tomer 1974

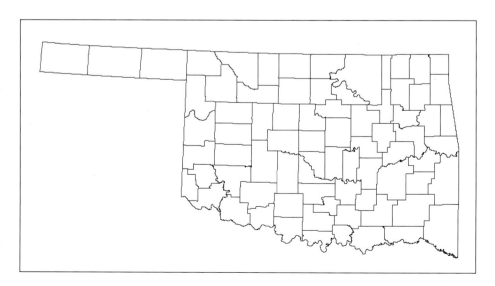

Black-and-white Warbler
Mniotilta varia

Mia R. Revels

The Black-and-white Warbler is one of the first warblers to return to Oklahoma in the spring. These "early birds" herald the beginning of spring migration. The male's song, a repetitive high-pitched *weesee,* is easy to learn and has been described as sounding like a squeaky wheel. It is the only warbler regularly found creeping along tree trunks and branches like a nuthatch.

Description: Both sexes are distinctively patterned in bold black-and-white stripes on head, most of body, and undertail coverts. Males can be distinguished from females by black throat and cheeks. Females and immatures have gray cheeks and a white throat. The male's high-pitched repetitive song is heard most fre-

quently in the early morning hours. Both sexes give sharp *chip* notes. This species is most likely to be confused with the Blackpoll Warbler, a transient species in Oklahoma. Male Blackpoll Warblers lack the black cheek and throat patch of the male Black-and-white Warbler; females are dull olive gray and do not possess sharply defined streaking.

Breeding Habitat: The Black-and-white Warbler breeds in mature and second-growth deciduous and mixed forests with thin understory. Often nests along slopes and ravines. A strong preference is shown for mature forest over early successional habitat.

Nest: Males and females may investigate potential nest

locations together. However, the well-concealed ground nest of leaves, bark strips, and grasses and lined with finer materials is built entirely by the female, usually at the base of a sapling or tree or under a fallen tree branch. The nest is very cryptic and is often tucked under an overhang of moss or fallen leaves.

NESTING ECOLOGY

Season: May–June. Single-brooded.
Eggs: 4–5; white, off-white, or pale bluish or greenish white, finely speckled with darker pigments that are often concentrated at larger end. Common host of Brown-headed Cowbirds.
Development: Incubation is by the female for 10–12 days. Young are provisioned by both sexes and fledge at 11–12 days.

DISTRIBUTION AND ABUNDANCE

Rangewide: A long-distance migrant that breeds in most of the eastern and central United States and much of Canada. Winters in Mexico, Central America, and northern South America.

Historical: Black-and-white Warblers have been described as common to uncommon summer residents in the eastern half of the state, rarer west, and as occasional migrants in the western half.
Current: The Black-and-white Warbler's preference for mature woodlands is demonstrated by its decreasing occurrence, and finally absence, moving from the eastern to the western half of the state. The low number of blocks scored as Confirmed is likely due to the difficulty of locating the cryptic nests of this ground-nesting species. Some of the blocks scored as Possible may be the result of birds singing during migration.

Population Trend: Breeding Bird Survey data for 1966–2000 show no conclusive trend rangewide (0.1 percent per year, P = 0.88) or in Oklahoma (0.3 percent per year, P = 0.86).

References: AOU 1998; Baicich and Harrison 1997; Baumgartner 1992; Baumgartner and Baumgartner 1992; Baumgartner and Howell 1948; Bent 1953; Carter 1992; Ehrlich et al. 1988; James 1971; Kricher 1995; Letson and Letson 1954; Nice 1931; Sauer et al. 2001; Sutton 1967

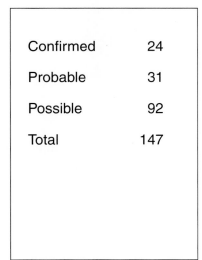

Confirmed	24
Probable	31
Possible	92
Total	147

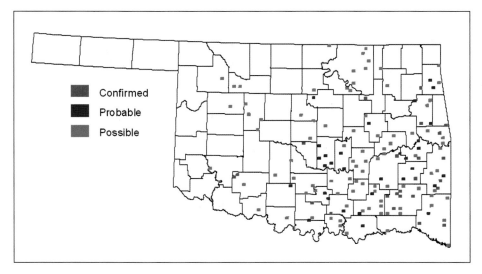

American Redstart

Setophaga ruticilla

Michael D. Bay

Courtesy of Arthur Morris / www.birdsasart.com

The "butterfly bird," as the American Redstart is sometimes called, is one of our most colorful warbler species. Males are black and orange, but do not acquire this plumage until after their first breeding season. First-year males resemble females and will breed in this plumage, but are generally less successful than older males.

Description: Adult males are black with orange patches on sides, wings, and tail. The belly and undertail are white. Females are gray above and white below with yellow patches in wings and tail. First-year males are similar to females but have black spotting on the breast. Not likely to be confused with any other

Oklahoma warbler. Song is variable, with one individual possessing 3–4 songs, which are frequently alternated during a singing session.

Breeding Habitat: Prefers open deciduous forests but also can be found in mixed woodlands and second-growth woodlands. May be limited by nest predators, competitors, and brood parasites in some heavily fragmented areas.

Nest: Open cup nest built of grasses, rootlets, and lichens and lined with fine materials. Usually higher than wide. Placed in the fork of a tree, usually between 3–6 m (10–20 ft) above ground.

NESTING ECOLOGY

Season: June–July. Probably single-brooded.

Eggs: Usually 3–4; white with brown markings. Frequent cowbird host, but occasionally buries cowbird eggs in the bottom of nest.

Development: Incubation is by the female for 12 days. Young are provisioned by both sexes and leave the nest after 9 days, but may be fed for up to 3 weeks.

DISTRIBUTION AND ABUNDANCE

Rangewide: Long-distant migrant, breeds from southeastern Alaska throughout much of Canada, the northern U.S. Rockies, and the eastern part of the United States. Absent from the southeastern coastal plain. Winters from Baja California and central Mexico south to Brazil.

Historical: Nesting primarily occurs only in eastern Oklahoma counties, where they are usually listed as common to uncommon. A rare or uncommon migrant throughout other parts of the state. Westernmost nesting records for Oklahoma come from Washington and Tulsa counties in the 1950s.

Current: The American Redstart is limited to a few eastern counties where its optimal habitats of deciduous woodlands or large forest tracts are likely to be found. Its rarity and localized distribution make it difficult to detect or sample using atlas project methods, so the extent of its range in Oklahoma is probably not well delineated here. Also, some individuals detected as Possible Breeders may actually have been migrants.

Population Trend: Breeding Bird Survey data for 1966–2000 show no conclusive trend rangewide (-0.6 percent per year. P = 0.36). No solid trend information is available for Oklahoma, but reported as being much more common near Spavinaw Lake (Mayes and Delaware counties) in the 1950s than in the 1970s.

References: Baker 1944; Baumgartner and Baumgartner 1992; DeGraaf and Rappole 1995; Ehrlich et al. 1988; Harrison 1984; Kendeigh 1945; Morse 1989; Rappole and Blacklock 1994; Sauer et al. 2001; Sherry and Holmes 1988, 1992, 1997; Weary et al. 1994

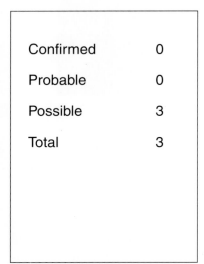

Confirmed	0
Probable	0
Possible	3
Total	3

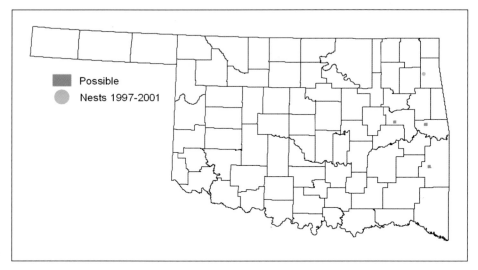

Possible
Nests 1997-2001

Prothonotary Warbler

Protonotaria citrea

Michael D. Bay

Courtesy of Bob Gress

The Prothonotary Warbler is the only cavity-nesting wood-warbler found in Oklahoma. This brilliant yellow bird received its name because its color was thought to be similar to the ceremonial yellow robes of a protonotarius, or official of the Roman Catholic Church. It is a bird of moist bottomland woods, where it is found near water.

Description: Males possess a yellow body, olive back, and blue-gray wings. The head is especially bright, approaching orange or a rich golden yellow. Females are similar but duller. The song is a series of repeated syllables on a single pitch that resembles *swee swee swee swee.*

Breeding Habitat: Prefers flooded bottomlands and riparian habitats. Seldom nests far from water. May be limited in some areas by availability of nest cavities or by competitors for cavities.

Nest: Open cup nest composed of moss, leaves, and twigs and constructed in a natural cavity, usually surrounded by water. This species will readily accept man-made cavities as well and has been recorded nesting in milk cartons, wooden nest boxes, coffee cans, mailboxes, sacks, and other makeshift cavities.

NESTING ECOLOGY

Season: May–June. Single- to double-brooded.
Eggs: Usually 5, sometimes 3–4; white, slightly tinted

with rose in addition to blotches of chestnut brown and gray. Often parasitized by the Brown-headed Cowbird, occurring more frequently than in most cavity nesters but possibly less frequently than in other wood-warblers.

Development: Incubation is by the female for 12–14 days. Young are provisioned by both sexes and fledge at 10–11 days, but continue to be fed by adults for another month.

DISTRIBUTION AND ABUNDANCE

Rangewide: Long-distant migrant, breeding in the eastern half of the United States north to Wisconsin and Minnesota, and wintering in the Yucatan Peninsula south to Columbia, Ecuador, and Venezuela.

Historical: Described as an uncommon to common summer resident of eastern regions and a rare and local summer resident west to Kay, Canadian, and Love counties.

Current: This warbler's preference for moist woodland areas near water confines much of its breeding distribution to eastern Oklahoma counties. However, suitable habitat in central Oklahoma and a few western counties evidently provides the species with scattered nesting opportunities.

Population Trend: Breeding Bird Survey data for 1966–2000 show a decline of 1.3 percent per year rangewide (P = 0.06), but show no conclusive trend in Oklahoma (-2.9 percent per year, P = 0.49).

References: Baumgartner 1992; Baumgartner and Baumgartner 1992; Blem and Blem 1991, 1992; Harrison 1984; Messerly 1979; Morse 1989; Petit 1989, 1999; Rappole and Blacklock 1994; Sauer et al. 2001; Sutton 1967; Walkinshaw 1941, 1953

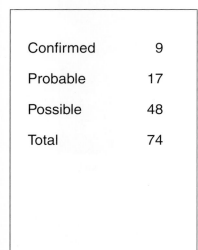

Confirmed	9
Probable	17
Possible	48
Total	74

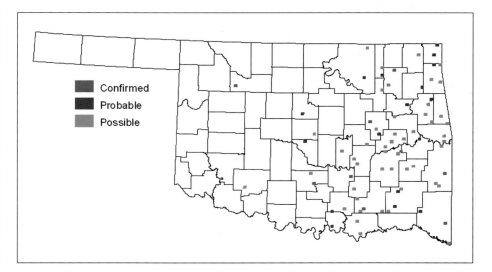

Worm-eating Warbler
Helmitheros vermivorus

Nathan R. Kuhnert

Courtesy of Steve Metz

The Worm-eating Warbler forages for caterpillars, as its name implies, in the breeding season, although it is a propensity it shares with most other wood warblers. It is uncommon and local in forests of eastern Oklahoma and is often sought by birders visiting these areas.

Description: Bold, dark lateral stripes on its buffy-orange head are distinctive. The back and wings are olive brown, and the breast is a rich buffy color. This species is inconspicuous to most observers except when singing its unmusical, flat, and very rapid, dry, trilled song that is strongest in the middle and weakest at the end. Its song is very similar to that of the Chipping

Sparrow, but is perhaps drier, higher, and more rapid. The song can also be confused with one variation of the Pine Warbler's song. Its call is a loud clear chip.

Breeding Habitat: Habitat consists of deciduous or mixed woodlands on gentle or steep slopes, along brushy ravines, and less commonly in swampy and drier mixed lowland woods. A dense, jungle-like understory is typical of most breeding habitats. Across the border into Arkansas it inhabits moist mature extensive forests with ample understory, ravines, and hillsides of the highlands. A common denominator of important habitat requirements seems to be extensive, unfragmented forest, thus this species can be used as an indicator of forest health. The Worm-eating Warbler has been found in dense stands of young pines in the Ouachitas of Arkansas and Oklahoma.

Nest: A cup of dead leaves, lined with fungi, moss, hair, or the stems of maple seeds. Nests are built by the female and well hidden on the ground, often under a shrub or sapling, among roots, or in a slight cavity.

NESTING ECOLOGY

Season: May–June. Single-brooded, but may replace lost clutches.
Eggs: Usually 4–5; white, unmarked, or marked with fine speckling and spotting. Frequent host to Brown-headed Cowbirds in some areas.
Development: Incubation is by the female for about 13 days. Young are provisioned by both sexes and leave the nest at 10–11 days.

DISTRIBUTION AND ABUNDANCE

Rangewide: Breeds primarily in the Appalachian states and is scattered in small isolated pockets across portions of the central Midwest before becoming more widespread again in the Ozark Plateau region and the Ouachita Mountains region of Arkansas and Oklahoma. Winters from eastern and southern Mexico south to Panama, and in the West Indies.

Historical: Described as a very rare and local resident in eastern Oklahoma counties. No nesting records are reported in Oklahoma ornithological literature, and breeding season records reported in extreme southeastern and northeastern Oklahoma are sparse. The scarcity of nest records may in part be attributed to its low population density and inconspicuous habits.
Current: The Worm-eating Warbler appears to be a rare breeder primarily in the oak-hickory forest association in far-southeastern Oklahoma. One report verified nesting in Cherokee County in northeastern Oklahoma in 2001. Its song is not strong compared to other songbirds and can be easily confused with the Pine Warbler, compounding the difficulty of verifying this species in a block.

Population Trend: Breeding Bird Survey data for 1966–2000 show no conclusive trend rangewide (0.9 percent per year, P = 0.29). No trend data are available for Oklahoma.

References: AOU 1998; Baicich and Harrison 1997; Baumgartner and Baumgartner 1992; Bent 1953; Dunn and Garrett 1997; Graber et al. 1983; Greenberg 1997; Hanners and Patton 1998; James and Neal 1986; Kuhnert 2001; Palmer-Ball 1996; Sauer et al. 2001; Sibley 2000; Stokes et al. 1997; Sutton 1967; Terres 1991

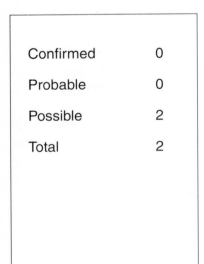

Confirmed	0
Probable	0
Possible	2
Total	2

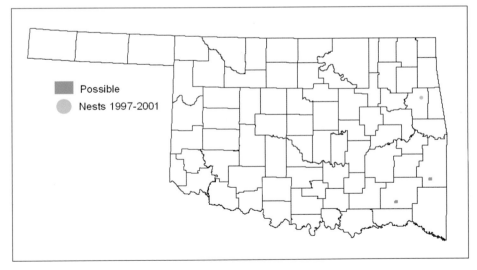

Possible
Nests 1997-2001

Swainson's Warbler

Limnothlypis swainsonii

John M. Dole

Courtesy of Bob Gress

The Swainson's Warbler is one of the visually least conspicuous members of a family filled with many brightly colored members. In Oklahoma, the Swainson's Warbler is uncommonly seen due to its limited range in the southeast, preference for dense swampy woods with ample understory, and secretive habits. Migrants are occasionally found north of their normal breeding range in the spring.

Description: Sexes similar. Olive-brown upperparts with a rufous crown, whitish supercilium and face, and dark eye line. Bill is long for a warbler. Song is a series of loud, slurred notes approximating *we-see-whip-poor-will.*

Breeding Habitat: Damp bottomland hardwoods with shaded and dense understory and canebrakes.

Nest: A bulky cup of dead leaves and other debris built by the female and lined with pine needles, cypress leaves, moss, grass stems, and occasionally hair. Placed 0.6–3 m (2–10 ft) above ground, usually in a branch fork in dense shrubs or trees.

NESTING ECOLOGY

Season: May–June. Single-brooded, but may replace lost clutches.

Eggs: 3–4; usually unmarked and white but may be tinted bluish green, pink, or buff. Known to be parasitized by the Brown-headed Cowbird, with the first such report coming from Oklahoma in 1917, when 2 of 6 nests contained cowbird eggs. Two of 4 nests found in 2001 were observed to be parasitized.

Development: Incubation is by the female for 13–15 days. Young are provisioned by both sexes and fledge at 10–12 days, but continue to be fed by adults for 2–3 weeks.

DISTRIBUTION AND ABUNDANCE

Rangewide: Breeds in the southeastern United States from southern Virginia, West Virginia, Kentucky, and Missouri west to eastern Texas and south to northern Florida. Winters primarily in the West Indies, but also in the Yucatan Peninsula of Mexico.

Historical: Formerly more common before its habitat was greatly reduced through lumbering and drainage. Described as a rare summer resident in Washington County in 1931; six nests were found along the Little Caney River in 1917. By 1967, Swainson's Warbler was described as a summer resident having been reported from McCurtain, Delaware, Washington, Tulsa, and Payne counties. A singing male was reported over a span of dates in Tulsa's Mohawk Park in spring and summer of 1950 and 1951. An adult feeding a large, fledged young was observed in McCurtain County in 1961.

Current: Now rare and local, known only from Little River National Wildlife Refuge in McCurtain County and other nearby locations. Four nests found in 2001 at this refuge during an intensive study are the first for the state since 1917. The very local distribution of this species resulted in no records in atlas blocks.

Population Trend: Breeding Bird Survey data for 1966–2000 show an increase of 2.9 percent per year rangewide (P = 0.07). No trend data are available for Oklahoma.

References: AOU 1998; Baicich and Harrison 1997; Baumgartner and Baumgartner 1992; Carter 1965; Curson et al. 1994; Dunn and Garrett 1997; Howell and Webb 1995; Kaufman 1996; Kirn 1918; Letson and Letson 1954; Meanley 1969, 1971a, 1971b; National Geographic Society 1999; Nice 1931; Revels, M. R., pers. comm.; Sallabanks et al. 2000; Sauer et al. 2001; Sutton 1967; Thomas et al. 1996

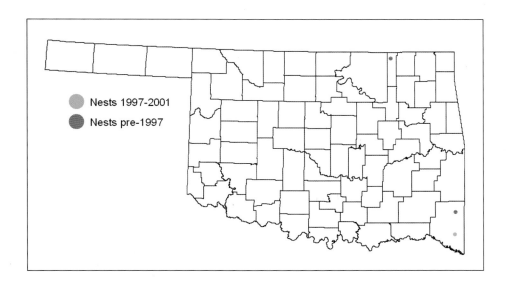

Nests 1997-2001
Nests pre-1997

Ovenbird
Seiurus aurocapillus

Nathan R. Kuhnert

The Ovenbird is named for its oven-like nest of leaves and grass, which is built on the forest floor. One of several long-distance Neotropical migrants that faces habitat loss on two fronts, it can be used as an indicator species of the quality of eastern North American forests due to its dependence on contiguous, mature hardwood stands. The Ovenbird is easy to hear, but less often seen. During early morning or late evening visits in the breeding season, the Ovenbird's spectacular and harmonious "flight song" resonates through the quiet forest air.

Description: A large olive-brown warbler with a pale orange crown extending from bill to nape, and with two lateral brownish-black stripes on both sides of crown. The underparts are white with bold, blackish-streaked spots on the lower throat, breast, and sides. It is most likely to be visually confused with both species of waterthrush. The song of the Ovenbird is comprised of chants that grow louder and louder, building to a crescendo, and can be expressed as *teacher-teacher-teacher-teacher-teacher* with an accent on the first syllable. Its song, when delivered without accents, can sound similar to both the Kentucky Warbler and the Carolina Wren. The "flight song" is comprised of varied and rambling notes.

Breeding Habitat: Large tracts of well-drained, mature

deciduous or mixed broadleaf-conifer forests. Prefers north-facing slopes or ravines with only modest ground cover of vegetation.

Nest: A rounded, domed structure (oven-like) placed in a small hollow on the forest floor, usually near a trail or woods road, and comprised of dead leaves, pine needles, grass, weed stems, rootlets, and moss. It is roofed with leaves and branches and has a small slit entrance on one side. The inner cup is lined with hair and fine rootlets.

NESTING ECOLOGY

Season: May–July. Single-brooded.

Eggs: 3–6; white, speckled and spotted blotches of brown. Frequent host to Brown-headed Cowbirds, but no records for Oklahoma.

Development: Incubation is by the female for 11–14 days. Young are provisioned by both sexes, leave the nest at 8–10 days, and reach independence in 20–30 more days.

DISTRIBUTION AND ABUNDANCE

Rangewide: Breeds throughout the eastern United States, southern Canada, and the northwestern United States to northern British Columbia. Winters in Mexico, Central America, and northern parts of South America.

Historical: Described as a rare and local summer resident of eastern counties. By 2000, described as summer resident of Delaware, Adair, LeFlore, and McCurtain counties. Formerly in Mayes County.

Current: The Ovenbird's specific habitat preference, weighted heavily on vegetation structure and topography, is met in the oak-hickory and oak-pine forest associations of the Ouachita Moutains in southeastern Oklahoma. Its song is highly audible in both frequency and volume, which should have led to a high detection rate in the sampled blocks wherever Ovenbirds were present.

Population Trend: Breeding Bird Survey data for 1966–2000 show an increase of 0.6 percent per year rangewide (P = 0.000), but show no conclusive trend in Oklahoma (-5.3 percent per year, P = 0.67).

References: AOU 1998; Baicich and Harrison 1997; Baumgartner and Baumgartner 1992; Bent 1953; Dunn and Garret 1997; Graber et al. 1983; Oklahoma Bird Records Committee 2000; Sauer et al. 2001; Sibley 2000; Stokes et al. 1997; Sutton 1967; Terres 1991; Van Horn and Donovan 1999

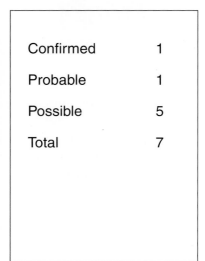

Confirmed	1
Probable	1
Possible	5
Total	7

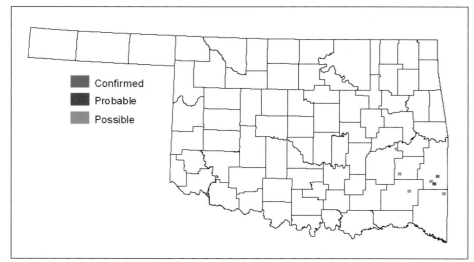

Louisiana Waterthrush
Seiurus motacilla

Bonnie L. Gall

Courtesy of Joseph A. Grzybowski

Lucky is the Oklahoma birder (such as this author) who lives close enough to a bubbly stream to be awakened in the early spring by the loud, distinctive song of the Louisiana Waterthrush. This warbler is one of the earliest to arrive in the spring, but its preference for wild places and flowing streams means that one has to venture to the remote and beautiful places of the state to see its bobbing stride and hear its upbeat song.

Description: Sexes similar. Dark back contrasts with whitish underparts and salmon-buff flanks. Bicolor eyeline, pale buff in front of eye and white behind. The legs are pink, the throat is white, and the breast is heavily streaked. Bobs slowly as it walks. Song is three or four loud slurred notes followed by a rapid jumble of notes. Call is a sharp *chink*. The similar Northern Waterthrush, a migrant in Oklahoma, often has a more buffy yellow eye line and a smaller bill, lacks contrast in color between flanks and underparts, and has a distinctly different song and call.

Breeding Habitat: Along wooded streams and in swamps with moving water in the eastern and central parts of the state.

Nest: A bulky mass of dead leaves in a hole in a steep bank of a stream or in overturned roots close to moving water. It is usually concealed by overhanging roots, weeds, or grass. The nest is reinforced with twigs, and the cup is lined with grasses, plants stems, or hair. Leaves in front of the nest make a pathway to the nest entrance.

NESTING ECOLOGY

Season: May–June. Single-brooded, but will replace lost clutches.
Eggs: Usually 4–6; creamy white and dotted or blotched with browns or grays. Frequent host to Brown-headed Cowbirds, but only one record known from Oklahoma.
Development: Incubation is by the female for 12–14 days. Young are provisioned by both sexes, fledge in about 10 days, and reach independence in 3–4 more weeks.

DISTRIBUTION AND ABUNDANCE

Rangewide: Breeds from Nebraska and eastern Texas eastward to the Atlantic Ocean. Winters in Mexico, Central America, and the Carribean.
Historical: Considered a common summer resident of eastern and central Oklahoma in appropriate habitat. Less common west to Major, Blaine, Caddo, and Comanche counties. One study in McCurtain County found a pair density of 0.21 pr/ha (8.6 pr/100 ac).
Current: Evidence of breeding or possible breeding for the Louisiana Waterthrush occurred throughout most of eastern and central Oklahoma. A preference for less accessible nesting habitat and the construction of well-camouflaged nests made this species difficult to locate and confirm. The patchiness of the distribution in the east may reflect these difficulties or may be influenced by atlas methodology. For example, evidence of nesting exists in Washington County in northeastern Oklahoma, but was not detected in atlas blocks in that county.

Population Trend: Breeding Bird Survey data for 1966–2000 show an increase of 0.8 percent per year rangewide (P = 0.07), but show no conclusive trend in Oklahoma (1.8 percent per year, P = 0.44).

References: Baumgartner 1992; Baumgartner and Baumgartner 1992; Bent 1963; Carter 1967; Dunn 1997; Eaton 1958; Harrison 1975; Johnsgard 1978; National Geographic Society 1999; Rickstrew 1975; Robinson 1995; Sauer et al 2001; Sutton 1967; Wolfe 1996a; Ziegler 1976

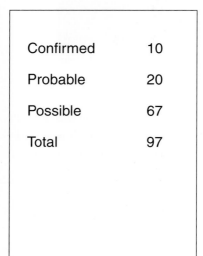

Confirmed	10
Probable	20
Possible	67
Total	97

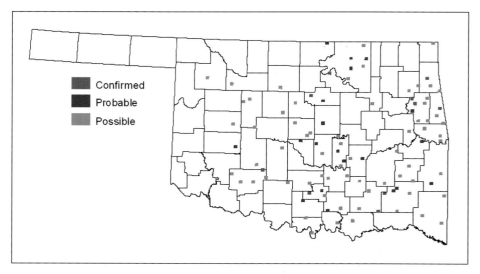

Kentucky Warbler
Oporornis formosus

Michael D. Bay

Courtesy of Arthur Morris / www.birdsasart.com

This ground-nesting warbler might be better named the Kentucky Wagtail due to its walking and tail-thrashing movements. A shy and cautious species that might otherwise escape notice if it were not for its loud singing. It is generally active at ground level but also forages above ground in low, dense vegetation.

Description: Sexes are similar with an olive green back and wings and a yellow throat and breast. A yellow eye ring extends to the bill and is sometimes referred to as yellow "spectacles." In addition, a black crown and black ear patch or mask are also distinctive. A similar species in Oklahoma, the Common Yellowthroat, also possesses a black mask, but it lacks the yellow spectacles. Song is a series of two-syllable phrases, somewhat similar to that of the Carolina Wren.

Breeding Habitat: Prefers deciduous woodlands with much shrubby understory, often near water.

Nest: Open cup situated on the ground or slightly above ground in the fork of a small sapling. Nest well concealed by understory vegetation.

NESTING ECOLOGY

Season: May–July. Usually single-brooded.
Eggs: 4–5; creamy white with brown blotchings Common host to the Brown-headed Cowbird.
Development: Incubation is by the female for 11–13 days. Young are provisioned by both sexes and fledge in 8–10 days, reaching independence about 3 weeks later.

DISTRIBUTION AND ABUNDANCE

Rangewide: Long-distance migrant, breeding from southeastern Nebraska, southwestern Wisconsin, central Ohio, and southern Pennsylvania south to east Texas and up through the Atlantic Coast states. Winters in southern Mexico south to Colombia and Venezuela.
Historical: Described as a common summer resident in eastern Oklahoma, but rarely encountered farther westward. Westernmost breeding records for Oklahoma are in Caddo County in 1867 and 1979.

Current: This species' preference for woodland habitat confines much of its Oklahoma distribution to the forested areas in the eastern half of the state. Though frequently active at or near ground level, its loud song and persistent singing make it easily detectible.

Population Trend: Breeding Bird Survey data for 1966–2000 show a decline of 1.0 percent per year rangewide (P = 0.01), but show no conclusive trend in Oklahoma (0.6 percent per year, P = 0.84).

References: Baumgartner 1992; Baumgartner and Baumgartner 1992; DeGraaf and Rappole 1995; Gibbs and Faaborg 1990; Harrison 1984; McDonald 1998; Morse 1989; Newell 1980; Nice 1931; Rappole and Blacklock 1994; Sauer et al. 2001; Shackford 1992a; Sutton 1967

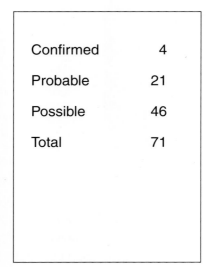

Confirmed	4
Probable	21
Possible	46
Total	71

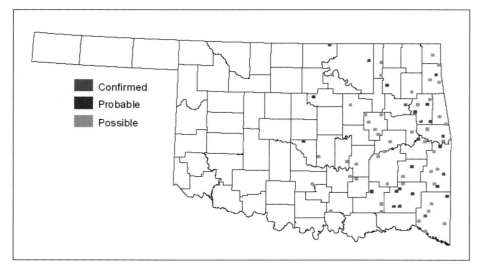

Common Yellowthroat
Geothlypis trichas

Richard A. Stuart

Courtesy of Bob Gress

One of the first birds of the New World to be described, this wren-like warbler is very secretive around the nest, making its nest one of the most difficult to find. The female slips off the nest and runs beneath the vegetation to pop up some distance away to eye and scold the intruder. More studies of its breeding biology are needed.

Description: The male Common Yellowthroat is characterized by his black "Lone Ranger" mask with a grayish-white border across the forehead and cheeks. He also has yellow undertail coverts. Both sexes have a yellow throat and upper breast with whitish abdomen. The female has an olive-brown face and a white eye ring. The primary song is an easily recognized *witchity-witchity-witchity-witch*. The black-masked Kentucky Warbler could be confused with the male yellowthroat, although Kentucky Warblers have yellow spectacles and a yellow belly.

Breeding Habitat: Grassy, weedy, or brushy locations in fields or woodland edges. Often found in moist areas because of the denser vegetation there, but can occur in drier areas with dense vegetation as well.

Nest: A well-camouflaged bulky cup sometimes constructed with a roof or dome and located within three feet of the ground or water surface. It is composed of grasses, plant fibers, leaves and moss and is lined with fine grass, plant fibers and, usually, hair.

NESTING ECOLOGY

Season: May–July. Probably double-brooded.

Eggs: 3–6, but usually 4; white, speckled and spotted with reddish-brown. Species is known to be parasitized by Brown-headed Cowbirds, including 3 of 5 Washington County nests in the early twentieth century.

Development: Incubation is by the female for about 12 days. Young are provisioned by both sexes and fledge at 9–10 days, but are not independent for another 3 weeks.

DISTRIBUTION AND ABUNDANCE

Rangewide: One of the most widespread of warblers, the Common Yellowthroat breeds across most of the United States and southern Canada, except in parts of the southwestern United States. It also breeds in central Mexico and winters from the southern United States south to northern South America.

Historical: Considered a summer resident in northern, southeastern, and central Oklahoma in 1931. Reported to be a decidedly local summer resident over most of the state by 1967, except in southwestern Oklahoma.

Current: A regular though uncommon breeder in the eastern part of Oklahoma, the Common Yellowthroat is much more locally distributed in the western half of the state. Some of the Possible Breeder blocks may indicate birds singing prior to the end of spring migration. The few confirmations underscore the difficulty of finding nests of this species in its favored habitats of thick grass and marshes.

Population Trend: Breeding Bird Survey data for 1966–2000 show a decline of 0.3 percent per year rangewide (P = 0.05) and an increase of 5.2 percent per year in Oklahoma (P = 0.05).

References: AOU 1998; Baicich and Harrison 1997; Baumgartner 1992; Baumgartner and Baumgartner 1992; Bent 1963; Guzy and Ritchison 1999; Harrison 1975, 1984; National Geographic Society 1999; Nice 1931; Peterson 1963; Sauer et al. 2001; Sibley 2000; Stokes and Stokes 1996; Sutton 1967

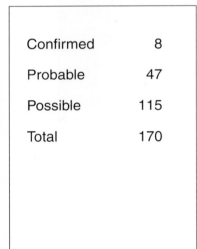

Confirmed	8
Probable	47
Possible	115
Total	170

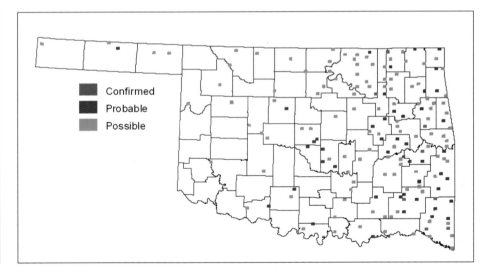

Hooded Warbler
Wilsonia citrina

Nathan R. Kuhnert

This strikingly bold warbler spends most of its life low in forest understory, except when the male perches higher to sing. Typically, it is only briefly glimpsed due to its reclusive habits. The Hooded Warbler requires extensive forest tracts and is an important indicator species of forest health.

Description: Adult males are olive green above and bright yellow below, with a black hood and throat contrasting with a bright yellow forehead and cheeks. The females are olive green above and bright yellow below and never have as complete and extensive a hood as adult males. Both sexes have extensive white in the outer three tail feathers, which is revealed in their habit of rapidly fanning the tail with a lateral movement.

This diagnostic behavioral trait can be used to separate it from the similar Wilson's Warbler which migrates through Oklahoma. The song is a short, loud series of whistled two-note phrases with an emphatic ending.

Breeding Habitat: Typically found in the undergrowth of mature deciduous forests and in wooded swamps, although it can also inhabit other forest types, especially those with an area greater than 15 ha (37 ac). Well-developed shrubby understory beneath these extensive forests is an important requirement. In western portions of its range, it is associated with thick bottomland woods in Oklahoma and wet, open woods in eastern Kansas.

Nest: A compact cup made of dead leaves, plant fibers, and down, bound with spider silk, and lined with fine grass. Often placed in shrub understory, vines, or saplings, from a few inches to 2 m (6 ft) above the ground.

NESTING ECOLOGY

Season: May–July. Usually double-brooded.
Eggs: 3–5; creamy white and speckled with brown spots. High rate of Brown-headed Cowbird nest parasitism. For Oklahoma, one report of an adult warbler feeding a cowbird in McCurtain County.
Development: Incubation is by the female for 12 days. Young are provisioned by both sexes and leave the nest at 8–9 days, reaching independence in another 4–5 weeks.

DISTRIBUTION AND ABUNDANCE

Rangewide: Breeds primarily in the eastern United States and mainly south of the Great Lakes region; reaches highest abundance in the southeast. Its western range extends to eastern Oklahoma and Kansas. Winters primarily on the Yucatan peninsula and adjacent regions of Mexico and Central America.
Historical: Summer resident only in the southeastern Oklahoma counties of Latimer, LeFlore, Pushmataha, and McCurtain. No nests known in Oklahoma, but young have been reported. Woodhouse in his nineteenth-century explorations commented that the Hooded Warbler was very common in Indian Territory, keeping along streams in the dense thickets. Two areas in McCurtain County where breeding records were common during the 1960s are now largely under water from dam construction.
Current: The Hooded Warbler's preference for moist and mature deciduous forest is revealed by the concentration of sightings in oak-pine forest associations of southeast Oklahoma, where annual rainfall exceeds 40 inches. The high proportion of blocks listed as Possible result from this species' highly audible song, coupled with the limitations of searching for nests in very dense stands of vegetation. While fledged young have previously been observed in Oklahoma, the first reported nests of this species in the state were found at Little River National Wildlife Refuge in 2001.

Population Trend: Breeding Bird Survey data for 1966–2000 show no conclusive trend rangewide (0.8 percent per year, P = 0.42) or in Oklahoma (-2.0 percent per year, P = 0.33).

References: AOU 1998; Baicich and Harrison 1997; Baumgartner and Baumgartner 1992; Bent 1953; Dunn and Garrett 1997; Evans and Stutchbury 1994; Graber et al. 1983; Oklahoma Bird Records Committee 2000; Revels, M. R., pers. comm.; Sauer et al. 2001; Sibley 2000; Stokes et al. 1997; Sutton 1967; Terres 1991; Woodhouse 1853

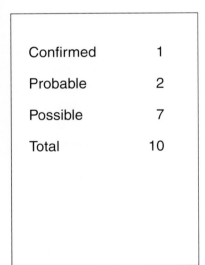

Confirmed	1
Probable	2
Possible	7
Total	10

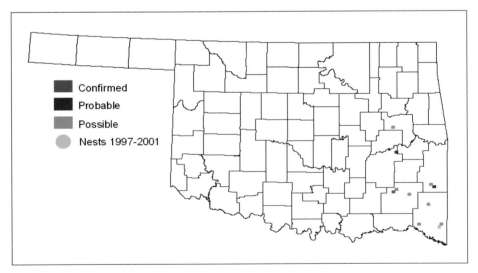

Confirmed
Probable
Possible
Nests 1997-2001

Yellow-breasted Chat

Icteria virens

Alan E. Versaw

Almost as difficult to see as they are easy to hear, Yellow-breasted Chats enliven thickets, brush, and forest edges throughout eastern Oklahoma. Although locally distributed through much of western Oklahoma, these flashy birds are encountered with diminishing frequency as one travels westward across the state. In the Panhandle, they are almost entirely absent as breeders. Most chats found in western Oklahoma represent the western subspecies, *Icteria virens auricollis,* distinguished by the male's brighter yellow breast and a longer tail in both sexes.

Description: A garish splash of yellow adorns the breast of both sexes. When singing from an exposed perch, the yellow breast and brilliant white spectacles bring instant recognition to the species. In many cases, however, an observer may gain only a furtive glimpse of the plain, olive-colored back and crown and perhaps be frustrated in attempts at identification. For those familiar with the shrieks, whistles, and rattles of the male chat, however, identification requires no visual contact. In this case, a relentless cacophony emanating from deep within a growth of tangles offers convincing evidence of the bird's presence.

Breeding Habitat: The Yellow-breasted Chat requires dense tangles and thickets for breeding. Tree branches and the tops of taller brush provide singing perches and launching sites for the flight song of the flamboyant male. Often, favored habitat is found on the edge of woodlands or in second growth following the clearing of a forested area. Throughout the west, including western Oklahoma, suitable habitat is found almost exclusively in riparian corridors. Breeding habitat in eastern Oklahoma is more broadly distributed, however, and less dependent on proximity to water.

Nest: Buried deep within a growth of tangles and standing a few feet above the ground, chat nests are exceedingly difficult to locate. The female constructs the outer layers of the nest from coarse grasses, forbs, and leaves. The inner cup, however, often enjoys a more comfortable construction of finer grasses and stems.

NESTING ECOLOGY

Season: May–July. Probably single-brooded.
Eggs: Usually 3–5; white or cream colored and spotted and blotched with reddish markings. Known Brownheaded Cowbird host, but size of chat nestlings allows them to compete more effectively with cowbird nestmates than other warbler species. The species is also known to destroy cowbird eggs and to abandon nests into which cowbird eggs have been deposited.
Development: Incubation is by the female for 11–12 days. Young are provisioned by both sexes and fledge at about 9 days.

DISTRIBUTION AND ABUNDANCE

Rangewide: The Yellow-breasted Chat breeds at least locally throughout most of the 48 contiguous states into the southern prairie provinces of Canada. Migration takes the birds south to the lower coastal areas of Mexico and Central America for winter.
Historical: Described as common but local in eastern regions; less common westward. Distribution has probably remained more or less constant.
Current: The dense tangles of vegetation required by Yellow-breasted Chats occur extensively throughout the eastern third of Oklahoma. West of that area, however, it occurs only locally, typically in conjunction with riparian corridors. As a result, the species is probably well sampled by the atlas protocol in eastern Oklahoma but subject to numerous "misses" in western Oklahoma where block selection bypassed prime habitat or atlas fieldworkers were unable to obtain permission to survey the isolated arteries of dense vegetation where chats may occur. Certainly, the species becomes less common in western Oklahoma but probably not so rare as the data would seem to indicate.

Population Trend: Breeding Bird Survey data for 1966–2000 show no conclusive trend rangewide (-0.1 percent per year, P = 0.61) or in Oklahoma (-1.1 percent per year, P = 0.41).

References: Baicich and Harrison 1997; Baumgartner and Baumgartner 1992; Curson et al. 1994; Dunn and Garrett 1997; Eckerle and Thompson 2001; Nice 1931; Sauer et al. 2001; Sutton 1967

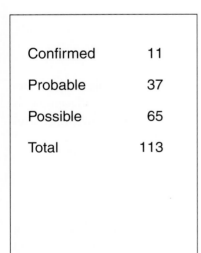

Confirmed	11
Probable	37
Possible	65
Total	113

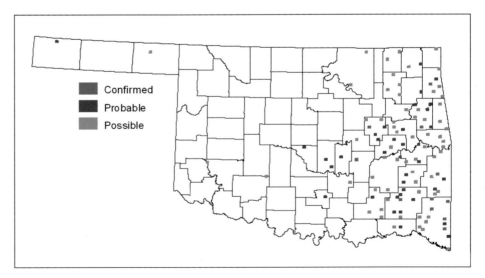

Summer Tanager
Piranga rubra

Michael D. Bay

Courtesy of Bob Gress

Asummer bird seen throughout much of the state, the brightly colored Summer Tanager is perhaps more common in the oak-pine wooded areas of eastern Oklahoma. It is known for eating bees and wasps, but it also eats fruits. More study of its breeding biology is needed.

Description: The full red plumage of a male Summer Tanager will be complete by late summer of its second year. Prior to this, second-year males will show some red feathers, but are mostly yellowish, as are the females. The song of the Summer Tanager has been compared to the American Robin, but is perhaps more musical and consists of 2–3 repeated phrases.

Breeding Habitat: Deciduous and mixed woodlands, preferring open, upland woods.

Nest: An open cup formed by the female from grasses and forbs and lined with finer grasses. Placement is usually on a horizontal branch of a hardwood anywhere between 1.8–12 m (6–40 ft) high.

NESTING ECOLOGY

Season: May–July. Possibly double-brooded.
Eggs: 3–4; pale blue, sometimes green with speckles of brown. Regularly parasitized by the Brown-headed Cowbird.

Development: Incubation is by the female for 11–12 days. Young are provisioned by both sexes and fledge at about 9–10 days, but continue to be fed by adults for about 3 weeks.

Hybridization: One report of hybridization with Scarlet Tanager was published in 1893; another report exists from Payne County, Oklahoma, in 1979 of a male Scarlet Tanager and an apparent female Summer Tanager raising 3 young.

DISTRIBUTION AND ABUNDANCE

Rangewide: A long-distant migrant that breeds from southeastern California to central Oklahoma and from eastern Nebraska to New Jersey south to the Gulf Coast. Wintering areas include Mexico to South America.

Historical: Common in eastern Oklahoma counties, primarily in oak-hickory and oak-pine forests. Rare in western Oklahoma. A few winter records exist for eastern counties.

Current: The Summer Tanager is primarily a woodland species, and its preference for this habitat can be seen in its common occurrence through the eastern half of the state. Its characteristic song and consistent singing make it easy to detect in atlas blocks.

Population Trend: Breeding Bird Survey data for 1966–2000 show no conclusive trend rangewide (-0.1 percent per year, P = 0.72) or in Oklahoma (-0.1 percent per year, P = 0.96).

References: Baumgartner and Baumgartner 1992; Bent 1965; DeGraaf et al. 1991; Ehrlich et al. 1988; Kastl 1980; Lowery 1974; Robbins et al. 1966; Sauer et al. 2001; Shy 1985

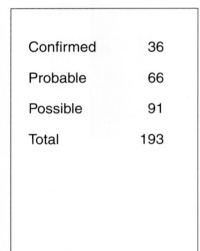

Confirmed	36
Probable	66
Possible	91
Total	193

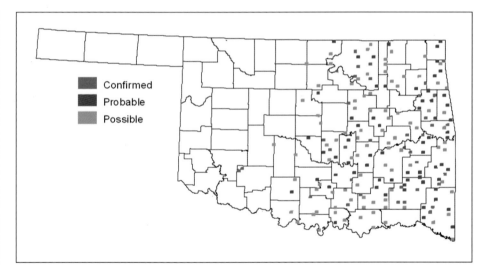

Scarlet Tanager
Piranga olivacea

Nathan R. Kuhnert

Courtesy of Arthur Morris / www.birdsasart.com

The male Scarlet Tanager's strikingly brilliant scarlet-red and velvet-black plumage is almost unrivaled among North American birds, although it is his characteristic call note that usually identifies his presence high in the tree canopy. Known as a species of the forest interior, the Scarlet Tanager is sensitive to forest fragmentation and has suffered high rates of predation and cowbird parasitism in small forest plots.

Description: The adult male in breeding plumage is bright red with shiny black wings and tail. The adult female is olive green above, olive yellow below, with dull, brownish-olive wings and a green-edged tail. Immature males resemble the adult female and can be confused with female and immature Summer Tanagers. Like the immature male, the female can also be confused with the Summer Tanager but is separated by her plain yellow, not orange-yellow, underparts, and espe-

cially by the unique call note. The Scarlet Tanager's hoarse and burry *CHIP-burrr* call is more distinctive than its short, buzzy, caroling, robin-like song that can also resemble the Summer Tanager, Rose-breasted Grosbeak, and Yellow-throated Vireo, which can all occur nearby.

Breeding Habitat: Inhabits a wide variety of deciduous and mixed deciduous-coniferous forest types, especially mature forest where oaks are common. It also occurs in young successional woodlands and even in wooded parks and roadside shade trees. In McCurtain County, it is known to nest in upland mature pine forest. The size of forest tract is an important habitat variable; estimated tract size needed to sustain a viable poulation is 10–12 ha (25–30 ac). Its habitat preference overlaps with the Summer Tanager, but it typically uses steeper slopes with higher canopy cover.

Nest: A shallow and loose saucer-shaped cup of twigs, grass, weed stems, and rootlets, which are lined with finer grasses, weed stems, and rootlets. Usually located well out on the limb and 4.5–18 m (15–59 ft) above ground.

NESTING ECOLOGY

Season: May–July. Single-brooded, but may renest if first nest is lost early in the breeding season.

Eggs: Usually 4; pale blue or pale green, minutely speckled or boldly spotted with brown. Regularly parasitized by the Brown-headed Cowbird; no definite records for Oklahoma.

Development: Incubation is by the female for 13–14 days. Young are provisioned by both sexes and fledge at 9–12 days, but continue to be fed by adults for 2 weeks.

Hybridization: One report of hybridization with Summer Tanager was published in 1893; another report exists from Payne County, Oklahoma, in 1979 of a male Scarlet Tanager and an apparent female Summer Tanager raising 3 young.

DISTRIBUTION AND ABUNDANCE

Rangewide: Long-distant Neotropical migrant. Breeding range centered in eastern North America coinciding with the range of the eastern deciduous forest. Northern range extends into extreme southeast Manitoba and southern Ontario, while southern range extends from extreme southeast Virginia across the south to extreme southeastern Oklahoma. Winters in northwestern South America.

Historical: Described as abundant in Indian Territory in the mid-1850s. Formerly bred in several eastern counties with appropriate habitat, but most recent nesting records come from LeFlore and McCurtain counties. Single nest records exist for Woodward and Payne counties. Occasionally occurs in central and western Oklahoma in migration.

Current: The Scarlet Tanager is primarily confined to the oak-pine and oak-hickory forest of the Ouachita Mountains in southeastern Oklahoma and to the western flanks of the Ozark Plateau in northeastern Oklahoma. The atlas results show a fairly dense distribution throughout these areas, indicating that this species is locally common in the region. Perhaps anomalies, two reports from Creek and Pontotoc counties may be best explained by the Scarlet Tanager's reputation for occasionally nesting far west of its normal range. The singing bird reported from Cimarron County is highly ususual so far west.

Population Trend: Breeding Bird Survey data for 1966–2000 show no conclusive trend rangewide (-0.2 percent per year, P = 0.37) or in Oklahoma (-4.0 percent per year, P = 0.56).

References: AOU 1998; Baicich and Harrison 1997; Baumgartner and Baumgartner 1992; Bent 1958; Gail et al. 1976; James and Neal 1986; Johnsgard 1979; Kastl 1980; Kuhnert 1998; McCormick 1893; Moorman 1986; Mowbray 1999; Project Tanager 1993; Robbins 1980; Roberts and Norment 1999; Ruley 2000; Sauer et al. 2001; Sibley 2000; Stokes et al. 1997; Sutton 1967; Terres 1991; Tomer 1974; Tyler 1986b

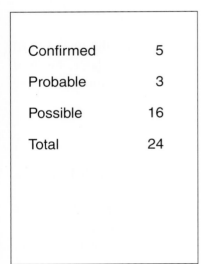

Confirmed	5
Probable	3
Possible	16
Total	24

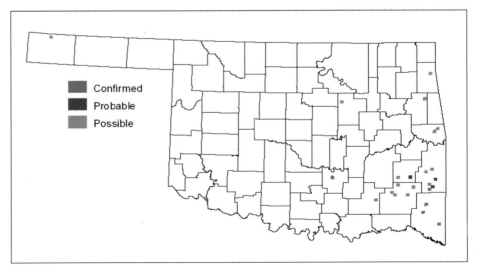

Green-tailed Towhee
Pipilo chlorurus

John S. Shackford

Courtesy of Michael Gray

The Green-tailed Towhee, usually found on the ground or in low, thick vegetation, is quite secretive and easily overlooked. This reticence adds to its charm. Diligence in seeking one out is also rewarded with the view of a trim, handsome bird. Only one nest is known for Oklahoma.

Description: The Green-tailed Towhee is generally grayish, with greenish on wings, tail, and back, a rufous crown, and a white throat. The face has an additional white malar stripe.

Breeding Habitat: Typically nests from about 1,400–3,200 m (4,600–10,500 ft) in arid foothills of chaparral, sagebrush, and scrub oaks, and in pine forests and river valleys. Prefers areas that are species-rich in shrubs.

Nest: Usually placed in low shrubs within 0.6 m (2 ft) of the ground. The nest is relatively large, made of twigs, grasses, and weed stems, and lined with fine rootlets and hair.

NESTING ECOLOGY

Season: May–July. Probably double-brooded, but little information is available.
Eggs: Usually 3–4; pale sky blue with reddish speckling. Rarely parasitized by Brown-headed Cowbirds.
Development: Incubation is by the female for about

12 days. Young are provisioned by both sexes and leave the nest in 11–12 days, but continue to be fed by adults for another 2 weeks.

DISTRIBUTION AND ABUNDANCE

Rangewide: Breeds from southeastern Washington State to central Montana south to northwestern New Mexico. Winters from central California to eastern Texas south through most of Mexico.

Historical: Closest known regular breeding area to Oklahoma is at Capulin Mountain, Union County, northeastern New Mexico. The single Oklahoma breeding record is a May 1982 nest containing three eggs in a concrete restroom facility at the Black Mesa State Park in Cimarron County. The nest was soon abandoned. The species is otherwise described as a rare migrant and casual visitant in Oklahoma, primarily in the western Panhandle. One other summer record exists, on 16 July 1968 at the Quartz Mountain State Park in Greer County.

Current: Because the Green-tailed Towhee is very rare, local, and secretive, it is poorly sampled by atlas methodology. It is (or was) an extremely rare breeder in the Black Mesa region of northwestern Cimarron County.

Population Trend: Breeding Bird Survey data for 1966–2000 show no conclusive trend rangewide (-0.1 percent per year, P = 0.83). No trend data are available for Oklahoma due to very low density and local occurrence.

References: AOU 1998; Baicich and Harrison 1997; Baumgartner and Baumgartner 1992; Bent 1968; Dobbs et al. 1998; Downs 1983; Johnsgard 1979; Parker 1973; Sauer et al. 2001; Sutton 1967; Terres 1980

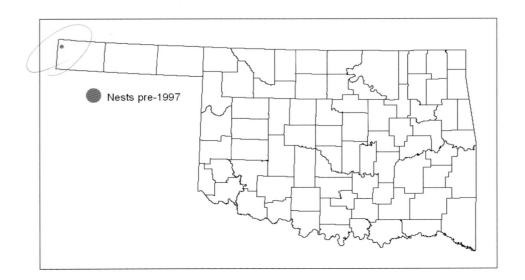

Nests pre-1997

Spotted Towhee
Pipilo maculatus

Dan L. Reinking

Although a common winter resident across most of the state, the Spotted Towhee reaches the eastern edge of its breeding range at the tip of the Oklahoma Panhandle. Despite its striking plumage and bright red eye, it can at times be hard to see because of its tendency to forage on the ground in dense cover. The Spotted Towhee was formerly considered conspecific with the Eastern Towhee.

Description: Very similar to but somewhat larger than the closely related Eastern Towhee, with black head, back, tail, and wings, and rufous flanks. Females are somewhat browner than males. Conspicuous white spotting on the wings and back help separate this species from the Eastern Towhee, as does its harsher and less musical song.

Breeding Habitat: Known only as a breeder from the Oklahoma Panhandle, where it has been found in shrubby thickets along streams or on the side of a mesa.

Nest: The only nest known from Oklahoma was found on the ground amid litter below some shrubby oaks. Nest typically consists of coarse plant materials lined with finer materials such as dry grass and pine needles.

NESTING ECOLOGY

Season: May–July. Possibly double-brooded.

Eggs: Usually 3–5; variably whitish, greenish, or pinkish with darker fine spots or speckles, often concentrated at the large end.

Development: Incubation is by the female for 12–14 days. Young are provisioned by both sexes and fledge at 9–11 days, but continue to be fed by adults for about 4 weeks.

DISTRIBUTION AND ABUNDANCE

Rangewide: Breeds from southwestern Canada, across the western third of the United States, south to northern Central America. Winters over much of the breeding range, as well as eastward across the southern Great Plains.

Historical: Considered a fairly common migrant and winter resident across the state. No nest records prior to the atlas project.

Current: The sole nest record for Oklahoma consists of a female flushed from a nest containing 4 eggs on 16 May 1997 east of Kenton in Cimarron County. Additionally, a territorial male was recorded in an atlas block along the Cimarron River in Cimarron County north of Boise City on 16 July 1999; an individual had previously been noted in this same block in 1997.

Population Trend: Breeding Bird Survey data for 1966–2000 show no conclusive trend rangewide (0.6 percent per year, P = 0.11). No trend data are available for Oklahoma.

References: AOU 1998; Baicich and Harrison 1997; Baumgartner and Baumgartner 1992; Greenlaw 1996a; Sauer et al. 2001; Sutton 1967; Wiggins, D. A. pers. comm.

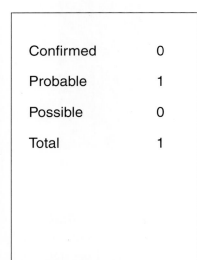

Confirmed	0
Probable	1
Possible	0
Total	1

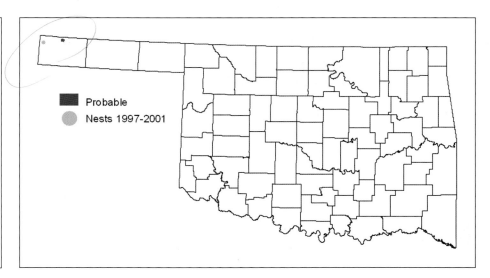

■ Probable
● Nests 1997-2001

Eastern Towhee
Pipilo erythrophthalmus

Mia R. Revels

Courtesy of Joseph A. Grzybowski

One of Oklahoma's most boldy patterned sparrows, the Eastern Towhee's song is also unmistakable and often described as *drink-your-teeeeeeee*. These birds spend much of their time on or near the ground, foraging with a distinctive two-footed scratching behavior. In fact, this noisy foraging method often helps to locate these birds in their cryptic shrubby habitat. They are very rare and local in northeastern Oklahoma during summer.

Description: Male Eastern Towhees have very striking coloration, with black head, back, wings, and tail, chestnut sides, and white underparts. Females have a similar color pattern, with brown replacing the black. White wing patches and a white-cornered tail are con-

spicuous in flight. In addition to the *drink-your-teeeeeeee* song of the male, both sexes produce the call for which the species was named, sometimes translated as *tow-hee* and other times as *chewink*. Eastern Towhees can be distinguished from their close relative, the Spotted Towhee, by their smaller size and the lack of spotting on their back.

Breeding Habitat: Eastern Towhees are edge-associated generalists that breed in shrubby areas, including open brushy fields, forest edges, stream sides, thickets, and along roads and trail edges. They prefer areas with dense, low cover and a well-developed litter layer. Larger trees may or may not be present.

Nest: A bulky open cup composed of leaves, bark, twigs, and grasses and lined with finer material is built by the female on or near the ground or in a small bush, 0–1.5 m (0–5 ft) high. Ground nests are typically placed in a depression, possibly made by the bird, with their edges flush with the ground.

NESTING ECOLOGY

Season: May–July. Single- or double-brooded.
Eggs: Usually 3–5; grayish or creamy white with dark speckles of varying color. Markings are often concentrated at the larger end. Commonly parasitized by Brown-headed Cowbirds, though not recorded in Oklahoma.
Development: Incubation is by the female for 12–13 days. Young are provisioned by both parents and fledge at 10–11 days, but continue to be fed for 3–4 weeks.

DISTRIBUTION AND ABUNDANCE

Rangewide: Breeding range extends from southern Manitoba to southern Maine and south to Florida and the Gulf Coast. Northern populations of the Eastern Towhee are short-distance migrants, while southern populations are resident.

Historical: Described as a very rare and local summer resident in northeastern Oklahoma. Nest records exist for Washington County in 1917, Tulsa County in 1922, and Delaware County in 1977 and 1978. Considered a rare to common migrant and winter resident throughout much of the eastern and central portions of the state.
Current: Present only in the northeastern corner of the state, Eastern Towhees are rare and locally distributed, making them difficult to detect by atlas project methods. Additionally, some blocks scored as Possible may be the result of birds observed on blocks prior to the end of migration.

Population Trend: Breeding Bird Survey data for 1966–2000 show a decline of 1.9 percent per year rangewide (P = 0.000). No trend data are available for Oklahoma.

References: AOU 1998; Baicich and Harrison 1997; Baumgartner 1979, 1990; Baumgartner and Baumgartner 1992; Ehrlich et al. 1988; Greenlaw 1996b; Morimoto and Wasserman 1991; Nice 1931; Sauer et al. 2001; Sutton 1967

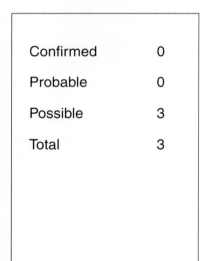

Confirmed	0
Probable	0
Possible	3
Total	3

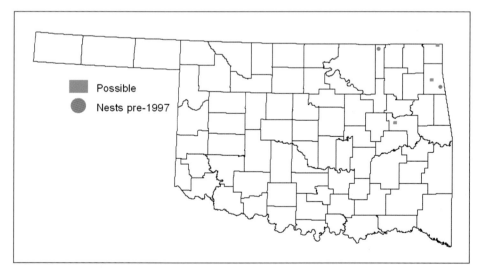

Possible
Nests pre-1997

Canyon Towhee
Pipilo fuscus

Sebastian T. Patti

A large, plain sparrow of the southwestern United States with a complicated taxonomic history, the Canyon Towhee was recently split from the similar appearing California Towhee based on its significantly different DNA composition. Probably the most adaptive of all the towhees, it is a resident bird found in a wide variety of habitats. It can be shy and retiring and very difficult to see in rugged areas; yet, in towns, villages, farms, and ranches, it can be a very tame "yard" bird.

Description: Sexes similar, gray brown with a rufous crown, an indistinct necklace of dark spots and streaks on the throat, and a distinct central breast spot. The undertail coverts are warm buff. The song is a series of six or seven monotone double syllables, often rendered as *chili-chili-chili-chili-chili-chili;* the call is a hoarse or rough two-syllable *sheddup.*

Breeding Habitat: Pinyon-oak-juniper woodlands, often with scattered dense shrubbery or cactus. Also found in grasslands with scattered mesquite, cholla, catclaw, or barberry, and in association with human ranches, farms, and villages. Generally found in drier areas and often near canyons and canyon walls.

Nest: A bulky cup constructed by the female alone of grasses and plant stems and lined with fine grasses. Usually placed low in a tree such as a mesquite, juniper, pinyon pine, or cholla cactus.

NESTING ECOLOGY

Season: Primarily May–June. Probably double-brooded.

Eggs: Usually 3; bluish white to pearl gray in color with brown or black and purple markings.

Development: Incubation is by the female alone for perhaps 11 days, but poorly known. Both sexes provision young. Fledging age poorly known; perhaps 10 days.

DISTRIBUTION AND ABUNDANCE

Rangewide: Resident from southeastern Colorado, south and west through most of New Mexico, the northwesternmost portion of the Oklahoma Panhandle, central and western Texas, and central and western Arizona, south through northern and central Mexico. Generally sedentary, but some lateral and altitudinal movement occurs at higher elevations and in the northern reaches of the species' range.

Historical: Described as a common resident of western Cimarron County.

Current: Limited to the "rougher" areas of northwestern Cimarron County, the Canyon Towhee seems to be a fairly common resident in the Black Mesa region of the state. The one confirmed breeding report was of a family group of 5 birds (3 heavily streaked juveniles barely capable of sustained flight, attended by 2 adults) found on a block north of Boise City on the Cimarron River in June 1997.

Population Trend: Breeding Bird Survey data for 1966–2000 show a decline of 1.4 percent per year rangewide (P = 0.08). No trend data are available for Oklahoma.

References: AOU 1998; Baicich and Harrison 1997; Baumgartner and Baumgartner 1992; Dillon 1998; Johnson and Haight 1996; Nice 1931; Oberholser 1974; Sauer et al. 2001; Sutton 1967; Tate 1923; Thompson and Ely 1992

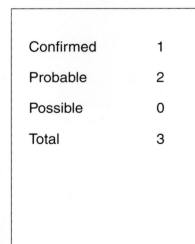

Confirmed	1
Probable	2
Possible	0
Total	3

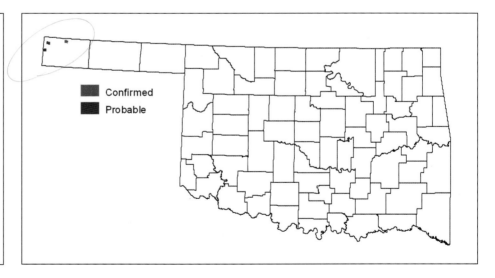

Cassin's Sparrow
Aimophila cassinii

William A. Carter and Mickle D. Duggan

Courtesy of Jim and Deva Burns / Natural Impacts

The three species of the genus *Aimophila* that are found in Oklahoma are difficult to identify in the field. All three are larger than most other Oklahoma nesting sparrows. All three have secretive habits except for their territorial songs. They are usually found in rather specific habitats and more often than not are located and identified by their distinctive songs. All live in pairs or family groups and are never found in large flocks.

Description: Sexes similar; fairly large, grayish sparrows without obvious distinctive markings. They have large bills, elongated bodies, pale lemon at bend of wing, and long rounded tails with white tips. Territorial males give a "flight song" that begins from an elevated perch with introductory notes given as the male rises upward 6–9 m (20–30 ft), followed by a trill while floating downward on set wings with head up, tail feathers spread, and legs dangling. This "skylarking" behavior is often the best clue for identification of this sparrow, as they are inconspicuous when not singing. Young are like adults but with faint streaking on breast and sides.

Breeding Habitat: Found in sparse shortgrass or mixedgrass prairies with scattered shrubs, yucca, and cactus, which are used as singing perches.

Nest: Cup of dry grass and weed stems constructed by the female and lined with finer grass blades, rootlets, and sometimes animal hair. Well hidden a few inches above ground in grass clumps or on the ground at the base of a bush or cactus.

NESTING ECOLOGY

Season: Primarily May–July, but highly variable in response to local weather conditions. Prolonged breeding season suggest double-broods, but late nestings may be renesting attempts.

Eggs: 3–5; unmarked and slightly glossy white. Infrequently parasitized by Brown-headed Cowbirds, but no evidence of parasitism known in Oklahoma.

Development: Not well documented, but incubation probably only by female for 11 days; fledging at 9–10 days; nestlings and fledglings provisioned by both parents.

DISTRIBUTION AND ABUNDANCE

Rangewide: Large annual fluctuations in numbers and range. May be absent from an area for several years then reappear, especially along eastern edge of range. During breeding season, found in suitable habitat in eastern Colorado, western Kansas, southeastern Arizona, New Mexico except the northwestern quarter, the western half of Oklahoma and Texas, and southward into Mexico. Northern populations migratory; winters from Texas and New Mexico south to central Mexico.

Historical: Migrant and summer resident in western part of the state from early April to mid-September, but few fall records exist. Occurs irregularly to Noble, Cleveland, Johnston, and Love counties, primarily in or following dry years, which keep cover to sparse levels preferred by this species.

Current: Cassin's Sparrows are expected in the shortgrass prairies of the High Plains and are readily detected by the "skylarking" territorial males. Localized populations are scattered in the mixedgrass prairies, but are less likely to be detected by atlas methodology.

Population Trend: Breeding Bird Survey data for 1966–2000 show a decline of 2.3 percent per year rangewide (P = 0.00), but show no conclusive trend in Oklahoma (-2.8 percent per year, P = 0.40).

References: AOU 1998; Baicich and Harrison 1997; Baumgartner and Baumgartner 1992; Dunning et al. 1999; Grula 1973; Johnsgard 1979; Kaufman 1996; Rising 1996a; Sutton 1967; Williams and LeSarrier 1968; Wolf 1977

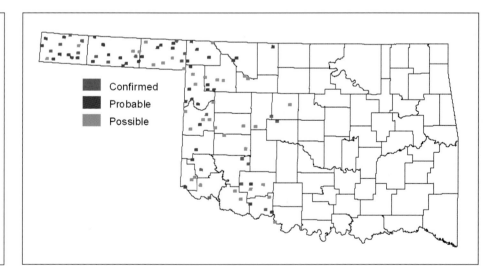

Confirmed	20
Probable	43
Possible	37
Total	100

Bachman's Sparrow
Aimophila aestivalis

William A. Carter and Mickle D. Duggan

Courtesy of James Flynn

Bachman's Sparrow is endemic to the pine forests of the southeastern United States and reaches its northwestern limit of distribution in eastern Oklahoma. Unique to this state is that the range of Bachman's Sparrow overlaps that of Rufous-crowned Sparrow and is within a short distance of the eastern edge of Cassin's Sparrow range. Rarely heard are the "complex" wren-like song and the barely audible "whisper" song of Bachman's Sparrows. The "typical" song, a three- to five-second plaintive whistle followed by a trill, usually gives notice of the presence of this species.

Description: Sexes similar. Bachman's Sparrows are fairly large sparrows, brownish above with red-brown streaks on the back. They have large bills, elongated bodies, yellow at the bend of the wing, and a long rounded tail. The crown is reddish brown with a grayish supercillary. Underparts are buffy with a whitish belly. Young are like adults but with faint streaking on underparts. Best located by listening for song, a clear whistle with a trill.

Breeding Habitat: Open woodlands with dense ground cover of bluestem grasses and early clearcuts with bluestem ground cover.

Nest: Domed or cup nest constructed with grasses by the female. Usually concealed in clumps of bluestem and utilizing grass of the clump to form the dome.

NESTING ECOLOGY

Season: April–July. Double-brooded.

Eggs: Usually 3–5; unmarked white, glossy, often with pale bluish cast. Infrequently parasitized by Brown-headed Cowbirds; for Oklahoma, just one known instance.

Development: Incubation is by the female for 12–14 days. Young are provisioned by both sexes and fledge at 9–10 days.

DISTRIBUTION AND ABUNDANCE

Rangewide: Both range and population size have fluctuated during the history of this species. Local populations fluctuate depending on habitat changes. Currently restricted to the southeastern states from North Carolina westward to the eastern edge of Oklahoma and Texas. Southern populations thought nonmigratory.

Historical: Considered a rare and local summer resident in southeastern and central counties from late March to mid-August, with few recorded fall records. There are three winter records, but winter status awaits further documentation.

Current: Atlas blocks in Osage and Creek counties, together with summer sight records from Atoka County that were not in atlas blocks, mark the northern and western edges of the known range of Bachman's Sparrow in Oklahoma. This sparrow is difficult to locate unless it is singing and without doubt occurs in other localities of eastern Oklahoma.

Population Trend: Breeding Bird Survey data for 1966–2000 show a decline of 2.8 percent per year rangewide (P = 0.01), but the population is considered to have undergone its largest decline from 1930 to 1960, prior to the BBS program. Listed as endangered by a number of states and considered a high conservation priority rangewide. Little reliable trend data are available for Oklahoma, but the speices may be expanding northward as a breeder.

References: AOU 1998; Baicich and Harrison 1997; Baumgartner and Baumgartner 1992; Carter 1970; Dunning 1993; Haggerty 1988, 1992; Kaufman 1996; Rising 1996a; Sauer et al. 2001; Sutton 1967; Weston 1968; Wolf 1977

Confirmed	4
Probable	2
Possible	2
Total	8

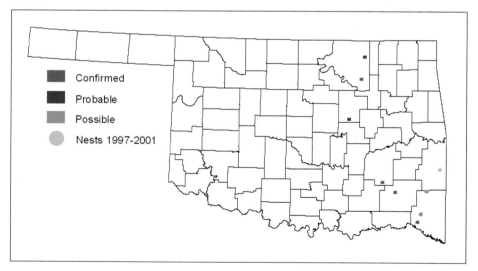

Confirmed
Probable
Possible
Nests 1997-2001

Rufous-crowned Sparrow
Aimophila ruficeps

William A. Carter and Mickle D. Duggan

Courtesy of Michael Gray

Unfamiliar to many casual birders because of its secretive habits and its preference for rocky, inaccessible areas, the Rufous-crowned Sparrow is nonetheless common in local areas, especially in western Cimarron County and parts of southwestern Oklahoma.

Description: Sexes similar. Fairly large sparrow with a long rounded tail. Rufous crown, white eye ring, and black malar line are key features. Pale gray below, with upperparts gray to brownish and darker on wings and tail. Young are like adults but with faint streaking on breast and sides. Vocalizations include a *deer deer deer deer* and a chatter, along with a single-note call.

Breeding Habitat: Prefers rocky outcrops with mixed-grasses and shrubs. More common in the dryer, western half of the state, but small, isolated colonies are found in eastern Oklahoma as well.

Nest: An open cup on or near the ground, usually in clumps of grass between rocks. The nest is composed of grasses and is lined with fine grass and sometimes animal hair.

NESTING ECOLOGY

Season: April–July. Probably single-brooded.

Eggs: Usually 3–4; unmarked, pale bluish-white. Infrequently parasitized by Brown-headed Cowbirds, but no evidence of parasitism known for nests in Oklahoma.

Development: Incubation is by the female for 11–13 days. Young are provisioned by both sexes and fledge at about 8–10 days, but continue to be fed by adults for an unknown period.

DISTRIBUTION AND ABUNDANCE

Rangewide: Resident in preferred habitat in much of the southwestern United States and Mexico.

Historical: Described as a resident of western Cimarron County and parts of southwestern and western Oklahoma; rare resident eastward in areas with rocky outcrops.

Current: The Rufous-crowned Sparrow's secretive habits and its preference for rocky outcrops and hillsides for nesting limit its detectability and distribution in Oklahoma. Rather common in the Black Mesa area of Cimarron County, the Arbuckle Uplift, and the southwestern corner of the state, the Rufous-crowned Sparrow is very localized elsewhere in Oklahoma.

Population Trend: Breeding Bird Survey data for 1966–2000 show no conclusive trend rangewide (-0.8 percent per year, P = 0.46) and a large decline of 9.6 percent per year in Oklahoma (P = 0.05), although the Oklahoma trend data are based on few survey routes.

References: AOU 1998; Baicich and Harrison 1997; Banta 1985; Baumgartner and Baumgartner 1992; Collins 1999; Kaufman 1996; Phillips 1968; Rising 1996a; Sauer et al. 2001; Sutton 1934, 1967; Wolf 1977

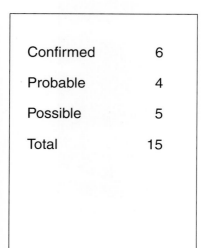

Confirmed	6
Probable	4
Possible	5
Total	15

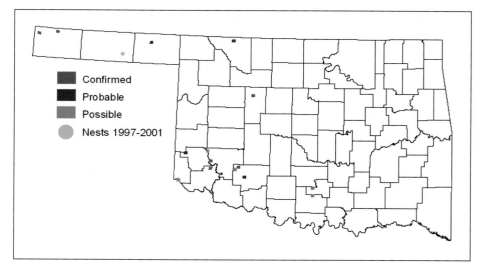

Chipping Sparrow
Spizella passerina

Joseph A. Grzybowski

Courtesy of Michael Gray

Many Oklahomans have probably observed flocks of Chipping Sparrows during spring migration periods foraging on the recently seeding grass of their lawns. Although a common migrant throughout Oklahoma, the Chipping Sparrow is less well recognized as an Oklahoma breeder. Many general guides ignore its admittedly local but statewide distribution. Its dry trill and small size do not draw much attention.

Description: A small sparrow, among our smallest, with a conspicuous rufous crown, black eye line, streaked brown back, slight pale wing bars, and largely gray face, underparts, and rump. Its tail is slightly forked (characteristic of its genus), the bill two toned (dark upper, light lower), and legs flesh colored. Sexes are similar. The song is a prolonged dry trill, building to a sustained intensity. This species can be mistakenly confused with American Tree Sparrow on Christmas Bird Counts, the latter being more likely at winter bird feeders.

Breeding Habitat: Prefers open or grassy woodland areas where ample ground-foraging opportunities along with low nesting cover exists. Parklands, open oak woods, older residential treed neighborhoods in eastern Oklahoma, and more mesic canyonland areas in west-central Oklahoma can provide suitable areas.

Nest: A loosely woven cup of rootlets, grasses, and other fine materials well concealed on supporting branches 1–7 m (3–24 ft) high, often in coniferous vegetation.

NESTING ECOLOGY

Season: Mid-April–July. Often double-brooded.
Eggs: Usually 4; pale blue, sparingly marked with spots and blotches. Regularly parasitized by Brown-headed Cowbirds.
Development: Incubation is by the female for 10–12 days. Young are provisioned by both sexes and fledge in 9–12 days. Adults tend young about 3 weeks after fledging.

DISTRIBUTION AND ABUNDANCE

Rangewide: Breeds across much of North America from east-central Alaska and southern Newfoundland to Georgia, through much of Mexico east to Nicaragua. Winters in the southern United States and Mexico; Central American populations sedentary.
Historical: Breeds in eastern Oklahoma, quite sparingly to central Oklahoma, and very locally in west-central Oklahoma, notably the Wichita Mountains and Caddo Canyonlands. Also breeds in northwestern

Cimarron County. A void in distribution has generally been recognized in western Oklahoma and much of the Panhandle, although local pockets may exist.
Current: Atlasing demonstrates a statewide distribution for Chipping Sparrows diminishing from east to west. This likely corresponds to the decrease in wooded areas with more open understories as one goes west. Fewer detections than might be expected were made in the Caddo Canyonlands. Voids appeared in the Osage Prairies and south-central and midwest-central areas (including Caddo County). Some observations, particularly in far-western Oklahoma and the Panhandle may be the result of birds recorded that were actually migrants. Breeding in the mesa country of northwestern Cimarron County apparently went undetected.

Population Trend: Breeding Bird Survey data for 1966–2000 show no conclusive trend rangewide (-0.1 percent per year, P = 0.60) or in Oklahoma (-2.4 percent per year, P = 0.49).

References: AOU 1998; Baicich and Harrison 1997; Baumgartner and Baumgartner 1992; Buech 1982; Middleton 1998; Nice 1931; Reynolds and Knapton 1984; Rising 1996a; Sauer et al. 2001; Sutton 1967

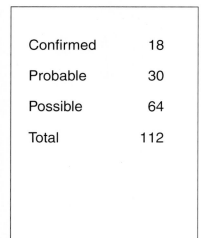

Confirmed	18
Probable	30
Possible	64
Total	112

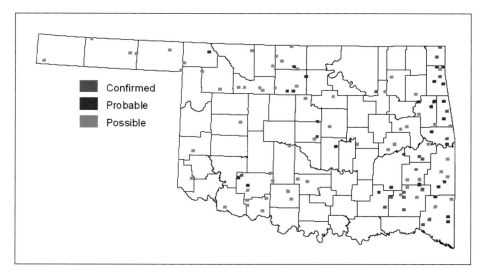

Brewer's Sparrow
Spizella breweri

Bonnie L. Gall

Courtesy of Jim and Deva Burns / Natural Impacts

This western sparrow just manages to make its presence known in the western part of the Oklahoma Panhandle where its preferred sagebrush habitat can be found. Records for Brewer's Sparrow in the state are very limited. Its drab appearance and preference for wide-open spaces make this species a challenging bird to document and study.

Description: A small sparrow with long, notched tail, small bill, rounded head, and complete white eye ring. It shows drab, grayish-brown upperparts, and a weak face pattern. The similar Clay-colored and Chipping sparrows usually have more distinct facial patterns and are more colorful in general. All three species, however, can be very similar in nonbreeding plumage. The song is described as a long series of fast variable trills and buzzes that can last for 10 to 15 seconds. There is also a short song (1.5–3 seconds) that consists of 1 to 3 buzzy trills. The call note is a weak *tsip* or *seep.*

Breeding Habitat: Shrublands, especially with sagebrush, and in pinyon-juniper woodland openings.

Nest: The nest is a compact cup of grasses and rootlets lined with fine grasses, sagebrush bark, and hair. Dark horsehair is very popular. Nests are frequently built within 20–45 cm (10–18 in) of the ground, primarily in large sagebrush or saltbushes. Adequate cover for the nest is important in nest site selection.

NESTING ECOLOGY

Season: May–July. If the first nest fails, replacement clutches are laid quickly. Frequently double-brooded.
Eggs: 3–4; pale blue green with dark brown or reddish spots. Eggs are indistinguishable from those of Chipping Sparrows.
Development: Incubation is mostly by the female for 10–14 days. Young are provisioned by both sexes and fledge at 6–9 days, but take several more days to attain flight.

DISTRIBUTION AND ABUNDANCE

Rangewide: A summer resident of the western Great Basin area of the United States, breeding in sagebrush and meadow areas, including parts of British Columbia and Alberta in Canada. The Brewer's Sparrow winters from southeastern California to southwestern Texas, and south throughout Baja California and the highlands of northern Mexico.

Historical: Most records for the state occur in Cimarron County in the western Panhandle during spring or fall migration. There are a few accidental records during migration from farther east, one in Woodward County and one in Cleveland County. In June 1957, 4 nests with young were found west of Boise City in Cimarron County.
Current: Not recorded during atlas project years.

Population Trend: Brewer's Sparrow populations are highly variable depending on habitat and year. Breeding Bird Survey data for 1966–2000 show a decline of 3.2 percent per year rangewide (P = 0.00). No trend data are available for Oklahoma.

References: Baumgartner and Baumgartner 1992; Harrison 1979; Johnsgard 1979; Kaufman 1990; National Geographic Society 1999; Paine 1968; Rotenberry et al. 1999; Sauer et al. 2001; Sibley 2000; Sutton 1967

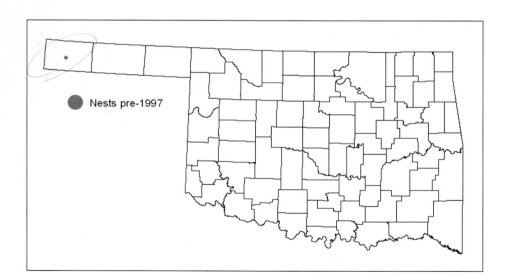

Nests pre-1997

Field Sparrow
Spizella pusilla

Dan L. Reinking

Courtesy of Joseph A. Grzybowski

The clear, distinctive song of the Field Sparrow announces its summer presence in open, brushy areas throughout most of Oklahoma. Birds in the western part of the Field Sparrow's range, including much of Oklahoma, tend to be larger, paler, and grayer than eastern Field Sparrows.

Description: Sexes are similar, with a brick-reddish crown, gray face, white eye ring, pink bill and legs, grayish or buffy breast, streaked back, and two white wing bars. During winter and early spring may be confused with American Tree Sparrow, which uses similar habitats but has a central dark breast spot and lacks the pink bill and legs of Field Sparrow. Chipping Sparrows have black and white eye stripes and black bills. Song is

a series of down-slurred whistles accelerating into a trill, much like the cadence of a ping-pong ball dropped onto a table, bouncing slowly at first and then more and more rapidly.

Breeding Habitat: Field Sparrows prefer, as their name suggests, weedy fields, pastures, prairie/woodland edges, roadside areas through open habitats, and woodland openings. Fires too frequent remove too much woody vegetation, while fires too infrequent allow a canopy to develop, both of which render an area unsuitable for this species. Field Sparrows do not nest near human habitation. Young birds may, to some extent, select their future breeding area during their first autumn of life.

Nest: A cup woven of coarse grasses and lined with smaller grasses and rootlets is built by the female while accompanied by the male. Early nests may be on the ground, while later nests may be up to 1 m (3 ft) high in small shrubs, blackberries, or forbs.

NESTING ECOLOGY

Season: April–July. Double- to triple-brooded.

Eggs: 3–5, with later clutches usually smaller than early ones. White or tinted pale blue or green, and finely marked with browns, reds, purples, or grays, usually concentrated at the large end and often forming a ring. Field Sparrows are regularly parasitized by Brown-headed Cowbirds (3 of 9 nests in Osage and Washington counties from 1992 to 1996), but often abandon such nests and are generally poor hosts.

Development: Incubation is by the female for 10–11 days or longer in cold weather when the onset of incubation may be delayed. Young are brooded by the female but fed by both sexes, typically leave the nest at 7–8 days, and reach independence at about 30 days. Fledglings may be divided between the male and female for feeding responsibility, or the male may feed all fledglings if the female begins another nest.

DISTRIBUTION AND ABUNDANCE

Rangewide: Field Sparrows breed from eastern Montana south through western Oklahoma and west-central Texas to south-central Texas, and eastward though northern Florida in the south to southern Maine in the north. The species is largely resident over much of its breeding range, but northern birds and even some southern birds do winter in areas south and west of their breeding range, including portions of northeastern Mexico.

Historical: Field Sparrow is found year round in the main body of the state, but some breeders move south for winter. It is described as more common in eastern and central Oklahoma, although very local in wooded areas of the southeast. Once considered a transient and winter visitant in the Panhandle, a few summer observations in Texas and Cimarron counties suggest the possibility of nesting.

Current: Centers of abundance for Field Sparrow include most of eastern and central Oklahoma, and northwestern Oklahoma, with reduced occurrence in the southwestern and Panhandle areas of the state. The loud, frequently repeated song of this species makes it hard to miss in a block.

Population Trend: Breeding Bird Survey data for 1966–2000 show a decline of 3.1 percent per year rangewide (P = 0.00), but show no conclusive trend in Oklahoma (-0.5 percent per year, P = 0.61).

References: Adams and Brewer 1981; AOU 1998; Baicich and Harrison 1997; Baumgartner and Baumgartner 1992; Best 1977a, 1977b, 1978, 1979; Carey et al. 1994; George M. Sutton Avian Research Center unpubl. data; Sauer et al. 2001; Sutton 1967

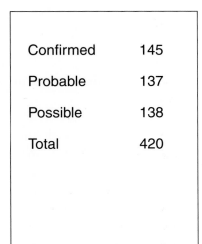

Confirmed	145
Probable	137
Possible	138
Total	420

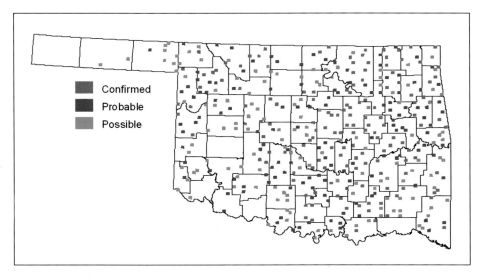

Lark Sparrow
Chondestes grammacus

Thomas G. Shane

Courtesy of Bill Horn

The Lark Sparrow is one species that has undergone major shifts in its breeding range in the past two centuries, shifts which continue today in response to the many changes humankind has made to the landscape of North America. For those of us living within its current breeding range, the little clown-faced sparrow appears to be a bundle of energy, whether it is the male courting, giving its turkey-like strut with tail raised and wings dropped, or during the feeding of fledglings with all their associated chatter.

Description: A fairly large sparrow with a distinctive black, white, and chestnut face, an unstreaked white breast with a central spot, and a long, rounded tail with very noticeable white corners. The song is a melodious array of rich trills, with a considerable range of pitch and volume.

Breeding Habitat: Open, dry woodlands, pastures, or grassy, park-like areas.

Nest: A cup of grasses and small twigs lined with finer grasses and occasionally hair, often placed in a small shrub or tree or on the ground next to a forb or in grass. Occasionally observed nesting a few feet up in small pines that are frequently planted around farmsteads. Occasionally uses an old nest of another species, especially mockingbirds, and has been observed sharing nests with mockingbirds.

NESTING ECOLOGY

Season: April–July. Double-brooded.

Eggs: 3–5; creamy white, with black to lilac spots and scrawls around the larger end. Brown-headed Cowbird parasitism in Oklahoma ranges from 19–46 percent, with ground nests being parasitized almost twice as frequently as above-ground nests.

Development: Incubation is by the female for 11–12 days. Young are provisioned by both sexes and fledge at 9–12 days.

DISTRIBUTION AND ABUNDANCE

Rangewide: A North American short-distance migrant breeding from northern Mexico to the prairie provinces of Canada and from California to Indiana. Winters in the southernmost United States and Mexico. Range expanded east with forest clearing in the 1800s, but is now retreating.

Historical: Described as common summer resident statewide, but more common west. Unlike the drastic changes in distribution at the east and west ends of its range, little change seems to have occurred in Oklahoma.

Current: The Lark Sparrow is a common nesting bird in Oklahoma and was confirmed as a breeder in all but two counties. The species was very easy to detect and confirm, from the time of courtship and copulation to the period when vocal families often congregate along county roads.

Population Trend: Breeding Bird Survey data for 1966–2000 show a decline of 3.5 percent per year both rangewide and in Oklahoma (P = 0.00 for both datasets).

References: AOU 1998; Baich and Harrison 1997; Baumgartner and Baumgartner 1992; Dechant, Sondreal, Johnson, Igl, Goldade, Parkin, and Euliss 1999; Martin and Parrish 2000; McNair 1984c, 1985; Newman 1970; Rising 1996a; Sauer et al. 2001; Sutton 1967; Wiens 1963

Confirmed	351
Probable	96
Possible	49
Total	496

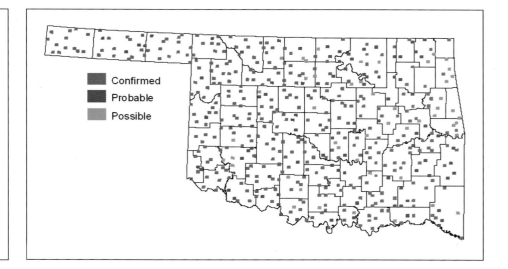

Black-throated Sparrow
Amphispiza bilineata

David A. Wiggins

Courtesy of Michael Gray

Easily identified by the colorful black, gray, and white plumage pattern on its face, the Black-throated Sparrow is a bird of arid western scrublands with low shrubs and little ground cover. At the margin of its range here in Oklahoma, it nests only in Cimarron County and rarely strays eastward.

Description: Male and female are similar, with a black throat patch and bold white stripes above and below the eye. Unlike most sparrows, the plumage is basically gray, with little to no brown coloration. Males sing a short song of high, tinkling notes.

Breeding Habitat: Desert scrub, with scattered bushes and small trees. In Oklahoma, they show a preference for arid scrub mixed with scattered mesquite trees.

Nest: Built by female alone. Woven of twigs, grasses, and leaves, and lined with hair. Typically in a low bush or in cholla cactus.

NESTING ECOLOGY

Season: May–June. May be double-brooded.
Eggs: Usually 3–4; unmarked pale blue. In New

Mexico, regularly parasitized by Brown-headed Cowbirds.

Development: Incubation about 12 days. Young are provisioned by both sexes and fledge at about 10 days.

DISTRIBUTION AND ABUNDANCE

Rangewide: Summer resident primarily around the Great Basin region of the western United States and to portions of northern Arizona and New Mexico. Resident along United States/Mexico border and south to central Mexico.

Historical: Reported as a common summer resident in northwestern Cimarron County in the early 1900s, but recorded only sporadically thereafter. Still fairly common in the 1970s in the Black Mesa region of northwestern Cimarron County. Nonbreeding records exist for Cleveland, Kiowa, Major, and Oklahoma counties, although the Major County observation was on 7 June 1982. Few actual nest records exist for Oklahoma.

Current: The only breeding evidence recorded during the atlas period was of a territorial male in extreme northwestern Cimarron County, in the same area where most historical breeding records have occurred. However, the Black-throated Sparrow is rare and local in Oklahoma, making it a difficult species to document with atlas methods. The few remaining pairs in Oklahoma are likely scattered in mesquite scrub in the Black Mesa region.

Population Trend: Breeding Bird Survey data for 1966–2000 show a decline of 4.1 percent per year rangewide (P = 0.00). No trend data are available for Oklahoma.

References: Baicich and Harrison 1997; Baumgartner and Baumgartner 1992; Isaacs 1980; Johnsgard 1979; Nice 1931; Robertson 1986; Shackford 1983; Sutton 1967; Tate 1923; Van Velzen 1968; Wiggins, D. A. pers. observ.

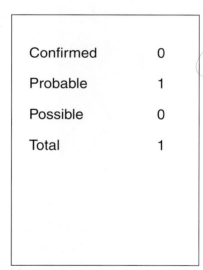

Confirmed	0
Probable	1
Possible	0
Total	1

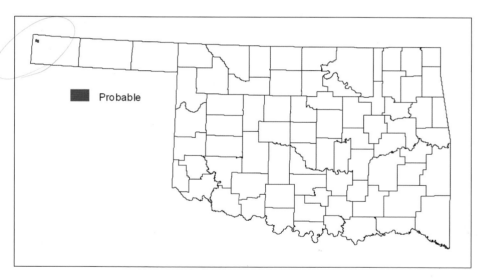

Probable

Lark Bunting
Calamospiza melanocorys

Thomas G. Shane

Courtesy of Bob Gress

The Lark Bunting is a large member of the Emberizidae family, with males acquiring a showy summer plumage and sometimes being dubbed the black-and-white Cadillac of the sparrow world. It nests in the Oklahoma Panhandle in most but not all years. The species is probably monogamous in Oklahoma; however, polygyny is common in the northern part of its range.

Description: The male in breeding plumage is black, and the female, in a more typical sparrow fashion, is light brown with a streaked breast; both have a white wing patch. The male sings from a perch or gives an aerial flight song, called the primary song, which is used to attract females and stake out a territory. Fairly unique to the bird world, the male has an additional flight song, called the aggressive flight song, which most often is performed with other males. Females will at times sing a subdued primary song while on the nest. A chitter call is given by both sexes while returning to or departing the nest.

Breeding Habitat: Short- and mixedgrass prairies, along with fallow fields. A key habitat characteristic is adequate plants capable of shading the nest, something very important since the black male sits on eggs and broods nestlings. Lark Buntings often nest in what appear to be colonies.

Nest: A cup of grasses and sometimes hair built on the

ground in a scrape and placed under a plant that is taller than the surrounding vegetation.

NESTING ECOLOGY

Season: May–July. Normally single-brooded.

Eggs: Usually 4–5; light blue and usually unmarked. Species is rarely parasitized in the southwestern part of its range by the Brown-headed Cowbird, but is regularly parasitized in the north.

Development: Incubation is by both sexes for 11–12 days. Young are provisioned by both sexes and fledge in 8–9 days.

DISTRIBUTION AND ABUNDANCE

Rangewide: A North American short-distance migrant breeding from the Texas Panhandle to the prairie provinces of Canada and wintering from the western half of Texas to southern Arizona south into the high plateau of northern Mexico.

Historical: Described as an irregular summer resident in the Panhandle, occurring somewhat farther east in winter and during migration. Has nested east to Grant and Garfield counties.

Current: Lark Buntings were found in the Panhandle region where their preferred habitat type, shortgrass prairie mixed with a few shrubs, is still in fair supply. Only occasionally does the species move farther east into the main body of the state to nest, something that did not occur during the atlasing period. Lark Buntings often move to the edges of county roads with their fledged young, making confirmation rates fairly high. There appears to be no major change in this species' somewhat erratic nesting pattern in Oklahoma. Being at the southern extreme of the species' breeding range here in Oklahoma, it occurs at a relatively low density.

Population Trend: Breeding Bird Survey data for 1966–2000 show a decline of 1.4 percent per year rangewide (P = 0.03) and a decline of 14.1 percent per year in Oklahoma (P = 0.03), although the species wanders from year to year and is irregular in Oklahoma, making trend analysis difficult.

References: AOU 1998; Baicich and Harrison 1997; Baumgartner and Baumgartner 1992; Davis 1988; Dechant, Sondreal, Johnson, Igl, Goldade, Zimmerman, and Euliss 1999; Dunn 1986; Helema 1974; Rising 1996a; Sauer et al. 2001; Shane 1974, 2000; Sutton 1967; Tyler 1985

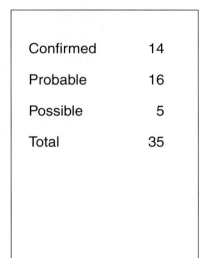

Confirmed	14
Probable	16
Possible	5
Total	35

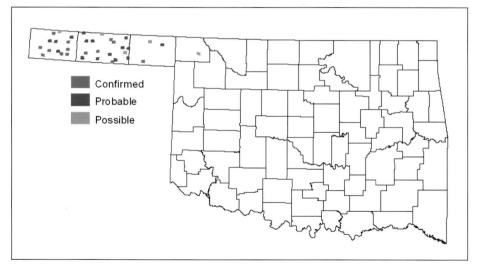

Grasshopper Sparrow
Ammodramus savannarum

Dan L. Reinking

Courtesy of Bill Horn

A rather inconspicuous species until one learns its two subtle and very different songs, the Grasshopper Sparrow is actually quite common in some areas of Oklahoma. While so named because of its insect-like song, the Grasshopper Sparrow does in fact rely heavily on grasshoppers for its summer diet, and it frequently removes the less digestible legs sequentially in homologous pairs before feeding its young.

Description: Like other sparrows in the genus *Ammodramus,* Grasshopper Sparrows are small, short tailed, and flat headed, and except for singing males, rather secretive. Sexes are similar, having a buffy breast, a white central crown stripe, white eye ring, and yel-

lowish spot in front of the eye. Two very different songs are commonly given, a dry, insect-like *tip-tup-azeeeeee* and a long series of high, musical, squeaky notes. This species may be confused with Henslow's Sparrow, which has a greenish cast to the head and nape, or with other members of their genus that migrate and/or winter in Oklahoma.

Breeding Habitat: Tall-, mixed-, and shortgrass prairies, pastures, and hayfields are used for nesting. Patchy areas of bare ground amid clumped vegetation are generally present in occupied habitat, and woody vegetation must be minimal. Grasshopper Sparrows prefer relatively short, sparse vegetation resulting from fire or grazing in moist tallgrass habitats such as those of central and eastern Oklahoma, but prefer more lush areas of vegetation in drier shortgrass habitats such as those found in western Oklahoma and the Panhandle.

Nest: A small, difficult to locate cup of grasses and stems woven by the female and placed on the ground in a depression under overhanging grasses or forbs, which often form a side entrance.

NESTING ECOLOGY

Season: May–July. Double-brooded.

Eggs: 3–6; white with brown or reddish speckles or blotches usually concentrated at larger end. Grasshopper Sparrows are occasionally parasitized by Brown-headed Cowbirds (6 percent of 273 nests in Osage and Washington counties, 1992–1996), but their nests may often be too well hidden.

Development: Incubation is by the female alone for about 12 days. Young are both brooded and fed by the female and typically leave the nest at 9 days.

DISTRIBUTION AND ABUNDANCE

Rangewide: Grasshopper Sparrows nest over most of the eastern two-thirds of the United States and in scattered regions of the west where suitable habitat exists. They reach peak breeding densities in western Kansas and portions of Colorado and South Dakota. A short-distance migrant, they winter along the Gulf Coast and in southern Arizona, Mexico, and Cuba.

Historical: Described as an uncommon and local summer resident throughout nearly all of Oklahoma, but rare or absent in eastern forested areas and in the western Panhandle.

Current: Grasshopper Sparrow abundance is highest from the Flint Hills of Osage County westward across Oklahoma and through the Panhandle. It was confirmed rather readily, perhaps due to the habit of adults carrying food perching on roadside barbed-wire fences before making deliveries to the nest. This species is absent in the heavily forested southeastern regions of Oklahoma.

Population Trend: Breeding Bird Survey data for 1966–2000 show a decline of 3.7 percent per year rangewide (P = 0.00), but show no conclusive trend in Oklahoma (0.1 percent per year, P = 0.97).

References: AOU 1998; Baicich and Harrison 1997; Baumgartner and Baumgartner 1992; Dechant et al. 1998; Easley 1983; George M. Sutton Avian Research Center unpubl. data; Kaspari 1991; National Geographic Society 1999; Norman 1982, 1987; Rohrbaugh et al. 1999; Sauer et al. 2001; Stewart 1990; Sutton 1967; Verser 1990; Vickery 1996; Wiens 1973

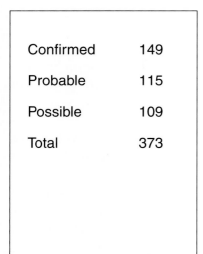

Confirmed	149
Probable	115
Possible	109
Total	373

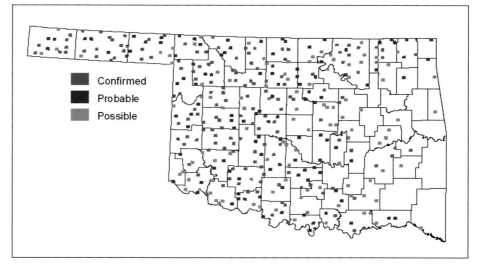

Henslow's Sparrow
Ammodramus henslowii

Dan L. Reinking

Courtesy of Bob Gress

Only recently established as a breeding species in Oklahoma, the Henslow's Sparrow population in and around the Tallgrass Prairie Preserve in Osage County now represents one of the largest local nesting populations in the United States. This increase in the western populations of Henslow's Sparrow has also occurred in Missouri, Kansas, and Nebraska.

Description: The Henslow's Sparrow is a large-billed, flat-headed, short-tailed grassland sparrow with thin, dark streaking on the breast, extensively reddish wings, and an olive-greenish cast to the head. The sexes are similar. Its song is an insect-like *ts-lick,* which, though unobtrusive, carries well and is given persistently during the nesting season, even during the nighttime hours. It

is most likely to be confused with Grasshopper Sparrow, which has an unstreaked breast and more distinct crown stripes and generally appears paler.

Breeding Habitat: Tallgrass prairie areas with a large amount of standing dead vegetation, a thickly matted litter layer, and relatively sparse woody vegetation are preferred. This species generally avoids areas burned within the previous two years and areas that have remained unburned for long periods, which results in significant encroachment of woody vegetation. Henslow's Sparrows require larger habitat patches than many grassland birds, perhaps 55 ha (136 ac) or more.

Nest: A well-concealed open cup (sometimes domed

over) woven of grass and placed on or near the ground, often in a thick clump of grass.

NESTING ECOLOGY

Season: May–August. Probably double-brooded.

Eggs: 3–5; creamy white or greenish white speckled with reddish brown. Occasionally parasitized by Brown-headed Cowbirds (2 of 24 nests in Osage County, 1992–1996).

Development: Incubation is by the female for 10–11 days. Young are provisioned by both sexes and fledge at 10–11 days.

DISTRIBUTION AND ABUNDANCE

Rangewide: A North American short-distance migrant, breeding locally in parts of the Northeast, Midwest, and Great Plains, and wintering along and near the Gulf and southern Atlantic coasts.

Historical: The Henslow's Sparrow is a recent addition to Oklahoma's breeding avifauna. A few scattered sight records exist for the 1920s through the 1960s, but the species was first confirmed by photographic documentation in Oklahoma in 1974 and first confirmed nesting in 1987 (both discoveries in Washington County). Starting in the late 1980s and especially throughout the 1990s, Henslow's Sparrows have been discovered locally in small numbers in several counties throughout northeastern Oklahoma. With the establishment of the Tallgrass Prairie Preserve in Osage County in the late 1980s, and the resulting preferred habitat conditions, this area began supporting hundreds if not thousands of Henslow's Sparrows annually.

Current: Although limited in its Oklahoma distribution to parts of northeastern and north-central Oklahoma, and despite its rather stringent habitat requirements, the number of blocks in which Henslow's Sparrow was recorded indicate that the species is locally common. Because of its local distribution, the extent of this species' range in Oklahoma is probably not well delineated by atlas project results. The small number of reports, as well as the extreme difficulty of finding nests of this species, account for the lack of confirmations. The Tallgrass Prairie Preserve in northern Osage County remains the stronghold of this species in Oklahoma, although the prescribed burning schedule there coincidentally rendered the atlas block within the preserve unsuitable for this species during the year in which that block was surveyed.

Population Trend: Breeding Bird Survey data for 1966–2000 show a decline of 7.5 percent per year rangewide (P = 0.00). Because of its very recent and local distribution in Oklahoma, trend data are not available. Declines in the northeastern United States may be mitigated by range expansions to the west and southwest.

References: AOU 1998; Baicich and Harrison 1997; Baumgartner and Baumgartner 1992; Goard 1974; Herkert 1994a, 1994b, 1998; Hyde 1939; Pruitt 1996; Reinking and Hendricks 1993; Reinking et al. 2000a; Rising 1996a; Sauer et al. 2001; Seibert and Loyd 1993; Sutton 1967; Verser 1990; Zimmerman 1993

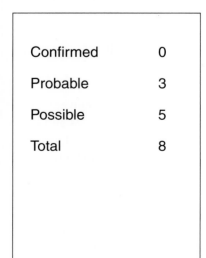

Confirmed	0
Probable	3
Possible	5
Total	8

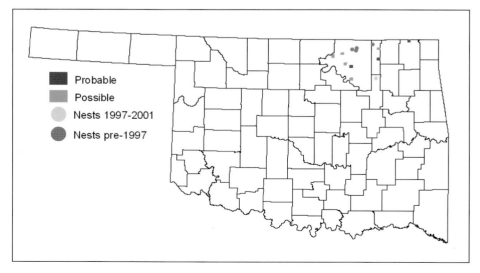

Northern Cardinal
Cardinalis cardinalis

Richard A. Stuart

Courtesy of Warren Williams

The Northern Cardinal, or "Redbird" as it is sometimes known, is one of the favorite yard and feeder birds in North America. In fragmented woodlands, it is one of the most common of breeding birds. The bright plumage and the cheerful song, which is sung by both sexes, appeal to most people, whether they are birders or not. It has been named the state bird in seven states.

Description: Both sexes have a distinct crest and a heavy, cone-shaped, reddish-orange bill. The male is red with black feathering around the bill and extending to the throat. The female is brownish on the back and underparts, with some red in the crest, wings, tail, and on the breast. Song is usually a loudly whistled *Whit-*

cheer whit-cheer whit-whit-whit-whit and the call note is a sharp chip.

Breeding Habitat: Forest edges, woodlands, grasslands with shrubs, parks, and yards.

Nest: A loosely built structure of twigs, stems, leaves, strips of bark, and grasses lined with fine grass and hair; constructed by the female. It is usually placed low in a bush, shrub, or tangle, usually below 3 m (10 ft).

NESTING ECOLOGY

Season: March–August. Double- or triple-brooded.
Eggs: Usually 2–3; whitish gray, blue, or green, densely

spotted and spattered with browns, grays, and purples. Frequently parasitized by Brown-headed Cowbirds.

Development: Incubation is by the female for 11–13 days. Young are provisioned by both sexes, fledge at about 9–10 days, and reach independence in 3–8 weeks.

DISTRIBUTION AND ABUNDANCE

Rangewide: Resident from New Brunswick, central Minnesota, extreme eastern Colorado, southeast, central, and southwestern New Mexico, and southeastern California southward to Honduras. It has been introduced into southwestern California, Hawaii, and Bermuda. It has expanded its range northward since the mid-1800s.

Historical: Described as common to abundant throughout most of the state, but uncommon and local in the Panhandle.

Current: Because the Northern Cardinal tolerates a wide variety of habitats, it is commonly found throughout most of the main body of the state. In the Oklahoma Panhandle it was found only locally in Beaver County. The visibility of fledglings and adults carrying food to young made for a high confirmation rate.

Population Trend: Breeding Bird Survey data for 1966–2000 show no conclusive trend rangewide (0.0 percent per year, P = 0.90), and an increase of 2.2 percent per year in Oklahoma (P = 0.00).

References: AOU 1998; Baicich and Harrison 1997; Baumgartner and Baumgartner 1992; Bent 1968; Halkin and Linville 1999; Harrison 1975; Kelley 1977; McGee 1975; National Geographic Society 1999; Newell 1990; Osborne 1992; Sauer et al. 2001; Stokes and Stokes 1996; Sutton 1967, 1973

Confirmed	324
Probable	133
Possible	51
Total	508

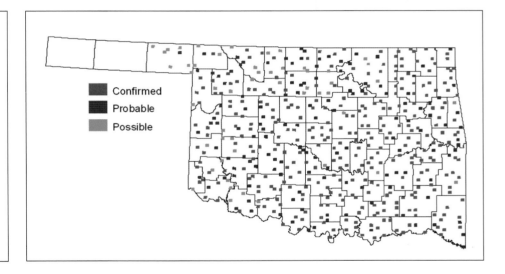

Confirmed
Probable
Possible

Rose-breasted Grosbeak
Pheucticus ludovicianus

David E. Fantina

Courtesy of Bob Gress

An uncommon spring migrant and rare breeder in eastern and central Oklahoma, the Rose-breasted Grosbeak is one of the most colorful and melodious breeding birds in the state. In the last half of the twentieth century it has become somewhat more common in the eastern and central portions of the state.

Description: The beautiful male Rose-breasted Grosbeak is unmistakable, with a bold black head and back, rose-colored breast and wing linings, white underparts, and a white rump. The female has yellow wing linings, an overall brown, streaked appearance, and shares the male's large triangular bill. The female Black-headed Grosbeak of the west is similar but is less heavily streaked. The male's song is a rich warble reminiscent of an American Robin or a Scarlet Tanager but somewhat more musical than either. The metallic call note, *chink*, is also diagnostic.

Breeding Habitat: Prefers open woods and wood edges, parks, and rural yards with shade trees.

Nest: A loose cup of twigs, grasses, and leaves built mainly by the female with some help from the male. Generally placed in the fork of a tree branch 1–6 m (3–20 ft) high. On rare occasions, a nest may be reused the following season.

NESTING ECOLOGY

Season: May–July. Double-brooded.
Eggs: Usually 4; greenish blue with dark blotches.
Development: Incubation is by both sexes for 12–14 days. Young are provisioned by both sexes and leave the nest at 9–12 days, but continue to be fed by adults for 3 weeks.
Hybridization: Known with Black-headed Grosbeak in the Great Plains.

DISTRIBUTION AND ABUNDANCE

Rangewide: A long-distance migrant breeding throughout much of eastern North America and central Canada, and generally wintering from Mexico to South America.
Historical: Prior to the 1950s the Rose-breasted Grosbeak was considered a transient in Oklahoma. It was first found breeding in 1954 in Ponca City.

Although still uncommon, it has since been reported nesting several times near Oklahoma City in the period 1957–1970 and in Washington County for several years in the 1970s.
Current: The Rose-breasted Grosbeak may continue to be a rare breeder in Oklahoma, but some of the blocks scored as Possible may represent migrants rather than breeders.

Population Trend: Breeding Bird Survey data for 1966–2000 show a decline of 0.8 percent per year rangewide (P = 0.01). No trend data are available for Oklahoma, except anecdotal suggestions of range expansion here in the past 50 years.

References: AOU 1998; Baicich and Harrison 1997; Baumgartner and Baumgartner 1992; Bent 1968; Friesen, Wyatt, and Cadman 1999; Sauer et al. 2001; Sutton 1967; Vacin 1968; Williams 1969

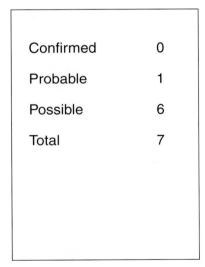

Confirmed	0
Probable	1
Possible	6
Total	7

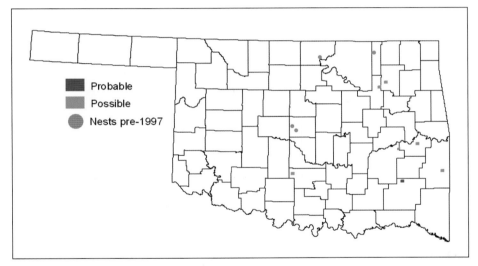

Probable
Possible
Nests pre-1997

Black-headed Grosbeak

Pheucticus melanocephalus

Dan L. Reinking

Courtesy of Michael Gray

Range maps depict the breeding range of the Black-headed Grosbeak as being tantalizingly close to the western end of the Oklahoma Panhandle. Although the species may be readily found in western Oklahoma in spring or fall migration, evidence of nesting in the state is scarce.

Description: Males have cinnamon underparts, a black head, and black wings with large white patches. Females are much paler in color. Both sexes have very thick bills common to grosbeaks. Rich, musical song is very similar to that of the Rose-breasted Grosbeak.

Breeding Habitat: Mature cottonwoods, hackberries,

and willows along streams, and shade trees around houses and towns.

Nest: An open, loose cup of twigs, plant stems, and pine needles, constructed by the female in the outer branches of a tree.

NESTING ECOLOGY

Season: Primarily May–June. Single-brooded.
Eggs: Often 3, but 2–5; greenish blue with reddish spotting.
Development: Incubation is by both sexes for 12–14 days. Young are provisioned by both sexes and leave the

nest at about 13 days, but cannot fly for another 2 weeks.

Hybridization: Known with Rose-breasted Grosbeak in the Great Plains.

DISTRIBUTION AND ABUNDANCE

Rangewide: Breeds across most of the western United States and southwestern Canada, and south through central Mexico to southern Mexico. Winters in Mexico.

Historical: Considered an uncommon migrant to casual visitant across western and central Oklahoma. A male was seen in Ponca City during the summers of 1954 through 1957, and was observed feeding two young in 1956, but it may have been paired with a female Rose-breasted Grosbeak.

Current: The sole record during atlas project years came from a block in Cimarron County in which a pair was observed in July acting agitated while a kestrel flew overhead. The female was seen twice carrying food into vegetation and leaving without it. Willows, cottonwoods, and hackberries were present along the Beaver River at this location.

Population Trend: Breeding Bird Survey data for 1966–2001 show no conclusive trend rangewide (1.0 percent per year, P = 0.14). No trend data are available for Oklahoma.

References: Baumgartner and Baumgartner 1992; Hill 1995; National Geographic Society 1999; Oklahoma Bird Records Committee 2000; Sutton 1967

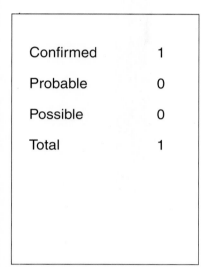

Confirmed	1
Probable	0
Possible	0
Total	1

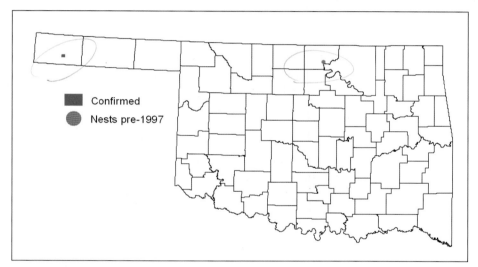

■ Confirmed
● Nests pre-1997

Blue Grosbeak
Guiraca caerulea

Alan E. Versaw

Courtesy of Michael Gray

The largest of the "blue buntings" in a state well populated with these handsome finches, the Blue Grosbeak also ranks as Oklahoma's most widely distributed member of this select group of birds. The nondescript females are seen only infrequently, but the males sing and offer their distinctive calls from the tops of roadside shrubs and tangles and occasionally even from fence posts. Though well equipped for eating seeds, they consume mostly grasshoppers and crickets during the few months of the year when they inhabit Oklahoma and are feeding young.

Description: Coloration of both male and female closely resembles the smaller Indigo Bunting. Male Blue Grosbeaks are most easily separated from Indigo Buntings by the proportionately larger bill, slightly duller shade of indigo, and the chestnut wing bars. Female Blue Grosbeaks have a heavier bill than Indigo Buntings, and also wear chestnut wing bars that may go unnoticed against the brownish tones of her body. While the male's song defies easy description, the loud and distinctive *chink* calls offered by both male and female provide a means of easy identification for this species.

Breeding Habitat: Overgrown fields or weedy edges of agricultural fields, roadside hedgerows, flood plains dominated by small trees, utility easements, forest edges, and the like each provide suitable breeding habitat for the Blue Grosbeak. Dominant tree and shrub types utilized by the grosbeak include willow, persimmon, hackberry, sumac, and wild plum. The structure, rather than the species of the trees and shrubs present, appears to be most important in determining suitability of habitat. Key elements may include dense, relatively low growth in semi-open areas.

Nest: An open cup generally constructed at low levels (usually less than 5 m or 16 ft high) in available trees or shrubbery. Perhaps the most notable feature of the nest is the species' propensity toward including scraps of paper or fabric, cellophane, snake skin, and other materials of similar texture in the nest's construction. May be lined with rootlets, hair, or grasses.

NESTING ECOLOGY

Season: May-August. Late summer development of insect populations may encourage breeding later in season. Often double-brooded.

Eggs: Usually 4; very pale blue, unmarked eggs. Heavily parasitized by cowbirds in most parts of range. Twenty of 33 nests (61 percent) found in Marshall County in the 1950s were parasitized. Four of 5 nests (80 percent) found in Osage County from 1992 to 1996 were parasitized.

Development: Incubation is by the female for 11–12 days. Young are provisioned mostly by the female at first, but after fledging at 9–10 days the male takes a more active role.

DISTRIBUTION AND ABUNDANCE

Rangewide: Except in the Great Plains states where it breeds north to North Dakota, the Blue Grosbeak is mostly restricted to, but widely distributed across, the southern half of the 48 states and Mexico. Fall migration returns the species to an area ranging from the southern two-thirds of Mexico nearly to the southeastern terminus of Central America.

Historical: Described as a summer resident statewide, more common east.

Current: Compared to its closest relatives, the Blue Grosbeak adapts nicely to a range of habitats. Even adaptability has its limits, however—a fact nicely illustrated by the range and distribution of the Blue Grosbeak within Oklahoma. Most abundant throughout the southeastern third of the state (excepting, of course, the densely forested corner of southeastern Oklahoma), the distribution and abundance of the species slowly, but perceptibly, diminishes the farther one travels northward and westward in the state. In the Panhandle, the Blue Grosbeak still occurs, but almost entirely in association with plantings of anthropogenic origin.

Population Trend: Breeding Bird Survey data for 1966–2000 show an increase of 0.9 percent per year rangewide (P = 0.00), but show no conclusive trend in Oklahoma (-1.0 percent per year, P = 0.22).

References: Baicich and Harrison 1997; Baumgartner and Baumgartner 1992; George M. Sutton Avian Research Center unpubl. data; Ingold 1993; Melcher 1998a; Melcher and Giesen 1996; Stabler 1959; Sutton 1967

Confirmed	106
Probable	153
Possible	151
Total	410

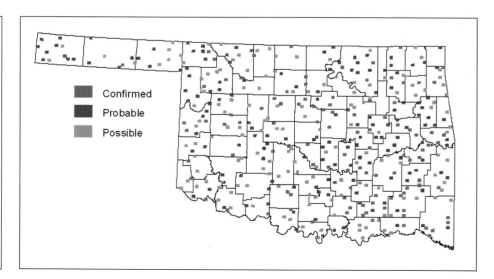

Lazuli Bunting

Passerina amoena

John M. Dole

Hybrid Lazuli / Indigo Bunting, Courtesy of Bill Horn

Lazuli Bunting, © Peter LaTourrette

The Lazuli Bunting typically occurs over much of Oklahoma as a rare and erratic migrant. Most regular in western Oklahoma, the species has bred in a few locations. It is a persistent singer throughout the breeding season. The Lazuli Bunting interbreeds occasionally with its close relative the Indigo Bunting.

Description: Adult males have blue upperparts and throat in breeding plumage. The back, wings, and tail are infused with brown. The breast is rusty colored and the belly is white. White wing bars are prominent. During the winter, males are much browner. Females are brown above with bluish rump, whitish belly, and buffy throat and breast. Immature birds resemble females; young males have variable amounts of blue by the first spring. Females are similar to female Indigo Buntings but have lighter underparts and are typically blue on the rump. Song is a fast warble.

Breeding Habitat: Brushy areas and deciduous woods, often along streams or nearby hillsides.

Nest: A cup of coarse, dry grass stems and leaves, bark strips, and rootlets. Lined with hair, rootlets, and fine grasses. Located in dense brush, vines, or small trees, 0.3–3 m (1–10 ft) high, normally less than 1 m (3 ft). Nest is constructed by the female.

NESTING ECOLOGY

Season: April–July. Usually double-brooded.

Eggs: Usually 3–4; unmarked pale blue, greenish blue, or white. Known to be a common Brown-headed Cowbird host in some parts of range.

Development: Incubation is by the female for about 12 days. Young are provisioned by both sexes and fledge in 9–11 days.

Hybridization: Not uncommon with Indigo Bunting; noted in south-central and western Oklahoma.

DISTRIBUTION AND ABUNDANCE

Rangewide: This western species ranges from southernmost western Canada to northern Baja California and northern Arizona and New Mexico. The eastern edge of the range is reached in the Dakotas, Nebraska, Colorado, and New Mexico. Occasionally breeds east of the indicated range as in Oklahoma. Winters from southeast Arizona and northwestern Mexico south to Oaxaca, Mexico.

Historical: This species was primarily limited to Cimarron County in the early part of the twentieth century; however, it has bred east to Arkansas on occasions since then. Although it nests more frequently in western Oklahoma, it is still erratic and may not breed every year. Most nest records are from the westernmost column of non-Panhandle counties, but summer records from Comanche County have increased in recent years; many hybrids with Indigo Bunting have been observed.

Current: The breeding range of this erratic nester is limited in Oklahoma, with few records found during the atlasing period. The only nesting confirmation occurred in Comanche County (but not in an atlas block) where a number of sight records have occurred over a period of several years. One Probable record was obtained in Cimarron County where the species is frequently seen, but usually only during migration. Other records scattered across four counties may be of late migrants.

Population Trend: Breeding Bird Survey data for 1966–2000 show no conclusive trend rangewide (1.0 percent per year, P = 0.14). No trend data are available for Oklahoma.

References: AOU 1998; Baicich and Harrison 1997; Baker and Boylan 1999; Baumgartner and Baumgartner 1992; Berry and Brock 1998; Emlen et al. 1975; Greene et al. 1996; Howell and Webb 1995; Kaufman 1996; National Geographic Society 1999; Nice 1931; Sauer et al. 2001; Sibley and Short 1959; Sutton 1934, 1938, 1967

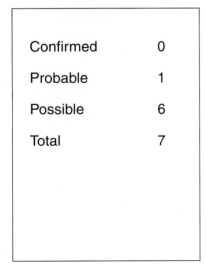

Confirmed	0
Probable	1
Possible	6
Total	7

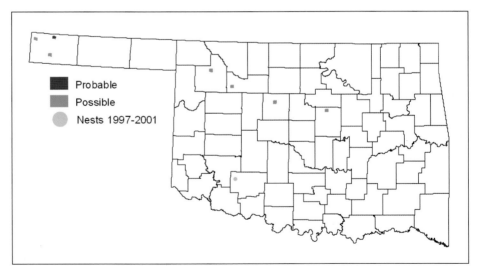

Indigo Bunting
Passerina cyanea

Michael D. Bay

Courtesy of Bill Horn

This handsomely colored bird could be the miniature version of the Blue Grosbeak, though lacking the chestnut wing markings of the latter. Like the grosbeak, the Indigo Bunting has benefited from clear-cutting of forests and abandonment of pastures, creating its preferred oldfield and woodland habitats.

Description: Males are uniform indigo blue, while females and immatures of both sexes are brown with some light streaking on the breast. Females and immature males might suggest a sparrow, but they lack the back streaking typical of most sparrow species. Males are commonly confused with the male Blue Grosbeak,

but the latter is larger, has a heavier beak, and two rusty wing bars. The song begins as a series of high-pitched notes that grow faint at the end.

Breeding Habitat: Prefers forest edges, brushy thickets, and oldfields. This species is one of the few Neotropical migrants that benefits from forest fragmentation.

Nest: An open cup of leaves, grasses, stems, and bark situated below 1 m (3 ft) in the branches of a shrub, bush, or low tree.

NESTING ECOLOGY

Season: May–July. Double-brooded.

Eggs: Usually 3–4; pale bluish white, sometimes pure white with faint specks of brown. Common host to the Brown-headed Cowbird.

Development: Incubation is by the female for 12–13 days. Young are provisioned mostly by the female, fledge in 9–10 days, and reach independence in about 3 weeks.

Hybridization: Indigo Bunting reaches its western-most limit in Oklahoma, where its range overlaps with its western cousin, the Lazuli Bunting. Hybrids have been observed in south-central and western Oklahoma.

DISTRIBUTION AND ABUNDANCE

Rangewide: Long-distant migrant, breeding from Saskatchewan south to central and southeastern Texas, parts of the Southwest, and east to the Gulf and Atlantic coasts. Winters in southern Mexico, south to Panama, and the Greater Antilles.

Historical: Described as common to abundant throughout central and eastern Oklahoma, less common in western Oklahoma, and rare in the Panhandle.

Current: The Indigo Bunting is a very common breeding resident with a statewide distribution. Its preference for a variety of habitat types, its frequent singing, and its visibility made it easily detected in atlas blocks.

Population Trend: Breeding Bird Survey data for 1966–2000 show a decline of 0.7 percent per year rangewide (P = 0.00), but show no conclusive trend in Oklahoma (1.0 percent per year, P = 0.38).

References: Baker and Boylan 1999; Baumgartner and Baumgartner 1992; Bay 1996; Bent 1968; Carey and Nolan 1979; DeGraaf and Rappole 1995; Delap 1971; Ehrlich et al. 1988; Emlen et al. 1975; Payne 1992; Sauer et al. 2001; Sibley and Short 1959; Sutton 1938, 1967; Thomas 1970

Confirmed	122
Probable	163
Possible	110
Total	395

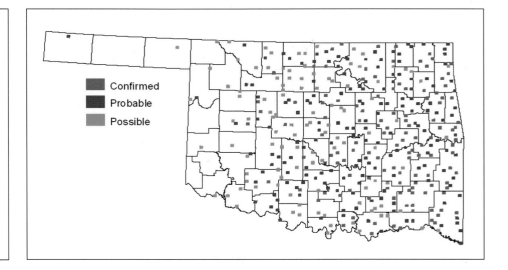

Painted Bunting
Passerina ciris

Michael D. Bay

Courtesy of Arthur Morris / www.birdsasart.com

The Painted Bunting is arguably the most attractive species found in North America; it is certainly one of the most colorful. No other North American species combines the colors of blue, red, and green so sharply defined as in the male of this species. Though brightly colored, it is frequently hard to see in the dense thickets it inhabits.

Description: The male has a blue head, red breast and rump, lime-green back, with dark wings and tail. The female and immature male have a bright yellow-green body with dark wings. The song consists of a series of rapid warbles.

Breeding Habitat: Thickets, forest edges, brushy old-fields, and other open areas with scattered brush and trees.

Nest: Open cup of grasses, forbs, and leaves, usually placed in a low bush, hedgerow, or woody vines.

NESTING ECOLOGY

Season: May–July. Double-brooded.
Eggs: 3–4; pale blue spotted with brown. Frequent host to the Brown-headed Cowbird. Thirteen of 45 nests (29 percent) in Marshall County in 1956 were parasitized.
Development: Incubation is by the female for 11–12 days. Young are provisioned by the female while in the

nest; male may feed young after fledging, which occurs at about 9–12 days.

DISTRIBUTION AND ABUNDANCE

Rangewide: Breeds from southern New Mexico and Missouri south to Mexico and east to Alabama. Disjunct population breeds along southern Atlantic Coast. Winters from central Florida south to the Bahamas as well as central Mexico south to Central America.

Historical: Described as an uncommon summer resident over much of the state, rare in the Ozarks and Panhandle, and more common in southeastern counties.

Current: The Painted Bunting is a very common breeding resident distributed throughout the main body of the state but tapering off rapidly in the more arid Panhandle, where brushy thickets and forest edge are less available.

Population Trend: Breeding Bird Survey data for 1966–2000 show a decline of 2.7 percent per year rangewide (P = 0.00), but show no conclusive trend in Oklahoma (0.3 percent per year, P = 0.67).

References: Baumgartner and Baumgartner 1992; Bent 1968; DeGraaf and Rappole 1995; DeGraaf et al. 1991; Ehrlich et al. 1988; Lowther et al. 1999; Parmelee 1959; Sauer et al. 2001; Sutton 1967, 1977; Tveten 1993

Confirmed	96
Probable	191
Possible	146
Total	433

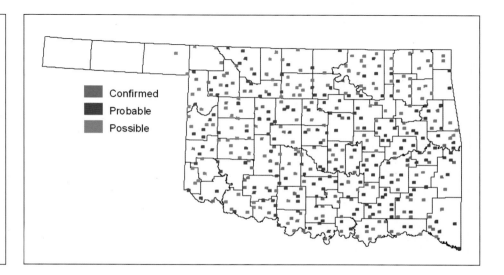

Confirmed
Probable
Possible

Dickcissel
Spiza americana

Dan L. Reinking

Courtesy of Colin Smith

One of the most common summer bird songs in Oklahoma's central and northeastern prairies is the dry, unmusical vocal effort of the Dickcissel. From wintering flocks in Venezuela that may number over one million birds, Dickcissels fan out over their Great Plains breeding grounds, sometimes extending their range eastward or westward depending on weather or habitat conditions.

Description: Male Dickcissels have a yellow breast, black bib, white throat, gray head with a yellowish eye stripe, and chestnut patches on the bends of the wings. Females are generally similar but not as bright and lack the black bib. The Dickcissel's song usually consists of three dry, rasping parts roughly corresponding to *dick*

dick dickcissel. The call is a buzzer-like *bzrrrt* and is usually given in flight. Dickcissels are not likely to be confused with other species, although their pattern of yellow and black is superficially similar to that of meadowlarks.

Breeding Habitat: Dickcissels select moderately tall, dense vegetation such as that often found in prairies, pastures, and oldfields, and in some years they also nest in roadside right-of-ways. Habitats with a moderate amount of forbs are preferred. Spring burning and grazing reduces nest success of Dickcissels in Oklahoma and Kansas tallgrass prairie, but does not affect density.

430

Nest: A cup woven of coarse grasses and lined with smaller grasses and rootlets is built by the female. Nests are generally elevated in forbs, shrubs, grasses, or trees. Of 887 nests found in Osage and Washington counties from 1992 to 1996, the mean height was 25 cm (10 in), with a range of 0–540 cm (0–18 ft).

NESTING ECOLOGY

Season: May–July. Probably occasionally double-brooded.

Eggs: 3–5, usually 4; light blue without markings. Dickcissels are regularly parasitized by Brown-headed Cowbirds (26 percent of 1,100 nests in Osage and Washington counties, 1992–1996).

Development: Incubation is by the female alone for about 12 days. Young are both brooded and fed by the female and typically leave the nest at 9–10 days.

DISTRIBUTION AND ABUNDANCE

Rangewide: Dickcissels nest throughout the Great Plains and regularly east to central Ohio and Tennessee. Numbers of breeding birds east to Virginia and Pennsylvania are variable from year to year, perhaps due to weather and vegetation conditions in their core breeding range. They reach peak breeding densities in eastern Kansas and adjacent states. A long-distance migrant, most Dickcissels winter gregariously in a relatively small area of central Venezuela.

Historical: Described as abundant but variable from year to year in central Oklahoma and local in suitable habitat within the largely forested areas of eastern Oklahoma. Also local and variable in the shinnery-oak country of Ellis and Roger Mills counties, as well as the Panhandle. Considered more common in western fringe areas in wet years.

Current: The Dickcissel is very common in open habitats across Oklahoma, except for forested portions of southeastern Oklahoma where its distribution is more restricted. Its distinctive, seemingly endlessly repeated song ensures that its presence does not go unrecorded in an atlas block.

Population Trend: Breeding Bird Survey data for 1966–2000 show a decline of 1.4 percent per year rangewide (P = 0.00) and an increase of 1.1 percent per year in Oklahoma (P = 0.02).

References: AOU 1998; Baicich and Harrison 1997; Baumgartner and Baumgartner 1992; Bergey 1976; Berry 1971; Crabb 1922, 1923; Dechant, Sondreal, Johnson, Igl, Goldade, Zimmerman, and Euliss 1999; Delap 1979, 1980; Ely 1957; George M. Sutton Avian Research Center unpubl. data; National Geographic Society 1999; Norman 1973, 1982, 1987; Overmire 1962, 1963; Ratzlaff 1989; Rohrbaugh et al. 1999; Sauer et al. 2001; Sutton 1967; Verser 1990; Zimmerman 1997

Confirmed	237
Probable	200
Possible	77
Total	514

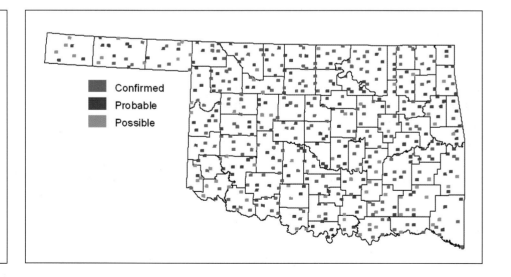

Red-winged Blackbird
Agelaius phoeniceus

Eugene A. Young

Courtesy of Warren Williams

The Red-winged Blackbird is perhaps the most abundant bird in the contiguous United States during the breeding season. It is well known during that time for the male's visual display, in which the brilliant red epaulets are shown off to their best advantage. It is also well known, and less well liked, for the large migrating and wintering flocks that can cause damage to crops in local areas.

Description: Males are mostly black, with bright red and yellow epaulets. Females and young males are typically mottled brown and black with heavy streaking on the underside, usually with some rufous, red, or pinkish in the wings, and rufous tones in the back. In flight,

all blackbirds can look similar, but call notes usually help separate species.

Breeding Habitat: Commonly found in a variety of wetlands, including farm ponds, low-lying fields and hayfields, old fields, and pastures; typically in cattails, bulrushes, sedges, tall forbs, and willows over water; occasionally in alfalfa or upland areas, especially tall grasses. Males generally arrive in the spring before females to establish territories.

Nest: A sturdy structure, usually within 1 m (3 ft) above water. Consists of a deep cup made of dried cattail leaves, reeds, and milkweed fibers, all woven around supports of nearby vegetation and lined with grass.

NESTING ECOLOGY

Season: April–July. Sometimes double-brooded.

Eggs: Usually 3–4; pale bluish green, scrawled, streaked or spotted with purplish-blackish areas, usually toward the wide end. Commonly parasitized by Brown-headed Cowbirds. Ninety of 468 nests (19 percent) were observed to be parasitized in Osage and Washington counties from 1992 to 1996. For over 100 nests observed in Marshall County in the 1950s and 1960s, the observed parasitism rate was only 0–2 percent.

Development: Incubation is by the female for 11–13 days. Young are provisioned by the female and sometimes the male as well and fledge at 10–11 days, but continue to be fed for another 2–5 weeks.

DISTRIBUTION AND ABUNDANCE

Rangewide: Breeds from southern Alaska east to Nova Scotia, and throughout North America, south through east and western Mexico to Central America. Northernmost populations move south for winter, with some birds present over most of the United States southward.

Historical: Described as a common summer resident throughout most of the state and abundant in migration and winter.

Current: The Red-winged Blackbird is common and widespread throughout Oklahoma, with the exception of the heavily wooded southeastern portion of the state. Easily recognized, prolific singing, and gregarious, conspicuous nesting habits account for the high proportion of blocks in which it was recorded and confirmed.

Population Trend: Breeding Bird Survey data for 1966–2000 show a decline of 1.0 percent per year rangewide (P = 0.00) and an increase of 1.8 percent per year in Oklahoma (P = 0.04).

References: Alberts 1978; AOU 1998; Baicich and Harrison 1997; Baumgartner and Baumgartner 1992; Clotfelter and Yasukawa 1999; Ely 1957; George M. Sutton Avian Research Center unpubl. data; Goddard and Board 1967; Sauer et al. 2001; Sibley 2000; Sutton 1967; Terres 1991; Thompson and Ely 1992; Tveten 1993; Wiens 1963; Yasukawa and Searcy 1995

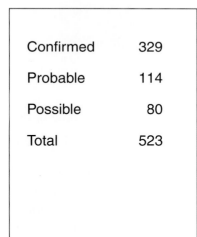

Confirmed	329
Probable	114
Possible	80
Total	523

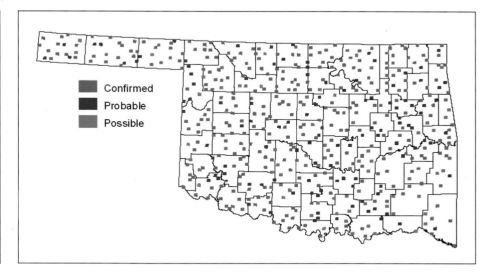

Eastern Meadowlark
Sturnella magna

Dan L. Reinking

One of the songbirds most familiar to rural Oklahomans, the Eastern Meadowlark is present year round and is frequently seen perched on fence posts or making short, low flights over its favored grassy habitats. Its songs and calls best distinguish it from its very similar western cousin.

Description: The Eastern Meadowlark is a chunky, short-tailed, long-billed grassland bird with a black V superimposed on a bright yellow breast. In flight, it shows extensive white in the outer tail feathers. The sexes are similar, although females are not as bright in color. Its song is a clear whistle of several syllables, and a frequently given call is a buzzy *drzzt*. It is almost identical to Western Meadowlark, but has more white

in the tail feathers, more white and less yellow in the malar region, and a simpler, less musical song.

Breeding Habitat: Tallgrass and mixedgrass prairies, pastures, hayfields, and old field areas with a high proportion of grass and low coverage of woody vegetation. Moderately grazed areas have higher breeding densities than heavily grazed or ungrazed areas. In places where ranges overlap, Eastern Meadowlarks inhabit wetter lowland areas, while Western Meadowlarks inhabit drier uplands.

Nest: A relatively large, domed structure woven of grass and stems by the female alone. Placed on the ground often in a small hollow, nests usually have a side rather than a top entrance, and sometimes have an entrance tunnel.

NESTING ECOLOGY

Season: April–July. Double-brooded.

Eggs: Usually 3–5; white, speckled or spotted with reddish or purplish brown mostly at the larger end. Occasionally parasitized by Brown-headed Cowbirds (6 percent of 631 nests in Osage and Washington counties from 1992 to 1996). Nest sharing or nest competition by females has also been noted in Oklahoma.

Development: Incubation by the female for 13–14 days. Young are provisioned by both sexes (but mostly by the female), fledge at 10–12 days, but are fed by parents for another 2 weeks.

Hybridization: Rare with Western Meadowlark. In Oklahoma, one confirmed record of a nest with 3 young tended by a male Western Meadowlark and a female Eastern Meadowlark exists for Cleveland County in 1965. Captive-raised Eastern and Western meadowlarks have mated successfully, but hybrid offspring produced infertile eggs.

DISTRIBUTION AND ABUNDANCE

Rangewide: A North American resident breeding from the northeastern United States, along the U.S.-Canadian border west to Minnesota, south through the central Great Plains through Texas, and west through southern New Mexico and Arizona. Also breeds in Mexico, Middle America, Cuba, and portions of South America. Mostly sedentary, Eastern Meadowlarks winter in all but the northernmost areas of the breeding range, where birds may move south in winter.

Historical: Described as common in eastern and central Oklahoma west to Major, Blaine, and Tillman counties; less common westward to Beaver County in low-lying areas bordering rivers. A rapid westward range expansion in southern Kansas and in Texas in the 1960s, mostly along flood plains of major watercourses, also occurred in Oklahoma.

Current: The Eastern Meadowlark is very common in open habitats throughout the main body of the state, but reaches the western edge of its Oklahoma range partway through the Panhandle. It was confirmed often, perhaps due to the visibility of fledglings or of adults carrying food.

Population Trend: Breeding Bird Survey data for 1966–2000 show a decline of 2.9 percent per year rangewide (P = 0.00) and a decline of 1.9 percent per year in Oklahoma (P = 0.00).

References: AOU 1998; Baicich and Harrison 1997; Baskett 1940; Baumgartner and Baumgartner 1992; Chapman 1900; George M. Sutton avian Research Center unpubl. data; Granfors et al. 1996; Griffin 1959; Hull 2000; Lanyon 1956a, 1956b, 1966, 1979, 1995; Ordal 1976; Risser et al. 1981; Rohrbaugh et al. 1999; Rohwer 1972a, 1972b, 1972c; Roseberry and Klimstra 1970; Sauer et al. 2001; Shackford 1990; Smith 1940; Sutton 1967; Sutton and Dickerson 1965; Wolfe 1996; Zimmerman 1993

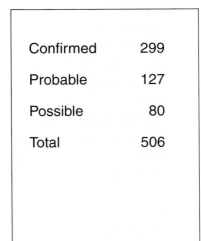

Confirmed	299
Probable	127
Possible	80
Total	506

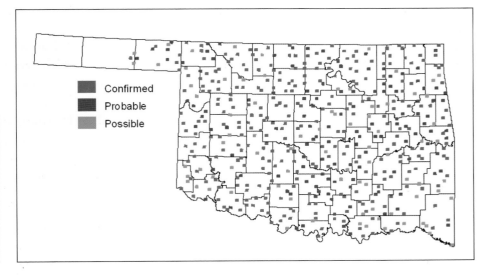

Western Meadowlark
Sturnella neglecta

Dan L. Reinking

Courtesy of Bob Gress

Lewis and Clark mentioned the Western Meadowlark, but John James Audubon felt it was a species that had been largely overlooked, and thus gave it its scientific name *neglecta*. No longer neglected, it has been declared the state bird of six states, the second most common choice. The Western Meadowlark is present year round in western and central Oklahoma and is best distinguished from the very similar Eastern Meadowlark by songs and calls.

Description: The Western Meadowlark is a chunky, short-tailed, long-billed grassland bird with a black V superimposed on a bright yellow breast. In flight, it shows white in the outer tail feathers. The sexes are similar, although females are not as bright in color. Its primary song is a melodious, clear whistle, and a frequently given call is a brief *chupp*. It is almost identical to Eastern Meadowlark, but has less white in the tail feathers, more yellow and less white in the malar region, and a more complex musical song.

Breeding Habitat: Grasslands, pastures, hayfields, and old field areas with a high proportion of grass and low coverage of woody vegetation. They generally respond positively to light or moderate grazing and negatively to heavy grazing. In places where ranges overlap, Western Meadowlarks inhabit drier uplands, while Eastern Meadowlarks inhabit wetter lowland areas.

Nest: A relatively large usually domed structure woven

of grass and stems by the female alone. Placed on the ground, nests usually have a side rather than a top entrance, and sometimes have an entrance tunnel which may be several feet long.

NESTING ECOLOGY

Season: April–July. Double-brooded.

Eggs: Usually 3–6; white, speckled or spotted with reddish or purplish brown mostly at the larger end. Occasionally parasitized by Brown-headed Cowbirds.

Development: Incubation is by female for 13–14 days. Young are provisioned by both sexes (but mostly by the female), fledge at 10–12 days, but are fed by the parents for another 2 weeks.

Hybridization: Rare with Eastern Meadowlark. In Oklahoma, one confirmed record of a nest with 3 young tended by a male Western Meadowlark and a female Eastern Meadowlark exists for Cleveland County in 1965. Captive-raised Eastern and Western meadowlarks mated successfully, but hybrid offspring produced infertile eggs.

DISTRIBUTION AND ABUNDANCE

Rangewide: A North American resident breeding from central Alberta south through all of the western United States through interior Mexico, and east to the Great Lakes. Absent in parts of southeastern Arizona. Mostly sedentary, Western Meadowlarks winter in all but the northernmost areas of the breeding range, where birds move south in winter.

Historical: Described as uncommon to abundant during the breeding season in western and central Oklahoma east to Grant, Canadian, Grady, and Cotton counties. Has been heard singing during the breeding season as far east as Payne, Oklahoma, Cleveland, and Marshall counties; very rare in far-eastern counties. More common in the east in winter.

Current: Western Meadowlarks were confirmed in nearly all Panhandle atlas blocks and were recorded throughout the western third of the state, diminishing in occurrence eastward through central Oklahoma. Many of the easternmost records may be birds recorded as singing prior to the end of postwinter movements.

Population Trend: Breeding Bird Survey data for 1966–2000 show a decline of 0.6 percent per year rangewide (P = 0.00) and a decline of 1.5 percent per year in Oklahoma (P = 0.00).

References: AOU 1998; Baicich and Harrison 1997; Baskett 1940; Baumgartner and Baumgartner 1992; Chapman 1900; Coffey 1977; Dechant et al. 1999; Griffin 1959; Lanyon 1956a, 1956b 1966, 1979, 1994; Ordal 1976; Rohwer 1972a, 1972b, 1972c; Smith 1940; Sutton 1967; Sutton and Dickerson 1965

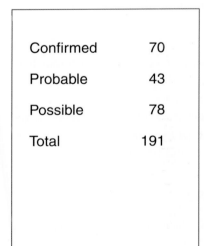

Confirmed	70
Probable	43
Possible	78
Total	191

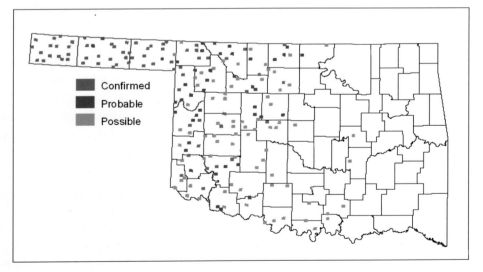

Yellow-headed Blackbird

Xanthocephalus xanthocephalus

John S. Shackford

Courtesy of Bill Horn

Most first-time observers, upon seeing a male Yellow-headed Blackbird, are stunned by such vibrancy of color in a "mere" blackbird. You may hear birdwatchers grumble about too many blackbirds—starlings (not a true blackbird), cowbirds, grackles, even Red-wings, but never Yellow-heads!

Description: The adult male is mostly black, but has a bright yellow head and throat, as well as white primary wing coverts. Females are generally a dark brown except for a wash of pale yellow on upper breast and throat which extends onto parts of the face. First winter males are similar to females.

Breeding Habitat: Cattail, reed, and bulrush marshes, often in large colonies.

Nest: Dead reeds, cattails, and other waterlogged vegetation wrapped around living cattails and reeds. Nest is lined with narrow leaves and fine grasses.

NESTING ECOLOGY

Season: May–June. Single-brooded, but lost clutches may be replaced.
Eggs: 3–7; grayish white, with fine dots and specks of gray and brown. Rarely parasitized by Brown-headed Cowbirds.

Development: Incubation is by the female for 12–13 days. Young are provisioned primarily by the female with some help by the male and fledge at 9–12 days, but continue to be fed for several more days.

DISTRIBUTION AND ABUNDANCE

Rangewide: Breeds throughout much of the western United States and Canada from northern Alberta to Minnesota, west to eastern Washington, Oregon, and California, and south to central New Mexico. Winters in the southwestern United States and Mexico.

Historical: Only 2 historical nest records exist for Oklahoma. One nest was in northwestern Cimarron County in 1914, and several nests and young were in a colony estimated at 25 adults at Optima Reservoir, Texas County, in 1986. The species is described as a recently established and locally common breeder in the Texas Panhandle.

Current: A rare nester in the Oklahoma Panhandle. Almost certainly, most of the birds seen during the breeding season are nonbreeding or migrating "stragglers."

Population Trend: Breeding Bird Survey data for 1966–2000 show an increase of 1.6 percent per year rangewide (P = 0.03). No trend data are available for Oklahoma.

References: AOU 1998; Baicich and Harrison 1997; Baumgartner and Baumgartner 1992; Bent 1965; Johnsgard 1979; Peterjohn and Sauer 1999; Sauer et al. 2001; Seyffert 2001; Shackford and Tyler 1987; Sutton 1967; Tate 1923; Terres 1980; Twedt and Crawford 1995

Confirmed	3
Probable	2
Possible	5
Total	10

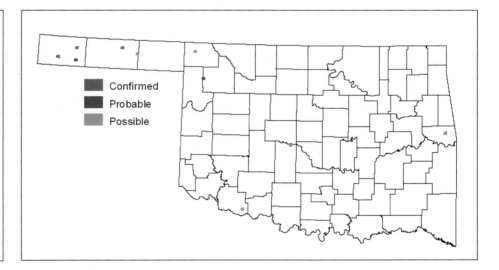

Confirmed
Probable
Possible

Brewer's Blackbird
Euphagus cyanocephalus

Sebastian T. Patti

Courtesy of Steve Metz

Afairly common blackbird in Oklahoma in winter, the Brewer's prefers open agricultural areas and cities and towns. It is migratory in the northern portions of its range and generally resident in the western and southern portions. During the twentieth century, the species experienced a significant range expansion, particularly in the eastern portion of the continent, possibly as a result of the expansion of ranching and agricultural activities. Some recent authors now suggest that the species may be contracting, as a possible result of competition with Common Grackles, and because of heavy cowbird parasitism. It is (or was) a rare breeder in Oklahoma.

Description: Adult males are glossy black all over with

a distinct purplish sheen (in good light) on the head, throat, and upper breast areas; rest of body with a greenish cast. Distinctive white irides. Adult females are uniformly gray-brown overall, usually with dark eyes. Call is a flat *tick* or *tuck*. The male's song is a squeaky, unremarkable, two-note *quee-see*. Lacks the long, keel-shaped tail of grackles.

Breeding Habitat: An adaptable species, the Brewer's Blackbird can be found in a variety of habitats from marshy wetlands and semiarid lands, to agricultural areas and towns and cities. Small trees and shrubs in proximity to water are favored nesting areas.

Nest: A large bulky cup that may be placed on the

ground, in low bushes or trees, or 5–9 m (18–30 ft) high in a tree or shrub. The nest is made of sticks, twigs, and grasses, often molded together with mud or manure. Somewhat colonial, the species often nests in loose groups of 5–20 pairs.

NESTING ECOLOGY

Season: The few records from Oklahoma range from May to September. Double-brooding is not uncommon in other parts of range. Colonies tend to be synchronous in breeding.

Eggs: 4–8, usually 5–6; greenish or bluish white with brown streaks or spots. Often parasitized by Brown-headed Cowbird.

Development: Incubation is by the female for 12–13 days. Young are provisioned by both sexes and fledge at 13 days, but are fed for another 12–13 days.

DISTRIBUTION AND ABUNDANCE

Rangewide: Breeds from central and southern British Columbia to the Great Lakes including northern Michigan and southern Ontario, west through much of Wisconsin and Minnesota, and south and west to include most of the western United States, to northwestern Baja California and southern Nevada, northeastern Arizona, and northern New Mexico. Generally migratory in the northern and eastern portions of the species' range and resident in western and southern areas.

Historical: Described as uncommon to common in central and western areas in winter and rare east. Nest records exist for Bryan (1883), Cimarron (1910), and Creek (1920) counties. Described as a summer resident in the Panhandle in 1931, but not in later publications.

Current: Although there are some older breeding records from the western part of the state, there are no recent confirmed records. This lack of breeding evidence is consistent with the contiguous parts of the Texas Panhandle. The species was recently confirmed breeding in southeastern Colorado, however, on two atlas blocks abutting Cimarron County, Oklahoma. Additional fieldwork may confirm the breeding of the species in the westernmost portions of the Panhandle. The one report during the atlas project involved a singing male on the westernmost atlas block in the state (abutting New Mexico). The Brewer's Blackbird apparently chased a male Brown-headed Cowbird from its territory.

Population Trend: Breeding Bird Survey data for 1966–2000 show a decline of 1.3 percent per year rangewide (P = 0.00). These data suggest a decline of 20.6 percent per year in Oklahoma for the same time period (P = 0.08), but this is based on only a few observations on two routes in Cimarron and Texas counties in the 1960s and 1970s dropping to no observations from the late 1980s onward.

References: AOU 1998; Baicich and Harrison 1997; Baumgartner and Baumgartner 1992; Bent 1958; Brewer et al. 1991; Melcher 1998b; Mumford and Keller 1984; Oberholser 1974; Sauer et al. 2001; Sutton 1967; Tate 1923; Thompson and Ely 1992

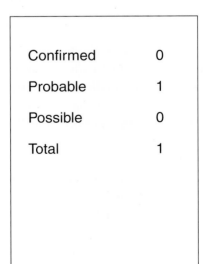

Confirmed	0
Probable	1
Possible	0
Total	1

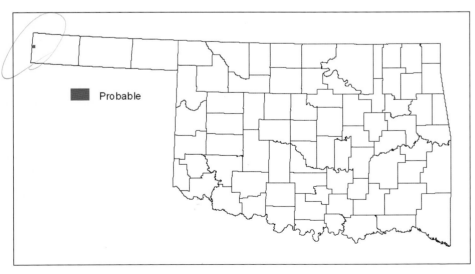

Probable

Common Grackle
Quiscalus quiscula

Eugene A. Young

A long-tailed, striking, gregarious species commonly associated with urban environments, Common Grackles have greatly expanded their range in the American west. As in many other bird species, magnetic material contained in their heads may assist with navigation.

Description: Both sexes are black with yellow eyes and have a long wedged-shaped tail often keeled in flight due to the outer tail feathers being shorter than the inner. Typically, the heads of males are glossy with purple sheens, while the body has a bronze sheen; females are duller brownish-black. Songs and calls are harsh and unmusical. Great-tailed Grackles are larger and longer tailed.

Breeding Habitat: Somewhat colonial, this species prefers wind breaks and shelterbelts, roadside parks, open and cultivated areas, and generally more mesic habitats. It breeds in towns, farmyards, open woods, and forest edges, utilizing shade trees and occasionally cattails over water.

Nest: Typically located on horizontal branches or in a tree crotch 0.2–22 m (0.7–72 ft) high; rarely in tree cavity. Nest is a bulky loose cup made of weed stems, twigs, grasses, rags, paper, or string, with an inner cup of mud and lined with feathers, hair, and grass.

NESTING ECOLOGY

Season: April–July. Usually single-brooded, but will replace lost nests.

Eggs: Often 4–6; pale greenish to light brown, blotched, scrawled, and spotted with brown, black, and purple. Rarely parasitized by Brown-headed Cowbirds; no evidence of cowbird parasitism in Oklahoma.

Development: Incubation is by the female for 11–15 days. Young are provisioned by both sexes and fledge in about 12–15 days, but continue to be fed for up to several weeks.

DISTRIBUTION AND ABUNDANCE

Rangewide: A short-distance migrant that is a summer resident in Canada east of the Rocky Mountains, the northeastern and northern United States, and the High Plains and is a permanent resident in the central and southeastern United States. Winter populations in the south are large because of influx of birds from more northerly latitudes.

Historical: Reported to be a summer resident through-

out most of the state but not found in southeastern Oklahoma and rare in the Panhandle in 1931. More recently considered a common summer resident throughout most of the state, less common and more local in the Panhandle, although the range appears to have spread westward. Less common in winter.

Current: The Common Grackle is both common and widespread throughout much of the state. Its conspicuous presence and breeding habits allow for a high number of Confirmed records, but it becomes scarce in forested habitats of southeastern Oklahoma.

Population Trend: Breeding Bird Survey data for 1966–2000 show a decline of 1.4 percent per year rangewide (P = 0.00), but show no conclusive trend in Oklahoma (0.5 percent per year, P = 0.70).

References: AOU 1998; Andrews and Righter 1992; Baicich and Harrison 1997; Baumgartner and Baumgartner 1992; Bent 1958; Bray et al. 1973; Edwards et al. 1992; Erskine 1971; Peer and Bollinger 1997; Sauer et al. 2001; Stokes and Stokes 1979, Sutton 1967, 1984a; Terres 1991; Thompson and Ely 1992; Tveten 1993; Watson and Royall 1978; Wilson et al. 1971

Confirmed	238
Probable	78
Possible	103
Total	419

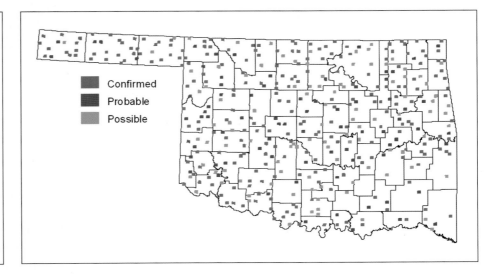

Great-tailed Grackle

Quiscalus mexicanus

John M. Dole

Courtesy of Colin Smith

This gregarious and conspicuous bird is a relatively recent arrival in Oklahoma, with the first sight records occurring in 1953 and the first breeding record in 1958. Since then it has become a common species in some areas of the state. The loud calls and screeching of the male Great-tailed Grackle can often be heard before the bird is seen. One call is reminiscent of sheets being torn in half. Formerly considered conspecific with Boat-tailed Grackle, the two were split after 1957.

Description: The male Great-tailed Grackle is glossy bluish-black with iridescent purple on the head, neck, and back. The tail is strikingly long and keel shaped. The female is smaller than the male, medium to blackish brown with lighter brown supercilium, throat, and chest. The iris is yellow on adult birds. The similar Common Grackle is smaller with a distinctly shorter tail and has a bronze-black body contrasting with an iridescent bluish head. Vocalizations consist of loud mechanical rattles and a variety of other sounds.

Breeding Habitat: Tall trees and shrubs near water, although birds can often be found foraging far from water, even in heavily developed areas.

Nest: Comprised of weed stems, coarse grasses, strips of bark, or plant fibers, lined with mud or dung. The inner cup is made of fine grasses, rootlets, feathers, and other soft materials. Nest is constructed by the female. Nests are located in tall marsh plants, shrubs, or trees in marshes or along watercourses and occasionally in shade trees near houses. Nest height is variable, but usually 1.5–4.5 m (5–15 ft) above the ground. In Oklahoma, Sutton noted that nests were 0.6–1.8 m (2–6 ft) up in willows, cattails, or bulrushes or 3.7–6.0 m (12–20 ft) up in junipers, pecans, black locusts, or other trees. Nesting is usually colonial and can occur in heron rookeries.

NESTING ECOLOGY

Season: April–July. Single- to double-brooded.
Eggs: Usually 3–4; tinted pale blue to pink, purple, or brown with numerous black, purple, or gray markings.
Development: Incubation is by the female for 13–14 days. Young are provisioned by the female and fledge at about 12–14 days but cannot fly well for another 2 weeks.

DISTRIBUTION AND ABUNDANCE

Rangewide: The Great-tailed Grackle breeds from southeastern Iowa, Missouri, Arkansas, and Louisiana west to California, and south through Mexico and Central America to northwest Venezuela and northwest Peru. Northernmost populations withdraw south during the winter.
Historical: This species has been expanding its range

north and west from Texas for several decades. First recorded in Oklahoma in 1953, and first known to nest here in 1958. By 1967 nesting had occurred in numerous counties. By 1992 the Great-tailed Grackle was considered to be locally common throughout the state. Populations decease during the winter in northern Oklahoma.
Current: The Great-tailed Grackle is widespread across the state but limited in number in the southeast. The local, colonial nature of this species restricted the number of blocks in which the species was recorded.

Population Trend: Breeding Bird Survey data for 1966–2000 show an increase of 3.5 percent per year rangewide (P = 0.04), but show no conclusive trend in Oklahoma (2.7 percent per year, P = 0.28). This species underwent a major range expansion from Texas during the twentieth century. Oklahoma populations increased until the 1980s and leveled off thereafter.

References: AOU 1998; Baicich and Harrison 1997; Baumgartner and Baumgartner 1992; Black 1970; Cook and Krehbiel 1987; Davidson 1969; Davis 1975; Delap 1980; Harden 1972; Howell and Webb 1995; Kaufman 1996; National Geographic Society 1999; Porter 1980; Sauer et al. 2001; Shackford 1981, 1983; Sutton 1967

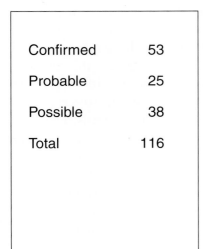

Confirmed	53
Probable	25
Possible	38
Total	116

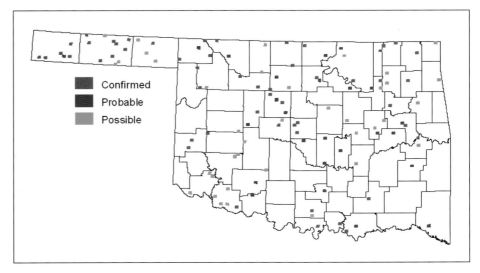

Brown-headed Cowbird
Molothrus ater

Kimberly S. Score

Courtesy of Bill Horn

The Brown-headed Cowbird's exploitative behavior of laying its eggs only in the nests of other birds makes it an unusual species. There are over 220 known host species, the majority being other passerines. A single female cowbird may lay up to 40 eggs per season. Some species, like the Yellow Warbler, have evolved strategies to counter brood parasitism; however, most hosts are victims that rear cowbird chicks at the expense of their own. Cowbirds are a serious threat to host species with small populations, like the Black-capped Vireo.

Description: Males have a handsome, glossy black body with contrasting brown head and neck. Females are drab brown-gray and are slightly smaller than males. The song consists of liquid gurgling notes followed by whistles. The Brown-headed Cowbird can be potentially confused with its icterid cousins, the blackbirds and grackles.

Breeding Habitat: Woodland edges, prairies, pastures, and residential areas are preferred over dense forest or open grassland. Cowbirds have distinct foraging and breeding habitats. As its name suggests, this species is commonly seen in association with cattle. Groups of cowbirds are frequently observed in pastureland near corrals or foraging close to grazing animals. The energetic requirements of commuting between foraging and breeding habitats limit the distance cowbirds travel to parasitize nests. Female cowbirds are known to commute more than 20 km (12 mi) one way, but cowbird abundance on breeding grounds decreases with distance from the preferred prairie/woodland ecotone.

Nest: Cowbirds do not build a nest or care for their own young. A single egg is laid, usually before sunrise, and within 30 seconds of arrival at a host's nest. A female cowbird will often remove or puncture a host's egg prior to laying her own. Eggs may be laid in nests of several host species throughout the season. This brood parasitism strategy is thought to have evolved in response to following wandering herds of bison, which did not allow time to build a nest and rear young in one location.

NESTING ECOLOGY

Season: April–July for egg laying.

Eggs: About 40 per season, laid one per day with occasional pauses. White with brown spotting concentrated at larger end of egg. One or more eggs per host nest. Nonexclusive preference for hosts with eggs smaller than its own.

Development: The incubation period may be 10–12 days, with the eggs often hatching before those of the host species. This strategy allows the larger cowbird chick to out-compete the host's chicks for food. Fledging occurs at 8–13 days.

DISTRIBUTION AND ABUNDANCE

Rangewide: Breeds from southern Northwest Territories south throughout most of Canada and all of the United States south to central Mexico, except southern Florida. Winters broadly across the eastern and southern United States and the Pacific Coast to southern Mexico.

Historical: Considered abundant in northeastern Oklahoma and uncommon in central Oklahoma in 1931. Described as a statewide summer resident, though less common in the Panhandle, in 1967. Considered uncommon to rare in winter, though locally abundant.

Current: As there is no shortage of livestock or fragmented habitat for foraging and breeding requirements, cowbirds are a ubiquitous species throughout Oklahoma. Breeding confirmations result from an observer discovering either a cowbird egg in the nest of another species or more often by witnessing the demands of a cowbird fledgling on the host parents.

Population Trend: Breeding Bird Survey data for 1966–2000 show a decline of 1.0 percent per year rangewide (P = 0.00) and a decline of 2.3 percent per year in Oklahoma (P = 0.00).

References: AOU 1998; Baicich and Harrison 1997; Baumgartner and Baumgartner 1992; Bent 1958; Byre and Kuhnert 1996; Carter 1981, 1992; Curson et al. 2000; Delap 1971; Elliott 1978; Fleischer 1986; Friedmann 1929, 1963, 1966, 1971; Friedmann et al. 1977; Friedmann and Kiff 1985; Goddard 1971; Goguen 1999; Goguen and Mathews 1998, 1999; Grzybowski 1994, 1995b; Grzybowski, Clapp, and Marshall 1986; Hellack 1969; Hill 1976; Johns 1974; Johnson and Temple 1990; Linz and Bolin 1982; Lowther 1977, 1985, 1993; Mayfield 1965; McGee and McGee 1972; Messerly 1998b; Neudorf and Sealy 1994; Newell 1980; Newman 1969, 1970; Nice 1921; Nice and Nice 1924; Norman 1982; Parmley 1978; Payne 1976; Pease and Grzybowski 1995; Purdue 1969; Reinking and Hendricks 1993; Reynolds 1973; Robinson et al. 1995; Rodgers 1973; Sauer et al. 2001; Scott 1991; Shackford 1987; Smith 1981; Sutton 1967; Thomas 1970; Thompson 1994; Wiens 1963; Wolfe 1994a, 1995, 1996a

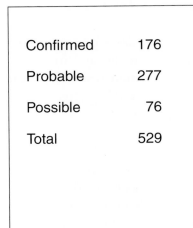

Confirmed	176
Probable	277
Possible	76
Total	529

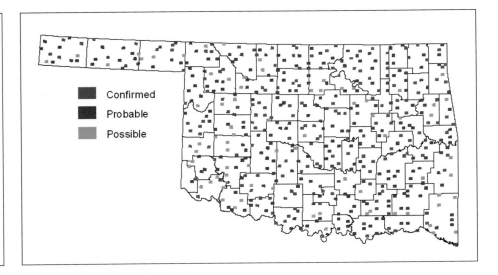

Orchard Oriole

Icterus spurius

Dan L. Reinking

Courtesy of Ike Raley

The smallest oriole in North America, the Orchard Oriole leaves its wintering grounds relatively late in the spring and returns as early as late summer. This makes its time in Oklahoma brief and limits it to raising one brood per season. Significant population declines in Oklahoma warrant further study of this interesting but not well-known species.

Description: Adult male Orchard Orioles are dark chestnut-orange with a black head, back, and upper breast. Immature males (those about one year of age) are olive above and mostly yellow below with a black throat. Females are olive above and yellow below, and can be distinguished from female orioles of other species by smaller size and uniformly yellowish under-parts, without orange tones or white areas. Song is a rapid outburst of whistles, slurred at the end.

Breeding Habitat: Areas with scattered trees, including suburban and rural yards, parks, and roadsides. Orchard Orioles prefer shorter, more dense trees than do Baltimore or Bullock's orioles. They often nest in riparian areas or along lake shores.

Nest: A cup usually attached to a twig fork at the end of a branch, from 2–15 m (6–49 ft) in height. Constructed of grasses and usually lined with fine grasses and vegetable down. Mesquite grass, gamma grass, and fibers from yucca and cacti may also be used in western Oklahoma. Orchard Orioles often nest in the same tree as Eastern Kingbirds and Scissor-tailed Flycatchers, perhaps for the nest protection the aggressive flycatchers provide.

NESTING ECOLOGY

Season: May–July. Single-brooded.

Eggs: 4–6; pale blue with scrawls and spots of blackish or purplish brown concentrated near the large end. Often parasitized by Brown-headed Cowbirds (24 percent of 49 nests in Osage County, 1992–1996).

Development: Incubation is by the female for 12–14 days. Young are provisioned by both sexes and fledge at 11–14 days.

DISTRIBUTION AND ABUNDANCE

Rangewide: Orchard Orioles nest across most of the eastern United States west to the central Great Plains and throughout central Mexico. They winter from southern Mexico south to northwestern Venezuela.

Historical: Described as a common summer resident in most areas of eastern and central Oklahoma, but less common in western Oklahoma and the Panhandle.

Current: The Orchard Oriole shows a statewide distribution, though it is less common in the western half of the main body of the state. Contrary to historical descriptions, it appears now to be fairly common in the Panhandle.

Population Trend: Breeding Bird Survey data for 1966–2000 show no conclusive trend rangewide (-0.6 percent per year, P = 0.45), but show a very large decline of 12.1 percent per year in Oklahoma (P = 0.00).

References: AOU 1998; Baicich and Harrison 1997; Baumgartner and Baumgartner 1992; George M. Sutton Avian Research Center unpubl. data; Johns 1974; Schaefer 1976; Scharf and Kren 1996; Sutton 1967; Tate 1926

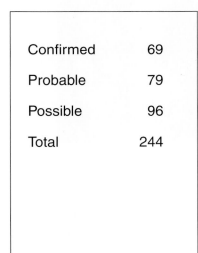

Confirmed	69
Probable	79
Possible	96
Total	244

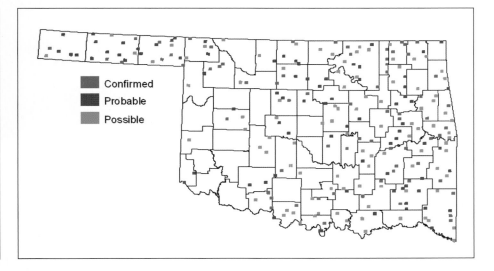

Baltimore Oriole
Icterus galbula

Mia R. Revels

The Baltimore Oriole is an active, colorful, and vociferous member of the breeding bird community in Oklahoma. It is easily observed during summer months in parks, campgrounds, and wooded urban areas. For a time combined with Bullock's Oriole as a single species, the Northern Oriole, the two are once again considered separate species.

Description: Males brightly colored, with black upper back, wings, and head; bright orange underparts; and large orange patches on a black tail. Females are similar, but with brownish-olive above, yellowish-orange below, and varying amounts of black on the head. White bars are conspicuous on the wings; males have one, females two. Both males and females sing their loud, clear song of four to eight whistled notes from high perches. Baltimore Orioles are most likely to be confused with their close relative, Bullock's Oriole. This situation is further complicated because the two species hybridize where their ranges overlap. These hybrids show intermediate characteristics.

Breeding Habitat: These adaptable birds breed in a wide variety of habitats, but prefer riparian areas, woodland edges, and open areas with scattered deciduous trees. They will also nest in parks, orchards, farmland, and wooded urban areas.

Nest: Built by the female, sometimes with material deliveries from the male, and attached by the rim at the end of a drooping branch 2–18 m (6–60 ft) high. The pouch-like suspended nest is woven from long plant fibers, string, hair, and moss and lined with fine grasses, hair, and cottony plant fibers. The nest opening is usually at the top, and there are frequently long fibers and other nest materials hanging free.

NESTING ECOLOGY

Season: May–July. Single-brooded, but may renest if first nest fails.

Eggs: Usually 4–5; pale bluish or grayish white with irregular brown blotches, sometimes unmarked. Infrequent Brown-headed Cowbird host; adult feeding cowbird chick was noted in Johnston County in 1968.

Development: Incubation is by the female for 12–14 days; young are brooded by the female but provisioned by both sexes and fledge at 12–14 days.

Hybridization: With Bullock's Oriole in central to western Oklahoma.

DISTRIBUTION AND ABUNDANCE

Rangewide: Long-distance migrant, breeding range widespread in North America east of the Rocky Mountains, and wintering from southern Mexico south through Central America. Some small populations of Baltimore Orioles winter in the southern United States.

Historical: Records indicate that the Baltimore Oriole was common only in the easternmost portion of Oklahoma prior to settlement of the plains in the early 1900s. Pioneers established settlements and planted trees as they moved across the grasslands, thus providing appropriate nesting habitat and allowing Baltimore Orioles to extend their range westward. Eventually, this westward expansion allowed their range to meet up with that of the primarily western Bullock's Oriole and extensive hybridization between the two species resulted, mostly west of Oklahoma City. Historically considered common in northern and central counties.

Current: Baltimore Orioles are common and widely distributed across the state except for the western portion of the Panhandle. Mirroring the historical impression, they were more often found in northern and central Oklahoma counties. The high number of reports for this species is likely due to the fact that these birds are easily observed and highly vocal, in addition to being fairly common.

Population Trend: Breeding Bird Survey data for 1966–2000 show a decline of 0.5 percent per year rangewide (P = 0.00) and a decline of 5.0 percent per year in Oklahoma (P = 0.00).

References: AOU 1998; Baicich and Harrison 1997; Baumgartner and Baumgartner 1992; Baumgartner and Howell 1948; Bent 1958; Ehrlich et al. 1988; Newman 1969; Nice 1931; Rising and Flood 1998; Sauer et al. 2001; Stokes 1983; Sutton 1938, 1967, 1968

Confirmed	79
Probable	72
Possible	101
Total	252

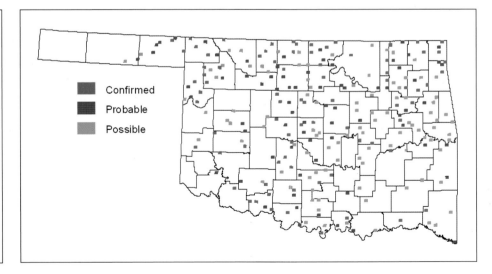

Bullock's Oriole
Icterus bullockii

Alan E. Versaw

Courtesy of Jim and Deva Burns / Natural Impacts

No bird lights up a spring morning quite like a male oriole, and in the Oklahoma Panhandle, that job is done by the Bullock's Oriole. Arriving in late April or early May, and departing by early August, the male Bullock's Oriole compensates for the brevity of his visits with eye-popping color.

Description: Both males and females resemble the closely related and more familiar Baltimore Oriole. Bullock's females tend to wear somewhat lighter colors than their cousins, with the yellow throat generally fading to white by the time it reaches the belly. The male, however, sports a black cap, eye line, and throat emblazoned over a bright orange face, in lieu of the plain, black head of a Baltimore. Male Bullock's replace the narrow white wing bar of the Baltimore with a brilliant white wing patch. The song of the Bullock's Oriole is harsher and less musical than that of the Baltimore Oriole. Together, the Panhandle and western Oklahoma neatly span the zone of hybridization, and intergrades between the two species may be expected west of Oklahoma City.

Breeding Habitat: In Oklahoma, the Bullock's Oriole is a bird of mature riparian corridors, especially those dominated by cottonwoods, as well as residential areas. Poplars rank as a particular favorite of the species when breeding occurs at ranch houses or in cities. Large mature trees are favored by the species and most nesting activity occurs near open water. Habitat preferences consistent with those of the Baltimore Oriole lead to hybridization.

Nest: The pendant nests of the Bullock's Oriole are made of whatever fibers are locally abundant, including string. The female performs most of the construction work, suspending the nest from a narrow branch high in the host tree. Most nests are found at heights of 3–7.5 m (10–25 ft), but may range much higher.

NESTING ECOLOGY

Season: April–July. Single-brooded except in Arizona, but will renest if an early nest is lost.

Eggs: Usually 4–5; pale bluish or grayish with purplish-brown splotches and lines. Reported as an infrequent cowbird host, but actual rate of parasitism may be hidden by tendency of this species to eject cowbird eggs from the nest. A nest with 1 oriole chick, 2 cowbird chicks, and 2 dead oriole chicks below was found in Cimarron County in 1911.

Development: Incubation is by the female for 11–14 days. Young are provisioned by both sexes and fledge at about 14 days.

Hybridization: With Baltimore Oriole in central to western Oklahoma.

DISTRIBUTION AND ABUNDANCE

Rangewide: Breeds from southwestern Canada across most of the western United States east to the western edge of the Great Plains. In winter, individuals return to central Mexico and Guatemala.

Historical: The Bullock's Oriole, as well as the Baltimore Oriole, appears to have benefited from permanent human settlement. Tree plantings in both east and west have enabled the birds to expand their ranges, and thus the zone of hybridization, into previously uninhabitable parts of the state. It is described as a summer resident in western Oklahoma, although Nice suggests its presence in southwestern Oklahoma began between 1902 and 1923.

Current: For the Bullock's Oriole, the "west" extends a bit farther east into Oklahoma than it does for most typically western species. Although the Bullock's Oriole competes with the Baltimore Oriole over much of its Oklahoma range, it occurs with remarkable regularity through the westernmost tier of counties. Atlas data suggest regular breeding activity extending still farther eastward along the Red River Valley, at least as far as Tillman County.

Population Trend: Breeding Bird Survey data for 1966–2000 show a decline of 1 percent per year rangewide (P = 0.01) and a decline of 6.4 percent per year for Oklahoma (P = 0.03).

References: Baicich and Harrison 1997; Baumgartner and Baumgartner 1992; Nice 1931; Rising 1983, 1996; Rising and Williams 1999; Sauer et al. 2001; Sutton 1967; Sutton 1968; Tate 1923

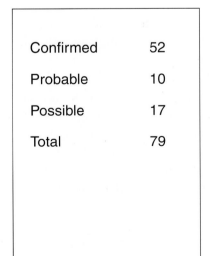

Confirmed	52
Probable	10
Possible	17
Total	79

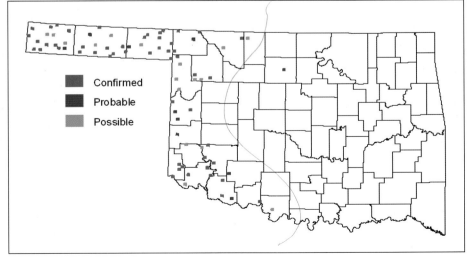

House Finch
Carpodacus mexicanus

Eugene A. Young

Courtesy of M. Frank Carl

The House Finch is originally a western U.S. species once marketed in pet stores as the "Hollywood Finch" because it was common in southern California. It was introduced into Long Island, New York, in 1941 when pet stores, fearing prosecution for selling wild birds, released their inventories. Since that time it has become established across most of the United States, with eastern populations meeting western populations in recent years.

Description: Males are similar to male Purple and Cassin's finches, but are usually smaller in size, duller rosy-red on the head, back, wings, and breast, and have brown-streaked flanks. Females are usually gray brown overall, with streaks on the breast and sides; they usu-

ally lack the prominent eye stripe of female Purple Finches. Occasionally male variants will have yellowish rather than red plumage highlights.

Breeding Habitat: Rangewide, uses arid scrub and brush, oak-juniper, pine-oak, chaparral, open woodlands, savanna, cholla cactus flats, riparian woods, and disturbed areas in urban settings, around buildings in towns, farmyards, houses, and campuses, and cultivated land. Usually nests near human habitation in Oklahoma.

Nest: In trees, especially evergreens, but also on ledges, in hanging baskets or hanging coconut shells, in old nests of other birds, in nest boxes, or occasionally on the ground. Structure is a cup of weeds, grass stems, leaves, rootlets, twigs, string, wool, and feathers, with similar finer material used for the lining; built by the female. Edge of nest develops a buildup of droppings since adults do not remove fecal sacs from about the fifth day on. Occasionally uses same nest for consecutive broods.

NESTING ECOLOGY

Season: April–July. Double- to triple-brooded.
Eggs: Variable but usually 4–5; bluish white, spotted or streaked with black or brown, usually toward the larger end. Infrequently parasitized by cowbirds.
Development: Incubation is by the female for 13–14 days. Young are provisioned with plant material, primarily weed seeds, by both sexes through regurgitation. Young fledge at about 14–16 days.

DISTRIBUTION AND ABUNDANCE

Rangewide: Formerly bred from southwest Canada, south through northern Idaho, north-central and southeastern Wyoming, southwest South Dakota, western Nebraska, west-central Kansas, western Oklahoma, south to Baja California. Now throughout the United States and southern Canada, spreading from introduced birds on Long Island, New York, in the 1940s. Generally nonmigratory, except in some introduced eastern populations.
Historical: Described in 1931 as a common resident in Cimarron County, where it moved into Oklahoma in 1919 with the first nesting records near Kenton in 1922. Expanding populations reached central and northern Oklahoma during the 1980s, although nest-

ing wasn't confirmed in Beaver County of the Oklahoma Panhandle until 1989, followed by nesting in the northwestern main body of the state in 1991 (Harper County), in central Oklahoma in 1992 (Cleveland County), and nesting in northeastern Oklahoma by 1993 (Mayes County, Washington County). Mode of distribution may be from both the east and west in Oklahoma, but these dates suggest an easterly movement from the west, similar to that observed in Kansas.
Current: The House Finch appears to be most concentrated in central and northeastern Oklahoma. This might be a reflection of its preference for being associated with human habitation. The nearly statewide distribution has been accomplished in a little over 70 years since it was first recorded nesting in the Oklahoma Panhandle.

Population Trend: Breeding Bird Survey data for 1966–2000 show no conclusive trend rangewide (1.5 percent per year, P = 0.11) and a huge increase of 42.7 percent per year in Oklahoma (P = 0.01), reflecting the recent and widespread colonization of the state by this species.

References: Aldrich and Weske 1978; AOU 1998; Baicich and Harrison 1997; Baumgartner and Baumgartner 1992; Beavers and Beavers 1989; Byre 1993; Coppedge 1994; Hill 1993; Mery 1991; Nice 1931; Oliphant and Brown 1984; Parmelee 1969; Reinking, D. L. pers. observ.; Robbins and Easterla 1992; Sauer et al. 2001; Sibley 2000; Skutch 1999; Sutton 1967; Tate 1925; Terres 1991; Thompson and Ely 1992; Tveten 1993; Tyler 1992a, 1992b

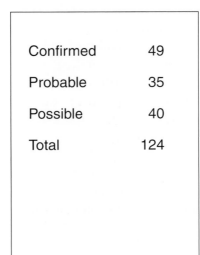

Confirmed	49
Probable	35
Possible	40
Total	124

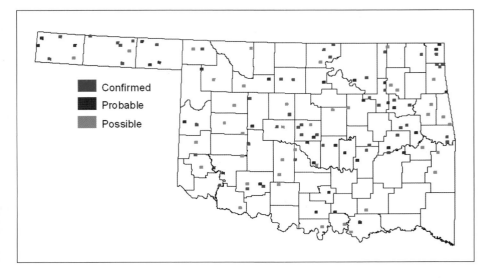

Pine Siskin

Carduelis pinus

Sebastian T. Patti

Courtesy of Bill Horn

A small finch, the Pine Siskin is easily separated from other members of its genus by its streaks and by yellow-edged flight feathers. The species is both opportunistic and adaptable and is well known to people who feed birds, especially during the winter months, because it is readily and easily attracted to feeding stations. Siskin distribution is irruptive in nature, and its opportunistic tendencies have led this species to linger and breed in wintering areas. There are only two reports of nesting for Oklahoma.

Description: Sexes generally similar, although males average more yellow in the flight feathers than females. The same size as the American Goldfinch, with which it often associates, the Pine Siskin's feathers are boldly streaked with dark brown on a brownish background. The tail is short and noticeably notched, and the wings are fairly long and pointed. Adult males show a prominent yellow wing stripe and considerable yellow in the tail feathers, as well. Call is an ascending, raspy *zshreeeeEE,* and the common flight call is an explosive *kleee-up.* Its slender, small bill is well suited to extracting small seeds, and it is adept at hanging upside-down and feeding on cones and small buds.

Breeding Habitat: Prefers open coniferous forests, but has adapted well to the spread of conifers, and now readily breeds in ornamental conifers planted in parks, cemeteries, and towns.

Nest: A flat, shallow saucer made of an outer structure of twigs, grasses, stems, barks, and roots, lined with finer materials such as fur, hair, feathers, or thistle down. Most authors believe that the female alone builds the nest, and the male accompanies the female as she gathers materials.

NESTING ECOLOGY

Season: April–June. Probably single-brooded.

Eggs: 3–4; pale bluish green. The species is occasionally parasitized by the Brown-headed Cowbird, but for most of its history its breeding range did not widely overlap with that of the cowbird.

Development: Incubation is by the female for 13 days. Young are provisioned by both sexes and fledge at 13–17 days. Young remain with parents and are generally dependent on them for up to 3 weeks after fledging.

DISTRIBUTION AND ABUNDANCE

Rangewide: Breeds from Alaska south and east to the Great Lakes and Maine, as well as in large parts of the western United States and Mexico. The species has bred south of this range, particularly following major invasion years or irruption cycles, and has expanded its breeding range during the twentieth century.

Historical: Described as an irregular, uncommon to common migrant and winter resident, and rare in east-ern forested parts of the state. One nest record exists from Cimarron County in 1911, and another nesting report came from Texas County in 1950.

Current: Pine Siskins were not reported during the atlas project period. Given the limited historical nesting of the species in the Panhandle, and more recent records from the Texas Panhandle, southeastern Colorado, and southwestern Kansas, observers should watch for evidence of this species nesting in the Panhandle from April through June.

Population Trend: Breeding Bird Survey data for 1966–2000 show no conclusive trend rangewide (1.1 percent per year, P = 0.68). No trend data are available for Oklahoma. Some authors have suggested that the expansion of silvaculture practices and the proliferation of bird feeding stations can help to explain this species' apparent recent range expansion. Because of the species' irruptive tendencies, however, it may be difficult to distinguish between short-term "irregularities" and true, long-term distributional changes.

References: AOU 1998; Barrett and Levad 1998; Baumgartner and Baumgartner 1992; Bolen 1989; Busby and Zimmerman 2001; Dawson 1997; Jacobs and Wilson 1997; Oberholser 1974; Porter 1984; Robbins and Easterla 1992; Sauer et al. 2001; Sibley 2000; Sutton 1967; Tate 1923; Thompson and Ely 1992

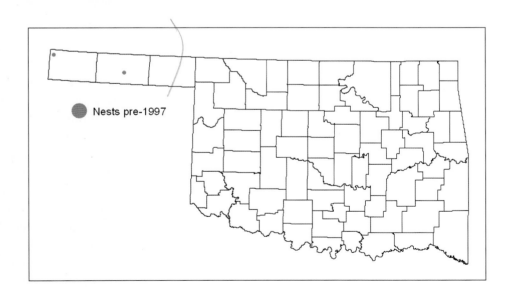

Nests pre-1997

Lesser Goldfinch
Carduelis psaltria

Sebastian T. Patti

A small social goldfinch of the western United States, the Lesser Goldfinch is usually seen in small flocks, often in the company of other finches. As with other members of its genus, the Lesser Goldfinch tends to be nomadic and irruptive. The back coloration of the species varies geographically and clinally. Birds in the western part of the range have greenish backs, those in the east have black backs; the blackest-backed birds are found in the southeastern portion of the bird's range. The species is a talented mimic, and researchers have recorded Lesser Goldfinches mimicking no fewer than 39 bird species, as well as some mammals.

Description: Adult males of the West Coast are green-backed with a black cap; to the east of this zone they are black-backed. Wings are black with a large white patch at the base of the primaries. Underparts are bright lemon yellow. Adult females have uniformly olive-green upperparts and light olive yellow underparts. Wings are similar to those of males, but white patch at base of primaries is much reduced. The common contact call is a distinctive, two-note *tee-yee*. The two notes are separate and unslurred. Female Lesser Goldfinches can be confused with female American Goldfinches; calls are distinctive, and undertail coverts in Lesser Goldfinches are usually yellowish as opposed to white.

Breeding Habitat: The Lesser Goldfinch is a highly adaptable species found in a wide variety of habitats.

Breeding areas include foothill woodlands, riparian woods, and brushy and residential areas. A source of water seems to be important, and cottonwoods and willows seem to be favored tree species.

Nest: A compact structure woven of plant materials and lined with hair, fur, cottonwood fibers, or some similar soft substance. Nest is usually concealed in dense foliage, in leaf clusters. Site selection and nest construction are performed by the female.

NESTING ECOLOGY

Season: June–August. Believed to be single-brooded, but failed first nests may be replaced.

Eggs: 4–5; pale bluish white.

Development: Incubation is by the female for 12–13 days. Young are provisioned by both sexes, are thought to fledge after 11 days, and are probably dependent on their parents for several weeks after fledging, as are young American Goldfinches. Only one record of parasitism by the Brown-headed Cowbird, and not in Oklahoma.

DISTRIBUTION AND ABUNDANCE

Rangewide: Resident from southwestern Washington, western Oregon, northern California, northern Utah and Colorado, northwestern Oklahoma, and central and southern Texas, south through Mexico and much of Central America to northern South America. Irregular breeder north and east of this range.

Historical: Described as a summer resident in Cimarron County in 1931. During the late 1960s and early 1970s, a number of birds occupied parts of Canadian and Caddo counties, and two nests were found at Red Rock Canyon State Park in 1970. By 1992 the species was described as a rare and local summer resident in Cimarron County and parts of southwestern Oklahoma.

Current: Lesser Goldfinches were located in a total of three blocks: in far-western Cimarron County (Confirmed), in Kiowa County (Probable), and in Comanche County (Possible). During the last several years, residents in Kenton (Cimarron County) have erected and filled bird feeders during the spring and the summer. This has attracted a number of finches, including Lesser Goldfinches, to this small town during these seasons. Although Kenton was not located in an atlas block, Kenton may be one of the best places to see this handsome species in Oklahoma.

Population Trend: Breeding Bird Survey data for 1966–2000 show no conclusive trend rangewide (-1.4 percent per year, P = 0.11). No trend data are available for Oklahoma.

References: AOU 1998; Baumgartner and Baumgartner 1992; Busby and Zimmerman 2001; Levad 1998; Newell 1985; Oberholser 1974; Sauer et al. 2001; Sutton 1967; Thompson and Ely 1992; Tyler 1979; Watt and Willoughby 1999

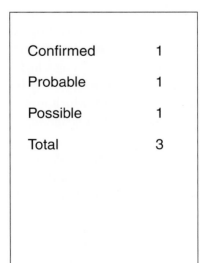

Confirmed	1
Probable	1
Possible	1
Total	3

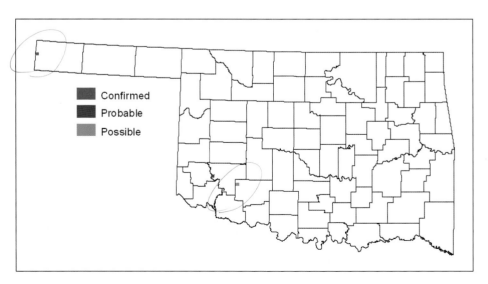

American Goldfinch
Carduelis tristis

Eugene A. Young

Courtesy of Warren Williams

Perhaps one of the best-known backyard birds in North America, the American Goldfinch can gather in flocks of hundreds of individuals at feeding stations during winter and migration. Goldfinches are commonly observed in open country dangling precariously from thistles, which they use for food and nesting, and from which they derive their Latin genus name coming from *carduus,* meaning thistle.

Description: In all plumages, both sexes have white to buffy wing bars and white undertail coverts. Females have brown wings while males have black wings, although males usually have yellow lesser wing coverts that are visible when the birds are perched. Male breeding plumage is characterized by a strikingly bright yellow-gold body, black wings, black forehead and cap, and black tail with white tips. Female, immature male, and winter male plumages are similar, consisting of brownish-gray to light yellow or olive-green upperparts, usually brighter around the head and face. Song a high-pitched repetitive musical phrase. This species may be confused with the Lesser Goldfinch, with which it may occur in the Panhandle and southwestern Oklahoma.

Breeding Habitat: A variety of open areas with trees and shrubs, often near water and associated with farm ponds and open riparian forests, agricultural fields with nearby edge habitat, early successional oldfields, and urban areas.

Nest: Built by the female in about 6 days, it is a tightly woven cup of strips of bark, plant fibers, catkins, plant down, cotton, wool, thistledown filaments, and cater-pillar and spider webbing, and is lined with plant down. It is usually placed in a tree, though occasionally in a forb, around 0.9–3 m (3–10 ft) high, although sometimes higher. Nests are usually placed in a shaded location. Construction is so tightly woven that young can drown from rain if parents are not brooding young.

NESTING ECOLOGY

Season: Late May–September, with most activity in late June–August. Single-brooded to double-brooded, but sometimes triple-brooded.

Eggs: Usually 5; smooth and slightly glossy, pale blue or greenish-blue, usually unmarked. Uncommonly and unsuccessfully parasitized by Brown-headed Cowbirds, due to the goldfinch's late nesting season and granivorous brood-rearing diet.

Development: Incubation is by the female alone for 11–14 days. Young are usually brooded by the female while the male brings all of the food for the first week, after which young are provisioned by both parents and leave the nest at 10–16 days. Once out of the nest, young are generally tended by the male while the female often starts a second brood. Parents feed young entirely on regurgitated seeds.

DISTRIBUTION AND ABUNDANCE

Rangewide: Breeds coast to coast from southern Canada south to northeast California, central Nevada, central Colorado, central Oklahoma, northeast Texas, northern Louisiana, central Alabama, central Georgia, and South Carolina. Winters in the same area, south to Mexico with populations generally shifting southward of their breeding range.

Historical: An uncommon to common summer resident that is less abundant during summer than winter. Uncommon to rare in southwestern Oklahoma in summer.

Current: Many observers finish their blocks prior to the late nesting of the American Goldfinch, which probably accounts for the low proportion of breeding confirmations. Goldfinches were detected less often in heavily wooded and more arid areas of the state.

Population Trend: Breeding Bird Survey data for 1966–2000 show a decline of 0.4 percent per year rangewide (P = 0.09), but show no conclusive trend in Oklahoma (-0.5 percent per year, P = 0.80).

References: AOU 1998; Baicich and Harrison 1997; Baumgartner and Baumgartner 1992; Bay 1996; Holcomb 1969; Middleton 1993; Nickell 1951; Sauer et al. 2001; Sibley 2000; Stokes and Stokes 1979, Sutton 1967; Terres 1991; Thompson and Ely 1992; Tveten 1993

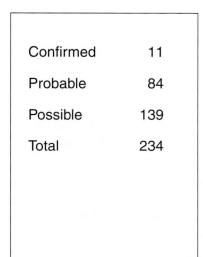

Confirmed	11
Probable	84
Possible	139
Total	234

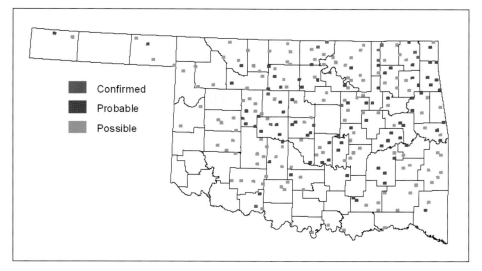

House Sparrow
Passer domesticus

Richard A. Stuart

Courtesy of Bill Horn

The House Sparrow is one of the most successful bird species in the world today. It has gained a poor reputation for being a dirty, noisy, and quarrelsome. It competes with native cavity-nesting species, often with detrimental results to these native competitors.

Description: The males are recognized by a gray crown, chestnut nape, white cheek, and black bib, while the females are known by their streaked back, buffy eye stripe, and unmarked, grayish-brown breast. The song and call notes are often monotonously repeated chips and chirps.

Breeding Habitat: In, near, and around buildings in both rural and urban areas, as well as near bridges or dams. Very often found wherever livestock are housed and fed.

Nest: House Sparrows use cavities, whether natural or man-made, in buildings, barns, sheds, rafters, nest boxes, walls, rock ledges, and dense trees. Nest size depends on the location and how much space is available. Nest is usually a ball, sometimes just a cup if in a birdhouse, of grasses and trash lined with feathers.

NESTING ECOLOGY

Season: March–July, but sometimes earlier or later. Multiple-brooded.

Eggs: 3–6; white or greenish and spotted with gray and brown.

Development: Incubation mostly by female for 10–14 days. Young are provisioned by both sexes and fledge at about 14 days, but continue to be fed by adults for another 7–10 days.

DISTRIBUTION AND ABUNDANCE

Rangewide: A native of Eurasia and North Africa, the House Sparrow has either been introduced or naturally occurs nearly worldwide, except on the Antarctic continent. In North America, about 100 birds were introduced from England to Brooklyn, New York, in 1851 and 1852 and have since expanded throughout the United States and much of Canada.

Historical: This species occupied Oklahoma from east to west beginning after 1886 and reached Kenton in Cimarron County by 1903. By 1930 it was considered an abundant resident statewide.

Current: Still an abundant statewide resident, the House Sparrow's willingness to nest in close association with commercial buildings and residences resulted in the high confirmation rate.

Population Trend: Breeding Bird Survey data for 1966–2000 show a decline of 2.5 percent per year rangewide (P = 0.00) and a similar decline of 2.2 percent per year in Oklahoma (P = 0.00).

References: AOU 1998; Baicich and Harrison 1997; Baumgartner and Baumgartner 1992; Harrison 1975; Lowther 1979; Lowther and Cink 1992; Marti 1973; National Geographic Society 1999; Nice 1931; North 1968; Peterson 1963; Robbins 1973; Sauer et al. 2001; Sibley 2000; Stokes and Stokes 1996; Sutton 1967

Confirmed	401
Probable	29
Possible	42
Total	472

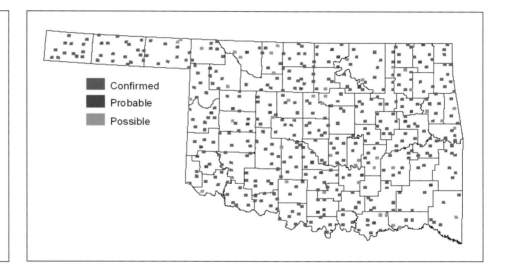

Appendix 1
Notes on Additional Oklahoma Bird Species

The following species include extinct, extirpated, irregular historical (>50 years prior to OBBA), introduced, and potential Oklahoma breeders not treated in the species accounts.

Swallow-tailed Kite (*Elanoides forficatus*). Extirpated. Described (Sutton 1967) as a former summer resident in eastern and central Oklahoma, last recorded in Oklahoma in 1910. More recently, one was seen by multiple observers in a LeFlore County atlas block on 26 April 1998. It is conceivable that this species could once again nest in Oklahoma in the coming years.

Gunnison Sage-Grouse (*Centrocercus minimus*). Extirpated. Sutton (1967) gives records from Woods County in 1902 and Cimarron County as recently as 1911 and 1920 (from Tate 1923).

Sharp-tailed Grouse (*Tympanuchus phasianellus*). Extirpated. Described by Sutton (1967) as a former resident of Cimarron and Texas counties, probably never very common. Described by Tate (1923) as "once numerous, now rare."

Sora (*Porzana carolina*). Potential but unconfirmed breeder. Sutton (1967) remarks on the existence of summer records but the lack of stronger breeding evidence. Two observers reported at least 5 Soras at a playa lake near Hooker, Oklahoma, in Texas County on 15 July 2001, suggesting the possibility of nesting.

Passenger Pigeon (*Ectopistes migratorius*). Extinct. Sutton (1967) reports on a nest record near Shawnee, Oklahoma, in 1881, but states that this species was not known to regularly nest in Oklahoma.

Monk Parakeet (*Myiopsitta monachus*). Introduced through escapes of caged birds. Native to South America. Baumgartner and Baumgartner (1992) report nest records for Norman and Tulsa. Nesting occurred near Altus, Oklahoma, in 2001.

Carolina Parakeet (*Conuropsis carolinensis*). Extinct. Described by Sutton (1967) as a former visitant and possible resident in eastern Oklahoma, but no confirmed evidence of nesting exists.

Lesser Nighthawk (*Chordeiles acutipennis*). Historical (probably accidental) breeder based on a specimen of a preflight juvenile collected in Tulsa County on 15 June 1933 and reported by Dickerman (1986).

Ivory-billed Woodpecker (*Campephilus principalis*). Probably extinct. Sutton (1967) reports that it once nested in bottomland woods of eastern Oklahoma as far north as Nowata County and as far west as Bryan and Atoka counties. A recent credible but undocumented sighting in Louisiana offers slim hope that the species may still exist.

Cave Swallow (*Petrochelidon fulva*). Potential but unconfirmed breeder. Flight-capable juveniles have been reported in Oklahoma in recent years. To be looked for primarily in southern Oklahoma.

Sage Thrasher (*Oreoscoptes montanus*). Historical (probably accidental) breeder. Described by Sutton (1967) as a transient and winter visitant, with one nest record from Cimarron County in 1920 reported by Tate (1923). Fairly common in the Panhandle in winter.

McCown's Longspur (*Calcarius mccownii*) Historical (probably accidental) breeder. Sutton (1967) reports nest records from Cimarron County in 1911 and 1914.

Appendix 2
Oklahoma Breeding Bird Atlas
Project Data Forms

BLOCK VISITATION DATA FORM (use one per atlas block)

NAME: _____   COUNTY: _____

ADDRESS: _____   BLOCK: _____

_____   YEAR: _____

PHONE: _____   Coverage goal: _____

E-MAIL: _____

VISIT	MONTH, DAY, TIMES	Total Party Hours	# of Parties
1 (required)			
2 (required)			
3			
4			
5			
6			
7			
8			
9			
10			
Total Party Hours (10 or more are needed):			

Breeding Codes (for more information see handbook)

Observed column (OB)	Probable column (PR)	Confirmed column (CO)
O Observed	M 7 or more singing males	DD Distraction Display
	P Pair (♂ and ♀)	PE Physiological Evidence
	T Territory Defense	NB Nest Building (all others)
Possible column (PO)	C Courtship	UN Used Nest (caution!)
X Singing male in suitable habitat	V Visiting potential nest site	ON Occupied Nest
	A Agitated behavior	NE Nest with Egg(s)
S Observed (♂ or ♀) in suitable habitat within Safe dates (Record the date on form)	N Nest building by wrens and woodpeckers	NY Nest with Young
		AY Attending Young
		FL Fledglings

Abundance Codes: A= 1-2   B= 3-30   C= >30

Please read instruction handbook before filling out data form.

Return form to: Oklahoma Breeding Bird Atlas
Sutton Avian Research Center
P.O. Box 2007
Bartlesville, OK 74005-2007

NAME_____ BLOCK_____ YEAR_____

Oklahoma Breeding Bird Atlas Project

SPECIES LIST (use a separate list for each atlas block!)

Species	OB	PO	PR	CO	AB
1. Pied-billed Grebe					
2. Eared Grebe*					
3. Anhinga*					
4. Double-crested Cormorant					
5. American Bittern*					
6. Least Bittern*					
7. Black-crowned Night-Heron					
8. Yellow-crowned Night-Heron					
9. Green Heron					
10. Little Blue Heron					
11. Cattle Egret					
12. Snowy Egret					
13. Great Egret					
14. Great Blue Heron					
15. White-faced Ibis*					
16. Canada Goose					
17. Mallard					
18. Northern Pintail*					
19. Northern Shoveler*					
20. Blue-winged Teal					
21. Cinnamon Teal*					
22. Wood Duck					
23. Ruddy Duck*					
24. Redhead*					
25. Hooded Merganser*					
26. King Rail*					
27. Purple Gallinule*					
28. Common Moorhen*					
29. American Coot					
30. Black-necked Stilt*					
31. Snowy Plover*					
32. Killdeer					
33. Mountain Plover*					
34. Long-billed Curlew*					

Species	OB	PO	PR	CO	AB
35. Spotted Sandpiper					
36. American Woodcock					
37. Upland Sandpiper					
38. Least Tern**					
39. Turkey Vulture					
40. Black Vulture					
41. Golden Eagle*					
42. Bald Eagle*					
43. Mississippi Kite					
44. White-tailed Kite*					
45. Northern Harrier					
46. Cooper's Hawk*					
47. Red-shouldered Hawk					
48. Broad-winged Hawk					
49. Red-tailed Hawk					
50. Swainson's Hawk					
51. Ferruginous Hawk					
52. Osprey*					
53. American Kestrel					
54. Prairie Falcon					
55. Greater Prairie-Chicken					
56. Lesser Prairie-Chicken					
57. Northern Bobwhite					
58. Scaled Quail					
59. Ring-necked Pheasant					
60. Wild Turkey					
61. Rock Dove					
62. Mourning Dove					
63. Yellow-billed Cuckoo					
64. Black-billed Cuckoo					
65. Greater Roadrunner					
66. Barn Owl					
67. Short-eared Owl*					
68. Long-eared Owl*					
69. Great Horned Owl					

*= fill out a special interest species (SIS) form late May-July; **= use SIS but do not disturb endangered species

Oklahoma Breeding Bird Atlas Project

Species	OB	PO	PR	CO	AB
70. Barred Owl					
71. Eastern Screech-Owl					
72. Western Screech-Owl*					
73. Burrowing Owl					
74. Chuck-will's-widow					
75. Whip-poor-will					
76. Common Poorwill					
77. Common Nighthawk					
78. Chimney Swift					
79. Ruby-throated Hummingbird					
80. Black-chinned Hummingbird*					
81. Belted Kingfisher					
82. Golden-fronted Woodpecker					
83. Red-bellied Woodpecker					
84. Northern Flicker					
85. Red-headed Woodpecker					
86. Lewis's Woodpecker*					
87. Downy Woodpecker					
88. Hairy Woodpecker					
89. Ladder-backed Woodpecker					
90. Pileated Woodpecker					
91. Eastern Kingbird					
92. Western Kingbird					
93. Cassin's Kingbird					
94. Scissor-tailed Flycatcher					
95. Great Crested Flycatcher					
96. Ash-throated Flycatcher					
97. Eastern Wood-Pewee					
98. Eastern Phoebe					
99. Say's Phoebe*					
100. Vermillion Flycatcher*					
101. Acadian Flycatcher					
102. Willow Flycatcher					
103. Horned Lark					
104. Tree Swallow*					

Species	OB	PO	PR	CO	AB
105. Purple Martin					
106. Bank Swallow					
107. N. Rough-winged Swallow					
108. Cliff Swallow					
109. Barn Swallow					
110. Western Scrub-Jay					
111. Pinyon Jay*					
112. Blue Jay					
113. Black-billed Magpie					
114. American Crow					
115. Fish Crow					
116. Chihuahuan Raven					
117. Common Raven					
118. Tufted Titmouse					
119. Juniper Titmouse					
120. Carolina Chickadee					
121. Verdin*					
122. Bushtit					
123. White-breasted Nuthatch					
124. Brown-headed Nuthatch					
125. House Wren					
126. Carolina Wren					
127. Bewick's Wren					
128. Sedge Wren*					
129. Canyon Wren					
130. Rock Wren					
131. Blue-gray Gnatcatcher					
132. Eastern Bluebird					
133. Mountain Bluebird					
134. Wood Thrush					
135. American Robin					
136. Loggerhead Shrike					
137. Gray Catbird					
138. Northern Mockingbird					
139. Brown Thrasher					

*= fill out a special interest species (SIS) form late May-July; **= use SIS but do not disturb endangered species

Oklahoma Breeding Bird Atlas Project

Species	OB	PO	PR	CO	AB
140. Curve-billed Thrasher					
141. Cedar Waxwing*					
142. European Starling					
143. Black-capped Vireo**					
144. White-eyed Vireo					
145. Yellow-throated Vireo					
146. Bell's Vireo					
147. Red-eyed Vireo					
148. Warbling Vireo					
149. Prothonotary Warbler					
150. Northern Parula					
151. Black-and-white Warbler					
152. Cerulean Warbler*					
153. Yellow-throated Warbler					
154. Prairie Warbler					
155. Pine Warbler					
156. Yellow Warbler					
157. Kentucky Warbler					
158. Hooded Warbler					
159. Worm-eating Warbler					
160. Swainson's Warbler*					
161. Ovenbird					
162. Louisiana Waterthrush					
163. Common Yellowthroat					
164. Yellow-breasted Chat					
165. American Redstart					
166. Rose-breasted Grosbeak*					
167. Northern Cardinal					
168. Blue Grosbeak					
169. Indigo Bunting					
170. Lazuli Bunting					
171. Painted Bunting					
172. Eastern Towhee*					

Species	OB	PO	PR	CO	AB
173. Canyon Towhee					
174. Grasshopper Sparrow					
175. Henslow's Sparrow*					
176. Lark Sparrow					
177. Bachman's Sparrow*					
178. Cassin's Sparrow					
179. Rufous-crowned Sparrow					
180. Field Sparrow					
181. Chipping Sparrow					
182. Dickcissel					
183. Lark Bunting					
184. Eastern Meadowlark					
185. Western Meadowlark					
186. Yellow-headed Blackbird*					
187. Red-winged Blackbird					
188. Brown-headed Cowbird					
189. Common Grackle					
190. Great-tailed Grackle					
191. Orchard Oriole					
192. Baltimore Oriole					
193. Bullock's Oriole					
194. Scarlet Tanager					
195. Summer Tanager					
196. House Sparrow					
197. American Goldfinch					
198. Lesser Goldfinch*					
199. House Finch					
TOTAL IN EACH CATEGORY:					

Return form to: Breeding Bird Atlas, Sutton Avian Research Center, P.O. Box 2007, Bartlesville, OK 74005-2007 (918) 336-7778

*= fill out a special interest species (SIS) form late May-July; **= use SIS but do not disturb endangered species

Colonial Nesting Birds Data Form
Oklahoma Breeding Bird Atlas Project
(Use one form per colony. Colonies need not be in an atlas block.)

Species _____	Number of birds _____	Number of nests _____	**Circle:** Eggs or chicks seen? None
Species _____	Number of birds _____	Number of nests _____	**Circle:** Eggs or chicks seen? None
Species _____	Number of birds _____	Number of nests _____	**Circle:** Eggs or chicks seen? None
Species _____	Number of birds _____	Number of nests _____	**Circle:** Eggs or chicks seen? None
Species _____	Number of birds _____	Number of nests _____	**Circle:** Eggs or chicks seen? None
Species _____	Number of birds _____	Number of nests _____	**Circle:** Eggs or chicks seen? None

County _____ Date(s) observed _____ Year _____

Specific Location (include miles and direction from nearest town) _____ Atlas block if in _____

Do you know any details of the history of this colony? _____

Do you know who owns the land? _____

Comments _____

_____ Observer & address

Return to: Breeding Bird Atlas, Sutton Avian Research Center, P.O. Box 2007, Bartlesville, OK 74005-2007

Special Interest Species
Oklahoma Breeding Bird Atlas Project

The Oklahoma Breeding Bird Atlas Project is a volunteer effort to document the breeding distribution of Oklahoma's nesting birds. Coverage of about 600 randomly selected blocks of land throughout Oklahoma forms the core of the project, but there are selected species for which we desire information regardless of their location in the state. If you see any of the following species between the last week of May and the end of July, *or* if you find evidence of any of these species nesting at other times, please fill out and return a Special Interest Species form. For more information contact: Breeding Bird Atlas, Sutton Avian Research Center, P.O. Box 2007, Bartlesville, OK 74005-2007. Phone (918) 336-7778. E-mail GMSARC@AOL.COM

Eared Grebe
Anhinga
American Bittern
Least Bittern
White-faced Ibis
Northern Pintail
Northern Shoveler
Cinnamon Teal
Ruddy Duck
Redhead
Hooded Merganser
King Rail
Purple Gallinule
Common Moorhen
Black-necked Stilt
Snowy Plover
Mountain Plover
Long-billed Curlew
Least Tern
Golden Eagle
Bald Eagle
White-tailed Kite
Cooper's Hawk
Osprey

Short-eared Owl
Long-eared Owl
Western Screech-Owl
Black-chinned Hummingbird
Lewis's Woodpecker
Say's Phoebe
Vermillion Flycatcher
Tree Swallow
Pinyon Jay
Verdin
Sedge Wren
Cedar Waxwing
Black-capped Vireo
Cerulean Warbler
Swainson's Warbler
Rose-breasted Grosbeak
Eastern Towhee
Black-throated Sparrow
Henslow's Sparrow
Bachman's Sparrow
Yellow-headed Blackbird
Lesser Goldfinch
and any other notably rare nesting species in Oklahoma

SPECIAL INTEREST SPECIES OBSERVATION FORM

(For <u>any</u> nesting <u>or</u> late May through July sightings of special interest species)

SPECIES_____ NAME_____

COUNTY_____ ADDRESS_____

SPECIFIC LOCATION_____ _____

_____ ATLAS BLOCK (if in)_____

_____ DATE_____YEAR_____

_____ NUMBER OBSERVED_____

Please provide as much of the following information as you can for this sighting:

Description (include details of <u>voice</u>, <u>size</u>, <u>shape</u>, <u>plumage</u>, etc., and compare to similar species): You may use the back of this form if you need more space.

Habitat (general):

Habitat (specific):

Behavior (and/or nest) (include any evidence of breeding):

Return form to: Oklahoma Breeding Bird Atlas
Sutton Avian Research Center
P.O. Box 2007
Bartlesville, OK 74005-2007

Oklahoma Breeding Bird Atlas Project
Block Upgrade Form

NAME: _____   COUNTY: _____

ADDRESS: _____   BLOCK: _____

_____   YEAR: _____

PHONE: _____   Total additional hours: _____

E-MAIL: _____

Use this form for any additions or upgrades to blocks you have worked on in previous years, including the following items:
1) adding a new species to a block
2) upgrading breeding **status*** for a species (going from **PO**ssible to **PR**obable, for example)
3) changing to a higher **code**** within a breeding status category (such as going from DD to FL in the **CO**nfirmed category, for example)
4) upgrading the amount of time spent atlasing in a block (even if you don't find anything new)

VISIT	MONTH, DAY, TIMES	PARTY HOURS	# PARTIES
extra 1			
extra 2			
extra 3			
extra 4			

SPECIES and DATE	NEW BREEDING *STATUS	NEW EVIDENCE **CODE

Return to: Breeding Bird Atlas, Sutton Avian Research Center, P.O. Box 2007, Bartlesville, OK 74005-2007

Bibliography

Adamcik, R. S., and L. B. Keith. 1978. Regional movements and mortality of Great Horned Owls in relation to snowshoe hare fluctuations. Can. Field-Nat. 92:228–234.

Adams, R. J., Jr., and R. Brewer. 1981. Autumn selection of breeding location by Field Sparrows. Auk 98:629–631.

Alberts, P. H. 1978. Habitat selection by breeding Red-winged Blackbirds. Wilson Bull. 90(4):619–634.

Aldrich, J. W. 1963. Geographic orientation of American *Tetraonidae.* J. Wildl. Manage. 27:529–545.

Aldrich, J. W., and A. J. Duvall. 1955. Distribution of American gallinaceous game birds. USFWS Circ. 34:1–23.

Allen, P. E. 1950. Road-runner in eastern Oklahoma. Condor 52:43.

Allen, T. T. 1961. Notes on the breeding behavior of the Anhinga. Wilson Bull. 73:115–125.

Allison, P. S., A. W. Leary, and M. J. Bechard. 1995. Observations of wintering Ferruginous Hawks (*Buteo regalis*) feeding on prairie dogs (*Cynomys ludovicianus*) in the Texas Panhandle. Tex. J. Sci. 47(3):235–237.

American Ornithologists' Union. 1998. The AOU Check-list of North American Birds. 7th ed. American Ornithologists' Union, Washington, D.C.

Anderson, S. H., and J. R. Squires. 1997. The Prairie Falcon. University of Texas Press, Austin.

Andrews, A., and R. Righter. 1992. Colorado Birds: A Reference to Their Distribution and Habitat. Denver Museum of Natural History, Denver, Colorado.

Angell, T. 1978. Ravens, Crows, Magpies, and Jays. University of Washington Press, Seattle.

Applegate, R. D., B. E. Flock, and S. Gough. 2001. Status of the Greater Prairie-Chicken in 2001. Grouse Partnership News 2:10.

Archibeque, A. M. 1987. Interior Least Terns nest on Sequoyah National Wildlife Refuge. U.S. Fish and Wildlife Service, Vian, Oklahoma.

Ault, J. W., III. 1977. American Coot breeding in Jackson County, Oklahoma. Bull. Okla. Ornithol. Soc. 10:23.

Ault, J. W., III. 1978. Early spring sighting of Common Nighthawk in Oklahoma. Bull Okla. Ornithol. Soc. 11(1):7.

Ault, J. W., III. 1982. A quantitative estimate of Barn Owl nesting habitat quality. M.S. thesis, Oklahoma State University, Stillwater.

Ault, J. W., III. 1984. The Curve-billed Thrasher in southwestern Oklahoma. Bull. Okla. Ornithol. Soc. 17:12–14.

Austin, J. E., and M. R. Miller. 1995. Northern Pintail (*Anas acuta*). *In* The Birds of North America, No. 163 (A. Poole and F. Gill, eds.). Academy of Natural Sciences, Philadelphia, and American Ornithologists' Union, Washington, D.C.

Baicich, P. J., and C. J. O. Harrison. 1997. A Guide to the Nests, Eggs, and Nestlings of North American Birds. Academic Press, San Diego, California.

Bailey, F. M. 1921. Handbook of Birds of the Western United States. Houghton Mifflin Co., New York.

Baker, B. K. 1998. Western Wood-Pewee. *In* Colorado Breeding Bird Atlas (H. E. Kingery, ed.). Colorado Bird Atlas Partnership and Colorado Division of Wildlife, Denver.

Baker, B. W. 1944. Nesting of the American Redstart. Wilson Bull. 56:83–90.

Baker, M. C., and J. T. Boylan. 1999. Singing behavior, mating associations and reproductive success in a population of hybridizing Lazuli and Indigo buntings. Condor 101(3):493–504.

Baker, M. F. 1953. Prairie-chickens of Kansas. Univ. Kans. Pub. No. 5:1–68.

Balgooyen, T. G. 1976. Behavior and ecology of the American Kestrel (*Falco sparverius L.*) in the Sierra Nevada of California. Univ. Calif. Publ. Zool. 103:1–88.

Baltosser, W. H., and S. M. Russell. 2000. Black-chinned Hummingbird (*Archilocus alexandri*). *In* The birds of North America, No. 495 (A. Poole and F. Gill, eds.). Academy of Natural Sciences, Philadelphia, and American Ornithologists' Union, Washington, D.C.

Banta, J. K. 1985. Early date for Rufous-crowned Sparrow nest in Oklahoma. Bull. Okla. Ornithol. Soc. 18:15–16.

Barclay, J. S., and R. W. Smith. 1977. The status and distribution of woodcock in Oklahoma. Pp. 39–50 *in* Proc. Sixth Woodcock Symp. (D. M. Keppie and R. B. Owen Jr., eds.). New Brunswick Dept. Nat. Resour., Fredericton.

Barlow, J. C. 1964. Natural history of the Bell's Vireo, *Vireo bellii* Audubon. Univ. Kans. Publ. 12:241–296.

Barrett, N. M., and R. Levad. 1998. Pine Siskin (*Carduelis pinus*). *In* Colorado Breeding Bird Atlas (H. E. Kingery, ed.). Colorado Bird Atlas Partnership and Colorado Division of Wildlife, Denver.

Baskett, T. S. 1940. The distribution of meadowlarks in Oklahoma. Proc. Okla. Acad. Sci. 20:27–31.

Batcheller, G. R. 1980. The ecology and behavior of Blue Jays in Oklahoma pecan orchards. M.S. thesis. Oklahoma State University, Stillwater.

Batcheller, G. R., J. A. Bissonette, and M. W. Smith. 1984. Towards reducing pecan losses to Blue Jays in Oklahoma. Wildl. Soc. Bull. 12:51–55.

Baumgartner, A. M. 1983. First nest of Red-breasted Nuthatch in Oklahoma. Bull. Okla. Ornithol. Soc. 16:12–13.

Baumgartner, A. M. 1989. Composition of Ruby-throated Hummingbird populations in northeast Oklahoma. Bull. Okla. Ornithol. Soc. 22(1):3–5.

Baumgartner, A. M., and F. M. Baumgartner. 1941. Rare water and shorebirds in north-central Oklahoma. Auk 58:576–578.

Baumgartner, F. M. 1938. Courtship and nesting of the Great Horned Owls. Wilson Bull. 50:274–285.

Baumgartner, F. M. 1939. Territory and population of the Great Horned Owl. Auk 56:274–282.

Baumgartner, F. M. 1979a. Additional summer records for the Rufous-sided Towhee in Oklahoma. Bull. Okla. Ornithol. Soc. 23:6–7.

Baumgartner, F. M. 1979b. Breeding of the Rufous-sided Towhee in Oklahoma. Bull. Okla. Ornithol. Soc. 12:9–11.

Baumgartner, F. M. 1988. A Blue-winged Warbler nest in Delaware County, Oklahoma. Bull. Okla. Ornithol. Soc. 21:15–16.

Baumgartner, F. M. 1992. Comparative ecology of warblers summering in the Oklahoma Ozarks. Bull. Okla. Ornithol. Soc. 25:9–15.

Baumgartner, F. M., and A. M. Baumgartner. 1944. Hawks and owls in Oklahoma 1939–1942: Food habits and population changes. Wilson Bull. 56:209–215.

Baumgartner, F. M., and A. M. Baumgartner. 1992. Oklahoma Bird Life. University of Oklahoma Press, Norman.

Baumgartner, F. M., and J. C. Howell. 1942. Notes on the numerical status and migration of the birds of the Lake Carl Blackwell project in north-central Oklahoma. Proc. Okla. Acad. Sci. 22:53–64.

Baumgartner, F. M., and J. C. Howell. 1948. The numerical and seasonal statuses of the birds of Payne County, Oklahoma. Proc. Okla. Acad. Sci. 27:45–59.

Baumgartner, F. M., and R. G. Lawrence. 1953. Breeding bird populations in Payne County, Oklahoma. Proc. Okla. Acad. Sci. 34:93–102.

Bay, M. D. 1996. Breeding birds in early successional oldfields: The effect of area on community structure. Proc. Okla. Acad. Sci. 76:67–73.

Bay, M. D. 1999. A review of the behavior and ecology of the Northern Parula (*Parula americana*) with notes from Oklahoma and Texas. Proc. Okla. Acad. Sci. 79:33–40.

Beal, K. G. 1978a. Immature Cooper's Hawk attempts to capture Roadrunner. Bull. Okla. Ornithol. Soc. 11:31.

Beal, K. G. 1978b. Year-round weather-dependent behavior of the Roadrunner (*Geococcyx californianus*). Ph.D. diss., Ohio State University, Columbus.

Beal, K. G. 1981. Winter foraging habits of the Roadrunner. Bull. Okla. Ornithol. Soc. 14:13–15.

Beason, R. C. 1995. Horned Lark (*Eremophila alpestris*). *In* The Birds of North America, No. 195 (A. Poole and F. Gill, eds.). Academy of Natural Sciences, Philadelphia, and American Ornithologists' Union, Washington, D.C.

Beason, R. C., and E. C. Franks. 1974. Breeding behavior of the Horned Lark. Auk 91(1):65–74.

Beavers, L., and E. Beavers. 1989. New House Finch records for western Oklahoma. Bull. Okla. Ornithol. Soc. 22:30–31.

Bechard, M. J., R. L. Knight, D. G. Smith, and R. E. Fitzner. 1990. Nest sites and habitats of sympatric hawks (*Buteo* spp.) in Washington. J. Field Ornithol. 61(2):159–170.

Bechard, M. J., and J. K. Schmutz. 1995. Ferruginous Hawk (*Buteo regalis*). *In* The Birds of North America, No. 172 (A. Poole and F. Gill, eds.). Academy of Natural Sciences, Philadelphia, and American Ornithologists' Union, Washington, D.C.

Bednarz, J. C. 1988. A comparative study of the breeding ecology of Harris and Swainson's Hawks in southeastern New Mexico. Condor 90(2):311–323.

Bednarz, J. C., D. Klem Jr., L. J. Goodrich, and S. E. Senner. 1990. Migration counts of raptors at Hawk Mountain, Pennsylvania, as indicators of population trends, 1934–1986. Auk 107:96–109.

Bellrose, F. C. 1976. Ducks, Geese, and Swans of North America. Stackpole Books, Harrisburg, Pennsylvania.

Bellrose, F. C. 1980. Ducks, Geese, and Swans of North America. 3rd edition. Stackpole Books, Harrisburg, Pennsylvania.

Bemis, C., and J. D. Rising. 1999. Western Wood-Pewee (*Contopus sordidulus*). *In* The Birds of North America, No. 451 (A. Poole and F. Gill, eds.). Academy of Natural Sciences, Philadelphia, and American Ornithologists' Union, Washington, D.C.

Benson, K. L. P., and K. A. Arnold. 2001. The Texas Breeding Bird Atlas. Texas A&M University System, College Station and Corpus Christi, TX. http://tbba.cbi.tamucc.edu (12 April 2002).

Bent, A. C. 1923. Life histories of North American Wild Fowl. Pt. 1. U.S. Natl. Mus. Bull. 126. Washington, D.C.

Bent, A. C. 1926. Life histories of North American marsh birds. U.S. Natl. Mus. Bull. 135, Washington, D.C.

Bent, A. C. 1927. Wilson's Phalarope. *In* Life Histories of North American Shore Birds. Pt. 1. Smithsonian Institution U.S. Natl. Mus. Bull. 142, United States Printing Office. Reprinted by Dover Publications, New York, 1962, pp. 28–37.

Bent, A. C. 1939. Life histories of North American wood-peckers. U.S. Natl. Mus. Bull. 174.

Bent, A. C. 1940. Life histories of North American cuckoos, goatsuckers, hummingbirds, and their allies. U.S. Natl. Mus. Bull. 176.

Bent, A. C. 1948. Life histories of North American nuthatches, wrens, thrashers, and their allies. U.S. Natl. Mus. Bull. 195, Washington, D.C.

Bent, A. C. 1950. Life histories of North American wagtails, shrikes, vireos, and their allies. U.S. Natl. Mus. Bull. 197.

Bent, A. C. 1953. Life histories of North American wood warblers. U.S. Natl. Mus. Bull. 203.

Bent, A. C. 1958. Life histories of North American blackbirds, orioles, tanagers, and their allies. U.S. Natl. Mus. Bull. 211.

Bent, A. C. 1961. Life Histories of North American Birds of Prey. Pt. 1 and 2. Dover Publications, New York.

Bent, A. C. 1962a. Life Histories of North American Shore Birds. Pt. 1 and 2. Dover Publications, New York.

Bent, A. C. 1962b. Life Histories of North American Wild Fowl. Pt. 2. Dover Publications, New York.

Bent, A. C. 1963a. Life Histories of North American diving birds. Dover Publications, New York.

Bent, A. C. 1963b. Life Histories of North American Flycatchers, Larks, Swallows, and Their Allies. Dover Publications, New York.

Bent, A. C. 1963c. Life Histories of North American Marsh Birds. Dover Publications, New York.

Bent, A. C. 1963d. Life Histories of North American Wood Warblers. Dover Publications, New York.

Bent, A. C. 1964a. Life Histories of North American Cuckoos, Goatsuckers, Hummingbirds and Their Allies. Pt. 1. Dover Publications, New York.

Bent, A. C. 1964b. Life Histories of North American Nuthatches, Wrens, Thrashers, and Their Allies. Dover Publications, New York.

Bent, A. C. 1964c. Life Histories of North American Petrels and Pelicans and Their Allies. Dover Publications, New York.

Bent, A. C. 1964d. Life Histories of North American Woodpeckers. Dover Publications, New York.

Bent, A. C. 1965a. Life Histories of North American Blackbirds, Orioles, Tanagers, and Their Allies. Dover Publications, New York.

Bent, A. C. 1965b. Life Histories of North American Wagtails, Shrikes, Vireos, and Their Allies. Dover Publications, New York.

Bent, A. C. 1968. Life Histories of North American Cardinals, Grosbeaks, Buntings, Towhees, Finches, Sparrows, and Their Allies. Dover Publications, New York.

Bergey, P. 1976. Dickcissel in winter in central Oklahoma. Bull. Okla. Ornithol. Soc. 9(4):34–35.

Berry, G. A. 1971. The nesting biology of the Dickcissel (Spiza americana) in north central Oklahoma. M.S. thesis. Oklahoma State University, Stillwater.

Berry, M. E., and C. E. Bock. 1998. Effects of habitat and landscape characteristics on avian breeding distribution in Colorado foothills shrub. Southwestern Naturalist 43(4):453–461.

Best, L. B. 1977a. Nestling biology of the Field Sparrow. Auk 94:308–319.

Best, L. B. 1977b. Territory quality and mating success in the Field Sparrow (Spizella pusilla). Condor 79:192–204.

Best, L. B. 1978. Field Sparrow reproductive success and nesting ecology. Auk 95:9–22.

Best, L. B. 1979. Effects of fire on a Field Sparrow population. Am. Midl. Nat. 101:434–442.

Bidwell, T. G., ed. 2002. Ecology and management of the Lesser Prairie-Chicken. OSU Ext. Circular E-970. Oklahoma Coop. Ext. Serv., Stillwater, Oklahoma.

Bidwell, T. G., ed. 2003. Ecology and Management of the Greater Prairie-Chicken. OSU Ext. Circular E-969. Okla. Coop. Ext. Serv. Stillwater, Oklahoma.

Bidwell, T. G., and A. D. Peoples. 1991. Habitat management for Oklahoma's prairie-chickens. OSU Extension Facts, No. 9004. 4pp.

Bidwell, T. G., C. B. Green, A. D. Peoples, and R. E. Masters. 1995. Prairie-Chicken Management in Oklahoma. OSU Ext. Circular E–945.

Birkhead, T. R. 1991. The Magpies: The Ecology and Behavior of Black-billed and Yellow-billed Magpies. Academic Press, London.

Black, E. A. 1979. American Kestrel possibly two-brooded in central Oklahoma. Bull. Okla. Ornithol. Soc. 12(4):29–30.

Black, J.H. 1970. Boat-tailed Grackles feeding spadefoot tadpoles to nestlings. Bull. Okla. Ornithol. Soc. 3(4):33–34.

Black, J. H. 1976. The lined snake as food for birds. Bull. Okla. Ornithol. Soc. 9(3):17–18.

Black, J. H. 1985. The lined snake as food for the Great Horned Owl. Bull. Okla. Ornithol. Soc. 18(2):14–15.

Blaha, R. J., P. Hendricks, M. R. Nelson, and M. D. Stewart. 1995. A Short-eared Owl nest in Osage County, Oklahoma. Bull. Okla. Ornithol. Soc. 28(3):26–28.

Blair, C. L., and F. Schitoskey Jr. 1982. Breeding biology and diet of the Ferruginous Hawk in South Dakota. Wilson Bull. 94(1):46–54.

Blair, W. F., and T. H. Hubbell. 1938. The biotic districts of Oklahoma. Am. Midl. Nat. 20:425–454.

Blem, C. R., and L. B. Blem. 1991. Nest box selection by Prothonotary Warblers. J. Field Ornithol. 6:299–307.

Blem, C. R., and L. B. Blem. 1992. Prothonotary Warblers nesting in nest boxes: Clutch size and timing in Virginia. Raven 63:15–20.

Boarman, W. I., and B. Heinrich. 1999. Common Raven (Corvus corax). In The Birds of North America, No. 476

(A. Poole and F. Gill, eds.). Academy of Natural Sciences, Philadelphia, and American Ornithologists' Union, Washington, D.C.

Bock, C. E., and L. W. Lepthien. 1975. Distribution and abundance of the Black-billed Magpie (*Pica pica*) in North America. Great Basin Nat. 35:269–272.

Bock, C. E., and L. W. Lepthien. 1976. Changing winter distribution and abundance of the Blue Jay, 1962–1971. Am. Midl. Nat. 96:232–236.

Bolen, E. G. 1979. Blue-winged x Cinnamon Teal hybrid from Oklahoma. Wilson Bull. 91:367–370.

Bolen, E. G., and D. L. Flores. 1993. The Mississippi Kite. University of Texas Press, Austin.

Bolen, H. D. 1989. The Birds of Illinois. Indiana University Press, Bloomington.

Boone, G. C. 1963. Ecology of the Red-bellied Woodpecker in Kansas. Master's thesis, University of Kansas, Manhattan.

Bowen, B. S., and A. D. Kruse. 1993. Effects of grazing on nesting by Upland Sandpipers in southcentral North Dakota. J. Wildl. Manage. 57(2):291–301.

Boyd, C. S., and T. G. Bidwell. 2001. Influence of prescribed fire on Lesser Prairie-Chicken habitat in shinnery oak communities in western Oklahoma. Wildl. Soc. Bull. 29:938–947.

Boyd, R. L. 1972. Breeding biology of the Snowy Plover at Cheyenne Bottoms Waterfowl Management Area, Barton County, Kansas. M.S. thesis, Emporia State University, Emporia, Kansas.

Boyd, R. L. 1991. First nesting record for the Piping Plover in Oklahoma. Wilson Bull. 103:305–308.

Boyle, S. 1998. Black-chinned Hummingbird (*Archilochus alexandri*). *In* Colorado Breeding Bird Atlas (H. E. Kingery, ed.). Colorado Bird Atlas Partnership and the Colorado Division of Wildlife, Denver.

Brackbill, H. 1970a. New light on the Mourning Dove. Maryland Birdlife (spring): 8–11.

Brackbill, H. 1970b. Tufted Titmouse breeding behavior. Auk 87:522–536.

Bradley, R. A. 1980. Vocal and territorial behavior in the White-eyed Vireo. Wilson Bull. 92:302–311.

Brandt, J. H. 1959. Unusual nesting observations in Colorado. Condor 61(1):56–57.

Bray, O. E., W. C. Royal Jr., J. L. Guarino, and J. W. DeGrazio. 1973. Migration and seasonal distribution of Common Grackles banded in North and South Dakota. J. Field Ornithol. 44(1):1–12.

Brennan, L. A. 1999. Northern Bobwhite (*Colinus virginianus*). *In* The Birds of North America, No. 397 (A. Poole and F. Gill, eds.). Academy of Natural Sciences, Philadelphia, and American Ornithologists' Union, Washington, D.C.

Brewer, R. 1961. Comparative notes on the life history of the Carolina Chickadee. Wilson Bull. 73(4):348–373.

Brewer, R., G. A. McPeek, and R. J. Adams. 1991. The Atlas of Breeding Birds of Michigan. Michigan State University Press, East Lansing.

Brewer, W. M., and W. D. Harden. 1975. American Kestrel banded in Oklahoma and recovered in Nebraska. Bull. Okla. Ornithol. Soc. 8(1):3–4.

Brigham, R. M. 1989. Roost and nest sites of Common Nighthawks: Are gravel roofs important? Condor 91(3):722–724.

Brown, B. T. 1993. Bell's Vireo (*Vireo bellii*). *In* The Birds of North America, No. 35 (A. Poole, P. Stettenheim, and F. Gill, eds.). Academy of Natural Sciences, Philadelphia, and American Ornithologists' Union, Washington, D.C.

Brown, B. T. 1994. Rates of brood parasitism by Brown-headed Cowbirds on riparian passerines in Arizona. J. Field Ornithol. 65:160–168.

Brown, C. R. 1986. Cliff Swallow colonies as information centers. Science 234:83–85.

Brown, C. R. 1997. Purple Martin (*Progne subis*). *In* The Birds of North America, No. 287 (A. Poole and F. Gill, eds.). Academy of Natural Sciences, Philadelphia, and American Ornithologists' Union, Washington, D.C.

Brown, C. R., and M. B. Brown. 1995. Cliff Swallow (*Hirundo pyrrhonota*). *In* The Birds of North America, No. 149 (A. Poole and F. Gill, eds.). Academy of Natural Sciences, Philadelphia, and American Ornithologists' Union, Washington, D.C.

Brown, C. R., and M. B. Brown. 1996. Coloniality in the Cliff Swallow: The Effect of Group Size on Social Behavior. University of Chicago Press, Chicago.

Brown, C. R., and M. B. Brown. 1998. Late record of the Purple Martin for Oklahoma. Bull. Okla. Ornithol. Soc. 31:33–34.

Brown, C. R., and M. B. Brown. 1999. Barn Swallow (*Hirundo rustica*). *In* The Birds of North–America, No. 452 (A. Poole and F. Gill, eds.). Academy of Natural Sciences, Philadelphia, and American Ornithologists' Union, Washington, D.C.

Brown, C. R., and S. D. Wolfe III. 1978. Post-breeding movements of Purple Martins in the Lake Texoma area. Bull. Okla. Ornithol. Soc. 11:22–23.

Brown, I. S. 1981. American Woodcock in Beckham County, Oklahoma. Bull. Okla. Ornithol. Soc. 14(4):32.

Brown, I. S. 1985. Successful nesting of the House Wren in western Oklahoma. Bull. Okla. Ornithol. Soc. 18:17–20.

Brown, L. 1976. Birds of Prey, Their Biology and Ecology. A & W Publishers, New York.

Brown, L., and D. Amadon. 1968. Eagles, Hawks, and Falcons of the World. McGraw-Hill Book Co., New York.

Brown, L., and D. Amadon. 1989. Eagles, Hawks and Falcons of the World. Vol. 1. Wellfleet Press, Secaucus, New York.

Brown, S., C. Hickey, B. Harrington, and R. Gill, eds. United

States Shorebird Conservation Plan. 2001. Manomet Center for Conservation Sciences. Manomet, Massachusetts.

Bruner, W. E. 1931. The vegetation of Oklahoma. Ecol. Monogr. 1:100–188.

Bryce, F. D. 1986. A Chuck-will's Widow nest in Comanche County, Oklahoma. Bull. Okla. Ornithol. Soc. 19(2):13.

Buck, P., and R. W. Kelting. 1962. A survey of the tall-grass prairie in northeastern Oklahoma. Southwest. Nat. 7:163–175.

Buckley, N. J. 1999. Black Vulture (*Coragyps atratus*). *In* The Birds of North America, No. 411 (A. Poole and F. Gill, eds.). Academy of Natural Sciences, Philadelphia, and American Ornithologists' Union, Washington, D.C.

Buech, R. R. 1982. Nesting ecology and cowbird parasitism of Clay-colored, Chipping, and Field sparrows in a Christmas tree plantation. J. Field Ornithol. 53:363–369.

Buehler, D. A. 2000. Bald Eagle (*Haliaeetus leucocephalus*). *In* The Birds of North America, No. 506 (A. Poole and F. Gills, eds.). Academy of Natural Sciences, Philadelphia, and American Ornithologists' Union, Washington, D.C.

Bull, E. L., and J. E. Jackson. 1995. Pileated Woodpecker (*Dryocopus pileatus*). *In* The Birds of North America, No. 148 (A. Poole and F. Gill, eds.). Academy of Natural Sciences, Philadelphia, and American Ornithologists' Union, Washington, D.C.

Bump, G. 1963. History and analysis of tetraonid introductions into North America. J. Wildl. Manage. 27:855–867.

Bunker, C. D. 1910. Habits of the Black-capt [sic] Vireo (*Vireo atricapillus*). Condor 12:70–73.

Burger, J. 1978. Competition between Cattle Egrets and native North American Herons, egrets, and ibises. Condor 80:15–23.

Busby, W. H., and J. L. Zimmerman. 2001. Kansas Breeding Bird Atlas. University Press of Kansas, Lawrence.

Butler, R. W. 1992. Great Blue Heron (*Ardea herodias*). *In* The Birds of North America, No. 25 (A. Poole and F. Gill, eds.). Academy of Natural Sciences, Philadelphia, and American Ornithologists' Union, Washington, D.C.

Butts, K. O. 1973. Life History and Habitat Requirements of Burrowing Owls in Western Oklahoma. M. Sc. thesis, Oklahoma State University, Stillwater.

Butts, K. O. 1976. Burrowing Owls wintering in the Oklahoma Panhandle. Auk 93:510–516.

Butts, K. O., and J. C. Lewis. 1982. The importance of prairie dog towns to Burrowing Owls in Oklahoma. Proc. Okla. Acad. Sci. 62:46–52.

Byre, V. J. 1993. First House Finch nests for Cleveland County, Oklahoma. Bull. Okla. Ornithol. Soc. 26(4):42–43.

Byre, V. J. 1995. Proximal nesting of Barred Owls, Great Horned Owls, and Red-shouldered Hawks in Cleveland County, Oklahoma. Bull. Okla. Ornithol. Soc. 28:22–24.

Byre, V. J. 2000. Productivity, habitat assessment, and management of Least Terns nesting along the Canadian River in central Oklahoma. Occasional Papers No. 8:1–13. Sam Noble Oklahoma Museum of Natural History, University of Oklahoma, Norman.

Byre, V. J., and N. R. Kuhnert. 1996. Notes on population density and nesting of Bell's Vireo along the Canadian River in central Oklahoma. Bull. Okla. Ornithol. Soc. 29(2):9–15.

Cabe, P. R. 1993. European Starling (*Sturnus vulgaris*). *In* The Birds of North America, No. 48 (A. Poole and F. Gill, eds.). Academy of Natural Sciences, Philadelphia, and American Ornithologists' Union, Washington, D.C.

Caccamise, D. F., L. M. Reed, J. Romanowski, and P. C. Stouffer. 1997. Roosting behavior and group territoriality in American Crows. Auk 114:628–637.

Cade, T. J. The Falcons of the World. 1982. Cornell University Press, Ithaca.

Caffrey, C. 1992. Female-biased delayed dispersal and helping in American Crows. Auk 109:609–619.

Caffrey, C. 1999. Feeding rates and individual contributions to feeding at nests in cooperatively breeding Western American Crows. Auk 116:836–841.

Caffrey, C. 2000a. Correlates of reproductive success in cooperatively breeding Western American Crows: If helpers help, it's not by much. Condor 102:333–341.

Caffrey, C. 2000b. Tool modification and use by an American Crow. Wilson Bull. 112:283–284.

Caffrey, C. 2001. Goal-directed use of objects by American Crows. Wilson Bull. 113(1):114–115.

Caffrey, C. 2002a. Catching Crows. North American Bird Bander. Oct.–Dec.: 137–145.

Caffrey, C. 2002b. Marking Crows. North American Bird Bander. Oct.–Dec.: 146–150.

Cairns, W. E. 1982. Biology and behavior of breeding Piping Plovers. Wilson Bull. 94:531–545.

Calder, W. A. 1967. Breeding behavior of the Roadrunner Geococcyx californianus. Auk 84:597–598.

Campo, J. J., B. C. Thompson, J. C. Barron, R. C. Telfair II, P. Durocher, and S. Gutreuter. 1993. Diet of Double-crested Cormorants wintering in Texas. J. Field Ornithol. 64:135–144.

Cannings, R. J., and T. Angell. 2001. Western Screech-Owl (*Otus kennicotti*). *In* The Birds of North America, No. 597 (A. Poole and F. Gill, eds.). Academy of Natural Sciences, Philadelphia, and American Ornithologists' Union, Washington, D.C.

Cannon, R. W. 1980. Current status and approaches to monitoring populations and status of Lesser Prairie-Chickens in Oklahoma. M.S. thesis, Oklahoma State University, Stillwater.

Cannon, R. W., and F. L. Knopf. 1978. Distribution and status of the Lesser Prairie-Chicken in western Oklahoma. Okla. Coop. Wildl. Res. Unit Progress Rep. 31:48–52.

Cannon, R. W., and F. L. Knopf. 1979. Lesser Prairie-Chicken response to range fires at the booming ground. Wildl. Soc. Bull. 7:44–46.

Cannon, R. W., and F. L. Knopf. 1980. Distribution and status of the Lesser Prairie-Chicken in Oklahoma. Pp. 71–74 in Proceedings Prairie Grouse Symposium (P. A. Vohs, and F. L. Knopf, eds.). Oklahoma State University, Stillwater.

Cannon, R. W., and F. L. Knopf. 1981a. Lek numbers as a trend index to prairie grouse populations. J. Wildl. Manage. 45:776–778.

Cannon, R. W., and F. L. Knopf. 1981b. Lesser Prairie-Chicken densities on shinnery oak and sand sagebrush rangelands in Oklahoma. J. Wildl. Manage. 45:521–524.

Cannon, R. W., F. L. Knopf, and L. R. Pettinger. 1982. Use of Landsat data to evaluate Lesser Prairie-Chicken habitats in western Oklahoma. J. Wildl. Manage. 46:915–922.

Carey, M., and V. Nolan Jr. 1979. Population dynamics of Indigo Buntings and the evolution of avian polygyny. Evolution 33:1180–1192.

Carey, M., D. E. Burhans, and D. A. Nelson. 1994. Field Sparrow (Spizella pusilla). In The Birds of North America, No. 103 (A. Poole and F. Gill, eds.). Academy of Natural Sciences, Philadelphia, and American Ornithologists' Union, Washington, D.C.

Carl, R. A. 1982. Life and death of a heronry. Bull. Okla. Ornithol. Soc. 15:22–23.

Carmichael, J. 1978. A Bald Eagle nest on the R. S. Kerr Reservoir. Bull. Okla. Ornithol. Soc. 11:4–7.

Carpenter, J. W., P. M. Kehde, and D. E. Watts. 1969. Observations at a Red-tailed Hawk nest. Bull. Okla. Ornithol. Soc. 2:25–26.

Carrie, N. R. 1999. Brown-headed Cowbird parasitism of Wood Thrush nests in eastern Texas. J. Field Ornithol. 70(2):263–267.

Carter, W. A. 1961. Breeding bird populations at Lake Carl Blackwell. Proc. Okla. Acad. Sci. 41:78–81.

Carter, W. A. 1965. Ecology of the summer nesting birds of the McCurtain Game Preserve. Ph.D. diss., Oklahoma State University, Stillwater.

Carter, W. A. 1967. Ecology of the nesting birds of McCurtain Game Preserve, Oklahoma. Wilson Bull. 79:259–272.

Carter, W. A. 1968a. Annotated list of summer birds of the McCurtain County Game Preserve, McCurtain County, Oklahoma. Proc. Okla. Acad. Sci. 47:60–66.

Carter, W. A. 1968b. Poor-will in Pontotoc County, Oklahoma. Bull. Okla. Ornithol. Soc. 1:19.

Carter, W. A. 1969. Span of breeding season of American Coot in Oklahoma. Bull. Okla. Ornithol. Soc. 2:13–14.

Carter, W. A. 1970. Nesting of Bachman's Sparrow in Oklahoma. Bull. Okla. Ornithol. Soc. 3(2):9–14.

Carter, W. A. 1972. New locality records for Brown-headed Nuthatch in southeastern Oklahoma. Bull. Okla. Ornithol. Soc. 5:23.

Carter, W. A. 1974. Pileated Woodpeckers desert nest after encounter with black rat snake. Bull. Okla. Ornithol. Soc. 7(1):6–8.

Carter, W. A. 1981. Nesting of the Eastern Bluebird in Pontotoc County, Oklahoma. Bull. Okla. Ornithol. Soc. 14(1):1–5.

Carter, W. A. 1992. Black-and-white Warbler nest failure in Pontotoc County, Oklahoma. Bull. Okla. Ornithol. Soc. 25:22–23.

Carter, W. A., and C. L. Fowler. 1983. Black-shouldered Kite in Oklahoma: 1860 and 1982. Bull. Okla. Ornithol. Soc. 16(2):9–11.

Cassidy, J. 1990. Book of North American Birds. Reader's Digest Association, Inc. New York.

Chace, J. E., A. Cruz, and A. Cruz Jr. 1997. Nesting success of the Western Wood-Pewee in Colorado. Western Birds 28:110–112.

Chapman, F. M. 1900. A study of the genus Sturnella. Bull. Am. Mus. Nat. Hist. 13:297–320.

Cicero, C. 2000. Oak Titmouse (Baeolophus inornatus) and Juniper Titmouse (Baeolophus ridgwayi). In The Birds of North America, No. 485 (A. Poole, P. Stettenheim, and F. Gill, eds.). Academy of Natural Sciences, Philadelphia, and American Ornithologists' Union, Washington, D.C.

Cimprich, D. A., and F. R. Moore. 1995. Gray Catbird (Dumatella carolinensis). In The Birds of North America, No. 167 (A. Poole and F. Gill, eds.). Academy of Natural Sciences, Philadelphia, and American Ornithologists' Union, Washington, D.C.

Cink, C. L. 1975. Mourning Dove incubates robin eggs. Kans. Ornithol. Soc. Bull. 26(4):19–21.

Clark, R. G., and R. D. Ohmart. 1985. Spread-wing posture of Turkey Vultures: Single or multiple functions? Condor 87:350–355.

Clements, J. F. 1978. Birds of the World: A Check List. The Two Continents Publishing Group, Ltd. New York.

Clotfelter, E. D., and T. Brush. 1995. Unusual parasitism by the Bronzed Cowbird. Condor 97:814–815.

Clotfelter, E. D., and K. Yasukawa. 1999. The effect of aggregated nesting on Red-winged Blackbird nest success and brood parasitism by Brown-headed Cowbirds. Condor 101(4):729–736.

Clover, P. C. 1981. Breeding of Hooded Merganser in Alfalfa County, Oklahoma. Bull. Okla. Ornithol. Soc. 14:28–29.

Coffey, B. B., Jr. 1977. Possible breeding of Western Meadowlark in northeastern Oklahoma. Bull. Okla. Ornithol. Soc. 10(2):14–15.

Collias, N. E., and E. C. Collias. 1984. Nest Building and

Bird Behavior. Princeton University Press, Princeton, New Jersey.

Collias, N. E., and L. R. Jahn. 1959. Social behavior and breeding success in Canada Geese (*Branta canadensis*) confined under semi-natural conditions. Auk 76:478–509.

Collins, P. W. 1999. Rufous-crowned Sparrow (*Aimophila ruficeps*). *In* The Birds of North America, No. 472 (A. Poole and F. Gill, eds.). Academy of Natural Sciences, Philadelphia, and American Ornithologists' Union, Washington, D.C.

Colvin, W. 1935a. Nesting of the American Raven in Cimarron County, Oklahoma. Auk 52:453–454.

Colvin, W. 1935b. Roadrunner nesting in Kansas. Auk 52:88.

Colvin, W. 1939. Cassin's Kingbird in Colorado and Oklahoma. Auk 56:85–86.

Colwell, M. A., and J. R. Jehl Jr. 1994. Wilson's Phalarope (*Phalaropus tricolor*). *In* The Birds of North America, No. 83 (A. Poole and F. Gills, eds.). Academy of Natural Sciences, Philadelphia, and American Ornithologists' Union, Washington, D.C.

Comer, C. W., and H. S. Cooksey. 1973. Nesting of a red-phased pair of screech-owls in central Oklahoma. Bull. Okla. Ornithol. Soc. 6:1–5.

Comer, C. W., and J. B. Freeland. 1980. Loggerhead Shrike observed killing Cardinal. Bull. Okla. Ornithol. Soc. 13(2):13–15.

Conant, S. 1972. Visual and acoustic communication in the Blue Jay, *Cyanocitta cristata* (Aves, Corvidae). Ph.D. diss., University of Oklahoma, Norman.

Conway, C. J. 1995. Virginia Rail (*Rallus limicola*). *In* The Birds of North America, No. 173 (A. Poole and F. Gill, eds.). Academy of Natural Sciences, Philadelphia, and American Ornithologists' Union, Washington, D.C.

Cook, W., and A. Krehbiel. 1987. When did the Great-tailed Grackle first invade northeastern New Mexico? Bull. Okla. Ornithol. Soc. 10(4):32–33.

Cooksey, H. S. 1968. Loggerhead Shrike kills cardinal. Bull. Okla. Ornithol. Soc. 1(2):20.

Copelin, F. F. 1958. Pinnated Grouse habitat management. ODWC, Fed. Aid in Wildl. Rest. Proj. W-062-R-02. 14pp.

Copelin, F. F. 1959a. Evaluation of the Greater Prairie-Chicken habitat management program (winter food plots), 1958–1959. ODWC Unpublished Report. Project W-062-R-03. 5pp.

Copelin, F. F. 1959b. Notes regarding the history and current status of the Lesser Prairie-Chicken in Oklahoma. Proc. Okla. Acad. Sci. 37:158–161.

Copelin, F. F. 1963. The Lesser Prairie-Chicken in Oklahoma. ODWC' Tech. Bull. No. 58pp.

Coppedge, B. R. 1994. First House Finch nests for northeastern Oklahoma. Bull. Okla. Ornithol. Soc. 27(3):22–24.

Cornell Laboratory of Ornithology. 1997. Cerulean Warbler Atlas Project. http://birds.cornell.edu/cewap/.

Cornell Laboratory of Ornithology. 1993. Project Tanager Eastern Region Training Tape.

Cornell Laboratory of Ornithology 2000. http://www.birds.cornell.edu/BOW/YELWAR/.

Couch, J. R., Jr. 1996. Landscape level patterns in breeding bird distributions in the western Ouachita Mountains. Ph.D. diss., Oklahoma State University, Stillwater.

Crabb, E. D. 1922. Observation on the behavior of a male Dickcissel (*Spiza Americana*) during the nesting period. Proc. Okla. Acad. Sci. 2:11–12.

Crabb, E. D. 1923. Notes on the nesting of a pair of Dickcissels (Spiza americana). Auk 40:606–609.

Crabb, E. D. 1924. A list of the woodpeckers found in Oklahoma prior to 1924. Proc. Okla. Acad. Sci. 4:28–29.

Crabb, E. D. 1930. The woodpeckers of Oklahoma. Publ. Okla. Biol. Survey 2(3):105–170.

Craig, W. 1943. The song of the wood pewee. New York State Mus. Bull. 334:1–186.

Cramp, S., and K. E. L. Simmons. 1977. Handbook of the Birds of Europe, the Middle East, and North Africa. Vol. 1: Ostriches to Ducks. Oxford University Press, Oxford, England.

Crawford, J. A. 1980. Status, problems, and research needs of the Lesser Prairie-Chicken. Pp. 1–7 *in* Proceedings Prairie Grouse Symposium (P. A. Vohs and F. L. Knopf, eds.). Oklahoma State University, Stillwater.

Crawford, J. A., and F. A. Stormer. 1980. A bibliography of the Lesser Prairie-Chicken, Gen. Tech. Rep. RM-80. Rocky Mountain Forest and Range Experimental Station, USDA Forest Service. 8pp.

Crocoll, S. T. 1994. Red-shouldered Hawk (*Buteo lineatus*). *In* The Birds of North America, No. 107 (A. Poole and F. Gill, eds.). Academy of Natural Sciences, Philadelphia, and American Ornithologists' Union, Washington, D.C.

Csada, R. D., and R. M. Brigham. 1992. Common Poorwill. *In* The Birds of North America, No. 32 (A. Poole, P. Stettenheim, and F. Gill, eds.). Academy of Natural Sciences, Philadelphia, and American Ornithologists' Union, Washington, D.C.

Cullen, S. A., J. R. Jehl Jr., and G. L. Nuechterlein. 1999. Eared Grebe (*Podiceps nigricollis*). *In* The Birds of North America, No. 433 (A. Poole and F. Gill, eds.). Academy of Natural Sciences, Philadelphia, and American Ornithologists' Union, Washington, D.C.

Curson, D. R., C. B. Goguen, and N. E. Mathews. 1998. Western Wood-Pewees accept cowbird eggs. Great Basin Nat. 58:90–91.

Curson, D. R., C. B. Goguen, and N. E. Mathews. 2000. Long-distance commuting by Brown-headed Cowbirds in New Mexico. Auk 117:795–799.

Curson, J., D. Quinn, and D. Beadle. 1994. Warblers of the Americas. Houghton Mifflin Co., Boston.

Custer, T. W., and C. Bunck. 1992. Feeding flights of breeding

Double-crested Cormorants at two Wisconsin colonies. J. Field Ornithol. 63:203–211.

Custer, T. W., G. W. Pendleton, and R. W. Roach. 1992. Determination of hatching date of eggs for Black-crowned Night-Herons, Snowy Egrets and Great Egrets. J. Field Ornithol. 63:145–154.

Davidson, S. L. 1969. Unsuccessful nesting of the Boat-tailed Grackle in Pontotoc County, Oklahoma. Bull. Okla. Ornithol. Soc. 2(1):8.

Davies, N. B. 2000. Cuckoos, cowbirds, and other cheats. T. & A. D. Poyser, Ltd., London.

Davis, D. W. 1985. Black-necked Stilts in Oklahoma during May and June. Bull. Okla. Ornithol. Soc. 18:13–14.

Davis, J. A. 1998. Intraspecific brood parasitism in Purple Martins. Bull. Okla. Ornithol. Soc. 31:29–33.

Davis, J. A., and C. R. Brown. 1999. Costs of coloniality and the effect of colony size on reproductive success in Purple Martins. Condor 101:737–745.

Davis, L. I., and F. S. Webster Jr. 1970. An intergeneric hybrid flycatcher (*Tyrannus x Muscivora*). Condor 72:37–42.

Davis, W. E., Jr. 1993. Black-crowned Night-Heron (*Nycticorax nycticorax*). In The Birds of North America, No. 74 (A. Poole and F. Gill, eds.). Academy of Natural Sciences, Philadelphia, and American Ornithologists' Union, Washington, D.C.

Davis, W. E., Jr., and J. A. Kushlan. 1994. Green Heron (*Butorides virescens*). In The Birds of North America, No. 129 (A. Poole and F.Gill, eds.). Academy of Natural Sciences, Philadelphia, and American Ornithologists' Union, Washington, D.C.

Davis, W. M. 1975. The Great-tailed Grackle in Oklahoma. Bull. Okla. Ornithol. Soc. 8(2):9–18.

Davis, W. M. 1970. Early June waterbird and shorebird records for the Oklahoma Panhandle. Bull. Okla. Ornithol. Soc. 3(2):14–15.

Davis, W. M. 1988. Diurnal fall migration of Lark Buntings in the Oklahoma Panhandle. Bull. Okla. Ornithol. Soc. 21:23–24.

Davis, W. M. 1989. Extraordinary aggregation of White-faced Ibises at a playa lake in Texas County. Bull. Okla. Ornithol. Soc. 22:27.

Davison, V. E. 1940. An 8-year census of Lesser Prairie-Chickens. J. Wildl. Manage. 4:55–62.

Dawson, W. R. 1997. Pine Siskin (*Carduelis pinus*). In The Birds of North America, No. 280 (A. Poole and F. Gill, eds.). Academy of Natural Sciences, Philadelphia, and American Ornithologists' Union, Washington, D.C.

de Hoyo, J., A. Elliot, and J. Sargatal, eds. 1992a. Cattle Egret. P. 415 *in* Handbook of the Birds of the World. Vol. 1. Lynx Edicions, Barcelona.

de Hoyo, J., A. Elliott, and J. Sargatal, eds. 1992b. Tricolor Heron. P. 410 *in* Handbook of the Birds of the World. Vol. 1. Lynx Edicions, Barcelona.

de Hoyo, J., A. Elliot, and J. Sargatal, eds. 1994. Pp. 542–543 *in* Handbook of the Birds of the World: New World Vultures to Guineafowl. Vol. 2. Lynx Edicions, Barcelona.

de Hoyo, J., A. Elliot, and J. Sargatal, eds. 1997. P. 606 *in* Handbook of the Birds of the World: Sandgrouse to Cuckoos. Vol. 4. Lynx Edicions, Barcelona.

Dechant, J. A., M. L. Sondreal, D. H. Johnson, L. D. Igl, C. M. Goldade, M. P. Nenneman, and B. R. Euliss. 1998. Effects of management practices on grassland birds: Grasshopper Sparrow. Northern Prairie Wildlife Research Center, Jamestown, North Dakota. Northern Prairie Wildlife Research Center Home Page. http://www.npwrc.usgs.gov/resource/literatr/grasbird/grasshop/grasshop.htm (Version 17FEB2000).

Dechant, J. A., M. F. Dinkins, D. H. Johnson, L. D. Igl, C. M. Goldade, B. D. Parkin, and B. R. Euliss. 1999. Effects of management practices on grassland birds: Upland Sandpiper. Northern Prairie Wildlife Research Center, Jamestown, North Dakota.

Dechant, J. A., M. L. Sondreal, D. H. Johnson, L. D. Igl, C. M. Goldade, B. D. Parkin, and B. R. Euliss. 1999 (revised 2000). Effects of management Ppactices on grassland birds: Lark Sparrow. Northern Prairie Wildlife Research Center, Jamestown, North Dakota.

Dechant, J. A., M. L. Sondreal, D. H. Johnson, L.D. Igl, C. M. Goldale, P. A. Rabie, and B. R. Euliss. 1999. Effects of management practices on grassland birds: Burrowing Owl. Northern Prairie Wildlife Research Center, Jamestown, North Dakota.

Dechant, J. A., M. L. Sondreal, D. H. Johnson, L. D. Igl, C. M. Goldade, J. L. Zimmerman, and B. R. Euliss. 1999. Effects of management practices on grassland birds: Dickcissel. Northern Prairie Wildlife Research Center, Jamestown, North Dakota. Northern Prairie Wildlife Research Center Home Page. http://www.npwrc.usgs.gov/resource/literatr/grasbird/dick/dick.htm (Version 17FEB2000).

Dechant, J. A., M. L. Sondreal, D. H. Johnson, L. D. Igl, C. M. Goldade, A. L. Zimmerman, and B. R. Euliss. 1999 (revised 2000). Effects of management practices on grassland birds: Lark Bunting. Northern Prairie Wildlife Research Center, Jamestown, North Dakota.

Dechant, J. A., M. L. Sondreal, D. H. Johnson, L. D. Igl, C. M. Goldade, A. L. Zimmerman, and B. R. Euliss. 1999. Effects of management practices on grassland birds: Western Meadowlark. Northern Prairie Wildlife Research Center, Jamestown, North Dakota. Northern Prairie Wildlife Research Center Home Page. http://www.npwrc.usgs.gov/resource/literatr/grasbird/weme/weme.htm (Version 17FEB2000).

Dechant, J. A., M. L. Sondreal, D. H. Johnson, L. D. Igl, C. M. Goldade, B. D. Parkin, and B. R. Euliss. 2001. Effects of management practices on grassland birds: Sedge Wren. Northern Prairie Wildlife Research Center, Jamestown, North Dakota. Northern Prairie Wildlife

Research Center Home Page.
http://www.npwrc.usgs.gov/resource/literatr/grasbird/se
wr/sewr.htm (Version 17FEB2000).

Dechant, J. A., M. L. Sondreal, D. H. Johnson, L. D. Igl,
C. M. Goldade, P. A. Rabie, and B. R. Euliss. 2001.
Effects of management practices on grassland birds:
Long-billed Curlew. Northern Prairie Wildlife Research
Center, Jamestown, North Dakota. Northern Prairie
Wildlife Research Center Home Page.
http://www.npwrc.usgs.gov/resource/literatr/grasbird/fpl
bcu/fplbcu.htm (Version 29FEB2000).

Dechant, J. A., M. L. Sondreal, D. H. Johnson, L. D. Igl,
C. M. Goldade, A. L. Zimmerman, and B. R. Euliss.
2001. Effects of management practices on grassland
birds: American Bittern. Northern Prairie Wildlife
Research Center, Jamestown, North Dakota. Northern
Prairie Wildlife Research Center Home Page.
http://www.npwrc.usgs.gov/resource/literatr/grasbird/am
bi/ambi.htm (Version 17FEB2000).

Dechant, J. A., D. H. Johnson, C. M. Goldade, J. O. Church,
and B. R. Euliss. 2002. Effects of management practices
on wetland birds: Eared Grebe. Northern Prairie Wildlife
Wildlife Research Center, Jamestown, North Dakota.
Northern Prairie Wildlife Research Center Home Page.
http://www.npwrc.usgs.gov/resource/literatr/wetbird/eag
r/eagr.htm (Version 04MAR2002).

Dechant, J. A., A. L. Zimmerman, D. H. Johnson,
C. M. Goldade, B. E. Jamison, and B. R. Euliss. 2002.
Effects of management practices on wetland birds:
American Avocet. Northern Prairie Wildlife Research
Center, Jamestown, North Dakota. Northern Prairie
Wildlife Research Center Home Page.
http://www.npwrc.usgs.gov/resource/literatr/wetbird/amav
/amav.htm (Version 04MAR2002).

DeGraaf, R. M., and J. H. Rappole. 1995. Neotropical
Migratory Birds. Cornell University Press, Ithaca, New
York.

DeGraaf, R. M., V. E. Scott, R. H. Hamre, L. Ernst, and
S. H. Anderson. 1991. Forest and Rangeland Birds of
the United States. Agriculture Handbook 688.

DeJong, M. J. 1996. Northern Rough-winged Swallow
(*Stelgidopteryx serripennis*). *In* The Birds of North
America, No. 234 (A. Poole and F. Gill, eds.). Academy
of Natural Sciences, Philadelphia, and American
Ornithologists' Union, Washington, D.C.

Delap, E. 1971. Indigo Bunting attending young cowbirds.
Bull. Okla. Ornithol. Soc. 4:19–20.

Delap, E. 1977. Flock of Short-eared Owls in Washington
County, Oklahoma. Bull. Okla. Ornithol. Soc.
10(4):33.

Delap, E. 1979a. Breeding of King Rail in Washington
County, Oklahoma. Bull. Okla. Ornithol. Soc.
12(2):14.

Delap, E. 1979b. Fourth winter record of Dickcissel in

Washington County, Oklahoma. Bull. Okla. Ornithol.
Soc. 13(1):6.

Delap, E. 1979c. Third winter record of Dickcissel in
Washington County, Oklahoma. Bull. Okla. Ornithol.
Soc. 12(4):34.

Delap, E. 1980. Breeding of Great-tailed Grackle in Osage
County, Oklahoma. Bull. Okla. Ornithol. Soc.
13(3):24.

Delap, E., and M. Droege. Unpublished records of the
Bartlesville Audubon Society. 1965–2000.

DeMaso, S. J., A. D. Peoples, S. A. Cox, and E. S. Parry. 1997.
Survival of Northern Bobwhite chicks in western
Oklahoma. J. Wildl. Manage. 61:846–853.

Derrickson, K. C., and R. Breitwisch. 1992. Northern
Mockingbird (*Mimus polyglottos*). *In* The Birds of North
America, No. 7 (A. Poole and F. Gill, eds.). The
Academy of Natural Sciences, Philadelphia; The
American Ornithologists' Union, Washington, D.C.

Desmond, M. J., and J. A. Savidge. 1999. Satellite burrow use
by Burrowing Owl chicks and its influence on nest fate.
Pp. 128–130 *in* Ecology and Conservation of Grassland
Birds of the Western Hemisphere (P. D. Vickery and
J. R. Herkert, eds.). Stud. Avian Biol. no. 19.

DeVore, N. 1979. Pileated Woodpecker sighted in Oklahoma
County, Oklahoma. Bull. Okla. Ornithol. Soc.
12(3):23.

Dexter, C. 1998. Ash-throated Flycatcher (*Myiarchus cineras-
cens*). *In* Colorado Breeding Bird Atlas (H. E. Kingery,
ed.). Colorado Bird Atlas Partnership and Colorado
Division of Wildlife, Denver.

Dickerman, R. W. 1986. Possible breeding of Lesser
Nighthawk in Tulsa County, Oklahoma. Bull. Okla.
Ornithol. Soc. 19:1–2.

Dillon, D. O. 1975. Late nesting of Yellow-billed Cuckoo in
Oklahoma. Bull. Okla. Ornithol. Soc. 8:28.

Dillon, M. B. 1998a. Canyon Towhee (*Pipilo fuscus*). *In*
Colorado Breeding Bird Atlas (H. E. Kingery, ed.).
Colorado Bird Atlas Partnership and Colorado Division
of Wildlife, Denver.

Dillon, M. B. 1998b. Curve-billed Thrasher (*Toxostoma curvirostre*). *In* Colorado Breeding Bird Atlas (H. E. Kingery,
ed.). Colorado Bird Atlas Partnership and Colorado
Division of Wildlife, Denver.

Dinkins, M. F., A. L. Zimmerman, J. A. Dechant,
B. D. Parkin, D. H. Johnson, L. D. Igl, C. M. Goldade,
and B. R. Euliss. 2001. Effects of management practices
on grassland birds: Horned Lark. Northern Prairie
Wildlife Research Center, Jamestown, North Dakota.
Northern Prairie Wildlife Research Center Home Page.
http://www.npwrc.usgs.gov/resource/literatr/grasbird/ho
la/hola.htm (Version 16JUN2000).

Dirck, M. 1986. Loggerhead Shrike takes American
Goldfinch. Bull. Okla. Ornithol. Soc. 19(4):29–30.

Dobbs, R. C., P. R. Martin, and T. E. Martin. 1998. Green-tailed Towhee (*Pipilo chlorurus*). *In* The Birds of North America, No. 368 (A. Poole and F. Gill, eds.). The Birds of North America, Inc. Philadelphia, Pennsylvania.

Dodson, M. M. 1954. Oklahoma Migratory Game Bird Study Report for 1949–1953. Oklahoma Game and Fish Department, P-RW-32-R.

Dolbeer, R. A. 1991. Migration patterns of Double-crested Cormorants east of the Rocky Mountains. J. Field Ornithol. 62:83–93.

Donaldson, D. D. 1966. Brush control and the welfare of Lesser Prairie-Chickens in western Oklahoma. Proc. Okla. Acad. Sci. 46:221–228.

Donaldson, D. D. 1969. Effect on Lesser Prairie-Chickens of brush control in western Oklahoma. Ph.D. diss., Oklahoma State University, Stillwater.

Downing, R. L. 1959. Significance of ground nesting by Mourning Doves in northwestern Oklahoma. J. Wildl. Manage. 23:117–118.

Downs, J. 1983. Green-tailed Towhee nest in Cimarron County, Oklahoma. Bull. Okla. Ornithological Society 16:7.

Drobney, R. D., J. H. Schulz, S. L. Sheriff, and W. J. Fuemmeler. 1998. Mourning Dove nesting habitat and nest success in central Missouri. J. Field Ornithol. 69(2):299–305.

Droege, M. M. 1987. Observations of Belted Kingfishers. Bull. Okla. Ornithol. Soc. 20:15–16.

Droege, M. M. 1989. A recent Cooper's Hawk nest in Osage County, Oklahoma. Bull. Okla. Ornithol. Soc. 22:13.

Droege, M. M. 1993. Late nesting of White-breasted Nuthatch in northeastern Oklahoma. Bull. Okla. Ornithol. Soc. 26(3):30–32.

Droege, M. M. 1996. First Long-eared Owl nest in northeastern Oklahoma. Bull. Okla. Ornithol. Soc. 29:20–21.

Dubowy, P. J. 1996. Northern Shoveler (*Anas clypeata*). *In* The Birds of North America, No. 217 (A. Poole and F. Gill, eds.). Academy of Natural Sciences, Philadelphia, and American Ornithologists' Union, Washington, D.C.

Duck, L. G., and J. B. Fletcher. 1943. A game type map of Oklahoma. A Survey of the Game and Furbearing Animals of Oklahoma. Oklahoma Dept. of Wildlife Conservation, Oklahoma City, Oklahoma.

Duck, L. G., and J. B. Fletcher. 1944. A survey of the game and furbearing animals of Oklahoma. Div. Wildl. Restoration and Res., Okla. Game and Fish Comm. State Bull. 3.

Duck, L. G., and J. B. Fletcher. 1945. The game types of Oklahoma: Introduction. *In*: State Bulletin No. 3, editor. A Survey of the Game and Furbearing Animals of Oklahoma. Oklahoma Dept. of Wildlife Conservation, Oklahoma City, Oklahoma.

Dugger, B. D., K. M. Dugger, and L. H. Fredrickson. 1994. Hooded Merganser (*Lophodytes cucullatus*). *In* The Birds of North America. No. 98, (A. Poole and F. Gill, eds.).

The Academy of Natural Sciences, Philadelphia, and The American Ornithologists' Union, Washington, D.C.

Dunk, J. R. 1995. White-tailed Kite (*Elanus leucurus*). *In* The Birds of North America, No. 178 (A. Poole and F. Gill, eds.). Academy of Natural Sciences, Philadelphia, and American Ornithologists' Union, Washington, D.C.

Dunkle, S. W. 1977. Swainson's Hawks on the Laramie plains, Wyoming. Auk 94(1):65–71.

Dunn, J. L., and K. L. Garrett. 1997. A Field Guide to Warblers of North America. Houghton Mifflin Co., Boston.

Dunn, L. E. 1984. Say's Phoebe nest in Beaver County, Oklahoma. Bull. Okla. Ornithol. Soc. 17(2):16.

Dunn, L. E. 1986. Nesting of Lark Bunting in Harper and Beaver counties, Oklahoma. Bull. Okla. Ornithol. Soc. 19(4):32.

Dunning, J. B. 1993. Bachman's Sparrow (*Aimophila aestivalis*). *In* The Birds of North America, No. 38 (A. Poole, P. Stettenheim, and F. Gill, eds.). Academy of Natural Sciences, Philadelphia, and American Ornithologists' Union, Washington, D.C.

Dunning, J. B., Jr., R. K. Bowers Jr., S. J. Suter, and C. E. Bock. 1999. Cassin's Sparrow (*Aimophila cassinii*). *In* The Birds of North America, No. 471 (A. Poole and F. Gill, eds.). Academy of Natural Sciences, Philadelphia, and American Ornithologists' Union, Washington, D.C.

Dusi, J. L. 1968. The competition between Cattle Egrets and Little Blue Herons. Ala. Birdlife 14:2–8.

Easley, W. 1983. Late nesting of Grasshopper Sparrow in Texas County, Oklahoma. Bull. Okla. Ornithol. Soc. 16(3):23–24.

Easterla, D. A. 1965. Range extension of the Fish Crow in Missouri. Wilson Bull. 77:297–298.

Eaton, S. W. 1958. A life history study of the Louisiana Waterthrush. Wilson Bull. 70:211–236.

Eaton, S. W. 1992. Wild Turkey. *In* The Birds of North America, No. 22 (A. Poole and F. Gill, eds.). Academy of Natural Sciences, Philadelphia, and American Ornithologists' Union, Washington, D.C.

Eckerle, K. P., and C. F. Thompson. 2001. Yellow-breasted Chat (*Icteria virens*). *In* The Birds of North America, No. 575 (A. Poole and F. Gill, eds.). Academy of Natural Sciences, Philadelphia, and American Ornithologists' Union, Washington, D.C.

Eckert, A. W., and K. E. Karalus. 1987. The Owls of North America. Weathervane Books, New York.

Eddelman, W. R., R. E. Flores, and M. L. Legare. 1994. Black Rail (*Laterallus jamaicensis*). *In* The Birds of North America, No. 123 (A. Poole and F. Gill, eds.). Academy of Natural Sciences, Philadelphia, and American Ornithologists' Union, Washington, D.C.

Edwards, H. H., G. D. Schnell, R. L. Dubois, and

V. H. Hutchison. 1992. Natural and induced remanent magnetism in birds. Auk 109:43–56.

Ehrlich, P. R., D. D. Dobkin, and D. Wheye. 1988. The Birders Handbook: A Field Guide to the Natural History of North American Birds. Simon and Schuster Inc., New York.

Ehrlich, P. R., D. D. Dobkin, and D. Wheye. 1992. Birds in Jeopardy. Stanford University Press.

Elliott, P. F. 1978. Cowbird parasitism in the Kansas tallgrass prairie. Auk 95:161–167.

Ellison, W. G. 1992. Blue-gray Gnatcatcher. *In* The Birds of North America, No. 23 (A. Poole, P. Stettenheim, and F. Gills, eds.). Academy of Natural Sciences, Philadelphia, and American Ornithologists' Union, Washington, D.C.

Ellsworth, D. L., R. L. Honeycutt, N. J. Silvy, K. D. Rittenhouse, and M. H. Smith. 1994. Mitochondrial-DNA and nuclear-gene differentiation in North American prairie grouse (genus *Tympanuchus*). Auk 111:661–671.

Ellsworth, D. L., R. L. Honeycutt, and N. J. Silvy. 1995. Phylogenetic relationships among North American grouse inferred from restriction endonuclease analysis of mitochondrial DNA. Condor 97:492–502.

Ely, C. A. 1957. Comparative Nesting Success of Certain South-central Oklahoma Birds. Unpubl. M.S. thesis, University of Oklahoma, Norman. 73 pp.

Ely, D. C. 1990. A pair of Pileated Woodpeckers in the Wichita Mountains Wildlife Refuge, Comanche County, Oklahoma. Bull. Okla. Ornithol. Soc. 23(3–4):24–25.

Emlen, J. T., Jr., 1954. Territory, nest building, and pair formation in the Cliff Swallow. Auk 71:16–35.

Emlen, S. T., J. D. Rising, and W. L. Thompson. 1975. A behavioral and morphological study of sympatry in the Indigo and Lazuli buntings of the Great Plains. Wilson Bull. 87:145–179.

England, A. S., M. J. Bechard, and C. S. Houston. 1997. Swainson's Hawk (*Buteo swainsoni*). *In* The Birds of North America, No. 265 (A. Poole and F. Gill, eds.). Academy of Natural Sciences, Philadelphia, and American Ornithologists' Union, Washington, D.C.

Engle, D. M., T. G. Bidwell, and M. E. Moseley. 1997. Invasion of Oklahoma rangelands and forests by eastern redcedar and ashe juniper. Oklahoma Coop. Ext. Serv., Oklahoma State University, Stillwater, Circ. E-947.

Engle, M. C. 1981. Mississippi Kite strikes human being. Bull. Okla. Ornithol. Soc. 13:21–22.

Erpino, M. J. 1968. Nest-related activities of Black-billed Magpies. Condor 70:154–165.

Erskine, A. J. 1971. Some new perspectives on the breeding ecology of Common Grackles. Wilson Bull. 83(4):352–370.

Esler, D. 1992. Habitat use by piscivorous birds on a power plant cooling reservoir. J. Field Ornithol. 63:241–249.

Eubanks, T. R. 1971. Unusual flight of Mississippi Kites in Payne County, Oklahoma. Bull. Okla. Ornithol. Soc. 4:33.

Evans, D. F. 1995. Lone Bank Swallow pair nesting in Logan County, Oklahoma. Bull. Okla. Ornithol. Soc. 28:15–16.

Evans, K. E. 1968. Characteristics and habitat requirements of the Greater Prairie-Chicken and Sharp-tailed Grouse—a review of the literature. USDA For. Serv., Conserv. Res. Rep. 12. Fort Collins, Colorado. 31pp.

Evans, L. J., and B. J. Stutchbury 1994. Hooded Warbler (*Wilsonia citrina*). *In* The Birds of North America, No. 110 (A. Poole and F. Gill, eds.). Academy of Natural Sciences, Philadelphia, and American Ornithologists' Union, Washington, D.C.

Farrand, J., Jr. 1983. The Audubon Society Master Guide to Birding. Alfred A. Knopf. New York.

Farrand, J., Jr. 1988. An Audubon Handbook: Western Birds. McGraw-Hill Book Co., New York.

Feirer, S. T., and R. S. Sheppard. 1999. First nesting record of the Tricolored Heron for Oklahoma. Bull. Okla. Ornithol. Soc. 32:4–5.

Felis, C. A. 1975. Nesting of American Coot in Comanche County, Oklahoma. Bull. Okla. Ornithol. Soc. 8:18–19.

Felis, C. A. 1976. Inca Dove in Caddo County, Oklahoma. Bull. Okla. Ornithol. Soc. 9:33–34.

Fischer, R. B. 1958. The Breeding Biology of the Chimney Swift *Chaetura pelagica*. State University of New York, Albany.

Fleischer, R. C. 1986. Brood parasitism by Brown-headed Cowbird in a simple host community in eastern Kansas. Kans. Ornithol. Soc. Bull. 37:21–29.

Flowers, T. L. 1985. Recent breeding of the Mountain Plover in Cimarron, Oklahoma. Bull. Okla. Ornithol. Soc. 18(2):9–12.

Force, E. R. 1929. The birds of Tulsa County, Oklahoma, and vicinity. Proc. Okla. Acad. Sci. 9:67–72.

Franson, J. C. 1994. Parathion poisoning of Mississippi Kites in Oklahoma. J. Raptor Res. 28:108–109.

Franzreb, K. E. 1989. Ecology and conservation of the endangered Least Bell's Vireo. Biol. Rept. 89. U.S. Fish and Wildl. Serv., Washington, D.C.

Frederick, P. C. 1997. Tricolored Heron (*Egretta tricolor*). *In* The Birds of North America, No. 306 (A. Poole and F. Gills, eds.). Academy of Natural Sciences, Philadelphia, and American Ornithologists' Union, Washington, D.C.

Frederick, P. C., and D. Siegel-Causey. 2000. Anhinga (*Anhinga anhinga*). *In* The Birds of North America, No. 522 (A. Poole and F. Gill, eds.). Academy of Natural Sciences, Philadelphia, and American Ornithologists' Union, Washington, D.C.

Freeman, J. 1993. American Crow predation on nestlings in Carter County, Oklahoma. Bull. Okla. Ornithol. Soc. 26:41.

Friedmann, H. 1929. The Cowbirds: A study in the biology of social parasitism. Charles C. Thomas, Springfield, Illinois & Baltimore, Maryland.

Friedmann, H. 1963. Host relationships of the parasitic cowbirds. U.S. Nat. Mus. Bull. 233.

Friedmann, H. 1966. Additional data on the host relations of the parasitic cowbirds. Smithsonian Misc. Coll., 149, no. 11.

Friedmann, H. 1971. Further information on the host relations of the parasitic cowbirds. Auk 88:239–255.

Friedmann, H., L. F. Kiff, and S. I. Rothstein. 1977. A further contribution to the knowledge of the host relations of the parasitic cowbirds. Smithson. Contrib. Zool. 235:1–75.

Friedmann, H., and L. F. Kiff. 1985. The parasitic cowbirds and their hosts. Proc. West. Found. Vert. Zool.

Friesen, L. E., V. E. Wyatt, and M. D. Cadman. 1999. Nest reuse by Wood Thrushes and Rose-breasted Grosbeaks. Wilson Bull. 111:132–133.

Friesen, L. E., M. D. Cadman, and R. J. MacKay. 1999. Nesting success of neotropical migrant songbirds in a highly fragmented landscape. Conserv. Biol. 13(2):338–346.

Frings, H., and M. Frings. 1976. Common Redpoll in central Oklahoma. Bull. Okla. Ornithol. Soc. 9(2):16.

Gail, A. E., C. F. Leck, and R. T. T. Forman. 1976. Avian distribution patterns in forest islands of different sizes in central New Jersey. Auk 93:356–364.

Gall, B. L. 1989. Carolina Chickadee trapped in nestbox. Bull. Okla. Ornithol. Soc. 22:15.

Gamble, L. R., and T. M. Bergin. 1996. Western Kingbird (*Tyrannus verticalis*). *In* The Birds of North America, No. 227 (A. Poole and F. Gill, eds.). Academy of Natural Sciences, Philadelphia, and American Ornithologists' Union, Washington, D.C.

Gammonley, J. H. 1996. Cinnamon Teal (*Anas cyanoptera*). *In* The Birds of North America, No. 209 (A. Poole and F. Gill, eds.). Academy of Natural Sciences, Philadelphia, and American Ornithologists' Union, Washington, D.C.

Gardali, T., and G. Ballard. 2000. Warbling Vireo (Vireo gilvus). *In* The Birds of North America, No. 551 (A. Poole and F. Gill, eds.). Academy of Natural Sciences, Philadelphia, and American Ornithologists' Union, Washington, D.C.

Garrison, B. A. 1999. Bank Swallow (*Riparia riparia*). *In* The Birds of North America, No. 414 (A. Poole and F. Gill, eds.). Academy of Natural Sciences, Philadelphia, and American Ornithologists' Union, Washington, D.C.

Garrison, N. 1978. First hummingbird nest for Pawnee County, Oklahoma. Bull. Okla. Ornithol. Soc. 11:15.

Garrison, N. 1986. Nesting Mississippi Kites. Outdoor Oklahoma 42:32–37.

Geary, D. 1986. Monitoring Greater and Lesser Prairie-Chicken. ODWC Project No. W-82-R-25, Study No. 1, Job 1.

Geary, D. 1986. Monitoring Greater and Lesser Prairie-Chicken. ODWC Project No. W-82-R-25, Study No. 1, Job 1.

Gehlbach, F. R. 1994. The Eastern Screech-Owl: Life History, Ecology, and Behavior in Suburbia and the Countryside. Texas A&M University Press, College Station.

Gehlbach, F. R. 1995. Eastern Screech-Owl (*Otus asio*). *In* The Birds of North America, No. 165 (A. Poole and F. Gill, eds.). Academy of Natural Sciences, Philadelphia, and American Ornithologists' Union, Washington, D.C.

Geluso, K. N. 1969. Food and survival problems of Oklahoma Roadrunners in winter. Bull. Okla. Ornithol. Soc. 2:5–6.

Geluso, K. N. 1970a. Feeding behavior of a Roadrunner in winter. Bull. Okla. Ornithol. Soc. 3(4):32.

Geluso, K. N. 1970b. Additional notes on food and fat of Roadrunners in winter. Bull. Okla. Ornithol. Soc. 3:6.

George M. Sutton Avian Research Center. 1995. A survey of raptor nests in the Panhandle region of Oklahoma. Unpubl. rept. to U.S. Fish and Wild. Serv., 15 pp.

George, J. C. 1969. North goes the Mocker. Audubon Magazine 71:48–49.

Ghalambor, C. K., and T. E. Martin. 1999. Red-breasted Nuthatch (*Sitta Canadensis*). *In* The Birds of North America, No. 459 (A. Poole and F. Gill, eds.). Academy of Natural Sciences, Philadelphia, and American Ornithologists' Union, Washington, D.C.

Gibbs, J. P., and J. Faaborg. 1990. Estimating the viability of Ovenbird and Kentucky Warbler populations in forest fragments. Conserv. Biol. 4:193–196.

Gibbs, J. P., S. Melvin, and F. A. Reid. 1992. American Bittern (*Botaurus lentiginosus*). *In* The Birds of North America, No. 179 (A. Poole and F. Gill, eds.). Academy of Natural Sciences, Philadelphia, and American Ornithologists' Union, Washington, D.C.

Giesen, K. M. 1998. The Lesser Prairie-Chicken (*Tympanuchus pallidicinctus*). *In* The Birds of North America, No. 364 (A. Poole and F. Gill, eds.). Academy of Natural Sciences, Philadelphia, and American Ornithologists' Union, Washington, D.C.

Gietzentanner, J. B. 1976. Scaled Quail in Custer County, Oklahoma. Bull. Okla. Ornithol. Soc. 9(1):6.

Giffs, J. P., F. A. Reid, and S. M. Melvin. 1992. Least Bittern. *In* The Birds of North America, No. 17 (A. Poole, P. Stettenheim, and F. Gill, eds.). Academy of Natural Sciences, Philadelphia, and American Ornithologists' Union, Washington, D.C.

Gill, F. B., R. A. Canterbury, and J. L. Confer. 2001. Blue-winged Warbler (*Vermivora pinus*). *In* The Birds of North America, No. 584 (A. Poole and F. Gill, eds.). Academy of Natural Sciences, Philadelphia, and American Ornithologists' Union, Washington, D.C.

Gilmer, D. S., and R. E. Stewart. 1984. Swainson's Hawk nesting ecology in North Dakota. Condor 86(1):12–18.

Giudice, J. H., and J. T. Ratti. 2001. Ring-necked Pheasant

(*Phasianus colchicus*). *In* The Birds of North America, No. 572 (A. Poole and F. Gill, eds.). Academy of Natural Sciences, Philadelphia, and American Ornithologists' Union, Washington, D.C.

Glass, C. R., P. Hendricks, M. J. Phillips, and T. L. Waltman. 1994. Common Poorwill nesting in Osage County, Oklahoma. Bull. Okla. Ornithol. Soc. 27(2):12–13.

Goard, D. M. 1973. Nest of Poor-will in Cimarron County, Oklahoma. Bull. Okla. Ornithol. Soc. 6:22.

Goard, D. M. 1974. Henslow's Sparrow in Oklahoma. Bull. Okla. Ornithol. Soc. 7(4):57–60.

Goddard, S. V. 1971. Size, migration pattern, structure of fall, early winter blackbird, starling populations in western Oklahoma. Wilson Bull. 83:371–382.

Goddard, S. V., and V. V. Board. 1967. Reproductive success of Red-winged Blackbirds in north-central Oklahoma. Wilson Bull. 79(3):283–289.

Goertz, J. W., and K. Rutherford. 1972. Adult Carolina Chickadee carries young. Wilson Bull. 84(2):205–206.

Goguen, C. B. 1999. Brown-headed Cowbird movements, habitat use, and impacts on hosts in a grazed and ungrazed landscape. Ph.D. diss., University of Wisconsin, Madison.

Goguen, C. B., and N. E. Mathews. 1998. Songbird community composition and nesting success in grazed and ungrazed pinyon-juniper woodlands. J. Wildl. Manage. 62:474–484.

Goguen, C. B., and N. E. Mathews. 1999. Review of the causes and implications of the association between cowbirds and livestock. Pp. 10–17 *in* Research and Management of the Brown-headed Cowbird in Western Landscapes (M. L Morrison, L. S. Hall, S. K. Robinson, S. I. Rothstein, D. C. Hahn, and T. D. Rich, eds.). Studies in Avian Biology No. 18.

Good, E. E. 1952. The life history of the American Crow (*Corvus brachyrhynchos Brehm*). Ph.D. diss., Ohio State University, Columbus.

Gooders, J., and T. Boyer. 1986. Ducks of North America. Facts On File, Inc., New York.

Goodrich, L. J., S. C. Crocoll, and S. E. Senner. 1996. Broad-winged Hawk (*Buteo platypterus*). *In* The Birds of North America, No. 218 (A. Poole and F. Gill, eds.). Academy of Natural Sciences, Philadelphia, and American Ornithologists' Union, Washington, D.C.

Goodwin, D. 1976. Crows of the World. Cornell University Press, Ithaca, New York.

Gowaty, P. A., and J. H. Plissner. 1998. Eastern Bluebird (*Sialia sialis*). *In* The Birds of North America, No. 381 (A. Poole and F. Gill, eds.). Academy of Natural Sciences, Philadelphia, and American Ornithologists' Union, Washington, D.C.

Graber, J. W. 1957. A bioecological study of the Black-capped Vireo (*Vireo atricapilla*). Ph.D. diss., University of Oklahoma, Norman.

Graber, J. W. 1961. Distribution, habitat requirements, and life history of the Black-capped Vireo (*Vireo atricapilla*). Ecol. Mono. 31:313–336.

Graber, J. W., R. R. Graber, and E. L. Kirk. 1983. Illinois Birds: Wood Warblers. Biological Notes No. 118. State of Illinois, Dept. of Energy and Natural Resources.

Graber, J. W., R. R. Graber, and E. L. Kirk. 1985. Illinois Birds: Vireos. Illinois Natural History Survey Biological Notes 124.

Granfors, D. A., K. E. Church, and L. M. Smith. 1996. Eastern Meadowlarks nesting in rangelands and Conservation Reserve Program fields in Kansas. J. Field Ornithol. 67(2):222–235.

Graul, W. D. 1971. Observations of a Long-billed Curlew nest. Auk 88(1):182–184.

Graul, W. D. 1975. Breeding biology of the Mountain Plover. Wilson Bull. 87:6–31.

Greenberg, R. 1997. Worm-eating Warbler Acrobat of the Aerial Leaf Litter. http://natzoo.si.edu/smbc/Featurebird/wema.htm 13 July 2001.

Greene, E., V. R. Meuhter, and W. Davidson. 1996. Lazuli Bunting (*Passerina amoena*). *In* The Birds of North America, No. 232 (A. Poole and F. Gills, eds.). Academy of Natural Sciences, Philadelphia, and American Ornithologists' Union, Washington, D.C.

Greenlaw, J. S. 1996a. Spotted Towhee (*Pipilo maculatus*). *In* The Birds of North America, No. 263 (A. Poole and F. Gill, eds.). Academy of Natural Sciences, Philadelphia, and American Ornithologists' Union, Washington, D.C.

Greenlaw, J. S. 1996b. Eastern Towhee (*Pipilo erythrophthalmus*). *In* The Birds of North America, No. 262 (A. Poole and F. Gill, eds.). Academy of Natural Sciences, Philadelphia, and American Ornithologists' Union, Washington, D.C.

Greer, J. K., and R. L. Gilstrap. 1970. Vertebrate remains in Barn Owl pellets. Bull. Okla. Ornithol. Soc. 3:25–29.

Griffin, D. N. 1959. The poisoning of meadowlarks with insecticides. Wilson Bull. 71:193

Griscom, L., and A. Sprunt. 1979. The Warblers of America. Doubleday, Garden City, New York.

Gross, A. O. 1932. Greater Prairie-Chicken. Pp. 242–263 *in* Life Histories of North American Gallinaceous Birds (A. C. Bent, ed.). U.S. Natl. Mus. Bull. 162.

Grover, P. B., and M. Grover. 1982. Breeding charadriiform birds of the Great Salt Plains. Bull. Okla. Ornithol. Soc. 15:11–14.

Grover, P. B., and F. L. Knopf. 1982. Habitat requirements and breeding success of charadriiform birds nesting at Salt Plains National Wildlife Refuge, Oklahoma. J. Field Ornithol. 53:139–148.

Grover, P. B., Jr. 1978. Notes on a heronry in northeastern Oklahoma. Bull. Okla. Ornithol. Soc. 11:18–19.

Grubb, T. C., Jr., and V. V. Pravosudov. 1994. Tufted Titmouse (*Baeolophus bicolor*). *In* The Birds of North America, No. 86 (A. Poole and F. Gill, eds.). Academy of Natural Sciences, Philadelphia, and American Ornithologists' Union, Washington, D.C.

Grula, J. 1973. Cassin's Sparrow in Noble County, Oklahoma. Bull. Okla. Ornithol. Soc. 6(2):11–12.

Grula, J. 1974. Acadian Flycatcher near Stillwater, Oklahoma. Bull. Okla. Ornithol. Soc. 7(2):14.

Grzybowski, J. A. 1980. Distribution of prairie-chicken harvest and hunters in Oklahoma. P. 86 *in* Proceedings Prairie Grouse Symposium (P. A. Vohs and F. L. Knopf, eds.). Oklahoma State University, Stillwater.

Grzybowski, J. A. 1981. Late nesting of Western Kingbird in Oklahoma. Bull. Okla. Ornithol. Soc. 14(4):33–34.

Grzybowski, J. A. 1983a. Curve-billed Thrasher in Cleveland County, Oklahoma. Bull. Okla. Ornithol. Soc. 16:22.

Grzybowski, J. A. 1983b. Western Screech-Owl: A "New" Species for Oklahoma. Bull. Okla. Ornithol. Soc. 16(3):17–20.

Grzybowski, J. A. 1987. First nesting record of Gadwall in Oklahoma. Bull. Okla. Ornithol. Soc. 20:5–6.

Grzybowski, J. A. 1994. First breeding record and summer records for the White-eyed Vireo in the Wichita Mountains, Oklahoma. Bull. Okla. Ornithol. Soc. 27:7–8.

Grzybowski, J. A. 1995a. Black-capped Vireo (*Vireo atricapillus*). *In* The birds of North America, No. 181 (A. Poole and F. Gill, eds.). Academy of Natural Sciences, Philadelphia, and American Ornithologists' Union, Washington, D.C.

Grzybowski, J. A. 1995b. Carolina Wrens fledge Brown-headed Cowbird chick. Bull. Okla. Ornithol. Soc. 28:6–7.

Grzybowski, J. A., R. B. Clapp, and J. T. Marshall Jr. 1986. History and current distribution of the Black-capped Vireo in Oklahoma. American Birds 40:1151–1161.

Grzybowski, J. A. , D. J. Tazik, and G. D. Schnell. 1994. Regional analysis of Black-capped Vireo breeding habitats. Condor 96:512–544.

Guzy, M. J., and G. Ritchison. 1999. Common Yellowthroat (*Geothlypis trichas*). *In* The Birds of North America, No. 448 (A. Poole and F. Gill, eds.). Academy of Natural Sciences, Philadelphia, and American Ornithologists' Union, Washington, D.C.

Haggerty, T. M. 1988. Aspects of the breeding biology and productivity of Bachman's Sparrow in central Arkansas. Wilson Bull. 100:247–255.

Haggerty, T. M. 1992. Effects of nestling age and brood size on nestling care in the Bachman's Sparrow (*Aimophila aestivalis*). Am. Midl. Nat. 128:115–125.

Haggerty, T. M., and E. S. Morton. 1995. Carolina Wren (*Thryothorus ludovicianus*). *In* The Birds of North America, No. 188 (A. Poole and F. Gill, eds.). Academy

of Natural Sciences, Philadelphia, and American Ornithologists' Union, Washington, D.C.

Haig, S. M. 1992. Piping Plover (*Charadrius melodus*). *In* The Birds of North America, No. 2 (A. Poole and F. Gill, eds.). Academy of Natural Sciences, Philadelphia, and American Ornithologists' Union, Washington, D.C.

Halkin, S. L. and S. U. Linville. 1999. Northern Cardinal (*Cardinalis cardinalis*). *In* The Birds of North America, No. 440 (A. Poole and F. Gill, eds.). Academy of Natural Sciences, Philadelphia, and American Ornithologists' Union, Washington, D.C.

Hall, G. A. 1996. Yellow-throated Warbler (*Dendroica dominica*). *In* The Birds of North America, No. 223 (A. Poole and F. Gill, eds.). Academy of Natural Sciences, Philadelphia, and American Ornithologists' Union, Washington, D.C.

Haller, K. W. 1972. Late nesting of Yellow-billed Cuckoo in southeastern Oklahoma. Bull. Okla. Ornithol. Soc. 5:19–20.

Haller, K. W. 1973. Double-crested Cormorants with head plumes sighted along south shore of Lake Texoma. Bull. Okla. Ornithol. Soc. 6:5–6.

Hamas, M. J. 1994. Belted Kingfisher (*Ceryle alcyon*). *In* The Birds of North America, No. 84 (A. Poole and F. Gill, eds.). Academy of Natural Sciences, Philadelphia, and American Ornithologists' Union, Washington, D.C.

Hamel, P. B. 2000. Cerulean Warbler (*Dendroica cerulea*). *In* The Birds of North America, No. 511 (A. Poole, P. Stettenheim, and F. Gill, eds.). Academy of Natural Sciences, Philadelphia, and American Ornithologists' Union, Washington, D.C.

Hamerstrom, F. N. 1986. Harrier: Hawk of the marshes. Smithsonian Institution Press, Washington, D.C.

Hamerstrom, F. N., and F. Hamerstrom. 1961. Status and problems of North American grouse. Wilson Bull. 73:284–294.

Hamerstrom, F. N., O. E. Mattson, and F. Hamerstrom. 1957. A guide to prairie-chicken management. Wisc. Conserv. Dep. Tech. Wildl. Bull. No. 15. 128pp.

Hanebrink, E. L. 1968. A comparison of three heronries in the Mississippi valley. Migrant 39:49–52.

Hanners, L. A., and S. R. Patton. 1998. Worm-eating Warbler (*Helmitheros vermivora*). *In* The Birds of North America, No. 367 (A. Poole, P. Stettenheim, and F. Gill, eds.). Academy of Natural Sciences, Philadelphia, and American Ornithologists' Union, Washington, D.C.

Hansen, H. A. 1965. The Giant Canada Goose. Southern Illinois University, Carbondale.

Harden, W. D. 1972a. Predation by hawks on bats at Vickery Bat Cave. Bull. Okla. Ornithol. Soc. 5(1):4–5.

Harden, W. D. 1972b. Recovery in north-central Oklahoma of Boat-tailed Grackle banded in central Oklahoma. Bull. Okla. Ornithol. Soc. 5:16.

Harden, W. D. 1977. Late nesting of Pied-billed Grebe in

Oklahoma. Bull. Okla. Ornithol. Soc. 10:21–22.

Hardy, J. W. 1958. The occurrence of the Inca Dove (*Scardafella inca*) in Kansas. Bull. Kans. Ornithol. Soc. 8:18–19.

Harlan, J. R. 1957. Grasslands of Oklahoma. Oklahoma State University, Stillwater.

Harris, H. R. 1986. Notes on a population of Bell's Vireos in Oklahoma County, Oklahoma. Bull. Okla. Ornithol. Soc. 19(4):30–31.

Harris, H. R. 1988. Lewis's Woodpecker in Logan County, Oklahoma. Bull. Okla. Ornithol. Soc. 21:19–20.

Harrison, H. H. 1975. A Field Guide to Birds' Nests in the United States East of the Mississippi River. Houghton Mifflin Co., Boston.

Harrison, H. H. 1979. A Field Guide to Western Birds Nests. Houghton Mifflin Co., Boston.

Harrison, H. H. 1984. Wood Warblers' World. Simon and Schuster, New York.

Hatch, J. J., and D. V. Weseloh. 1999. Double-crested Cormorant (*Phalacrocorax auritus*). *In* The Birds of North America, No. 441 (A. Poole and F. Gill, eds.). Academy of Natural Sciences, Philadelphia, and American Ornithologists' Union, Washington, D.C.

Haug, E. A., B. A. Millsap, and M. S. Martell 1993. Burrowing Owl (*Speotyto cunicularia*). *In* The Birds of North America, No. 61 (A. Poole and F. Gill. eds.). Academy of Natural Sciences, Philadelphia, and American Ornithologists' Union, Washington, D.C.

Hayman, P., J. Marchant, and T. Prater. 1986. Shorebirds: An Identification Guide. Houghton Mifflin Co., New York.

Heck, B. A. 1991. Nesting of the Anhinga in McCurtain County, Oklahoma. Bull. Okla. Ornithol. Soc. 24:13–14.

Heck, B. A. 1994. Anhinga nesting update in McCurtain County, Oklahoma. Bull. Okla. Ornithol. Soc. 27(4):26–27.

Heck, B. A. 1999. Breeding record of the Tree Swallow in McCurtain County, Oklahoma. Bull. Okla. Ornithol. Soc. 32:6–7.

Heck, B. A. 2001. First nesting attempt of the Inca Dove for Oklahoma. Bull. Okla. Ornithol. Soc. 34:4.

Heck, B. A., and W. D. Arbour. 2001. First nesting records of the Black-bellied Whistling-Duck in southeastern Oklahoma. Bull. Okla. Ornithol. Soc. 34:17.

Heflebower, C. C., and E. V. Klett. 1980. A killer hailstorm at the Washita Refuge. Bull. of the Okla. Ornithol. Soc. 13:27.

Hefley, H. M. 1937. Ecological studies on the Canadian River floodplain in Cleveland County, Oklahoma. Ecological Monographs 7:346–402.

Heitmeyer, M. E. 1986. Post-breeding distribution and habitat use of wading birds in Oklahoma, USA. Waterbirds 9:163–170.

Heitmeyer, M. E., and P. A. Vohs Jr. 1984. Characteristics of wetlands used by migrating dabbling ducks in Oklahoma, USA. Wildfowl 35:61–70.

Helema, F. 1974. Breeding of Lark Bunting in Garfield County, Oklahoma. Bull. Okla. Ornithol. Soc. 7(2):16.

Hellack, J. J. 1969. Successful nesting of Bell's Vireo in Johnston County, Oklahoma. Bull. Okla. Ornithol. Soc. 2:7–8.

Hellack, J. J. 1974. Spring arrival of Little Blue Heron in Oklahoma. Bull. Okla. Ornithol. Soc. 7:5.

Henderson, E. 1933. Birds and Mammals of Texas County, Oklahoma. Master's thesis, University of Kansas, Lawrence.

Hendricks, D. P. 1972. A persistent pair of Carolina Wrens. Bull. Okla. Ornithol. Soc. 5(2):14–15.

Hendricks, D. P. 1975. Copulatory behavior of a pair of Yellow-billed Cuckoos. Auk 92:151.

Hepp, G. R., and F. C. Bellrose. 1995. Wood Duck (*Aix sponsa*). *In* The Birds of North America, No. 169 (A. Poole and F. Gill, eds.). Academy of Natural Sciences, Philadelphia, and American Ornithologists' Union, Washington, D.C.

Herbert, L. 1997. First nesting for Cedar Waxwing in eastern Oklahoma. Bull. Okla. Ornithol. Soc. 30:33–34.

Herkert, J. R. 1994a. The effects of habitat fragmentation on midwestern grassland bird communities. Ecological Applications 4(3):461–471.

Herkert, J. R. 1994b. Breeding bird communities of midwestern prairie fragments: The effects of prescribed burning and habitat area. Nat. Areas J. 14:128–135.

Herkert, J. R. 1998. Effects of management practices on grassland birds: Henslow's Sparrow. Northern Prairie Wildlife Research Center, Jamestown, North Dakota.

Herkert, J. R., D. E. Kroodsma, and J. P. Gibbs. 2001. Sedge Wren (*Cistothorus platensis*). *In* The Birds of North America (A. Poole and F. Gill, eds.). Academy of Natural Sciences, Philadelphia, and American Ornithologists' Union, Washington, D.C.

Hicks, E. C. 1978. Black Rail sighted in Osage County, Oklahoma. Bull. Okla. Ornithol. Soc. 11(3):21.

Hier, R. H. 1999. History and hunting the Greater Prairie-Chicken: A rich tradition. Pp. 163–167 in The Greater Prairie-Chicken: A National Look (W. D. Svedarsky, R. H. Hier, and N. J. Silvy, eds.). Univ. Minn. Misc. Publ. 99–19999. Minn. Ag. Exp. Sta., St. Paul.

Hill, G. E. 1993. House Finch (*Carpodacus mexicanus*). *In* The Birds of North America, No. 46 (A. Poole and F. Gill, eds.). Academy of Natural Sciences, Philadelphia, and American Ornithologists' Union, Washington, D.C.

Hill, G. E. 1995. Black-headed Grosbeak (*Pheucticus melanocephalus*). *In* The Birds of North America, No. 143 (A. Poole and F. Gill, eds.). Academy of Natural Sciences, Philadelphia, and American Ornithologists' Union, Washington, D.C.

Hill, L. A. 1985. Breeding ecology of Interior Least Terns,

Snowy Plovers, and American Avocets at Salt Plains National Wildlife Refuge, Oklahoma. M.S. thesis, Oklahoma State University, Stillwater.

Hill, L. A. 1992. Status of the Least Tern and Snowy Plover on the Red River, 1991. U.S. Fish and Wildlife Service, Tulsa, Oklahoma.

Hill, L. A. 1993. Status and Distribution of the Least Tern in Oklahoma. Bull. Okla. Ornithol. Soc. 26(2):9–24.

Hill, R. A. 1976. Host-parasite relationships of the Brown-headed Cowbird in a prairie habitat of west-central Kansas. Wilson Bull. 88:555–565.

Hines, J. E., and G. J. Mitchell. 1984. Parasitic laying in nests of Gadwalls. Can. J. Zool. 62:627–630.

Hitchcock, R. R., and R. E. Mirarchi. 1984. Duration of dependence of wild fledgling Mourning Doves on parental care. J. Wildl. Manage. 48:99–108.

Hoagland, B. W. 2000. The vegetation of Oklahoma: A classification for landscape mapping and conservation planning. Southwest. Nat. 45:385–420.

Hoagland, B. W., I. Butler, and F. L. Johnson. 1999. Ecology and vegetation of the cross timbers in Kansas, Oklahoma and Texas. In The Savanna, Barren and Rock Outcrop Communities of North America (R. C. Anderson, Anderson, R. C., J. Fralish, and J. Baskin, eds.). Cambridge University Press.

Hoagland, B. W., and S. L. Collins. 1997. Heterogeneity in shortgrass prairie vegetation: The role of playa lakes. J. Veg. Sci. 8:277–286.

Hobbet, S., and R. Hobbet. 1988. A Pileated Woodpecker nest in Woodward County, Oklahoma. Bull. Okla. Ornithol. Soc. 21(2):11–12.

Holcomb, L. C. 1969. Breeding biology of the American Goldfinch in Ohio. J. Field Ornithol. 40(1):26–44.

Holmgren, M. 1981. Wood Duck and Vermilion Flycatcher in far-western Oklahoma. Bull. Okla. Ornithol. Soc. 14:13–14.

Holt, D. W., and S. M. Leasure. 1993. Short-eared Owl (Asio flammeus). In The Birds of North America, No. 62 (A. Poole and F. Gill, eds.). Academy of Natural Sciences, Philadelphia, and American Ornithologists' Union, Washington, D.C.

Hopp, S. L., A. Kirby, and C. A. Boone. 1995. White-eyed Vireo (Vireo griseus). In The Birds of North America, No. 168 (A. Poole and F. Gill, eds.). Academy of Natural Sciences, Philadelphia, and American Ornithologists' Union, Washington, D.C.

Horak, G. J. 1985. Kansas Prairie-Chickens. KFGC publication, Wildl. Bull. No. 3.

Horak, G. J., and R. D. Applegate. 1998. Greater Prairie-Chicken management. Kans. School Nat. 45(1):1–15.

Horton, R. E. 2000. Distribution and abundance of Lesser Prairie-Chicken in Oklahoma. Prairie Nat. 32:189–195.

Horton, R. E., and D. H. Wolfe. 1999. Status and management of the Greater Prairie-Chicken in Oklahoma.

Pp. 105–111 in The Greater Prairie-Chicken: A National Look (W. D. Svedarsky, R. H. Hier, and N. J. Silvy, eds.). Univ. Minn. Misc. Publ. 99–19999. Minn. Ag. Exp. Sta., St. Paul.

Horvath, O. 1963. Contributions to nesting ecology of forest birds. M.S. Forestry, University of British Columbia, Canada.

Howell, J. C. 1950. Notes on certain Oklahoma birds. Proc. Okla. Acad. Sci. 29:35–37.

Howell, S. N. G., and S. Webb. 1995. A Guide to the Birds of Mexico and Northern Central America. Oxford University Press, Oxford, England.

Howes-Jones, D. 1985a. Nesting habits and activity patterns of Warbling Vireos, Vireo gilvus, in southern Ontario. Can. Field-Nat. 99:484–489.

Howes-Jones, D. 1985b. The complex song of the Warbling Vireo. Can. J. Zool. 63:2756–2766.

Howes-Jones, D. 1985c. Relationships among song activity, context, and social behavior in the Warbling Vireo. Wilson Bull. 97:4–20.

Hoyt, S. F. 1957. The ecology of the Pileated Woodpecker. Ecology 38(2):246–256.

Hughes, J. M. 1996. Greater Roadrunner (Geococcyx californianus). In The Birds of North America, No. 244 (A. Poole and F. Gills, eds.). Academy of Natural Sciences, Philadelphia, and American Ornithologists' Union, Washington, D.C.

Hughes, J. M. 1999. Yellow-billed Cuckoo (Coccyzus americanus). In The Birds of North America, No. 418 (A. Poole and F. Gill, eds.). Academy of Natural Sciences, Philadelphia, and American Ornithologists' Union, Washington, D.C.

Hughes, W. 1952. Snowy Egret and Little Blue Heron breeding in Oklahoma. Wilson Bull. 64:160.

Hull, S. D. 2000. Effects of management practices on grassland birds: Eastern Meadowlark. Northern Prairie Wildlife Research Center, Jamestown, North Dakota. Northern Prairie Wildlife Research Center Home Page. Http://www.npwrc.usgs.gov/resource/literatr/grasbird/fpeame/fpeame.htm (Version 16JUN2000).

Humann, A. 2001. Long-tailed Tits (Bushtit). In The Sibley Guide to Bird Life and Behavior. Alfred A. Knopf, New York.

Hume, R. 1991. Owls of the World. Parkgate Books, London, England.

Hunt, W. H. 1986. Successful late nesting of House Wren in Grady County, Oklahoma. Bull. Okla. Ornithol. Soc. 19:13–14.

Husak, M. S., and T. C. Maxwell. 1998. Golden-fronted Woodpecker (Melanerpes aurifrons). In The Birds of North America, No. 373 (A. Poole and F. Gill, eds.). Academy of Natural Sciences, Philadelphia, and American Ornithologists' Union, Washington, D.C.

Husak, M. S., and T. C. Maxwell. 2000. A review of twentieth-century range expansion and population trends of the Golden-fronted Woodpecker (*Melanerpes aurifrons*): Historical and ecological perspectives. Tex. J. Sci. 52:275–284.

Hyde, A. S. 1939. The life history of Henslow's Sparrow, *Passerherbulus henslowi* (Audubon). Misc. Publ. No. 41, Mus. of Zoology, University of Michigan, Ann Arbor.

Ingold, J. L. 1993. Blue Grosbeak (*Guiraca caerulea*). *In* The Birds of North America, No. 79 (A. Poole and F. Gill, eds.). Academy of Natural Sciences, Philadelphia, and American Ornithologists' Union, Washington, D.C.

Isaacs, W. S. 1980. Second Black-throated Sparrow record for central Oklahoma. Bull. Okla. Ornithol. Soc. 13:34–35.

Isley, L. D. 1979. Successful nesting of the Bald Eagle in east-central Oklahoma. Bull. Okla. Ornithol. Soc. 12:1–4.

Isley, L. D. 1982. Second successful nesting of Bald Eagle in Oklahoma. Bull. Okla. Ornithol. Soc. 15:5–7.

Isley, L. D., and J. W. Lish. 1986. Nesting and summer records for Ospreys in Oklahoma. Bull. Okla. Ornithol. Soc. 19(1):2–3.

Isted, D. 1978. Second King Rail breeding record for Payne County, Oklahoma. Bull. Okla. Ornithol. Soc. 11:20–21.

Jackson, B. J. S., and J. A. Jackson. 2000. Killdeer (*Charadrius vociferous*). *In* The Birds of North America, No. 517 (A. Poole and F. Gill, eds.). Academy of Natural Sciences, Philadelphia, and American Ornithologists' Union, Washington, D.C.

Jackson, J. A. 1976. A comparison of some aspects of the breeding ecology of Red-headed and Red-bellied woodpeckers in Kansas. Condor 78:67–76.

Jackson, J. A. 1983. Nesting phenology, nest site selection, and reproductive success of Black and Turkey vultures. *In* Vulture Biology and Management,. S. R. Wilbur and J. A. Jackson, eds. University of California Press, Berkeley.

Jackson, J. A. 1994. Red-cockaded Woodpecker (*Picoides borealis*). *In* The Birds of North America, No. 85 (A. Poole and F. Gill, eds.). Academy of Natural Sciences, Philadelphia, and American Ornithologists' Union, Washington, D.C.

Jackson, J. A. 2001. Water witch. Wildfowl Carving Magazine 17(2):51–64.

Jackson, J. A., and W. E. Davis Jr. 1998. Range expansion of the Red-bellied Woodpecker. Bird Observer 26:4–12.

Jackson, J. A., R. N. Conner, and B. J. S. Jackson. 1986. The effects of wilderness on the endangered Red-cockaded Woodpecker. Pp. 71–78 *in* Wilderness and Natural Areas in the Eastern United States: A Management Challenge (D. L. Kulhavy and R. N. Conner, eds.). Center for Applied Studies, School of Forestry, Stephen F. Austin State University, Nacogdoches, Texas.

Jacobs, B., and J. D. Wilson. 1997. Missouri Breeding Bird Atlas. Missouri Department of Conservation, Jefferson City.

Jacobs, K. F. 1958. A drop-net trapping technique for Greater Prairie-Chickens. Proc. Okla. Acad. Sci. 38:154–157.

Jacobs, K. F. 1959. Restoration of the Greater Prairie-Chicken. ODWC publication.

Jacobs, K. F. 1960. Distribution of Scaled Quail (*Callipepla squamata*) in Oklahoma. Final Rep., Proj. W-65-R-S, Okla. Dept. Wildl. Conserv.

Jacobs, K. F. 1968. Capture of a prairie-chicken by a Prairie-Falcon. Bull. Okla. Ornithol. Soc., 1:8–9.

James, D. A., and J. A. Neal. 1986. Arkansas Birds: Their Distribution and Abundance. University of Arkansas Press. Fayetteville.

James, E. 1823. Account of an Expedition from Pittsburgh to the Rocky Mountains, Performed in the years 1819 and 1820, Under the Command of Major Stephen H. Long (2 vol.). Carey and Lea, Philadelphia, PA.

James, F. C. 1971. Ordination of habitat relationships among breeding birds. Wilson Bull. 83:215–236.

James, J. D., and J. E. Thompson. 2001. Black-bellied Whistling-Duck (*Dendrocygna autumnalis*). *In* The Birds of North America, No. 578 (A. Poole, P. Stettenheim, and F. Gills, eds.). Academy of Natural Sciences, Philadelphia, and American Ornithologists' Union, Washington, D.C.

Jamison, B. E., J. A. Dechant, D. H. Johnson, L. D. Igl, C. M. Doldade, and B. R. Euliss. 2002. Effects of management practices on grassland birds: Lesser Prairie-Chicken. Northern Prairie Wildlife Research Center, Jamestown, North Dakota. 29 pp.

Jenkins, M. A., and S. K. Sherrod. 1993. Recent Bald Eagle nest records in Oklahoma. Bull. Okla. Ornithol. Soc. 26(3):25–28.

Jenkins, M. A., and S. K. Sherrod. 1994. Additional information on Bald Eagle breeding in Oklahoma. Bull. Okla. Ornithol. Soc. 27(4):28.

Jenkinson, M.A., and R. M. Mengel. 1970. Ingesting stones by goatsuckers. Condor 72:236–237.

Jennings, R. G. 1983. Possible courtship feeding of Yellow-billed Cuckoo. Bull. Okla. Ornithol. Soc. 16:14.

Johns, M. A. 1971. Successful nesting of the House Wren in Cleveland County, Oklahoma. Bull. Okla. Ornithol. Soc. 4:9–11.

Johns, M. A. 1974. Late date for Orchard Oriole and cowbird it had fledged. Bull. Okla. Ornithol. Soc. 7(2):16.

Johnsgard, P. A. 1968. Waterfowl: Their Biology and Natural History. University of Nebraska Press, Lincoln.

Johnsgard, P. A. 1973. Pinnated Grouse. Pp. 274–299 *in* Grouse and quails of North America. University Nebraska Press, Lincoln. 553pp.

Johnsgard, P. A. 1978. Ducks, Geese, and Swans of the World. University of Nebraska Press, Lincoln.

Johnsgard, P. A. 1979. Birds of the Great Plains, Breeding Species and Their Distribution. University of Nebraska Press, Lincoln.

Johnsgard, P. A. 1988. North American Owls. Smithsonian Institution Press, Washington, D.C.

Johnsgard, P. A. 1990. Hawks, Eagles, and Falcons of North America: Biology and Natural History. Smithsonian Institution Press, Washington, D.C.

Johnsgard, P. A. 1993. Cormorants, Darters, and Pelicans of the World. Smithsonian Institution Press, Washington, D.C.

Johnsgard, P. A. 1997. The Hummingbirds of North America. 2nd ed. Smithsonian Institution Press, Washington, D.C.

Johnson, H. L., and C. E. Duchon. 1995. Atlas of Oklahoma Climate. University of Oklahoma Press, Norman.

Johnson, L. S. 1998. House Wren (*Troglodytes aedon*). *In* The Birds of North America, No. 380 (A. Poole and F. Gill, eds.). Academy of Natural Sciences, Philadelphia, and American Ornithologists' Union, Washington, D.C.

Johnson, R. G., and S. A. Temple. 1990. Nest predation and brood parasitism of tallgrass prairie birds. J. Wildl. Manage. 54:106–111.

Johnson, R. R., and L. Haight. 1996. Canyon Towhee (*Pipilo fuscus*). *In* The Birds of North America, No. 264 (A. Poole and F. Gill, eds.). Academy of Natural Sciences, Philadelphia, and American Ornithologists' Union, Washington, D.C.

Johnston, R. F. 1960. Behavior of the Inca Dove. Condor 62:7–24.

Johnston, R. F. 1992. Rock Dove. *In* The Birds of North America, No13. (A. Poole, P. Stettenheim, and F. Gill, eds.). Academy of Natural Sciences, Philadelphia, and American Ornithologists' Union, Washington, D.C.

Jones, R. E. 1960. The life-form concept applied to prairie-chicken habitat in Oklahoma. Proc. Okla. Acad. Sci. 40:134–136.

Jones, R. E. 1961. A comparative study of the habitats of the Lesser and Greater Prairie-Chickens. Okla. Coop. Wildl. Res. Unit Quart. Rep. 14:21–24.

Jones, R. E. 1963a. A comparative study of the habits of the Lesser and Greater Prairie-Chickens. Ph.D. diss. Oklahoma State University, Stillwater. 160pp.

Jones, R. E. 1963b. Identification and analysis of Lesser and Greater Prairie-Chicken habitat. J. Wildl. Manage. 27:757–778.

Jones, R. E. 1964a. The specific distinctness of the Greater and Lesser Prairie-Chickens. Auk 81:65–73.

Jones, R. E. 1964b. Habitat used by Lesser Prairie-Chickens for feeding related to seasonal behavior of plants in Beaver County, Oklahoma. Southwest Nat. 9:111–117.

Jones, S. L. 1998. Canyon Wren (*Catherpes mexicanus*). *In* Colorado Breeding Bird Atlas (H. E. Kingery, ed.). Colorado Bird Atlas Partnership and Colorado Division of Wildlife, Denver.

Jones, S. L., and J. S. Dieni. 1995. Canyon Wren (*Catherpes mexicanus*). *In* The Birds of North America, No. 197 (A. Poole and F. Gill, eds.). Academy of Natural Sciences, Philadelphia, and American Ornithologists' Union, Washington, D.C.

Jones, S. R. 1998. Cassin's Kingbird (*Tyrannus vociferans*). *In* Colorado Breeding Bird Atlas (H. E. Kingery, ed.). Colorado Bird Atlas Partnership and Colorado Division of Wildlife, Denver.

Josef, R. 1996. Loggerhead Shrike (*Lanius ludovicianus*). *In* The Birds of North America, No. 231 (A. Poole and F. Gill, eds.). Academy of Natural Sciences, Philadelphia, and American Ornithologists' Union, Washington, D.C.

Joyner, D. E. 1977. Behavior of Ruddy Duck broods in Utah. Auk 94:343–349.

Joyner, D. E. 1983. Parasitic egg laying in Redheads and Ruddy Ducks in Utah: Incidence and success. Auk 100:717–725.

Kahl, R. B., T. S. Baskett, J. A. Ellis, and J. N. Burroughs. 1985. Characteristics of summer habitats of selected nongame birds in Missouri. University of Missouri-Columbia. Agric. Exp. Stn. Rs. Bull. 1056.

Kamp, M. B., and J. Loyd. 2001. First breeding records of the Black-bellied Whistling-Duck for Oklahoma. Bull. Okla. Ornithol. Soc. 34:13–17.

Kaspari, M. 1991. Prey preparation as a way that Grasshopper Sparrows (*Ammodramus savannarum*) increase the nutrient concentration of their prey. Behav. Ecol. 2:234–241.

Kastl, M. 1980. Scarlet Tanager nesting in north-central Oklahoma. Bull. Okla. Ornithol. Soc. 13:1–4.

Kaufman, K. 1996. Lives of North American birds. Houghton Mifflin Co., Boston.

Kaufman, K. 2000. Birds of North America. Houghton Mifflin Co., New York.

Keir, J. R., and D. D. L. R. Wilde. 1976. Observations of Swainson's Hawk nesting in northeastern Illinois. Wilson Bull. 88(4):658–659.

Kelley, M. 1977. A late nesting of the Cardinal. Bull. Okla. Ornithol. Soc. 10(3):19–21.

Kelly, J. F., S. M. Pletschet, and D. M. Leslie Jr. 1993. Habitat associations of Red-cockaded Woodpecker cavity trees in an old-growth forest of Oklahoma. J. Wildl. Manage. 57:122–128.

Kelly, J. F., S. M. Pletschet, and D. M. Leslie Jr. 1994. Decline of the Red-cockaded Woodpecker (Picoides borealis) in southeastern Oklahoma. Am. Midl. Nat. 132:275–283.

Kendeigh, S. C. 1945. Nesting behavior of wood warblers. Wilson Bull. 57:145–162.

Kennedy, E. D., and D. W. White. 1997. Bewick's Wren (*Thryomanes bewickii*). *In* The Birds of North America, No. 315 (A. Poole and F. Gill, eds.). Academy of Natural Sciences, Philadelphia, and American Ornithologists' Union, Washington, D.C.

Keppie, D. M., and R. M. Whiting Jr. 1994. American Woodcock (*Scolopax minor*). *In* The Birds of North

America, No. 100 (A. Poole and F. Gill, eds.). Academy of Natural Sciences, Philadelphia, and American Ornithologists' Union, Washington, D.C.

Kilham, L. 1974. Early breeding season behavior of Downy Woodpeckers. Wilson Bull. 84:407–18.

Kilham, L. 1989. The American Crow and the Common Raven. Texas A&M University Press, College Station.

Kingery, H. E., ed. 1998. Colorado Breeding Bird Atlas. Colorado Bird Atlas Partnership and Colorado Division of Wildlife, Denver.

Kirn, A. J. 1918. Observations of Swainson's Warbler. Oologist 35(6):97–98.

Knopf, F. L. 1996. Mountain Plover (*Charadrius montanus*). *In* The Birds of North America, No. 211 (A. Poole and F. Gill, eds.). Academy of Natural Sciences, Philadelphia, and American Ornithologists' Union, Washington, D.C.

Knopf, F. L., and J. R. Rupert. 1999. Use of cultivated fields by breeding Mountain Plovers in Colorado. Pp. 81–86 *in* Ecology and Conservation of Grassland Birds of the Western Hemisphere (P. D. Vickery and J. R. Herkert, eds.). Studies in Avian Biology 19.

Koenen, M. T. 1995. Breeding ecology and management of Least Terns, Snowy Plovers and American Avocets. M.S. thesis, Oklahoma State University, Stillwater.

Koenen, M. T., M. Oliphant, J. Key, and E. Key. 1994. First nesting record of Black-necked Stilts for Oklahoma. Bull. Okla. Ornithol. Soc. 27:1–4.

Koenen, M. T., B. R. Winton, R. S. Shepperd, and D. M. Leslie Jr. 1996. Species composition of a ciconiiform rookery in north-central Oklahoma. Bull. Okla. Ornithol. Soc. 29:3–6.

Kricher, J. C. 1995. Black-and-white Warbler (*Mniotilta varia*). *In* The Birds of North America, No. 158 (A. Poole and F. Gill, eds.). Academy of Natural Sciences, Philadelphia, and American Ornithologists' Union, Washington, D.C.

Kuenning, R. R. 1998. Lewis's Woodpecker. *In* Colorado Breeding Bird Atlas (H. E. Kingery, ed.). Colorado Bird Atlas Partnership and Colorado Division of Wildlife, Denver.

Kuhnert, N. R. 1998. Overview of landbird monitoring program work in LeFlore County. Note sent to the U.S. Forest Service, Idabel, Oklahoma. 11pp.

Kuhnert, N. R. 2001. An overview of landbird monitoring program work in LeFlore County. Note sent to the U.S. Forest Service, Idabel, Oklahoma. 3 pp.

Kushlan, J. A. 1973. Least Bittern nesting colonially. Auk. 90:685–686.

Kushlan, J. A., and K. L. Bildstein. 1992. White Ibis. *In* The Birds of North America, No. 9 (A. Poole, P. Stettenheim, and F. Gills, eds.). Academy of Natural Sciences, Philadelphia, and American Ornithologists' Union, Washington, D.C.

Lack, D. B., L. W. Oring, and S. J. Maxson. 1985. Mate and nutrient limitation of egg-laying in a polyandrous shorebird. Ecology 66:1513–1524.

Lane, D., and A. Jaramillo. 2000. Identification of *Hylocichla/Catharus* thrushes. Birding 32(2):121–135.

Langford, J. O. 1970. Premature departure from nest of young Common Ravens. Bull. Okla. Ornithol. Soc. 3:23–24.

Lanyon, W. E. 1956a. Ecological aspects of the sympatric distribution of meadowlarks in the north-central states. Ecology 37(1):98–108.

Lanyon, W. E. 1956b. Territory in the meadowlarks, genus *Sturnella*. Ibis 98:485–489.

Lanyon, W. E. 1966. Hybridization in meadowlarks. Bull. Am. Mus. Nat. Hist. 134:1–26.

Lanyon, W. E. 1979. Hybrid sterility in meadowlarks. Nature 279:557–558.

Lanyon, W. E. 1994. Western Meadowlark (*Sturnella neglecta*). *In* The Birds of North America, No. 104 (A. Poole and F. Gill, eds.). Academy of Natural Sciences, Philadelphia, and American Ornithologists' Union, Washington, D.C.

Lanyon, W. E. 1995. Eastern Meadowlark (*Sturnella magna*). *In* The Birds of North America, No. 160 (A. Poole and F. Gill, eds.). Academy of Natural Sciences, Philadelphia, and American Ornithologists' Union, Washington, D.C.

Lanyon, W. E. 1997. Great-crested Flycatcher (*Myiarchus crinitus*). *In* The Birds of North America, No. 300 (A. Poole and F. Gill, eds.). Academy of Natural Sciences, Philadelphia, and American Ornithologists' Union, Washington, D.C.

Laubhan, M. K., and F. A. Reid. 1991. Characteristics of Yellow-crowned Night-Heron nests in lowland hardwood forests of Missouri. Wilson Bull. 103:486–491.

Lauckhart, J. B., and J. W. McKean. 1956. Chinese Pheasants in the Northwest. Pp. 43–89 *in* Pheasants in North America. Stackpole Comp., Harrisburg, Penn.

Leppla, R. R., and D. H. Gordon. 1978. Predation by Loggerhead Shrikes. Bull. Okla. Ornithol. Soc. 11(4):33.

LeSchack, C. R., S. K. McKnight, and G. R. Hepp. 1997. Gadwall (*Anas strepera*). *In* The Birds of North America, No. 283 (A. Poole and F. Gill, eds.). Academy of Natural Sciences, Philadelphia, and American Ornithologists' Union, Washington, D.C.

Leslie, D. M., J. S. Shackford, A. Woodward, S. Fuhlendorf, and C. B. Greene. 1999. Landscape-level evaluation of the decline of the Lesser Prairie-Chicken in Oklahoma, Texas, and New Mexico. ODWC Final Report, grant no. AP-96-201W. 63pp.

Letson, O. W., and E. Letson. 1954. New and unusual birds for Tulsa County, Oklahoma. Proc. Okla. Acad. Sci. for 1952, 33:136–137.

Levad, R. 1998. Lesser Goldfinch (*Carduelis psaltria*). *In*

Colorado Breeding Bird Atlas (H. E. Kingery, ed.). Colorado Bird Atlas Parnership and Colorado Division of Wildlife, Denver.

Lewis, W. E. 1930. Water birds in a dry land. Wilson Bull. 42:36–44.

Ligon, J. D. 1970. Still more responses of the Poor-will to low temperatures. Condor 72:496–498.

Lincer, J. L., and K. Steenhof, eds. 1997. The Burrowing Owl, Its Biology and Management: Including the Proceedings of the First International Symposium. Raptor Research Report Number 9.

Lindsay, H. L. 1985. Common Poorwill in Tulsa County, Oklahoma. Bull. Okla. Ornithol. Soc. 18:6–7.

Linz, G. M., and S. B. Bolin. 1982. Incidence of Brown-headed Cowbird parasitism on Red-wing Blackbirds. Wilson Bull. 94:93–95.

Lish, J. W. 1974. Apparent predation by Golden Eagle at Great Blue Heron colony. Bull. Okla. Ornithol. Soc. 7:4.

Lish, J. W., and S. K. Sherrod. 1986. A history of Bald Eagle nesting activity in Oklahoma. Proc. Okla. Acad. Sci. 66:15–20.

Little, E. L. 1939. The vegetation of the Caddo County canyons, Oklahoma. Ecology 20:1–10.

Little, E. L. 1980. Baldcypress (*Taxodium distichum*) in Oklahoma. Proc. Okla. Aca. Sci. 60:105–107.

Little, E. L. 1996. Forest Trees of Oklahoma. 14th ed. Oklahoma Department of Agriculture, Forestry Services.

Logan, T. H. 1970. A study of Rio Grande Wild Turkey by radio telemetry (in western Oklahoma). Fed. Aid in Fish and Wildlife Restoration Project W-86-R.

Lokemoen, J. T., and H. F. Duebbert. 1976. Ferruginous Hawk nesting ecology and raptor populations in northern South Dakota. Condor 78(4):464–470.

Long, M. P., and C. I. Long. 1997. Breeding records of Tree Swallows at Grand Lake, Oklahoma. Bull. Okla. Ornithol. Soc. 30:21–23.

Looney, M. W. 1972. Predation on bats by hawks and owls. Bull. Okla. Ornithol. Soc. 5(1):1–4.

Lowery, G. H. 1974. Louisiana Birds. Louisiana State University Press, Baton Rouge.

Lowther, P. E. 1977. Old cowbird breeding records from the Great Plains region. Bird-banding 48:358–369.

Lowther, P. E. 1979. The nesting biology of House Sparrows in Kansas. Kans. Ornithol. Soc. Bull. 30:23–26.

Lowther, P. E. 1985. Catalog of Brown-headed Cowbird hosts from Iowa. Proc. Iowa Acad. Sci. 92:95–99.

Lowther, P. E. 1993. Brown-headed Cowbird (*Molothrus ater*). *In* The Birds of North America, No. 47 (A. Poole and F. Gill, eds.). Academy of Natural Sciences, Philadelphia, and American Ornithologists' Union, Washington, D.C.

Lowther, P. E. 2001. Ladder-backed Woodpecker (*Picoides scalaris*). *In* The Birds of North America, No. 565 (A.

Poole and F. Gill, eds.). Academy of Natural Sciences, Philadelphia, and American Ornithologists' Union, Washington, D.C.

Lowther, P. E., C. Celada, N. K. Klein, C. C. Rimmer, and D. A. Spector. 1999. Yellow Warbler (*Dendroica petechia*). *In* The Birds of North America, No. 454 (A. Poole, P. Stettenheim, and F. Gill, eds.). Academy of Natural Sciences, Philadelphia, and American Ornithologists' Union, Washington, D.C.

Lowther, P. E., and C. L. Cink. 1992. House Sparrow (*Passer domesticus*). *In* The Birds of North America, No. 12 (A. Poole and F. Gill, eds.). Academy of Natural Sciences, Philadelphia, and American Ornithologists' Union, Washington, D.C.

Lowther, P. E., D. E. Kroodsma, and G. H. Farley. 2000. Rock Wren (Salpinctes obsoletus). *In* The Birds of North America, No. 486 (A. Poole and F. Gill, eds.). Academy of Natural Sciences, Philadelphia, and American Ornithologists' Union, Washington, D.C.

Lowther, P. E., S. M. Lanyon, and C. W. Thompson. 1999. Painted Bunting (*Passerina ciris*). *In* The Birds of North America, No. 398 (A. Poole and F. Gill, eds.). Academy of Natural Sciences, Philadelphia, and American Ornithologists' Union, Washington, D.C.

Loyd, J. 1987. An Osprey carrying mammalian prey. Bull. Okla. Ornithol, Soc. 20(4):31.

Lunk, W. A. 1962. The Rough-winged Swallow: A Study Based on Its Breeding Biology in Michigan. Publ. Nuttall Ornithol. Club, 4, Cambridge, Massachusetts.

MacWhirter, R. B., and K. L. Bildstein. 1996. Northern Harrier (*Circus cyaneus*). *In* The Birds of North America, No. 210 (A. Poole and F. Gill, eds.). Academy of Natural Sciences, Philadelphia, and American Ornithologists' Union, Washington, D.C.

Maddock, M., and D. Geering. 1994. Range expansion and migration of the Cattle Egret. Ostrich 65(2):191–203.

Madge, S., and H. Burn. 1988. Waterfowl: An Identification Guide to the Ducks, Geese, and Swans of the World. Houghton Mifflin Co., Boston.

Marks, J. S., D. L. Evans, and D. W. Holt. 1994. Long-eared Owl (*Asio otis*), *In* The Birds of North America, No. 133 (A. Poole and F. Gills, eds.). Academy of Natural Sciences, Philadelphia, and American Ornithologists' Union, Washington, D.C.

Marti, C. D. 1973. House Sparrows feeding young at night. Wilson Bull. 85(4):483.

Marti, C. D. 1974. Feeding ecology of four sympatric owls. Condor 76:45–61.

Marti, C. D. 1992. Barn Owl (*Tyto alba*). *In* The Birds of North America, No. 1 (A. Poole, P. Stettenheim, and F. Gill, eds.). Academy of Natural Sciences, Philadelphia, and American Ornithologists' Union, Washington, D.C.

Marti, C. D., P. W. Wagner, and K. W. Denne. 1979. Nest

boxes for the management of Barn Owls. Wildl. Soc. Bull. 7:145–148.

Martin, J. M., and R. W. Storer. 1999. Pied-billed Grebe (*Podilymbus podiceps*). *In* The Birds of North America. No. 410 (A. Poole and F. Gill, eds.). Academy of Natural Sciences, Philadelphia, and American Ornithologists' Union, Washington, D.C.

Martin, J. W., and J. R. Parrish. 2000. Lark Sparrow (*Chondestes grammacus*). *In* The Birds of North America, No. 488 (A. Poole and F. Gill, eds.). Academy of Natural Sciences, Philadelphia, and American Ornithologists' Union, Washington, D.C.

Martin, S. A. 1978. Density and distribution of the Greater Prairie-Chicken in Oklahoma. Okla. Coop. Wildl. Res. Unit, Semi-annual Prog. Rept. 31:53–56.

Martin, S. A. 1980. Current status and approaches to monitoring populations and habitats of Greater Prairie-Chickens in Oklahoma. M.S. thesis. Oklahoma State University, Stillwater.

Martin, S. A., and F. L. Knopf. 1980. Distribution and numbers of Greater Prairie-Chickens in Oklahoma. Pp. 68–70 in Proceedings Prairie Grouse Symposium (P. A. Vohs and F. L. Knopf, eds.). Oklahoma State University, Stillwater.

Mason, K. 1983. Late fall sightings of Mississippi Kite. Bull. Okla. Ornithol. Soc. 16(1):4.

Masters, R. E., J. E. Skeen, and J. Whitehead, 1994. Preliminary fire history of McCurtain County Wilderness Area and implications for Red-cockaded Woodpecker management. *In* Proc. Red-cockaded Woodpecker Symposium III: Species Recovery, Ecology, and Management (D. L. Kulhavy, R. G. Hooper, and R. Costa, eds.). Nacogdoches, Texas.

Masters, R. E., J. E. Skeen, and J. A. Garner. 1989. Red-cockaded Woodpecker in Oklahoma: An update of Wood's 1974–77 study. Proc. Okla. Acad. Sci. 69:27–31.

Matiasek, J. J. 1998. Nest-site selection and breeding behavior of the migratory Rock Wren (*Salpinctes obsoletus*) in western Kansas. M.S. thesis, Fort Hays State University, Hays, Kansas.

Matray, P. F. 1974. Broad-winged hawk nesting and ecology. Auk 91:307–24.

Matthews, G. W. 1974. Vermilion Flycatcher in Washington County, Oklahoma. Bull. Okla.

Mayfield, H. 1965. The Brown-headed Cowbird with old and new hosts. Living Bird 4:13–28.

Mays, L. P. 1971. Early nesting of Black Vulture in Oklahoma. Bull. Okla. Ornithol. Soc. 4:3–4.

Mays, L. P. 1987. Late nesting of Purple Martin in central Oklahoma. Bull. Okla. Ornithol. Soc. 20:31–32.

Mazur, K. M., and P. C. James. 2000. Barred Owl (*Strix varia*). *In* The Birds of North America, No. 508 (A. Poole and F. Gill, eds.). Academy of Natural Sciences, Philadelphia, and American Ornithologists' Union, Washington, D.C.

McCarty, J. P. 1996. Eastern Wood-Pewee (*Contopus virens*). *In* The Birds of North America, No. 245 (A. Poole and F. Gill, eds.). Academy of Natural Sciences, Philadelphia, and American Ornithologists' Union, Washington, D.C.

McCormick, L. M. 1893. A hybrid tanager. Auk 10:302–303.

McDonald, M. V. 1998. Kentucky Warbler (*Oporornis formosus*). *In* The Birds of North America, No. 324 (A. Poole and F. Gill, eds.). Academy of Natural Sciences, Philadelphia, and American Ornithologists' Union, Washington, D.C.

McGaha, H. R. 1998. Late nesting date for the Carolina Wren in Oklahoma. Bull. Okla. Ornithol. Soc. 31(1):8.

McGee, L. E. 1975. Early nesting of cardinal in southwestern Oklahoma. Bull. Okla. Ornithol. Soc. 8(1):6–7.

McGee, L. E. 1978. Eastern Phoebe three-brooded in southwestern Oklahoma. Bull. Okla. Ornithol. Soc. 6:7–8.

McGee, L. E. 1980. American Kestrel nest in Comanche County, Oklahoma. Bull. Okla. Ornithol. Soc. 13(2):11–12.

McGee, L. E. 1990. First Common Poorwill nest for Comanche County, Oklahoma. Bull. Okla. Ornithol. Soc. 23:13–14.

McGee, J. M., and L. E. McGee. 1972. Blue Jay destroys cowbird-parasitized nest of Painted Bunting. Bull. Okla. Ornithol. Soc. 5:12–13.

McGee, L. E., and F. Neeld. 1972. The western limits of the Pileated Woodpecker's range in Oklahoma. Bull. Okla. Ornithol. Soc. 5(1):5–7.

McHargue, L. A. 1981. Black Vulture nesting, behavior, and growth. Auk 56:472–474.

McKnight, D. E. 1974. Dry-land nesting by Redheads and Ruddy Ducks. J. Wildl. Manage. 38:112–119.

McMahon, D. J., III. 1989. A summer record for the Osprey in Sequoyah County, Oklahoma. Bull. Okla. Ornithol. Soc. 22:13–14.

McMahon, J. 1989. Unusually high number of Short-eared Owls in northeastern Oklahoma in winter. Bull. Okla. Ornithol. Soc. 22(1):7.

McNair, D. B. 1984a. Breeding biology of the Fish Crow. Oriole 49:21–32.

McNair, D. B. 1984b. Clutch size and nest placement in the Brown-headed Nuthatch (*Sitta pusilla*). Wilson Bull. 96:296–301.

McNair, D. B. 1984c. Reuse of other species' nests by Lark Sparrows. Southwest. Nat. 29:506–509.

McNair, D. B. 1985. A comparison of oology and nest record card data in evaluating the reproductive biology of Lark Sparrows, *Chondestes grammacus*. Southwest. Nat. 30:213–224.

Meanley, B. 1969. Prenesting and nesting behavior of the Swainson's Warbler. Wilson Bull. 81:246–257.

Meanley, B. 1971a. Additional notes on prenesting and nesting behavior of the Swainson's Warbler. Wilson Bull. 83:194.

Meanley, B. 1971b. Natural History of the Swainson's Warbler. North American Fauna No. 69. U.S. Dept. Interior, Washington, D.C.

Meanley, B. 1992. King Rail. In The Birds of North America, No. 3 (A. Poole, P. Stettenheim, and F. Gill, eds.). Academy of Natural Sciences, Philadelphia, and American Ornithologists' Union, Washington, D.C.

Melcher, C. 1998a. Blue Grosbeak (Guiraca caerulea). In Colorado Breeding Bird Atlas (H. E. Kingery, ed.). Colorado Bird Atlas Partnership and Colorado Division of Wildlife, Denver.

Melcher, C. 1998b. Brewer's Blackbird (Euphagus cyanocephalus). In Colorado Breeding Bird Atlas (H. E. Kingery, ed.). Colorado Bird Atlas Partnership and Colorado Division of Wildlife, Denver.

Melcher, C., and K. Giesen. 1996. Blue Grosbeaks: A response to habitat changes and a late nesting record. J. Colo. Field Ornithol. 30(4):158–160.

Melhop, P., and P. Tonne. 1994. Results of surveys for the Southwestern Willow Flycatcher. U.S. Army Corps of Engineers, Albuquerque, New Mexico.

Melvin, S. L., D. E. Gawlik, and T. Scharff. 1999. Long-term movement patterns for seven species of wading birds. Waterbirds 22(3):411–416.

Mengel, R. M., and Henkinson, M. A. 1971. Vocalizations of the chuck-will's-widow and some related behavior. Living Bird 10:171–83.

Mery, I. S. 1991. House Finch nests in coconut half-shell in Elk City. Scissortail 41:27–28.

Mery, S. C. 1976. Oklahoma fall records for the Yellow-throated Warbler. Bull. Okla. Ornithol. Soc. 9:34.

Messerly, E. H. 1969. Recent nesting of American Coot in Cimarron County, Oklahoma. Bull. Okla. Ornithol. Soc. 2(4–5).

Messerly, E. H. 1972. Late nesting of Eastern Kingbird in Wagoner County, Oklahoma. Bull. Okla. Ornithol. Soc. 5(3):21.

Messerly, E. H. 1979. Early nest of Prothonotary Warbler in Washington County, Oklahoma. Bull. Okla. Ornithol. Soc. 12:15–16.

Messerly, E. H. 1984. Pied-billed Grebe with young in Alfalfa County, Oklahoma. Bull. Okla. Ornithol. Soc. 17:4–5.

Messerly, E. H. 1998a. Albert J. B. Kirn and his work in Oklahoma. Bull. Okla. Ornithol. Soc. 31(2):9–20.

Messerly, E. H. 1998b. Carolina Wren feeds fledgling Brown-headed Cowbird. Bull. Okla. Ornithol. Soc. 31:34.

Middleton, A. L. A. 1993. American Goldfinch (Carduelis tristis). In The Birds of North America, No. 80 (A. Poole and F. Gill, eds.). Academy of Natural Sciences, Philadelphia, and American Ornithologists' Union, Washington, D.C.

Middleton, A. A. 1998. Chipping Sparrow (Spizella passerina). In The Birds of North America, No. 334 (A. Poole and F. Gill, eds.). Academy of Natural Sciences,

Philadelphia, and American Ornithologists' Union, Washington, D.C.

Mirarchi, R. E., and T. S. Baskett. 1994. Mourning Dove (Zenaida macroura). In The Birds of North America, No. 117 (A. Poole and F. Gill, eds.). Academy of Natural Sciences, Philadelphia, and American Ornithologists' Union, Washington, D.C.

Mitchell, H. D. 1954. An unusual Killdeer nesting. Kingbird 4(3):66–68.

Mitchell, T. L. 1993. Tool use by a White-breasted Nuthatch. Bull. Okla. Ornithol. Soc. 26(1):6–7.

Mock, D. W. 1976. Pair formation displays of the Great Blue Heron. Wilson Bull. 88:185–230.

Mock, D. W. 1978. Pair formation displays of the Great Egret. Condor 80:159–172.

Mock, D. W., and B. J. Ploger. 1987. Parental manipulation of optimal hatch asynchrony in Cattle Egrets: An experimental study. Anim. Behav. 35:150–160.

Moldenhauer, R. R., and D. L. Regelski. 1996. Northern Parula (Parula americana). In The Birds of North America, No. 215 (A. Poole, P. Stettenheim, and F. Gill, eds.). Academy of Natural Sciences, Philadelphia, and American Ornithologists' Union, Washington, D.C.

Montaperto, T. 1988. First Northern Harrier nest in southwestern Oklahoma. Bull. Okla. Ornithol. Soc. 21(2):12–13.

Moore, G. A. 1927. Birds of Payne County. Proc. Okla. Acad. Sci. 7:98–102.

Moore, J. E., and P. V. Switzer. 1998. Preroosting aggregations in the American Crow, Corvus brachyrhynchos. Can. J. Zool. 76:508–512.

Moore, S. T. 1984. Snake predation of Pileated Woodpecker nestlings. Bull. Okla. Ornithol. Soc. 17(4):32–33.

Moore, W. S. 1995. Northern Flicker (Colaptes auratus). In The Birds of North America, No. 166 (A. Poole and F. Gill, eds.). Academy of Natural Sciences, Philadelphia, and American Ornithologists' Union, Washington, D.C.

Moorman, Z. 1986. Nesting of Scarlet Tanager in Woodward County, Oklahoma. Bull. Okla. Ornithol. Soc. 19(2):15–16.

Morimoto, D. C., and F. E. Wasserman. 1991. Dispersion patterns and habitat associations of Rufous-sided Towhees, Common Yellowthroats, and Prairie Warblers in the southeastern Massachusetts pine barrens. Auk 108:264–276.

Morrison, R. I. G., R. E. Gill, B. A. Harrington, S. Skagen, G. W. Page, C. E. Gratto-Trevor, and S. M. Haag. 2001. Estimates of shorebird populations in North America. CWS Occasional Paper No. 104. 64 pp. Canadian Wildlife Service, Ottawa.

Morse, D. H. 1989. American Warblers. Harvard University Press, Cambridge, Massachusetts.

Mote, K. D., R. D. Applegate, J. A. Bailey, K. E. Giesen,

R. Horton, and J. L. Sheppard, tech. eds. 1999. Assessment and conservation strategy for the Lesser Prairie-Chicken (*Tympanuchus pallidicinctus*). Kans. Dept. of Wildl. and Parks, Emporia, Kansas.

Mousley, H. 1934. A study of the home life of the Northern Crested Flycatcher. Auk 51:207–216.

Mowbray, T. B. 1999. Scarlet Tanager (*Piranga olivacea*). *In* The Birds of North America, No. 479 (A. Poole, P. Stettenheim, and F. Gill, eds.). Academy of Natural Sciences, Philadelphia, and American Ornithologists' Union, Washington, D.C.

Mueller, A. J. 1992. Inca Dove (*Columbina inca*). *In* The Birds of North America, No. 28 (A Poole, P. Stettenheim, and F. Gill, eds.). Academy of Natural Sciences, Philadelphia, and American Ornithologists' Union, Washington, D.C.

Mumford, R. E., and C. F. Keller. 1984. The Birds of Indiana. Indiana University Press, Bloomington.

Murphy, M. T. 1994. Breeding patterns of Eastern Phoebes in Kansas: Adaptive strategies or physiological constraints? Auk 111(3):617–633.

Murphy, M. T. 1996. Eastern Kingbird (*Tyrannus tyrannus*). *In* The Birds of North America, No. 253 (A. Poole and F. Gill, eds.). Academy of Natural Sciences, Philadelphia, and American Ornithologists' Union, Washington, D.C.

Muzny, P. L. 1982. Two concurrent nestings of Chuck-will's-widow in McClain County, Oklahoma. Bull. Okla. Ornithol. Soc. 15(2):15.

National Geographic Society. 1983. Birds of North America. National Geographic Society, Washington, D.C.

National Geographic Society. 1999. Field Guide to the Birds of North America, 3rd ed. National Geographic Society, Washington, D.C.

Neeld, F. 1972. Late nesting of Greater Roadrunner in Carter County, Oklahoma. Bull. Okla. Ornithol. Soc. 25:21.

Neeld, F. 1993. Tree Swallows nesting in Stephens County, Oklahoma. Bull. Okla. Ornithol. Soc. 26:40–41.

Nelson, D. L. 1998. Chihuahuan Raven (*Corvus cryptoleucus*). *In* Colorado Breeding Bird Atlas (H. E. Kingery, ed.). Colorado Bird Atlas Partnership and Colorado Division of Wildlife, Denver.

Neudorf, D. L., and S. G. Sealy. 1994. Sunrise nest attentiveness in cowbird hosts. Condor 96:162–169.

Newell, D. B. 1990. Second record of Northern Cardinal in Cimarron County, Oklahoma. Bull. Okla. Ornithol. Soc. 23(2):15–16.

Newell, J. G. 1969. The Cattle Egret in central Oklahoma. Bull. Okla. Ornithol. Soc. 2(2):11–12.

Newell, J. G. 1979. Breeding of Tree Swallow in Cimarron County, Oklahoma. Bull. Okla. Ornithol. Soc. 12:24.

Newell, J. G. 1980. Breeding of Kentucky Warbler in Red Rock Canyon, Caddo County, central Oklahoma. Bull. Okla. Ornithol. Soc. 13:15–16.

Newell, J. G. 1981. Whip-poor-will in Oklahoma City. Bull. Okla. Ornithol. Soc. 14(3):23–24.

Newell, J. G. 1985. A temporary colony of Lesser Goldfinches in central Oklahoma. Bull. Okla. Ornithol. Soc. 18:1–4.

Newell, J. G., and G. M. Sutton. 1982. The Olivaceous Cormorant in Oklahoma. Bull. Okla. Ornithol. Soc. 15:1–5.

Newman, G. A. 1969. Baltimore Oriole parasitized by Brown-headed Cowbird in Oklahoma. Bull. Okla. Ornithol. Soc. 2:23.

Newman, G. A. 1970. Cowbird parasitism and nesting success of Lark Sparrows in southern Oklahoma. Wilson Bull. 82:304–209.

Nice, M. M. 1921. A white cowbird (*Molothrus ater ater*). Wilson Bull. 33:145–146.

Nice, M. M. 1922. A study of the nesting of Mourning Dove. Auk 39:457–474.

Nice, M. M. 1923. Nesting records from 1920 to 1922 from Norman, Oklahoma. Proc. Okla. Acad. Sci. 3:61–67.

Nice, M. M. 1924. Extension of range of the Robin and Arkansas Kingbird in Oklahoma. Auk 41:565–568.

Nice, M. M. 1927. The bird life of a forty-acre tract in central Oklahoma. Proc. Okla. Acad. Sci. 7:75–93.

Nice, M. M. 1929. The fortunes of a pair of Bell's Vireos. Condor 31:13–20.

Nice, M. M. 1931. The Birds of Oklahoma. Rev. ed. Publ. Okla. Biol. Surv., 3(1). 224 pp.

Nice, M. M. 1938. American Egret and Anhinga nesting in Oklahoma. Auk 55:121–122.

Nice, M. M., and L. B. Nice. 1924. The Birds of Oklahoma. Univ. of Okla. Bull., New Series 20.

Nice, M. M., and L. B. Nice. 1925. Some bird observations in Cleveland County in 1924. Proc. Okla. Acad. Sci. 5:104–107.

Nickell, W. P. 1951. Studies of Habitats, Territory and Nests of the Eastern Goldfinch. Auk 68:447–470.

Nighswonger, P. F. 1977. Recovery of a five-year-old Swainson's Hawk. Bull. Okla. Ornithol. Soc. 10(2):12.

Nolan, V. 1978. The ecology and behavior of the Prairie Warbler *Dendroica discolor*. Ornithol. Monogr. 26:1–595.

Norman, J. L. 1971. Late fledging of Barn Owl in northeastern Oklahoma. Bull. Okla. Ornithol. Soc. 4:6–7.

Norman, J. L. 1973. Oklahoma winter records for the Dickcissel. Bull. Okla. Ornithol. Soc. 6(4):32–33.

Norman, J. L. 1976. Birds killed at a TV tower near Coweta, Oklahoma. Bull. Okla. Ornithol. Soc. 9(3):20.

Norman, J. L. 1977. First Oklahoma breeding record for Hooded Merganser. Bull. Okla. Ornithol. Soc. 10:22–23.

Norman, J. L. 1982. The Coweta TV tower kill. Bull. Okla. Ornithol. Soc. 15(3):19–22.

Norman, J. L. 1987. Synopsis of birds killed at the Coweta, Oklahoma, TV tower, 1974–1984. Bull. Okla. Ornithol. Soc. 20(3):17–22.

Norman, J. L., and E. Hayes. 1988. Black-bellied Whistling-Duck: A new species for Oklahoma. Bull. Okla. Ornithol. Soc. 21(4):25–26.

North, C. A. 1968. A study of the House Sparrow populations and their movements in the vicinity of Stillwater, Oklahoma. Ph.D. diss., Oklahoma State University, Stillwater.

Norton, P. W. 1973a. A cormorant colony on Robert S. Kerr Reservation. Bull. Okla. Ornithol. Soc. 5:17–20.

Norton, P. W. 1973b. Recent breeding of Anhinga in Oklahoma. Bull. Okla. Ornithol. Soc. 6:12–13.

Oberholser, H. C. 1921. The geographic races of *Cyanocitta cristata*. Auk 38:83–89.

Oberholser, H. C. 1974. The Bird Life of Texas. University of Texas Press, Austin.

Offutt, G. C. 1965. Behavior of the Tufted Titmouse before and during the nesting season. Wilson Bull. 77:382–387.

O'Halloran, K. A. 1987. Habitat used by Brown-headed Nuthatches. Bull. Tex. Ornithol. Soc. 20:7–13.

O'Halloran, K. A., and R. N. Conner. 1987. Habitat used by Brown-Headed Nuthatches. Bull. Tex. Ornithol. Soc. 20:7–13.

Oklahoma Bird Records Committee. 2000. Date Guide to the Occurrences of Birds in Oklahoma. Oklahoma Ornithological Society, Tulsa, Oklahoma.

Oklahoma Climatological Survey. 2002. Oklahoma Climate Data. http://climate.ocs.ou.edu.

Oklahoma Wildlife Federation. 1991. Oklahoma Backroads. Oklahoma Wildlife Federation. Oklahoma City, Oklahoma.

Olendorff, R. R. 1974. A courtship flight of the Swainson's Hawk. Condor 76(2):215.

Oliphant, M., and I. S. Brown. 1984. Eastward expansion of the House Finch's range in Oklahoma. Bull. Okla. Ornithol. Soc. 17:9–12.

Oliver, G. V., Jr. 1970. Black ratsnake predation upon nesting Barn and Cliff swallows. Bull. Okla. Ornithol. Soc. 3:17–20.

Ordal, J. M. 1976. Effect of sympatry on meadowlark vocalizations. Condor 78:100–101.

Oring, L. W. 1969. Summer biology of the Gadwall at Delta, Manitoba. Wilson Bull. 81:44–53.

Oring, L. W., and W. M. Davis. 1966. Shorebird migration at Norman, Oklahoma: 1961–1963. Wilson's Bull. 78:166–174.

Oring, L. W., E. M. Gray, and J. M. Reed. 1997. Spotted Sandpiper. *In* The Birds of North America, No. 289 (A. Poole and F. Gill, eds.). Academy of Natural Sciences, Philadelphia, and American Ornithologists' Union, Washington, D.C.

Oring, L. W., D. B. Lank, and S. J. Maxson. 1983. Population studies of the polyandrous Spotted Sandpiper. Auk 100:272–285.

Orr, R. T. 1948. Nesting behavior of the Poor-will. Auk 65:46–54.

Ortenburger, A. I., and E. L. Little Jr. 1930. Notes on a collection of birds from western Oklahoma. Publ. Univ. Okla. Biol. Surv. 2:189–194.

Ortenburger, R. D. 1926. Bird records from southern Oklahoma. Proc. Okla. Acad. Sci. 6:193–196.

Osborne, June. 1992. The Cardinal. University of Texas Press, Austin.

Otteni, L. C., E. G. Bolen, and C. Cottam. 1972. Predator-prey relationships and reproduction of the Barn Owl in southern Texas. Wilson Bull. 84:434–438.

Overmire, T. G. 1962. Nesting of the Dickcissel in Oklahoma. Auk 79:115–116.

Overmire, T. G. 1963. The effects of grazing on habitat utilization of the Dickcissel (*Spiza americana*) and Bell's Vireo (*Vireo bellii*) in north central Oklahoma. Ph. D. diss. Oklahoma State University, Stillwater. 57 pp.

Owen, R. D., and B. E. Leuck. 1978. Verdin nest in Harmon County, Oklahoma. Bull. Okla. Ornithol. Soc. 11:24.

Page, G. W., J. S. Warriner, J. C. Warriner, and P. W. C. Paton. 1995. Snowy Plover (*Charadrius alexandrinus*). *In* The Birds of North America, No. 154 (A. Poole and F. Gill, eds.). Academy of Natural Sciences, Philadelphia, and American Ornithologists' Union, Washington, D.C.

Paine, R. T. 1968. Brewer's Sparrow. *In* Life Histories of North American Cardinals, Grosbeaks, Buntings, Towhees, Finches, Sparrows, and Allies, Pt. 2 (A. C. Bent and collaborators, ed. O. L. Austin Jr.). U.S. Natl. Mus. Bull. No. 237, Dover Publications, New York.

Palmer, R. S., ed. 1962. Handbook of North American Birds Volume 1 Loons through Flamingos. Yale University Press, New Haven, Connecticut.

Palmer, R. S., ed. 1976. Handbook of North American Birds, Vol. 2. Yale University Press, New Haven, Connecticut.

Palmer, R. S., ed. 1988. Handbook of North American Birds, Vol. 4: Diurnal raptors, Pt. 1. Yale University Press, New Haven, Connecticut.

Palmer-Ball, B. L., Jr. 1996. The Kentucky Breeding Bird Atlas. University Press of Kentucky, Lexington.

Parker, J. W. 1973. Green-tailed Towhee in Oklahoma in summer. Bull. Okla. Ornithol. Soc. 6:24.

Parker, J. W. 1976. Growth of the Swainson's Hawk. Condor 78(4):557–558.

Parker, J. W. 1999. Mississippi Kite (*Ictinia mississippiensis*). *In* The Birds of North America, No. 402 (A. Poole and F. Gill, eds.). Academy of Natural Sciences, Philadelphia, and American Ornithologists' Union, Washington, D.C.

Parker, J. W., and J. C. Ogden. 1979. The recent history and status of the Mississippi Kite. American Birds 33:119–129.

Parker, T. A, III. 1973. First Snow Bunting specimen for Oklahoma. Bull. Okla. Ornithol. Soc. 6(4):33.

Parmelee, D. F. 1959. The breeding behavior of the Painted Bunting in southern Oklahoma. Bird Banding 30:1–18.

Parmelee, D. F. 1968. An Oklahoma nest of the Common Raven. Bull. Okla. Ornithol. Soc. 1:21–23.

Parmelee, D. F. 1969. Early nesting of the House Finch in Oklahoma. Bull. Okla. Ornithol. Soc. 2:16.

Parmley, D. C. 1974. Late fall date for Eastern Kingbird in Oklahoma. Bull. Okla. Ornithol. Soc. 7(4):64.

Parmley, D. C. 1978. Scissor-tailed Flycatcher parasitized by cowbird in Oklahoma. Bull. Okla. Ornithol. Soc. 11(2):15–16.

Parry, G., and R. Putman. 1979. Birds of Prey. Simon and Schuster, New York.

Parsons, K. C., and T. L. Master. 2000. Snowy Egret (*Egretta thula*). *In* The Birds of North America, No. 489 (A. Poole and F. Gill, eds.). Academy of Natural Sciences, Philadelphia, and American Ornithologists' Union, Washington, D.C.

Paton, P. W. C. 1999. A closer look at the Snowy Plover. Birding 31:238–244.

Payne, R. B. 1970. Second recorded nesting of Golden-fronted Woodpecker in Oklahoma. Bull. Okla. Ornithol. Soc. 3(2):16.

Payne, R. B. 1976. The clutch size and numbers of eggs of Brown-headed Cowbirds: Effects of latitude and breeding season. Condor 78:337–342.

Payne, R. B. 1992. Indigo Bunting. *In* The Birds of North America, No. 4 (A. Poole, P. Stettenheim, and F. Gill, eds.). Academy of Natural Sciences, Philadelphia, and American Ornithologists' Union, Washington, D.C.

Peacock, F. I. 1969. Late fledging of Tufted Titmouse in Oklahoma. Bull. Okla. Ornithol. Soc. 2(1):6–7.

Pearson, T. G. 1936. Birds of America. Garden City Books, Garden City, New York.

Pease, C. M., and J. A. Grzybowski. 1995. Assessing the consequences of brood parasitism and nest predation on a seasonal fecundity in passerine birds. Auk 112:343–363.

Peer, B. D., and E. K. Bollinger. 1997. Common Grackles (*Quiscalus quiscula*). *In* The Birds of North America, No. 271 (A. Poole and F. Gill, eds.). Academy of Natural Sciences, Philadelphia, and American Ornithologists' Union, Washington, D.C.

Perrins, C., and C. J. O. Harrison. 1979. Birds: Their Life, Their Ways, Their World. Reader's Digest Association, Inc. Pleasantville, New York.

Peterjohn, B. G., and J. R. Sauer. 1995. Purple Martin population trends from the North American Breeding Bird Survey, 1966–1994. Purple Martin Update 6(2):2–8.

Peterjohn, B. G., and J. R. Sauer. 1999. Population status of North American grassland birds from the North American Breeding Bird Survey 1966–1996. *In* Ecology and Conservation of Grassland Birds of the Western Hemisphere: Studies in Avian Biology (P. D. Vickery and J. R. Herkert, eds.). Allen Press, Lawrence, Kansas.

Peterson, R. T. 1963. A Field Guide to the Birds of Texas. Houghton Mifflin Co., Boston.

Peterson, R. T. 1996. North American Birds. Peterson Multimedia Guides TM. Houghton Mifflin Co., Boston.

Petit, L. J. 1989. Breeding biology of Prothonotary Warblers in riverine habitat in Tennessee. Wilson Bull. 101:51–61.

Petit, L. J. 1999. Prothonotary Warbler (*Protonotaria citrea*). *In* The Birds of North America, No. 408 (A. Poole and F. Gill, eds.). Academy of Natural Sciences, Philadelphia, and American Ornithologists' Union, Washington, D.C.

Pettingill, O. S., Jr. 1936. The American Woodcock (*Philohela minor*). Mem. Boston Soc. Nat. History. 9:196–391.

Phillips, A. R. 1968. *Aimophila ruficeps eremoeca* (Brown) Rock Rufous-crowned Sparrow. Pp. 981–990 *in* Life Histories of North American Cardinals, Grosbeaks, Buntings, Towhees, Finches, Sparrows and Their Allies (A. C. Bent, O. L. Austin Jr., and collaborators, eds.). U.S. Nat. Mus. Bull. 237.

Phillips, A. R. 1986. The Known Birds of North and Middle America. Pt. 1. Denver Museum of Natural History, Denver, Colorado.

Pianalto, F. R. 1993. Attacks by adult Least Terns on chicks. Bull. Okla. Ornithol. Soc. 26:36–37.

Platt, S. 1974. Mid-October hawk migration in Payne County, Oklahoma. Bull. Okla. Ornithol. Soc. 7(3):55.

Ploger, B. J., and D. W. Mock. 1986. Role of sibling agression in food distribution to nestling Cattle Egrets (*Bubulcus ibis*). Auk 103:768–776.

Pogue, D., and J. A. Grzybowski. 1997. Erratum. Bull. Okla. Ornithol. Soc. 30(1):11.

Porter, R. A. 1980. Great-tailed Grackle colony in Washington County, Oklahoma. Bull. Okla. Ornithol. Soc. 13(3):18–20.–Porter, R. A. 1984. Summer records for Pine Siskin in Washington and Delaware counties, Oklahoma. Bull. Okla. Ornithol. Soc. 17:33–34.

Ports, M. 1974. Mourning Dove as possible prey of Short-eared Owl. Bull. Okla. Ornithol. Soc. 7(4):63.

Ports, M. 1979. Spotted Sandpiper breeding in Texas County, Oklahoma. Bull. Okla. Ornithol. Soc. 12:20–21.

Poulin, R. G., S. D. Grindal, and R. M. Brigham. 1996. Common Nighthawk (*Chordeiles minor*). *In* The Birds of North America, No. 213 (A. Poole and F. Gill, eds.). Academy of Natural Sciences, Philadelphia, and American Ornithologists' Union, Washington, D.C.

Powders, V. N. 1986. Pileated Woodpecker in Woodward County, Oklahoma. Bull. Okla. Ornithol. Soc. 19(4):27–28.

Power, H. W., and M. P. Lombardo. 1996. Mountain Bluebird (*Sialia currucoides*). *In* The Birds of North America, No. 222 (A. Poole and F. Gill, eds.). Academy of Natural Sciences, Philadelphia, and American Ornithologists' Union, Washington, D.C.

Pratt, H. M. 1970. Breeding biology of Great Blue Herons and Common Egrets in central California. Condor 72(4):407–416.

Pravosudov, V. V., and T. C. Grubb Jr. 1993. White-breasted Nuthatch (*Sitta carolinensis*). *In* The Birds of North America, No. 54 (A. Poole and F. Gill, eds.). Academy of Natural Sciences, Philadelphia, and American Ornithologists' Union, Washington, D.C.

Preston, C. R., and R. D. Beane. 1993. Red-tailed Hawk (*Buteo jamaicensis*). *In* The Birds of North America, No. 52 (A. Poole and F. Gills, Eds). Academy of Natural Sciences, Philadelphia, and American Ornithologists' Union, Washington, D.C.

Price, J., S. Droege, and A. Price. 1995. The Summer Atlas of North American Birds. Academic Press, London.

Project Tanager Eastern Region Training Tape. 1993. Laboratory of Ornithology, Cornell University, Ithaca, New York.

Pruitt, L. 1996. Henslow's Sparrow Status Assessment. U.S. Fish and Wildlife Service, Bloomington, Indiana.

Pulich, W. M. 1988. The Birds of North Central Texas. Texas A&M University Press, College Station.

Purdue, J. R. 1969. Robin a victim of cowbird parasitism. Bull. Okla. Ornithol. Soc. 2:30.

Purdue, J. R. 1976. Adaptations of the Snowy Plover on the Great Salt Plains, Oklahoma. Southwest. Nat. 21:347–357.

Pyle, P. 1997. Identification Guide to North American Birds, Pt. 1. Slate Creek Press, Bolinas, California.

Ramsey, R. L. 1970. Woodpecker nest failures in creosoted utility poles. Auk 87:367–369.

Raney, E. C. 1939. Robin and Mourning Dove use same nest. Auk 56:337–338.

Rappole, J. H., and G. W. Blacklock. 1994. Birds of Texas. Texas A&M University Press, College Station.

Ratzlaff, A. 1986. Breeding of Eared Grebe in Kingfisher County, Oklahoma. Bull. Okla. Ornithol. Soc. 19:9–11.

Ratzlaff, A. 1989. Early spring record for Dickcissel in Comanche County, Oklahoma. Bull. Okla. Ornithol. Soc. 22(2):16.

Ray, G. E. 1973. Early nesting of Mourning Dove in southwestern Oklahoma. Bull. Okla. Ornithol. Soc. 6:6–7.

Ray, R. E. 1973. Nesting of American Coot in Lincoln County, Oklahoma. Bull. Okla. Ornithol. Soc. 6:21.

Regosin, J. V. 1993. Mourning Dove and Scissor-tailed Flycatcher nests in close proximity. Bull. Okla. Ornithol. Soc. 26:5.

Regosin, J. V. 1994a. Cooper's Hawk preys on Scissor-tailed Flycatcher nestling. Bull. Okla. Ornithol. Soc. 27:28.

Regosin, J. V. 1994b. Scissor-tailed Flycatchers eject Brown-headed Cowbird eggs. J. Field. Ornithol. 65:508–511.

Regosin, J. V. 1998. Scissor-tailed Flycatcher (*Tyrannus forficatus*). *In* The Birds of North America, No. 342 (A. Poole and F. Gills, eds.). Academy of Natural Sciences, Philadelphia, and American Ornithologists' Union, Washington, D.C.

Regosin, J. V., S. Orr, and J. Sarnat. 1991. Recent breeding records for the Northern Harrier in southwestern Oklahoma. Bull. Okla. Ornithol. Soc. 24(4):29–30.

Regosin, J. V., and S. Pruett-Jones. 1995. Aspects of breeding biology and social organization in the Scissor-tailed Flycatcher. Condor 97:154–164.

Reinking, D. L., compiler. 1997. Handbook for Atlasers. Unpubl. handbook.

Reinking, D. L., compiler. 1998. Rev. ed. Handbook for Atlasers. Unpubl. handbook.

Reinking, D. L., and D. P. Hendricks. 1993. Occurrence and nesting of Henslow's Sparrows in Oklahoma. Bull. Okla. Ornithol. Soc. 26:33–36.

Reinking, D. L., D. A. Wiedenfeld, D. H. Wolfe, and R. W. Rohrbaugh Jr. 2000a. Distribution, habitat use, and nesting success of Henslow's Sparrow in Oklahoma. Prairie Nat. 32:219–232.

Reinking, D. L., D. H. Wolfe, and D. A. Wiedenfeld. 2000b. Effects of livestock grazing on bird abundance and vegetation structure in shortgrass prairie. Bull. Okla. Ornithol. Soc. 33:29–36.

Renken, R. B., and E. P. Wiggers. 1993. Habitat characteristics related to Pileated Woodpecker densities in Missouri. Wilson Bull. 105(1):77–83.

Repenning, R. W., and R. F. Labisky. 1985. Effects of even-age timber management on bird communities of the longleaf pine forest in northern Florida. J. Wildl. Manage. 49:1088–1098.

Reynolds, A. 1973. White-eyed Vireo observed feeding fledged cowbird. Bull. Okla. Ornithol. Soc. 6:23.

Reynolds, J. D., and R. W. Knapton. 1984. Nest-site selection and breeding biology of the Chipping Sparrow. Wilson Bull. 96:488–493.

Rice, E. L. 1960. The microclimate of a relict stand of sugar maple in Devil's Canyon in Canadian County, Oklahoma. Ecology 41:445–452.

Rice, E. L. 1965. Bottomland forests of north-central Oklahoma. Ecology 46:708–714.

Rice, E. L., and W. T. Penfound. 1959. The upland forests of Oklahoma. Ecology 40:592–608.

Rickstrew, M. 1975. A Louisiana Waterthrush nest in Ghost Hollow. Bull. Okla. Ornithol. Soc. 8:3–5.

Rickstrew, M. 1976. A hummingbird nest in Ghost Hollow. Bull. Okla. Ornithol. Soc. 9:12–13.

Riggs, C. D., and K. Starks . 1951. Canada Geese nesting at Lake Texoma, Oklahoma. Proc. Okla. Acad. Sci. 32:33–36.

Rising, J. D. 1983. The progress of oriole "hybridization" in Kansas. Auk 100:885–897.

Rising, J. D. 1996a. A guide to the Identification and Natural History of the Sparrows of the United States and

Canada. Academic Press, New York.

Rising, J. D. 1996b. The stability of the oriole hybrid zone in western Kansas. Condor 98:658–663.

Rising, J. D., and N. J. Flood. 1998. Baltimore Oriole (*Icterus galbula*). *In* The Birds of North America, No. 158 (A. Poole and F. Gill, eds.). Academy of Natural Sciences, Philadelphia, and American Ornithologists' Union, Washington, D.C.

Rising, J. D., and P. L. Williams. 1999. Bullock's Oriole (Icterus bullockii). *In* The Birds of North America, No. 416 (A. Poole and F. Gill, eds.). Academy of Natural Sciences, Philadelphia, and American Ornithologists' Union, Washington, D.C.

Risser, P. G., E. C. Birney, H. D. Blocker, S. W. May, W. J. Parton, and J. A. Wiens. 1981. The true prairie ecosystem. U.S. International Biological Program Synthesis Series, No. 16. Hutchinson Ross Publishing Co., Stroudsburg, Pennsylvania. 557 pages.

Robbins, C. S. 1973. Introduction, spread, and present abundance of the House Sparrow in North America. Ornithol. Monogr. 14:3–9.

Robbins, C. S. 1980. Effect of forest fragmentation on breeding bird populations in the piedmont of the mid-Atlantic region. Atlantic Nat. 33:31–36.

Robbins, C. S., B. Bruun, and H. S. Zim. 1966. Birds of North America. Golden Press, New Robbins, C. S., B. Bruun, H. S. Zim, and A. B. Singer. 1983. A Guide to Field Identification of North American Birds. Golden Press, New York.

Robbins, M. B., and D. A. Easterla. 1992. Birds of Missouri: Their Distribution and Abundance. University of Missouri Press, Columbia.

Roberts, C., and C. J. Norment. 1999. Effects of plot size and habitat characteristics on breeding success of Scarlet Tanagers. Auk 116:73–82.

Roberts, J. S. 1971. Recovery in South America of a Snowy Egret banded as a nestling in Oklahoma. Bull. Okla. Ornithol. Soc. 4:26.

Robertson, J. H. 1986. Black-throated Sparrow in Major County, Oklahoma. Bull. Okla. Ornithol. Soc. 24:16.

Robertson, R. J., B. J. Stutchbury, and R. R. Cohen. 1992. Tree Swallow (*Tachycineta bicolor*). *In* The Birds of North America, No. 11 (A. Poole, P. Stettenheim, and F. Gill, eds.). Academy of Natural Sciences, Philadelphia, and American Ornithologists' Union, Washington, D.C.

Robinson, J. A., L. W. Oring, J. P. Skorupa, and R. Boettcher. 1997. American Avocet (*Recurvirostra americana*). *In* The Birds of North America, No. 275 (A. Poole and F. Gill, eds.). Academy of Natural Sciences, Philadelphia, and American Ornithologists' Union, Washington, D.C.

Robinson, J. A., J. M. Reed, J. P. Skorupa, and L. W. Oring.

1999. Black-necked Stilt (*Himantopus mexicanus*). *In* The Birds of North America, No. 449 (A. Poole and F. Gill, eds.). Academy of Natural Sciences, Philadelphia, and American Ornithologists' Union, Washington, D.C.

Robinson, S. K., S. I. Rothstein, M. C. Brittingham, L. J. Petit, and J. A. Grzybowski. 1995. Ecology and behavior of cowbirds and their impact on host populations. Pp. 428–460 *in* Ecology and Management of Neotropical Migratory Birds: A Synthesis and Review of Critical Issues (T. E. Martin and D. M. Finch, eds.). Oxford University Press, New York.

Robinson, T. R., R. R. Sargent, and M. B. Sargent. 1996. Ruby-throated Hummingbird (*Archilochus colubris*). *In* The Birds of North America, No. 204 (A. Poole and F. Gill, eds.). Academy of Natural Sciences, Philadelphia, and American Ornithologists' Union, Washington, D.C.

Robinson, W. D. 1995. Louisiana Waterthrush (*Seiurus motacilla*). *In* The Birds of North America, No. 151 (A. Poole and F. Gill, eds.). Academy of Natural Sciences, Philadelphia, and American Ornithologists' Union, Washington, D.C.

Rodewald, P. G., and R. D. James. 1996. Yellow-throated Vireo (*Vireo flavifrons*). *In* The Birds of North America, No. 247 (A. Poole and F. Gill, eds.). Academy of Natural Sciences, Philadelphia, and American Ornithologists' Union, Washington, D.C.

Rodewald, P. G., J. H. Withgott, and K. G. Smith. 1999. Pine Warbler (*Dendroica pinus*). *In* The Birds of North America, No. 438 (A. Poole and F. Gill, eds.) Academy of Natural Sciences, Philadelphia, and American Ornithologists' Union, Washington, D.C.

Rodgers, J. A., and H. T. Smith. 1995. Little Blue Heron (*Egretta caerulea*). *In* The Birds of North America, No. 145 (A. Poole and F. Gill, eds.). Academy of Natural Sciences, Philadelphia, and American Ornithologists' Union, Washington, D.C.

Rodgers, L. 1973. First Oklahoma record of House Sparrow fledging a cowbird. Bull. Okla. Ornithol. Soc. 6:15–16.

Rogers, C. M. 1953. The vegetation of the Mesa de Maya region of Colorado, New Mexico, and Oklahoma. Lloydia 16:257–291.

Rohrbaugh, R. W., Jr., D. L. Reinking, D. H. Wolfe, S. K. Sherrod, and M. A. Jenkins. 1999. Effects of prescribed burning and grazing on nesting and reproductive success of three grassland passerine species in tallgrass prairie. Pp. 165–170 *in* Ecology and conservation of grassland birds of the Western Hemisphere (P. D. Vickery and J. R. Herkert, eds.). Studies in Avian Biology 19.

Rohwer, S. A. 1969. Spring specimens of Baird's Sparrow from northeastern New Mexico. Bull. Okla. Ornithol. Soc. 2(4):30–31.

Rohwer, S. A. 1971. Molt and annual cycle of the Chuck-will's-widow, *Caprimulgus carolinensis*. Auk 88(3):485–519.

Rohwer, S. A. 1972a. Distribution of meadowlarks in the central and southern Great Plains and the desert grasslands of eastern New Mexico and west Texas. Trans. Kans. Acad. Sci. 75(1):1–19.

Rohwer, S. A. 1972b. A multivariate assessment of interbreeding between the meadowlarks, Sturnella. Syst. Zool. 21:313–338.

Rohwer, S. A. 1972c. Significance of sympatry to behavior and evolution of Great Plains meadowlarks. Evolution 27:44–57.

Rohwer, S. A., and J. Butler. 1977. Ground foraging and the rapid molt in the Chuck-will's-widow. Wilson Bull. 89:165–166.

Romagosa, C. M., and T. McEneaney. 1999. Eurasian Collared-Dove in North America and the Caribbean. North American Birds 53:348–353.

Romero, F. S., and A. Romero. 1971. Spring arrival date for Broad-winged Hawk in Oklahoma. Bull. Okla. Ornithol. Soc. 4(2):16–17.

Root, R. B. 1969. The behavior and reproductive success of the Blue-gray Gnatcatcher. Condor 71:16–31.

Roseberry, J. L., and W. D. Klimstra. 1970. The nesting ecology and reproductive performance of the Eastern Meadowlark. Wilson Bull. 82(3):243–267.

Rosenberg, K. V., S. E. Barker, and R. W. Rohrbaugh. 2000. An Atlas of Cerulean Warbler Populations, Final Report to the USFWS: 1997–2000 Breeding Seasons. Cornell Lab of Ornithology, Ithaca, New York.

Rosenfield, R. N. 1984. Nesting biology of Broad-winged Hawks in Wisconsin. Raptor Res. 18:6–9.

Rosenfield, R. N., and J. Bielefeldt. 1993. Cooper's Hawk (*Accipiter cooperii*). *In* The Birds of North America, No. 75 (A. Poole and F. Gills, eds.). Academy of Natural Sciences, Philadelphia, and American Ornithologists' Union, Washington, D.C.

Rotenberry, J. T., M. A. Patton, and K. L. Preston. 1999. Brewer's Sparrow (*Spizella breweri*). *In* The Birds of North America, No. 390 (A. Poole and F. Gills, eds.). Academy of Natural Sciences, Philadelphia, and American Ornithologists' Union, Washington, D.C.

Roth, R. R., M. S. Johnson, and T. J. Underwood. 1996. Wood Thrush (*Hylocichla mustelina*). *In* The Birds of North America, No. 246 (A. Poole and F. Gills, eds.). Academy of Natural Sciences, Philadelphia, and American Ornithologists' Union, Washington, D.C.

Rue, L. L. 1973. Game birds of North America. Outdoor Life. New York, Evanston, San Francisco, London. 490pp.

Ruley, D. A. 2000. Petition Under the Endangered Species to List the Cerulean Warbler *Dendrocia* as a Threatened Species. Filed with the U.S. Fish and Wildlife Service, October 31, 2000.

Ryan, M. R., L. W. Burger, D. P. Jones, and A. P. Wywialowski. 1998. Breeding ecology of Greater Prairie-Chickens (*Tympanuchus cupido*) in relation to prairie landscape configuration. Am. Midl. Nat. 140:111–121.

Ryder, R. A., and D. E. Manry. 1994. White-faced Ibis (*Plegadis chihi*). *In* The Birds of North America, No. 130 (A. Poole and F. Gill, eds.). Academy of Natural Sciences, Philadelphia, and American Ornithologists' Union, Washington, D.C.

Ryser, F. A., Jr. 1985. Birds of the Great Basin. University of Nevada Press, Reno.

Sallabanks, R., and F. C. James. 1999. American Robin (*Turdus migratorius*). *In* The Birds of North America, No. 462 (A. Poole and F. Gill, eds.). Academy of Natural Sciences, Philadelphia, and American Ornithologists' Union, Washington, D.C.

Sallabanks, R., J. R. Walters, and J. A. Collazo. 2000. Breeding bird abundance in bottomland hardwood forests: Habitat, edge, and patch size effects. Condor 102(4):748–758.

Sallee, G. W. 1974. Marsh Hawks observed feeding peaceably with Bald Eagles. Bull. Okla. Ornithol. Soc. 7(4):62.

Sallee, G. W. 1980. Breeding of Black-billed Magpie in northeastern Oklahoma. Bull. Okla. Ornithol. Soc. 13:4–5.

Sallee, G. W. 1982. Mixed heronries of Oklahoma. Proc. Okla. Acad. Sci. 62:53–56.

Sands, J. L. 1968. Status of the Lesser Prairie-Chicken. Audubon Field Notes 22:454–456.

Sauer, J. R., J. E. Hines, and J. Fallon. 2001. The North American Breeding Bird Survey, Results and Analysis, 1996–2000. USGS Patuxent Wildlife Research Center. Laurel, Maryland.

Sauer, J. R., S. Orsillo, and B. G. Peterjohn. 1994. Population status and trends of grouse and prairie-chickens from the North American Breeding Bird Survey and Christmas Bird Count. Trans. No. Am. Wildl. and Nat. Resources Conf. 59:439–448.

Saunders, G. B., Jr. 1926. A census of the song and insectivorous birds of Oklahoma County for 1924–1925. Proc. Okla. Acad. Sci. 6:63–70.

Schaefer, V. H. 1976. Geographic variation in the placement and structure of oriole nests. Condor 78:443–448.

Scharf, W. C., and J. Kren. 1996. Orchard Oriole (*Icterus spurius*). *In* The Birds of North America, No. 255 (A. Poole and F. Gill, eds.). Academy of Natural Sciences, Philadelphia, and American Ornithologists' Union, Washington, D.C.

Schemnitz, S. D. 1961. Ecology of the Scaled Quail in the Oklahoma Panhandle. Wildl. Monogr. 8, 47 pp.

Schemnitz, S. D. 1964. Comparative ecology of Bobwhite and Scaled Quail in the Oklahoma Panhandle. Am. Midl. Nat. 71:429–433.

Schemnitz, S. D. 1994. Scaled Quail (*Callipepla squamata*). *In* The Birds of North America, No. 106 (A. Poole and F.

Gill, eds.). Academy of Natural Sciences, Philadelphia, and American Ornithologists' Union, Washington, D.C.

Schorger, A. W. 1966. The Wild Turkey: Its History and Domestication. University of Oklahoma Press, Norman.

Schroeder, M. A., and L. A. Robb. 1993. Greater Prairie-Chicken. *In* The Birds of North America, No. 36 (A. Poole and F. Gill, eds.). Academy of Natural Sciences, Philadelphia, and American Ornithologists' Union, Washington, D.C.

Schukman, J. M. 1974. Comparative Nesting Ecology of the Eastern Phoebe (*Sayornis phoebe*) and Say's Phoebe (*Sayornis saya*) in west-central Kansas. M.S. thesis, Fort Hays State University, Kansas.

Schukman, J. M., and B. O. Wolf. 1998. Say's Phoebe (*Sayornis saya*). *In* The Birds of North America, No. 374 (A. Poole and F. Gill, eds.). Academy of Natural Sciences, Philadelphia, and American Ornithologists' Union, Washington, D.C.

Schweitzer, S. H., and D. M. Leslie Jr. 1994. Abundance and conservation of endangered interior least terns nesting on salt flat habitat. Annual Report, Salt Plains National Wildlife Refuge, Work Order No. 11:1–134.

Schweitzer, S. H., and D. M. Leslie Jr. 1996. Foraging patterns of the Least Tern (*Sterna antillarum*) in north-central Oklahoma. Southwest. Nat. 41:307–314.

Schweitzer, S. H., D. M. Finch, and D. M. Leslie Jr. 1998. The Brown-headed Cowbird and its riparian-dependant hosts in New Mexico. General Technical Report RMRS-GTR-1. Fort Collins, Colorado: U.S. Dept. of Agriculture, Forest Service, Rocky Mountain Research Station.

Schwilling, M. D., and C. W. Comer. 1972. Recent nesting of Mountain Bluebird in Cimarron County, Oklahoma. Bull. Okla. Ornithol. Soc. 5(2):15–16.

Scott, C. M. 1978. On early nesting of the American Coot in Oklahoma, with comments on incubation period and chick mortality. Bull. Okla. Ornithol. Soc. 11:21–22.

Scott, D. M. 1991. The time of day of egg laying by the Brown-headed Cowbird and other icterines. Can. J. Zool. 69:2093–2099.

Scweitzer, S. H. 1994. Abundance and conservation of endangered interior Least Terns nesting on salt flat habitat. Ph.D. diss., Oklahoma State University, Stillwater.

Sealy, S. G. 1996. Evolution of host defenses against brood parasitism: Implications of puncture-ejection by a small passerine. Auk 113:346–355.

Sedgewick, J. A. 2000. Willow Flycatcher (*Empidonax traillii*). *In* The Birds of North America, No. 533 (A. Poole and F. Gill, eds.). Academy of Natural Sciences, Philadelphia, and American Ornithologists' Union, Washington, D.C.

Sedgewick, J. A., and F. L. Knopf. 1988. A high incidence of Brown-headed Cowbird parasitism of Willow Flycatchers. Condor 90:253–256.

Seibel, R. 1977. Breeding of Common Gallinule in Grant County, Oklahoma. Bull. Okla. Ornithol. Soc. 10:12.

Seibert, P. 1991. Nesting status of the Pied-billed Grebe in Tulsa County, Oklahoma. Bull. Okla. Ornithol. Soc. 24:4–5.

Seibert, P. 1995. Early nesting date for Great Horned Owl in Oklahoma. Bull. Okla. Ornithol. Soc. 28:21–22.

Seibert, P., and J. Loyd. 1993. Henslow's Sparrow in Tulsa County, Oklahoma. Bull. Okla. Ornithol. Soc. 26(4):43.

Selander, R. K., and D. R. Giller. 1959. Interspecific relations of woodpeckers in Texas. Wilson Bull. 71(2):104–124.

Seyffert, K. D. 1972. Discovery of the Verdin in southwestern Oklahoma. Bull. Okla. Ornithol. Soc. 5:9–12.

Seyffert, K. D. 1989a. Breeding Status of the Black-necked Stilt in the Texas Panhandle. Bull. Okla. Ornithol. Soc. 22:10–13.

Seyffert, K. D. 1989b. Common Moorhens nesting in the Texas Panhandle. Bull. Okla. Ornithol. Soc. 22:23–24.

Seyffert, K. D. 2001. Birds of the Texas Panhandle. Texas A&M University Press, College Station.

Shackelford, C. E., and R. N. Conner. 1997. Woodpecker abundance and habitat use in three forest types in eastern Texas. Wilson Bull. 109:614–629.

Shackelford, C. E., R. E. Brown, and R. N. Conner. 2000. Red-bellied Woodpecker (*Melanerpes carolinus*). *In* The Birds of North America, No. 500 (A. Poole and F. Gill, eds.). Academy of Natural Sciences, Philadelphia, and American Ornithologists' Union, Washington, D.C.

Shackford, J. S. 1980. Breeding of Ruddy Duck in Oklahoma. Bull. Okla. Ornithol. Soc. 13:9–11.

Shackford, J. S. 1981. An important marshy pond in Kingfisher County, Oklahoma. Bull. Okla. Ornithol. Soc. 14:20.

Shackford, J. S. 1982a. Eight Mallard broods in Cimarron County, Oklahoma, one date, one locality. Bull. Okla. Ornithol. Soc. 15:23–24.

Shackford, J. S. 1982b. Third Black-throated Sparrow record for central Oklahoma. Bull. Okla. Ornithol. Soc. 16:7–8.

Shackford, J. S. 1983. Great-tailed Grackle breeding in Cimarron County, Oklahoma. Bull. Okla. Ornithol. Soc. 16(2):16.

Shackford, J. S. 1984a. Cooper's Hawk nests in Cimarron County, Oklahoma. Bull. Okla. Ornithol. Soc. 17:15.

Shackford, J. S. 1984b. Early spring record for Cattle Egret in Oklahoma. Bull. Okla. Ornithol. Soc. 17:7.

Shackford, J. S. 1987. Possible Cowbird parasitism of Yellow-breasted Chat in Cimarron County, Oklahoma. Bull. Okla. Ornithol. Soc. 20:3–4.

Shackford, J. S. 1988. First Eared Grebe nests for Oklahoma. Bull. Okla. Ornithol. Soc. 21:1–2.

Shackford, J. S. 1989. A Curve-billed Thrasher nest in Texas County, Oklahoma. Bull. Okla. Ornithol. Soc. 22:28–29.

Shackford, J. S. 1990. Early nesting of Eastern Meadowlark in Oklahoma County, Oklahoma. Bull. Okla. Ornithol. Soc. 23(2):14–15.

Shackford, J. S. 1991. Breeding ecology of the Mountain Plover in Oklahoma. Bull. Okla. Ornithol. Soc. 24(2):9–13.

Shackford, J. S. 1992a. Kentucky Warbler nest in Oklahoma County, Oklahoma. Bull. Okla. Ornithol. Soc. 25:5–6.

Shackford, J. S. 1992b. Yellow-throated Vireo nest in Cimarron County, Oklahoma. Bull. Okla. Ornithol. Soc. 25(2):15–16.

Shackford, J. S. 1994. Nesting of Long-billed Curlews on cultivated fields. Bull. Okla. Ornithol. Soc. 27(3):17–20.

Shackford, J. S. 1995. Melanistic Mountain Plover in Cimarron County, Oklahoma. Bull. Okla. Ornithol. Soc. 28:4–5.

Shackford, J. S. 1996. The importance of shade to breeding Mountain Plovers. Bull. Okla. Ornithol. Soc. 29(3):17–21.

Shackford, J. S., and E. M. Grigsby. 1993. Mountain Bluebird nests in Cimarron County. Bull. Okla. Ornithol. Soc. 26(1):7.

Shackford, J. S., and W. D. Harden. 1993. Possible excavations in mesquite by Downy and Red-bellied woodpeckers. Bull. Okla. Ornithol. Soc. 26(4):37–38.

Shackford, J. S., and J. D. Tyler. 1987. A nesting Yellow-headed Blackbird colony in Texas County, Oklahoma. Bull. Okla. Ornithol. Soc. 20:9–12.

Shackford, J. S., and W. D. Harden. 1989. Ash-throated Flycatcher nesting in central Oklahoma. Bull. Okla. Ornithol. Soc. 22:22–23.

Shane, T. G. 1974. Nest placement by Lark Buntings. Bird Watch 2:1–3.

Shane, T. G. 2000. Lark Bunting (*Calamospiza melanocorys*). *In* The Birds of North America, No. 543 (A. Poole and F. Gill, eds.). Academy of Natural Sciences, Philadelphia, and American Ornithologists' Union, Washington, D.C.

Shannon, C. W. 1921. Some personal observations on the habits of the Butcher Shrike. Proc. Okla. Acad. Sci. 1:34.

Sheffield, S. R. 1993. Courtship displays between and Eastern and Western Kingbird in Cimarron County, Oklahoma. Bull. Okla. Ornithol. Soc. 26(1):5–6.

Sheffield, S. R. 1996. Recent records for the Barn Owl in north-central Oklahoma. Bull. Okla. Ornithol. Soc. 24:22–23.

Sheffield, S. R. 1998. Nest defense and prolonged incubation in the Rio Grande Wild Turkey. Bull. Okla. Ornithol. Soc. 31:25–28.

Sheffield, S. R., and M. Howery. 2001. Current status, distribution, and conservation of the Burrowing Owl in Oklahoma. J. Raptor Res. 35:351–356.

Sheldon, W. G. 1967. The Book of the American Woodcock. University of Massachusetts Press, Amherst.

Shepperd, R. S. 1996. White-faced Ibises nest at Salt Plains National Wildlife Refuge, Oklahoma. Bull. Okla. Ornithol. Soc. 29:1–2.

Sherrod, S. K. 1972. Aggressive behavior of Starling at Yellow-shafted Flicker nest site. Bull. Okla. Ornithol. Soc. 5:7–8.

Sherry, T. W., and R. T. Holmes. 1988. Habitat selection by breeding American Redstarts in response to a dominant competitor, the Least Flycatcher. Auk 105:350–364.

Sherry, T. W., and R. T. Holmes. 1992. Population fluctuations in a long distance Neotropical migrant: Demographic evidence for the importance of breeding season events in the American Redstart. Pp. 431–442 *in* Ecology and Conservation of Neotropical Migrant Landbirds (J. M. Hagen III and D. W. Johnston, eds.). Smithsonian Institution Press, Washington, D.C.

Sherry, T. W., and R. T. Holmes. 1997. American Redstart (*Stegophaga ruticilla*). *In* The Birds of North America, No. 277 (A. Poole and F. Gill, eds.). Academy of Natural Sciences, Philadelphia, and American Ornithologists' Union, Washington, D.C.

Shirley, J. C. 1928. A biological survey of Garfield County. Proc. Okla. Acad. Sci. 7:103–104.

Shurtleff, L. W., and C. Savage. 1996. The Wood Duck and the Mandarin. University of California Press, Berkeley.

Shy, E. 1985. Songs of Summer Tanagers (*Piranga rubra*): Structure and geographical variation. Am. Midl. Nat. 114:112–124.

Sibley, C. G., and L. L. Short Jr. 1959. Hybridization of the buntings (Passerina) of the Great Plains. Auk 76:443–463.

Sibley, D. A. 2000. National Audubon Society The Sibley Guide to Birds. Chanticleer Press, New York.

Sidle, J. G., J. J. Dinan, M. P. Dryer, J. P. Rumanick Jr., and J. W. Smith. 1988. Distribution of the Least Tern in interior North America. American Birds 42:195–201.

Silver, W. H. 1952. Birds of the state fish hatchery near Durant, Oklahoma. Proc. Okla. Aca. Sci. 33:66–69.

Simons, T. S., S. K. Sherrod, M. W. Collopy, and M. A. Jenkins. 1988. Restoring the Bald Eagle. Am. Sci. 76:253–260.

Skutch, A. F. 1999. Helpers and Birds' Nests: A Worldwide Survey of Cooperative Breeding and Related Behavior. University of Iowa Press, Iowa City.

Slack, R. S. 1973. Sparrow Hawk preys on young Killdeer. Bull. Okla. Ornithol. Soc. 6(3):20–21.

Sloane, S. A. 1996. Incidence and origins of supernumeraries at Bushtit (*Psaltriparus minimus*) nests. Auk 113:757–770.

Sloane, S. A. 2001. Bushtit (*Psaltriparus minimus*). *In* The Birds of North America, No. 598 (A. Poole and F. Gill, eds.). Academy of Natural Sciences, Philadelphia, and American Ornithologists' Union, Washington, D.C.

Smith, C. C. 1940. The effect of overgrazing and erosion upon the biota of the mixed-grass prairie of Oklahoma. Ecology 21:381–397.

Smith, C. R., ed. Handbook for Atlasing American Breeding Birds. 1990. Laboratory of Ornithology and Department of Natural Resources, Cornell University, and Vermont Institute of Natural Science, Woodstock, Vermont.

Smith, J. I. 1987. Evidence of hybridization between Red-bellied and Golden-fronted woodpeckers. Condor 89(2):377–386.

Smith, K. 1991. Brown Thrashers harass fledgling Loggerhead Shrikes. Bull. Okla. Ornithol. Soc. 24(4):34–35.

Smith, K. G. 1978. Range extension of the Blue Jay into western North America. Bird-Banding 49:208–214.

Smith, K. G., M. W. Davis, T. E. Kienzle, W. Post, and R. W. Chinn. 1999. Additional records of fall and winter nesting by Killdeer in southern U.S. Wilson Bull. 111(3):424–426.

Smith, K. G., J. H. Withgott, and P. G. Rodewald. 2000. Red-headed Woodpecker (*Melanerpes erythrocephalus*). *In* The Birds of North America, No. 518 (A. Poole and F. Gill, eds.). Academy of Natural Sciences, Philadelphia, and American Ornithologists' Union, Washington, D.C.

Smith, M. F. 1981. Carolina Wren nest in hole in bank. Bull. Okla. Ornithol. Soc. 14(2):15–16.

Smith, P. W. 1987. The Eurasian Collared-Dove arrives in the Americas. American Birds 41:1370–1379.

Smith, R. W. 1974. Occurrence of the American Woodcock in Oklahoma. M.S. thesis, Oklahoma State University, Stillwater.

Smith, W. P. 1942. Nesting habits of the Eastern Phoebe. Auk 59(3):410–417.

Snow, C. S. 1994. A third Oklahoma Brown Thrasher nest on the ground. Bull. Okla. Ornithol. Soc. 27(2):16.

Snyder, J. W., E. C. Pelren, and J. A. Crawford. 1999. Translocation histories of prairie grouse in the United States. Wildl. Soc. Bull. 27:428–432.

Snyder, N. F. R., and H. A. Snyder. 1991. Raptors: North American Birds of Prey. Voyageur Press, Inc., Stillwater, Minnesota.

Spencer, O. R. 1943. Nesting habits of the Black-billed Cuckoo. Wilson Bull. 55:11–22.

Stabler, R. M. 1959. Nesting of the Blue Grosbeak in Colorado. Condor 61:46–48.

Stahlecker, D. W., and H. J. Griese. 1977. Evidence of double brooding by American Kestrels in the Colorado high plains. Wilson Bull. 89(4):618–619.

Stalmaster, M. V. 1987. The Bald Eagle. Universe Books, New York.

Stancill, W. J., D. M. Leslie Jr., and R. F. Raskevitz. 1989. Waterfowl Production on Grand Lake and Associated Wetlands in Northeast Oklahoma. Proc. Okla. Acad. Sci. 69:33–38.

Stancill, W. J., R. F. Raskevitz, and D. M. Leslie Jr. 1988.

Species composition of a mixed ardeid colony on Grand Lake, Oklahoma. Proc. Okla. Acad. Sci. 62:53–56.

Stauffer, D. F., and L. B. Best. 1980. Habitat selection by cavity-nesting birds of riparian habitat in Iowa. Wilson Bull. 94:329–337.

Steenhof, K. 1998. Prairie Falcon (*Falco mexicanus*). *In* The Birds of North America, No. 346 (A. Poole and F. Gill, eds.). Academy of Natural Sciences, Philadelphia, and American Ornithologists' Union, Washington, D.C.

Stephens, H. A. 1980. The Great Blue Heron in Kansas. Trans. Kans. Acad. Sci. 83:161–186.

Stevenson, J. 1936. Bird notes from Oklahoma. Wilson Bull. 48:132–133.

Stewart, M. E. 1989. Eastern Screech-Owl in McCurtain County, Oklahoma. Bull. Okla. Ornithol. Soc. 22:7–8.

Stewart, M. E. 1990. Impaled Grasshopper Sparrow in Jefferson County, Oklahoma. Bull. Okla. Ornithol. Soc. 23(2):16.

Stewart, M. E., and J. D. Tyler. 1989. Additional Eastern Screech-Owl records for southeastern Oklahoma. Bull. Okla. Ornithol. Soc. 22:14–15.

Stewart, P. A. 1980. Population trends of Barn Owls in North America. Am. Birds 34:698–700.

Stewart, P. A. 1982. Migration of Blue Jays in eastern North America. N. Amer. Bird Bander 7:107–112.

Stokes, D. W., and L. Q. Stokes. 1979. A Guide to Bird Behavior. Vol. 1. Little, Brown and Co., Boston.

Stokes, D. W., and L. Q. Stokes. 1983. A Guide to Bird Behavior. Vol. 2. Little, Brown and Co., Boston.

Stokes, D. W., and L. Q. Stokes. 1989. A Guide to Bird Behavior. Vol. 3. Little, Brown and Co., Boston, Massachusetts.

Stokes, D. W., and L. Q. Stokes. 1996. Stokes Field Guide to Birds—Eastern Region. Little, Brown and Co., Boston.

Stokes D. W., L. Q. Stokes, and L. Elliot. 1997. Stokes Field Guide to Bird Songs. Time Warner Audio Books, New York. 3 cassettes.

Stoleson, S. H., and D. M. Finch. 1999. Unusual nest sites for Southwestern Willow Flycatchers. Wilson Bull. 111:574–575.

Stotts, V. D. 1975. The age at first flight for young American Ospreys. Wilson Bull. 87(2):277–278.

Stouffer, P. C., and D. F. Caccamise. 1991. Roosting and diurnal movements of radio-tagged American Crows. Wilson Bull. 103:387–400.

Straight, C. A., and R. J. Cooper. 2000. Chuck-will's-widow (*Caprimulgus carolinensis*). *In* The Birds of North America, No. 499 (A. Poole and F. Gill, eds.). Academy of Natural Sciences, Philadelphia, and American Ornithologists' Union, Washington, D.C..

Strawn, S. 1992. Green leaf collecting by nesting Purple Martins. Bull. Okla. Ornithol. Soc. 25:4–5.

Sullivan, R. S. 1976. Oklahoma records for the Black Rail. Bull. Okla. Ornithol. Soc. 9:9–10.

Sutton, G. M. 1915. Suggestive methods of bird-study: Pet Road-runners. Bird Lore 17:57–61.

Sutton, G. M. 1922. Notes on the Road-runner at Fort Worth, Texas. Wilson Bull. 34:2–20.

Sutton, G. M. 1934. Notes on the birds of the western Panhandle of Oklahoma. Ann. Carnegie Mus. 24:1–50.

Sutton, G. M. 1936a. Food Capturing Tactics of the Least Bittern. Auk. 53:74–75.

Sutton, G. M. 1936b. Notes from Ellis and Cimarron counties, Oklahoma. Auk 53:431–434.

Sutton, G. M. 1938a. Oddly plumaged orioles from western Oklahoma. Auk 55:1–6.

Sutton, G. M. 1938b. Some findings of the Semple Oklahoma expedition. Auk 55:501–508.

Sutton, G. M. 1939. The Mississippi Kite in spring. Condor 41:41–53.

Sutton, G. M. 1940. *Geococcyx californianus* (Lesson), Roadrunner. Pp. 36–51 *in* Life Histories of North American Cuckoos, Goatsuckers, Hummingbirds, and Their Allies (A. C. Bent, ed.) U.S. Natl. Mus. Bull. No. 176.

Sutton, G. M. 1944. The kites of the genus *Ictinia*. Wilson Bull. 56:3–8.

Sutton, G. M. 1948. The Curve-billed Thrasher in Oklahoma. Condor 50:40–43.

Sutton, G. M. 1949. Studies of the nesting birds of the Edwin S. George Reserve. Pt. 1: the vireos. Misc. Publ. Univ. Mich. 74:5–36.

Sutton, G. M. 1964. On plumages of the young Lesser Prairie-Chicken. Southwest. Nat. 9:1–5.

Sutton, G. M. 1967. Oklahoma Birds. University of Oklahoma Press, Norman.

Sutton, G. M. 1968a. Curve-billed Thrasher in Jackson County, southwestern Oklahoma. Bull. Okla. Ornithol. Soc. 1:19.

Sutton, G. M. 1968b. The natal plumage of the Lesser Prairie-Chicken. Auk 85:679.

Sutton, G. M. 1968c. Young Curve-billed Thrasher attended by adult Brown Towhee. Auk 85:127–128.

Sutton, G. M. 1969. A Chuck-will's-widow in postnuptial molt. Bull. Okla. Ornithol. Soc. 2(2):9–11.

Sutton, G. M. 1972. Winter food of a central Oklahoma Roadrunner. Bull. Okla. Ornithol. Soc. 5:30.

Sutton, G. M. 1973. Early nesting of the Cardinal in central Oklahoma. Bull. Okla. Ornithol. Soc. 6(1):8.

Sutton, G. M. 1977a. Fifty common birds of Oklahoma and the southern Great Plains. University of Oklahoma Press, Norman.

Sutton, G. M. 1977b. The Lesser Prairie-Chicken's inflatable neck sacs. Wilson Bull. 89:521–522.

Sutton, G. M. 1978. Wood Duck nesting in Norman, Oklahoma. Bull. Okla. Ornithol. Soc. 11:13–14.

Sutton, G. M. 1979. Is the American Kestrel two-brooded in Oklahoma? Bull. Okla. Ornithol. Soc. 12(4):30–31.

Sutton, G. M. 1984a. Common Grackle nest in tree cavity. Bull. Okla. Ornithol. Soc. 17(2):15–16.

Sutton, G. M. 1984b. The Red-bellied Woodpeckers fail again. Bull. Okla. Ornithol. Soc. 17(1):1–3.

Sutton, G. M. 1985. European Starlings lining nest or roosting quarters in fall. Bull. Okla. Ornithol. Soc. 18:7–8.

Sutton, G. M. 1986a. Birds Worth Watching. University of Oklahoma Press, Norman.

Sutton, G. M. 1986b. Dichromatism of the Screech Owl in Central Oklahoma. Bull. Okla. Ornithol. Soc. 19(3):17–20.

Sutton, G. M. 1986c. Nests of Western Kingbirds in pines. Bull. Okla. Ornithol. Soc. 19(1):5–6.

Sutton, G. M. and G. W. Dickerson. 1965. Interbreeding of the Eastern and Western meadowlarks in central Oklahoma. Southwest. Nat. 10(4):307–310.

Sutton, G. M., and J. D. Tyler. 1978. Ash-throated Flycatcher and Loggerhead Shrike nesting in same tree. Bull. Okla. Ornithol. Soc. 11(3):22–23.

Sutton, G. M., and J. D. Tyler. 1979. On the behavior of American Kestrels nesting in town. Bull. Okla. Ornithol. Soc. 12(4):25–29.

Svedarsky, W. D., R. H. Hier, and N. J. Silvy. 1999. The Greater Prairie-Chicken: A National Look. Minn. Agricultural Experiment Station, Univ. Minn. Misc. Publ. 187pp.

Svensson, L., P. J. Grant, K. Mullarney, and D. Zetterstrom. 1999. Birds of Europe. Princeton University Press, New Jersey.

Tanner, W. D., Jr., and G. O. Hendrickson. 1956. Ecology of the King Rail in Clay County, Iowa. Iowa Bird Life 26:54–56.

Tarvin, K. A., and G. E. Woolfenden. 1999. Blue Jay (*Cyanocitta cristata*). *In* The Birds of North America, No. 469 (A. Poole and F. Gill, eds.). Academy of Natural Sciences, Philadelphia, and American Ornithologists' Union, Washington, D.C.

Tate, R. C. 1923. Some birds of the Oklahoma Panhandle. Proc. Okla. Acad. Sci. 3:41–51.

Tate, R. C. 1924. Favorite foods of some Oklahoma birds. Proc. Okla. Acad. Sci. 4:33–35.

Tate, R. C. 1925a. The House Finch in the Oklahoma Panhandle. Condor 27:176.

Tate, R. C. 1925b. Some materials used in nest construction by certain birds of the Oklahoma Panhandle. Proc. Okla. Acad. Sci. 5:103–104.

Tate, R. C. 1927. The American Magpie in the Oklahoma Panhandle. Condor 29:244–245.

Tate, R. C. 1933. Notes on the further extension in range of the American Magpie in the Oklahoma Panhandle. Proc. Okla. Acad. Sci. 13:10.

Taylor, M. A., and F. S. Guthery. 1980. Status, ecology, and management of the Lesser Prairie-Chicken. U.S. For. Serv. Gen. Tech. Rep. RM-77. Rocky Mt. Forest and

Range Exper. Sta., Fort Collins, Colorado.

Taylor, W. K.. 1972. Mobbing of a Fish Crow by passerines. Wilson Bull. 84(1):98.

Telfair, R. C., II. 1994. Cattle Egret (*Bubulcus ibis*). *In* The Birds of North America, No. 113 (A. Poole and F. Gills, eds.). Academy of Natural Sciences, Philadelphia, and American Ornithologists' Union, Washington, D.C.

Telfair, R. C., II, and M. L. Morrison. 1995. Neotropic Cormorant (*Phalacrocorax brasilianus*). *In* The Birds of North America, No. 137 (A. Poole and F. Gill, eds.). Academy of Natural Sciences, Philadelphia, and American Ornithologists' Union, Washington, D.C.

Terres, J. K. 1980. The Audubon Society Encyclopedia of North American Birds. Alfred A. Knopf, Inc. New York.

Terres, J. K. 1991. The Audubon Society Encyclopedia of North American Birds. Wings Books, New York.

Thomas, B. G., E. P. Wiggers, and R. L. Clawson. 1996. Habitat selection and breeding status of Swainson's Warblers in southern Missouri. J. Wildl. Manage. 60(3):611–616.

Thomas, F. D. 1970. Indigo Bunting as host to Brown-headed Cowbird in Oklahoma. Bull. Okla. Ornithol. Soc. 3:34–35.

Thompson, B. C., J. A. Jackson, J. Burger, L. A. Hill, E. M. Kirsch, and J. L. Atwood. 1997. Least Tern (*Sterna antillarum*). *In* The Birds of North America, No. 290 (A. Poole and F. Gill, eds.). Academy of Natural Sciences, Philadelphia, and American Ornithologists' Union, Washington, D.C.

Thompson, F. R., III. 1994. Temporal and spatial patterns of breeding Brown-headed Cowbirds in the midwestern United States. Auk 111:979–990.

Thompson, M. C. 1961. Observations on the nesting success of the Barn Swallow in south-central Kansas. Bull. Kans. Ornithol. Soc. 12:9–11.

Thompson, M. C., and C. Ely. 1989. Birds in Kansas. Vol. 1. University of Kansas Museum of Natural History, Lawrence, Kansas.

Thompson, M. C., and C. Ely. 1992. Birds in Kansas. Vol. 2. University of Kansas Museum of Natural History, Lawrence, Kansas.

Thurow, T. L., and C. M. White. 1983. Nest site relationship between the Ferruginous Hawk and Swainson's Hawk. J. Field Ornithol. 54(4):401–406.

Tobalske, B. W. 1997. Lewis's Woodpecker (*Melanerpes lewis*). *In* The Birds of North America, No. 284 (A. Poole and F. Gill, eds.). Academy of Natural Sciences, Philadelphia, and American Ornithologists' Union, Washington, D.C.

Todd, F. S. 1996. Natural History of the Waterfowl. Ibis Publishing Co., Vista, California.

Toepfer, J. E. 1988. Ecology of the Greater Prairie-Chicken as related to reintroduction. Ph.D. diss., Montana State University, Bozeman.

Toepfer, J. E., R. L. Eng, and R. K. Anderson. 1990. Translocating prairie grouse: What have we learned? Trans. No. Am. Wildl. Conf. 55:569–579.

Tomer, J. S. 1955. Notes on a heron rookery in northeastern Oklahoma. Wilson Bull. 67:134–135.

Tomer, J. S. 1967. Cattle Egret nesting in northeastern Oklahoma. Wilson Bull. 79:245.

Tomer, J. S. 1974. The ornithological work of S. W. Woodhouse in Indian Territory. Bull. Okla. Ornithol. Soc. 7(3):17–54.

Tomer, J. S. 1983. Nesting of Vermilion Flycatcher in Cimarron County, Oklahoma. Bull. Okla. Ornithol. Soc. 16:1–3.

Tomer, J. S. 1997. The first listing of Oklahoma birds. Bull. Okla. Ornithol. Soc. 30(2–3):14–21.

Trewartha, G. 1968. An Introduction to Climate. McGraw-Hill, New York. 408 pp.

Trost, C. H. 1994. Black-billed Magpie (*Pica pica*). *In* The Birds of North America, No. 389 (A. Poole and F. Gills, eds.). Academy of Natural Sciences, Philadelphia, and American Ornithologists' Union, Washington, D.C.

Turner, B. J. 1971. Early nesting of Killdeer in Oklahoma. Bull. Okla. Ornithol. Soc. 4:27.

Tveten, J. L. 1993. The Birds of Texas. Shearer Publishing, Fredericksburg, Texas.

Twedt, D. J., and R. D. Crawford. 1995. Yellow-headed Blackbird (*Xanthocephalus xanthocephalus*). *In* The Birds of North America, No. 192 (A. Poole and F. Gill, eds.). Academy of Natural Sciences, Philadelphia, and American Ornithologists' Union, Washington, D.C.

Tweit, R. C. 1996. Curve-billed Thrasher (*Toxostoma curvirostre*). *In* The Birds of North America, No. 235 (A. Poole and F. Gill, eds.). Academy of Natural Sciences, Philadelphia, and American Ornithologists' Union, Washington, D.C.

Tweit, R. C., and J. C. Tweit. 2000. Cassin's Kingbird (*Tyrannus vociferans*). *In* The Birds of North America, No. 534 (A. Poole and F. Gill, eds.). Academy of Natural Sciences, Philadelphia, and American Ornithologists' Union, Washington, D.C.

Tyler, J. D. 1968a. Distribution and vertebrate associates of the black-tailed prairie dog in Oklahoma. Ph.D. diss., University of Oklahoma, Norman.

Tyler, J. D. 1968b. Early nesting of White-necked Raven in Oklahoma. Bull. Okla. Ornithol. Soc. 1:11.

Tyler, J. D. 1972. American Woodcock in Comanche County, Oklahoma, in winter. Bull. Okla. Ornithol. Soc. 5(4):29.

Tyler, J. D. 1974. Inca Dove in Jackson County, Oklahoma. Bull. Okla. Ornithol. Soc. 7:63–64.

Tyler, J. D. 1979a. Birds of southwestern Oklahoma. Contrib. Stovall Mus. Nat. Hist. No. 2., Norman, Oklahoma.

Tyler, J. D. 1979b. Late date for nesting of Scissortail in Oklahoma. Bull. Okla. Ornithol. Soc. 12:23.

Tyler, J. D. 1979c. Nest of Lewis's Woodpecker in Cimarron

County, Oklahoma. Bull. Okla. Ornithol. Soc. 12:14–15.

Tyler, J. D. 1981. The Swainson's Hawk in southwestern Oklahoma. Bull. Okla. Ornithol. Soc. 14(2):11–12.

Tyler, J. D. 1983. Notes on Burrowing Owl food habits in Oklahoma. Southwest. Nat. 28:100–102.

Tyler, J. D. 1985. The Lark Bunting in Oklahoma. Bull. Okla. Ornithol. Soc. 28:25–28.

Tyler, J. D. 1986a. Curve-billed Thrasher eggs eaten by western coachwhip. Bull. Okla. Ornithol. Soc. 19:14–15.

Tyler, J. D. 1986b. First record of Scarlet Tanager in southwestern Oklahoma. Bull. Okla. Ornithol. Soc. 19:6.

Tyler, J. D. 1987. An invasion of Northern Shrikes in Cimarron County, Oklahoma. Bull. Okla. Ornithol. Soc. 20(1):7–8.

Tyler, J. D. 1991a. From the editor. Bull. Okla. Ornithol. Soc. 24:24.

Tyler, J. D. 1991b. Vertebrate prey of the Loggerhead Shrike in Oklahoma. Proc. Okla. Acad. Sci. 71:17–20.

Tyler, J. D. 1992a. First House Finch nests for southwest Oklahoma. Bull. Okla. Ornithol. Soc. 25:7–8.

Tyler, J. D. 1992b. History of the House Finch in Oklahoma, 1919–1991. Proc. Okla. Acad. Sci. 72:33–35.

Tyler, J. D. 1992c. Nesting ecology of the Loggerhead Shrike in southwestern Oklahoma. Wilson Bull. 104(1):95–104.

Tyler, J. D. 1993. Cedar Waxwings in Cherokee County, Oklahoma, during June. Bull. Okla. Ornithol. Soc. 26:7–8.

Tyler, J. D. 1994a. Average arrival and departure dates for some breeding birds in southwestern Oklahoma, 1938–92. Proc. Okla. Acad. Sci. 74:47–48.

Tyler, J. D. 1994b. How early does the Great Blue Heron nest in Oklahoma? Bull. Okla. Ornithol. Soc. 27(4):25–26.

Tyler, J. D. 1994c. How often do Brown Thrashers nest on the ground in Oklahoma? Bull. Okla. Ornithol. Soc. 27(1):4–6.

Tyler, J. D. 1994d. The Least Bittern in southwestern Oklahoma. Bull. Okla. Ornithol. Soc. 27(4):29.

Tyler, J. D. 1994e. Nest-site selection by Loggerhead Shrikes in southwestern Oklahoma. Proc. Okla. Acad. Sci. 74:43–45.

Tyler, J. D., and F. J. Bechtold. 1996. Statuses of four avian species in southwestern Oklahoma. Bull. Okla. Ornithol. Soc. 29(4):27–34.

Tyler, J. D., and L. E. Dunn. 1984. A pair of Say's Phoebes with nine young. Bull. Okla. Ornithol. Soc. 17(1):7–8.

Tyler, J. D., and T. McKee. 1991. Early nighthawk records for north-central Texas and southwestern Oklahoma. Bull. Okla. Ornithol. Soc. 24(3):21–22.

Tyler, J. D., and K. C. Parkes. 1992. A hybrid Scissor-tailed Flycatcher x Western Kingbird specimen from western Oklahoma. Wilson Bull. 78:104, 178–181.

Tyler, J. D., S. J. Orr, and J. K. Banta. 1989. The Red-shouldered Hawk in southwestern Oklahoma. Bull. Okla. Ornithol. Soc. 22(3):17–21.

Tyler, W. M. 1965. Cedar Waxwing. In Life Histories of North American Wagtails, Shrikes, Vireos, and Their Allies (A. C. Bent, ed.). U.S. Natl. Mus. Bull. 197, Dover Publications, New York.

U.S. Fish and Wildlife Service. 1985. Interior population of the Least Tern determined to be endangered. Federal Register 50:21784–21792.

U.S. Fish and Wildlife Service. 1990. Recovery plan for the interior population of the Least Tern (Sterna antillarum). U.S. Fish and Wildlife Service, Twin Cities, Minnesota.

U.S. Fish and Wildlife Service. 1991. Black-capped Vireo (Vireo atricapillus) recovery plan. U.S. Fish Wildlife Service, Austin, Texas.

U.S. Fish and Wildlife Service and Canadian Wildlife Service. 1989. 1989 status of waterfowl and fall flight forecast. U.S. Fish and Wildlife Service, Washington, D.C.

U.S. Fish and Wildlife Service. 1998. Twelve-month administrative finding on petition to list the Lesser Prairie-Chicken (Tympanuchus pallidicinctus) as threatened. Tulsa Ecol. Services, USFWS, Tulsa, OK. 65pp.

U.S. Fish and Wildlife Service. 2001. Twelve-month finding for a petition to list the Yellow-billed Cuckoo (Cocyzus americanus) in the western continental United States. Federal Registry 66:38611–38626.

Udvardy, M. D., and J. Farrand Jr. 1997. National Audubon Society Field Guide to North American Birds Western Region. Alfred A. Knopf, New York, New York.

United States Shorebird Conservation Plan. 2001. Editors S. Brown, C. Hickey, B. Harrington and R. Gill. Manomet Center for Conservation Sciences. Manomet, Massachusetts.

Vacin, V. J. 1968. Summering of Rose-breasted Grosbeak near Oklahoma City, Oklahoma. Bull. Okla. Ornithol. Soc. 1:16–18.

Vacin, V. J. 1972. Red-breasted Nuthatch observed in central Oklahoma in June carrying suet to two other Red-breasted Nuthatches. Bull. Okla. Ornithol. Soc. 5:13–14.

Van Den Bussche, R. A., S. R. Hoofer, D. A. Wiedenfeld, D. H. Wolfe, and S. K. Sherrod. 2003. Genetic variation within and among fragmented populations of Lesser Prairie-Chickens (Tympanuchus pallidicinctus). Molecular Ecology 12:675–683.

Van Horn, M. A., and T. M. Donovan. 1999. Ovenbird (Seiurus aurocapillus). In The Birds of North America, No. 88 (A. Poole, P. Stettenheim, and F. Gill, eds.). Academy of Natural Sciences, Philadelphia, and American Ornithologists' Union, Washington, D.C.

Van Tyne, J. 1948. Home range and duration of family ties in the Tufted Titmouse. Wilson Bull. 60:121.

Van Velzen, W. T. 1968. Black-throated Sparrow in Kiowa County, Oklahoma. Bull. Okla. Ornithol. Soc. 1:26.

Vance, D. R., and R. L. Westemeier. 1979. Interactions of pheasants and prairie-chickens in Illinois. Wildl. Soc. Bull. 7:221–225.

Verbeek, N. A. M., and C. Caffrey. 2002. American Crow (*Corvus brachyrhynchos*). *In* The Birds of North America, No. 647 (A. Poole and F. Gill, eds.). Academy of Natural Sciences, Philadelphia, and American Ornithologists' Union, Washington, D.C.

Verser, D. W. 1990. Henslow's Sparrow in northeast Oklahoma. Bull. Okla. Ornithol. Soc. 23(2):9–12.

Vickery, P. D. 1996. Grasshopper Sparrow (*Ammodramus savannarum*). *In* The Birds of North America, No. 239 (A. Poole and F. Gill, eds.). Academy of Natural Sciences, Philadelphia, and American Ornithologists' Union, Washington, D.C.

Vierling, K. T. 1997. Habitat selection of Lewis's Woodpeckers in southeastern Colorado. Wilson Bull. 109:121–130.

Voelker, G., and S. Rohwer. 1998. Contrasts in scheduling of molt and migration in Eastern and Western Warbling-vireos. Auk 115:142–155.

Voelker, W. G. 1979. Early nesting of Great Horned Owl in Oklahoma. Bull. Okla. Ornithol. Soc. 12:5–6.

Vohs, P. A., and F. L. Knopf, eds. 1980. Proceedings prairie grouse symposium. Oklahoma State University, Stillwater. 66pp.

Walkinshaw, L. H. 1941. The Prothonotary Warbler: A comparison of nesting conditions in Tennessee and Michigan. Wilson Bull. 53:3–21.

Walkinshaw, L. H. 1953. Life history of the Prothonotary Warbler. Wilson Bull. 65:152–168.

Walters, M. 1994. Bird's Eggs. Dorling Kindersley, London.

Watson, J. E., and W. C. Royall Jr. 1978. Dispersal of Common Grackles banded in south-central Oklahoma. Bull. Okla. Ornithol. Soc. 11:26–28.

Watt, D. J., and E. J. Willoughby. 1999. Lesser Goldfinch (*Carduelis psaltria*). *In* The Birds of North America, No. 392 (A. Poole and F. Gill, eds.). Academy of Natural Sciences, Philadelphia, and American Ornithologists' Union, Washington, D.C.

Watts, B. D. 1995. Yellow-crowned Night-Heron (*Nyctinassa violacea*). *In* The Birds of North America, No. 161 (A. Poole and F. Gill, eds.). Academy of Natural Sciences, Philadelphia, and American Ornithologists' Union, Washington, D.C.

Weary, D. M., R. E. Lemon, and S. Perreault. 1994. Different responses to different song types in American Redstarts. Auk 111:730–734.

Webb, W. D., and J. D. Tyler. 1988. Hybridization of Northern Bobwhites and Scaled Quail in Oklahoma and Texas. Bull. Okla. Ornithol. Soc. 21(1):3–5.

Webster, J. D. 1990. Breeding pair of Vermilion Flycatchers in Cimarron County, Oklahoma. Bull. Okla. Ornithol. Soc. 23:25–27.

Weeks, H. P., Jr. 1994. Eastern Phoebe (*Sayornis phoebe*). *In*

The Birds of North America, No. 94 (A. Poole and F. Gill, eds.). Academy of Natural Sciences, Philadelphia, and American Ornithologists' Union, Washington, D.C.

Weller, M. W. 1958. Observations on the incubating behavior of a Common Nighthawk. Auk 75(1):48–59.

Weller, M. W. 1961. Breeding biology of the Least Bittern. Auk 73:11–35.

Weske, J. S. 1973. Nest of Poor-will in Cimarron County, Oklahoma. Bull. Okla. Ornithol. Soc. 6:22.

Weske, J. S. 1974. Acadian Flycatcher summering in Alfalfa County, Oklahoma: A re-identification. Bull. Okla. Ornithol. Soc. 7(2):14–15.

Westemeier, R. L. 1980. Greater Prairie-Chicken status and management, 1968–1979. Pp. 8–17 *in* Proceedings Prairie Grouse Symposium (P. A. Vohs and F. L. Knopf, eds.). Oklahoma State University, Stillwater.

Westemeier, R. L., and S. Gough. 1999. National outlook and conservation needs for Greater Prairie-Chickens. Pp. 169–187 in The Greater Prairie-Chicken: A National Look (W. D. Svedarsky, R. H. Hier, and N. J. Silvy, eds.). Univ. Minn. Misc. Publ. 99–19999. Minn. Ag. Exp. Sta., St. Paul.

Westemeier, R. L., J. E. Buhnerkempe, W. R. Edwards, J. D. Brawn, and S. A. Simpson. 1998. Parasitism of Greater Prairie-Chicken nests by Ring-necked Pheasants. J. Wildl. Manage. 62:854–863.

Westmoreland, D., and L. B. Best. 1987. What limits Mourning Doves to a clutch of two eggs? Condor 89(3):486–493.

Westmoreland, D., L. B. Best, and D. E. Blockstein. 1986. Multiple brooding as a reproductive strategy: Time conserving adaptations in Mourning Doves. Auk 103(1):196–203.

Weston, F. M. 1964. Blue-gray Gnatcatcher. Pp. 344–363 *in* Life Histories of North American Thrushes, Kinglets, and Their Allies (A. C. Bent, ed.). U.S. Natl. Mus. Bull. No. 196, Dover Publications, New York.

Weston, F. M. 1968. *Aimophila aestivalis* (Audubon) Bachman's Sparrow. Pp. 956–975 *in* Life Histories of North American Cardinals, Grosbeaks, Buntings, Towhees, Finches, Sparrows, and Their Allies (A. C. Bent, O. L. Austin Jr., and collaborators). U.S. Nat. Mus. Bull. 237.

Wheeler, B. K., and W. S. Clark. 1999. A Photographic Guide to North American Raptors. Academic Press, San Diego, California.

White, C. M., and T. L. Thurow. 1985. Reproduction of Ferruginous Hawks exposed to controlled disturbance. Condor 87(1):14–22.

Whittier, J. B., B. R. Winton, and D. M. Leslie Jr. 1999. Common Nighthawk nesting on an exposed alkaline flat. Bull. Okla. Ornithol. Soc. 32(4):29–31.

Whittle, H. G. 1923. Recent experiences with nesting catbirds.

Auk 40:603–606.

Wiedenfeld, D. A., and M. M. Swan. 2000. Louisiana Breeding Bird Atlas. Louisiana Sea Grant College Program, Baton Rouge.

Wiedenfeld, D. A., D. H. Wolfe, J. E. Toepfer, L. M. Mechlin, R. D. Applegate, and S. K. Sherrod. 2002. Survey for reticuloendotheliosis viruses in wild populations of Greater and Lesser Prairie-Chickens. Wilson Bull. 114(1):142–144.

Wiens, J. A. 1963. Aspects of cowbird parasitism in southern Oklahoma. Wilson Bull. 75(2):130–139.

Wiens, J. A. 1965. Nest parasitism of the Dickcissel by the Yellow-billed Cuckoo in Marshall County, Oklahoma. Southwest. Nat. 10:142.

Wiens, J. A. 1973. Pattern and process in grassland bird communities. Ecol. Monogr. 50:237–270.

Wiggins, D. A. 1979. The Plain Titmouse in Oklahoma. Bull. Okla. Ornithol. Soc. 11:9–11.

Wilbur, S. R., and J. A. Jackson. 1983. Vulture Biology and Management. University of California Press, Berkeley.

Wildlife Habitat Management Institute. 1999. Lesser Prairie-Chicken (Tympanuchus pallidicinctus). Fish and Wildlife Management Leaflet No. 6. NRCS, WHMI, Madison, MS. 8pp.

Wilhelm, E. J., Jr. 1960. The Fish Crow in easternmost Oklahoma. Wilson Bull. 72:405.

Williams, F. C., and A. L. LeSarrier. 1968. Aimophila cassinii (Woodhouse) Cassin's Sparrow. Pp. 981–990 in Life Histories of North American Cardinals, Grosbeaks, Buntings, Towhees, Finches, Sparrows, and Their Allies (A. C. Bent, O. L. Austin Jr., and collaborators). U.S. Nat. Mus. Bull. 237.

Williams, J. L. 1973. Black ratsnake nest-predation on Wood Duck in Oklahoma. Bull. Okla. Ornithol. Soc. 6:15.

Williams, M. P. 1969. Wintering of Rose-breasted Grosbeak in Okmulgee County, Oklahoma. Bull. Okla. Ornithol. Soc. 2:23–24.

Williamson, M. 1973. Cattle Egret in Payne County, Oklahoma. Bull. Okla. Ornithol. Soc. 6(2):13–14.

Wilmore, S. B. 1977. Crows, Jays, Ravens and Their Relatives. Paul S. Eriksson, Middlebury, Vermont.

Wilson, M. F., R. D. St. John, R. L. Lederer, and S. Muzos. 1971. Clutch size in Grackles. Bird-banding 42:28–35.

Wilson, P. W. 1981. Successful nesting of the Bank Swallow in Oklahoma. Bull. Okla. Ornithol. Soc. 14:9–11.

Wilson, P. W. 1995. Short-eared Owl nests unsuccessfully in northeast Oklahoma. Bull. Okla. Ornithol. Soc. 28(3):24–26.

Winkler, H., D. A. Christie, and D. Nurney. 1995. Woodpeckers: An Identification Guide to the Woodpeckers of the World. Houghton Mifflin Co., Boston.

Winn, R. 1998. Common Raven (Corvus corax). In Colorado Breeding Bird Atlas (H. E. Kingery, ed.). Colorado Bird

Atlas Partnership and Colorado Division of Wildlife, Denver.

Winternitz, B. L. 1998a. American Avocet (Recurvirostra americana). Pp. 174–175 in The Colorado Breeding Bird Atlas (H. E. Kingery, ed.). Colorado Bird Atlas Partnership and Colorado Division of Wildlife, Denver.

Winternitz, B. L. 1998b. Ladder-backed Woodpecker (Picoides scalaris). In Colorado Breeding Bird Atlas (H. E. Kingery, ed.). Colorado Bird Atlas Partnership and Colorado Division of Wildlife, Denver.

Winton, B. R., and D. M. Leslie Jr. 1997. Breeding ecology of American Avocets (Recurvirostra americana) in north-central Oklahoma. Bull. Okla. Ornithol. Soc. 30:25–32.

Winton, B. R., and D. M. Leslie Jr. 1999. Relative abundance and diversity of ciconiiforms in north-central Oklahoma. Proc. Okla. Acad. Sci. 79:41–44.

Withgott, J. H. 1991. Pre-migratory roosting behavior of Scissor-tailed Flycatchers in Oklahoma. Bull. Okla. Ornithol. Soc. 24:18–21.

Withgott, J. H., and J. A. McMahon. 1993. Conspecific harassment of a leucistic Barn Swallow. Bull. Okla. Ornithol. Soc. 26:38–39.

Withgott, J. H., and K. G. Smith. 1998. Brown-headed Nuthatch (Sitta pusilla). In The Birds of North America, No. 349 (A. Poole and F. Gill, eds.). Academy of Natural Sciences, Philadelphia, and American Ornithologists' Union, Washington, D.C.

Witmer, M. C., D. J. Mountjoy, and L. Elliot. 1997. Cedar Waxwing (Bombycilla cedrorum). In The Birds of North America, No. 309 (A. Poole and F. Gill, eds.). Academy of Natural Sciences, Philadelphia, and American Ornithologists' Union, Washington, D.C.

Wolf, B. O., and S. L. Jones. 2000. Vermilion Flycatcher (Pyrocephalus rubinus). In The Birds of North America, No. 484 (A. Poole and F. Gill, eds.). Academy of Natural Sciences, Philadelphia, and American Ornithologists' Union, Washington, D.C.

Wolf, L. L. 1977. Species relationships in the avian genus Aimophila. Ornithol. Monogr. 23.

Wolfe, D. H. 1994a. Brown-headed Cowbirds fledge from Barn Swallow and American Robin nests. Wilson Bull. 106:764–766.

Wolfe, D. H. 1994b. Yellow-billed Cuckoo hatched in Mourning Dove nest. Bull. Okla. Ornithol. Soc. 27:29–30.

Wolfe, D. H. 1995. Brown-headed Cowbird parasitism of Northern Mockingbirds in Oklahoma. Bull. Okla. Ornithol. Soc. 28(1):7–8.

Wolfe, D. H. 1996a. Brown-headed Cowbirds fledge from a Louisiana Waterthrush nest. Bull. Okla. Ornithol. Soc. 29:15–16.

Wolfe, D. H. 1996b. Nest competition in Eastern Meadowlarks. Bull. Okla. Ornithol. Soc. 29(1):6–7.

Womack, E. 1994. Notable recaptures of banded Ruby-throated Hummingbirds. Bull. Okla. Ornithol. Soc. 27(4):30–31.

Wood, D. A. 1975. Status, habitat, home range, and notes on the behavior of the Red-cockaded Woodpecker in Oklahoma. M.S. thesis, Oklahoma State University, Stillwater.

Wood, D. A. 1983a. Foraging and colony habitat characteristics of the Red-cockaded Woodpecker in Oklahoma. Pp. 51–58 in Red-cockaded Woodpecker Symposium II Proceedings. State of Florida Game and Fresh Water Fish Commission, Tallahassee, Florida.

Wood, D. A. 1983b. Observations on the behavior and breeding biology of the Red-cockaded Woodpecker in Oklahoma. Pp. 92–94 in Red-cockaded Woodpecker Symposium II Proceedings (D. A. Wood, ed.). State of Florida Game and Fresh Water Fish Commission, Tallahassee, Florida.

Wood, D. S., and G. D. Schnell. 1984. Distributions of Oklahoma Birds. University of Oklahoma Press, Norman.

Wood, G. K., and D. M. Leslie Jr. 1992. Breeding biology of Interior Least Terns on the Arkansas River below Keystone Dam, summer 1992. Report prepared for U.S. Army Corps Eng., Tulsa.

Wood, S. 1982. First nest of Whip-poor-will for Oklahoma. Bull. Okla. Ornithol. Soc. 15(3):24.

Woodhouse, S. W. 1853. Birds. Pp. 58–105 in Report of an expedition down the Zuni and Colorado rivers, by Capt. Lorenzo Sitgreaves. Washington, D.C.: R. Armstrong, Public Printer.

Woodward, A. J., S. D. Fuhlendorf, D. M. Leslie Jr., and J. S. Shackford. 2001. Influence of landscape composition and change on Lesser Prairie-Chicken (Tympanuchus pallidicinctus) populations. Am. Midl. Nat. 145:261–274.

Yasukawa, K., and W. A. Searcy. 1995. Red-winged Blackbird (Agelaius phoeniceus). In The Birds of North America, No. 184 (A. Poole and F. Gill, eds.). Academy of Natural Sciences, Philadelphia, and American Ornithologists' Union, Washington, D.C.

Young, E. A., and M. C. Thompson. 1995. Notes on some large concentrations of migrating birds in south-central Kansas. Kans. Ornithol. Soc. Bull. 46(4):30–32.

Zahm, G. R. 1976. A Chimney Swift nest in a garage. Bull. Okla. Ornithol. Soc. 9:10–12.

Ziegler, R. L. 1976. Louisiana Waterthrush nest in Blaine County. Bull. Okla. Ornithol. Soc. 9:16.

Zimmerman, J. L. 1979. Ten-year summary of the Kansas Breeding Bird Survey: Trends. Kans. Ornithol. Soc. Bull. 30:17–19.

Zimmerman, J. L. 1993. Birds of Konza: The Avian Ecology of the Tallgrass Prairie. University of Kansas Press, Lawrence.

Zimmerman, J. L. 1997. Avian community responses to fire, grazing, and drought in the tallgrass prairie. Pp. 167–180 in Ecology and conservation of Great Plains vertebrates (F. L. Knopf and F. B. Samson, eds.). Springer-Verlag, New York.

Zink, R. M., and R. C. Blackwell-Rago. 2000. Species limits and recent population history in the Curve-billed Thrasher. Condor 102:881–886.

Species Index

Author Credits

Photographer Credits

Western Species

☆ W. Screech Owl – rare
  Burrowing Owl
  Common Poorwill
  Black-chinned Hummingbird – SW
☆ Lewis Woodpecker – rare – SW
  Golden-fronted Woodpecker – SW
  Ladder-backed Woodpecker – SW
☆ W Wd Pewee – rare
(☆) Says Phoebe
  Ash-throated Flyc – SW
☆ Cassin's Kingbird – rare
☆ W Scrub Jay – rare
☆ Pinyon Jay – rare
☆ Bl-Bill Magpie
(☆) Chihuahuan Raven
☆ Common Raven – rare
☆ Juniper Titmouse – rare – SW
  Verdin – SW – rare
☆ Bushtit – rare
  Rock Wren
  Canyon Wren
☆ Mtn Blue Bird – rare
  Curve-bill Thrasher
☆ GT Towhee – rare
☆ Spotted Towhee – rare
☆ Canyon Towhee
  Cassin's Sp
☆ Brewer's Sp – rare
☆ Bl-th Sp – rare
(☆) Lark Bunting
☆ Bl-hd Grosbeak
☆ Lesser Gldf – rare
☆ Pine Siskin – rare
  Bullock's Oriole
☆ Brewer's Blackbird – rare
  W Meadowlark
  Lazuli Bunting – rare
  YH Blackbird

Gr. Roadrunner – SW
☆ Wilson's Phalarope
  Am Avocet
☆ Mtn Plover
  Gambel Quail
(☆) Les Pr Chicken
☆ Pr Falcon – rare
☆ Gol Eagle – rare
(☆) Fer Hawk
(☆) LB Curlew